S0-CFH-861

45天突破版
TOEFL词汇
词根+联想
记忆法

俞敏洪 ● 编著

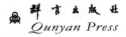

群言出版社
Qunyan Press

图书在版编目(CIP)数据

TOEFL 词汇词根＋联想记忆法：45 天突破版 / 俞敏洪编著. —北京：群言出版社，2009（2012.9 重印）
ISBN 978-7-80256-062-8

Ⅰ. T⋯　Ⅱ. 俞⋯　Ⅲ. 英语—词汇—记忆术—高等教育—自学参考资料　Ⅳ. H313

中国版本图书馆 CIP 数据核字（2009）第 137550 号

TOEFL 词汇词根＋联想记忆法：45 天突破版

出 版 人　范　芳
责任编辑　孙春红
封面设计　大愚设计
出版发行　群言出版社（Qunyan Press）
地　　址　北京东城区东厂胡同北巷 1 号
邮政编码　100006
网　　站　www.qypublish.com
读者信箱　bj62605588@163.com
总 编 办　010－65265404　65138815
编 辑 部　010－65276609　65262436
发 行 部　010－62605588　62605019

经　　销　新华书店
读者服务　010－65220236　65265404　65263345
法律顾问　中济律师事务所
印　　刷　北京四季青印刷厂

版　　次　2012 年 9 月第 1 版第 8 次印刷
开　　本　880mm×1230mm　1/32
印　　张　16.5
字　　数　560 千
书　　号　ISBN 978-7-80256-062-8
定　　价　45.00 元

［版权所有　侵权必究］

如有缺页、倒页、脱页等印装质量问题，请拨打服务热线：010－62605166。

新东方图书策划委员会

主任　俞敏洪

委员　（按姓氏笔画为序）

王　强　　包凡一

仲晓红　　沙云龙

陈向东　　张洪伟

邱政政　　汪海涛

周成刚　　徐小平

谢　琴　　窦中川

前　言

　　词汇向来是学习英语的基石，更是应对所有考试的关键。如果把英语学习比作建造大厦的话，词汇便是深埋于地下的基石，虽不浮于表面，但决定了这座语言大厦的坚固与否。词汇量的匮乏严重影响并制约着一个人听、说、读、写等各方面能力的发展，更会成为各种英语考试的障碍。不掌握一定数量的词汇，任何技巧都犹如隔靴搔痒，难有成效。新托福考试更是对词汇的掌握和运用提出了新的挑战。

　　俗话说"好马配好鞍"，背单词也需要一本好书。那么何谓"一本好书"？简而言之，一本好书应该具有行之有效的单词记忆方法、合理的单词安排结构以及实用有趣的内容。而"词根＋联想"学习法是经广大学习者验证的系统高效的学习方法。因此，本书以词根、词缀记忆法为主体，利用单词的分拆、同义词和形近词的比较，以及词与词之间的联系，并配合幽默的插图形成了一套实用、有趣的记忆方法，帮助考生高效记忆单词。本书特色如下：

一、重点词汇"一网打尽"，单词无序胜有序

　　本书以新托福考试为依据，选取了约 3,900 个核心单词及 670 多个核心词组，并补充大量的派生词及相关单词，共收录约 8,000 个常用单词，将新托福考试重点单词"一网打尽"。此外，本书为部分单词配以同义词，并将已考过的同义词打上 * 号标记，大大丰富了考生的词汇量，并有助于考生理解单词词义。

　　本书打破了从 A 到 Z 常规的按字母顺序排列单词的方式，打乱原有单词顺序，将核心单词分成 45 个单元，以全新的乱序编排带来学习的新体验。考生可以每天学习一个单元，用 45 天的时间攻克新托福词汇。

二、"词根＋联想"，词汇障碍一扫而光

　　与中文的偏旁部首类似，英文单词由大量的词根、词缀构成。掌握常见的词根、词缀，即可以此为支点，拓展记忆海量单词。例如：

　　词根：voc, voke = to call（喊叫），voice（声音）

　　　　　provoke = pro-（向前）+ voke（喊叫）→ 冲向前喊叫 → 激怒

　　　　　revoke = re-（回）+ voke（喊叫）→ 唤回 → 撤回

　　　　　evoke = e-（出）+ voke（喊叫）→ 喊到外面 → 唤起

　　　　　vocal = voc-（声音）+ -al（有…性质）→ 声音的

　　考生在掌握词根 voc, voke 的意思后，配合常见的词缀 pro-, re-, e-, -al 等就可以轻松记住单词词义。考试中即使遇到生词，也能够从其结构推导出大概的意思，例如 circumspect 这个词，由常见词根 spect(看见)和前缀 circum-组成。考生对前缀 circum- 可能不熟悉，但 circuit(一圈；电路)是常见单词，由此可以推断出 circum-与"周"、"绕"等意思相关。circum- 与 spect 组合即包含"四周"与"看"的意思，"向四周查看"是十分谨慎的态度，由此结合上下文不难推出 circumspect 的词义：慎重的。

　　因此，通过词根、词缀的学习，记忆单词将不再是乏味的，而将成为妙趣横生的"拼字游戏"。

　　此外，本书通过将长词分拆、形近词对比、同音词和发音相似的单词串联等

方法为学习单词"减负"。分拆是将长难词分拆为几个简单的部分,利用联想的语句帮助考生推导出词义,例如 realm 的记忆法是：real（真正的）+ m → 真正的好东西(如音乐、艺术等)无国界 → 领域；王国。形近词对比是将较难的词与较简单的形近词放在一起,利用简单单词记忆复杂单词,从而达到事半功倍的效果,例如 ripe 的记忆法：稻熟(ripe)米(rice)香。

三、插图助记,开启轻松记忆之旅

除文字助记方法外,本书为单词配以 200 余幅生动有趣的插图,为考生营造轻松的记忆氛围。例如：

survive [səˈvaɪv] *vi.* 幸免,幸存

【记】词根记忆：sur + vive（生命）→ 在(事故)下面活下来 → 幸存

survive

【例】The tailed toad may not *survive* without special efforts of conservationists. 没有生态环境保护者付出的特殊努力,有尾蟾蜍可能无法生存。

【派】survival(*n.* 生存,幸免); survivor(*n.* 幸存者,生还者)

四、原汁原味例句,模拟考试语境

与多数国内考试相比,新托福考试的文章在难度和长度上都更具挑战性。因此,本书为单词增加了真题场景。这样考生在学习单词时,即可熟悉考试环境,直观了解考查要点,为进一步复习打下扎实的基础。

五、实用项目设置,直击新托福考点

本书还设计了实用的项目,为考生"揭密"新托福考点。【搭】中收录了托福常考的固定短语及词组,帮助考生克服对单词"只知其意,不知用法"的难题；【派】中补充了主词条的派生词,横向拓宽词汇量；【参】中补充了丰富的形近词、近义词、反义词、同类词等,考生可将这些单词串联记忆,提高效率。

与其他学习过程一样,背单词也是一项艰苦的任务,是对我们脑力与意志力的挑战。但当我们目标明确,勇往直前的时候,其中的辛苦就会变得微不足道。希望考生都有水的精神,抱定奔流入海的目标,一路前行。

对于还在考试路上奋进的各位考生,我无法相助其他,唯有通过本书为考生铺就新托福备考之路,祝各位取得理想的成绩,顺利进入自己理想的大学。

最后,感谢世纪友好的金利、关晓蕙、李馨源、王锋、汪欣欣、李素素、张大川等各位编辑,是他们的工作使得本书能够与大家见面。

编者

使用说明

单元前的词根、词缀预习表帮助考生掌握常用词根、词缀，迅速扩大词汇量。

星号标记已考同义词，复习有的放矢。

幽默有趣的插图解释单词含义，帮助考生记忆的同时增加了学习的趣味性。

核心单词表 *Word List 1* MP3-01

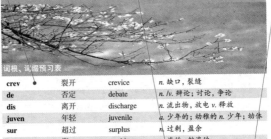

词根、词缀预习表

crev	裂开	crevice	*n.* 缺口，裂缝
de	否定	debate	*n. /v.* 辩论；讨论，争论
dis	离开	discharge	*n.* 流出物，放电 *v.* 释放
juven	年轻	juvenile	*a.* 少年的；幼稚的 *n.* 少年；幼体
sur	超过	surplus	*n.* 过剩，盈余
mari	海	maritime	*a.* 海的，航海的
pre	前	predominant	*a.* 支配的，主要的
radi	光线	radiation	*n.* 辐射
sol	独自	solo	*a.* 单独的 *n.* 独奏曲
tend	伸展	tendency	*n.* 倾向，趋向

acute [ə'kjuːt] *a.* 极度的；(事情)激烈的(*intense)，剧烈的；敏锐的(keen)；严重的
【记】分拆联想：a + cut(切) + e → 一刀切 → 极度的；激烈的
【例】It is urgent that the *acute* problem of air pollution in the city be solved. 该城市空气污染这一严重问题亟待解决。

deceive [dɪ'siːv] *v.* 欺骗(trick)
【记】词根记忆：de (变坏) + ceive (拿，抓) → 用不好的手段拿 → 欺骗
【例】Mary *deceived* the interviewer about her past experience. 玛丽就她过去的经历欺骗了面试官。
【派】deceptive(*a.* 欺骗性的)

deceive

tow [to] *v. /n.* 拖，牵引(pull)
【记】联想记忆：拉(tow)弓(bow)射箭
【例】Could you please give me a *tow*? 你能拉我一把吗?

tow

☐ acute ☐ deceive ☐ tow

编写大量词根记忆法，考生可举一反三，达到事半功倍的效果。

联想记忆通过单词的分拆、谐音和词与词之间的联系将难词化简、联想成串，轻松高效地记忆单词。

每页底部设置返记菜单，考生结束每页学习后可以及时地进行复习和自测，有助于对单词的全面掌握。

发音记忆是一种记忆单词的快捷方法，辅助记忆成效显著。

与托福考试难度相当的例句可以帮助考生记忆单词、熟悉考试难度。

丰富派生词，横向扩充词汇量。

hazard [ˈhæzəd] *n.* 危险(*danger); 风险(risk)

【记】发音记忆："骇人的" → 危险

【例】Cora reefs have always been one of the greatest *hazards* to ships sailing in tropical seas. 珊瑚暗礁对在热带海洋航行的船只来说向来是最大的威胁之一。

【派】hazardous(*a.* 危险的，冒险的)

virus [ˈvaɪrəs] *n.* 病毒

【记】发音记忆："娃弱死" → 小孩子身体弱，被病毒感染死掉了 → 病毒

【例】The *virus* replicates by attaching to a cell and injecting its nucleic acid. 病毒附着在细胞上，并往其中输入核酸来实现复制。

radiate [ˈreɪdɪeɪt] *v.* 发出(热量); 辐射

【记】词根记忆：radi(光线) + ate → 发出光线 → 发出(热量); 辐射

【派】radiation(*n.* 辐射); radiator(*n.* 暖气装置); radial(*a.* 放射状的); radiant(*a.* 光芒四射的)

radiate

compel [kəmˈpel] *v.* 驱使(drive)

【记】词根记忆：com + pel(驱使) → 驱使

【例】Beads come in shapes, colors, and materials that almost *compel* one to handle them and to sort them. 珠子的形状、色彩和材料各异，驱使人们把玩挑选。

【派】compelling(*a.* 引人注目的)

【参】dispel(*vt.* 驱散); impel(*vt.* 推动); repel(*vt.* 击退); expel(*v.* 开除)

intelligence [ɪnˈtelɪdʒəns] *n.* 智力; 聪明

【记】来自intelligent(*a.* 聪明的; 理智的)

【搭】intelligence quotient 智商; an intelligence agent 情报员

【例】Scientists think dolphin has a higher *intelligence* than ordinary mammals. 科学家认为海豚的智商比普通哺乳动物的要高。

【派】intelligencer(*n.* 情报员)

convince [kənˈvɪns] *v.* 使确信，说服(persuade, assure)

【记】词根记忆：con(全部) + vince(征服，克服) → 彻底征服对方 → 使确信

【例】She *convinced* the man to apply to graduate school. 她说服了这名男子向研究院提出申请。

【派】convincing(*a.* 令人信服的); unconvincing(*a.* 不令人信服的)

MP3

□ hazard　　□ virus　　□ radiate　　□ compel　　□ intelligence　　□ convince

配有 249 分钟录音 MP3 光盘一张，对所有英文单词以及中文释义进行了朗读。视、听两种感官的结合能有效提高对单词的理解能力和记忆效果。

归纳常考的词组和搭配，帮助考生抓住考试的重点。

针对听力、阅读，归纳、精选词汇。

目　录

核心单词表

Word List　1 ……………………………………………………… 1

Word List　2 ……………………………………………………… 12

Word List　3 ……………………………………………………… 24

Word List　4 ……………………………………………………… 36

Word List　5 ……………………………………………………… 48

Word List　6 ……………………………………………………… 60

Word List　7 ……………………………………………………… 71

Word List　8 ……………………………………………………… 82

Word List　9 ……………………………………………………… 93

Word List　10 ……………………………………………………… 103

Word List　11 ……………………………………………………… 114

Word List　12 ……………………………………………………… 125

Word List　13 ……………………………………………………… 136

Word List　14 ……………………………………………………… 147

Word List　15 ……………………………………………………… 158

Word List　16 ……………………………………………………… 169

Word List　17 ……………………………………………………… 180

Word List　18 ……………………………………………………… 191

Word List　19 ……………………………………………………… 202

Word List　20 ……………………………………………………… 213

Word List　21 ……………………………………………………… 223

Word List　22 ……………………………………………………… 234

Word List　23 ……………………………………………………… 245

Word List 24 ·································· 256

Word List 25 ·································· 266

Word List 26 ·································· 276

Word List 27 ·································· 287

Word List 28 ·································· 299

Word List 29 ·································· 310

Word List 30 ·································· 321

Word List 31 ·································· 331

Word List 32 ·································· 342

Word List 33 ·································· 353

Word List 34 ·································· 364

Word List 35 ·································· 375

Word List 36 ·································· 386

Word List 37 ·································· 396

Word List 38 ·································· 407

Word List 39 ·································· 418

Word List 40 ·································· 428

Word List 41 ·································· 440

Word List 42 ·································· 451

Word List 43 ·································· 461

Word List 44 ·································· 472

Word List 45 ·································· 484

索引 ·································· 495

核心单词表　*Word List 1*

词根、词缀预习表

crev	裂开	crevice	*n.* 缺口，裂缝
de	否定	debate	*n./v.* 辩论；讨论，争论
dis	离开	discharge	*n.* 流出物，放电 *v.* 释放
juven	年轻	juvenile	*a.* 少年的；幼稚的 *n.* 少年；幼体
sur	超过	surplus	*n.* 过剩，盈余
mari	海	maritime	*a.* 海的，航海的
pre	前	predominant	*a.* 支配的，主要的
radi	光线	radiation	*n.* 辐射
sol	独自	solo	*a.* 单独的 *n.* 独奏曲
tend	伸展	tendency	*n.* 倾向，趋向

accomplishment [ə'kɑːmplɪʃmənt] *n.* 成就；完成

【例】A: Let me tell you, I'm really happy I got that scholarship, but I wish my parents would stop bragging to everybody.

B: What, that's quite an *accomplishment*. If you ask me, I think you deserve a little bit recognition.

A：让我来告诉你吧，得到奖学金真让我开心，但是我希望父母别再向每个人炫耀这件事了。

B：是吗，这的确了不起。如果你问我的话，我觉得你应该得到一些赞誉。

acronym ['ækrənɪm] *n.* 首字母缩写词（abbreviation）

【记】词根记忆：acro(高) + nym(名称) → 把高出小写字母的大写字母放在一起 → 首字母缩写词

acute [ə'kjuːt] *a.* 极度的；(事情)激烈的(*intense)，剧烈的；敏锐的(keen)；严重的

【记】分拆联想：a + cut(切) + e → 一刀切 → 极度的；激烈的

【例】It is urgent that the *acute* problem of air pollution in the city be solved. 该城市空气污染这一严重问题亟待解决。

adhere [əd'hɪr] *vi.* 黏附(*stick)；坚持(cling)

【记】词根记忆：ad(加强) + her(黏附) + e → 黏附；坚持

【例】Some of sizable ice crystals *adhere* to each other to create a cluster of ice crystals or a snowflake. 一些大小相当的冰晶体粘附在一起，形成一簇冰晶体或一片雪花。

【派】adhesion (*n.* 黏附；黏附力；黏连(物))

aggression [ə'greʃn] *n.* 侵略(invasion)；敌对的情绪或行为

【记】词根记忆：ag + gress(走) + ion → 走到别的国家 → 侵略

【例】Within this colony, there is little *aggression* among ants from different nests. 在这个蚁群当中，来自不同蚁巢的蚂蚁之间很少有攻击行为。

artistic [ɑːr'tɪstɪk] *a.* 艺术(家)的(aesthetical)

【例】We'll see many *artistic* works depicting the major events of her life. 我们将看到描写她一生主要事件的艺术作品。

【派】artistically(*ad.* 艺术地)

【参】artistry(*n.* 艺术技巧)

awareness [ə'wernəs] *n.* 知道，注意(*realization)

【记】来自aware(*a.* 知道的，意识到的)

【搭】self-awareness自我意识；public awareness公共意识

balance ['bæləns] *vt.* 使平衡，使均衡(equilibrate)
n. 天平，称；平衡(equilibrium)；差额；余款

【记】联想记忆：bal(看作ball，球) + ance → 球操选手需要很好的平衡能力 → 平衡

【搭】lose one's balance 失去平衡；balance oneself 保持自身平衡；a balance of nature 自然平衡；maintain balance 保持平衡

【例】Winds are the natural way of *balancing* uneven distribution of air pressure over the earth. 风是平衡地球气压分配不均的自然方式。// A *balanced* meal consists of five key elements: proteins, carbohydrate, fats, vitamins and minerals. 平衡的膳食包括五个关键的要素：蛋白质、碳水化合物、脂肪、维生素和矿物质。

【派】counterbalance(*n.* 平衡力 *vt.* 使平衡)；well-balanced(*a.* 营养均衡的)

brochure [broʊ'ʃʊr] *n.* 小册子(pamphlet, booklet)

careless ['kerləs] *a.* 粗心的，疏忽的(negligent)

【例】The police claimed that the serious traffic accident resulted from a *careless* driver. 警方声称一名粗心的司机导致了这起严重的交通事故。

| adhere | aggression | artistic | awareness | balance | brochure |
| careless |

【派】carelessly(*ad.* 不注意地；粗心地)

chimpanzee [ˌtʃɪmpæn'zi:] *n.* 黑猩猩

collective [kə'lektɪv] *a.* 集体的，共同的(common)
【例】The decision, made by the board of directors, is the result of *collective* agreement. 董事会做出决定的结果是集体同意。

conductivity [ˌkɑːndʌk'tɪvəti] *n.* 传导性
【例】The nerve cells exhibit to a great degree the phenomena of *conductivity.* 神经细胞在很大程度上展示出传导性的现象。

congestion [kən'dʒestʃən] *n.* 拥塞(clog)
【记】来自congest(*v.* 充满，充塞)
【派】congested (*a.* 拥挤的)
【参】conversion(*n.* 转化；换算)

convince [kən'vɪns] *v.* 使确信，说服(persuade, assure)
【记】词根记忆：con(全部) + vince(征服，克服) → 彻底征服对方 → 使确信
【例】She *convinced* the man to apply to graduate school. 她说服了这名男子向研究生院提出申请。
【派】convincing(*a.* 令人信服的)；unconvincing(*a.* 不令人信服的)

council ['kaʊnsl] *n.* 理事会，委员会
【记】Security Council (联合国)安理会

crevice ['krevɪs] *n.* 缺口，裂缝(gap)
【记】词根记忆：crev(裂开) + ice → 裂缝

crossing ['krɔːsɪŋ] *n.* 横越，交叉口
【搭】level crossing=grade crossing (铁路、公路交汇的)平交道口；平面交叉；a river crossing 河流交叉口
【参】crossroad(*n.* 十字路口)；intersection(*n.* 十字路口，交叉口)

curriculum [kə'rɪkjələm] *n.* [*pl.* curricula] 课程(course)

debate [dɪ'beɪt] *n. /v.* 辩论(argue)；讨论，争论(discuss, dispute)
【记】词根记忆：de(否定) + bat(打，击) + e → 否定并打击对手 → 辩论
【例】The two parties are *debating* politics on the radio. 两党派正在广播电台就政治议题进行辩论。
【派】debatable(*a.* 有争执的)

deficiency [dɪ'fɪʃnsi] *n.* 不足，缺乏(lack)
【记】来自deficient(*a.* 不足的，缺乏的)
【搭】deficiency symptom 营养缺乏症状
【例】Vitamin D *deficiency* can lead to serious bone diseases. 缺乏维生素D会导致严重的骨骼疾病。

☐ chimpanzee	☐ collective	☐ conductivity	☐ congestion	☐ convince	☐ council
☐ crevice	☐ crossing	☐ curriculum	☐ debate	☐ deficiency	

【参】sufficiency(*n.* 充足)

◦ **devotion** [dɪ'voʊʃn] *n.* 热爱；投入(passion)；献身，奉献(dedication)

【记】来自devote(*vt.* 将…奉献给；把…专用于)

【例】We all appreciated the new employee's *devotion* of much time to the project. 我们都感激这位新员工，他对项目投入了大量时间。

◦ **discharge** ['dɪstʃɑːrdʒ] *n.* 流出物；放电 [dɪs'tʃɑːrdʒ] *v.* 释放(release)

【记】词根记忆：dis(离开) + charge(充电) → 放电

【例】Are you in any pain or is there any *discharge* in your ears? 你有痛感吗？你耳朵里是否有分泌物？//If too much volcanic heat is *discharged*, the crater's ice pack will melt away entirely. 如果释放出过多火山热量，火山口的冰层就会完全融化。

dispute [dɪ'spjuːt] *n.* 争论(*argument)；纠纷 *v.* 争论(debate)

【记】词根记忆：dis(不) + put(思考) + e → 思考不同 → 争论

【例】The village chief dealt with land *disputes* and religious affairs. 村长负责处理土地纠纷和宗教事务。//It would be hard to *dispute* that he manipulated space extremely well. 他对空间的操控非常娴熟，这一点难以辩驳。

【参】disrepute(*n.* 坏名声)

diverse [daɪ'vɜːrs] *a.* 不同的(*different)；多样的(*varied, various)

【记】词根记忆：di(离开) + vers(转) + e → 转开 → 不同的

diverse

【例】The researcher observed babies and their mothers in six *diverse* cultures. 研究人员观察了属于6个不同文化的婴儿及其母亲。

◦ **doctrine** ['dɑːktrɪn] *n.* 教条，教义(dogma, teachings)；学说(theory)

【例】For a while in the United States, laisser faire was a popular *doctrine*. 自由主义在美国有一段时期曾经是风靡一时的学说。

endless ['endləs] *a.* 无止境的(everlasting, eternal)

enforce [ɪn'fɔːrs] *v.* 实施，执行(carry out)；强迫(compel)

【记】分拆联想：en（使…）+ force（力量）→ 使有力量 → 实施，执行

【例】Dr. White *enforces* strict deadlines on lab work. 怀特博士对实验室的工作执行着严格的期限。

| ☐ devotion | ☐ discharge | ☐ dispute | ☐ diverse | ☐ doctrine | ☐ endless |
| ☐ enforce | | | | | |

a **essentially** [ɪˈsenʃəli] *ad.* 本质上，基本上(basically)

【例】We all know what an advertisement is, and it's *essentially* a message that announces something for sale. 我们都知道广告是什么，其本质就是一则宣布某物出售的信息。//The moon and the earth are composed of *essentially* the same minerals. 月球和地球基本上是由相同的矿物质组成的。

expire [ɪkˈspaɪər] *vi.* 到期；去世

【记】联想记忆：ex + pire(看作spire，呼吸)→没了呼吸→去世

【例】Ronald has to renew his passport because it is *expired*. 罗纳德的护照过期了，他不得不去续签。

【参】aspire(*v.* 热望，立志)；perspire(*v.* 出汗，流汗)

fare [fer] *n.* 费用(charge) *v.* 进展(evolve)

【例】How are you *faring* with your project? 你的项目进展如何？

flat [flæt] *a.* 平(坦)的(smooth) *n.* 平地，平面

【例】In ancient times, many people believed the earth was a *flat* disc. 古时候很多人认为地球是个扁平的圆盘。

【派】flattish(*a.* 稍平的)

forward [ˈfɔːrwərd] *ad.* 向前，前进 *a.* 向前的，前部的；进步的 *v.* 转交，转递

【搭】look forward to sth./doing 期盼…

【例】A: I'm pretty excited. The outdoor club is going hiking this weekend.

B: Yes. Finally, I've been looking *forward* to it all year.

A：我特别激动。户外俱乐部在这个周末要去远足。

B：是啊。终于成行了，我都盼了有一年了。

向前向前向前～
我们的队伍向太阳～

forward

foul [faʊl] *a.* 污秽的，肮脏的(disgusting, filthy)

【记】联想记忆：邪恶的(foul)心灵(soul)

【例】The teachers were all shocked by the boy's *foul* language and behaviors. 老师们都被这个男孩的污言秽语和不良行径惊呆了。

a **glow** [gloʊ] *v.* 发光(*shine)

【派】glowing(*a.* 白热的；通红的；发亮的)

gym [dʒɪm] *n.* 健身房；体育馆

【搭】go to the gym 去健身

【例】A: Have you been to the new *gym* since it opened?

B: Are you kidding? Tomorrow is the deadline for my project.

essentially	expire	fare	flat	forward	foul
glow	gym				

A：新健身房开放之后你去过没有？

B：你在开玩笑吗？明天是我的项目的截止日期。

A: Can you please tell me where I'd find *gym* shoes?

B: Yes, they'd be in the sportswear department at the back of the store.

A：你能告诉我哪里能找到运动鞋吗？

B：当然，在商店后面的运动装专区。

honest [ˈɑːnɪst] *a.* 诚实的；正直的(upright)；老实的

【搭】to be honest 老实说，实话实说

【例】To be *honest,* I haven't read the science fiction you borrowed me last week. 实话实说，我还没读你上周借给我的那本科幻小说。

A: Umm... are you going to try some of this chocolate pudding? It's incredible.

B: Well, to be *honest* with you, I've never been a big fan of chocolate.

A：嗯…你想尝点巧克力布丁吗？太好吃了。

B：算了，说实话，我向来都不怎么爱吃巧克力。

improve [ɪmˈpruːv] *v.* 改善，改进，增进；好转，进步

【例】A: Emh, coffee in this restaurant is really *improved*. They must have changed suppliers.

B: Really? You can taste differences?

A：嗯，这个饭店的咖啡的确更好喝了。他们肯定换了供应商。

B：真的吗？你能品尝出不同？

【参】approve(*v.* 赞成，批准)

interest [ˈɪntrəst] *n.* 兴趣；利息；[常pl.]权益，利益(benefit)

【例】Chisholm was known for advocating the *interests* of the urban poor. 齐泽姆因维护城市贫民的利益而闻名。

investigate [ɪnˈvestɪɡeɪt] *vt.* 研究；调查(*check, probe)

【记】分拆联想：invest(投资)+i+gate(大门)→想入投资大门先做市场调查→研究；调查

【例】The program will *investigate* how the brain functions and malfunctions. 这个项目将研究大脑如何运作以及如何失控。

【派】investigation(*n.* 调查，研究)

juvenile [ˈdʒuːvənl] *n.* 少年；【生】幼体 *a.* 少年的；未成熟的；幼稚的

【记】词根记忆：juven(年轻)+ile(…的)→年轻的→幼体

【参】larva(*n.* 幼虫)

load

load [loʊd] *n.* 负荷(量)，负担(*weight) *vt.* 装载；使负担(burden)

【例】Leslie has a heavier course *load* than usual this term. 莱斯利这个学期的课业负担比往常重。//They *loaded* my suitcases on the last plane. 他们把我的行李箱装上了最后一架飞机。

log [lɔːg] *n.* 圆木；木材(timber, wood)

manage [ˈmænɪdʒ] *v.* 操纵，控制；管理(*preside over, *administer)

【记】词根记忆：man(手) + age(行为) → 用手做 → 操纵，控制

【例】She wasn't able to *manage* the project well. 她没有能力管理好这个项目。

【派】manageable(*a.* 易管理的；易处理的)；management(*n.* 管理)

maritime [ˈmærɪtaɪm] *a.* 海的；航海的

【记】词根记忆：mari(海) + time → 海的；航海的

【例】The peopling of the Pacific Islands has been described as the greatest feat of *maritime* colonization in human history. 太平洋岛屿上的人口定居被称为人类历史上海洋殖民最伟大的壮举。

mat [mæt] *n.* 垫子(rug, cushion)；草席

【记】联想记忆：头上戴帽子(hat)，下面坐垫子(mat)

obstruct [əbˈstrʌkt] *vt.* 妨碍，阻塞(impede, block)

【记】词根记忆：ob(反) + struct(建造) → 反建造 → 妨碍，阻塞

【例】Skyscrapers and television reception *obstruct* air traffic. 摩天大楼和电视接收装置妨碍空中交通。

【派】obstruction(*n.* 阻碍，障碍物)；unobstructed(*a.* 畅通的)

overcharge [ˌoʊvərˈtʃɑːrdʒ] *v.* 讨价过高，索价过高；使过量装填；渲染，夸张 *n.* 过高的要价；过重的负担；超载

【记】词根记忆：over(过度) + charge(收费) → 索价过高

【例】Some car mechanics, if they think that someone doesn't know much about cars, might try to *overcharge* that person. 一些汽车修理工如果认为某人对车不太了解，就会设法多收这个人的钱。

partly [ˈpɑːrtlɪ] *ad.* 部分地，不完全地

【例】Many young people quit school and go to work *partly* because they live in poverty. 很多年轻人辍学就业的部分原因是生活贫困。

pollen [ˈpɑːlən] *n.* 花粉

predominant [prɪˈdɑːmɪnənt] *a.* 支配的；主要的(dominant, principal)

【记】分拆联想：pre(前) + dominant(统治的) → 在前面统治的 → 支配的

【例】Dark blue is the *predominant* color in the prince's room. 深蓝色是王子房间里的主要颜色。

【派】predominantly(*ad.* 主要地；大多数)

| □ log | □ manage | □ maritime | □ mat | □ obstruct | □ overcharge |
| □ partly | □ pollen | □ predominant | | | |

prevalent [ˈprevələnt] *a.* 流行的，普遍的(*common, universal)

【记】词根记忆: pre(前) + val(强壮的) + ent → 走在前面且强有力的 → 流行的

【例】Colds are *prevalent* in the winter. 感冒在冬天流行。

protagonist [prəˈtægənɪst] *n.* (戏剧、故事、小说中的)主角; 领导者

【记】词根记忆: prot(首先) + agon(打，行动) + ist → 首先行动者 → 领导者

【参】stooge(*n.* 配角，陪衬)

radiation [ˌreɪdiˈeɪʃn] *n.* 辐射

【记】词根记忆: radi(光线) + ation(表状态) → 光线呈放射状 → 辐射

【搭】solar radiation 太阳辐射; radiation therapy 放射疗法

【例】Because it spends a lot of time in the intense tropical sun, the grass mouse has also evolved two separate safeguards against the sun's ultraviolet *radiation*. 由于草鼠长时间待在强烈的热带阳光下，它演化出了两套防止紫外线辐射的安全措施。//When the quartz crystal in a heater vibrates at a particular frequency, its energy is turned into infrared *radiation*. 加热器中的石英晶体以某个频率振动时，其能量就能转化为红外辐射。

rehabilitate [ˌriːəˈbɪlɪteɪt] *v.* 使恢复原状，修复(restore)

【记】词根记忆: re(再，重新) + hab(拥有) + ilit + ate → 重新拥有 → 使恢复原状，修复

【例】San Antonio's leaders *rehabilitated* existing structures. 圣安东尼奥的领导人们修复了现存的结构。

【派】rehabilitation(*n.* 恢复，复原)

renovate [ˈrenəveɪt] *vt.* 修复(restore)

【记】词根记忆: re(重新) + nov(新的) + ate → 重新焕然一新 → 修复

【例】They have completely *renovated* the restaurant. 他们已经彻底整修了这家饭店。

【派】renovation(*n.* 修复，整修)

sapphire [ˈsæfaɪər] *n.* 蓝宝石

scatter [ˈskætər] *v.* 分散，驱散(*irregularly distribute, disperse)

【例】Over 25,000 islands are *scattered* across the surface of the Pacific. 太平洋上散布着超过2.5万座岛屿。

【派】scattered(*a.* 分散的)

sensual [ˈsenʃuəl] *a.* 感觉的; 感官的

【记】词根记忆: sens(感觉) + ual → 感觉的

prevalent	protagonist	radiation	rehabilitate	renovate	sapphire
scatter	sensual				

【例】The purpose of a poem need not inform the reader of anything, but rather to evoke feelings, to create a *sensual* pleasing experience. 诗不需要让读者了解什么，其目的应该是激发情感，产生感官上的愉悦体验。

shellfish [ˈʃelfɪʃ] *n.* 贝；有壳的水生动物

【例】*Shellfish* always attach themselves to huge rocks. 贝类经常将自己贴附在大石块上。

shuttle [ˈʃʌtl] *n.* 航天飞机

【搭】space shuttle（往返于地球和太空站之间运载人和物资的）航天飞机

sodium [ˈsoʊdiəm] *n.* 【化】钠

solo [ˈsoʊloʊ] *a.* 单独的(sole) *n.* 独奏(曲)

【记】词根记忆：sol(独自) + o → 独奏

【派】soloist(*n.* 独奏者；独唱者)

spice [spaɪs] *n.* 香料，调味品(season, flavor)

【派】spicy(*a.* 辣的；有风味的)

stretch [stretʃ] *v.* 延伸，拉长(*extend) *n.* 一段路程；延伸

【搭】stretch out 开始大踏步走；伸手

【例】The whole 150-mile *stretch* is influenced by tides from the Atlantic Ocean. 整个150英里的路程受到大西洋潮汐的影响。

strive [straɪv] *vi.* 奋斗，努力(struggle)；力求

【记】分拆联想：s + trive(看作drive，动力) → 奋斗需要动力

【搭】strive for 奋斗，争取

【例】Like all artists, jazz musicians *strive* for an individual style. 爵士音乐家如同所有艺术家一样，都力求体现个人风格。

【参】stride(*v.* 大步走)

stylistic [staɪˈlɪstɪk] *a.* 格式上的；体裁上的

surplus [ˈsɜːrpləs] *n.* 过剩，盈余(excess)

【记】词根记忆：sur(超过) + plus(加；多余的) → 过剩

【例】*Surpluses* of food could also be bartered for other commodities. 剩余的食品也能用来交换其他的商品。

sweep [swiːp] *v.* 打扫(clean)；席卷 *n.* 摆动(swing)

【例】The students in the laboratory helped *sweep* up the glass. 实验室里的学生帮着把玻璃擦干净了。

syllable [ˈsɪləbl] *n.* 音节

【记】分拆联想：syll(音似：say) + able (可以…的) → 可以说出来的 → 音节

□ shellfish	□ shuttle	□ sodium	□ solo	□ spice	□ stretch
□ strive	□ stylistic	□ surplus	□ sweep	□ syllable	

temporary ['tempəreri] *a.* 暂(临)时的(*existing)

【记】词根记忆: tempor(时间) + ary → 时间很短 → 暂时的

【例】She must have been a *temporary* worker. 她肯定是个临时工。

【派】temporarily(*ad.* 临时地, 暂时地)

tendency ['tendənsi] *n.* 倾向, 趋向(inclination, trend)

【记】词根记忆: tend(伸展) + ency → 向…伸展 → 倾向, 趋向

【例】There has been a *tendency* to romanticize the accomplishments of the Group. 现今存在一种将该集团的成就传奇化的倾向。

term [tɜːrm] *n.* 学期(semester); 期限; 期间; 条件, 条款(clause); 术语 *v.* 把…称作

【搭】in terms of 按照, 依据; 在…方面

【例】If you compare the earth and the moon in *terms* of substance, you will find the moon isn't much like the earth. 如果从物质的角度比较地球和月球, 你会发现月球和地球不太像。

tow [toʊ] *v. /n.* 拖, 牵引(pull)

【记】联想记忆: 拉(tow)弓(bow)射箭

【例】Could you please give me a *tow*? 你能拉我一把吗?

tow

trial ['traɪəl] *n.* 审讯; 试验, 考验(test)

【记】联想记忆: 加紧审讯(trial), 追查踪迹(trail)

【搭】trial class 实验课; bring sb. to trial 审判某人; clinical trials 临床实验; medical trials 医学实验

【例】A: Would you like to try the new seafood restaurant tonight? I hear it's very good.

B: I have to give a presentation tomorrow and I need to do a *trial* run.

A: 你今晚想去新开的海鲜餐厅吗? 我听说那里很不错。

B: 我明天要做个报告, 今晚需要演练一次。

A: I've got to give my oral presentation in class tomorrow and I'm so nervous.

B: Maybe you just need a *trial* run. Why don't you use me as your audience?

A: 我明天得在课堂上做口头报告, 心里很紧张。

B: 你试着演练一次没准就不紧张了。为什么不把我当作你的听众呢?

unearth [ʌn'ɜːrθ] *vt.* 掘出(dig out)

【例】They did *unearth* the bones of a 45-foot-long dinosaur. 他们的确挖掘出了有着45英尺身长的恐龙的骨骼。

varnish ['vɑːrnɪʃ] *vt.* 上清漆

【记】联想记忆：擦亮(burnish)之后涂上清漆(varnish)

【例】The main task of the limners was to *varnish* furniture. 画匠的主要任务是给家具上清漆。

【派】varnished(*a.* 上过清漆的)

wipe [waɪp] *v./n.* 擦，揩，抹

【搭】wipe out 抹掉，擦去，除去；消灭，毁灭

【例】A: Professor Jones, last night when I was putting the finishing touches on my paper, that electrical storm completely *wiped* out my computer files. Do you think I could have another day to retype it?

B: I'm sorry, Steven. I'm leaving for a conference tomorrow and I'll be away for two weeks. I suppose you could send it to me there.

A：琼斯教授，昨天晚上我就快写完论文了，可那场雷暴把我电脑里的文件全部破坏了。您能宽限一天让我重新打一遍吗？

B：听到这个消息很为你感到难过，斯蒂文。我明天要外出两周开会。我想你可以给我寄过去。

The people who get on in this world are the people who get up and look for circumstances they want, and if they cannot find them, make them.

在这个世界上取得成功的人，都努力去寻找他们想要的机会，如果找不到时，他们就自己创造机会。 ——萧伯纳(*Bernard Shaw*)

Word List 2 🔘 MP3-02

词根、词缀预习表

abili	能	ability	*n.* 能力
cord	心	accord	*n.* 一致,符合
ceive	拿	deceive	*v.* 欺骗
ign	点燃	igneous	*a.* 火的;[地](指岩石)火成的
inter	在…之间	interpret	*v.* 解释
leg	法律	legitimate	*a.* 合法的,正当的
liter	文字	literacy	*n.* 识字,有文化
mon	单个	monarch	*n.* 君主
mut	变	mutual	*a.* 相互的;共有的
para	类似	parallel	*a.* 相似的;平行的

ability [əˈbɪləti] *n.* 能力,才干(capacity)

【记】词根记忆:abili(能)+ ty(名词)→ 能力

【搭】have the ability to do sth. 有做…事的能力;academic ability 学习能力,研究能力

【例】You will be given the *ability* to recognize your own apprehension, to analyze and to draw a conclusion. 你将被给予能力来认识自己的见解,进行分析并得出结论。

【派】able(*a.* 有才能的,能干的)

【参】liability(*n.* 责任,义务;倾向;债务,负债);reliability(*n.* 可靠性)

accord [əˈkɔːrd] *n.* 一致,符合(agreement)

【记】词根记忆:ac + cord(心)→ 使双方都称心 → 一致,符合

【例】An *accord* with the labor union was reached at about midnight. 大约在午夜的时候与工会达成了一致。

【参】concord(*n.* 和谐)

additive [ˈædətɪv] *a.* 添加的;加法的 *n.* 添加剂

【记】分拆联想:add(加)+ itive → 添加的;添加剂

【搭】food without additives 不含添加剂的食品

affection [əˈfekʃn] *n.* 喜爱(fondness)；影响(influence)

【记】来自affect(*v.* 影响，感染)

【派】affectionate(*a.* 爱的，挚爱的)

alike [əˈlaɪk] *a.* 相同的，相似的(same, similar)

【记】词根记忆：a(加强) + like(相似的) → 相似的

【搭】look alike 看起来像

【派】alikeness(*n.* 相像)

alternately [ˈɔːltərnətli] *ad.* (指两种事物)交替地，轮流地；间隔地，每隔一个地

【搭】alternately spaced 交互排列

【例】The two traditional methods can be used *alternately* during the manufacturing process. 这两种传统方法可以在生产过程中交替使用。

behaviorism [bɪˈheɪvjərɪzəm] *n.* 行为主义

【例】Many people consider John Watson to be the founder of *behaviorism*. 很多人认为约翰·沃森是行为主义的创始人。

biologist [baɪˈɑːlədʒɪst] *n.* 生物学家

【例】Cantor, at the age of 50, had a world-wide reputation as a cell *biologist*. 坎托在50岁的时候成为了举世闻名的细胞生物学家。

【参】anthropologist (*n.* 人类学家)；archaeologist (*n.* 考古学家)；sociologist(*n.* 社会学家)

budget [ˈbʌdʒɪt] *n.* 预算

【例】They should ask for an increase in the *budget*. 他们应该要求增加预算。

calendar [ˈkælɪndər] *n.* (日、月)历；日程表

【记】分拆联想：cal(看作call，叫) + end(尽头) + ar → 一年到头对日子的叫法 →(日、月)历

【例】It's an exhibition of wildlife art *calendar* from about a hundred years ago. 这是一个关于大约100年前的野生动物艺术日历的展览。

coil [kɔɪl] *n.* 卷，线圈(wire) *vt.* 盘绕(to wind into rings or spirals)

【记】分拆联想：c + oil(油) → 油烧开了就出现一圈一圈的波纹 → 线圈

联想记忆：硬币(coin)和线圈(coil)都是圆的

colleague [ˈkɑːliːg] *n.* 同事，同僚

【记】分拆联想：col(共同) + league(联盟) → 工作于同一个联盟 → 同事

colleague

☐ affection	☐ alike	☐ alternately	☐ behaviorism	☐ biologist	☐ budget
☐ calendar	☐ coil	☐ colleague			

13

composer [kəmˈpoʊzər] *n.* 作曲家

【例】He doesn't know many *composers* of classical music. 他并不了解多少古典音乐的作曲家。//The director got a South African *composer* to write songs with a distinct African sound. 导演找了一位南非作曲家来创作带有独特非洲风格的歌曲。

composition [ˌkɑːmpəˈzɪʃn] *n.* 成分(component)；构成(composing)；作品，作文(works, writing)

【搭】mineral composition 矿物成分

【参】decomposition(*n.* 分解)

dairy [ˈderi] *n.* 牛奶场；奶制品

【记】和daily(*ad.* 每天)一起记

【搭】dairy product 乳制品；dairy cattle 乳牛；dairy farming 乳品业

deadline [ˈdedlaɪn] *n.* 最后期限，截止时间

【记】组合词：dead(死) + line(线) → 最后期限

deal [diːl] *n.* 数量，程度；交易(transaction, business)；份量 *v.* 处理(handle)；给予；做买卖，经营

【搭】a good deal (of) 许多；deal with 处理；deal in 经营

【例】A: I just got this car and already it's falling apart. First, one of the door handles fell off and now the inside light won't go on when you open the door.

B: Hey, what's the big *deal*? Falling apart is when your car needs a new engine, like mine does.

A: 我这辆车刚买就快散架了。先是一个门把手掉了，现在打开车门时里面的灯也不亮了。

B: 嗨，这有什么大不了的？车需要新发动机的时候才算散架，就像我的车一样。

Today we'll *deal* with music played by small jazz bands. 今天我们来了解小型爵士乐队演奏的音乐。//When the water hit the nearly vertical face of the seawall, it carries back a great *deal* of sand. 当海水撞击到海堤几乎垂直的表面时，卷回了大量的沙子。

【派】dealer(*n.* 经销商)；dealing(*n.* 行为；交易)

deceive [dɪˈsiːv] *v.* 欺骗(trick)

【记】词根记忆：de（变坏）+ ceive（拿，抓）→ 用不好的手段拿 → 欺骗

deceive

【例】Mary *deceived* the interviewer about her past experience. 玛丽就她过去的经历欺骗了面试官。

【派】deceptive(*a.* 欺骗性的)

distant [ˈdɪstənt] *a.* 远离的，遥远的(faraway, remote)；疏远的

【记】词根记忆：dis(分开) + tant → 分开了的 → 疏远的

【派】distance(*n.* 距离)

【参】instant(*a.* 立即的)

dramatic [drəˈmætɪk] *a.* 引人注目的(*striking)；戏剧性的(theatrical)；生动的(vivid)

【记】来自drama(*n.* 戏剧)

【例】He made a *dramatic* shift from the classical tradition to the arts and crafts movement. 他做出了一个从古典传统到工艺美术运动的戏剧性转变。//*Dramatic* activities require the use of costumes. 戏剧活动需要使用戏装。

【派】dramatically(*ad.* 戏剧性地，引人注目地)

erosion [ɪˈroʊʒn] *n.* 腐蚀，磨损，侵蚀(corrosion)；削弱，减少

【记】词根记忆：e + ros(咬) + ion → 咬掉 → 腐蚀

【搭】swale erosion 洼地侵蚀；the erosion of coastal area 沿海地区的减少

【例】Your professor has asked me to talk to you today about the topic that should be of real concern to civil engineers: the *erosion* of the US beaches. 你的教授让我今天和你谈谈土木工程师真正应该关心的问题：美国海岸遇到的侵蚀。

explosive [ɪkˈsploʊsɪv] *a.* 爆炸(性)的，爆发(性)的；使人冲动的，导致猛烈爆发的 *n.* 爆炸物，炸药

【搭】an explosive situation 一触即发的形势；an explosive news 爆炸性新闻

【例】The balloon's inflated with helium unlike the original, which was filled with hydrogen and unbeknown to the pilot, potentially *explosive*. 充满氦气的气球与原本充满氢气的气球不同，飞行员不知道这有可能爆炸。

forestall [fɔːrˈstɔːl] *vt.* 预防，预先阻止

【记】词根记忆：fore (前面；预先) + stall(停止) → 预先停止 → 预防

fume [fjuːm] *n.* 臭气；烟；激怒 *v.* 熏；冒烟

【记】词根记忆：fum(烟) + e → 烟

igneous [ˈɪgniəs] *a.* (地理)火的，火成的

【记】词根记忆：ign(点燃) + eous → 火的

immutable [ɪˈmjuːtəbl] *a.* 不变的(*unchangeable)

【记】词根记忆：im(不，无) + mut(变化) + able → 不变的

distant	dramatic	erosion	explosive	forestall	fume
igneous	immutable				

【例】Adjustments in various places show that this standard is not *immutable*. 不同地方的调整显示这个标准并非是一成不变的。

impetus ['ɪmpɪtəs] *n.* 促进，推动（impulse）

【记】词根记忆：im（在…内）+ pet（追求）+ us → 内心追求 → 促进

【例】The danger of the fire gave an *impetus* to the use of more durable material. 火灾的危险推动了更耐火材料的使用。

indicate ['ɪndɪkeɪt] *vt.* 指出，表明（*point）

【记】词根记忆：in + dic（说）+ ate → 说出 → 指出，表明

indicate

【例】When speaking before a group, a person's tone may *indicate* unsureness or fright, confidence or calm. 在一群人面前说话时，一个人的语气可能显示出犹疑、恐惧、自信或镇静。

【派】indication（*n.* 指标；迹象）；indicative（*a.* 指示的）；indicator（*n.* 指示器）

industry ['ɪndəstri] *n.* 勤奋；工业；行业

【例】H. D.'s *industry* and literary achievement are lust beginning to be recognized and appreciated. HD的勤奋和文学成就开始得到人们的认可和赏识。

intelligence [ɪn'telɪdʒəns] *n.* 智力；聪明

【记】来自intelligent（*a.* 聪明的；理智的）

【搭】intelligence quotient 智商；an intelligence agent 情报员

【例】Scientists think dolphin has a higher *intelligence* than ordinary mammals. 科学家认为海豚的智商比普通哺乳动物的要高。

【派】intelligencer（*n.* 情报员）

interpret [ɪn'tɜːrprɪt] *v.* 解释（explain）；理解（comprehend）；表现

【记】词根记忆：inter（在…之间）+ pret → 在两种语言中间说 → 解释

【例】It is difficult for babies to *interpret* emotions. 让婴儿理解情感很难。

【派】interpretation（*n.* 解释；艺术处理）；interpretive（*a.* 解释的；理解的）

intriguing [ɪn'triːgɪŋ] *a.* 引起兴趣（或好奇心）的，吸引人的（*fascinating，*attractive）

【例】The urban life seemed particularly *intriguing* to those raised in rural isolation. 城市生活似乎对在农村偏远地区长大的人来说特别吸引人。

justify [ˈdʒʌstɪfaɪ] *v.* 证明…是正当的

【例】An important task for both of these presidents was to *justify* for their citizens just why the war was necessary. 这两个总统的一项重要任务是向他们的公民证明为何战争是必要的。

legislative [ˈledʒɪsleɪtɪv] *n.* 立法机关 *a.* 立法的；立法机关的

【例】Members of congress have to spend most of their time in Washington taking care of their *legislative* duties. 国会议员大部分时间要待在华盛顿履行立法职责。

legitimate [lɪˈdʒɪtɪmət] *a.* 合法的(legal)；正当的 *v.* (使)合法

【记】词根记忆：leg(法律) + itim* + ate → 合法的；正当的

【例】A: It's the third time this week my roommate had a party in our room. This is really starting to affect my class work. I wonder if I should talk to someone at the housing office about changing rooms.

B: Sounds like you've got a *legitimate* reason. You two are just not compatible at all.

A: 这是我的室友本周在宿舍开的第三次派对了。这真的开始影响我的功课了。我想是否应该和住宿办谈谈换宿舍的事情。

B: 听起来好像你有个正当的理由。你俩根本就处不到一块儿。

literacy [ˈlɪtərəsi] *n.* 识字，有文化，读写能力

【记】词根记忆：liter(文字) + acy → 识字，有文化

床前明月光

有学问

literacy

【例】Franklin's newspaper was especially significant because *literacy* was increasing at the time. 富兰克林的报纸特别重要，因为当时识字的人在增多。

locomotion [ˌloukəˈmouʃn] *n.* 移动(remotion)；运动(movement)

【记】词根记忆：loco(地方) + mot(动) + ion → 从一个地方移动到另一个地方 → 移动；运动

【例】The pterosaurs rely on wind power for their *locomotion*. 翼龙依靠风力来移动。//A great deal can be learned from the actual traces of ancient human *locomotion*. 从古人迁徙的实际路线那里可以了解到很多信息。

longitude [ˈlɑːndʒətuːd] *n.* 经度

【记】联想记忆：long(长) + itude → 连接南北两极的长线叫经线 → 经度

【搭】longitude zone 经度带

【例】Each of the satellites is constantly sending out signals, and each signal contains important information that can be used to determine the *longitude*, latitude and elevation at any point on the earth's surface. 每颗卫星都在一直发送信号，每个信号都包含着重要的信息，这些信息可以用来确定地球表面任何一点的经纬度和海拔。
【参】attitude(*n.* 观点，态度); latitude(*n.* 纬度); altitude(*n.* 海拔，高度)

lower [ˈloʊər] *vt.* 降低(reduce) *a.* 较低的；下级的，下等的(inferior)
【例】Your heart rate is *lowered*. 你的心率降低了。//The study of *lower* animals gives insight into the form and structure of the nervous system of higher animals. 研究低等动物给人们了解高等动物神经系统的形状和结构提供了洞察的机会。
【参】lowering(*a.* 昏暗的)

marked [mɑːrkt] *a.* 显著的(*noticeable, pronounced)
【派】markedly(*ad.* 显著地，明显地)
【例】Crows have *marked* preferences for certain kinds of foods. 乌鸦对某些食物有明显的偏好。
【参】marker(*n.* 标记；里程碑)

modulate [ˈmɑːdʒəleɪt] *v.* 调节(temper, adjust)
【记】词根记忆：mod(方式)＋ulate → 改变方式 → 调节
【例】The ability to *modulate* a chemical signal is limited, compared with communication by visual or acoustic means. 与视觉或听觉交流相比，调节化学信号的能力是受到限制的。

monarch [ˈmɑːnərk] *n.* 君主(ruler, emperor)；大花蝶
【记】词根记忆：mon(单个)＋arch(统治者) → 个人统治 → 君主
【搭】monarch butterfly 黑脉金斑蝶
【派】monarchy(*n.* 君主政体；君主国)

motto [ˈmɑːtoʊ] *n.* 座右铭，箴言，格言(proverb)
【记】词根记忆：mot(动)＋to(给予) → 给予动作的指示 → 座右铭，箴言
【例】The economists' *motto* was laisser faire at that time. 经济学家们当时的座右铭是自由主义。

mutual [ˈmjuːtʃuəl] *a.* 相互的；共有的(joint, common)
【记】词根记忆：mut(变)＋ual → 改变是相互作用的结果 → 相互的；共有的

【例】It is this intense *mutual* engagement that elicits the display of skill and shapes the emerging performance. 正是这种强烈的互动，才使技能展示出来，塑造出逐渐成形的表演。

【派】mutually(*ad.* 互相地)

overall [ˌouvərˈɔːl] *a.* 全面的，综合的 [ˈouvərɔːl] *n.* (套头)工作服，工装裤

【记】组合词: over(从头到尾) + all(所有的) → 全面的，综合的

【例】A creative architect can find ways to incorporate natural landscape into the *overall* design. 富有创意的建筑师可以找到把自然景观融合进整体设计的方法。//In the experiment, the *overall* growth of algae and the number of species dropped. 在实验中，藻类的整体生长和物种的数量都降低了。

overlook [ˌouvərˈluk] *vt.* 俯瞰; 忽略(disregard, neglect); 检查(inspect)

【记】来自词组look over(从⋯上面看; 检查，察看)

【例】We'll have our lunch in a garden restaurant *overlooking* a small park. 我们将在一个能够俯瞰小公园的花园酒店共进午餐。//She overlooked my paper by mistake. 她因为失误而忽略了我的论文。

parallel [ˈpærəlel] *n.* 纬线 *a.* 平行的; 相似的(*similar) *vt.* 与⋯平行，比较

【记】词根记忆: para(类似) + llel → 相似的; 平行的

【派】unparalleled(*a.* 空前的)

paramount [ˈpærəmaunt] *a.* 至上的，极为重要的(foremost)

【记】分析联想: par + amount(数量) → 在量上超过别的 → 极为重要的

【例】Tradition is *paramount*, and change comes infrequently and slowly. 传统是至高无上的，变化的出现并不频繁，也很缓慢。

participant [pɑːrˈtɪsɪpənt] *n.* 参与者，参赛者

【记】联想记忆: parti(看作party, 晚会) + cip(抓，拿) + ant → 抓去参与派对的人 → 参与者

【例】The black man was a leading *participant* in the movement to end slavery. 这位黑人是结束奴隶制运动的一位主要参与者。

pendant [ˈpendənt] *n.* 垂饰，下垂物

【记】词根记忆: pend(悬挂) + ant → 悬挂着的东西 → 垂饰

【例】Some of the Pomo people's baskets were completely covered with shell *pendants*. 一些波莫人的篮子上挂满了贝壳垂饰。

planet [ˈplænɪt] *n.* 行星

【派】planetary(*a.* 行星的)

plausible ['plɔːzəbl] *a.* 似有道理的，似乎正确的(specious)

【记】词根记忆：plaus(鼓掌) + ible → 值得鼓掌的 → 似有道理的

【例】Well, as *plausible* as it sounds, it's only a theory. 这听起来似乎有道理，不过还只是个理论。

plot [plɑːt] *n.* 情节(clue) *v.* 计划(project)；划分

【例】Over the same period, another 550,000 lots were *plotted* outside the city limits but within the metropolitan area. 在同一时期，在市区之外大都会区以内的区域又划分出了55万块地。

precipitate [prɪ'sɪpɪteɪt] *vt.* 促成(cause)；降水 *vi.* 猛地落下

【记】词根记忆：pre(预先) + cipit(落下) + ate → 提前落下 → 促成

【例】Water dissolves, transports, and *precipitates* many chemical compounds. 水溶解、运送化合物并使之沉降。

【派】precipitation(*n.* 降水；降雨量)

radiate ['reɪdieɪt] *v.* 发出(热量)；辐射

【记】词根记忆：radi(光线) + ate → 发出光线 → 发出(热量)；辐射

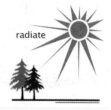
radiate

【派】radiation(*n.* 辐射)；radiator(*n.* 暖气装置)；radial(*a.* 放射状的)；radiant(*a.* 光芒四射的)

remnant ['remnənt] *n.* 残余物(remains)；遗留的痕迹

【记】可能是remain(*v.* 剩余，残存)的变体

【例】Most astronomers agree that comets are primordial *remnants* from the formation of the solar system. 多数天文学家认为彗星是太阳系形成时产生的原始残余物。

removal [rɪ'muːvl] *n.* 除去(elimination)；移动

【例】The field of "sanitary science" is concerned with waste *removal*, water purification and so on. 卫生科学领域研究废物处理、水净化等问题。

renaissance ['renəsɑːns] *n.* 复兴，再生(revival)

【记】词根记忆：re (重新) + naiss (=nas出生) + ance → 重新出生 → 再生

【搭】the Renaissance(欧洲14世纪至16世纪的)文艺复兴

retire [rɪ'taɪər] *vi.* 退休，引退

【记】词根记忆：re(反) + tire(劳累) → 不再劳累 → 退休

【例】My grandfather was a consultant in the company before he *retired*. 我祖父退休之前是公司的顾问。

【派】retirement(*n.* 退休)；retiree(*n.* 退休人员)

☐ plausible	☐ plot	☐ precipitate	☐ radiate	☐ remnant	☐ removal
☐ renaissance	☐ retire				

rod [rɑːd] *n.* 杆，棒(bar)
【记】联想记忆：拿着木棒(rod)打劫(rob)
【例】The fireplace had pivoting metal *rods* to hang pots. 壁炉有绕轴旋转的金属棒来悬挂锅。

salon [səˈlɑːn] *n.* (营业性的)厅，院，室，店
【记】发音记忆："沙龙"
【搭】hair salon 美发厅

scar [skɑːr] *n.* 疤痕(seam) *v.* (给…)留下伤痕(blemish)
【记】分拆联想：s + car(汽车) → 被汽车撞了一下 → 留下伤痕
【搭】scar tissue 疤痕组织
【例】Thousands of mine disposal sites *scarred* the coal-rich regions. 成千的矿井处理场给煤炭蕴藏丰富的地区留下了"疤痕"。

shipwright [ˈʃɪpraɪt] *n.* 造船者；造船工人；修船工
【记】组合词：ship(船) + wright(建造人，制作人) → 造船者

sloth [sloʊθ] *n.* 树懒
【记】分拆联想：slo(看作slow, 慢的) + th → 行动缓慢 → 树懒
【搭】ground sloth 地懒
【派】slothful(*a.* 懒惰的)

solitary [ˈsɑːləteri] *a.* 孤独的(lonely)；单独的(single, individual)
【记】词根记忆：solit(单独) + ary → 孤独的

specialize [ˈspeʃəlaɪz] *v.* 专攻；使专用于
【搭】specialize in 擅长于；专攻
【派】specialization(*n.* 专门化，特殊化)

specimen [ˈspesɪmən] *n.* 范例；标本(sample)
【记】词根记忆：speci(种类) + men → (将各种类生物制作成标本→)范例；标本

spectator [ˈspekteɪtər] *n.* 观众(audience)
【记】词根记忆：spect (看) + ator → 旁观者 → 观众

spill [spɪl] *v.* 溢出，溅出(overflow) *n.* 溅；溢出的东西
【记】分拆联想：s + pill(药丸) → 药丸洒了一地 → 溢出，溅出
【例】She's not upset about the *spill*. 溢出的东西并没有令她不安。

state [steɪt] *n.* 情况(condition)；国家(nation)；州(province) *v.* 陈述(express)
【派】statehood(*n.* 州的状态或地位)；stately[*ad./a.* 庄重地(的)；宏伟地(的)]；statement(*n.* 陈述，声明)

stem [stem] *n.* 茎，干(trunk) *v.* 起源；发自(originate)

【例】Her dance *stemmed* from her soul and spirit. 她的舞蹈源自她的灵魂和精神。

string [strɪŋ] *n.* 弦；细绳，带子

【记】分拆联想：st + ring(铃) → 系铃铛用的小绳 → 细绳

【搭】string music 弦乐队

【派】stringed(*a.* 有弦的)

sturdy ['stɜːrdi] *a.* (身体)强壮的；结实的(strong)；(物)稳固的(stable)

【记】联想记忆：身体强健(sturdy)是学习(study)的本钱

substantial [səb'stænʃl] *a.* 实质的，真实的；坚固的，结实的；富裕的；可观的

【例】The price reductions in winter clothes are pretty *substantial*. 冬季服装减价幅度非常大。

【派】substantially(*ad.* 主要地；实质上；重大地)

【参】substance(*n.* 物质)

towering ['taʊərɪŋ] *a.* 高耸的(topping)

【记】分拆联想：tower(塔) + ing → 像塔一样的 → 高耸的

【例】*Towering* skyscrapers cast long shadows at dusk. 耸入云霄的摩天大楼在黄昏时分投射出长长的影子。

versus ['vɜːrsəs] *prep.* 与…相对

【记】词根记忆：vers(转向) + us → 转向我们 → 与…相对，常缩写成vs，如：国际米兰 vs 尤文图斯

versus
宿命的对决

【例】When the scientists looked at the shoot *versus* the root surface, they found that the shoot surface, with all of its leaves, had a total surface area of about five square meters. 科学家们对比芽部和根部表面时发现，将所有叶片面积计算在内，芽表面的总表面积大约有5平方米。

worth [wɜːrθ] *n.* 价值(value) *a.* 值…的，价值…的，值得…的

【例】A: We are thinking of taking the kids to the new aquarium this weekend. Do you think it's *worth* the trip?

B: I've heard good things about it. I hope I get a chance to go myself soon.

A：我们想这个周末带孩子去新的水族馆。你觉得那里值得一去吗？

B：我听人们说那里不错。我希望我很快有机会去一次。

| stem | string | sturdy | substantial | towering | versus |
| worth | | | | | |

wrap [ræp] *vt.* 包装；裹（make up, pack）

【搭】wrap up 全神贯注；完成

【例】Are you ready to start studying for the test yet or to *wrap* up in that TV show? 你准备好开始复习考试了吗，还是要专心看那个电视节目？ //Let's *wrap* up the job and go home. 我们把工作干完回家吧。

The failures and reverses which await men—and one after another sadden the brow of youth—add a dignity to the prospect of human life, which no Arcadian success would do.

尽管失败和挫折等待着人们，一次次地夺走青春的容颜，但却给人生的前景增添了一份尊严，这是任何顺利的成功都不能做到的。

——亨利·大卫·梭罗（*Henry David Thoreau*）

Word List 3  MP3-03

词根、词缀预习表

mit	送	admit	v. 承认；接纳
pel	驱使	compel	v. 驱使
prehend	抓住	comprehend	v. 理解，领会
sent	感觉	consent	v./n. 同意，赞成
ordin	顺序	coordinate	vt. 协调，相配合
crus	十字	crusade	n. 十字军(远征)
ex	外	external	a. 外部的，位于外表的
in	进入	infest	vt. 骚扰；大批滋生
para	辅助	parameter	n. 参数，参量
super	在…的上面	superior	a. 更高的

accent ['æksent] *n* 口音；重音(stress)

【记】词根记忆：ac(加强) + cent(百) → 说一百遍 → 强调 → 重音

【例】Anyone with a foreign *accent*, even a child, was discriminated in the district. 有外国口音的人，哪怕是孩子，都会在这个地区受到歧视。

admit [əd'mɪt] *vt.* 承认(confess)；接纳(*let in)

【记】词根记忆：ad + mit(送) → 能送进去 → 接纳

【例】I must *admit* that my performance was bad. 我必须承认我的表现不佳。

【派】admittedly(*ad.* 诚然；公认地)

alkali ['ælkəlaɪ] *n.* 碱

【派】alkaline(*a.* 含碱的，碱性的)

asymmetrical [ˌeɪsɪ'metrɪkl] *a.* 不均匀的；不对称的(unbalanced, uneven)

【搭】an asymmetrical haircut 不对称发型

authority [ə'θɔːrəti] *n.* 权威人士；权力(power)；当局

【记】词根记忆：author(特权) + ity → 权力；当局

accent　　admit　　alkali　　asymmetrical　　authority

【例】He's an *authority* on energy sources. 他是能源方面的权威人士。//Your professor should have the *authority* to get something done about it. 你的教授应该有权让人对此采取措施。

bargain ['bɑːrgən] *n.* 廉价货；交易；契约，合同 *v.* 议价；成交

【记】联想记忆：bar(障碍) + gain(获得) → 高价是得到物品的障碍，所以要讨价还价 → 议价

【例】A: Did you buy any of the sweaters that were on sale?

B: Buy any? I got five of them. They were such a good *bargain*.

A：你买打折的运动衫了吗？

B：买了吗？我买了五件。这太值了。

A: Frank is certainly in a good mood.

B: The *bargain* he got on his new stereo made him very happy.

A：弗兰克心情真不错。

B：他买的新音响很划算，这让他很高兴。

A: I thought this shirt was a great deal but I washed it once and it's shrunk so much that I can't wear it.

B: Some *bargain*. You should ask for a refund.

A：我本以为这件衬衫很值，可洗了一次就缩水，没法穿了。

B：真是廉价货。你应该要求退款。

bony ['bouni] *a.* 瘦骨嶙峋的

【记】和bonny(*a.* 美丽的)一起记

【例】The three-toed sloth has hook-like claws at the ends of its long *bony* arms. 三趾树懒瘦长的手臂末端长有钩子状的爪子。

brief [briːf] *a.* 简短的；短暂的(fleeting, short)

【例】They are having a *brief* staff meeting. 他们正在开一个简短的员工会议。

【派】briefing(*n.* 简报；作战指示)；briefly (*ad.* 简要地，简短地)

brief

buddy ['bʌdi] *n.* 密友，伙伴(companion)

【搭】buddy system各负责另一人之安全的两人同行制

【例】We'll use a *buddy* system throughout the ride. 我们将在整个驾车程中实行一项伙伴制度。

catastrophe [kə'tæstrəfi] *n.* 突如其来的大灾难(disaster, tragedy)

【记】词根记忆：cat(看作cad，落下) + astro(星星) + phe → 星星坠落，大难临头 → 大灾难

【参】apostrophe(*n.* 省略符号)

| bargain | bony | brief | buddy | catastrophe |

classic ['klæsɪk] *a.* 经典的；典型的(typical) *n.* 经典作品(a work of enduring excellence)；[*pl.*]古典文学

coarse [kɔːrs] *a.* 粗(糙)的(*rough)

【记】分拆联想：coar(看作coal, 煤炭)＋se → 煤炭是很粗糙的 → 粗(糙)的

communicate [kə'mjuːnɪkeɪt] *vt.* 通信，沟通；传达，传播(express, convey)

【例】They will use satellites to communicate with mountain climbers. 他们将使用卫星与登山者进行联络。

【派】communication(*n.* 交流；通讯；传播)

compare [kəm'per] *v.* 比较，相比，对比；比作

【记】联想记忆：com(一起)＋pare(看作pair, 对) → 把这对放在一起看 → 比较

【搭】compare with 与…比较，对照；compare to 比喻为，把…比作；with compare 无与伦比

【例】*Compared* to lunar space suits, Martian space suits will require smaller air tanks; and to allow for freer movement; the elbow and knee areas of the space suits will also be altered. 与登月太空服相比，火星太空服所需的气罐更小，穿着活动更加自由，其肘部和膝部也将有所改变。

compel [kəm'pel] *v.* 驱使(drive)

【记】词根记忆：com＋pel(驱使) → 驱使

【例】Beads come in shapes, colors, and materials that almost *compel* one to handle them and to sort them. 珠子丰富各异的形状、色彩和材料，驱使人们把玩挑选。

【派】compelling(*a.* 引人注目的)

【参】dispel(*vt.* 驱散)；impel(*vt.* 推动)；repel(*vt.* 击退)；expel(*v.* 开除)

comprehend [ˌkɑːmprɪ'hend] *v.* 理解，领会(understand, grasp)

【记】词根记忆：com(全部)＋prehend(抓住) → 全部抓住 → 理解，领会

【例】He needed to look up some words in order to *comprehend* the novel. 他需要查一些词才能理解这部小说。

【派】comprehensible(*a.* 可理解的)；comprehensive(*a.* 全面的；综合的)

concentrate ['kɑːnsntreɪt] *v.* 集中，专心(focus)；浓缩 *n.* 浓缩物

【记】词根记忆：con(共同)＋centr(中心)＋ate → 共同聚集在一个中心 → 集中

classic　coarse　communicate　compare　compel　comprehend　concentrate

【搭】concentrate on 集中，全神贯注于

【例】A: What is that you are listening to? The beat's so strong that I can't *concentrate* on my work.

B: No problem. I can switch over to something lighter.

A: 你在听什么？节奏太强了，我都无法专心做功课。

B: 没问题。我可以换个节奏更轻柔的音乐。

consent [kənˈsent] v. /n. 同意，赞成（approve, agree）

【记】词根记忆：con（共同）+ sent（感觉）→ 有共同的感觉 → 同意，赞成

【例】We are fortunate that he's *consented* to share some of his experiences with us. 我们很幸运，他已经同意与我们分享他的一些经历了。

consideration [kənˌsɪdəˈreɪʃn] n. 考虑，思考；体谅，照顾；需要考虑的事；理由

【例】The government should give careful *consideration* to issues of food safety. 政府应该仔细考虑食品安全的问题。

contrast [ˈkɑːntræst] n. 对比，对照

[kənˈtræst] v. 对比，对照（compare, balance）

contrast

【例】Because of these *contrasts*, "popular" may be viewed as clearly different from "folk". 由于这些对比，"流行"被看成与"民俗"明显不同的词。//The passage is organized by *contrasting* the meanings of two related words. 这段话是通过对比两个相关字的意思而组织起来的。

coordinate [koʊˈɔːrdɪneɪt] vt. 协调，相配合（harmonize, cooperate）

【记】词根记忆：co + ordin（顺序）+ ate → 按顺序 → 协调，相配合

【例】Political parties in the United States help to *coordinate* the campaigns of their members that mark election years. 美国的政党帮助配合其候选人在选举年的竞选。

copious [ˈkoʊpiəs] a. 丰富的，富饶的

【记】分拆联想：copi（看作copy）+ ous → 能拷贝很多 → 丰富的

【例】Scientists support the theory of relativity with *copious* evidence. 科学家们用大量证据支持相对论。

count [kaʊnt] v. 数，计算（calculate）；算入；看作，认为 n. 计数，计算

【搭】count on 算上；lose count (of) 数不清；不知道

【例】I'm *counting* on you to make notes from the history lecture. 我正指望着你记历史课的笔记呢。

☐ consent　☐ consideration　☐ contrast　☐ coordinate　☐ copious　☐ count

A: Ever since your girlfriend moved to Bridgeport, you are always driving there. How many trips a week do you make anyway?

B: I have lost *count*. But I can do it with my eyes closed.

A：自打你女朋友搬到布里奇波特，你就总是开车去那里。你一个礼拜去几次啊？

B：我都数不清了。不过我闭着眼睛就能做到。

A: I got an invitation to a financial planning seminar. And I don't want to go alone.

B: *Count* me in. I need all the help to manage my money.

A：我收到邀请去参加一个财务规划研讨会。我不想自己一个人去。

B：把我算上。我需要理财方面的各种帮助。

【参】mount(*n.* 山 *vi.* 上马)

crusade [kruːˈseɪd] *n.* 十字军(远征)；运动(movement) *v.* 加入十字军，投身正义运动

【记】词根记忆：crus(十字) + ade → 十字军

【例】They came to perceive the war as a kind of democratic *crusade* against southern society. 他们逐渐把战争视为对抗南方城市的一种民主运动。

cushion [ˈkʊʃn] *n.* 垫子(pillow) *v.* 缓冲(to protect against force or shock)

【记】发音记忆："苦行" → 苦行僧盘腿在垫子上打坐

【搭】air-cushion vehicle 气垫船

【例】The carpet *cushioned* the fall of the vase. 地毯缓冲了花瓶的坠落。

custom [ˈkʌstəm] *n.* [常*pl.*] 进口税(duties)；海关

【搭】customs duties 进口税；customs commissioner 税务司

【参】customary(*a.* 合乎惯例的)

detectable [dɪˈtektəbl] *a.* 可发觉的；可看穿的(apparent)

draw [drɔː] *vt.* 吸引(attract, entice)

edifice [ˈedɪfɪs] *n.* 高大的或宏伟的建筑物

【记】分拆联想：edi (看作edit, 编辑) + fice (看作office, 办公室) → 编辑的办公室 → 高大的或宏伟的建筑物

【例】The White House is the oldest public *edifice* in Washington D.C. 白宫是华盛顿特区最古老的公共建筑。

emphasize [ˈemfəsaɪz] *vt.* 强调，着重；重读(*stress)

【记】分拆联想：em + phas(看作phrase, 用短语表达) + ize → 用短语表达是为了强调 → 强调，着重

【例】The story *emphasized* the courage of one man made him a hero in our history books. 我们历史书中的这个故事强调了一个人的勇气能使其成为英雄。

【参】emphasis(*n.* 强调, 重点)

engine ['endʒɪn] *n.* 引擎, 发动机

【派】engineer(*n.* 工程师); engineering(*n.* 工程学)

envelop [ɪn'veləp] *vt.* 包围(*surround, encircle)

【例】More dense atmosphere gradually *enveloped* Earth. 更加浓厚的大气逐渐覆盖了地球。

【派】envelope(*n.* 包层; 信封)

episode ['epɪsoʊd] *n.* 一段时期(period); (电视剧的)一集; 一段情节

【搭】Glacial episode 冰河时代

【例】I missed the first *episode* of the new TV show, but I hope to watch a later one. 我错过了新电视节目的第一集, 不过我希望观看下一集。

equation [ɪ'kweɪʒn] *n.* (数学)等式, 方程式; 相等; 均衡

【记】词根记忆: equ(相等, 平等) + ation → 等式

【例】As economists put it, the industry forms a crucial part of a country's economic *equation*.
正如经济学家所言, 工业是一个国家经济均衡的关键部分。

【参】equal(*a.* 平等的)

external [ɪk'stɜːrnl] *a.* 外部的, 位于外表的(exterior)

【记】词根记忆: ex(外) + ternal → 外部的

fade [feɪd] *v.* 褪色; 凋谢(wither); 消失(*disappear from, vanish)

【搭】fade away 逐渐凋谢; 慢慢减弱

【例】I've heard the printing really *fades* when you wash them. 我听说印花一洗真的会褪色。

fellowship ['feloʊʃɪp] *n.* 友谊(friendship); 奖学金(scholarship)

【例】I heard Joan was turned down for the graduate *fellowship*. 我听说琼未能申请到研究生奖学金。

fierce [fɪrs] *a.* 凶猛的, 残忍的(cruel); 狂热的, 强烈的; 激烈的, 猛烈的(violent)

【记】和force(*v.* 强制, 强迫)一起记

engine	envelop	episode	equation	external	fade
fellowship	fierce				

【例】 Human population near the equator have evolved dark skin over many generations because of exposure to the *fiercest* rays of the sun. 由于暴露在最强烈的日光下,赤道附近的人们经过很多代人的演化有了深色的皮肤。

flint [flɪnt] *n.* 燧石,打火石

【记】 分拆联想: f + lint(看作 line,线)→ 打火石产生的火光如同一条线 → 打火石

forefront ['fɔːrfrʌnt] *n.* 最前沿；中心(spotlight)

【记】 fore(前面)+ front(前面)→ 前面的前面 → 最前沿

【例】 I know many of you are already at the *forefront* of the work place technology. 我知道你们很多人已经处于车间技术的前沿领先水平。

freeze [friːz] *vt.* 使结冰,使凝固

【搭】 freeze over(水池、湖等)结冰；freeze up(机器、引擎中的水)结冰(使机器无法工作)

【例】 Jack caught a fish and dropped it beside him on the ice and it *froze* solid. 杰克捉到一条鱼,随手扔在了身旁的冰上,结果鱼冻得硬邦邦的。//I was really happy to be writing a detective story. But after the first few pages, I sort of *froze* up mentally. 我很高兴能写侦探小说。但是只写了几页我脑子就不转了。

grind [graɪnd] *vt.* 打磨(polish)；磨(碎),碾(碎)(*crush)

【记】 联想记忆: 将一块大(grand)石头磨碎(grind)

【例】 The windmill has been used to pump water and *grind* grains. 磨坊被用来泵水和碾谷子。

【派】 grinder(*n.* 磨工)

groom [gruːm] *v.* 将(动物的)皮毛弄干净；使做好准备；使…整洁

【例】 Mother chimpanzees care for and *groom* their young. 黑猩猩母亲照顾子女,并把它们的皮毛弄干净。//All trails have to be checked daily to make sure they are *groomed* probably. 所有的道路都得每天检查,确保其已清理整洁。

heading ['hedɪŋ] *n.* 标题

horde [hɔːrd] *n.* 一大群(crowd, swarm)

【例】 There are *hordes* of traders at the jumble sale today. 今天的旧货义卖会上有很多交易者。

inactive [ɪn'æktɪv] *a.* 不活动的；怠惰的(idle)

【例】 Although the states dominated economic activity during this period, the federal government was not *inactive*. 尽管这个时期各州政府掌控着经济活动,但联邦政府也并非无所作为。

| flint | forefront | freeze | grind | groom | heading |
| horde | inactive | | | | |

infest [ɪnˈfest] *vt.* 骚扰；大批滋生

【记】词根记忆：in(进入) + fest(匆忙)→(繁殖)得很快 → 大批滋生

【搭】be infested with 多得成灾

【派】infestation(*n.* 滋生，出没)

interior [ɪnˈtɪriər] *n./a.* 内部(的)(inner) *n.* [the~]内陆(inland)

【记】词根记忆：inter(在…之间) + ior → 内部的

【例】If a volcano erupts, some of the Earth's *interior* heat escapes to the surface. 如果火山喷发，地球内部的一些热量就会逃逸到地表。

jog [dʒɑːg] *vi.* 慢跑

【记】联想记忆：一边慢跑(jog)一边遛狗 (dog)

【例】Let's *jog* for another mile. 我们再慢跑 一英里吧。

Latin [ˈlætn] *a.* 拉丁的，拉丁文的 *n.* 拉丁语

【例】The term virus is derived from the *Latin* word for poison or slime. Virus(病毒)这个词起源于拉丁文毒药或黏液。

mammal [ˈmæml] *n.* 哺乳动物

【记】分拆联想：mamma(妈妈) + l → 靠吃妈妈的奶长大 → 哺乳 动物

【例】Desert-adapted *mammals* have the further ability to feed normally when extremely dehydrated. 适应沙漠的哺乳动物极度脱水时也能 正常哺乳。

【派】mammalian(*a.* 哺乳动物的，哺乳纲的)

melanin [ˈmelənɪn] *n.* 黑色素

【例】The skin of the grass mouse contains lots of *melanin*, or dark pigments. 草鼠的皮肤包含很多黑色素。

nomadic [noʊˈmædɪk] *a.* 游牧的

【记】来自nomad(游牧民，流浪者) + ic → 游牧的

【例】Some hunters continued the old pastoral and *nomadic* ways. 一 些猎户继续过着牧人游牧似的古老生活。

notorious [noʊˈtɔːriəs] *a.* 众所周知的；臭名昭著的，声名狼藉的

【记】词根记忆：not(知道) + or(说，口) + ious(…的) → 众口一 词，无人不知 → 众所周知的；声名狼藉的

【搭】be notorious for 因为…而臭名昭著

【例】The short story showed what was kind and what was evil through the contrast between two brothers, one famous and one *notorious*. 这

| ☐ infest | ☐ interior | ☐ jog | ☐ Latin | ☐ mammal | ☐ melanin |
| ☐ nomadic | ☐ notorious | | | | |

个短篇小说通过对比一个著名另一个臭名昭著的兄弟俩，显示出何为善恶。

parameter [pə'ræmɪtər] *n.* 参数，参量

【记】词根记忆：para（辅助）+ meter（测量）→ 辅助测量 → 参数，参量

【例】We must work within the *parameters* of budget and time this year. 我们今年必须按照预算和时间的规定工作。

pathology [pə'θɑːlədʒi] *n.* 反常，变态(abnormality)

【记】词根记忆：path（病）+ ology → 反常，变态

【例】The boundary lines between normality and *pathology* are often clearly delineated by medical science. 正常与反常的界限往往由医学来清楚地描述。

phenomena [fə'nɑːmɪnə] *n.* [*pl.*] 现象

【记】词根记忆：phen(=phan 出现) + omena → 现象

【例】Many foreigners are curious about the cultural *phenomena* when they first pay a visit to America. 很多外国人初次拜访美国时都会对其文化现象感到困惑。

【派】phenomenal(*a.* 显著的；现象的)；phenomenon(*n.* 现象)

plaster ['plæstər] *n.* 灰浆，石膏 *v.* 在…上抹灰泥

【记】联想记忆：plaste（看作paste，粘贴）+ r → 贴石膏 → 在…上抹灰泥

【例】These rough places on the wall could be *plastered* over. 可以在墙面的这些粗糙之处抹上灰泥。

policy ['pɑːləsi] *n.* 政策，方针；保险单

【记】联想记忆：警察(police)贯彻国家方针(policy)

【搭】insurance policy 保险单

quench [kwentʃ] *vt.* 淬火；熄灭(exinguish, put out)；解渴(slake, satisfy one's thirst)

【记】联想记忆：quen（看作queen，女王）+ ch → 扑灭女王的嚣张气焰 → 熄灭

【搭】quench one's thirst 解渴；quench a fire/flames 灭火

【例】Mineral water is the best way to *quench* one's thirst. 矿泉水是解渴的最佳方式。

【派】quenchable(*a.* 可熄灭的)；quencher(*n.* 淬火，骤冷)；quenching(*n.* 淬火，熄灭)

renew [rɪ'nuː] *vt.* 使续期；重建(reestablish)

【例】Ronald has to *renew* his passport because it is expired. 罗纳德的

□ parameter	□ pathology	□ phenomena	□ plaster	□ policy	□ quench
□ renew					

护照过期了，他不得不去续签。

【派】renewable(*a.* 可再生的); renewed(*a.* 更新的); renewal(*n.* 更新; 复兴)

ripen ['raɪpən] *v.* 成熟

【记】来自ripe(*a.* 成熟的)

【例】The fruit turns from green to yellow to red as it *ripens*. 水果成熟时颜色会由绿转黄再变红。

【派】ripener(*n.* 催熟剂)

roost [ruːst] *n.* 栖息处, 鸟巢 *v.* 栖息(alight, perch)

【搭】rule the roost 当家

【例】Curses come home to *roost*. 诅咒他人, 应验自身。

【派】rooster(*n.* 公鸡)

salmon ['sæmən] *n.* 鲑鱼, 大马哈鱼

【记】词根记忆: sal(跳) + mon → 在水中欢快跳跃 → 鲑鱼, 大马哈鱼

script [skrɪpt] *n.* 脚本; 文字体系(writing, manuscript)

【记】本身为词根, 意为: 写

【搭】cuneiform script 楔形文字

sheer [ʃɪr] *a.* 陡峭的(steep); 绝对的(absolute)

【记】联想记忆: 绵羊(sheep)在陡峭的(sheer)山坡上吃草

sheer

【例】The decade of the 1870's was a period in which the *sheer* number of newspapers doubled. 在19世纪70年代, 报纸的绝对数量增长了一倍。

spiral ['spaɪrəl] *a.* 螺旋形的(helical) *v.* 盘旋(coil, twist)

【记】来自spir(e)(螺旋) + al → 螺旋形的

【搭】spiral galaxy 漩涡星云; spiral thread 螺旋丝

【例】Particles *spiral* back and forth between the Earth's magnetic poles. 粒子在地球磁极之间来回盘旋。

staff [stæf] *n.* 全体职工, 工作人员(crew, personnel)

【记】联想记忆: 一个明星(star)后面都跟着一群工作人员(staff)

【例】A congressional representative needs a large *staff*. 一名国会代表需要一大批工作人员。

steady ['stedi] *a.* 牢固的(firm); 稳定的(constant, fixed)

【记】分拆联想: st + eady(看作ready, 有准备的) → 事先有准备, 心里就有底 → 稳定的

ripen	roost	salmon	script	sheer	spiral
staff	steady				

【派】steadily(*ad.* 稳定地)

strata [ˈstreɪtə] *n.* 地层(复数)

superior [suːˈpɪriər] *a.* (级别或地位)更高的；(质量或价值)更好的

【记】词根记忆：super(在…上面)＋ior→更高的

【例】Natural vitamins are *superior* to synthetic ones. 天然维生素优于合成维生素。

【派】superiority(*n.* 优越，优等)

surrender [səˈrendər] *v.* 投降

【记】分拆联想：sur(在…下面)＋render(放弃)→把(枪)放到下面放弃抵抗→投降

【例】The murderer finally *surrendered* to the police. 凶犯最终向警方投降。

suspension [səˈspenʃn] *n.* 悬架；暂停(pause)

【搭】suspension bridge 吊桥

【例】The *suspension* of trading on the Grain Exchange was justified. 谷物交易所暂停交易是有道理的。

therapy [ˈθerəpi] *n.* 治疗，疗法(treatment of illness)

【记】词根记忆：therap(照看，治疗)＋y→治疗，疗法

【例】In the third era of nutritional history, vitamin *therapy* began to fall into disrepute. 在营养史上的第三个阶段，维生素疗法的名声开始变坏。

tile [taɪl] *v.* 铺瓦于 *n.* 瓦，瓦片

unadorned [ˌʌnəˈdɔːrnd] *a.* 未装饰的，朴实的(plain, unembellished)

【例】The works written by the female poet are all *unadorned* and simple. 这位女诗人的作品朴实简练。

unprecedented [ʌnˈpresidentɪd] *a.* 空前的(unexampled)

【记】分拆联想：un(不)＋precedent(先例)＋ed→空前的

【例】These innovations in manufacturing boosted output and living standards to an *unprecedented* extent. 这些生产创新把产量和生活标准提高到了前所未有的程度。

utilize [ˈjuːtəlaɪz] *v.* 利用(make use of)

【记】词根记忆：util(用)＋ize→利用

【例】The body takes in and *utilizes* food substances. 身体吸收并利用食物成分。

【派】utilization(*n.* 利用)

vigorous [ˈvɪɡərəs] *a.* 精力充沛的(*energetic)；有力的(strong)

【记】来自vigor(*n.* 活力)

【例】The small group of the survivors was to become a *vigorous*, self-sustaining island population. 这一小群幸存者成为了岛屿上精力充沛、自给自足的居民。

【派】vigorously(*ad.* 精力旺盛地)

To a manager, the most important is to do what he should do. No matter how excellent his plans are, or how sound theories he advocates, they are nothing but merely some illusions if not put into practice.

对于经营者来说，最重要的，就是为其所当为。不论拥有多么杰出的构想，口中说着多么堂皇的理论，如果不能将其实行，充其量不过是画饼而已。

——松下幸之助(*Konosuke Matsushita*)

Word List 4

词根、词缀预习表

tire	梳理	attire	*n.* 穿着，服饰
bust	燃烧	combustible	*a.* 可燃的，易燃的
prehend	抓住	comprehend	*v.* 理解，领会
counter	相反地	counterpart	*n.* 相对物
deca	十	decade	*n.* 十年
duc	引导	ductile	*a.* 易延展的
homo	同类的	homogeneous	*a.* 同类的，同质的
loc	地点	locate	*vt.* 使坐落于；找出，定位
maxim	大；高	maximum	*a.* 最高的
orn	装饰	ornament	*n.* 装饰物

adventure [ədˈventʃər] *n.* 奇遇；冒险活动

【记】发音记忆：ad + venture（音似："玩车"）→ 飙车 → 冒险活动

【例】He has had many *adventures* along the way—lost instruments, miss connections, no hotel room, and so on. 他一路上经历了很多冒险——仪器丢了，失去了联系，没住上旅馆等等。

【派】adventurer(*n.* 冒险家)；adventurous(*a.* 喜欢冒险的)

analogy [əˈnælədʒi] *n.* 类比，类推；类似物

【记】词根记忆：ana(并列) + log(说话) + y → 放在一起说 → 类比，类推

【例】The teacher made an *analogy* between the lens of a camera and the lens of an eye. 老师把相机的镜头类比为眼球的晶体。

【派】analogous(*a.* 类似的)

apply [əˈplaɪ] *v.* 申请，请求；适用，应用，运用

【记】词根记忆：ap(加强；一再) + ply(重叠) → 一再重叠，反复使用 → 应用

【搭】apply to 适用于…；与…有关；应用；apply for 申请；apply to the customs 报关

☐ adventure ☐ analogy ☐ apply

【例】I would like to *apply* for one of the security guard positions you advertised in the local paper. 我想申请你在本地报纸上刊登的保安职位。

A: I heard you were thinking of *applying* for a job as a camp counselor.

B: Yeah, do you know if they need anyone at that place where you worked last summer?

A: 我听说你想申请一份营地管理员的工作。

B: 是的，你知道去年夏天你工作过的那个地方是否需要人手吗？

【派】applicant(*n.* 申请者，请求者)

【参】supply(*v.* 提供)

appraisal [əˈpreɪzl] *n.* 评价，估价(assessment, evaluation)

【记】词根记忆：ap(加强) + prais(价值，赞扬) + al → 给以价值 → 评价

【例】All the evidences have proved my *appraisal* to be correct. 所有的证据都表明我的评价是正确的。

appraisal

artifact [ˈɑːrtɪfækt] *n.* 人工制品；[常*pl.*]史前古器物

【记】词根记忆：arti(技巧) + fact(制作) → 用技巧制作出的东西 → 人工制品

assure [əˈʃʊr] *vt.* 确保(guarantee)；使确信(convince)

【记】词根记忆：as + sure(确定的) → 确保；使确信

【例】People who're dieting need a variety of foods to *assure* a constant supply of nutrients their bodies need. 节食的人需要各种食物，以确保身体所需的营养能得到持续供应。//She *assured* him that the chapter was finished. 她向他保证这一章写完了。

【参】ensure(*vt.* 保证)；insure(*vt.* 给…保险)；secure(*a.* 安全的)

attire [əˈtaɪər] *n.* 穿着，服饰(clothing, dress)

【记】词根记忆：at + tire(梳理) → 梳洗打扮 → 穿着，服饰

【参】attic(*n.* 阁楼，顶楼)

biochemical [ˌbaɪoʊˈkemɪkl] *a.* 生物化学的

【例】Enzymes are what make many of the body's *biochemical* reactions possible. 酶使身体的很多生化反应成为可能。//There are two reasons that enzymes are so effective at enabling *biochemical* reactions. 酶之所以能如此有效地促使生化反应，原因有两个。

☐ appraisal   ☐ artifact   ☐ assure   ☐ attire   ☐ biochemical

catalyst ['kætəlɪst] *n.* 催化剂

【记】词根记忆：cata(下面) + lyst(分开，分解) → 起分解作用 → 催化剂

【参】analyst(*n.* 分析家)

cohesion [koʊ'hi:ʒn] *n.*【物理】内聚力；凝聚力；团结，结合(*unity)

【搭】cohesion-tension theory 内聚力(学)说

combustible [kəm'bʌstəbl] *a.* 可燃的，易燃的(flammable)

【记】词根记忆：com + bust(燃烧) + ible → 易燃的

【例】Burning would also stop when the *combustible* substance was emptied of all its phlogiston. 把易燃物里的燃素全部提取出来，燃烧也会停止。

【参】blockbuster(*n.* 巨型炸弹)

complain [kəm'pleɪn] *v.* 抱怨；申诉

【记】联想记忆：com(加强) + plain(平常的) → 太过平淡的生活让人抱怨 → 抱怨

【搭】complain about 抱怨；申诉…；complain to 向…抱怨

【例】My mother always *complains* that her knee hurts just before a storm. 我母亲总是抱怨每到暴风雨前膝盖都会疼。//One day, a customer came into a drugstore *complaining* of a headache and asked for a bottle of cola syrup. 一天，一名顾客走进药店，说自己头疼，想买一瓶可乐糖浆。

counterpart ['kaʊntərpɑ:rt] *n.* 相对物，极相似之人或物(one remarkably similar to another)；副本(duplicate)

【记】词根记忆：counter(相反的) + part(部分) → 相对的那一部分 → 相对物

【例】These female writers, like most of their male *counterparts*, were amateur historians. 这些女性作家和多数男性作家一样，都是业余历史学家。

data ['deɪtə] *n.* 数据

【记】联想记忆：数据(data)与日(date)更新

【搭】analyzing the data 分析数据；computer data base 计算机数据库；data process 数据程序

【例】If the computer doesn't break down again, the *data* will be available to us soon. 如果电脑不再死机，我们就能很快得到数据。

decade ['dekeɪd] *n.* 十年

【记】词根记忆：deca(十) + de → 十年

☐ catalyst	☐ cohesion	☐ combustible	☐ complain	☐ counterpart	☐ data
☐ decade					

dimensional [daɪˈmenʃənl] *a.* 空间的

【例】One distinctive feature of Moore's sculpture is his use of holes or opening to emphasize that he is indeed working in a three *dimensional* medium. 摩尔的雕塑作品有一个鲜明的特色，那就是他使用洞口来强调他是在一个三维的环境中进行创作的。

diplomatic [ˌdɪpləˈmætɪk] *a.* 外交的，从事外交的；策略的(tactful)，有手腕的

【记】来自diplomat(*n.* 外交家，外交官)

【例】Betty really lost her temper at that meeting. She has to learn to be a lot more *diplomatic* than that. 贝蒂在那次会议上真的发脾气了。她应该学着更讲究一些策略。

diplomatic

disposal [dɪˈspoʊzl] *n.* 垃圾倾倒；处置(get rid of)

【搭】garbage disposal 垃圾处理

【例】Environmentalists think recycling should be promoted as the best answer to waste *disposal*. 环保主义者认为应该促进回收利用，这是处理废物的最佳方案。

documentation [ˌdɑːkjumenˈteɪʃn] *n.* 文件(file)

【例】The researcher is faced with the problem of primary materials that have little *documentation*. 这个研究人员面临的问题是原始资料很少有文件记载。

ductile [ˈdʌktaɪl] *a.* 易延展的(plastic)

【记】词根记忆：duct(引导) + ile → 易引导的 → 易延展的

【例】Another unusual feature of glass is the manner in which its viscosity changes as it turns from a cold substance into a hot, *ductile* liquid. 玻璃具有另一个不寻常的特性，那就是当其从冰冷的固态变成炽热的、易延展的液体时，其黏性就发生变化。

engage [ɪnˈgeɪdʒ] *v.* (使)从事于，(使)参加，(使)忙着；(使)订婚；聘用(employ)

【记】联想记忆：en(使…) + gage(挑战) → 使迎接挑战 → 使从事于

【搭】engage in 从事于…

【例】How are we going to classify a typical politician or business person who *engages* in unethical practices? 我们如何分类做事不道德的典型政客或商人？

【派】engaged(*a.* 忙碌的)

enrich [ɪn'rɪtʃ] *vt.* 使充实；使肥沃(fertilize)

【记】词根记忆：en(使…) + rich(充足的；肥沃的) → 使充实；使肥沃

【例】Plant growth greatly *enriched* our atmosphere with oxygen. 植物的生长大大丰富了大气中的氧气。

【派】enrichment(*n.* 肥沃)

epidemic [ˌepɪ'demɪk] *n.* 流行(popularity)；流行病

【记】词根记忆：epi(在…周围) + dem(人民) + ic → 在人民周围 → 流行

【例】The terrible *epidemic* killed most of the people it infected. 可怕的流行病害死了受感染的大部分人。

evaporation [ɪˌvæpə'reɪʃn] *n.* 蒸发；消失

expertise [ˌekspɜːr'tiːz] *n.* 专门知识(或技能等)(skill)

【记】来自 expert(*n.* 专家)

exploration [ˌeksplə'reɪʃn] *n.* 勘探，探测；探索

【例】A small group of explorers had just completed a month-long *exploration* of the region that is now called Yellow Stone. 一小队探险者刚在这个现在称为黄石的地区完成为期一个月的探索。

explore [ɪk'splɔːr] *vt.* 探险(adventure)；探究(*probe for, search)

【例】We'll *explore* through lecture and discussion what prominent political thinkers had to say about the topic. 我们将通过讲课和讨论的方式来探究著名政治思想家对这个话题的看法。

【派】explorer(*n.* 探险家)；exploration(*n.* 探索)；exploratory(*a.* 探险的，探测的)

extension [ɪk'stenʃn] *n.* 延长(期限)(postponement)；延伸(部分)(*supplement)

【例】The woman asked for an *extension* on the application deadline. 这个女子要求延长申请的截止期限。

【参】extensive(*a.* 大量的，广泛的)

figurative ['fɪɡərətɪv] *a.* 比喻的，借喻的；象征的；用修辞方法的

【记】来自 figure(外形，象征) + ative → 象征性的 → 比喻的

【例】Before I go on to the biochemical specifics of how this works, let me provide a *figurative* example. 我先打一个比方，然后再具体解释这如何发生了生化作用。

forage ['fɔːrɪdʒ] *n.* 草料(*feed, fodder) *v.* 搜寻粮秣(*search for food)

【记】分拆联想：for(为了) + age(年龄) → 为了年龄(成长)寻找草料 → 草料；搜寻

□ enrich	□ epidemic	□ evaporation	□ expertise	□ exploration	□ explore
□ extension	□ figurative	□ forage			

【例】Many ants *forage* across the countryside in large numbers. 很多蚂蚁成群结队地在田野上搜寻食物。

haunt [hɔːnt] *vt.* 萦绕在心头 *n.* 常去的地方

【记】联想记忆：姑妈(aunt)常去的地方(haunt)是商店

【例】People were *haunted* by the prospect that unprecedented change in the nation's economy would bring social chaos. 国民经济前所未有的变化将导致社会动乱的可能性萦绕在人们心头。

homogeneous [ˌhoʊmə'dʒiːniəs] *a.* 同类的，同质的(*uniform)

【记】词根记忆：homo(同类的) + gene(基因) + ous → 基因相同 → 同类的

【例】In a small community, behavioral norms are more likely being *homogeneous* than in a large city. 在小社区，行为规范可能比大城市更加统一。

hurricane ['hɜːrəkən] *n.* 飓风，风暴(storm)

【记】分拆联想：hurri(看作hurry，匆忙) + cane → 来去很匆忙的风 → 飓风

【参】cyclone(*n.* 暴风，龙卷风); typhoon(*n.* 台风)

imply [ɪm'plaɪ] *vt.* 意味着，暗示(suggest)

【记】词根记忆：im(进入) + ply(重叠) → 重叠表达 → 暗示

【例】Noise, in the technical sense, *implies* a random chaotic disturbance that is usually unwanted. 从技术层面讲，噪音就是通常令人讨厌的任意杂乱的干扰。

intoxication [ɪnˌtɑːksɪ'keɪʃn] *n.* 醉，醉酒

【记】来自intoxicate(*v.* 使醉)，in(使) + toxic(毒) + ate → 使中毒 → 使醉

【搭】water intoxication 水中毒

【例】At a depth of 5 atmospheres nitrogen causes symptoms resembling alcohol *intoxication*. 在5个大气压的深度，氮会导致类似醉酒的症状。

猫在哪里！
intoxication

label ['leɪbl] *n.* 标签(tag) *v.* 标记(mark)

【记】分拆联想：lab(实验室) + el → 实验室里的试剂瓶上贴有标签 → 标签；标记

【例】Other chimpanzees have learned to use numerals to *label* quantities of items and do simple sums. 其他黑猩猩已经学会了使用数字来标记物品的数量，并做简单的加法运算。

locate ['loʊkeɪt] *vt.* 使坐落于（situate）；找出，定位（orient）

【记】词根记忆：loc（地点）+ ate → 找到地点 → 找出，定位

【例】Her hotel is *located* far from the conference center. 她的酒店距会议中心很远。//She'd be able to *locate* where the man was seated. 她能够找到那个男子的座位。

【派】location（*n.* 位置；场所）

logical ['lɑːdʒɪkl] *a.* 符合逻辑的，合理的（reasonable）

【例】The apartment's room arrangement was not *logical*. 公寓房间的格局不合理。

maintenance ['meɪntənəns] *n.* 维护，保养（upkeep）

【记】词根记忆：main（手）+ ten（拿住）+ ance → 用手拿住 → 维护，保养

【例】Bones are made of dynamic living tissue that requires continuous *maintenance* and repair. 骨头由活跃的活组织构成，需要不断的保养和修护。

manifest ['mænɪfest] *v.* 表明，证明（indicate, show）*n.* 显示（indication）

【记】词根记忆：mani（手）+ fest（打）→ 用手打开 → 显示

【例】The contradiction *manifested* itself in the employment situation. 这个矛盾在就业形势中显示了出来。

【派】manifestation（*n.* 显示，表明）

material [mə'tɪriəl] *n.* 材料（stuff）；[常 *pl.*] 原料 *a.* 物质的；身体上的（physical）；重要的（crucial）

【搭】raw materials 原料

mathematics [ˌmæθə'mætɪks] *n.* 数学（math）

【例】She had no formal education in *mathematics*. 她没有受过有关数学的正规教育。

maximum ['mæksɪməm] *a.* 最（大、高、多）的，最大限度的（*peak, highest）*n.* 最大量（an upper limit）

【记】词根记忆：maxim（大，高）+ um → 最高的，最大限度的

【例】The *maximum* speed of this car is 150 miles per hour. 这辆车的最大时速为150英里。

memo ['memoʊ] *n.* 备忘录

【例】Please write a *memo* to be attached to the notice board when inviting your colleagues to join in the training program. 邀请你的同事参与培训项目时，请写一份备忘录贴在公告板上。

☐ locate	☐ logical	☐ maintenance	☐ manifest	☐ material	☐ mathematics
☐ maximum	☐ memo				

mold [mould] *n.* 霉菌(fungus); 模型(type) *vt.* 塑造(shape, figure)

【例】The higher the clay content in a sample, the more refined and durable the shapes into which it can be *molded*. 样品中黏土含量越高, 其所能塑成的形状就越精细和持久。

neoclassical [ˌniːoʊˈklæsɪkl] *a.* 新古典主义的

【例】The *neoclassical* sculptors seldom held a mallet or chisel in their own hands. 新古典主义的雕塑家很少亲自手持槌棒或凿子。

【派】neoclassicism(*n.* 新古典主义)

original [əˈrɪdʒənl] *a.* 最初的, 原始的(initial) *n.* 原件

【派】originality(*n.* 创意, 新奇); originally(*ad.* 独创地; 最初)

【参】aboriginal(*a.* 土著的)

ornament [ˈɔːrnəmənt] *n.* 装饰(物、品)(decoration, adornment)

【记】词根记忆: orn(装饰)+ ament → 装饰(物)

【例】The *ornaments* on the Christmas tree shined and sparkled. 圣诞树上的装饰品闪闪发光。

【派】ornamental(*a.* 装饰性的, 装饰用的)

outline [ˈaʊtlaɪn] *n.* 轮廓(profile); 概要(summarization) *v.* 描绘; 略述

【记】分拆联想: out(外面的)+ line(线条)→ 外面的线条 → 轮廓; 概要

【例】She hasn't prepared the course *outline* yet. 她还没有准备好课程的概要。//Anne *outlined* the primary points of her speech. 安妮略述了她演说的要点。

oyster [ˈɔɪstər] *n.* 牡蛎, 蚝

【记】联想记忆: 妹妹(sister)爱吃牡蛎(oyster)

paddle [ˈpædl] *n.* 脚蹼

【记】分拆联想: pad(动物的肉趾, 如鸭蹼)+ dle → 鳍状肢 → 脚蹼

【例】John accidentally dropped his *paddle* in the lake. 约翰不小心把桨掉到了湖里。

【派】paddler(*n.* 划桨者)

perception [pərˈsepʃn] *n.* 感觉, 察觉; 认识, 观念

【记】来自perceive(*v.* 感知, 觉察)

【例】All the statues along the road seems perfectly designed for the grand religious *perception* the local people often had there. 路旁所有的雕像似乎完全是为迎合当地人拥有的宏大宗教观念而设计的。

【参】exception(*n.* 例外)

☐ mold	☐ neoclassical	☐ original	☐ ornament	☐ outline	☐ oyster
☐ paddle	☐ perception				

perceptive [pərˈseptɪv] *a.* 有感知的；有洞察力的

【例】A *perceptive* scholar questioned the professor's theory. 一位有洞察力的学者质疑这个教授的理论。

【参】perception(*n.* 理解；感知); perceptual(*a.* 知觉的)

pretentious [prɪˈtenʃəs] *a.* 自负的(boastful); 做作的

【例】Self-image can be indicated by a tone of voice that is confident, *pretentious*, shy, aggressive, or outgoing. 自我形象能够通过自信、做作、羞涩、挑衅或开朗的语气显示出来。

proceed [proʊˈsiːd] *vi.* 进行(progress); 发生(occur)

【记】词根记忆: pro(向前) + ceed(前进) → 向前前进 → 进行；发生

【例】As one *proceeds* toward the Southeast, broadleaf vegetation becomes dominant. 越往西南地区走，宽叶植被越多。

puncture [ˈpʌŋktʃər] *v.* 刺穿(*pierce, penetrate)

【记】词根记忆: punct(点) + ure → 戳出一个点 → 刺穿

【例】The tire *punctured* a mile from home. 在离家一英里的地方车胎被刺穿了。

rebel [rɪˈbel] *vt.* 造反

[ˈrebl] *n.* 叛逆者

【例】She insists she never started out to be a *rebel*. 她坚持认为自己并非一开始就是个叛逆者。

【派】rebellion(*n.* 叛乱); rebellious(*a.* 反叛的)

recall [rɪˈkɔːl] *vt.* 回忆(起)，回想起(recollect) *n.* 记忆

【例】I seem to *recall* that the festival got started in the 1930s. 我好像记得20世纪30年代才开始庆祝这个节日。

relevance [ˈreləvəns] *n.* 有关，相关(性)；切题；重大关系，意义；实用性

【记】词根记忆: re（一再）+ lev（举）+ ance → 一再列举 → 重要的 → 重大关系

【例】As you prepare to become elementary school teachers, you'll be hearing a lot of discussion about the *relevance* of teaching penmanship. 在准备成为小学老师时，你会听到很多关于是否应该教授书法的讨论。

remains [rɪˈmeɪnz] *n.* 剩余，残余；遗骸

resistant [rɪˈzɪstənt] *a.* 抵抗的，有抵抗力的

【搭】be resistant to 抵抗…

【例】Scientists found that a number of damaging insects were *resistant* to pesticide. 科学家们发现许多害虫对杀虫剂有抵抗力。

resistant

perceptive	pretentious	proceed	puncture	rebel	recall
relevance	remains	resistant			

rural ['rʊrəl] *a.* 乡村的，农村的(country)；田园的

【记】词根记忆：rur(乡村) + al(…的) → 乡村的

【例】Composers often write the music in *rural* communities. 作曲家们经常在乡村创作音乐。

rustic ['rʌstɪk] *a.* 用粗糙的木材制作的

【记】词根记忆：rust(乡村) + ic → 乡村风味的 → 用粗糙的木材制作的

【例】The *rustic* floor is quite dirty. 木地板非常脏。

sculpt [skʌlpt] *vt.* 雕刻(carve)

【派】sculptor(*n.* 雕刻家)；sculptural(*a.* 雕刻的，雕刻般的)

selective [sɪ'lektɪv] *a.* 选择的，选择性的；精挑细选的

【记】词根记忆：se + lect(选择) + ive → 选择的

【例】I wouldn't mind going to that university. It has an excellent reputation for commercial art, but I have a feeling that it's very *selective*. 我不介意去那所大学。它在商业美术方面有良好的声誉，但我觉得它非常挑剔。

shrink [ʃrɪŋk] *vi.* 收缩，缩小(dwindle)

【记】联想记忆：童话里面说喝(drink)了巫婆的药水就能将身体缩小(shrink)

【例】The crystals *shrink* and become more compact. 晶体收缩后会变得更加紧凑。

【派】shrinkage(*n.* 收缩)

sledding ['sledɪŋ] *n.* 滑雪(skee)

spontaneous [spɑːn'teɪniəs] *a.* 自发的，自然产生的(instinctive, unplanned)

【记】词根记忆：spont(自然) + aneous → 自然产生的，自发的

【搭】spontaneous generation 自然发生

【派】spontaneously(*ad.* 自然地，自发地)

sticky ['stɪki] *a.* 黏的，有黏性的

【记】来自stick(*v.* 粘，粘贴)

【例】A: My fingers are *sticky* from that candy bar. Do you mind if I use the restroom to wash up before we leave?

B: No, I'll be over at the bus stop.

A: 我的手指被巧克力糖果条弄得发黏。出发之前我去洗手间把手洗干净，你不介意吧？

B: 没关系。我在车站等你。

superficial [ˌsuːpər'fɪʃl] *a.* 肤浅的，表面的(surface)

【记】词根记忆：super(在…上面) + fic(做) + ial → 只在上面做 → 表面的

| rural | rustic | sculpt | selective | shrink | sledding |
| spontaneous | sticky | superficial | | | |

45

synthetic [sɪnˈθetɪk] *a.* 合成的，人造的(artificial) *n.* [常*pl.*] 合成物质

【记】词根记忆：syn(共同，相同) + thet(放) + ic → 放到一起的 → 合成的

【搭】synthetic product 合成产品

throw [θroʊ] *v.* 扔，抛，投(fling)

【搭】throw up 扬起，猛地举起或抬起

【例】A: Should I help clean up by *throwing* away these newspapers?

B: I want to clip a couple of articles first.

A: 我帮你清理一下，把这些报纸扔了吧？

B: 我想先剪几篇文章。

【参】grow(*v.* 生长，成长)

trade [treɪd] *n.* 贸易，商业；职业，行业 *v.* 经商，交易；对换

【搭】international trade 国际贸易；the drug trade 毒品交易；the slave trade 奴隶贸易；make a trade 做交易；restraint of trade 贸易管制

【例】A: This is the second time this month that my boss's asked me to work extra hours. I am glad to get a bigger paycheck, but I just don't want her to give me such a heavy schedule.

B: Better watch your step. A lot of people would like to *trade* places with you.

A: 这已经是我的老板本月第二次要求我加班了。多发工资我很高兴，但是我不想让她把我的工作安排得这么满。

B: 你还是小心为好。很多人都巴不得和你换位置。

About 200 years ago, the United States' economy was growing quickly, mainly because of a booming *trade* in grain and cotton. 大约200年前，美国经济迅速发展，主要是因为谷物和棉花的贸易兴旺。

【参】trace(*v.* 追踪)；fade(*v.* 褪色；枯萎)

undergraduate [ˌʌndərˈgrædʒuət] *n.* 大学肄业生(以别于graduate研究生)；本科生

【例】You might give a little more explanation about your unique *undergraduate* background. 你不妨稍微再解释一下你独特的本科背景。

vanish [ˈvænɪʃ] *vi.* 消失(disappear, fade)，灭绝(die out)

【记】词根记忆：van(空) + ish → 消失，灭绝

【例】Some oyster beds have *vanished* entirely. 一些牡蛎养殖场彻底消失了。

venom ［ˈvenəm］ *n.* (蛇的)毒液(poison)
【记】词根记忆：ven(来)+om → 带来痛 → 蛇的毒液会带来痛 →
(蛇的)毒液

venture ［ˈventʃər］ *n.* 冒险，投机(gamble) *v.* 冒险(risk)
【记】发音记忆："玩车" → 玩车一族追求的就是冒险 → 冒险
【例】The whole *venture* seemed so impractical and foolish. 整个冒险
似乎特别不切实际和愚蠢。//The monarch butterfly produces as
many as four generations a year, each one of which *ventures* a little
farther north. 黑脉金斑蝶一年产下四批后代，每一代都朝着北方挺
进一段距离。
【派】venturesome(*a.* 好冒险的)

veto ［ˈviːtoʊ］ *n.* 否决(权)，禁止(prohibition) *vt.* 否决
【记】在拉丁文中veto的意思是"我不准"(I forbid)，在英语里则表
示"否决"或"否决权"
【搭】pocket veto 搁置否决权；veto message 否决通知书
【例】Often, lawmakers simply revised the *vetoed* bill and passed it
again. 立法者往往修改被否决的议案，然后再次通过。

vibration ［vaɪˈbreɪʃn］ *n.* 振动，颤动(libration, quiver)
【搭】sympathetic vibration 共振
【例】Seismic waves are *vibrations* caused by earthquakes. 地震波指
地震产生的振动。
【参】vibrancy(*n.* 活泼；振动)

vicinity ［vəˈsɪnəti］ *n.* 邻近，附近
【记】词根记忆：vicin(邻近)+ity → 邻近的地区 → 邻近，附近
【例】It's concluded that Pierre and his companions did in fact reach
the near *vicinity* of the North Pole on April 6th, 1909. 结论表明，皮埃
尔及其同伴的确于1909年4月6日到达了北极附近地区。

Word List 5

词根、词缀预习表

ail	小病	ailment	n. 轻病, 小病
simil	相同	assimilate	vt. 吸收知识; 吸收; 使同化, 使相似
audi	听	audio	a. 声音的
cred	相信	credential	n. 证明书
fin	范围	define	v. 定义; 解释
note	意义	denote	v. 表示
ert	动	inert	a. 惰性的
labor	工作	laboratory	n. 实验室
litho	石	lithosphere	n. 岩石圈
pose	指出	propose	vt. 建议; 计划

ailment ['eɪlmənt] n. 轻病, 小病(sickness, illness)

【记】词根记忆: ail(小病)+ ment → 小病

【例】Thanks to the medical reforms, the poor man got timely treatment for his *ailment*. 多亏了医疗改革, 这个穷人的疾病得到了及时的医治。

assimilate [ə'sɪməleɪt] vt. 吸收知识; 消化, 吸收; 使同化

【记】词根记忆: as + simil(相同)+ ate(使…)→ 使相同 → 使同化

【例】Such kinds of foods are *assimilated* much more easily than others. 这种食物比其他食物更容易吸收。

【派】assimilation(n. 消化, 吸收; 融合, 同化)

assimilate

audio ['ɔːdioʊ] a. 音频的(acoustic); 声音的(vocal)

【记】词根记忆: audi(听)+ o → 听到声音 → 声音的

【例】She bought some *audio* equipment. 她购买了一些音频设备。

☐ ailment	☐ assimilate	☐ audio

axis ['æksɪs] *n.* 轴(shaft)

【参】ax(*n.* 斧头)

cable ['keɪbl] *n.* 缆绳；电缆(wire)；电报(telegraph)

【搭】wire cable 多股缆；钢丝绳

chubby ['tʃʌbi] *a.* 丰满的，圆胖的(plump, fat)

【参】skinny(*a.* 瘦得皮包骨一样的)；slim(*a.* 苗条的)

committee [kə'mɪti] *n.* 委员会(council)

【搭】curriculum committee 课程编制委员会；advisory committee 咨询委员会

commute [kə'mjuːt] *v.* 坐公交车上下班

【记】词根记忆：com(共同) + mut(改变) + e → 换乘公共的车 → 坐公交车上下班

【例】More and more people live far from the old city center and still *commute* there for work. 越来越多的人住在远离老市中心的地方，不过他们仍然乘公交车去那里上班。

【派】commuter(*n.* 经常往返者；通勤者)

【参】telecommuter(*n.* 远程电脑工程师)

consult [kən'sʌlt] *v.* 请教；商议(counsel)；参考，翻阅(refer to)

【记】和insult(*v.* 侮辱)一起记

【例】She is *consulting* with the reference librarian. 她正在向参考书阅览室的图书管理员请教。

【派】consultant(*n.* 顾问)

【参】result(*n.* 结果)；assault(*n.* 攻击，袭击)

converse [kən'vɜːrs] *vi.* 交谈(talk, discuss)

【例】Pairs of deaf people are able to *converse* freely over television. 成对的听障人士能够通过电视自由交谈。

corrosive [kə'rousɪv] *a.* 腐蚀(性)的(tending or having the power to corrode)

【例】Chlorine is a *corrosive* gas that has sharp odor. 氯气是一种味道刺鼻的腐蚀性气体。

courageous [kə'reɪdʒəs] *a.* 勇敢的，有胆量的(brave)

【记】分拆联想：courage(勇气) + ous(…的) → 有勇气的 → 勇敢的

【参】righteous(*a.* 正直的)

cousin ['kʌzn] *n.* 堂(或表)兄弟，堂(或表)姐妹

【例】My *cousin*, who is a geography teacher, helped us plan our trip. 我的堂兄是地理老师，他帮助我们筹划旅行。

axis	cable	chubby	committee	commute	consult
converse	corrosive	courageous	cousin		

credential [krə'denʃl] *n.* 证明书（certificate），文凭（diploma），资格（qualification）

【记】词根记忆：cred（相信）＋ential → 让人相信的东西 → 证明书

【例】None of the people who applied for the job has the required *credentials*. 申请这个工作的人都不具备所需的资格。

define [dɪ'faɪn] *v.* 定义；解释（explain）

【记】词根记忆：de＋fin（范围）＋e → 划定范围 → 定义

【例】As the roles men and women played in society became more rigidly *defined*, so did the roles they played in the home. 随着男性和女性在社会中的角色限定越来越严格，他们在家庭中的角色也会是如此。

【派】redefine(*v.* 重新定义)

【参】confine(*vt.* 限制)

denote [dɪ'noʊt] *v.* 表示（show），意味着

【记】词根记忆：de＋note（意义）→ 给予意义 → 表示，意味着

【例】In sculpture, the term "modelling" *denotes* a way of shaping clay, wax, or other pliable materials. 雕塑艺术中"塑形"一词表示使黏土、蜡或其他可塑的材料成形的方式。

【参】connote(*v.* 意味着；暗示)；notify(*v.* 通知)

detergent [dɪ'tɜːrdʒənt] *n.* 清洁剂

【记】词根记忆：de＋terg（擦）＋ent → 能擦去污渍的东西 → 清洁剂

device [dɪ'vaɪs] *n.* 装置，设备（equipment, apparatus）；手法（technique）

【例】Allegory is a literary *device* by which another level of meaning is concealed within what is usually a story. 寓言是一种文学手法，通过这种手法把另外一层意思通常隐藏在一个故事里面。

【参】devise(*vt.* 设计)

dominant ['dɑːmɪnənt] *a.* 支配的（predominant），统治的；占优势的（important, outweighing）

【记】词根记忆：domin(=dom支配)＋ant → 占支配地位的 → 支配的

【搭】a dominant power in the world 世界头号强国；dominant position 支配地位；dominant philosophy 主流哲学；dominant theme 主题，主旨；dominant in sth. 主宰…

【例】Aristotle considered an object downward or upward motion to be the result of *dominant* nature of the object. 亚里士多德认为，物体的上下运动是由物体本身所具有的支配性所产生的结果。

【派】predominant(*a.* 卓越的；支配的)

estimate [ˈestɪmeɪt] *vt.* 估计(*judge, *reckon); 估价(value)

[ˈestɪmət] *n.* 估计; 估价

【例】One of these migrating swarms was *estimated* to contain 124 billion locusts. 据估计，这些迁徙的蝗虫中的一批有1240亿只。

【派】underestimate(*v./n.* 低估)

excavation [ˌekskəˈveɪʃn] *n.* 挖掘

facilitate [fəˈsɪlɪteɪt] *vt.* 推动, 促进(impulse)

【例】Government's trade policies *facilitated* the exporting of agricultural products. 政府的贸易政策推动了农产品的出口。

fellow [ˈfeloʊ] *n.* 家伙; 同事(colleague) *a.* 同道的

【例】Monet and his 29 *fellow* artists adopted the same name as a badge of their unity. 莫奈和29位艺术家同行采用了同样的名字，以示团结。

foremost [ˈfɔːrmoʊst] *a.* 最著名的; 最重要的(*leading, chief)

【记】组合词: fore(前面) + most(最) → 最前面的 → 最重要的; 最著名的

【例】He is one of the *foremost* pianists of our day. 他是我们这个时代最著名的钢琴家之一。

frenzy [ˈfrenzi] *n.* 狂暴(fury)

【记】词根记忆: fren(=phren心灵) + zy → 有关心灵 → 内心疯狂 → 狂暴

【例】Adams lamented the role that the new *frenzy* for business was playing in eroding traditional values. 新的商业狂热侵蚀了传统价值观，这让亚当斯痛惜不已。

【参】frenetic(*a.* 发狂的)

friction [ˈfrɪkʃn] *n.* 摩擦; 冲突(clash, conflict)

【记】联想记忆: 润滑油的功能(function)是减小摩擦(friction)

【例】The forward movement of a small animal is seriously reduced by the air *friction*. 小动物向前的运动因受到空气的摩擦而减缓。

hardware [ˈhɑːrdwer] *n.* 五金制品

【记】组合词: hard(硬的, 坚固的) + ware(器皿) → 五金制品

【例】Relatively little *hardware* was used during this period. 这个时期五金制品使用得相对较少。

【参】kitchenware 厨房用具; stoneware 瓷器

imprint [ɪmˈprɪnt] *vt.* 铭记, 牢记 (engrave) [ˈɪmprɪnt] *n.* 印记, 印痕 (*trace)

【记】分拆联想: im(进入) + print(印) → 深深地印入 → 印记, 印痕

【例】Did you see the deep *imprint* of the big toe? 你看到大脚趾所留下的深深的印痕了吗？

induce [ɪnˈduːs] *vt.* 引起，导致(*cause)；诱使

【记】词根记忆：in(使)＋duc(引导)＋e→引起，导致

【例】The marine biologists could *induce* oysters to spawn not only in the summer but also in the fall. 海洋生物学家可以诱使牡蛎在夏、秋两季均产卵。

【派】inducement(*n.* 引诱；劝诱)；inducible(*a.* 可诱导的，可诱发的)

【参】educe(*vt.* 得出)；deduce(*vt.* 推论)

inert [ɪˈnɜːrt] *a.* 惰性的(inactive)

【记】词根记忆：in(不)＋ert(动)→不动的→惰性的

【搭】inert element 惰性元素

【例】Viruses are *inert* outside living cells, but within the appropriate cells they can replicate. 病毒在活体细胞外呈惰性，但是在合适的细胞里它能够复制。

infection [ɪnˈfekʃn] *n.* 感染；传染病

【记】来自infect(*v.* 传染，感染)

【例】He had an ear *infection*. 他耳部感染了。

intense [ɪnˈtens] *a.* 强烈的(*extreme)；热切的(*acute)；极度的；认真的

【例】The metal burned with an *intense* flash. 金属燃烧时发出了强烈的闪光。//It was the result of *intense* study. 这是认真研究的结果。

【派】intensity(*n.* 强度)；intensive(*a.* 密集的；精耕细作的)；intensively(*ad.* 集约地；集中地)

intuitive [ɪnˈtuːɪtɪv] *a.* 直觉的

【例】What does make them good is having an *intuitive* feeling for how the music works. 他们之所以优秀，是因为对音乐如何发挥作用拥有直觉。

isolated [ˈaɪsəleɪtɪd] *a.* 分离的，隔绝的(secluded)；独一无二的(unique)

【记】来自isolate(*v.* 分离)

【例】The oceanic islands of the Pacific are some of the most *isolated* places on Earth. 太平洋上的海岛是地球上最与世隔绝的地方。//A folk culture is small, *isolated* and cohesive. 民俗文化的规模小，独一无二且有凝聚性。

【参】isolation(*n.* 孤立；隔绝)

jelly [ˈdʒelɪ] *n.* 果冻

【记】分拆联想：j + elly（看作belly，胃）→ 果冻吃多了会胃胀 →
果冻

【参】jellyfish(*n.* 海蜇)

jolt [dʒoʊlt] *vt.* 使震惊(*shock) *n.* 震动(shake)

【记】联想记忆：防止房门震动(jolt)时用门闩(bolt)将其固定

【例】The high rate of species extinctions in these environments is
jolting. 这些环境里物种灭绝率之高令人震惊。//The eel in the tank
behind me can produce a strong *jolt* of electricity to stun its prey. 我背
后鱼缸里的鳗鱼可以产生强烈的电流来击昏其捕食对象。

laboratory [ˈlæbrətɔːri] *n.* 实验室

【记】词根记忆：labor(工作) + atory(地点) → 工作的地方 → 实验室

lament [ləˈment] *vt.* 抱怨(*complain)

【记】分拆联想：lam(看作lame，瘸的) + ent → 瘸了腿所以抱怨 →
抱怨

leftover [ˈleftoʊvər] *n.* [常*pl.*] 剩余物；剩饭菜

【例】There weren't many *leftovers* from yesterday. 昨天没有剩下多
少菜。

lithosphere [ˈlɪθəsfɪr] *n.* 岩石圈(the outer part of the solid earth)

【记】词根记忆：litho(石) + sphere(范围，领域) → 岩石的范围 →
岩石圈

【例】The *lithosphere* is divided into a few dozen plates of various
sizes and shapes. 岩石圈分为尺寸和形状不同的十几个岩层。

manufacture [ˌmænjuˈfæktʃər] *v./n.* (大量) 制造，加工 (produce, process)；
[*pl.*] 制造品，产品(product)

【记】词根记忆：manu(手) + fact(制作) + ure → 用手制作 → 制
造，加工

【例】Those companies rely on high accuracy scales to *manufacture*
and package medicine. 这些公司依靠高精度秤来生产和包装药品。//
Automobile *manufacturers* are under pressure to develop cars that do
not pollute. 汽车制造商们正面临着开发无污染汽车的压力。

【派】manufactured(*a.* 人造的)；manufacturer (*n.* 制造商)

opposed [əˈpoʊzd] *a.* 反对的

【例】The have *opposed* views on the question. 在这个问题上他们持
相反的观点。

【派】opposing(*a.* 相反的，对立的)；opposition(*n.* 反对，敌对)；
oppose(*v.* 反对)

overhaul ['ouvərhɔːl] *n.* 仔细检查（examination）

【记】分拆联想：over + haul（拉，拖）→ 全部拉上来修理 → 仔细检查

【例】The citizens demanded an *overhaul* of the corrupt government. 公民要求全面治理腐败的政府。

overtime ['ouvərtaɪm] *a.* 超时的，加班的 *ad.* 加班地

【例】My boss keeps asking me to work *overtime*. 我的老板不断要求我加班。

A: Do you have to work *overtime* on your job?

B: Every so often I do.

A：你的工作要加班吗？

B：偶尔要加班。

overtime

pack [pæk] *vt.* 捆扎，塞满（stuff）*n.* 包裹（parcel）

【例】It is time to *pack* up my gloves and boots. 该把我的手套和靴子打包了。

【派】packing(*n.* 包装)；packer(*n.* 包装机)

pay [peɪ] *v.* 支付，付出；给予（注意）；值得；进行（访问等）*n.* 工资，薪金

【搭】pay for sth. 付…的款

【例】If you can see the movie on television, why *pay* for it? 如果你能在电视上看电影，那为什么还要掏钱看呢？

【参】repay(*v.* 偿还)

perfect ['pɜːrfɪkt] *a.* 完美的，理想的（*ideal, flawless）

[pə'fekt] *vt.* 使完美；使熟练

【例】Practice makes *perfect*. 熟能生巧。

【派】perfection(*n.* 完美)；perfectly(*ad.* 完美地；完全)

photodissociation [foutoudɪˌsouʃi'eɪʃn] *n.* 光解（作用）

【例】The sun split water vapor into hydrogen and oxygen during a process called *photodissociation*. 太阳在光解过程中把水蒸气分解为氢气和氧气。

pigeon ['pɪdʒɪn] *n.* 鸽子

【记】发音记忆："批准" → 禽流感期间，养鸽子也要经过批准 → 鸽子

poetry ['pouətri] *n.* 诗歌，诗集

【记】来自poet(*n.* 诗人)

【搭】modern poetry 现代诗

【例】A: Will you come to my *poetry* reading next week?

B: I'll be out of town then.

A：你下周会来我的诗歌朗诵会吗？

B：我那时候会出城。

principle ［'prɪnsəpl］*n.* 原则(fundamental)；原理(theory)

【记】词根记忆：prin(第一) + cip(取) + le → 须第一位选取的 → 原则；原理

【例】What is the *principle* idea of the laisser faire policy? 自由放任政策的核心思想是什么？

【参】principal(*n.* 负责人)

profound ［prə'faʊnd］*a.* 深远的(deep-seated)；知识渊博的(having intellectual depth and insight)；深奥的(difficult to understand)

【记】联想记忆：pro(在…前) + found(创立) → 有超前创见性的 → 深远的

【例】The transition to settled life also had a *profound* impact on the family. 向稳定生活的转变对这个家庭也有着深远的影响。

【派】profoundly(*ad.* 深度地)

promote ［prə'moʊt］*vt.* 促进；提升(boost, advance)；宣传(advertise)

【记】词根记忆：pro(向前) + mote(动) → 向前动 → 促进

【例】In the early decades of the United States, the agrarian movement *promoted* the farmer as society's hero. 美国建国之初的几十年，农业运动把农民提升为社会的英雄。

【派】promotion(*n.* 晋升；提升；宣传)

prompt ［prɑːmpt］*vt.* 促进，推动(accelerate, incite)；发扬(develop)

【记】词根记忆：pro(向前) + mpt → 使…向前 → 促进，推动

【例】Bob's dislike for hot weather *prompted* him to move north. 鲍勃不喜欢炎热的天气，这促使他迁往北方。

【派】promptly(*ad.* 迅速地)

propose ［prə'poʊz］*vt.* 建议(suggest)；计划(project)

【记】词根记忆：pro(提前) + pose(指出) → 提前计划，提出建议 → 建议；计划

【例】A number of schemes were *proposed* for sending pictures by Internet. 人们提出数个用网络发送图片的方案。

【派】proposal(*n.* 提案，建议)

reactor ［ri'æktər］*n.* 反应堆

【记】词根记忆：react(反应) + or → 发生反应的东西 → 反应堆

【搭】reactor pot 反应堆容器

【例】Impurities are washed out with methanol, I think, before this gas is sent on to *reactors* where it's changed into oil. 我认为，这种气体在被送往反应器转变为油之前，其杂质就用甲醇清洗干净了。

realization [ˌriːələˈzeɪʃn] *n.* 实现 (fulfillment)；意识 (awareness)

【例】Expectation is better than *realization*. 期望比实现更美好。

recession [rɪˈseʃn] *n.* 萧条时期

【记】词根记忆：re (反) + cess (行走) + ion → 经济向后走 → 萧条时期

reliable [rɪˈlaɪəbl] *a.* 可靠的，可信赖的 (dependable, trustworthy)

【记】来自 rely (*v.* 信赖)

【例】The majority of companies are willing to look for employees who are *reliable* and hard-working. 大部分公司愿意雇用可靠并勤劳的员工。

【派】reliability (*n.* 可靠性)

remarkable [rɪˈmɑːrkəbl] *a.* 显著的，值得注意的；非凡的 (*extraordinary, incredible)

【例】The newer ones experienced *remarkable* growth, which reflected basic changes in the economy. 新生事物经历了显著的增长，这反映了经济的基本变化。

【派】remarkably (*ad.* 显著地)

replenish [rɪˈpleniʃ] *vt.* 添加；补充 (supplement)

【记】词根记忆：re (重新) + plen (满) + ish → 重新添满 → 添加；补充

【例】The body needs to be *replenished* with nutrient in order to maintain a high level of energy throughout the day. 身体需要补充营养才能在全天保持高级别的活力。

response [rɪˈspɑːns] *n.* 回答；反应，响应

【派】responsive (*a.* 响应的)

revolution [ˌrevəˈluːʃn] *n.* 革命

【记】词根记忆：re + volut (滚；卷) + ion → 不断向前席卷而来的 → 革命

【派】revolutionary (*a.* 革命的)；revolutionize (*vt.* 使彻底变革)

scurry [ˈskɜːri] *v.* 急跑 (*rush, scamper)

【记】词根记忆：s + cur (跑) + ry → 急跑

sensible [ˈsensəbl] *a.* 明显的 (perceptible)；明智的 (advisable)；切合实际的 (practical)

【记】词根记忆：sens (感觉) + ible → 感觉到的 → 明显的

realization	recession	reliable	remarkable	replenish	response
revolution	scurry	sensible			

simulate [ˈsɪmjuleɪt] *vt.* 模仿，模拟(imitate)

【记】词根记忆：simul(类似) + ate(使…) → 使某物类似于某物 → 模仿

【例】The computer program *simulated* the effects of aging. 电脑程序模拟了变老的效果。

simulate

sluggish [ˈslʌɡɪʃ] *a.* 行动迟缓的(slow); 不活泼的(lethargic, inactive)

【记】词根记忆：slugg(=slug偷懒) + ish → 偷懒的 → 行动迟缓的

【搭】a sluggish market 不景气的市场

【例】I have taken some tablets that can make people feel rather *sluggish*. 我吃了一些会让人感到行动迟缓的药片。

【派】sluggishly(*ad.* 行动迟缓地); sluggishness(*n.* 萧条; 呆滞)

soft [sɔːft] *a.* 柔软的(delicate); 柔和的(mild, gentle); 不含酒精的

【搭】soft tissue 软组织; soft spot 弱点; 软弱不振的企业; soft focus 软焦点(照片)

【派】soften[*v.* (使)变柔软]; softness(*n.* 柔和; 柔软)

squash [skwɑːʃ] *n.* 南瓜(pumpkin)

【记】分拆联想：squ + ash(灰) → 给南瓜施点灰，会长得更大 → 南瓜

stuck [stʌk] *a.* 粘在(上面)的; 遇到困难(干不下去)的

【搭】get stuck 坚持(某种想法或信念)不动摇

【例】A: I hear you're really happy with your new car. I bet it's a lot better than the last one you got *stuck* with, the one you bought from Cathy.

B: I'm sure I've made a good choice this time.

A: 我听说你对新车很满意。我打赌它肯定比你上次从凯茜那里买的车强。

B: 我肯定这次我做了正确的选择。

A: I can't get this window open. It's really *stuck*.

B: Why don't you try using this screwdriver and see if that works?

A: 我打不开这扇窗户。卡得很死。

B: 你为何不试着用这把螺丝刀看能否撬开?

subsequent [ˈsʌbsɪkwənt] *a.* 随后的(*later); 并发的(successive)

【记】词根记忆：sub(下面) + sequ(跟随) + ent → 随后的

【例】*Subsequent* reforms have made these notions seem quite out-of-date. 随后的改革使这些观念显得颇为过时。

【派】subsequently(*ad.* 后来，随后)

【参】consequent(*a.* 作为结果的)

substantiate [səbˈstænʃieɪt] *vt.* 证实(*verify)

【记】词根记忆：substant(事实；物质)＋iate → 用事实来证明 → 证实

【例】The hypothesis was *substantiated* soon afterward by the discovery. 这个假设很快被这个发现证实了。

【参】substantial(*a.* 可观的，大量的)；substantive(*a.* 真实的；有实质的)

suburb [ˈsʌbɜːrb] *n.* 郊区

【记】词根记忆：sub(靠近)＋urb(城市) → 靠近城市的地方 → 郊区

【派】suburban(*a.* 郊外的，偏远的)；suburbanite(*n.* 郊区居民)；suburbanization(*n.* 近郊化；郊区建造)

supreme [suːˈpriːm] *a.* 最高的；最重要的(*most outstanding)

【记】词根记忆：supre(=super超过)＋me → 超越我的 → 最高的

【搭】supreme court 最高法院

【派】supremacy(*n.* 至高无上，霸权)；supremely(*ad.* 至高无上地，崇高地)

trace [treɪs] *vt.* 追溯；探索(explore)；描摹(describe) *n.* 痕迹(*imprint)；微量

【例】The Anasazi family was matrilinear, that is, descent was *traced* through the female. 阿那萨奇人的家庭是母系家庭，也就是说通过女性来传宗接代。//Scientists believe that when the oceans were young, they contained only a *trace* of salt. 科学家们认为，海洋在刚形成的时候只包含少量的盐分。

vague [veɪg] *a.* 模糊的(obscure)

【记】词根记忆：vag(=vaga流浪)＋ue → 思路总是在四处流浪 → 模糊的

【例】A *vague* air of mystery envelops them. 一种模糊的神秘感笼罩着他们。//The language of the charters was *vague*. 宪章中的语言含混不清。

【派】vaguely(*ad.* 含糊地)；vagueness(*n.* 含糊，不明确)

vast [væst] *a.* 巨大的，大量的；范围广的(large, broad, extensive)

【记】联想记忆：东方(east)地大(vast)物博

【搭】in vast numbers 大量的；the vast majority 绝大多数

【派】vastness(*n.* 巨大)；vastly(*ad.* 广大地)

virus [ˈvaɪrəs] *n.* 病毒

【记】发音记忆："娃弱死" → 小孩子身体弱，被病毒感染死掉了 → 病毒

substantiate	suburb	supreme	trace	vague	vast
virus					

【例】The *virus* replicates by attaching to a cell and injecting its nucleic acid. 病毒附着在细胞上，并往其中输入核酸来实现复制。

visual [ˈvɪʒuəl] *a.* 视觉的；看得见的

【记】词根记忆：vis(看) + ual(…的) → 视觉的

【搭】visual aids 直观教具；visual arts 视觉艺术；visual image 可视图像

【例】Without Julie's photograph, no *visual* record of the work would exist. 如果没有朱莉的照片，就不会存在这个视觉记录作品了。

【派】visualize(*v.* 想象，设想)；visually(*ad.* 视觉上地)

watercourse [ˈwɔːtərkɔːrs] *n.* 水道，河道

To pursue something, you should advance in regular order. Be sure never to be overhasty. Sometimes, the more eagerly you want to reach it, the farther it will be away from you.

对任何事物的追求都要循序渐进，不可操之过急。有些时候，你追得越急，它反而离你越远。

——李俊琪(*Li Junqi*)

Word List 6 🔘 MP3-06

词根、词缀预习表

lev	轻	alleviate	v. 减轻，缓和
celest	天空	celestial	a. 天空的
flagel	鞭子	flagellum	n. 鞭毛
cred	相信	credential	n. 证明书
glaci	冰	glacial	a. 冰期的
stitut	建立	institute	vt. 设立，制定
journ	日	journal	n. 日记，日志
sense	意义	nonsense	n. 胡说，废话
not	标识	notation	n. 符号
rupt	断	rupture	v. (使)破裂

agreeable [ə'griːəbl] a. 使人愉快的(pleasant)；欣然同意的(willing)

【记】来自agree(v. 同意，赞成)

【例】We find Bob *agreeable* most of the time. 我们发现鲍勃大部分时间都比较随和。//They were most *agreeable* on the subject of voting rights. 他们非常愿意谈论选举权这个话题。

allegiance [ə'liːdʒəns] n. 忠诚，效忠(loyalty, devotion)；忠贞；拥戴

【记】词根记忆：al + leg(法律) + iance → 法律需要人人拥护 → 忠诚

【例】Some chants showed people's *allegiance* to religious leaders or symbols. 一些咏唱表现了人们对宗教领袖或宗教信条的忠诚。

alleviate [ə'liːvieɪt] v. 减轻，缓和(relieve)

【记】词根记忆：al(加强) + lev(轻) + iate(使…) → 使…轻 → 减轻，缓和

【例】The drug *alleviated* the pain of Mary's broken leg. 这个药缓解了玛丽断腿的痛苦。

☐ agreeable   ☐ allegiance   ☐ alleviate

angular [ˈæŋgjələr] *a.* 有角的，尖角的

annoyed [əˈnɔɪd] *a.* 生气的（angry）

【例】She's *annoyed* with the man. 她在生这个男人的气。

【参】annoying(*a.* 恼人的，讨厌的)

architect [ˈɑːrkɪtekt] *n.* 建筑师

【记】词根记忆：archi(=archy统治) + tect(遮蔽) → 统治建造人类遮身之所的人 → 建筑师

【派】architecture(*n.* 建筑；建筑学); architectural(*a.* 建筑上的)

ascending [əˈsendɪŋ] *a.* 上升的，向上的（*climbing）

【例】The architects laid out a system of public roads with stone staircases for *ascending* cliff faces. 建筑师用石台阶设计了公用道路系统，以攀登岩壁。

bounce [baʊns] *v./n.* (使)弹，(使)反弹

【例】The basketball *bounced* off the backboard and missed the basket. 篮球从篮板上弹了回来，没进篮筐。//Your little nephew is growing by leaps and *bounce*. 你的小侄子长得很快。

cabin [ˈkæbɪn] *n.* 小屋（hut, cottage）

carp [kɑːrp] *n.* 鲤鱼

celestial [səˈlestʃl] *a.* 天空的（*astronomical, heavenly）

【记】词根记忆：celest(天空) + ial → 天空的

【搭】celestial body 天体

【例】Stars may be spheres, but not every *celestial* object is spherical. 星星可能是球体，但并非每个天体都是球形的。

ceremony [ˈserəmoʊni] *n.* 典礼，仪式；礼节

【记】分拆联想：cere(蜡) + mony → 古代典礼上蜡烛是少不了的 → 典礼

【搭】graduation ceremony 毕业典礼

【派】ceremonial(*a.* 仪式的；正式的 *n.* 仪式)

colonial [kəˈloʊniəl] *a.* 殖民(地)的

【记】来自colony(*n.* 殖民地)

【例】A: Hey, Teresa! Thanks for agreeing to help me review all this history material.

B: No problem, Bob. So do you want to start with the stuff missed yesterday? They are part about urban problems in the *colonial* period.

A: 嗨，特蕾莎！谢谢你同意帮我复习所有这些历史材料。

B: 没问题，鲍勃。你想开始补昨天漏掉的材料吗？部分内容是关于殖民时期的城市问题的。

comparable [ˈkɑːmpərəbl] *a.* (with, to)可比较的，类似的(similar, like)；比得上的(capable of or suitable for comparison)

【例】The potters replaced the imports with *comparable* domestic goods. 制陶工人用类似的国内产品替代了进口品。

complementary [ˌkɑːmplɪˈmentri] *a.* 补充的；互补的

【搭】complementary colors 互补色

congressional [kənˈgreʃənl] *a.* 代表大会的，会议的；国会的；最高立法机关的

【搭】congressional representative 国会代表；Congressional Medal of Honor 国会荣誉勋章；Congressional Record 国会报告

【例】William was given the *Congressional* Medal of Honor because of his great bravery during the war. 威廉因其战争期间的英勇表现被授予了国会荣誉勋章。

cornerstone [ˈkɔːrnərstoʊn] *n.* 墙角石，奠基石；柱石；基础

【例】Homer was the poet that laid down the *cornerstone* of western literature. 荷马是西方文学的奠基诗人。

crew [kruː] *n.* 全体船员；全体工作人员

【记】发音记忆："可入" → 限工作人员进入，闲人免进 → 全体工作人员

crow [kroʊ] *n.* 乌鸦

department [dɪˈpɑːrtmənt] *n.* 系，学部；部，局，处，科，部门(section)

【例】I read in the campus newspaper that your roommate was named the top student in the history *department*. 我在校报上看到你的室友被评为了历史系优等生。

A: I'm counting on my library science professor to get me a job in the cataloging *department* this summer.

B: I'm not sure it's up to him.

A：我正指望我的图书馆学教授今年夏天能在编目部给我找个工作。

B：我不能肯定这是否由他决定。

deserve [dɪˈzɜːrv] *v.* 应得；值得(be entitled to)

【记】词根记忆：de + serve(服务) → 充分享受服务 → 应得；值得

【例】The man *deserves* the grade he received. 这个人获得的等级是他应得的。

【派】deserved(*a.* 应得的)；deserving(*a.* 理应获得的)；undeserved(*a.* 不应得的)

【参】desert(*n.* 沙漠)

☐ comparable	☐ complementary	☐ congressional	☐ cornerstone	☐ crew	☐ crow
☐ department	☐ deserve				

desire [dɪˈzaɪər] v. 想要，渴望(long for) n. 愿望，欲望(appetite)

desire

【例】Customers generally discussed the silver objects they *desired*. 顾客们大致地讨论了一下他们想要的银制品。

【派】desired(a. 渴望的)；desirable(a. 值得要的)

digression [daɪˈgreʃn] n. 离题，扯到枝节上；题外话，枝节内容

【例】Although this might seem to be a *digression*, the professor is using an example to explain why plants that are grown in water must have gas bubbled through the water. 表面看来这好像是题外话，实际上教授是在用这个例子来解释水生植物为何必须在水中产生气泡。

director [dəˈrektər] n. 导演；主管，负责人(principal)

disadvantage [ˌdɪsədˈvæntɪdʒ] n. 缺点(drawback)；不利(handicap)

【记】词根记忆：dis(不) + advantage(优点) → 不是优点 → 缺点；不利

【派】disadvantageous(a. 不利的)

distinguish [dɪˈstɪŋgwɪʃ] v. 区别，辨别(*discriminate, differentiate)；出名

【记】词根记忆：di(分开) + sting(刺) + uish → 将刺挑出来 → 区别，辨别

【搭】distinguish from 区别，识别；distinguish oneself 使出名

【例】These three kinds of meteorites can usually be *distinguished* by density. 这三种陨星通常可以通过密度来区别。

【派】distinguishable(a. 可区别的)；distinguished(a. 著名的)；distinguishing(a. 有区别的)

eccentric [ɪkˈsentrɪk] a. 古怪的；反常的(odd, abnormal) n. 古怪的人

【记】词根记忆：ec(出) + centr(中心) + ic → 偏离中心的 → 古怪的(人)

【例】She began to dress only in white—a habit that added to her reputation as an *eccentric*. 她开始只穿白衣服——这个习惯使人们越发觉得她古怪。

【派】eccentricity(n. 古怪)

eligible [ˈelɪdʒəbl] a. 符合条件的，合格的(qualified)

【记】词根记忆：e + lig(=lect选择) + ible → 能被选择出来的 → 合格的

【例】Members of the Academy and Institute are not *eligible* for any cash prizes. 研究院的成员没有资格获得奖金。

【派】ineligible(a. 没有资格的)

desire	digression	director	disadvantage	distinguish	eccentric
eligible					

file [faɪl] *n.* 档案；行列 *v.* 归档(categorize)；提出

【例】I don't want to *file* all those letters. 我不想把所有这些信都归档。//Gould *filed* a patent application. 古尔德申请了专利。

flagellum [fləˈdʒeləm] *n.* [*pl.* flagella] 鞭毛

【记】词根记忆：flagel(鞭子) + lum → 鞭节，鞭毛

【例】Many bacteria lack *flagella* and cannot move about by their own power. 很多细菌没有鞭毛，不能靠自身的力量移动。

fold [foʊld] *n.* 褶皱(pleat) *v.* 合拢(bend)

【例】Many butterflies can suddenly disappear from view by *folding* their wings. 很多蝴蝶合起翅膀就能突然从眼前消失。

foolish [ˈfuːlɪʃ] *a.* 愚蠢的

【搭】look foolish 看起来蠢；a foolish person 蠢人；foolish behavior 愚蠢的行为；it is foolish to do sth. 做…很愚蠢

【例】Maybe some respondents' answers sound *foolish*, but the disturbing traffic problem needs solving as soon as possible. 或许有些回应者的回答听起来愚蠢，但是交通问题很烦人，需要尽快解决。

【派】fool(*n.* 愚人)；foolishly(*ad.* 愚笨地；无聊地)

fungi [ˈfʌŋiː] *n.* [*pl.* fungus] 真菌

【记】发音记忆："房盖" → 真菌的形状像房盖

【例】Eatable mushroom, a kind of *fungi*, has a high value of nutrition and is good for our health. 可食用的蘑菇是一种真菌，具有很高的营养价值，有益健康。

【参】bacteria(*n.* 细菌)；virus(*n.* 病毒)

glacial [ˈgleɪʃl] *a.* 冰期的；冰河时代的

【记】词根记忆：glaci(冰) + al → 冰期的

【例】A glacier maintains the same shape throughout the *glacial* process. 冰川在整个冰河期都保持同样的形状。

【派】glaciated(*a.* 受到冰川作用的)

grab [græb] *vt.* (随便地或匆匆地)取或拿(clutch)

【记】联想记忆：螃蟹(crab)用钳子抓(grab)人

【例】I'll *grab* a snack at the break. 我会在休息期间吃点东西。

grasp [græsp] *vt.* 抓住(seize)

【例】Their hands and feet are designed for holding and *grasping* branches. 他们的手和脚是用来抓握树枝的。

improvise [ˈɪmprəvaɪz] *vt.* 即席创作；临时准备

【记】词根记忆：im(不) + pro(在前) + vise(看) → 没有预先看过 → 即席创作

□ file	□ flagellum	□ fold	□ foolish	□ fungi	□ glacial
□ grab	□ grasp	□ improvise			

【例】The musical arrangement was normally *improvised* in the greatest hurry. 乐曲通常都是在很匆忙的情况下即席创作出来的。

【派】improvisation(*n.* 即席创作；即兴作品)

inconspicuous [ˌɪnkən'spɪkjuəs] *a.* 不显眼的(unapparent)

【例】It is said that the grand spectacle of a comet develops from a relatively small and *inconspicuous* chunk of ice and dust. 据说巨大的彗星开始只是由较小而不起眼的冰和灰尘组成的块状物。

institute ['ɪnstɪtuːt] *n.* 研究所，学院 *vt.* 设立；制定(establish)

【记】词根记忆：in + stitut(建立) + e → 设立；制定

【例】The government *instituted* a 35-hour workweek. 政府制定了每周工作35小时的制度。

【派】institution(*n.* 社会公共机构)

journal ['dʒɜːrnl] *n.* 定期刊物，杂志；日记，日志

【记】词根记忆：journ(日) + al → 日记，日志

【例】By 1892, for example, the circulation of the *Ladies' Home Journal* had reached an astounding 700,000. 例如，到1892年，《女士居家杂志》的发行量令人吃惊，已达到了70万份。

【派】journalism(*n.* 新闻业，新闻工作)；journalist(*n.* 新闻工作者)

landmark ['lændmɑːrk] *n.* (显而易见的)路标，地标；<喻>里程碑

【记】组合词：land(陆地) + mark(标志) → 地上的标志 → 路标

【搭】landmark and historic sites 风景名胜

【例】You should really keep this map with you for the first couple of weeks, at least until you'll become familiar with the buildings and *landmarks*. 最初几周你应该保留这张地图，至少等你熟悉了建筑物和地标之后。

loose [luːs] *a.* 松散的，宽松的；不牢固的(unstable)

【记】和lose(*v.* 失去)一起记

【例】I'm going to fix some *loose* shutters on my house. 我打算修理那下家里一些不牢固的百叶窗。

loose

【派】loosely(*ad.* 松散地)；loosen(*v.* 解开，放松，松开)

lost and found *n.* 失物招领

【搭】lost-and-found case 失物招领箱；lost-and-found office 失物招领处

【例】A: Excuse me, did anybody find a black umbrella after the last show? I left it under my chair.

B: As a matter of fact, we did. Check it at the ticket counter. That's where we turn in the *lost-and-found* items.

A：对不起，上次演出之后有谁看到一把黑色的伞了吗？我把它忘在座位下面了。

B：我们的确发现了一把。你去售票柜台看看。失物都交到那里了。

lush [lʌʃ] *a.* 茂盛的（flourishing）

【例】Severin began to paint large, *lush* still lifes of flowers, fruit, or both. 塞弗兰开始创作花卉、水果或两者兼而有之的大幅葱翠静物写生。

【派】lushness（*n.* 草木茂盛）

【参】blush（*v./n.* 脸红）；slush（*n.* 烂泥）

mental ['mentl] *a.* 精神的（spiritual）；智力的（intellectual）

【派】mentally（*ad.* 智力上地；精神上地）

moist [mɔɪst] *a.* 潮湿的（damp, humid）；多雨的（rainy）

【记】联想记忆：薄雾（mist）中湿漉漉的（moist）城市

【例】Warm and *moist* air from the Pacific Ocean is forced upward as it crosses the Sierra Nevada. 来自太平洋的暖湿气流在经过内华达山脉时被迫向上移动。

【派】moisten（*vt.* 使湿润）

nationalism ['næʃnəlɪzəm] *n.* 民族主义

nominee [ˌnɑːmɪ'niː] *n.* 被提名的候选人；被任命者

【例】Both political parties wanted Dwight D. Eisenhower as their presidential *nominee*. 两个政党都想让德怀特·D·艾森豪威尔当他们的总统候选人。

nonsense ['nɑːnsens] *n.* 胡说；废话（rubbish）

【记】词根记忆：non（不）＋ sense（意义）→ 无意义的话 → 废话

notation [noʊ'teɪʃn] *n.* 符号

【记】词根记忆：not（标识）＋ ation → 标记法

otherwise ['ʌðərwaɪz] *ad.* 另外；用别的方法；在其他方面 *conj.* 要不然，否则

【记】联想记忆：other（其他的）＋ wise → 在其他方面

【例】A: I'm looking for a gift for a friend of mine, any suggestions?

B: Well, I have to know a little bit about your friend first. It's hard for me to say *otherwise*.

A：我想给一个朋友买礼物，有什么建议吗？

B：嗯，我得先了解一下你的朋友。不然我很难提出什么建议。

A: What did you think of the lecture? Isn't that professor something?

□ lush	□ mental	□ moist	□ nationalism	□ nominee	□ nonsense
□ notation	□ otherwise				

B: She was pretty impressive. Too bad about the weather though; *otherwise* I'm sure there would've been a lot more people.

A: 你觉得讲座如何? 那个教授挺了不起吧?

B: 她的确令人留下了很深的印象。如果天气好会有更多听众的。

【参】likewise(*ad.* 同样地)

palate ['pælət] *n.* 上腭
【记】分拆联想: pal + ate(eat的过去式) → 用来帮助吃 → 上腭

physical ['fɪzɪkl] *a.* 身体的(corporal); 物理的; 物质的(substantial) *n.* 体检
【记】词根记忆: physic(医学) + al → 医学活动 → 体检
【搭】physical attribute 物理特性; 身体素质
【派】physically(*ad.* 身体上; 物理方面)

postcard ['poʊstkɑːrd] *n.* 明信片

president ['prezɪdənt] *n.* 总统; (大学)校长; 总经理
【派】presidential(*a.* 总统的)

quilt [kwɪlt] *n.* 棉被 *vt.* 制成棉被
【记】联想记忆: 静静地(quiet)躺在被子里(quilt), 真是享受
【例】The bedcover was *quilted* in a flower design. 床罩上设计了花的图案。
【派】quilted(*a.* 中间夹有轻软之物的)

rancher ['ræntʃər] *n.* 牧场主; 牛仔(cowboy)
【例】Rodeos at agricultural fairs began so popular that *ranchers* and business people began to organize rodeos as independent events, separate from fairs. 农展会的骑术表演变得如此流行, 以至于大农场主和商人们开始组织与展会分开的独立骑术表演。

rare [rer] *a.* 稀有的, 罕见的(*infrequent); (肉类)半熟的
【记】联想记忆: 稀有的(rare)东西要小心(care)对待
【例】They are a *rare* breed. 它们是稀有品种。//I prefer my meat *rare*. 我的肉要半熟的。
【派】rarely(*ad.* 很少地, 罕有地); rarefied(*a.* 稀薄的); rarity(*n.* 稀有)

raw [rɔː] *a.* 未加工过的
【例】What does the author imply about the *raw* materials used to make glass? 作者对制造玻璃的原材料有什么暗示?

reddish ['redɪʃ] *a.* 微红的
【例】They often appear as a solid *reddish* mass when viewed from a ship or from the air. 从船上或空中看过去, 它们通常像是一块微红的实体。

| palate | physical | postcard | president | quilt | rancher |
| rare | raw | reddish | | | |

67

refreshing [rɪˈfreʃɪŋ] *a.* 使人耳目一新的（*unusual）; 提神的

【记】分拆联想：refresh(使精神振作) + ing → 使精神振作的 → 提神的

【例】It's so *refreshing* to feel the wind in my hair and the water on my face. 吹拂着头发的风和脸上的水令人精神一振。

【参】refreshment(*n.* 提神之物; [常 pl.] 茶点)

rescue [ˈreskjuː] *vt./n.* 营救, 搭救(save)

【记】分拆联想：res(看作rest, 休息) + cue(线索) → 放弃休息紧追线索, 进行营救 → 营救, 搭救

【例】We only try to *rescue* the most valuable first edition books in our collection. 我们只努力抢救收藏中最珍贵的首版书。

resign [rɪˈzaɪn] *v.* 辞去, 辞职

【记】词根记忆：re(不) + sign(标记; 签名) → 不再签到 → 辞去, 辞职

【搭】resign from 从…辞职; resign one's seat/post/position 辞职

resign

【例】Aged 15, Edward *resigned* himself to the fact that he'd never be a first-class musician. 爱德华15岁就自认为无法成为一名一流音乐家。

【派】resignation(*n.* 辞职; 放弃)

rupture [ˈrʌptʃər] *v.* (使)破裂(*burst)

【记】词根记忆：rupt(断) + ure → 破裂

【例】The change in volume may cause the lungs to distend and even *rupture*. 容量的变化可能会导致肺肿胀甚至破裂。

schedule [ˈskedʒuːl] *n.* 时刻表, 日程表(timetable, agenda) *vt.* 安排, 预定(assign, appoint)

【记】源自拉丁语scheda(纸莎草的叶子), 后与法语cedule融合进入英语, 词义也转变为时刻表和日程表

【例】I tentatively *schedule* to meeting for Thursday to go over your inventory report. 我暂时安排在周四开会审查你的库存报告。

【派】scheduled(*a.* 预定的); scheduling(*n.* 日程安排); reschedule(*v.* 重新计划)

scholar [ˈskɑːlər] *n.* 学者(academician)

【记】源于意为"闲暇"的希腊语schole, 指一个真正的学者要有闲暇时间看书治学、思考问题、进行学术讨论

【派】scholarly(*a.* 学术的, 学术性的); scholarship(*n.* 奖学金)

seal [si:l] *n.* 海豹 *v.* 密封(fasten, close)

【记】分拆联想：sea(海洋)+l(看作love，爱)→喜欢的海洋动物→海豹

【例】The oven was *sealed* shut until the bread was fully baked. 烤箱一直密封到面包烤熟为止。

【派】sealed(*a.* 密封的)

sheath [ʃi:θ] *n.* 鞘，外壳(holder, scabbard)

shelter ['ʃeltər] *n.* 掩蔽处，庇护所(harbor, shield) *v.* 保护(protect)，避难

【记】分拆联想：shel(看作shell，壳)+ter→像壳一样的地方→庇护所

【例】They use the canopy of the trees for *shelter* from heat and cold. 他们把树冠用作罩棚，来避暑防寒。

【派】sheltered(*a.* 遮蔽的，受庇护的)

spacecraft ['speɪskræft] *n.* 宇宙飞船

【记】组合词：space(太空)+craft(技术)→用太空技术造出的机器→宇宙飞船

【搭】a manned spacecraft 载人宇宙飞船

spherical ['sferɪkl] *a.* 球的；球状的

【例】The Greeks knew that during eclipses of the moon, the earth was between the sun and the moon, and they saw that during these eclipses, the earth's shadow on the moon was always round. They realized that this could be true only if the earth was *spherical.* 希腊人知道月食的时候地球在太阳和月亮之间，他们发现这期间地球在月亮上的影子总是圆的，于是意识到只有地球是个球体时才可能这样。

stable ['steɪbl] *a.* 稳定的，安定的(steady, balanced)

【记】词根记忆：st(站，立)+able→能够屹立不倒→稳定的，安定的

【派】stability(*n.* 稳定性)；stabilize(*vt.* 使稳定)；unstable(*a.* 不稳定的)

sympathetic [ˌsɪmpə'θetɪk] *a.* 有同情心的；【物】和应的

【搭】sympathetic vibration 共振

【例】He is *sympathetic* and understanding. 他富有同情心，善解人意。

tally ['tæli] *n.* 记账，计算

【搭】tally method 记账方法

【例】The cowboy kept a *tally* book for keeping count of the cattle. 牛仔保留着一个计数簿来统计牛的数量。

seal	sheath	shelter	spacecraft	spherical	stable
sympathetic	tally				

tenement [ˈtenəmənt] *n.* 廉租公寓

【记】分拆联想: ten(十个) + e + men(人) + t → 十个人住一间屋子 → 廉租公寓

【例】The *tenements* lacked both running water and central heating. 廉租公寓既没有自来水, 也没有集体供暖。

tissue [ˈtɪʃuː] *n.* 【生】[常 *pl.*] 组织

【搭】soft tissue 软组织

vacant [ˈveɪkənt] *a.* 空的(empty); 闲置的(unused)

【记】词根记忆: vac(空) + ant(…的) → 空的

【例】There are still *vacant* rooms. 现在仍然有空房间。

【派】vacancy(*n.* 空处, 空缺)

vacant

Is the lavatory vacant?

verse [vɜːrs] *n.* 诗歌(poetry); 韵文(rhyme)

【记】词根记忆: vers(转) + e → 诗歌的音节百转千回 → 诗歌

【例】Walt Whitman originated a distinctive form of free *verse*. 沃尔特·惠特曼创造了一种独特的自由诗体。

waste [weɪst] *v.* 浪费, 消耗 *a.* 无用的, 废弃的; 荒芜的 *n.* 浪费; 废物

【例】A: Growing up we never had a TV. Even now I'm not used to watching it much.

B: Well, it's kind of like reading. Some things you find are great, but a few are real *waste* of time. You have to pick and choose.

A: 我们从小就没有电视。现在我还不怎么习惯看电视。

B: 嗯, 这有点像读书。你会发现有些内容不错, 但是有的真就是浪费时间。你要有所挑选。

zealous [ˈzeləs] *a.* 狂热的(crazy)

【记】来自zeal(*n.* 热心, 热诚)

【例】Wilton also made a lead equestrian image of King George III that was created in New York in 1770 and torn down by *zealous* patriots six years later. 1770年, 威尔顿在纽约也用铅制作了乔治三世国王骑马的塑像, 6年后被狂热的爱国者给捣毁了。

tenement	tissue	vacant	verse	waste	zealous

Word List 7

词根、词缀预习表				
alter	改变状态	alternate	*a.* 交替的
aqui	水	aquifer	*n.* 含水土层
awe	敬畏	awesome	*a.* 使人敬畏的
card	心	cardiac	*a.* 心脏的
cent	百	centennial	*n.* 百年纪念
verge	转	converge	*v.* 会聚，聚合
ethn	种族	ethnology	*n.* 人种学
femin	女人	feminist	*n.* 女权主义者
prim	最初的	primal	*a.* 最初的；主要的

accounting [əˈkaʊntɪŋ] *n.* 会计学

acidity [əˈsɪdəti] *n.* 酸度，酸性
【参】alkali(*n.* 碱)；alkaline(*a.* 碱性的)

acting [ˈæktɪŋ] *a.* 代理的(representative) *n.* 演戏，表演
【例】She will play the *acting* coach. 她将担任代理教练这一角色。

adoption [əˈdɑːpʃn] *n.* 采用
【记】来自adopt(*v.* 采用；收养)
【搭】adoption of 对…的采用
【例】With the *adoption* of new technology, there has been a great improvement in work efficiency. 新技术的采用使工作效率大大提高了。
【派】adoptive(*a.* 采用的)

alarm [əˈlɑːrm] *n.* 闹钟；警报(alert) *vt.* 使惊恐(startle)
【记】分拆联想：al + arm（武器）→ 用武器来惊吓 → 使惊恐
【例】She never wakes up before her *alarm* goes off. 闹钟不响她就醒不来。//Ecologists

alarm

would probably be *alarmed* by the scientists' findings. 科学家们的发现可能会使生态学家们感到惊恐。

【派】alarming(*a.* 令人担忧的); alarmist(*n.* 杞人忧天者)

alternate [ˈɔːltərnət] *a.* 交替的(by turns), 轮流的(*rotate, in turn)

【记】词根记忆：alter(改变状态) + nate → 交替改变的 → 轮流的

【搭】the alternate rise and fall of sea level 海面的交替涨落

【派】alternately(*ad.* 交替地; 间隔地); alternation(*n.* 交替, 轮流)

angiosperm [ˈændʒɪoʊspɜːrm] *n.* 被子植物

【例】In the last class we talked about the classification of trees and we ended up with a basic description of *angiosperm*. 上一节课我们谈到了树木的分类, 结束时我们对被子植物进行了概述。

aquifer [ˈækwɪfər] *n.* 含水土层

【记】词根记忆：aqui(=aqu水) + fer(带) → 带来水的地方 → 含水土层

【例】An *aquifer* is an underground layer of rock or sediment that has pores or holes in it. 含水土层是指地下有小孔或洞的岩石或沉积物层。

arboreal [ɑːrˈbɔːriəl] *a.* 树栖的; 树的(tree-dwelling; treelike)

【记】词根记忆：arbor(树) + eal → 树的

aurora [ɔːˈrɔːrə] *n.* 极光

【记】注意：aurore(*a.* 朝霞色的)

available [əˈveɪləbl] *a.* 可得到的(*accessible, obtainable); 可利用的(improvable); 有空的(free)

【例】Evening wear isn't *available* in those shops. 这些商店不卖晚装。//I'll be *available* on Tuesday and Friday afternoons to discuss your papers with you. 我周四和周五下午有空和你讨论你的论文。

【派】availability(*n.* 可用性); unavailable(*a.* 不可获得的)

awesome [ˈɔːsəm] *a.* 使人敬畏的; 使人惊惧的

【记】词根记忆：awe(敬畏) + some(充满…的) → 使人敬畏的

【例】The image of gods and kings on the surface of the columns was a little bit *awesome*. 柱子上神和国王的形象有点令人敬畏。

【参】handsome(*a.* 英俊的); wholesome(*a.* 卫生的, 健康的)

bacon [ˈbeɪkən] *n.* 咸肉, 熏肉

【记】即超市中卖的"培根"

【搭】bring home the bacon 成功; 赚钱糊口

【例】There is nothing I like better to get me started in the morning than a big breakfast. Eggs, *bacon*, home-fried potatoes... 早上吃一顿

alternate	angiosperm	aquifer	arboreal	aurora	available
awesome	bacon				

丰盛的早餐最能让我精力充沛地开始新的一天。鸡蛋、咸肉、家制的炸土豆…

balcony [ˈbælkəni] *n.* 包厢(loge)

【记】发音记忆："包给你" → 把整个包厢都"包给你" → 包厢

blush [blʌʃ] *vi.* 脸红，羞愧(flush)

【记】和flush[*vi.*(脸)发红]一起记

break [breɪk] *v.* 打破，折断，破碎；使中止，打断；破坏，违反 *n.* 打断，中止；休息时间

【搭】break... out into... 把…弄散组成…

【例】This is our last chance to take a *break* before finals. 这是决赛之前我们中间休息的最后一次机会。

A: Have you finalized your plans for spring *break* yet?

B: Well, I could visit some friends in Florida, or go to my roommate's home. It's a tough choice.

A：你春季休假的计划定下来没有？

B：嗯，我可能会去看望佛罗里达的一些朋友，或者去我室友的家里。二者很难选择。

buckle [ˈbʌkl] *n.* 皮带扣环 *v.* 扣紧(fasten)；变曲

【例】Two plates continued to float and therefore *buckled* to form a mountain chain. 两个板块继续漂移，碰撞后形成了山脉。

cardiac [ˈkɑːrdiæk] *a.* 心脏的(of or relating to the heart)；心脏病的

【记】词根记忆：card(心) + iac → 心脏的

【搭】cardiac muscle 心肌

centennial [senˈteniəl] *n.* 百年纪念(a 100th anniversary or its celebration)

【记】词根记忆：cent(百) + enn(年) + ial → 百年纪念

【例】The country was celebrating the *centennial* of Lincoln's birth. 这个国家在庆祝林肯诞辰100周年。

chagrin [ʃəˈɡrɪn] *n.* 懊恼，失望(disappointment)

【记】联想记忆：cha(拼音：茶) + grin(苦笑) → 喝茶苦笑 → 失望，懊恼

clog [klɑːɡ] *vt.* 障碍，阻塞(congest, jam)

【记】联想记忆：圆木(log)一般很重，放在c后自然是妨碍(clog)了

collaborator [kəˈlæbəreɪtər] *n.* 合作者

collide [kəˈlaɪd] *vi.* 碰撞；冲突(conflict)

【例】What happens when electrons and gas *collide* in space? 电子和气体在空间中撞击时会发生什么？

【派】collision(*n.* 碰撞)

| balcony | blush | break | buckle | cardiac | centennial |
| chagrin | clog | collaborator | collide | | |

comet ['kɑːmət] *n.* 彗星

【记】分拆联想：come（来）+ t → 很多年才来一次的星星 → 彗星

content [kən'tent] *a.* 满足的（satisfied）

['kɑːntent] *n.* [常 *pl.*] 内容（matter），容量（capacity）

【例】Those people were quite *content* to reunion in the more sumptuous, single-family homes. 这些人颇满足于在更华丽的独户住房重聚。

【派】discontented（*a.* 不满意的，不满足的）

【参】contend（*v.* 斗争）

converge [kən'vɜːrdʒ] *v.* 会聚，聚合（assemble, aggregate）

【记】词根记忆：con + verge（转）→ 转到一起 → 会聚，聚合

【例】Small pieces of floating ice *converge* and form icebergs. 小块的浮冰聚集在一起就形成冰山。

【派】convergence（*n.* 集中，聚合）

cost [kɔːst] *n.* 成本，费用，代价（expense）*v.* 价值为，花费

【搭】cost sb. an arm and a leg 昂贵的

【例】I decided to call landlord on how much the apartment would *cost*. 我决定给房东打电话，问这间公寓的租金是多少。

A: My boss says the company will pay for any college *costs* if I take advanced degree.

B: That's a benefit you wouldn't have if you had taken the other job offer.

A：我的老板说，如果我继续深造的话，公司将负担所有大学费用。

B：如果当初你选择了另外那份工作，你就得不到这样的好处了。

【参】post（*v.* 邮寄）；most（*a.* 最多的）

costume ['kɑːstuːm] *n.* 服饰（dress）*vt.* 装束

curl [kɜːrl] *v.* （使）卷曲，蜷缩（crouch）*n.* 卷发；卷曲状；卷曲物

【记】和 hurl（*v.* 用力投掷）一起记

【搭】curl up 卷起，撅起；蜷曲，蜷缩

【例】Although these bats sleep during the day, they do so *curled* up with their heads exposed to the sun. 尽管这些蝙蝠白天睡觉，它们还是会蜷起身体而将头暴露在阳光之下。

【参】hurl（*v.* 猛投，猛掷）

desolate [ˈdesələt] *a.* 荒凉的(deserted)

【记】词根记忆: de + sol(孤独) + ate → 偌大的平原上只长着几棵孤零零的树 → 荒凉的

【例】At the South Pole lies Antarctica, the coldest and most *desolate* region on Earth. 南极洲在南极, 是地球上最寒冷荒凉的地区。

【参】solitude(*n.* 孤独); solo(*n.* 独唱)

detest [dɪˈtest] *v.* 憎恶(hate)

【记】分拆联想: de + test(测试) → 有的学生十分憎恶测试 → 憎恶

【例】My sister *detests* rock music. 我的妹妹讨厌摇滚乐。

【参】attest(*v.* 证明); testify(*v.* 证实); contest(*v.* 争论, 争辩)

economy [ɪˈkɑːnəmi] *n.* 经济(制度); 节俭, 节约(thrift, saving)

【派】economize(*vi.* 节俭); economic(*a.* 经济学的; [*pl.*] *n.* 经济学); economical(*a.* 经济的; 节约的)

emerald [ˈemərəld] *n.* 绿宝石

emotion [ɪˈmoʊʃn] *n.* 感情; 情绪(sentiment, feeling)

【记】词根记忆: e + mot(动) + ion → 波动的东西 → 感情; 情绪

ethnology [eθˈnɑːlədʒi] *n.* 人种学, 民族学

【记】词根记忆: ethn(种族) + ology(学科) → 人种学, 民族学

【例】*Ethnology* is a branch of anthropology that deals with how various cultures developed. 民族学是人类学的分支, 研究各种文化是如何发展的。

exceed [ɪkˈsiːd] *v.* 超过, 超出(*surpass, *go beyond)

【记】词根记忆: ex(出) + ceed(走) → 走出去 → 超过, 超出

【例】The circulation of weekly magazines *exceeded* that of newspapers in that period. 在那个时期, 周刊的发行量超过了报纸。

【派】exceeding(*a.* 超过的); exceedingly(*ad.* 非常)

expect [ɪkˈspekt] *v.* 预期; 期望, 指望(anticipate)

【例】Economists *expect* the global economy to drop by 2% this year. 经济学家预期今年全球经济下降2%。

A: I wonder where the books I ordered are. I *expected* to receive the package several days ago.

B: Maybe you'd better check it with the company. They could be temporarily out of stock.

A: 我不知道我订购的书到哪里了。我本来指望几天前收到包裹的。

B: 你或许应该和公司联系一下, 他们可能暂时缺货。

【参】inspect(*v.* 检查); aspect(*n.* 方面)

expressive [ɪkˈspresɪv] *a.* 有表现力的, 富有表情的, 生动的

【搭】expressive leadership 社会情感型领导

【派】expressively(*ad.* 表现地); expressiveness(*n.* 表现, 表示)

feminist [ˈfemənɪst] *n.* 女权主义者

【记】词根记忆: femin(女人) + ist → 女权主义者

【例】Certain *feminists* showed a keen sense of history by keeping records of activities in which women were engaged. 某些女权主义者展示出了敏锐的历史感, 记录了妇女参与的各种活动。

financial [faɪˈnænʃl] *a.* 财政的, 金融的

【记】来自 finance(*n.* 财政)

【搭】financial plan 金融计划

【派】financially(*ad.* 财政上, 金融上)

forerunner [ˈfɔːrʌnər] *n.* 先驱者, 开路人; 先兆, 预兆

【例】Harriet was an important *forerunner* to the realistic movement that became popular later in the 19th century. 哈里特是 19 世纪末流行的现实主义运动中的一位重要先驱者。

hike [haɪk] *v./n.* 徒步旅行(walkabout); 远足

【记】联想记忆: 穿着耐克(Nike)鞋徒步旅行(hike)

【例】Her sister's children love to *hike* in the mountains. 她姐姐的孩子喜欢去山里徒步旅行。

hurry [ˈhɜːri] *n./v.* 匆忙

【搭】hurry up 快点, (使)赶快, 迅速完成; in a hurry 赶时间, 匆忙地, 急于

hurry

【例】A: Hey, Dan, do you think you might *hurry* up just a bit? You've been from that sandwich counter forever. And you know, I've got class in ten minutes, and so do you, by the way...

B: Sorry, oh, I just wish they didn't give me so many choices.

A: 喂, 丹, 你能快点吗? 你在那个三明治柜台停这么久了。要知道, 我 10 分钟后有课, 你也有, 再说了…

B: 哦, 对不起, 他们要是不给我那么多选择就好了。

identity [aɪˈdentəti] *n.* 身份(status); 特性(characteristic)

【记】分拆联想: i(我) + dent(牙齿) + ity(表性质) → 我通过牙齿来确定身份 → 身份

【例】The *identity* of the author is unknown. 作者的身份不为人所知。// The hardness of the mineral often gives a clue to its *identity*. 矿物的硬度常常是了解其特性的线索。

expressive feminist financial forerunner hike hurry
identity

impending [ɪmˈpendɪŋ] *a.* 即将发生的；迫近的

【记】来自impend(*v.* 即将发生)

【例】Some members of the flock warn others of *impending* dangers. 鸟群中的一些成员警告其他成员即将来临的危险。

inaccessible [ˌɪnækˈsesəbl] *a.* 难到达的，不可及的(unreachable)；不能得到的 (unattainable)

【记】词根记忆：in(不) + accessible(易达到的)→难达到的

【例】In the west only a small part of region has been surveyed because most of the lands are *inaccessible*. 在西部只有一小部分地区得到了勘察，因为多数地区人们难以到达。

indicative [ɪnˈdɪkətɪv] *a.* 指示的；预示的

【记】词根记忆：in + dic (说) + ative → 说出预言 → 预示的；指示的

【例】The teacher's presence is *indicative* of his wish to help us on the project. 老师亲临现场预示着他愿意帮助我们搞这个项目。

inventory [ˈɪnvəntɔːri] *n.* 详细目录，存货清单；库存(stock)

【记】分拆联想：in(进来) + vent(来) + ory(物) → 进来对库存货物进行清查 → 存货清单

【例】In the 1800's store owners sold everything from a needle to a plow, trusted everyone, and never took *inventory*. 19世纪的店主从针到犁什么都卖，他们相信每一个人，从来不搞存货清单。

keen [kiːn] *a.* 灵敏的，敏锐的(sharp)

【例】Their *keen* senses of hearing and smell have made some types of dogs valuable in hunting and tracking and as security guards. 某些种类的狗因听觉和嗅觉灵敏而在狩猎、追踪和看门方面很有利用价值。

【派】keenly(*ad.* 敏锐地)

landmass [ˈlændmæs] *n.* 地块；大片陆地

【记】组合词：land + mass → 大片陆地

【例】*Landmasses* occupy only one-third of the Earth's surface. 陆地只占地球表面的三分之一。

latent [ˈleɪtnt] *a.* 潜在的，隐伏的(hidden)

【记】分拆联想：late(晚) + nt → 潜伏在夜晚的窃贼 → 潜在的，隐伏的

【搭】latent heat 潜在热

【例】The term "*latent* heat" refers to the energy that has to be used to convert liquid water to water vapor. "潜在热"这个词指用来把液体水转换成水蒸气的能量。

layer ['leɪər] *n.* 层，层次

【记】来自lay(层面) + er → 层，层次

【例】The filling was a soft *layer* of wool which had been cleaned and separated. 填充物是已经清洗并分拣好了的柔软的羊毛。

manner ['mænər] *n.* 方式，风格(way, style)；[*pl.*] 礼貌(courtesy)；习惯 (habit)

【例】It was the *manner* of expressing the satiric method that made them interesting and entertaining. 正是表现嘲讽的风格使其有趣并令人愉悦。

【派】mannerism(*n.* 独特的风格、形式)

method ['meθəd] *n.* 方法(*means)；秩序(system)

【派】methodical(*a.* 有办法的；有条不紊的)；methodology(*n.* 方法论)

minimize ['mɪnɪmaɪz] *v.* 将…减到最少(to reduce to a minimum)；最小化

【记】词根记忆：minim(小) + ize → 最小化

【例】They also took steps to *minimize* damage to product. 他们也采取了措施把对产品的损失减到最少。

monumental [ˌmɑːnjuˈmentl] *a.* 纪念碑的；不朽的(enduring, imperishable)

【记】来自monument(纪念碑) + al → 纪念碑的；不朽的

【例】The concert was a *monumental* tribute to the orchestra's first conductor. 这场音乐会是对管弦乐队首位指挥的不朽颂词。

neutron ['nuːtrɑːn] *n.* 中子

【记】词根记忆：neutr(=neither两者都不) + on(物) → 中子

orchid ['ɔːrkɪd] *n.* 兰花

【记】分拆联想：or + chid(看作child，儿童) → 儿童天真纯洁得像兰花 → 兰花

patient ['peɪʃnt] *a.* 有耐心的，能忍耐的 *n.* 病人，患者

patient

【例】A: Where have you been? I was just about to give up on you.

B: Sorry, my bus was delayed. But I'm glad you were *patient*. It would have been hard for us to find another time to meet this week.

A: 你去哪里了？我正打算不等你了。

B: 对不起，我乘的公交车被耽误了。但是我很高兴你有耐心。本周咱们再找时间见面可能会很困难。

【参】patent(*n.* 专利权)

☐ layer	☐ manner	☐ method	☐ minimize	☐ monumental	☐ neutron
☐ orchid	☐ patient				

penmanship ['penmənʃɪp] *n.* 书法(calligraphy); 书写的技巧或风格

【例】*Penmanship* was often taught as a separate subject from the first grade. 书法通常从一年级开始就被作为一个独立的科目来教授。

permission [pərˈmɪʃn] *n.* 允许, 同意(consent)

【记】词根记忆: per(贯穿, 自始至终)+ miss(送)+ ion → 机密自始至终都不允许发送 → 允许

【搭】special permission 特许; permission slip 请假条; to ask for permission 请求同意

【例】A: I'm really disappointed; there are a couple of required courses I have to take before I can take the history class I'm interested in.

B: Don't be disappointed yet. You may be able to get special *permission* from the professor.

A: 我真的很失望; 要想修我感兴趣的历史课, 我首先要上几门必修的课程。

B: 先别失望。你可以从教授那里得到特殊许可。

plow [plaʊ] *n.* 犁(plough) *vt.* 耕作(cultivate, till)

【例】Most of the iron meteorites are found by farmers *plowing* their fields. 多数铁陨星是农民在犁地的时候发现的。

preponderance [prɪˈpɑːndərəns] *n.* 优势(superiority, dominance)

【记】来自preponderant(*a.* 占优势的)

【例】The New World butterflies make up the *preponderance* of examples because they are the most familiar species. 在这些标本中新大陆的蝴蝶占多数, 因为它们是最为人所熟知的物种。

primal ['praɪml] *a.* 最初的(original); 主要的(chief)

【记】词根记忆: prim(最初的)+ al → 最初的

【例】The Sun is far less radiant today than the *primal* Sun. 现在的太阳远远没有最初的太阳那么亮。

project ['prɑːdʒekt] *n.* 方案(scheme); 项目(item)

[prəˈdʒekt] *v.* 放映(show, screen); 规划(plan, figure)

【记】词根记忆: pro(向前)+ ject(扔)→ 向前投影 → 放映

【派】projecting(*a.* 突出的, 伸出的); projector(*n.* 放映机)

propel [prəˈpel] *vt.* 推进, 驱使(push, drive)

【记】词根记忆: pro(向前)+ pel(推)→ 推进

【例】The small plants and animals float about or weakly *propel* themselves through the sea. 小植物和动物要么漂浮着, 要么就在海中轻轻地推动自己前行。

【派】propellant(*n.* 推进物)

quotation [kwoʊˈteɪʃn] *n.* 引文，引语，语录；报价，牌价

【记】来自quote(*v.* 引用)

ranch [ræntʃ] *n.* 大牧场

【记】联想记忆：马在大牧场(ranch)里尽情地驰骋(ran)

【派】rancher(*n.* 牧场主)

rash [ræʃ] *n.* 疹，皮疹

【记】分拆联想：r + ash(灰) → 秘方，出疹子时糊上点草木灰就好了 → 皮疹

remodel [ˌriːˈmɑːdl] *v.* 重新塑造，改造(remake)

【例】The Philadelphia Museum of Art was *remodeled.* 费城艺术博物馆被重新改造了。

render [ˈrendər] *vt.* 给予(give)；致使(cause)

【例】Rapid ecological change may *render* an environment hostile to a species. 生态的快速变化会使环境对物种产生威胁。

【派】rendering(*n.* 表现，描写)

sacrificial [ˌsækrɪˈfɪʃl] *a.* 供奉(品)的，献祭(品)的，牺牲(品)的

【搭】sacrificial ceremony 祭祀仪式

【例】The temple located in the city is the largest surviving *sacrificial* temple in the world. 这座城市里的庙宇是世界上现存最大的祭祀庙宇。

score [skɔːr] *n.* 得分，分数(mark)；乐谱(*musical composition) *v.* 评分(grade)

【记】联想记忆：s + core(核心) → 考试的核心是得分 → 得分

【例】The game was tied until John *scored* the winning point. 约翰得分赢得比赛之前是平局。

silicon [ˈsɪlɪkən] *n.* 硅

【搭】silicon chip 硅片；silicon resin 硅树脂

simply [ˈsɪmpli] *ad.* 简单地(clearly)；简直；只不过(little more than)

【例】This vertical movement of the fieldstone is not *simply* an artifact of soil erosion. 卵石的垂直运动并非只是土壤侵蚀的结果。

【参】simplicity(*n.* 简单；朴素)；simplify(*v.* 简化)；simplistic(*a.* 简单化的)

sphere [sfɪr] *n.* 球(体)(ball, globe)

【记】本身为词根，意为：球

【派】spherical(*a.* 球状的)

quotation	ranch	rash	remodel	render	sacrificial
score	silicon	simply	sphere		

transcend [træn'send] *vt.* 超越(exceed, surpass)

【记】词根记忆：trans(越过)+(s)cend(爬)→超越

【例】Murray's essays *transcended* the boundaries of her world in recognizing the need for training women to earn their own living. 莫里的论文超越了她所在的视野，认识到了培训女性使其自谋生计的需要。

【参】transport(*v.* 传送，运输)

triangle ['traɪæŋgl] *n.* 三角(形)

【记】词根记忆：tri(三)+angle(角)→三角

【搭】equilateral triangle 等边三角形

【例】They calculated the length of *triangle* sides. 他们计算出了三角形边的长度。

typical ['tɪpɪkl] *a.* 典型的；有代表性的(representative)

【记】来自type(典型)+ical→典型的

【例】Hard work was so *typical* of immigrants and pioneers who settled the American Midwest. 勤奋是在美国中西部定居的移民和拓荒者的典型特点。

A: What's keeping Kevin? He said last night he'd meet us here by 2 o'clock and it's already 2:30.

B: It's so *typical* of him, isn't it? Just watch, he's going to show up in 5 minutes with some wild excuses.

A: 凯文怎么还不到？他昨晚说两点在这里和我们见面，现在已经两点半了。

B: 他就是这个样子，不是吗？你看好了，五分钟后他露面时准会给出一些荒诞的借口。

【派】typically(*ad.* 典型地，有代表性地)

viral ['vaɪrəl] *a.* 病毒(性)的

【记】和virus(*n.* 病毒)一起记

【例】The cell begins to manufacture *viral* proteins rather than its own. 细胞开始制造病毒的蛋白质，而不是自己的蛋白质。

Word List 8 ⊙ MP3-08

词根、词缀预习表

ann	年	annual	a. 每年的
struct	建立	construct	v. 建造
term	边界	determine	v. 确定
semin	种子	disseminate	v. 散布，传播
nutri	滋养	nutrition	n. 营养；营养学
vi	道路	viable	a. 可行的
magn	大	magnificent	a. 极好的

administer [əd'mɪnɪstər] *vt.* 管理(*manage)；执行(execute)

【记】分拆联想：ad(做) + minister(大臣) → 做一个大臣要精于管理 → 管理

【例】Prof. Andrews has agreed to *administer* the exam. 安德鲁斯教授已同意了进行考试。

【派】administration(*n.* 管理；当局)；administrative(*a.* 管理的，行政的)；administrator(*n.* 管理者，行政官)

along [ə'lɔːŋ] *ad.* 向前地；一起 *prep.* 沿着

【搭】come along 与…一起

【例】A: I think we should hold our committee meeting in one of the meeting rooms of the library. So far, there're 8 of us who plan to come.

B: Wow, if there were more than four, I'd say that we have it over at my place, but with 8 of us, I guess I'd have to get *along* with your suggestion.

A: 我认为我们应该在图书馆的一个会议室举行委员会会议。目前有我们8个人打算参加。

B: 哦，如果多于4个人，我建议在我那里开会。但是有8个人，我想还是听从你的建议。

A: What a relationship Steven and his father have!

B: Don't they? I only hope my daughter and I can get *along* like that when she's Steven's age.

A: 史蒂文和他父亲的关系多融洽啊!

B: 难道不是吗? 我只希望我女儿到了史蒂文的年纪, 能和我像他们父子那样相处。

A: I noticed you haven't been getting *along* well with your roommate lately.

B: You got that right. And it's going to be a long time before I feel comfortable with him again.

A: 我注意到你最近和室友关系不太好。

B: 你说对了。我和他的关系再次好转还需要很长时间。

amount [əˈmaʊnt] *n.* 总额(sum, quantity) *vi.* 总计达(totalize)

【例】By 1913 Seattle had 25 parks *amounting* to 1,400 acres. 到1913年, 西雅图共有25个公园, 总面积达1400英亩。

annual [ˈænjuəl] *a.* 每年的(yearly); 一年一度的

【记】词根记忆: ann(年) + ual(…的) → 每年的

【例】Earth Day has become an *annual* international event. 地球日已经成为了年度国际活动。

【派】annually(*ad.* 一年一次地)

apologize [əˈpɑːlədʒaɪz] *vi.* 道歉

【记】词根记忆: apo(远) + log(说话) + ize → 觉得过意不去, 远远地说话 → 道歉

【搭】apologize to sb. 向…道歉; apologize for(doing) sth. 因(做)…而道歉

【例】Our sports center *apologizes* to every customer who makes a complaint about service. 我们的体育中心向每一位对服务投诉的客户道歉。

astute [əˈstuːt] *a.* 机敏的, 精明的(shrewd, judicious)

【记】来自拉丁文astus(灵活)

【搭】an astute politician 机敏的政治家; astute investments 精明的投资

【例】It is *astute* to sell the stocks just before prices go down. 股价下跌之前清仓是精明的。

【派】astutely(*ad.* 敏捷地, 伶俐地); astuteness(*n.* 机敏, 精明)

bind [baɪnd] *v.* 使结合, 绑(tie, fasten); 装订

【记】发音记忆: "绑的" → 绑; 装订

【例】The glue used in the *binding* loses its strength. 装订用的胶没有黏性了。

【参】bookbinding(*n.* 装订)

block [blɑːk] *vt.* 阻塞(back up) *n.* 一块；街区

【例】He should stop *blocking* the doorway. 他不应该堵着门口。// The supermarket is just down the *block*. 超市就在这个街区南边。

bud [bʌd] *n.* 芽，蓓蕾

【记】联想记忆：在泥土(mud)中发芽(bud)

canal [kəˈnæl] *n.* 运河

【记】发音记忆："可难哦"→古代劳动人民靠双手开挖运河很困难→运河

champion [ˈtʃæmpiən] *n.* 冠军(winner, victor)；拥护者(defender, protector) *vt.* 支持

【例】One popular candidate *champions* tax reform. 一位受欢迎的候选人支持税收改革。

champion

chill [tʃɪl] *n.* 寒冷，寒意(coldness)

【记】分拆联想：c + hill(小山)→山上高处不胜寒→寒冷

construct [kənˈstrʌkt] *v.* 建造(build)；创立(found)

【记】词根记忆：con(加强) + struct(建立)→建造；创立

【例】The Anasazi lived in houses *constructed* of adobe and wood. 阿那萨奇人居住在泥砖和木头建造的房子里。

【派】reconstruct(*v.* 重建，改造)

consumption [kənˈsʌmpʃn] *n.* 消耗(量)，消费(量)；食用(*eating)

【例】All produce should be washed carefully before *consumption*. 所有的农产品在食用之前都应该仔细清洗。

creativity [ˌkriːeɪˈtɪvəti] *n.* 创造(力)

【例】Some jazz bands started relying on the *creativity* of the instrumentalist to attract audiences. 一些爵士乐队开始依靠乐器演奏家的创意来吸引听众。

cuneiform [ˈkjuːnɪfɔːrm] *a.* 楔形的 *n.* 楔形文字

current [ˈkɜːrənt] *a.* 当前的(ongoing) *n.* (液体、气体的)流(stream)；趋势(tendency)

【派】currently (*ad.* 现在；普遍地)；concurrent (*a.* 同时发生的)；currency(*n.* 货币)

democrat [ˈdeməkræt] *n.* [Democrat] 美国民主党人

【派】democracy(*n.* 民主，民主政治)

□ block	□ bud	□ canal	□ champion	□ chill	□ construct
□ consumption	□ creativity	□ cuneiform	□ current	□ democrat	

detect [dɪˈtekt] *v.* 发现，察觉(*discover)；探测(explore)

【记】词根记忆：de(去掉) + tect (=cover遮盖) → 去除遮盖 → 发现，察觉

【例】These experiments were designed to *detect* consciousness. 这些实验用来探测意识。

【派】detectable(*a.* 可发觉的)；detector(*n.* 探测器)

determine [dɪˈtɜːrmɪn] *v.* 确定(*dictate)；(使)决定(decide)

【记】词根记忆：de + term(边界) + ine → 确定各自的边界 → 确定

【例】We are *determined* to make our recycling program work. 我们决心使我们的再循环项目发挥作用。

【派】determinant (*a.* 决定的)；determination (*n.* 决心；决定)；indeterminate(*a.* 不确定的)

disseminate [dɪˈsemɪneɪt] *v.* 散布，传播(*spread)

【记】词根记忆：dis(分开) + semin(种子) + ate → 散布，传播

【例】The film *disseminated* an image of the good life in Southern California. 影片展现了南加州美好生活的景象。

Easter [ˈiːstər] *n.* 复活节

elegant [ˈelɪɡənt] *a.* 雅致的，高雅的

【例】The glass objects of this style are *elegant* in outline. 这种风格的玻璃物体轮廓雅致。

【派】elegance(*n.* 典雅，雅致)

engaging [ɪnˈɡeɪdʒɪŋ] *a.* 迷人的(charming)

【记】来自engage(*v.* 从事；吸引)

【例】Fanny Buice had an *engaging* personality that delighted audiences for nearly half a century. 范妮·布斯个性迷人，在将近半个世纪里一直给观众带来欢笑。

【参】engagement(*n.* 结合)

enormous [ɪˈnɔːrməs] *a.* 巨大的，极大的(*remarkable, massive)

【记】词根记忆：e(出) + norm(规范) + ous(…的) → 超出规范的 → 巨大的

enrollment [ɪnˈroʊlmənt] *n.* 登记，注册；入学

【例】A: I read that the *enrollment* in the School of Business is on the rise!

B: Well, that's been a trend for several years now.

A: 我获悉商学院的招生人数在增加！

B: 嗯，这个趋势已经持续好几年了。

extend [ɪkˈstend] *v.* 延长，延伸(*stretch, *increase)

【记】词根记忆：ex(出) + tend(伸展) → 延长；延展

【例】It *extends* the scientist's thinking beyond the known facts. 这使科学家的思维超越了已知的事实。

extreme [ɪk'striːm] *a.* 极度的(*intense) *n.* 极端(uttermost)

【例】I want to know how animals survive in *extreme* temperatures. 我想知道动物如何在极端温度下生存。

【派】extremely(*ad.* 极端地，非常地); extremity(*n.* 极端)

fasten ['fæsn] *vt.* 强加于(impose); 使固定(fix); 系(tie)

【例】The lighthouses in the Northeast are *fastened* to the surrounding rock. 东北的灯塔都固定在周围的岩石上。

film [fɪlm] *n.* 电影(movie); 胶卷; 薄膜 *v.* (把…)拍成电影

【搭】develop film 冲照片

【例】A: Do you have your *film* festival schedule with you? I'd like to find out what's playing this weekend.

B: I passed it on to my roommate, but there should be more in the bookstore. I can pick one up for you next time there.

A: 你有电影节的日程表吗? 我想看看周末上演什么电影。

B: 我传给室友看了, 不过书店里应该还有。下次去书店我可以给你取一份。

A: Mary, did you drop off the roll of *film* for developing?

B: No. I got Susan to do it.

A: 玛丽, 你把胶卷拿去冲洗了吗?

B: 没有, 我让苏珊送去了。

fitness ['fɪtnəs] *n.* 健康(the quality or state of being fit)

flamboyant [flæm'bɔɪənt] *a.* 艳丽的, 炫耀的

【记】联想记忆: flam(火) + boy(男孩) + ant(蚂蚁) → 男孩和蚂蚁高举火把 → 炫耀的

【例】The President's *flamboyant* lifestyle was well known among the citizens. 总统炫耀的生活方式在民众当中广为人知。

folklore ['foʊklɔːr] *n.* 民间传说

【记】组合词: folk(乡民) + lore(传说, 学问) → 民间传说

【例】Nancy Ward, a Cherokee leader of the 1700's, became a legendary figure in Tennessee *folklore*. 18世纪切诺基人的领袖南希·沃德成为了田纳西民间故事中的传奇人物。

generalization [ˌdʒenrələ'zeɪʃn] *n.* 概括

genetic [dʒə'netɪk] *a.* 基因的, 遗传(学)的

【记】来自gene(基因) + tic → 基因的

【例】What type of amber is probably the most valuable for *genetic* research? 哪种类型的琥珀可能对基因研究最有价值?

extreme	fasten	film	fitness	flamboyant	folklore
generalization	genetic				

hatch [hætʃ] *vt.* 孵化, 孵出

【记】分拆联想: hat（帽子）+ ch → 像扣上一顶帽子一样孵卵 → 孵化

【例】The young spiders *hatch* in mid-spring or early summer. 年轻的蜘蛛在仲春或初夏孵卵。

incessantly [ɪnˈsesntli] *ad.* 不断地（continually）

instruction [ɪnˈstrʌkʃn] *n.* 教导；〔常 pl.〕用法说明（directions）; 指示（indication）

【搭】instruction manual 使用说明手册

【例】The students must follow all *instructions* exactly. 学生必须准确遵守所有的指示。

juice [dʒuːs] *n.* 汁, 液

lack [læk] *n. /v.* 缺乏, 不足（deficiency）

【搭】lack of jobs 缺少工作; lack of 缺乏, 没有

【例】Studies show that *lack* of patience has a serious impact on one's success. 研究显示缺乏耐心对一个人的成功有严重的影响。//It's the *lack* of moisture that causes the problem. 正是缺少水分才导致了这个问题。

【参】lake(*n.* 湖)

larva [ˈlɑːrvə] *n.* [*pl.* larvae] 幼虫

【记】发音记忆: 近似于"lover" → 幼虫是两条虫子爱情的结晶 → 幼虫

【例】These eggs develop into *larvae*, which can swim freely. 这些卵发育成可以自由游动的幼虫。

lease [liːs] *n.* 租约; 租期

【记】分拆联想: l + ease(安心) → 有了租约所以安心 → 租约

【例】Her *lease* ends after graduation. 她的租约毕业后到期。

magnificent [mægˈnɪfɪsnt] *a.* 极好的（wonderful）; 华丽的（gorgeous）; 高尚的（lofty）

【记】词根记忆: magn(大) + ifi + cent → 华丽的; 高尚的

【例】Financier Andrew Mellon donated most of his *magnificent* art collection to the National Gallery of Art. 金融家安德鲁·梅隆把他收藏的大部分精美艺术品捐献给了国家艺术馆。//The temple is so grand and *magnificent* with so many features. 这座寺庙规模宏大、华丽壮观, 有很多特色。

hatch	incessantly	instruction	juice	lack	larva
lease	magnificent				

melodie [ˈmeɪləˈdiː] *n.* 小旋律歌曲（song）

【例】The music included sad melodies. 音乐包含伤感的旋律。

meteorologist [ˌmiːtɪəˈrɑːlədʒɪst] *n.* 气象学者

musician [mjuˈzɪʃn] *n.* 音乐家，乐师

normally [ˈnɔːrməli] *ad.* 通常地（usually），正常地

【例】A: Those were such funny stories Tom told last night. He was like a totally different guy.

B: Yeah, really. He is *normally* so serious.

A：汤姆昨晚讲的故事太逗了。他简直像换了个人一样。

B：没错，他平常很严肃的。

A: Do you want to go running down by the lake after psychology class? I really like to take advantage of the beautiful weather this afternoon.

B: Well, *normally* I begin to gather with my study group then, but I guess I can skip that just this once.

A：心理学的课结束之后你想去湖边跑步吗？今天下午天气这么好，我真想利用一下。

B：好的，我通常那时候要和学习小组聚会，不过我想可以缺席一次。

nutrition [nuˈtrɪʃn] *n.* 营养；营养学

【记】词根记忆：nutri（滋养）+ tion → 营养；营养学

【例】Vitamin D is important to human *nutrition* because it helps the body to absorb Calcium. 维生素D帮助人体吸收钙，对人的营养很重要。

【派】nutritional（*a.* 营养的）；nutritionist（*n.* 营养学家）；malnutrition（*n.* 营养不良）；nutritious（*a.* 有营养成分的，营养的）

omit [əˈmɪt] *v.* 省略，删去；遗漏，忽略（neglect）

【记】联想记忆：om（音似："呕"）+ it（它）→ 把它呕出去 → 省略

【搭】omit doing/to do 忘记做某事

【例】You'd better check the name list again to make sure there is no one *omitted* from it. 你最好再查看一下名单，确保没有遗漏任何人。

【参】vomit（*v.* 呕吐）

orientation [ˌɔːriənˈteɪʃn] *n.* 方向，定位（direction）；介绍性指导

【例】My job is providing *orientation* for new campus staff. 我的工作是让新的校园员工熟悉环境。

pore [pɔːr] *n.* 气孔，小孔（*hole）

【搭】pore space 孔隙

portrait ['pɔːrtrət] *n.* 肖像，画像（picture）；描写（description）

【记】词根联想：por + trait（特点，特性）→ 描绘某人的特点 → 肖像

【搭】portrait painting 肖像画

【派】portraitist(*n.* 肖像画家)；portraiture(*n.* 画像)

prefer [prɪ'fɜːr] *v.* 更喜欢，宁愿

【例】A: Do you want the windows open or closed?

B: I almost always *prefer* fresh air, if possible.

A：你想让窗户开着还是关着？

B：如果可能，我几乎总是想要新鲜空气。

A: There is nothing I like better to get me started in the morning than a big breakfast. Eggs, bacon, home-fried potatoes. . .

B: Not me! All that fatty food will give me a stomachache. I *prefer* something light, like fruit or a yogurt.

A：早上吃一顿丰盛的早餐最能让我精力充沛地开始新的一天。鸡蛋、咸肉、家里炸的土豆……

B：我可不行！这些油腻的食物会让我胃痛。我想吃清淡的早餐，比如水果或者酸奶。

prerequisite [ˌpriː'rekwəzɪt] *n.* 先决条件，前提（precondition）

【记】分拆联想：pre(预先) + requisite(必不可少的) → 预先必不可少的条件 → 先决条件

【例】There is plenty room, but there is a *prerequisite*. 空间很大，但是有一个先决条件。

prolific [prə'lɪfɪk] *a.* 多产的（*productive, *fruitful*)；富有创造力的

【记】分拆联想：pro(许多) + lif(看作life, 生命) + ic → 产生许多生命 → 多产的

【例】The beds of former lakes are also *prolific* sources of fossils. 过去湖泊的湖底也是化石组成的丰富来源。

【派】prolifically(*ad.* 多产地；丰富地)

punctual ['pʌŋktʃuəl] *a.* 严守时刻的（being on time）

【例】Fred is never *punctual*. 弗雷德从不守时。

regardless [rɪ'ɡɑːrdləs] *ad.* (of)不顾，不管（no matter what）

【记】来自regard(关心) + less → 不关心的 → 不顾，不管

【例】Chicago would become a great city *regardless* of the disadvantageous characteristics of the available site. 尽管其可用位置具有不利的因素，芝加哥仍将会成为一个伟大的城市。

【参】disregard(*vt.* 不理会)

relative [ˈrelətɪv] *a.* 相对的；有关的(related) *n.* 亲属

【例】She has produced a surprising amount of fictions in a *relative* short time. 她在相对较短的时间里创作了大量的小说。

relative

俺表兄

representative [ˌreprɪˈzentətɪv] *n.* 代表，代理人 *a.* 典型的(typical)，有代表性的

【搭】representative of …的代表；sales representative 销售代表

【例】You've all been selected as *representatives* to plan the graduation ceremonies. 你们都已被选为了代表来筹划毕业典礼。// Remember, as a *representative*, you'll have a lot of responsibilities. 要记住，作为代表你会有很多责任。

reschedule [riːˈskedʒuːl] *vt.* 重订…的时间表

【例】The international conference had to be *rescheduled* due to several countries' absence. 由于数个国家缺席，这次国际会议不得不重新安排时间。

A: I have an appointment with Dr. Stevens at 3 o'clock tomorrow. But something's come up I'd like to *reschedule*. Uh, any chance I can get in by the end of this week?

B: Well, we just had a cancellation for Friday. After that, the doctor will be out of the office for 2 weeks.

A: 明天3点我和史蒂文斯博士有个约会。但是我临时有事，想重新安排。我这个周末见他行吗？

B: 嗯，我们刚取消了周五的一个约会。稍后的两周，博士都不在办公室。

rust [rʌst] *n.* 锈，铁锈；【植】锈病 *v.* (使)生锈；(使)变迟钝；(使)能力荒废

【记】联想记忆：铁不磨一定(must)会生锈(rust)

【派】rusty(*a.* 生锈的；生疏的)

saturate [ˈsætʃəreɪt] *vt.* 使充满，浸透(fill, soak)

【记】词根记忆：satur(足够) + ate(使…) → 使足够 → 使充满

【例】The ocean *saturates* the atmosphere with water. 海洋使大气层充满水份。

【派】saturated(*a.* 饱和的，渗透的)

screen [skriːn] *n.* 屏幕 *vt.* 审查(censor)

【例】She methodically *screened* and cultured scores of soil samples, which she then sent to her partner. 她有条不紊地筛选培养了几十个土壤样品，然后派人送给了她的合伙人。

selection [sɪˈlekʃn] *n.* 选择（choice）；精选（assortment）

selection

skyscraper [ˈskaɪskreɪpər] *n.* 摩天大楼
【记】组合词：sky(天) + scrape(摩擦) + r → 可以擦到天 → 摩天大楼

sled [sled] *n.* 雪橇（sledge）

slumber [ˈslʌmbər] *n.* [常 *pl.*] 睡眠（sleep, doze）
【记】分拆联想：s + lumber(木材) → 睡得像根木头 → 睡眠

smoothly [ˈsmuːðli] *ad.* 顺利地（successfully）；平稳地

stereo [ˈsteriou] *n.* 立体声系统（装置）*a.* 立体声的
【记】分拆联想：stere(立方米) + o → 立体的 → 立体声的
【例】He wonders what kind of *stereo* equipment the woman has. 他想知道这个女子有哪种立体声设备。

strand [strænd] *n.* (线等的)股，缕；线（thread）
【记】联想记忆：只有一股绳(strand)是站(stand)不起来的
【搭】strand wire 绞合线，绳索

summarize [ˈsʌməraɪz] *v.* 概括，总结（generalize）
【记】来自summary(概略) + ize(使…化) → 概括
【搭】summarize of …的总结
【例】The authors, as a rule, *summarize* their views at the beginning of each passage. 作为规则，作者们要在每个段落开始的地方概括他们的观点。

suspect [səˈspekt] *vt.* 怀疑，猜想（speculate） [ˈsʌspekt] *a.* 可疑的（questionable）
【例】Most paleontologists *suspect* that abrupt changes in climate led to the mass extinctions. 多数古生物学家猜想气候的突然变化导致了动物大规模灭绝。// The phlogiston theory became *suspect*, and eventually was replaced by new ideas. 燃素理论遭人置疑，最终被新的概念所替代了。
【派】suspicion(*n.* 怀疑)；suspicious(*a.* 多疑的，可疑的)

swan [swɑːn] *n.* 天鹅
【记】联想记忆：天鹅(swan)游泳(swam, swim的过去式)

tend [tend] *v.* 趋向（incline），往往是；照料，看护
【记】本身为词根：伸 → 趋向
【搭】tend to do 趋向做…
【例】Children *tend* to be influenced by their parents' behaviour and habits. 孩子们往往受到父母的行为和习惯的影响。
【派】tendency(*n.* 趋向，趋势)
【参】tent(*n.* 帐篷)

selection	skyscraper	sled	slumber	smoothly	stereo
strand	summarize	suspect	swan	tend	

tolerate [ˈtɑːləreɪt] *vt.* 忍受（*endure, withstand*）

【例】I won't *tolerate* your foolish behavior anymore. 我不再容忍你愚蠢的行为了。

tuition [tuˈɪʃn] *n.* 学费（schooling）

【例】She can't afford to pay her *tuition*. 她负担不起学费。

underscore [ˌʌndərˈskɔːr] *v.* 强调（stress, emphasize）

【例】These excesses *underscore* a feature of residential expansion related to the growth of mass transportation. 这些过多之量强调了住宅扩展的特点，这与大规模运输的发展有关。

viable [ˈvaɪəbl] *a.* 可行的（feasible）

【记】词根记忆：vi(道路)＋able → 有路的 → 可行的

【例】Bessemer's process for converting iron into steel made the material more commercially *viable*. 贝西默把铁转化成钢的过程使这个原料在商业上更加可行了。

【派】viability(*n.* 可行性；生存能力)

volcano [vɑːlˈkeɪnoʊ] *n.* 火山

【记】分拆联想：vol(意志)＋can(会)＋o(看作no, 不) → 火山爆发不以人的意志为转移 → 火山

【例】How often a *volcano* is likely to erupt? 一座火山可能多长时间爆发一次？

【派】volcanic(*a.* 火山的)；volcanism(*n.* 火山作用)

【参】iceberg 冰山

warehouse [ˈwerhaʊs] *n.* 仓库，货栈（storehouse）

【记】组合词：ware(器皿)＋house(房屋) → 放器皿的房子 → 仓库

【例】A: Hi, I hope you can help me. I need the 2nd edition of *The United States Government* for my class on Monday afternoon. But I only see the 1st edition on the shelf. And I've already checked the other bookstores around here.

B: Yes. Someone else asked about this book earlier. I've called the *warehouse* and they are shipping copies to us. We should have them Monday morning.

A：你好，希望你能帮我个忙。我周一下午的课需要使用《美国政府》的第二版，可在书架上我只见到了第一版。我已经在周围的其他书店找过了。

B：好的，早些时候有别人问过这本书。我已经给库房打电话了，他们正在给我们发货。周一早上应该就能到书店。

Word List 9 MP3-09

词根、词缀预习表

bene	善, 好	benefit	*n.* 利益, 好处
memor	记住	commemorate	*v.* 纪念
cosm	宇宙	cosmos	*n.* 宇宙
spoil	损坏	despoil	*v.* 夺取, 掠夺
grad	行走	gradual	*a.* 逐渐的
lumin	光	illuminate	*v.* 照亮
sist	站	insist	*v.* 坚持要求
micro	小	micro	*n.* 显微镜
sub	在下面	subway	*n.* 地铁
terr	地	territory	*n.* 领土, 领域

access ['ækses] *n.* 通道 (approach); (接近或享用的) 机会 (opportunity)
vt. 存取; 使用; 接近
【例】Finding a water route across the continent was to gain easy *access* to the gold and other riches of the Northwest. 找到横穿大陆的水路就能容易获得西北地区的黄金和其他财富。

accredit [ə'kredɪt] *vt.* 授权 (authorize, commission)
【记】词根记忆: ac + credit (信任) → 十分信任 → 授权
【例】The dean in our department will *accredit* you as his assistant soon. 我们的系主任将很快授权你当他的助理。

advanced [əd'vænst] *a.* 先进的 (progressive); 高级的 (exclusive)
【例】They were an *advanced* agricultural people who used irrigation to help grow their crops. 他们这个民族拥有先进的农业, 利用灌溉促进作物生长。
【参】advancement (*n.* 进步)

adverse ['ædvɜːrs] *a.* 负面的 (negative, contrary); 不利的 (unfavorable)
【记】词根记忆: ad (坏) + vers (转) + e → 负面的; 不利的
【搭】adverse effect 反作用

☐ access   ☐ accredit   ☐ advanced   ☐ adverse

【例】The Group of Seven welcomed *adverse* criticism because it would help them to improve as artists. 七人组欢迎负面的批评，因为这能帮助他们提高艺术素养。//They could grow crops despite *adverse* weather. 尽管天气不利，他们也能种植作物。

【派】adversely(*ad.* 不利地，有害地)；adversity(*n.* 逆境)

【参】averse(*a.* 不愿意的)

afford [əˈfɔːrd] *vt.* 买得起；冒险做；提供(*provide, supply)

【记】分拆联想：af + ford(看作 Ford, 福特家族) → 财大气粗 → 买得起

【例】Most landless Americans could not *afford* the necessary tools and provisions. 多数无地的美国人买不起所需的工具和给养。

【派】affordable(*a.* 负担得起的)

annoying [əˈnɔɪɪŋ] *a.* 使人颇为生气或烦恼的

【例】There were many spelling errors in the text of that book. It was really *annoying*. 那本书里有很多拼写错误，真讨厌。

appreciation [əˌpriːʃɪˈeɪʃn] *n.* 欣赏；口味，兴趣(recognition；taste)

【例】European ladies once showed great *appreciation* of hats decorated with ostrich feather. 欧洲女士曾经十分热衷鸵鸟毛装饰的帽子。

assembly [əˈsembli] *n.* 集会；装配，安装

【搭】assembly line 装配线，流水线；assembly of …的集会

【例】People in the country used to fight for freedom of speech and freedom of *assembly*. 这个国家的人们过去常常为言论和集会的自由而斗争。

benefit [ˈbenɪfɪt] *n.* 利益，好处 *v.* (使)受益(profit)

【记】词根记忆：bene(善，好) + fit → 利益；有助于

【例】He has *benefited* from the woman's help. 他已从这个女子的帮助中受益。

captivity [kæpˈtɪvəti] *n.* 囚禁，拘留(confinement)

【记】词根记忆：capt(抓住) + ivity(表) → 被抓住 → 囚禁

championship [ˈtʃæmpiənʃɪp] *n.* [常*pl.*] 锦标赛

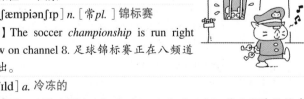

captivity

【例】The soccer *championship* is run right now on channel 8. 足球锦标赛正在八频道播出。

chilled [tʃɪld] *a.* 冷冻的

【例】The *chilled* drink refreshed us on the hot day. 热天里冷饮使我们精神抖擞。

☐ afford ☐ annoying ☐ appreciation ☐ assembly ☐ benefit ☐ captivity
☐ championship ☐ chilled

clue [kluː] *n.* 线索(*information, hint); 提示(cue)

column ['kɑːləm] *n.* 圆柱(pillar); 专栏; 长列(a long row)

commemorate [kə'meməreɪt] *v.* 纪念; 庆祝(celebrate, honor)

【记】词根记忆: com(共同) + memor(记住) + ate → 纪念

【例】Thank you for coming here this morning to *commemorate* the first balloon voyage in the United States. 感谢大家今天上午前来庆祝美国首次热气球旅行。

component [kəm'poʊnənt] *n.* 成分，组成部分 (*part, element) *a.* 构成的 (*constituent)

【记】词根记忆: com(共同) + pon(放置) + ent → 放到一起(的东西) → 成分

【例】Community service is an important *component* of education here at our university. 社区服务是我们这所大学教育体系中的重要组成部分。

【参】opponent(*a.* 对立的)

cosmos ['kɑːzmoʊs] *n.* 宇宙(universe)

【记】词根记忆: cosm(宇宙) + os → 宇宙

critic ['krɪtɪk] *n.* 评论家，批评家(detractor)

【参】criticism(*n.* 评判; 批评); criticize(*v.* 批评; 评论)

dehydrate [diː'haɪdreɪt] *vt.* 使脱水(dry, desiccate)

【记】词根记忆: de(去掉) + hydr(水) + ate(使) → 使脱水

【例】The little girl's body had *dehydrated* dangerously with the high temperature. 小姑娘的身体缺水，体温很高，十分危险。

【派】dehydration(*n.* 脱水, 干燥)

despoil [dɪ'spɔɪl] *v.* 夺取，掠夺(pillage)

【记】词根记忆: de(加强) + spoil(损坏) → 抢夺时不断地被损害 → 掠夺

【搭】despoil sb. of rights 剥夺某人的权利

【例】The foreign soldiers *despoiled* the small town of all its treasures. 外国士兵掠夺了小镇所有的财宝。

【派】despoiler(*n.* 掠夺者)

diction ['dɪkʃn] *n.* 措辞，用语(expression)

【记】词根记忆: dict(说话) + ion → 措辞，用语

【例】To practice *diction* by oneself is useful. 自己练习措辞十分有用。

【参】dictation(*n.* 听写)

dim [dɪm] *a.* 模糊的(faint)；暗淡的(pale)

【参】dime(*n.* 一角硬币)

elaborate [ɪˈlæbərət] *a.* 精心计划（制作）的(*detailed)，复杂精美的(*ornate, complex)

【记】分拆联想：e(出) + labor(劳动) + ate(使) → 辛苦劳动做出来 → 精心制作的

【例】They developed *elaborate* ceremonies and religious rituals to bring rain. 他们设计了复杂的典礼和宗教仪式来求雨。

【派】elaborately(*ad.* 精巧地)；elaboration(*n.* 详尽阐述)

engulf [ɪnˈɡʌlf] *v.* 吞没(merge)

【记】词根记忆：en(进入) + gulf(海湾；深渊) → 进入深渊 → 吞没

engulf

eternal [ɪˈtɜːrnl] *a.* 永恒的，不朽的(lasting)；不断的

【记】联想记忆：外部(external)世界是永恒的(eternal)诱惑

【例】They represent humans in an *eternal* struggle with the forces of nature. 他们是与自然界持续斗争的人们的代表。

fair [fer] *a.* 公平的，合理的 (disinterested, reasonable) *n.* 展览会(exhibition)；集市

【例】That shop has *fair* prices. 那个商店的商品价格合理。

fairly [ˈferli] *ad.* 相当地(rather)；公正地(impartially)

【例】Moore's design was *fairly* successful. 摩尔的设计相当成功。

feudal [ˈfjuːdl] *a.* 封建（制度）的

【记】来自feud(*n.* 世仇；封地)

【例】Although based on *feudal* models, the colony of Pennsylvania developed a reputation for a progressive political and social outlook. 尽管基于封建的模式，宾夕法尼亚的殖民地还是享有政治和社会前景不断进步的声誉。

function [ˈfʌŋkʃn] *n.* 机能；功能；作用(*serve)

【参】multifunctional(*a.* 多功能的)；malfunction(*n.* 故障)

gradual [ˈɡrædʒuəl] *a.* 逐渐的，逐步的(little by little)

【记】词根记忆：grad（行走）+ ual（…的）→ 渐进的行走 → 逐渐的，逐步的

【例】They grow by the *gradual* transformation of snow into glacier ice. 雪在逐渐转化为冰川冰时，它们自己也在增长。

【派】gradually(*ad.* 逐渐地，逐步地)

□ dim	□ elaborate	□ engulf	□ eternal	□ fair	□ fairly
□ feudal	□ function	□ gradual			

heed [hiːd] *n.* 注意(attention); 留心(notice)

【记】联想记忆：需要(need)的东西格外注意、留心(heed)

【例】The small investors paid little *heed* to future land users. 规模小的投资人很少关注未来的土地使用者。

hibernation [ˌhaɪbərˈneɪʃn] *n.* 冬眠(dormancy); 进入冬眠状态

【记】来自hibernate(*v.* 冬眠)

【例】Mammals vary their body temperatures during *hibernation*. 哺乳动物在冬眠时体温会发生变化。

hollow [ˈhɑːloʊ] *a.* 空心的; 虚伪的(false) *n.* 山谷(valley) *vt.* 挖空

【例】The man is destroyed by his own *hollow* values. 此人被自己虚伪的价值观给毁了。

horizon [həˈraɪzn] *n.* 地平线(skyline); [常 *pl.*] 眼界，视野(sight, eyeshot)

【记】分拆联想：ho + riz(看作rise, 升起) + on → 太阳从地平线上升起 → 地平线

【例】The farmers' broader *horizons* and greater self-respect were reflected to some degree in their behavior. 农民更开阔的视野和更强烈的自尊在一定程度上通过其行为反映了出来。

illuminate [ɪˈluːmɪneɪt] *v.* 照亮(lighten)

【记】词根记忆：il(加强) + lumin(光) + ate → 加强光亮 → 照亮

【例】The light *illuminates* the scales of the fish in the bottom of the boat. 灯照亮了船底鱼的鳞片。

【派】illuminating(*a.* 照亮的; 启蒙的)

implement [ˈɪmplɪment] *vt.* 执行，实施(carry out) [ˈɪmplɪmənt] *n.* [常 *pl.*] 工具(*tool)

【记】词根记忆：im(使…) + ple(满) + ment → 使圆满 → 执行，实施

【例】It took the company a year to *implement* the plan. 公司用了一年时间来实施这个计划。//They began using improved *implements*. 他们开始使用改良的工具。

【派】implementation(*n.* 执行)

incense [ˈɪnsens] *n.* 熏香

【记】词根记忆：in(使) + cense(=cand光亮的) → 发着亮光燃烧中的 → 熏香

【搭】incense burner 香炉

insist [ɪnˈsɪst] *v.* 坚持要求(demand), 坚决主张

【记】词根记忆：in(里面) + sist(站) → 一直站在里面 → 坚决主张

【搭】insist on 坚持

heed	hibernation	hollow	horizon	illuminate	implement
incense	insist				

【例】A: Jane *insists* she's coming to my graduation.

B: But she has to work that week, doesn't she?

A：简坚持来参加我的毕业典礼。

B：但是她不是那一周要上班吗？

【派】insistence(*n.* 坚持，坚持主张)

【参】consist(*v.* 由…组成); persist(*v.* 坚持)

launch [lɔ:ntʃ] *vt.* 使开始；发射(project)

【记】和lunch(*n.* 中餐)一起记

【例】The United States government *launched* a series of weather satellites in 1966. 美国政府在1996年发射了一系列气象卫星。

linguist ['lɪŋgwɪst] *n.* 语言学家

【记】词根记忆：lingu(语言) + ist → 语言学家

【例】Historical *linguists* study how languages evolve over time. 历史语言学家研究的是随着时间的流逝语言是如何演变的。

longevity [lɔ:n'dʒevəti] *n.* 长寿(long life)

【记】词根记忆：long(长) + ev(时间) + ity → 活得时间长 → 长寿

【搭】longevity of …的寿命

【例】A balanced diet, enough sleep as well as positive attitude towards everything contribute to *longevity*. 均衡的膳食、充足的睡眠以及对万事积极的态度有助于人长寿。

longevity

【派】longevous(*a.* 长寿的)

management ['mænɪdʒmənt] *n.* 经营，管理；管理部门

【记】联想记忆：man(人) + age(年纪) + ment → 一般管理人员都年龄较长，富有经验 → 管理

【搭】political management 政治管理

【例】I want to talk today about the political *management* of the war on both sides, the north under Lincoln, and the south under Davis. 今天我想谈谈内战中北方林肯和南方戴维斯双方的政治管理。//The level of *management* is vital to the development of a company. 管理水平对公司的发展至关重要。

medal ['medl] *n.* 奖牌，奖章(medallion)

【记】联想记忆：奖牌(medal)是金属(metal)做的

medieval [ˌmedi'i:vl] *a.* 中世纪的(of, relating to the Middle Ages)

【记】词根记忆：medi(中间) + ev(时间) + al → 中世纪的

【例】The museum had an exhibit of *medieval* armor last month. 博物馆上个月展出了中世纪的铠甲。

meteorology [ˌmiːtiəˈrɑːlədʒi] *n.* 气象学(aerography)

【记】词根记忆：meteor(陨石；天气) + ology(学科) → 古代根据流星判断天气 → 气象学

【派】meteorological(*a.* 气象学的)；meteorologist(*n.* 气象学者)

microscope [ˈmaɪkrəskoup] *n.* 显微镜

【记】词根记忆：micro(小) + scope(看) → 用来看小东西 → 显微镜

【派】microscopic(*a.* 用显微镜可见的；极小的)

mock [mɑːk] *v.* 嘲笑(ridicule)

【记】联想记忆：和尚(monk)没头发常受到嘲笑(mock)

【例】These achievements were *mocked* by the artistic elite of Paris as expensive and ugly follies. 巴黎艺术精英嘲笑这些成就是昂贵和丑陋的罪恶。

【参】mockingbird(*n.* 嘲鸟)

nourishment [ˈnɜːrɪʃmənt] *n.* 营养品

【例】The food produced by our company is not only a *nourishment* but also is convenient in our daily life. 我们公司生产的食品不仅是营养品，在日常生活中食用起来也很方便。

numerous [ˈnuːmərəs] *a.* 许多的(many)；无数的(countless)

【记】词根记忆：numer (计数) + ous → 不计其数的 → 许多的；无数的

【例】Cosmic rays consist of rapidly moving particles of *numerous* different kinds. 宇宙射线包括移动迅速的无数种粒子。

obscure [əbˈskjʊr] *a.* 暗的，朦胧的(dim)；模糊的，晦涩的 *vt.* 使暗，使不明显

【记】词根记忆：obs(看作ob，强调) + cur(流) + e → 流下的泪水模糊了她的视线 → 模糊的

【例】The path we had taken became more *obscure* in the heavy rain. 我们走的路在大雨中变得更加模糊了。

phenomenon [fəˈnɑːmɪnən] *n.* 现象；特殊的事物

【例】A similar *phenomenon* has also occurred in other parts of the animal kingdom. 在动物世界的其他部分也出现了类似的现象。

【派】phenomenal(*a.* 显著的)

pit [pɪt] *n.* 深坑(*hole, cavity)，矿井(mine) *vt.* 使竞争

【记】联想记忆：猪(pig)拱了个大坑(pit)

【例】The champion was *pitted* against the young contender. 冠军与年轻的竞争者对垒。

plumage ['pluːmɪdʒ] *n.* 鸟类羽毛(feathers)

【例】The bird's *plumage* has turned grey over one night. 这只鸟的羽毛在一夜之间变成了灰色。

porcelain ['pɔːrsəlɪn] *n.* 瓷器, 瓷(china)

【记】发音记忆: "跑四邻" → 卖瓷器需要跑四邻八方 → 瓷器

【例】The small shop around the corner sells various *porcelain* ware. 拐角处的小商店卖各种瓷器。

portion ['pɔːrʃn] *n.* 部分(part, share)

【记】分拆联想: port(看作part, 部分) + ion → 部分

【例】Why do squirrels eat only a *portion* of each acorn they retrieve? 松鼠为什么只吃它们重新得到的一部分橡子?

postpone [poʊ'spoʊn] *vt.* 使延期, 推迟(delay)

【记】词根记忆: post(在后面) + pone(放) → 放在后面 → 推迟

【例】The meeting has been *postponed* until further notice. 会议推迟了, 召开时间有待进一步通知。

presidency ['prezɪdənsi] *n.* 职位(position); 任期(term)

【例】The Whig party decided to nominate him for the *presidency*. 辉格党决定提名他为总统候选人。

productivity [ˌprɑːdʌk'tɪvəti] *n.* 生产力(fertility)

【记】来自product(产物, 产品) + ivity → 生产力

proponent [prə'poʊnənt] *n.* 支持者(*supporter); 倡导者(advocate)

【记】词根记忆: pro(向前) + pon(放) + ent → 处在前面的人 → 倡导者

【例】*Proponents* of the worksheet procedure believe that it will yield optimal, that is, the best decisions. 支持工作表程序的人认为, 这会得出最佳的决定。

【参】component(*n.* 成分)

protein ['proʊtiːn] *n.* 蛋白质

【记】分拆联想: pro(很多) + tein(看作tain, 保持) → 维持生命之物 → 蛋白质

recognize ['rekəgnaɪz] *vt.* 认出, 识别(identify); 认可(acknowledge)

【例】She didn't *recognize* the man because of his haircut. 她没有认出这个男子, 因为他理发了。

【派】recognition (*n.* 认出; 承认; 表彰); recognizable (*a.* 可辨认的); recognized(*a.* 公认的)

salamander ['sæləmændər] *n.* 火蜥蜴

☐ plumage	☐ porcelain	☐ portion	☐ postpone	☐ presidency	☐ productivity
☐ proponent	☐ protein	☐ recognize	☐ salamander		

seep [siːp] *v.* 漏出，渗漏(pass through slowly, ooze)

【记】联想记忆：啤酒渗出(seep)发出哔哔声(beep)

【派】seepage(*n.* 渗漏)

senate ['senət] *n.* 参议院(parliament)

【记】词根记忆：sen(老的) + ate(表人，职位) → 资格老的人组成的领导班子 → 上院

【派】senator(*n.* 参议员)

session ['seʃn] *n.* 会议；开庭(sitting)

【例】She'll probably be too tired to walk to the *session*. 她可能太累了，无法走到参议院。

shortage ['ʃɔːrtɪdʒ] *n.* 不足，缺乏(scarcity, deficiency)

【记】来自short(缺乏) + age → 不足，缺乏

skip [skɪp] *v.* 跳(jump, leap)；不出席(absent)；逃学(play hooky)

【例】I'd like to *skip* the meeting, but I can't just not go. 我不想参加这个会议，但是还不能不去。

slice [slaɪs] *vt.* 切(片) *n.* 薄片(flake)；片断(segment)

【记】分拆联想：sl + ice(冰) → 把冰块切碎 → 切(片)

slip [slɪp] *v.* 滑(过、落)(slide) *n.* (木、纸)片；滑倒

【记】分拆联想：s + lip(嘴唇) → 从唇边滑落 → 滑(过，落)

【派】slipper(*n.* 拖鞋)；slippery(*a.* 光滑的)

status ['steɪtəs] *n.* 身份，地位(rank, position)；情况(condition)

【例】A woman's *status* was changed by marriage. 一个女人的地位因婚姻而改变。//I wonder what the *status* of the storm is now. 我想知道风暴的情况如何。

strain [streɪn] *n.* 张力 *vt.* 扭伤(sprain)

【记】本身为词根，意为：拉紧

【例】You might *strain* your shoulder. 你可能会扭伤你的肩膀。

stride [straɪd] *n.* 大步；步法(pace)

【记】分拆联想：st + ride (骑自行车) → 走得像骑自行车一样快 → 大步

subway ['sʌbweɪ] *n.* 地铁(underground)

【记】词根记忆：sub(在下面) + way(路) → 在下面的路 → 地铁

session

stride

surge [sɜːrdʒ] *v.* 汹涌奔腾 *n.* 汹涌,澎湃;猛涨(*sharp increase)

【记】本身为词根,意为:升起,立起

【例】In June 1986, the glacier *surged* ahead as much as 47 feet a day. 1986年6月,冰川每天最远向前挺进47英尺。// The movement of *surge* glaciers can be prevented. 猛涨的冰川运动可以被阻止。

【派】upsurge(*n.* 高涨,高潮)

terminus ['tɜːrmɪnəs] *n.* (火车、汽车)终点站(terminal, end)

territory ['terətɔːri] *n.* 领土,领域(domain)

【记】词根记忆: terr(地) + it + ory(表地点)→ 领土,地域

【例】How did spiders defend their *territory*? 蜘蛛如何捍卫其领地?

thereby [ˌðer'baɪ] *ad.* 因此,从而

【搭】thereby doing sth. 从而做…

topsoil ['tɑːpsɔɪl] *n.* 表层土

【记】分拆联想: top(顶上的) + soil(土地)→ 表层土

【例】The fieldstones remain in a frozen layer of *topsoil*. 大卵石仍然在冻土表层里。

transit ['trænzɪt] *n.* 运输(线)(transport);转变

【记】词根记忆: trans(改变) + it → 改变它的地点 → 运输

【搭】mass transit 公共交通

unpredictable [ˌʌnprɪ'dɪktəbl] *a.* 不可预知的

【记】分拆联想: un(无) + predict(预言) + able → 不可预知的

【例】Their major discovery illustrated how *unpredictable* consequences can come from rather modest beginnings. 他们的重要发现表明了貌似平常的初始是如何产生预想不到的结果的。

【派】unpredictability(*n.* 不可预知性)

The fireworks that jump high and go far are beautiful.

凡是能冲上去的,能散发出来的焰火,都是美丽的。

——安徒生(*Andersen*)

☐ surge ☐ terminus ☐ territory ☐ thereby ☐ topsoil ☐ transit
☐ unpredictable

Word List 10 MP3-10

tribute	给予	distribute	v. 分配，分发
junct	连接	junction	n. 交叉点，汇合点
manu	手	manual	a. 手工的
mel	甜	melody	n. 悦耳的旋律
popul	人	populate	v. 居住于
rod	咬	rodent	n. 啮齿类动物
pose	提出	suppose	vt. 假设
vig	生命	vigilance	n. 警戒
voc	声音	vocal	a. 声音的

abort [ə'bɔːrt] n. 中止计划(任务)；夭折(cancel)

【记】分拆联想：ab(相反) + ort(看作ori, 升起, 开始)→ 还没开始就中止

【例】I've wasted almost a year on an *abort*. 我在一个中途失败的行动上浪费了几乎一年的时间。

acidic [ə'sɪdɪk] a. 酸的, 酸性的

【派】acidity(n. 酸度, 酸性)

adequate ['ædɪkwət] a. 适当的(proper)；足够的(*sufficient)

【记】词根记忆：ad(加强) + equ(平等) + ate(…的)→ 比平等多的 → 足够的

【例】There is little evidence that people lacked *adequate* wild food resources. 很少有证据表明人们缺少足够的野生食物来源。

【派】adequately(ad. 充分地)；inadequate(a. 不充分的, 不足的)

adorn [ə'dɔːrn] vt. 装饰, 装扮(*decorate, beautify)

【记】词根记忆：ad + orn(装饰)→ 装饰, 装扮

【例】Children *adorned* themselves with beads. 儿童用珠子来装扮自己。

【派】adornment(n. 装饰)；unadorned(a. 朴实的)

【参】ardor(n. 热情)；adore(v. 崇拜)

approve [ə'pruːv] *vt.* 批准（pass, ratify）*vi.* 赞成（assent）

【记】分拆联想：ap（一再）+ prove（证实）→ 一再证实是好的 → 批准；赞成

【例】The advisor has already *approved* the man's class schedule. 指导教师已经批准了此人的课程安排。//He doesn't *approve* of the dean's plan. 他不赞成院长的计划。

【派】approval（*n.* 赞成；批准）；disapproval（*n.* 不赞成）

atomic [ə'tɑːmɪk] *a.* 原子的；原子能的（nuclear）

【记】来自atom（*n.* 原子）

【搭】atomic energy 原子能

【例】Atoms that have different *atomic* numbers generally behave differently. 具有不同原子数的原子一般表现也不同。

bacteria [bæk'tɪriə] *n.* 细菌

【记】联想记忆：bac(看作back，背后) + ter + ia(病) → 总是偷偷（背后）让人得病的东西 → 细菌

【搭】bacteria infection 细菌感染

【例】A: Now we have lots of antibiotics that kill *bacteria*.

B: Well, penicillin kills *bacteria*, but not all antibiotics do.

A: 现在我们有很多杀死细菌的抗生素。

B: 是啊，盘尼西林杀死细菌，但是并非所有的抗生素都能做到这一点。//Like the other microbes, *bacteria* are single-cells. 跟其他微生物一样，细菌是单一细胞。

breathing ['briːðɪŋ] *n.* 呼吸（respiration）

【例】When you feel nervous, the best way to relax is deep *breathing* exercises. 当你感觉紧张时，最好的放松方式是练习深呼吸。

bubble ['bʌbl] *n.* (气、水)泡 *v.* 起泡

【记】象声词：指水冒泡的声音

bulb [bʌlb] *n.* 植物的球茎，球形物；灯泡

cluster ['klʌstər] *n.* 串，丛；群（*group）*vt.* 丛生；使成群（*concentrate, assemble）

【记】词根记忆：clust(=clot凝成块) + er → 凝块 → 使成群

consume [kən'suːm] *vt.* 消耗，消费（spend, use up）；大吃大喝（waste）

consume

【记】分拆联想：con(加强) + sume(取) → 把钱全部取出消费，吃喝 → 消费

【例】How much of a day's total calories should be *consumed* at breakfast? 早餐应该摄入一天所需总热量的多少？

| ☐ approve | ☐ atomic | ☐ bacteria | ☐ breathing | ☐ bubble | ☐ bulb |
| ☐ cluster | ☐ consume | | | | |

debris [dəˈbriː] *n.* 废墟，残骸(ruin, remains)；碎片(fragment)
【记】分拆联想：de(向下) + bris(看作brick，砖)→砖都向下倒去→废墟

destined [ˈdestɪnd] *a.* 注定的(doomed)
【例】They were *destined* never to meet again. 他们注定再也无法见面了。
【参】destination(*n.* 目的地)

distribute [dɪˈstrɪbjuːt] *v.* 分配，分发(parcel out)；散布(scatter, spread)
【记】词根记忆：dis(分开) + tribute(给予)→分开给→分配，分发
【例】Professor Burke will *distribute* calculators to the students. 伯克教授将分发计算器给学生。
【派】distributed (*a.* 分布式的)；distribution (*n.* 分发，分配)；distributor(*n.* 发行人)

dolphin [ˈdɑːlfɪn] *n.* 海豚

drill [drɪl] *v.* 钻(孔)，打眼(bore) *n.* 钻(孔)；操练(practice)
【记】分拆联想：dr(看作dry，干燥的) + ill(生病)→操练让人口干舌燥，差点生病
【例】The first oil well was *drilled* by E. L. Drake, a retired railroad conductor. 第一口油井是E·L·德雷克钻的，此人是一名退休的铁路列车长。

elementary [ˌelɪˈmentri] *a.* 初级的(primary)
【搭】elementary school 小学

engraving [ɪnˈɡreɪvɪŋ] *n.* 雕刻术；版画(print)
【记】来自engrave(*v.* 雕刻)

entitle [ɪnˈtaɪtl] *vt.* 使有权(做某事)
【记】词根记忆：en(使…) + title(头衔，权利)→使有权
【例】Most students buy meal contracts, which *entitle* them to twenty meals a week at any of the cafeterias. 多数学生购买用餐合同，这使他们有权每周在任意一个餐厅用餐20次。
【派】entitled(*a.* 名为…的)

expansion [ɪkˈspænʃn] *n.* 扩张，膨胀；张开，伸展
【记】来自expand(*v.* 扩大)
【例】The graph on the wall shows the *expansion* of international business in the company. 墙上的图标显示了公司国际业务的增长。
【参】extent(*n.* 长度，广度)

exposure [ɪkˈspoʊʒər] *n.* 显露；曝光
【记】来自expose(*v.* 揭露)

【例】Vaccines for some rare diseases are given only to persons who risk *exposure* to the disease. 某些罕见疾病的疫苗只给有可能接触这些疾病的人。

【参】extension(*n.* 延长)；expansion(*n.* 扩充)

farce [fɑːrs] *n.* 闹剧，滑稽剧

flexible ['fleksəbl] *a.* 易曲的，柔软的(pliable)；灵活的(elastic)

【记】词根记忆：flex(弯曲) + ible → 易曲的，柔软的

【例】Sea anemones have *flexible* bodies. 海葵的身体柔软。//She can't offer the man a *flexible* schedule. 她无法给这个男子一个灵活的时间表。

【派】flexibly(*ad.* 易曲地)；flexibility(*n.* 弹性；灵活性)；inflexible(*a.* 不可弯曲的)

fulfill [fʊl'fɪl] *v.* 履行(perform, execute)；符合(accord with)

【记】分拆联想：ful(看作full，充满的) + fil(看作fill，装满了) → 做得圆满 → 履行，实现

【例】He has *fulfilled* his graduation requirements. 他已经符合毕业要求了。

gender ['dʒendər] *n.* 性别(sex)

【记】和tender(*a.* 温柔的)一起记

genius ['dʒiːniəs] *n.* 天才(talent)；天赋(endowment)

【记】希腊神话中的一种守护精灵，他不但引导人的命运，而且左右人的个性。后来genius的词义逐渐转变为"天生智慧很高的人"。

【例】They insisted that *The Iliad* and *The Odyssey* could have been the work of single poetic *genius*. 他们坚持认为《伊利亚特》和《奥德赛》可能是一个天才诗人的作品。//Human beings may benefit from their own inventive *genius*. 人类可以从他们自己的发明天才中受益。

gospel ['gɑːspl] *n.* 信条(principle)；福音音乐

【记】来自《圣经·新约》中的福音书(Gospel)，可能来自god + spell → 上帝的话 → 信条

【例】Mahalia Jackson's powerful, joyous *gospel* music style had gained her an international reputation. 马哈莉亚·杰克逊有力欢快的福音音乐风格使她享誉世界。

hamper ['hæmpər] *vt.* 妨碍(*hinder)

【记】发音记忆："寒迫" → 饥寒交迫 → 妨碍

【例】The development of a scientific approach to chemistry was *hampered* by several factors. 几个因素阻碍了研究化学的科学方法的发展。

hygiene [ˈhaɪdʒiːn] *n.* 卫生 (sanitation)

【记】在希腊神话中有一个女神叫Hygeia, 被人奉为健康女神, 她的名字所基于的希腊词根hygies含有"健康的"之意, 现在作为医学术语, 表示"卫生, 卫生学, 保健"

【搭】personal hygiene 个人卫生

ideology [ˌaɪdiˈɑːlədʒi] *n.* 思想体系; 意识形态

【记】分拆联想: ideo (看作idea, 思想) + logy (…学) → 思想体系

【例】Gradually, economic reality overcame *ideology*. 经济现实逐渐克服了意识形态。

inconvenient [ˌɪnkənˈviːniənt] *a.* 不方便的 (inappropriate); 让人不舒服的 (uncomfortable)

【记】in + convenient (方便的) → 不便的

【例】The campus bus runs at really *inconvenient* time. 校园巴士运行的时间真不方便。//It was *inconvenient* to carry anything in pants pockets while riding. 开车时裤子口袋装什么东西都不方便。

infrared [ˌɪnfrəˈred] *a.* 红外线的

【记】词根记忆: infra (在…下) + red (红色) → 在红色之下 → 红外线的

【例】The quartz crystal's energy is turned into *infrared* radiation. 石英晶体的能量可以转换成红外辐射。

invasion [ɪnˈveɪʒn] *n.* 侵入, 侵略

【记】词根记忆: in (进入) + vas (走) + ion → 走进来 → 侵略

【例】An *invasion* of the introduced species had threatened the development of agriculture. 引入物种的入侵威胁了农业的发展。

junction [ˈdʒʌŋkʃn] *n.* 交叉点, 汇合处 (intersection)

【记】词根记忆: junct (连接) + ion → 交叉点, 汇合处

【例】A major railroad *junction* in Illinois, Decatur has become an important commercial hub for the region's farm products and livestock. 德卡图尔是伊利诺斯州的一个主要铁路枢纽, 现在已经成了该地区农产品和牲畜交易的重要商业中心。

laureate [ˈlɔːriət] *n.* 戴桂冠的人

【搭】poet laureate 桂冠诗人

literary [ˈlɪtəreri] *a.* 文学 (上) 的

【记】词根记忆: liter (文字) + ary → 文字上的 → 文学的

【例】Mark Twain drew on his own experiences and used dialect and common speech instead of *literary* language. 马克·吐温从亲身经历取材, 使用方言和普通话而不是文学语言进行写作。

【参】literacy (*n.* 有文化); illiterate (*a.* 缺乏教育的)

hygiene	ideology	inconvenient	infrared	invasion	junction
laureate	literary				

mammoth [ˈmæməθ] *n.* 猛犸象 *a.* 巨大的（huge）

【记】发音记忆：原指古代的猛犸象，十分巨大

mania [ˈmeɪnɪə] *n.* 狂热（craze, madness）

【记】联想记忆：man（男人）+ ia（病）→ 男人病 → 狂热

【例】The *mania* for architectural reconstruction had largely subsided by the 1950's and 1960's. 建筑改造的热潮在20世纪50年代和60年代就大大消退了。

mammoth

manual [ˈmænjuəl] *a.* 手工的（by hand）*n.* 手册，指南（guidebook, handbook）

【记】词根记忆：manu（手）+ al（…的）→ 手工的

【例】I am good at *manual* tasks, but I don't do math well. 我擅长手工，但是数学不好。//She'll give the man her instruction *manual*. 她将把她的指导手册给这名男子。

melody [ˈmelədi] *n.* 悦耳的旋律

【记】词根记忆：mel（甜）+ ody（唱）→ 悦耳的旋律

【例】Ragtime is a kind of music that has a strongly syncopated *melody* and a regularly accented accompaniment. 拉格泰姆音乐是一种有强烈的切分旋律以及音调起伏均匀的伴奏的音乐。

【派】melodious（*a.* 声调优美的，悦耳的）

moral [ˈmɔːrəl] *a.* 道德的（ethical）；精神的（spiritual）*n.* [常 *pl.*] 道德（ethics）

【派】morality（*n.* 道德）；moralism（*n.* 道德教育，道德准则）；moralistic（*a.* 道德观念的）

muggy [ˈmʌgi] *a.* （指天气）闷热而潮湿的

【例】A: I was expecting another hot, *muggy* day.

B: But the wind's cooled things off, hasn't it?

A：我本来以为这又是炎热潮湿的一天。

B：但是风已经使天气凉爽了，是不是？

naive [naɪˈiːv] *a.* 天真的（innocent）；纯朴的（artless）

【记】联想记忆：native（原始的，土著的）减去 t → 比土著人懂得还要少 → 天真的；纯朴的

【例】Her expression is neither *naive* nor instinctive. 她的表情既不天真也不是出于本能。//His works produced *naive* pictures of country life. 他的作品描绘了一幅幅淳朴的乡村生活图景。

☐ mammoth	☐ mania	☐ manual	☐ melody	☐ moral	☐ muggy
☐ naive					

narrate [nə'reɪt] v. 叙述(relate)

【例】The passage is organized by *narrating* a story about excellent teachers. 本段叙述了一个优秀教师的故事。

【派】narration(n. 叙述); narrator(n. 叙述者)

notion ['nouʃn] n. 概念，观念(concept); 想法(thought)

【记】词根记忆: not(知道) + ion(性质) → 知道了 → 有了概念和想法 → 概念; 想法

【例】Subsequent reforms have made these *notions* seem quite out-of-date. 后来的改革使这些观念看上去颇为落伍。

offer ['ɔːfər] v. 提供(provide, supply)

【搭】take a job offer 得到工作; offer sth. to sb. 向…提供…

【例】A: It's so thoughtful of you to *offer* to drop me off at the train station. Are you sure it's not out of your way?

B: Not at all. The station is really close to where I'm going.

A: 你真体贴人，要把我送到火车站。你肯定这不会让你绕路吧?

B: 完全不会。车站离我要去的地方很近。

outbreak ['autbreɪk] n. 发作; 爆发(beginning, eruption, explosion)

【记】来自词组break out 突发，爆发

【搭】the outbreak of war 战争的爆发

【例】With the *outbreak* of natural disaster, there has been a massive epidemic sweeping over the region. 随着自然灾害的爆发，一场大规模的流行病横扫了这个地区。

overload [,ouvər'loud] vt. 使超载，使过载; 使(电路等)超过负荷; 装填…过满; 使负担过重 ['ouvərloud] n. 超载; 负荷过多; 过满装填，过重负担

【例】Car drivers usually *overload* their cars. 卡车一般都超载。

partial ['pɑːrʃl] a. 不完全的(incomplete)

【记】来自part(部分) + ial → 部分的 → 不完全的

【派】partially(ad. 部分地); impartially(ad. 公平地)

populate ['pɑːpjuleɪt] v. 居住于(inhabit); 移民(migrate)

【记】词根记忆: popul(人) + ate(使…) → 使人在某处安家 → 居住于

【例】The town is heavily *populated* by immigrants. 该镇居住着很多外来移民。

【派】population(n. 人口; 人口密度)

| ☐ narrate | ☐ notion | ☐ offer | ☐ outbreak | ☐ overload | ☐ partial |
| ☐ populate | | | | | |

prevailing [prɪ'veɪlɪŋ] *a.* 普遍的（*most frequent, universal）；流行的（popular）

【记】来自 prevail（流行）+ ing → 流行的

【搭】prevailing wind 【气】盛行风（a wind from the direction that is predominant or most usual at a particular place or season）

【例】The *prevailing* winds in the Great Basin are from the west. 大盆地的盛行风来自西部。

prohibitively [prə'hɪbətɪvli] *ad.* （价格）极高地（extremely）

【例】The cost of equipping and operating many thousands of conventional weather stations was *prohibitively* high. 上千个传统气象站的装备运营成本极高。

proofread ['pruːfriːd] *vt.* 校对，校正（revise）

【记】组合词：proof（验证）+ read（读）→ 校对，校正

【例】Beth missed several errors while *proofreading* her paper. 贝斯校对她的论文时漏掉了几处错误。

protest ['proʊtest] *n.* 抗议，反对

[prə'test] *v.* 抗议，反对（object）

【记】分拆联想：pro（很多）+ test（测验）→ 考试太多，遭到学生反对、抗议；注意不要和 protect（*v.* 保护）相混

【例】The students have been *protesting* against the increasing tuition. 学生们一直在抗议学费上涨。

quota ['kwoʊtə] *n.* 定额（ration）

【例】The club president announced that each member has a *quota* of ten tickets to sell for the talent show. 俱乐部主席宣布每个成员有销售业余歌手演唱会 10 张票的定额。

rampant ['ræmpənt] *a.* 猖獗的，蔓生的（wild, extravagant）

【记】来自 ramp（蔓延）+ ant → 蔓生的，猖獗的

【搭】rampant inflation 无法控制的通货膨胀

【例】Due to the climate, the serious disease is *rampant* in this region. 由于气候原因，这种严重的疾病在这个地区不断地蔓延。

ratio ['reɪʃioʊ] *n.* 比，比率（proportion）

【记】本身为词根，意为：推定；理由，理性

recital [rɪ'saɪtl] *n.* 独奏会

【参】solo（*n.* 独唱）

reckless ['rekləs] *a.* 轻率的，鲁莽的（*irresponsible, rash）

【记】来自 reck（顾忌）+ less → 无所顾忌的 → 轻率的

restoration [ˌrestə'reɪʃn] *n.* 恢复；翻新

【例】The common citizens in the country demand a *restoration* of the right to vote. 这个国家的普通民众要求恢复选举权。

prevailing	prohibitively	proofread	protest	quota	rampant
ratio	recital	reckless	restoration		

rodent [ˈroʊdnt] *n.* 啮齿目动物

【记】词根记忆: rod（咬）+ ent → 喜欢用牙咬的动物 → 啮齿目动物

【参】edentate(*n.* 贫齿类动物)

scholarship [ˈskɑːlərʃɪp] *n.* 奖学金; 学问, 学识

【搭】full scholarship 全额奖学金; get a scholarship to the university 得到这个大学的奖学金

scuba [ˈskuːbə] *n.* 水中呼吸器

【记】分拆联想: s + cuba（音似: 哭吧）→ 潜水时丢了水中呼吸器只有哭吧 → 水中呼吸器

【搭】scuba-diving 佩戴水肺的潜水

sedimentary [ˌsedɪˈmentri] *a.* 沉积的, 沉淀性的(precipitable)

【例】Stratigraphy is the description of strata in *sedimentary* rock. 地层学的主要内容是描述沉积岩层。

sewerage [ˈsuːərɪdʒ] *n.* 排水系统(waste, drainage)

shower [ˈʃaʊər] *n.* 淋浴(器)(bath); 阵雨

【例】He got out of the *shower* to answer the phone. 他从淋浴里出来去接电话。

silt [sɪlt] *n.* 淤泥(sullage)

【记】联想记忆: 小心别坐上(sit)淤泥(silt)

stripe [straɪp] *n.* 条纹, 斑纹

【记】和strip(*n.* 条)一起记

suppose [səˈpoʊz] *vt.* 假设, 推测(presume)

【记】词根记忆: sup + pose（提出）→ 提出 → 假设

suppose

【例】Now, *suppose* you got a bag and you put a bunch of locks in it. 现在假设你有一个袋子, 你往里面放了一串锁。

【派】supposed（*a.* 假定的）; supposedly（*ad.* 按照推测, 想象上）; supposition(*n.* 假设)

【参】purpose(*n.* 目的); propose(*vt.* 建议)

symptom [ˈsɪmptəm] *n.* 症状; 征兆(sign)

【例】Much of the focus of the education was on the recognition of vitamin deficiency *symptoms*. 教育的重点是辨识缺乏维生素的症状。

tension [ˈtenʃn] *n.* 紧张(stress); 拉紧(tightness); 张力

【记】词根记忆: tens(伸展)+ ion → 伸展出的状态 → 拉紧

【搭】tension spring 拉伸弹簧

【例】The expressive leaders are attempting to minimize the *tension* and conflict. 富有表现力的领导人正在试图最大限度地减少紧张和冲突。//Four strings are stretched at high *tension*. 四根绳子拉得非常紧。

【参】tensile(*a.* 可拉长的，可伸长的)；tense(*a.* 紧张的，绷紧的)

treadmill [ˈtredmɪl] *n.* 踏车

【记】联想记忆：tread(踩踏) + mill(磨坊) → 在磨坊里踩踏车 → 踏车

tributary [ˈtrɪbjəteri] *n.* 支流(branch) *a.* 支流的

【记】词根记忆：tribut(给予) + ary → 支流

undertaking [ˌʌndərˈteɪkɪŋ] *n.* 事业，企业(enterprise)

【例】A: Professor Johnson, for my sociology project this term I'm thinking of interviewing all the residents in town on their TV viewing habit.

B: Well that's quite an *undertaking* for such a short-time project. Maybe you should take a little while to think about what that would entail before making your final decision.

A：约翰逊教授，关于这个学期社会学的项目，我想就看电视的习惯这一主题采访镇里的所有居民。

B：对这样的短期项目而言这是件大事。或许在最终决定之前你应该花时间想想这需要做哪些工作。

unparalleled [ʌnˈpærəleld] *a.* 空前的；无比的(unequaled, matchless)

【记】分拆联想：un(无) + parallel(平行) + ed → 没有东西可以与之平行 → 无比的

【例】Chicago possesses an almost *unparalleled* situation in economy development. 芝加哥在经济发展方面具有几乎无与伦比的环境。

vertical [ˈvɜːrtɪkl] *a.* 垂直的，竖直的(upright, erect)

【记】联想记忆：电影《垂直极限》的英文名 *Vertical Limit*

【例】There are both horizontal and *vertical* movements in air. 空气中既有水平运动也有垂直运动。

【派】vertically(*ad.* 垂直地)

vigilance [ˈvɪdʒɪləns] *n.* 警戒，警惕(watchfulness, alertness, caution)

【记】词根记忆：vig (生命) + il + ance → 有生命的，活动的 → 不睡 → 警惕

【例】The police cannot afford to relax their *vigilance* for a minute. 警方一刻也不敢放松警惕。

【派】vigilant(*a.* 警惕着的)

vocal ['voʊkl] *a.* 声音的, 有声的(phonic)

【记】词根记忆: voc(声音) + al(…的) → 声音的

【搭】vocal cords 声带

【派】vocalize(*v.* 发出声音)

wane [weɪn] *v.* 衰退(decline)

【记】联想记忆: 天鹅(swan)的数量在减少(wane) → 衰退

【例】Not only had household production *waned*, but technological improvements were rapidly changing the rest of domestic work. 不仅家庭作坊的数量减少了, 而且技术的进步也在迅速改变其他的家庭工作。

To be assured of your victory, you must have overwhelming advantage, strength and momentum to impress your opponents. However, without necessary tactics, you are easily to be reckless.

要想有必胜的把握, 就得建立绝对优势, 以绝对的力量压制对手, 以绝对的气势震慑对手。但是, 如果离开了必要的策略, 就成了蛮干。

——李嘉诚(*Li Jiacheng*)

Word List 11 MP3-11

词根、词缀预习表

plaud	鼓掌	applaud	vi. 鼓掌喝彩
fer	带来，拿来	confer	vt. 授予
cept	拿，抓	deception	n. 欺骗
dict	讲话；命令	dictate	v. 规定；决定
act	行动	enact	vt. 制定
curs	跑	excursion	n. 远足
gene	产生；基因	genesis	n. 起源
psycho	精神	psychology	n. 心理学
re	反	revolt	n./v. 起义，反抗
seg	切割	segregate	vt. 隔离；分离

absorb [əb'sɔːrb] vt. 吸收(take in, engage)

【记】分拆联想：ab(离去) + sorb(吸收) → 吸收

【例】This gamma radiation is *absorbed* by atoms inside the Sun. 这种伽马射线被太阳内部的原子吸收。//Mary is so smart that she just *absorbs* any book she reads. 玛丽真聪明，读什么书都能领会。

【派】absorbent(a. 能吸收的)；absorbed(a. 全神贯注的)

acknowledge [ək'nɑːlɪdʒ] v. 承认，确认(recognize, admit)；对…表示感谢(express gratitude)

【记】分拆联想：ac + know(知道) + ledge → 大家都知道了，所以不得不承认 → 承认

【例】Bill *acknowledged* his failure to complete the job. 比尔承认了未能完成工作。//I *acknowledged* Tom for all of his help with the project. 我对汤姆为这个项目提供的帮助表示了感谢。

ambitious [æm'bɪʃəs] a. 有雄心的，野心勃勃的(aspiring, enterprising)

【记】来自ambition(n. 雄心)

【例】According to the survey, many *ambitious* college students want to be their own boss after graduation. 根据调查，很多雄心勃勃的大学生想在毕业后自己当老板。

amenity [əˈmenəti] *n.* [*pl.*] 生活福利设施, 娱乐场所; 愉快, 适意

【记】联想记忆: a + men(人) + ity → 为人民服务 → 生活福利设施

【搭】public amenities 公共设施

【例】The little dog immediately found the *amenity* of its new surroundings. 小狗立即发现了新环境的娱乐设施。

applaud [əˈplɔːd] *vi.* 鼓掌喝彩(cheer); 称赞(acclaim)

【记】词根记忆: ap(加强) + plaud(鼓掌) → 鼓掌喝彩; 称赞

【例】The audience stood up and *applauded*. 观众们起立鼓掌。

avalanche [ˈævəlæntʃ] *n.* 雪崩(snowslide), 山崩(landslide)

bald [bɔːld] *a.* 光秃的(uncovered, hairless)

【搭】bald eagle 秃鹰

【例】He's *bald* and doesn't need a haircut. 他是秃头, 不需要理发。

【参】bold(*a.* 大胆的)

barrier [ˈbæriər] *n.* 栅栏(fence); 屏障(obstruction)

【记】分拆联想: bar(栅栏) + rier → 栅栏; 屏障

【例】The earth's magnetosphere is a *barrier* to the solar winds. 地球的磁气圈阻挡了太阳风。

bolster [ˈboulstər] *n.* 垫子, 枕垫 *vt.* 支持(support)

【例】The miners *bolstered* their morale by shouting slogans. 矿工们通过喊口号提高士气。

cargo [ˈkɑːrgou] *n.* 货物(freight)

【记】分拆联想: car(汽车) + go(走) → 汽车运走的东西 → 货物

carve [kɑːrv] *vt.* 切(cut, slice); 雕刻(*incise)

【例】The flutes are *carved* from a length of soft, straight-grained wood. 笛子是由一根直纹软木刻制而成的。

【派】carving(*n.* 雕刻, 雕刻品); carver(*n.* 雕刻匠)

ceramic [səˈræmɪk] *n.* [常*pl.*] 陶(瓷)器

【记】分拆联想: c + era(时代, 时期) + mic → 古时中国以陶器而闻名 → 陶(瓷)器

【例】Rockingham ware was one of the most important American *ceramics* of the nineteenth century. 罗金厄姆陶器是美国19世纪最重要的陶瓷产品之一。

【参】metalwork 金属制品；textile 纺织品；handcraft 手工

commitment [kəˈmɪtmənt] *n.* 承诺(promise)；支持(support)；允许(permission)；致力，献身(devotion)

【例】Bill has a *commitment* to donate $3,000 to the charity. 比尔承诺为慈善机构捐赠3000美元。//Lisa displays a lot of *commitment* to her job. 丽萨对工作十分投入。

conclude [kənˈkluːd] *v.* 作出结论；使…完毕(complete, end)

【例】The story *concludes* with the heroine's death. 这个故事以女主角之死而结束。//Newman *concluded* that walking on Mars will probably be easier than walking on the moon. 纽曼得出了结论，在火星上行走可能比在月球上轻松。

【派】inconclusive(*a.* 非决定性的)

confer [kənˈfɜːr] *vt.* 授予(award)

【记】词根记忆：con(共同) + fer(带来，拿来) → 授予；注意不要和infer(*v.* 推断)相混淆

【例】In the family, traditional cultural patterns *confer* leadership on one or both of the parents. 在家庭中，传统文化模式把领导权授予了父母中的一方或父母双方。

crawl [krɔːl] *v./n.* 缓慢(或费力)地行进，爬行(creep)

【记】分拆联想：c + raw(生疏的) + l → 对地形生疏，开车就要缓慢地行进 → 缓慢地行进，爬行

【例】I'm so out of shape. I might have to *crawl* the rest of the way. 我状态太差，可能剩下的路要爬着回去了。//This ordinary backyard dirt is *crawling* with microbes. 这种寻常的后院泥土上爬满了微生物。

deception [dɪˈsepʃn] *n.* 骗局，诡计，欺骗，欺诈

【记】词根记忆：de(坏) + cept(拿，抓) + ion → 拿坏的东西来以次充好 → 欺骗

destructive [dɪˈstrʌktɪv] *a.* 破坏性的(ruinous)

【搭】destructive power 破坏力

【例】The *destructive* power of fungi is impressive. 真菌的破坏力令人印象深刻。

dictate [ˈdɪkteɪt] *v.* 规定(regulate)；决定(*determine)

【记】词根记忆：dict(讲话，命令) + ate → 规定；决定

【例】The quality of the hinterland *dictated* the pace of growth of the cities. 内地的质量决定了城市的发展速度。

【参】abdicate(*v.* 退位)

□ commitment	□ conclude	□ confer	□ crawl	□ deception	□ destructive
□ dictate					

division [dɪ'vɪʒn] *n.* 划分(partition); 除法

【记】来自divide(*v.* 划分; 除)

【例】All meteorites are assigned to three broad *divisions* on the basis of two kinds of material. 所有的陨星都根据两种材料划分为三大类。

editorial [ˌedɪ'tɔːriəl] *n.* 社论 *a.* 社论的

【例】Did you read the *editorial* in the paper about the mayor's speech? 你读了报纸上关于市长演讲的社论了吗?

electrode [ɪ'lektroʊd] *n.* 电极

【例】If you put *electrodes* on the throat and measure muscle activity, you will discover that when people are thinking, there is muscular activity in the throat. 如果你把电极放到喉咙上测量肌肉活动的话, 你会发现人们思考时喉部肌肉在活动。

【参】electronic(*a.* 电子的); electrical(*a.* 电的, 有关电的)

emit [i'mɪt] *vt.* 发出(*give off, *produce); 放射(radiate)

【记】词根记忆: e(出) + mit(放出) → 发出; 放射

【例】The plants react by *emitting* a chemical signal, which acts like a call for help. 植物们的反应是发出化学信号, 就像呼唤求助一样。

enactment [ɪ'næktmənt] *n.* 制定(*establishment)

【记】词根记忆: en(进入) + act(行动) + ment → 制定行动计划 → 制定

erect [ɪ'rekt] *a.* 直立的(upright) *vt.* 建立(establish)

【记】词根记忆: e + rect(竖, 直) → 直立的; 建立

【例】Many buildings in this style were *erected* nationwide through government programs during the Depression. 在大萧条时期, 很多这种风格的建筑物通过政府立项在全国各地修建起来。

excursion [ɪk'skɜːrʒn] *n.* 远足(hike)

【记】词根记忆: ex + curs(跑) + ion → 跑出去 → 远足

【例】The society's activities also included organized sketching *excursions* along the Hudson River. 这个社团的活动也包括沿着哈德逊河进行的有组织的写生远足活动。

exhaust [ɪg'zɔːst] *vt.* 耗尽(drain) *n.* 废气; 排气管

【例】He returned from the gym, too *exhausted* to eat dinner. 他从健身房回来后精疲力竭, 连饭都懒得吃了。

【派】exhaustive(*a.* 彻底的); exhausted(*a.* 精疲力竭的, 耗尽的); inexhaustible(*a.* 无穷无尽的); exhausting(*a.* 使用尽的)

division	editorial	electrode	emit	enactment	erect
excursion	exhaust				

favor ['feɪvər] *n.* 好意；喜爱

【搭】do sb. a favor 帮忙；owe sb. a favor 欠某人的情；in favor of 支持…

【例】A: I was wondering if you could do me a *favor*.

B: Sure. What?

A: 我在想你能否帮我一个忙？

B: 没问题。什么事？

【参】flavor(*n.* 风味)

favored ['feɪvərd] *a.* 有利的(profitable)；受优待的，首选的(*preferred)

【例】Here are the *favored* locations for processing raw materials prior to export. 这里是出口前加工原材料的有利地点。//*Favored* recreations includes fishing, hunting, skating, and swimming. 首选的娱乐活动包括钓鱼、捕猎、滑冰和游泳。

ferment [fər'ment] *vt.* 使发酵

【记】词根记忆：ferm(=ferv 热)+ ent → 生物发酵过程中会产生热量 → 使发酵

【例】Yogurt contains a higher percentage of lactic acid than other *fermented* milks. 酸奶比其他发酵的奶制品含有更多的乳酸。

【派】fermenter(*n.* 发酵物)；fermentation(*n.* 发酵)

fertile ['fɜːrtl] *a.* 肥沃的(rich)；能繁殖的(productive)

【记】词根记忆：fert(=fer 带来，结果)+ ile → 可带来果实的 → 能繁殖的

【例】The soil near the forts is very *fertile*. 城堡附近的泥土非常肥沃。

【派】fertility(*n.* 肥沃，富饶；多产)；infertile(*a.* 贫瘠的)

fertilizer ['fɜːrtəlaɪzər] *n.* 肥料，化肥

【记】来自 fertile(*a.* 肥沃的)

【搭】spread fertilizer 施肥

【例】If you are growing things in water, you can add the *fertilizer*. 如果你在水里种东西，你可以往水里加肥料。

forecast ['fɔːrkæst] *vt./n.* 预报(predict)；预测(to calculate the future)

【记】分拆联想：fore(前面)+ cast(扔)→ 预先扔下 → 预料

【例】Severe weather conditions have been *forecasted* following these mild days. 这几天风和日丽，不过预报说之后的天气就会变得恶劣。

genesis ['dʒenəsɪs] *n.* 起源(origin)

【记】词根记忆：gene (产生，基因)+ sis → 基因是生命产生的起源 → 起源

favor	favored	ferment	fertile	fertilizer	forecast
genesis					

healing [ˈhiːlɪŋ] *a.* 有治疗功用的(*curative)

【记】来自heal(*v.* 治疗, 治愈)

inactivate [ɪnˈæktɪveɪt] *vt.* 使不活动, 使不活跃

【记】分拆联想: in(不) + activate(使活动) → 使不活动

【例】Glycoproteins in plant cell walls may *inactivate* enzymes that degrade cell walls. 植物细胞壁的糖蛋白可以抑制酶的活动, 这种酶可以损害细胞壁。

insult [ɪnˈsʌlt] *vt./n.* 侮辱, 凌辱(*affront, humiliate)

【记】分拆联想: in(在…内) + sult(看作salt, 盐) → 灌盐水 → 侮辱

【例】He *insulted* her by calling her a stupid fool. 他侮辱了她, 说她是个傻瓜。

invertebrate [ɪnˈvɜːrtɪbrət] *n.* 无脊椎动物

【记】in(无) + vertebrate(脊椎动物) → 无脊椎动物

【参】vertebrate(*n.* 脊椎动物)

latter [ˈlætər] *a.* 后面的, 后者的; 后期的

【例】This *latter* form is what is generally meant when one uses the term "satellite city". 后面这种形式就是人们使用"卫星城"这个词一般所指的意思。

listless [ˈlɪstləs] *a.* 倦怠的, 无精打采的(downhearted)

【记】分拆联想: list(名单) + less → 榜上无名所以没精打采 → 无精打采的

【例】A bird in heavy molt often seems *listless* and unwell. 换羽厉害的鸟往往看上去无精打采并且不舒服。

mature [məˈtʃʊr] *a.* 成熟的(ripe); 深思熟虑的(deliberate) *v.* (使)成熟(to become fully developed or ripe)

【记】联想记忆: 自然(nature)中的n更换成m就是成熟的(mature)

【例】The best gardeners are very *mature*. 最优秀的园丁非常成熟。// Orchid seeds take up eighteen months to *mature* before they sprout. 兰花籽发芽之前需要18个月才成熟。

mechanist [ˈmekənɪst] *n.* 机械论者

【例】The modern scientist tends to be a *mechanist*. 现代科学家往往是个机械论者。

merchandise [ˈmɜːrtʃəndaɪs] *n.* [总称]商品, 货物(goods, commodities)

【记】词根记忆: merc(贸易) + hand(掌管) + ise → 他掌管着一家经营进出口商品贸易的公司 → 商品

minority [maɪˈnɔːrəti] *n.* 少数(fewness); 少数民族

【记】来自minor(较小的) + ity → 少数

healing　inactivate　insult　invertebrate　latter　listless
mature　mechanist　merchandise　minority
119

【例】Unfortunately, based on the general response, you and I are definitely in the *minority*. 不幸的是，基于一般的反应，你我肯定属于少数。

orbit [ˈɔːrbɪt] *n.* 轨道(track)

【派】orbital(*a.* 轨道的)

packed [pækt] *a.* 拥挤的(crowded)；压紧的(compressed)

【例】The subway sure is *packed* this morning. 今天早上地铁里真挤。

parking [ˈpɑːrkɪŋ] *n.* 机动车停放；停车场

【搭】parking sticker 停车许可证；parking meter(投币式)计时停车计费器；parking lot 停车场

【例】We're organizing a rally on Thursday afternoon to get the administration to reconsider the *parking* lot plan. 我们正在组织周四下午的集会，让当局重新考虑停车场计划。

A: Excuse me, but do you happen to have some change for the *parking* meter?

B: No. But if you go into the restaurant you'll probably be able to change a dollar bill.

A: 对不起，你有可以投到停车计费表的零钱吗？

B: 没有。不过你如果去饭店，或许能换一美元的零钱。

pave [peɪv] *v.* 铺(cover)；密布(densely cover)

【例】The sky was *paved* with clouds. 天空乌云密布。

personal [ˈpɜːrsənl] *a.* 个人的，私人的(private, individual)；亲自的

【例】He doesn't like to ask *personal* questions. 他不喜欢提私人问题。

【派】personalize(*v.* 使人性化，使人格化)；personally(*ad.* 个人地)

preliminary [prɪˈlɪmɪneri] *a.* 预备的，初步的(*primary)

【记】词根记忆：pre(预先) + limin(=lumin 光) + ary → 预先透光的 → 预备的

【例】I'll expect a *preliminary* draft of each paper two weeks before the final due date. 我期望在截止日期之前两周得到每份论文的初稿。

psychology [saɪˈkɑːlədʒi] *n.* 心理学(the science of mind and behavior)；心理(mentality)

【记】词根记忆：psycho(精神) + logy → 精神方面的学科 → 心理学

【搭】clinical psychology 临床心理学

【派】psychological(*a.* 心理的，精神上的)；psychologist(*n.* 心理学家)

receptacle [rɪˈseptəkl] *n.* 容器(container)

【记】词根记忆：re + cept(取，抓) + acle(物) → 用来盛装物体以备取用的东西 → 容器

rehearse [rɪˈhɜːrs] *vt.* 预演，排练

【记】分拆联想：re(一再) + hear(听) + se → 导演在一旁一遍遍地听并看她们排练 → 排练

【例】We *rehearse* only one night a week. 我们一周只排练一晚上。

【派】rehearsal(*n.* 排练，排演)

reliever [rɪˈliːvər] *n.* 救济者；缓解物

【搭】pain reliever 止痛药

【例】A: Oh my god, you still don't look too good. Didn't you take the pain *reliever* I gave you?

B: Yeah, an hour ago. Because I've got a headache that just won't quit.

A：哦，天哪！你看上去气色还是不太好。你没有用我给你的止痛剂吗？

B：一个小时以前用的。只不过是因为我的头痛是不会轻易就好的。

resist [rɪˈzɪst] *vt.* 抵抗(withstand)；耐(热等)

【记】词根记忆：re(反) + sist(站) → 反过来站 → 抵抗

【例】It *resists* breaking when heated. 加热时它能够防裂。

【派】resistance(*n.* 反抗；阻力；电阻)；resistant(*a.* 抵抗的)

revolt [rɪˈvoʊlt] *v.* 反叛(rebel) *n.* 起义(uprise)；反抗

【记】词根记忆：re(反) + volt(转) → 反过来转 → 反叛

revolt

【例】The Imagists *revolted* against earlier poets' emphasis on the classics. 意象派诗人反感早期诗人对于古典文学的注重。//It caused a prison *revolt*. 这导致了监狱暴乱。

rhythm [ˈrɪðəm] *n.* 节奏，韵律

【记】本身为词根，意为：节奏

【派】rhythmical(*a.* 有韵律的，有节奏的)

ribbon [ˈrɪbən] *n.* (打印机等的)色带；带状物

【记】分拆联想：rib(肋骨) + bon(看作bone，骨头) → 狭长的像肋骨 → 带状物

【例】I went through a whole box of paper and a printer *ribbon* just trying to get my resume right. 我为了让简历好看一些而用了整整一箱纸和一条打印色带。

【派】ribbonlike(*a.* 带状的)

☐ receptacle	☐ rehearse	☐ reliever	☐ resist	☐ revolt	☐ rhythm
☐ ribbon					

segregate ['segrɪgeɪt] *vt.* 隔离；分离(separate)
【记】词根记忆：seg(切割) + reg + ate → 隔离
【例】They are easily *segregated* from sand and silt. 它们可以轻易地从沙子和淤泥中分离出来。

significant [sɪg'nɪfɪkənt] *a.* 有意义的；重要的，重大的(noteworthy, important)
【记】词根记忆：sign(记号) + i + fic(做) + ant → 值得做记号的 → 有意义的
【搭】significant difference 显著的差异；significant change 重大转变
【例】The experimental result shows that there are no *significant* differences between the two groups of students. 实验结果显示，这两组学生之间没有显著的差异。
【派】significantly(*ad.* 值得注目地；相当地)

skeptical ['skeptɪkl] *a.* 怀疑的(suspicious)
【派】skepticism(*n.* 怀疑论)

solution [sə'lu:ʃn] *n.* 溶液(liquor)；解答，解决(办法)
【记】词根记忆：solut(松的) + ion → 让其充分松开 → 溶液

soprano [sə'prɑ:nou] *n.* 女高音
【记】分拆联想：so(看作son，声音) + prano(看作piano，钢琴) → 声音超过钢琴 → 女高音

spun [spʌn] *a.* 拉成丝的
【搭】spun glass 玻璃纤维

sterile ['sterəl] *a.* 贫瘠的(barren)；无菌的(germfree)
【派】sterilize(*v.* 杀菌)

subtle ['sʌtl] *a.* 细微的，微妙的(*slight)
【例】This interdependence is sometimes *subtle*, sometimes obvious. 这种相互依赖性有时细微，有时明显。

survey ['sɜ:rveɪ] *n.* 调查
【例】A *survey* is a study, generally in the form of an interview or a questionnaire. 调查通常是采访或问卷形式的研究。
【派】surveyor(*n.* 测量员)

swallow ['swɑ:lou] *n.* 燕子 *v.* 吞，咽
【记】分拆联想：s + wall(墙) + ow → 燕子在墙角垒窝 → 燕子
【例】Chew your food properly before *swallowing* it. 吞咽食物之前要好好咀嚼。

thorn [θɔ:rn] *n.* 刺，荆棘
【记】分拆联想：t + horn(角) → 尖尖的角 → 刺，荆棘

| □ segregate | □ significant | □ skeptical | □ solution | □ soprano | □ spun |
| □ sterile | □ subtle | □ survey | □ swallow | □ thorn | |

【例】*Thorns* are imitated as a means of protection by some of the tropical species. 某些热带物种模仿荆棘来保护自己。

【派】thorny(*a.* 多刺的)

thrive [θraɪv] *vi.* 茂盛(flourish); 苗壮成长(grow vigorously)

【记】分拆联想: th + rive(看作river, 河) → 河两边的树木一般都比较茂盛 → 茂盛

【例】Fungi *thrive* in a wide variety of environments. 真菌在多种环境中繁衍。//Why have ants been able to *thrive* for such a long time?为什么蚂蚁能苗壮成长这么久?

trash [træʃ] *n.* 无价值之物, 废物(rubbish)

【记】分拆联想: tr + ash(灰) → 像灰尘一样微不足道 → 废物

【搭】trash can 垃圾桶

【例】Most people don't like to take the time to separate their *trash*. 多数人不喜欢花时间把垃圾分类。

troupe [truːp] *n.* 剧团

【记】联想记忆: 部队(troop)里的一群(group)人组建了一个剧团(troupe)

【例】Cheryl usually doesn't travel with the dance *troupe*. 谢里尔一般不和舞蹈团一同旅行。

twine [twaɪn] *n.* 细绳(rope, string)

【记】联想记忆: 大家应该像Twins(著名女生演唱组合)一样拧成一股绳(twine), 共闯天下

【例】The reaper gathered the stalks and bound them with *twine*. 收割者把秸秆收了起来, 并用细绳绑住了。

utmost [ˈʌtməʊst] *a.* 最大限度的(extreme)

【记】分拆联想: ut(看作at) + most(最多) → 到达最多 → 最大限度的

【例】The clay used in prehistoric pot making was invariably selected with the *utmost* care. 史前制造锅罐所用的黏土往往都是精挑细选的。

vacancy [ˈveɪkənsi] *n.* (未被占用的)空余住处; 空位, 空缺(opening); 头脑空虚

【记】词根记忆: vac(空的) + ancy(状态) → 处于空的状态 → 空缺

【例】A: My parents want to come visit next weekend, but I've checked every hotel in this area and they all seem to be full.
B: Well, why not call the Cliffside inn? It's not so near the campus but it's always got a few *vacancies*.

| ☐ thrive | ☐ trash | ☐ troupe | ☐ twine | ☐ utmost | ☐ vacancy |

A：我的父母想在下周末来看我，我问过这个地区的所有宾馆，好像都客满了。

B：那你为何不给Cliffside旅店打电话？那离校园不是很近，但是总会有几个空房间。

valid ['vælɪd] *a.* 有根据的(well-founded); 有效的(effective)

【记】词根记忆：val(价值) + id → 有价值的 → 有效的

【例】The data in your report seems to be *valid* to me. 你报告里的数据在我看来好像是有根据的。//The main point of the passage is that oral narratives are a *valid* form of literature. 这个段落的主要观点是口述是一种有效的文学形式。

【派】validate(*vt.* 证实，确认); validity(*n.* 根据; 合法性)

vapor ['veɪpər] *n.* (蒸)气，水汽(steam)

【记】发音记忆："外喷" → 蒸汽都是向外喷的

【派】vaporization(*n.* 蒸发)

verbal ['vɜːrbl] *a.* 口头的(oral, spoken)

【记】词根记忆：verb(字，词) + al → 字，词由口而出 → 口头的

【搭】verbal agreement 口头协议

voyage ['vɔɪɪdʒ] *n.* 旅行(travel); 航程(journey, sail)

【记】词根记忆：voy(路) + age → 旅行; 航程

voyage
路~在~脚~下~

【例】According to the original records of the flight, the *voyage* lasted 46 minutes. 根据飞行的原始记录，航行持续了46分钟。//The ship has gone on over 100 *voyages.* 这艘船已经航行过100多次了。

【派】voyager(*n.* 航行者，航海者)

yield [jiːld] *v.* 出产(*provide) *n.* 产量(output)，收益(income)

【记】联想记忆：这片田地(field)出产(yield)西瓜

【例】His well begins to *yield* 20 barrels of crude oil a day. 他的油井每天开始产20桶原油。//Crop *yields* have increased dramatically. 农作物产量已显著增长。

☐ valid   ☐ vapor   ☐ verbal   ☐ voyage   ☐ yield

Word List 12

词根、词缀预习表

nounce	讲话，说出	announce	vt. 宣布
auct	提高	auction	n. 拍卖
corp	团体	corps	n. 军团
pict	描画	depict	v. 描写，描绘
in	在…里面	inner	a. 内部的
trepid	惊恐的	intrepid	a. 勇敢的
tric	复杂	intricate	a. 错综复杂的
local	地方	locality	n. 地点，位置
mono	单个	monotonous	a. 单调的
nav	船	navigation	n. 航海，航空

addition [ə'dɪʃn] *n.* (增)加，加法；附加(物)

【记】词根记忆：add(加) + ition → 加，加法

【搭】in addition to 另外，还有

【例】In *addition* to exercising regularly, eating a good breakfast is considered by many health experts to be a significant part of a successful way of reduction plan. 除了按时锻炼，吃好早餐被很多健康专家认为是减肥计划成功方式的重要部分。

【派】additive(*a.* 添加的 *n.* 添加剂)

address [ə'dres] *n.* 地址；讲话(speech)

v. 作(正式)讲话；写姓名地址

【例】Dean Williams was invited by the college president to *address* the faculty. 威廉姆斯系主任收到了学院院长的邀请给教职员工讲话。

adhesive [əd'hi:sɪv] *a.* 带黏性的 *n.* 胶合剂

【记】词根记忆：ad + hes(=her黏) + ive → 带黏性的；胶合剂

【例】It's considered one of the strongest *adhesives* in nature. 这被认为是大自然中最强的胶合剂。

☐ addition   ☐ address   ☐ adhesive

advisable [əd'vaɪzəbl] *n.* 可取的，适当的

【记】advise(建议，劝告) + able(能…的) → 能够听取别人的劝告是明智的 → 可取的

【例】A: Do I have to book the seat in advance?

B: Oh, yes, it's *advisable*.

A：我需要提前订座吗？

B：是的，建议你这么做。

【派】advisability(*n.* 适当；明智)

alchemist ['ælkəmɪst] *n.* 炼金术士

announce [ə'naʊns] *vt.* 宣布(*herald, proclaim)；通告(notify)

【记】词根记忆：an + nounce(讲话，说出) → 说出来 → 宣布；通告

【派】announcement(*n.* 宣告；发表)；announcer(*n.* 广播员；播音员)

auction ['ɔːkʃn] *n.* 拍卖

【记】词根记忆：auct(提高) + ion → 提高价格 → 拍卖

【例】*Auctions* are another popular form of occasional trade. 拍卖是偶然性交易的另一种流行形式。

auction

cellist ['tʃelɪst] *n.* 大提琴家

【参】fiddler(*n.* 拉小提琴的人，小提琴家)

cereal ['sɪriəl] *n.* 谷类(食品)

【记】分拆联想：ce + real(真正的) → 真正的粮食 → 谷类

check/cheque [tʃek] *n.* 支票 *v.* 检查

【搭】check in 登记，报到；check out 付账后离开；检验，校验；check up on 验证

【例】A mass of foreign tourists cash a *check* at the big bank. 很多外国游客在这家大银行把支票兑换成现金。//I have to get a *check* cashed to pay my bookstore bill. 我得兑现一张支票来支付书店的账单。

A: These are terrible light bulbs. I keep having to replace the one in this lamp.

B: What about *checking* the wiring in the lamp?

A：这些灯泡太差。我得不停地给这个灯换灯泡。

B：检查灯里的线路怎么样？

commit [kə'mɪt] *vt.* 承诺(promise)；负责(obligate)；犯(错)

【例】The college is *committed* to selecting more faculty members. 学院致力于选择更多的教职成员。

【派】committed(*a.* 忠于…的)

☐ advisable	☐ alchemist	☐ announce	☐ auction	☐ cellist	☐ cereal
☐ check/cheque	☐ commit				

complacence [kəm'pleɪsns] *n.* 自满，满足（satisfaction）

compress [kəm'pres] *vt.* 压缩（condense）；缩短（shorten）

【记】词根记忆：com + press（压）→ 压缩；缩短

【例】Some geologists think that the Earth's interior contains a highly *compressed* ball of incandescent gas. 一些地质学家认为地球内部包含着高度压缩的白炽气团。//She compressed two days' work into one. 她把两天的工作时间缩短成了一天。

【派】compressed（*a.* 被压缩的）；compression（*n.* 压缩，浓缩）；compressible（*a.* 可压缩的）

compute [kəm'pjuːt] *vt.* 计算（calculate, reckon）

【记】词根记忆：com（加强）+ put（思考；认为）+ e → 一再思考 → 计算

construction [kən'strʌkʃn] *n.* 构造（structure）；建筑

【搭】metal-frame construction 金属框架建筑

【例】Because of the real risk of losing beaches, many geologists support a ban on all types of stabilizing *construction* on shore lines. 由于丧失海滩的实际风险，很多地质学家对禁止在海岸线建造各类固定建筑这一法令表示支持。

A: The *construction* company just built some new apartments near campus, but a one-bedroom rents for five hundred dollars a month.

B: That's a bit beyond the reach of most students.

A：建筑公司在校园附近刚刚修建了一些新公寓楼，但是一间卧室的月租为500美元。

B：多数学生可负担不起这个租金。

【参】instruction（*n.* 说明，指令）

corps [kɔːr] *n.* 军团，兵团

【记】词根记忆：corp（团体）+ s → 团队 → 军团

depict [dɪ'pɪkt] *v.* 描写，描述（*present, *describe）；描绘（portray）

【记】词根记忆：de（加强）+ pict（描画）→ 描写；描绘

【例】The Impressionists want to *depict* what they see in nature. 印象派画家想描绘他们眼中的自然。

【派】depiction（*n.* 描写，叙述）

eminent ['emɪnənt] *a.* 显著的；杰出的（outstanding, distinguished）

【记】词根记忆：e（出）+ min（突出）+ ent → 显著的；杰出的

【派】preeminent（*a.* 卓越的）

【参】imminent（*a.* 逼近的）；prominent（*a.* 卓越的，显著的）

fantasy ['fæntəsi] *n.* 想象，幻想(imagination, illusion)

【记】热门游戏《最终幻想》的英文名称*Final Fantasy*

【例】Science fiction is a mixture of science and *fantasy*. 科幻小说融合了科技和幻想。

【参】fantastic(*a.* 极好的)

fascinating ['fæsineitiŋ] *a.* 迷人的，醉人的

【搭】a fascinating shop window display 吸引人的商店橱窗陈列

【例】Jane's novels provided a *fascinating* account of social life in seventeen-century England. 简的小说提供了17世纪英国社会生活的迷人记录。

【参】charming(*a.* 迷人的)

fashionable ['fæʃnəbl] *a.* 流行的，时髦的；上流社会的

【例】It's becoming *fashionable* to wear miniskirt again while it was out of fashion two decades ago. 二十年前迷你裙不再时髦，现在又重新流行了。

flu [fluː] *n.* 流行性感冒

【搭】come down with flu 感冒；catch a flu 得了流行性感冒

【例】I've got a typical *flu*. I'm usually miserable for a week and it ends up ruining my holidays. 我患了典型流感。我一般要难受一个礼拜，因此我的假期就毁了。

glossy ['glɑːsi] *a.* 光滑的(slick)

【记】来自gloss(*n.* 光泽的表面；光彩)

granite ['grænit] *n.* 花岗岩

【记】词根记忆：gran(=grain颗粒) + ite → 颗粒状石头 → 花岗岩

【例】This building is made of white *granite* and marble. 这座建筑是由白花岗岩和大理石建造而成的。

graphite ['græfait] *n.* 石墨

【记】词根记忆：graph(写；图) + ite → 用来写字、画画的东西 → 石墨

guarantee [ˌɡærən'tiː] *vt.* 保证(pledge)；担保(assure)

【记】分拆联想：guar(看作guard, 保卫) + antee → 保卫国家是为了保证国家的安全 → 保证

【例】We have a priority service that would *guarantee* delivery in three days. 我们提供优先服务，保证三天内到货。

| ☐ fantasy | ☐ fascinating | ☐ fashionable | ☐ flu | ☐ glossy | ☐ granite |
| ☐ graphite | ☐ guarantee | | | | |

hazard [ˈhæzərd] *n.* 危险(*danger); 风险(risk)

【记】发音记忆: "骇人的" → 危险

【例】Cora reefs have always been one of the greatest *hazards* to ships sailing in tropical seas. 珊瑚暗礁对在热带海洋航行的船只来说向来是最大的威胁之一。

【派】hazardous(*a.* 危险的, 冒险的)

herald [ˈherəld] *n.* 信使(messenger) *vt.* 预示(foreshadow); 宣布(*announce)

【记】分拆联想: her + ald(看作old, 老的) → 她带来老人的告诫 → 信使

【例】America's War of Independence *heralded* the birth of three modern nations. 美国的独立战争预示着三个现代国家的诞生。

hockey [ˈhɑːki] *n.* 曲棍球; 冰球

【记】联想记忆: 一只猴子(monkey)在玩曲棍球(hockey)

【例】Why didn't you go to the *hockey* finals last weekend? 上个周末你怎么没有去看冰球决赛?

humid [ˈhjuːmɪd] *a.* 潮湿的(damp); 湿润的(wettish)

【记】分拆联想: hum(嗡嗡声) + id → 蚊虫总有嗡嗡的声音, 而潮湿的地方多蚊虫 → 潮湿的

【例】The southwestern coastal region has a *humid* mild marine climate. 西南沿海地区有着湿润的温带海洋气候。

【派】humidity(*n.* 湿度)

identify [aɪˈdentɪfaɪ] *vt.* 识别(*spot, recognize); 鉴定(judge)

【例】This odor allows ants to *identify* intruders. 这个气味可以让蚂蚁识别入侵者。

【派】identifiable(*a.* 可识别的); identification(*n.* 辨认, 鉴别)

illustration [ˌɪləˈstreɪʃn] *n.* 例证; 插图

incongruity [ˌɪnkɑːnˈgruːəti] *n.* 不一致, 不和谐(incompatibility, disharmony)

【记】in(不) + congruity(一致, 和谐) → 不一致, 不和谐

inner [ˈɪnər] *n./a.* 内部(的); 内心(的)

【记】词根记忆: in(在…里面) + ner → 内部的; 内心的

【例】The drama reflected the frustrations *inner* of the dramatist. 这个戏剧反应了剧作家内心的挫败感。

【参】innermost(*a.* 最里面的)

hazard	herald	hockey	humid	identify	illustration
incongruity	inner				

intrepid [ɪnˈtrepɪd] *a.* 勇敢的, 无畏的(fearless)

【记】词根记忆: in(不) + trepid(惊恐的) → 毫不惊恐的 → 勇敢的, 无畏的

intrepid

【例】Nellie gained a reputation as a daring, *intrepid* journalist. 内莉赢得了勇敢无畏记者的名声。

intricate [ˈɪntrɪkət] *a.* 错综复杂的(*complex)

【记】词根记忆: in + tric(复杂) + ate → 错综复杂的

【例】A city is more *intricate* than a village. 城市比村庄更加错综复杂。

locality [loʊˈkæləti] *n.* 地点(site), 位置(position)

【记】词根记忆: local(地方) + ity → 地点, 位置

【例】Nomadic hunter and gatherer societies move on when they have exhausted each *locality*. 游牧狩猎者和采集者团队在耗尽每个地点的资源后就迁移到另一处。

【参】location(*n.* 位置, 场所)

luster [ˈlʌstər] *n.* 光彩, 光泽(gloss)

【记】本身为词根, 意为: 光亮

【例】Turquoise is opaque with waxy *luster*, varying in color from greenish gray to sky blue. 绿宝石不透明, 具有柔软的光泽, 颜色从绿灰到天蓝都有。

magnesium [mægˈniːziəm] *n.* 镁

modify [ˈmɑːdɪfaɪ] *vt.* 修改, 更改(*change, alter)

【例】Water precipitates many chemical compounds and is constantly *modifying* the face of the Earth. 水使很多化合物沉淀, 并在不断改变地球的表面。

【派】modified(*a.* 改良的, 修正的); modification(*n.* 改变, 修正)

monotonous [məˈnɑːtnəs] *a.* 单调的; 因单调而使人厌倦的(*boring, *tedious)

【记】词根记忆: mono(单个) + ton(声音) + ous → 一个声音 → 单调的

【例】Factory work is less creative and more *monotonous*. 工厂的工作缺乏创意, 更多的是单调。

motivate [ˈmoʊtɪveɪt] *vt.* 激励(*stimulate, impel); 激发(inspire)

【记】词根记忆: mot(动) + iv + ate(使…) → 使向前运动 → 激励; 激发

【例】The students need to be *motivated*. 学生需要激励。

【派】motivated(*a.* 有动机的, 由…推动的); motivation(*n.* 动机; 刺激)

| intrepid | intricate | locality | luster | magnesium | modify |
| monotonous | motivate |

mythology [mɪˈθɑ:lədʒi] *n.* 神话学，神话
【派】mythological(*a.* 神话的；虚构的)

navigation [ˌnævɪˈgeɪʃn] *n.* 航海，航空；导航，领航
【记】词根记忆：nav(船) + ig + ation(行为；状态) → 开船 → 航海
【搭】navigation tools 航用具；electronic navigation system 电子导航系统
【例】Critics persisted in raising questions about his *navigation* and the distances the explorer claimed to have covered. 批评家坚持就这位探险家的航行及其宣称走过的距离提出了疑问。
【参】negotiation(*n.* 谈判)

ooze [uːz] *v.* 渗出(leak, seep) *n.* 淤泥(silt)
【记】分拆联想：oo(像气体渗出时冒的泡泡) + ze → 渗出
【例】The resin *oozes* out of the tree and the spider or leaf gets encased in it. 树脂从树里渗出来，蜘蛛或树叶就被裹在了里面。

organic [ɔːrˈgænɪk] *a.* 有机的
【搭】organic chemistry 有机化学
【参】organism(*n.* 生物体，有机体)

outfit [ˈaʊtfɪt] *n.* 全套服装
【记】分拆联想：out(外面的) + fit(合适的) → 里里外外都合适用的 → 全套服装
【例】I wish these shoes matched my *outfit*. 我希望这些鞋子与我的全套服装相配。

outspoken [aʊtˈspoʊkən] *a.* 直言不讳的，坦率的(frank)

overdue [ˌoʊvərˈduː] *a.* 过期未付的；逾期的；过度的，过火的；迟到的，延误的
【记】词根记忆：over(过度) + due(预期的) → 超过期限的 → 逾期的
【例】I have to take these magazines back to the library—they're *overdue*. 我得把这些杂志带到图书馆去还了——它们超期了。

pastel [pæˈstel] *a.* 柔和的(bland, soft)；彩色蜡笔的
【记】词根记忆：paste(糨糊) + l → 用糊状物制作的彩笔 → 彩色蜡笔的
【搭】pastel shades 柔和的色彩
【例】*Pastel* colors are always restful to our eyes. 柔和色总能让我们的眼睛得到休息。
【派】pastelist(*n.* 粉笔着色画家)

persist [pərˈsɪst] *vi.* 坚持(stick to)；持续(*continue)
【记】词根记忆：per(始终) + sist(坐) → 始终坐着 → 坚持；继续

【例】John won't give up. He *persists* in repeating his opinion. 约翰不愿放弃。他坚持重复自己的观点。//These myths *persisted* and provided material for art and drama. 这些神话流传了下来, 给美术和戏剧提供了素材。

【派】persistence(*n.* 坚持); persistent(*a.* 持久稳固的)

【参】subsist(*v.* 生存); consist(*vi.* 由…组成)

pleasing ['pliːzɪŋ] *a.* 令人高兴的, 愉快的(attractive, comfortable)

【搭】a pleasing performance 令人愉快的表演; pleasing experience 愉悦的经历; pleasing to the eye 赏心悦目的

【例】The arrangement of the furniture and facilities formed a *pleasing* atmosphere in the mall. 家具和设施的布置在商场营造出了愉快的氛围。

【派】pleasingly (*ad.* 令人高兴地)

portable ['pɔːrtəbl] *a.* 轻便的, 便携的

【记】词根记忆: port(拿, 运) + able → 可以拿的 → 轻便的

【例】He designed a *portable* camera. 他设计了一个便携式照相机。

【派】portability(*n.* 可携带, 轻便)

prevail [prɪ'veɪl] *vi.* 居主导地位, 流行(predominate, fashion)

【记】词根记忆: pre(前) + vail(=val 力量) → 力量在别人之前 → 居主导地位

【例】Most goods are handmade, and a subsistence economy *prevails*. 多数商品都是手工制作的, 自给自足式的经济占主导地位。

proclaim [prə'kleɪm] *vt.* 宣布, 声明(declare, announce); 显示(display)

【记】词根记忆: pro + claim(叫, 喊) → 在前面喊 → 宣布

【例】Advocates of organic foods frequently *proclaim* that such products are safer and more nutritious than others. 有机食品的支持者经常宣称这种产品比其他食品更加安全和有营养。

【参】exclaim(*v.* 惊呼)

refurbish [riː'fɜːrbɪʃ] *vt.* 重新装饰(redecorate)

【记】词根记忆: re(重新) + furbish(磨光, 磨亮) → 重新装饰

【例】Once the hotel's *refurbished*, it could start to attract people to our town again. 酒店重新装饰之后, 就可以开始吸引人们再次来我们的镇子。

religion [rɪ'lɪdʒən] *n.* 宗教, 信仰(belief)

【记】词根记忆: re(一再) + lig(绑) + ion → 绑缚思想的巨大力量 → 宗教

【派】religious(*a.* 宗教的)

remind [rɪˈmaɪnd] vt. 提醒（inform）; 使想起

【例】He'll drive more slowly only if you *remind* him. 你只有提醒他，他才会开慢点。//The reason why Dutch settlers planted tulips in their gardens was that tulips *reminded* them of home. 荷兰移民在花园种植郁金香的原因是郁金香使他们想起了家乡。

report [rɪˈpɔːrt] n. 报告，汇报; 传说; 传阅 v. 报告，汇报，报到

【搭】weather report 天气预报

【例】A: I've been working on this *report* all day. And I've still got 12 pages to write. At this rate, I'll never get it done by tomorrow.

B: Oh, that's right. You weren't in class today, so you probably haven't heard that the deadline has been extended a week.

A: 我一整天都在写这个报告。还有12页要写。按照这个速度，到明天之前我肯定写不完。

B: 哦，没错。你今天没上课，所以可能没听说最后期限延长了一周。

A: Do you know where I can get a copy of that *report*?

B: How about the dean's office?

A: 你知道我在哪里能弄到那份报告吗?

B: 去系主任办公室看看怎么样?

resonance [ˈrezənəns] n. 共振; 共鸣

【记】来自resonant (a. 洪亮的; 引起共鸣的)

【例】The musical tone of an electric guitar is created not by the *resonance* of the body of the guitar but by electronical amplification. 电吉他的乐音不是靠吉他本身的共振产生，而是靠电子扩音器。

resume [rɪˈzuːm] v. (中断后)重新开始 (*begin again)

[ˈrezəmeɪ] n. 简历

【记】词根记忆: re (重新) + sume (拿起) → 重新拿出行动 → 重新开始

【例】She left the hospital and *resumed* her classes. 她离开医院，重新开始上课了。

reunion [ˌriːˈjuːniən] n. 团圆，重聚

【记】词根记忆: re (重新) + union (联合) → 重新联合在一起 → 团圆，重聚

【搭】a family reunion 家庭团聚

【例】A: Where are you going next Monday?

B: California. We're having a family *reunion*. It's my grandmother's ninetieth birthday, so all the cousins and aunts and uncles are going. She planned the whole thing herself.

A：下周一你去哪里？

B：加利福尼亚。我们有个家庭聚会，是我奶奶的90岁生日，因此所有的堂兄妹、姑姑和叔叔都要去。这完全是由她自己一手操办的。

semester ［sɪ'mestər］ *n.* 学期（term）

【记】分拆联想：se（看作see，看）+ mester（看作master，老师）→在新学期又能看到老师了 → 学期

sewage ［'suːɪdʒ］ *n.* 污水；污物

spark ［spɑːrk］ *v.* 激发（blaze）；引起（bring about）*n.* 火花，火星（flash）

【记】分拆联想：s + park（公园）→ 公园是情侣们约会擦出感情火花的地方 → 火花

【例】I'll *spark* some interest on campus. 我会在校园激发一些兴趣。

越洗越脏

sewage

squid ［skwɪd］ *n.* 鱿鱼

stratigraphy ［strə'tɪɡrəfi］ *n.* 地层学；地层学中的岩石组成

【例】Scientists can identify the living age of some species by studying *stratigraphy*. 科学家们可以通过研究岩石组成来确定一些物种的生存年代。

strip ［strɪp］ *vt.* 剥夺，剥掉（remove）*n.* 条，带状物

【记】分拆联想：s（音似：死）+ trip（旅行）→ 死亡剥夺了人在尘世的时间之旅 → 剥夺

【搭】comic strip 连环漫画，连环图画；strip away 揭掉，去掉

stun ［stʌn］ *vt.* 使晕倒，使震惊

【记】联想记忆：太阳（sun）里面多了一个t，使人震惊（stun）

【派】stunning（*a.* 令人惊叹的；极好的）

stunt ［stʌnt］ *vt.* 阻碍…的正常发育 *n.* 特技（表演）

【记】分拆联想：stun（震惊）+ t → 受到震惊 → 惊险动作，特技（表演）

suffragist ［'sʌfrədʒɪst］ *n.* 妇女政权论者

【例】In 1916, United States *suffragist* Alice Paul founded the National Woman's Party dedicated to establishing equal rights for women. 1916年，美国妇女政权论者爱丽丝·保罗建立了全美女性党，致力于为女性争取平等的权利。

technological ［ˌteknə'lɑːdʒɪkl］ *a.* 技术的，工艺的（technical）

【记】来自technology（*n.* 技术）

【搭】scientific and *technological* advances 科技进步

134

□ semester	□ sewage	□ spark	□ squid	□ stratigraphy	□ strip
□ stun	□ stunt	□ suffragist	□ technological		

tedium ［ˈtiːdiəm］ *n.* 单调乏味(boredom)

【例】Their ancestors had traditionally relieved the *tedium* of life. 他们的祖先按照传统方式调剂了生活的乏味。

【派】tedious(*a.* 单调乏味的, 沉闷的)

threaten ［θretn］ *vt.* 恐吓, 威胁(menace); 预示(危险)

【搭】threaten sb with death 以死来威胁…

【例】The American elm has been *threatened* by a dangerous disease. 美国榆树已受到一种危险疾病的威胁。//The landlord is *threatening* to evict us for not paying the full rent. 因为我们未能支付全额房租, 房东威胁要把我们赶出去。

thwart ［θwɔːrt］ *vt.* 阻碍(baffle, frustrate)

【例】The Rosetta Stone *thwarted* scholars' efforts for several decades until the early nineteenth century. 罗塞塔石碑使学者们的努力受挫几十年, 直至19世纪初为止。

underlying ［ˌʌndərˈlaɪɪŋ］ *a.* 潜在的(latent); 基础的(basal)

【记】分拆联想: under(在…下) + lying(躺着的) → 在下面躺着的 → 潜在的

【例】An interviewer can go beyond written questions and probe for a subject's *underlying* feelings and reasons. 面试官可以不局限于书面问题而去了解受试者潜在的情感和理智。

vary ［ˈveri］ *v.* 改变, 变化(change, alter)

【例】Orthoclases *vary* in color from white to pink to red. 正长石颜色不一, 从白色到粉色再到红色都有。

【派】varied(*a.* 各式各样的); varying(*a.* 改变的, 变化的)

vegetative ［ˈvedʒɪteɪtɪv］ *a.* 植物的; 有生长力的

【搭】vegetative reproduction 营养生殖

【例】For this kind of plant, botanists still depend on *vegetative* reproduction. 对于这种植物, 植物学家仍然依靠于营养生殖。

wagon ［ˈwægən］ *n.* 四轮马车; 货车(carriage)

【参】coach(*n.* 四轮大马车); stagecoach(*n.* 公共马车)

wither ［ˈwɪðər］ *v.* 枯萎(fade, perish); 衰退(decline)

【例】Some of the elm's leaves have *withered* and turned yellow. 一些榆树叶已经枯萎变黄了。

Word List 13  MP3-13

词根、词缀预习表

ment	思考；神智	comment	*n./vi.* 评论
gnos	知道	diagnose	*v.* 诊断
frig	冷	frigid	*a.* 寒冷的
hemi	半	hemisphere	*n.* 半球
pharma	药；毒	pharmacy	*n.* 药店
sanct	神圣	sanctuary	*n.* 圣所，圣殿
multi	多	multiply	*v.* 增加，繁殖

addictive [əˈdɪktɪv] *a.* 上瘾的，沉醉的，醉心的
【记】来自addict(*vt.* 使沉溺，使上瘾)
【例】It is said that Marijuana is psychologically though not physically *addictive.* 据说大麻使人心理而非生理上瘾。

agency [ˈeɪdʒənsi] *n.* 代理处；（政府等的)专门行政部门
【搭】travel agency 旅行社；government agency 政府机构
【参】agent(*n.* 代理人；作用物)

airborne [ˈerbɔːrn] *a.* 空气传播的
【记】分拆联想：air(空气) + born(出生) + e → 空气传播的
【例】You increase your exposure to *airborne* viruses just when your body's resistance is already low from all the running around you do. 你跑来跑去，使身体抵抗力下降，这增加了你暴露给空气传播病毒的可能性。

alien [ˈeɪliən] *a.* 不同的(different, foreign) *n.* 外星人；组织之外的人
【例】Someone introduced an *alien* plant into the Florida swamp. 有人向佛罗里达的沼泽引入了一种外来植物。//Many movies have been made about *aliens* coming to earth. 很多电影都是关于造访地球的外星人的。

☐ addictive ☐ agency ☐ airborne ☐ alien

anxious [ˈæŋkʃəs] *a.* 渴望的(eager, keen); 担忧的(worried)

【例】Workers were a bit *anxious* about the safety of the machines bought abroad at first. 工人们起初有点儿担忧从国外购买的机器的安全性。

atmosphere [ˈætməsfɪr] *n.* 大气, 空气(*air); 气氛(tone)

【记】分拆联想: atmo + sphere(球体) → 围绕地球的空气 → 大气

【派】atmospheric(*a.* 大气的, 空气的)

attractive [əˈtræktɪv] *a.* 吸引人的(*tempting, *appealing, *inviting), 有魅力的(*intriguing, charming)

【例】American children's books are almost always *attractive* and interesting to children. 美国的儿童读物趣味盎然, 总能吸引孩子们。

【派】attractiveness(*n.* 魅力, 吸引力); unattractive(*a.* 不引人注意的)

audience [ˈɔːdiəns] *n.* 听众(listener); 观众(spectator)

【记】词根记忆: audi(听) + ence → 听众; 观众

【参】inaudible(*a.* 听不见的, 不可闻的)

bark [bɑːrk] *n.* 树皮

beverage [ˈbevərɪdʒ] *n.* 饮料

bold [bould] *a.* 大胆的(*daring)

【记】分拆联想: b + old(年长) → 年长的人胆大心细 → 大胆的

【例】The employee paid for his *bold* remark by getting extra work. 这位员工为他的口无遮拦付出了加班的代价。

care [ker] *n.* 小心, 谨慎(caution), 注意; 关怀, 操心, 照料 *v.* 关心; 介意(mind), 计较

【搭】care for 喜欢; 为…操心; 照顾, 照料; take care of 照顾, 照料

【例】Many experts think that the government should take measures to improve medical *care*. 很多专家认为政府应该采取措施改善医疗。

A: You said you wanted to borrow my camera for Prof. Wilson's assignment. Well, here it is.

B: I know this is precious to you, and I'll take good *care* of it. I hate using other people's things, especially expensive equipment like this.

A: 你说过你想借我的相机来完成威尔逊教授布置的作业。好, 你拿去用吧。

B: 我知道这对你来说很珍贵, 我会小心使用的。我不喜欢用别人的东西, 尤其像这种贵重的设备。

【参】fare(*n.* 费用); mare(*n.* 母马)

comment [ˈkɑːment] *n./vi.* 评论(review); 注释(remark, note)

【记】词根记忆: com(共同) + ment(思考; 神智) → 一起思考 → 评论

【例】The teacher *comments* on his musical training at the Juilliard School. 老师评价了他在朱利亚德学校的音乐培训。

common [ˈkɑːmən] *a.* 普通的, 平常的(ordinary); 共同的, 公共的

【记】联想记忆: com(共同) + mon(提醒) → 对大家的提醒 → 共同的

【搭】common use 广泛使用, 普遍使用; common sense 常识; 公众意识; in common 共用, 共有, 共同

【例】The term plankton covers a wide variety of freely floating plants and animals from microscopic one-celled organisms to large ones such as the *common* jellyfish. 浮游生物这个词包含各种自由浮动的动植物, 从极微小的单细胞的生物到如普通水母那么大的动物。

A: So, you and Julia are no longer roommates. I'm not surprised. You two never did things very compatible.

B: Yeah, well... It's not that we didn't get along... We just didn't have much in *common*.

A: 这么说你和茉莉亚不再是室友了。我不感到奇怪。你们俩做事做不到一块去。

B: 是的……并非我们合不来……我们就是没什么共同点。

comply [kəmˈplaɪ] *v.* 服从, 遵守(conform, submit)

【记】词根记忆: com + ply(重) → 观点重合 → 服从

【例】A good citizen *complies* with the laws of the country. 好公民服从国家的法律。

comprise [kəmˈpraɪz] *vt.* 包含(include); 由…组成(*consist of)

【记】词根记忆: com (共同) + pris (握取) + e → 被握在一起 → 包含

【例】The Earth *comprises* three principal layers. 地球主要由三层构成。

【参】compromise(*n.* 妥协)

conceal [kənˈsiːl] *vt.* 隐蔽, 隐瞒(*cover)

【记】分拆联想: con + ceal(看作 seal, 密封) → 密封起来 → 隐蔽, 隐瞒

【例】Those shallow puddles are often *concealed* by leaves and dust. 这些浅水坑经常被树叶和灰尘所隐藏。

conceal

conduct [ˈkɑːndʌkt] *n.* 行为(behavior)

[kənˈdʌkt] *vt.* 引导(guide); 传导(transmit); 进行(progress)

【例】He found the copper used was not effective in *conducting* heat.

他发现所使用的铜在导热方面没有效果。//I'll be *conducting* my psychology experiment this Saturday. 我将在本周六开展我的心理实验。

contour ['kɑːntʊr] *n.* 轮廓(outline)；等高线；周线

【例】Ground plans and *contour* maps of the Earth can be drawn from aerial photographs. 可以用空中拍摄的相片来绘制地球的平面图和等高线地形图。

crab [kræb] *n.* 蟹

【记】分拆联想：cr(看作cry，叫) + ab → 被蟹的ab两个大钳子夹住了，痛得直叫 → 蟹

crumple ['krʌmpl] *v.* 把…弄皱；起皱(rumple)

【搭】crumple up 起褶

【例】Jane *crumpled* the letter up, torn it into pieces and in the end threw it on the fire. 简把信揉成一团，撕成碎片，最后扔进火里。

【派】uncrumple(*vt.* 使恢复平整)

depot ['diːpoʊ] *n.* 货站，仓库(depository, storehouse)

deserted [dɪ'zɜːrtɪd] *a.* 荒废的(obsolete)；无人的(void)

【记】来自desert(*v.* 放弃，遗弃)

【例】Downtown shopping areas became *deserted* after the war. 市中心购物区在战后被废弃了。

diagnose [ˌdaɪəg'noʊs] *v.* 诊断

【记】词根记忆：dia(穿过) + gnos(知道) + e → 古时通过望、闻、问、切诊断病情，透过表面看实质 → 诊断

【派】diagnosis(*n.* 诊断)

diagnose

dilate [daɪ'leɪt] *v.* 膨胀，扩大(expand)

【记】词根记忆：di + late(放) → 放开 → 扩大

【搭】dilate on/upon 详述；铺张

【参】dilute(*v.* 冲淡，稀释)

diversification [daɪˌvɜːrsɪfɪ'keɪʃn] *n.* 多样化

【例】Accompanying that economic growth was a structural change that featured increasing economic *diversification*. 伴随经济增长的是结构变化，其特点为经济更加多元化。

dot [dɑːt] *vt.* 星罗棋布于(scatter across) *n.* 点，圆点

【记】和pot(*n.* 壶)一起记

【例】The fantastic island, *dotted* with tropical plants, attracts tens of thousands of tourists abroad every year. 长满了热带植物的奇异海岛每年都吸引着成千上万的国外游客。

contour	crab	crumple	depot	deserted	diagnose
dilate	diversification	dot			

effective [ɪˈfektɪv] *a.* 有效的, 生效的; 给人深刻印象的, 显著的

【记】来自effect(*n.* 影响, 效果)

【搭】effective measures 有效措施; an effective remedy 有效药物

【例】A: I am going to tell that neighbor of mine to turn down that music once and for all.

B: I see why you are angry. But I've always found that the polite route is the most *effective*.

A: 我要告诉我的邻居, 把那个音乐声彻底关小。

B: 我明白你为什么发火了。但是我总是发现礼貌的处理办法最有效。

【派】ineffective(*a.* 无效的); effectively(*ad.* 有效地); effectiveness (*n.* 效力)

expressly [ɪkˈspresli] *ad.* 特意地, 专门

【记】来自express(*v.* 表达 *a.* 特别的)

facility [fəˈsɪləti] *n.* [常*pl.*] 设备, 工具(instrument, equipment)

【例】The dormitories have limited cooking *facilities*. 宿舍里只有很有限的烹饪设备。

field [fiːld] *n.* 田, 田野; 运动场; 领域, 方面(area); (电, 磁等)场

【搭】field study 野外研究

【例】A: Oh, I am so angry. My biology professor would not even let me try to explain why I missed the *field* trip. He just gave me a zero.

B: That seemed unfair. I would feel that way too if I were you.

A: 哦, 我真生气。我的生物学教授甚至不让我解释为何没有参加实地考察旅行就给了我个零分。

B: 这好像不太公平。如果我是你, 我也会有同感。

finch [fɪntʃ] *n.* 雀类

【记】分拆联想: fin(鳍, 鱼翅) + ch(音似: 翅) → 雀类和鱼类都有翅 → 雀类

frigid [ˈfrɪdʒɪd] *a.* 寒冷的(freezing, wintry); 冷淡的(cold, icy)

【记】词根记忆: frig(冷) + id(…的) → 寒冷的

【例】The *frigid* ground in the far north acts as a remarkable preservative for animal fossils. 遥远的北方的寒冷地表成为动物化石很好的防腐剂。

furnace [ˈfɜːrnɪs] *n.* 暖气锅炉; 熔炉(oven, kiln)

【记】分拆联想: fur(毛皮) + nace → 坐在暖气锅炉旁边就像披着温暖的毛皮 → 暖气锅炉

【搭】blast furnace 鼓风炉

☐ effective	☐ expressly	☐ facility	☐ field	☐ finch	☐ frigid
☐ furnace					

gasoline ['gæsəli:n] *n.* 汽油(petrol)

【记】词根记忆：gaso(=gas气) + line → 汽油

【例】Henry Ford constructed a one-cylinder *gasoline* motor in 1982. 亨利·福特于1982年制造了一辆单缸汽车。

generalize ['dʒenrəlaɪz] *vt.* 概括，归纳(sum up, conclude)

【记】来自general(概括的) + ize → 概括，归纳

【例】Algebra *generalizes* certain basic laws. 代数学总结某些基本法则。

【派】generalization(*n.* 归纳，概括；推广)；generalized(*a.* 广泛的，普遍的)

given ['gɪvn] *a.* 特定的(specified)；假定的(supposed)

【例】A few birds awake at any *given* moment to give the alarm. 一些鸟可以随时醒来报警。

hay [heɪ] *n.* 干草(stover)

【搭】hay stack 干草堆

hemisphere ['hemɪsfɪr] *n.* (地球或天体的)半球；大脑的半球(*side)

【记】词根记忆：hemi(半) + sphere(球) → 半球

【例】Columbus returned to Spain from the western *hemisphere*. 哥伦布从西半球返回西班牙。

hay

hieratic [haɪə'rætɪk] *a.* 僧侣的，僧侣用的

imitation [ˌɪmɪ'teɪʃn] *n.* 模仿，仿效(mock)；仿制；仿造品(fake)

【记】来自imitate(*v.* 模仿，仿效)

【搭】in imitation of 为了仿效…；the illegal imitation 伪造

【例】The increasing popularity of winter cycling can be attributed to the creation of mountain bike and its subsequent *imitations*. 冬季骑车越来越流行是因为创造出了山地车以及随后的仿制品。

【派】imitate(*v.* 模仿)

immature [ˌɪmə'tʃʊr] *a.* 未成熟的(unripe)

【记】词根记忆：im(不) + mature(成熟的) → 未成熟的

【例】This tomato plant is still *immature*. 这株西红柿仍然不成熟。

impressive [ɪm'presɪv] *a.* 给人深刻印象的(*stunning)

【记】来自impress(*v.* 给…以深刻印象)

【例】The destructive power of fungi is *impressive*. 真菌的破坏力是令人惊叹的。

inheritance [ɪnˈherɪtəns] *n.* 遗产(heritage)

【例】Demon and his twin brother entered on their *inheritance* when they were only 21. 德蒙和他的孪生兄弟仅21岁时就继承了遗产。

interactive [ˌɪntərˈæktɪv] *a.* 交互式的

【派】interactivity(*n.* 交互)

【参】intercourse(*n.* 交往，交流)

lace [leɪs] *n.* 蕾丝；缎带

【记】发音记忆

【例】Fine handmade *lace* is traditionally made of linen thread. 精美的手工蕾丝传统上由麻线制成。

latitude [ˈlætɪtuːd] *n.* 纬度；[常*pl.*] 纬度地区

【记】词根记忆：lati(阔)＋tude → 两个纬度之间的区域很广阔 → 纬度

【例】Each aurora hangs like a curtain of light stretching over the polar regions and into the higher *latitudes*. 每束极光像窗帘一样挂在极地地区，并延伸至高纬度地区。

【参】longitude(*n.* 经度，经线)；altitude(*n.* 高度)；gratitude(*n.* 感激)

lay [leɪ] *v.* 下(蛋)；放置

【例】Turtles travel miles through the sea to *lay* eggs on an island. 海龟在海里游数英里到岛上产卵。//They *laid* the injured woman down on the grass. 他们把受伤的女人平放在草地上。

legislature [ˈledʒɪsleɪtʃər] *n.* 立法机关

【记】来自legislat(e)(制定法律)＋ure → 立法机关

【例】Senators are designated by their respective state *legislatures* rather than by the voters themselves. 参议员由各自的州立法机构指定，而不是由选民自己决定。

march [mɑːrtʃ] *n.* 进行曲 *v.* 前进，行进

【例】The band played a military *march*. 乐队演奏了军队进行曲。//The front ranks *marched* toward the enemy line. 前锋朝敌方的防线行进了。

marvel [ˈmɑːrvl] *n.* 奇异的事物；奇迹(wonder)

【记】分拆联想：mar(毁坏)＋vel(音似：well) → 遭到毁坏再重建好，真是奇迹 → 奇迹

【派】marvelous(*a.* 不可思议的)

metric [ˈmetrɪk] *a.* 米制的；公制的

【记】词根记忆：metr(计量，测量)＋ic(…的) → 米制的；公制的

【例】The woman could use his *metric* ruler. 这个女子可以使用他的米尺。

□ inheritance	□ interactive	□ lace	□ latitude	□ lay	□ legislature
□ march	□ marvel	□ metric			

metropolitan [ˌmetrə'pɑːlɪtən] *a.* 主要都市的，大城市的

modeling ['mɑːdəlɪŋ] *n.* 立体感(表现法)(third dimension)；造型(术)

【例】In sculpture the term "*modeling*" denotes a way of shaping clay, wax, or other pliable materials. 雕塑艺术中"造型"一词表示使黏土、蜡或其他可塑材料成形的方式。

monitor ['mɑːnɪtər] *n.* 显示器 *vt.* 监控(watch)；调节(regulate)

【例】Have you had experience *monitoring* alarm systems? 你有监控警报系统的经验吗？

multiply ['mʌltɪplaɪ] *v.* 增加；繁殖(increase, breed)

【记】词根记忆：multi(多) + ply(表动词) → 变多 → 增加；繁殖

【例】Mosquitoes seem to *multiply* quickly. 蚊子好像繁殖得很快。

【派】multiplication(*n.* 乘法)

mythical ['mɪθɪkl] *a.* 神话的(legendary)；虚构的

【例】The history of her life has also become somewhat *mythical*. 她的生活史好像也有点神话色彩。

offspring ['ɔːfsprɪŋ] *n.* 子孙，后代(descendant)

【记】分拆联想：off(出来) + spring(春天) → 像春天一样带来希望 → 子孙，后代

pamphlet ['pæmflət] *n.* 小册子(booklet, brochure)

【记】来自拉丁文pamphilus，是一首爱情名诗，pam(=pan全部) + phil(爱) + us → 表达爱情

【参】chapbook 小本诗歌集或故事书

pause [pɔːz] *v./n.* 中止，暂停(suspend)

【搭】pause to do 停顿做…

【例】A *pause* gives the listener time to think about what was just said. 停顿给听众时间去思考刚才说的话。

petition [pə'tɪʃn] *n.* 请愿书，申请书，诉状 *v.* (向…)请愿，正式请求(appeal)

【记】词根记忆：pet(寻求) + ition → 寻求(帮助) → 请愿书，申请书

【搭】sign a petition 签请愿书

【例】A *petition* signed by 3,000 hospital doctors was handed to the Minister of Health. 一份由3000名医院医生签署的请愿书被递交给了卫生部长。

petroleum [pə'trouliəm] *n.* 石油

【记】词根记忆：petro(石) + leum → 石油

【参】petrifaction[*n.* 石化(作用)；化石]

pharmacy [ˈfɑːrməsi] n. 药店(drugstore)

【记】词根记忆: pharma(药, 毒)+ cy → 药店

【参】pharmacology(n. 药理学); pharmacist(n. 药剂师)

preserve [prɪˈzɜːrv] vt. 保护, 保存(*protected from destruction)

【记】分拆联想: pre(前面)+ serve(服务)→ 提供在前面做保护的服务 → 保护, 保存

【例】Welcome to the Forewinds Historical Farm where traditions of the past are *preserved* for visitors like you. 欢迎来到 Forewinds 历史农庄, 这里为你这样的游客保留了过去的传统。

【派】preservation(n. 保护, 保存); well-preserved(a. 保存很好的)

priority [praɪˈɔːrəti] n. 在先; 优先权(privilege)

【记】来自 prior(在前的)+ ity → 在先

【例】The system gives *priority* to the students who have been here the longest. 该制度给在这里时间最久的学生以优先权。

puzzle [ˈpʌzl] n. 难题, 谜(riddle), 迷惑 v. (使)迷惑; (使)为难

【搭】jigsaw puzzle 七巧板, 智力拼图; be puzzled by 被…为难住

【例】For a while, the zookeepers were *puzzled* by the accident, but they finally discovered what happened. 动物园管理员一度被这件事所困惑, 但是他们最终发现了来龙去脉。

A: You were right about the *puzzle* you lent me last week. It really is a challenge. I want to try to get it myself though. So I'm going to work on it a little longer.

B: Well, if you get really stuck, remember I'm only a phone call away.

A: 你说的没错, 你上周提供给我的难题的确是个挑战。不过我想自己解出来。所以我要再研究一段时间。

B: 好的, 如果你真的解不出来, 记住随时给我打电话。

【派】puzzlement(n. 困惑)

recognition [ˌrekəgˈnɪʃn] n. 承认(admission); 认出, 辨认; 赞扬

【记】来自 recognize(vt. 认出; 承认)

【搭】social recognition 社会认同

recurring [rɪˈkɜːrɪŋ] a. 往复的, 再次发生的(repeated, recurrent, repetitious)

【例】Some scientists believe one can control over *recurring* bad dreams. 一些科学家认为一个人可以控制反复做的噩梦。

refraction [rɪˈfrækʃn] n. 折光, 折射(deflection)

retreat [rɪˈtriːt] vi. 退却, 撤退(retire) n. 退却; 隐退处

【例】She and her tribe had to abandon their lands and *retreat* to Canada. 她和她的部落不得不放弃他们的土地, 撤退到了加拿大。

Those log buildings are the mountain *retreats* of wealthy New Yorkers. 那些圆木建筑是富有的纽约人的山间隐居所。

reveal [rɪ'viːl] *vt.* 暴露，揭露(disclose)；展现(*show)

【记】分拆联想：re(相反) + veal(看作veil，面纱) → 除去面纱 → 暴露，揭露

【例】Glassmakers did not want to *reveal* the methods they used. 玻璃工人不想展示他们所使用的方法。

sanctuary ['sæŋktʃueri] *n.* 动物保护区；避难所(shelter, refuge)；圣所，圣殿

【记】词根记忆：sanct(神圣) + uary(地方) → 神圣的地方 → 圣所，圣殿

【搭】natural sanctuary 自然保护区

sanctuary
禁猎区

【例】Hunters are forbidden from hunting in wildlife *sanctuaries* of this region. 狩猎者被禁止在这一带的野生动物保护区捕猎。

sketch [sketʃ] *n.* 草稿(draft)；草图；素描 *vt.* 给…速写(*draw)

【派】sketching(*n.* 草图)

stanza ['stænzə] *n.* (诗)节，段

substantive [səb'stæntɪv] *a.* 真实的(actual)；有实质的(substantial)

target ['tɑːrgɪt] *n.* 目标(aim)，对象，靶子 *vt.* 把…作为目标

【记】发音记忆："他击的" → 是他击中目标的 → 目标

【搭】target sth. at/on sb./sth. 把…作为…的目标；sth. be targeted at/on sb./sth. …被作为目标

【例】A: Joe, I thought your article on the school newspaper was right on *target*. You certainly convinced me anyway.

B: Thanks Mary. Unfortunately, based on the general response, you and I are definitely in the minority.

A: 乔，我觉得你在校报发表的文章一语中的。你肯定说服我了。

B: 谢谢玛丽。不幸的是，根据总体的反应，你和我肯定是少数。//

A: About this survey on the quality of life in the dorm I feel sort of awkward because, well, I'm not really comfortable here. Are you sure you want me to fill out this survey form?

B: It's people like you who can help us *target* areas for improvement.

A: 关于这个宿舍生活质量的调查，我觉得有点尴尬，因为我在这里不是很舒服。你肯定你想让我填写这个调查表吗？

B: 正是像你这样的人才能帮助我们找到改进的地方。

【派】targeted(*a.* 作为目标的，作为对象的)

unity [ˈjuːnəti] *n.* 统一，联合（unification, combination）

【记】词根记忆：uni（单一）＋ty → 统一，联合

【例】Monet and his 29 fellow artists in the exhibit adopted the same name as a badge of their *unity*. 莫内和29位艺术家同行采用了同样的名字，以示团结。

unravel [ʌnˈrævl] *v.* 弄清楚（*discover）

【记】分拆联想：un（打开，解开）＋ravel（纠缠）→ 解开纠缠 → 弄清楚

【例】Genetic engineering helps researchers *unravel* the mysteries of previously incurable diseases. 遗传工程帮助研究人员揭开此前不治之症的谜。

veil [veɪl] *vt.* 隐藏，遮蔽 *n.* 面纱（cover, hide）

【记】联想记忆：邪恶的（evil）人总是试图掩饰自己，像蒙着面纱（veil）

【搭】draw a veil over sth. 遮盖…

【例】Even nowadays, most women in this region wear *veils* in public places. 时至今日，该地区多数妇女仍然在公众场合蒙着面纱。

【派】veil-like(*a.* 似面纱的)

I have already anticipated that nothing will be simple. I know beforehand what I will encounter, so what can I complain?

我已经预料到一切都不会是轻而易举的。我事先就明白我将遭遇到什么，所以，我有什么可抱怨的呢？ ——迈克尔·舒马赫（*Michael Schumacher*）

Word List 14

词根、词缀预习表

absent	缺席	absenteeism	n. 旷课；旷工
dia	通过，穿过	diagnose	v. 诊断
cave	空；洞	concave	a. 凹的
sign	标出	designate	vt. 指定，任命
fract	碎裂	fraction	n. 小部分
volve	卷	involve	vt. 牵涉；包含
optim	最好	optimistic	a. 乐观的
pend	挂	suspend	vt. 吊，挂

abrasion [əˈbreɪʒn] *n.* 表面磨损

【记】词根记忆：ab（离去）+ ras（=rad 摩擦）+ ion → 表面磨损

【例】*Abrasion* due to daily wear alters the surface features of beads. 由于日常佩戴导致的磨损改变了珠子的表面特征。

【参】abrasive(*n.* 磨料 *a.* 研磨的)

absenteeism [ˌæbsənˈtiːˌɪzəm] *n.* 旷课；旷工(absence)

【记】词根记忆：absent（缺席）+ ee（人）+ ism → 旷课；旷工

【例】Johnson was fired because of his habitual *absenteeism.* 约翰逊因为经常旷工而被开除了。

acclaim [əˈkleɪm] *vt. /n.* 喝彩(applaud)；称赞(*praise)

【记】词根记忆：ac （一再）+ claim （大叫）→ 不断大叫 → 喝彩；称赞

【例】These artists achieved widespread popular success and *acclaim.* 这些艺术家取得了广泛的成功，获得了广泛的赞誉。

【派】acclaimed(*a.* 受赞誉的)

【参】exclaim(*v.* 呼喊)；declaim(*v.* 巧辩)；reclaim(*vt.* 要求归还；开垦)

astronomy [əˈstrɑːnəmi] *n.* 天文学

【记】词根记忆：astro（星星）+ nom（名字）+ y → 研究星星名字的

学科 → 天文学

【派】astronomical(a. 天文学的；天体的)；astronomer(n. 天文学家)

boundary [ˈbaʊndri] n. 分界线；边界(bound, border)

【记】分拆联想：bound(界限) + ary(表场所) → 场所之间的界限 → 分界线；边界

【例】The neighbors had a long-standing disagreement over the *boundary* line. 邻居们就分界线存在着长期的分歧。

brass [bræs] n. 黄铜(器)；铜管乐器

【记】和grass(n. 草)一起记

candidate [ˈkændɪdət] n. 候选人(nominee)

【例】The crowd was overwhelmed by the *candidate's* speech. 人群被候选人的演说震撼了。

coincide [ˌkoʊɪnˈsaɪd] vi. 一致(agree, accord)；相巧合

【记】词根记忆：co(共同) + in + cide(切) → 共同切分 → 一致

【派】coincidence(n. 巧合)；coincident(a. 一致的；巧合的)

colony [ˈkɑːləni] n. 殖民地(settlement)；(生物)群体(community)

【记】分拆联想：col(共同) + on(在…上) + y(表场所) → 他们合作将那片土地变为自己的殖民地 → 殖民地

【派】colonist(n. 殖民者)；colonial(a. 殖民的；殖民地的)

comic [ˈkɑːmɪk] a. 滑稽的，喜剧的(funny, laughable)

【例】There are many *comic* characters in this play. 这部戏剧中有很多喜剧人物。

comprehensive [ˌkɑːmprɪˈhensɪv] a. 全面的，综合的

【记】联想记忆：com + prehen(看作prehend，抓住) + sive → 全部抓住 → 全面的，综合的

【例】Our customers are supplied with a *comprehensive* range of service. 我们给顾客提供一系列的全方位服务。

concave [kɑːnˈkeɪv] a. 凹的

【记】词根记忆：con + cave(空；洞) → 洞是凹进去的 → 凹的

【搭】concave lens 凹透镜

cooperation [koʊˌɑːpəˈreɪʃn] n. 合作，协作

【搭】be in cooperation with 与…合作；play in cooperation with 与…一起玩

【例】There is an urgent need to strengthen international *cooperation* during the financial crisis. 在经济危机期间迫切需要加强国际合作。

curious [ˈkjʊriəs] a. 好奇的；求知的(inquisitive)

【搭】a curious glance 好奇的眼光

□ boundary	□ brass	□ candidate	□ coincide	□ colony	□ comic
□ comprehensive	□ concave	□ cooperation	□ curious		

【例】Researchers are *curious* to find that the disease results from an uncertain virus. 研究人员好奇地发现这种疾病源自一种不确定的病毒。

decode [ˌdiːˈkoʊd] *vt.* 译解(interpret)

【例】The Rosetta Stone was found by scholars trying to *decode* ancient languages. 罗塞塔石碑是由试图破译古代语言的学者们发现的。

demanding [dɪˈmændɪŋ] *a.* 苛求的(rigorous); 费力的

【记】来自demand(*v.* 要求, 需要)

【例】His current schedule is also very *demanding*. 他当前的日程安排也非常费力。

demanding

designate [ˈdezɪɡneɪt] *vt.* 指定(name, appoint); 任命(nominate)

【记】词根记忆: de + sign(标出) + ate → 标出来 → 指定

【例】The founders stipulated that senators be *designated* by their respective state legislatures rather than by the voters themselves. 建国者们规定参议员由各自的州立法机构指定, 而不是由选民自己决定。

【派】designated(*a.* 指定的); designation(*n.* 指定)

diversity [daɪˈvɜːrsəti] *n.* 多样性(variety)

【搭】biological diversity 生物差异; species diversity 物种多样性

【例】The author argues that there is more *diversity* of life in the sea than in the rain forests. 作者辩称海洋里的生物比雨林里的更加多样化。

dogged [ˈdɔːɡɪd] *a.* 顽强的; 顽固的(persevering)

【记】联想记忆: dog(狗) + ged → 像狗一样顽强 → 顽强的

【例】The researcher has been *dogged* by failure over the past year; now he is working hard to pull out. 这名研究人员过去一年一直被失败所累; 现在他正努力恢复心情。

donation [doʊˈneɪʃn] *n.* 捐赠, 捐款(endowment)

【记】词根记忆: don(给予) + ation → 给出去 → 捐款

【搭】blood donation 献血

【例】Many generous people made a voluntary *donation* to victims in the earthquake. 很多慷慨的人自愿向地震受害者捐了款。

【派】donor(*n.* 捐助者)

dormitory [ˈdɔːrmətɔːri] *n.* 宿舍(hostel)

【记】词根记忆: dorm(睡眠) + itory → 睡觉的地方 → 宿舍

【搭】dormitory room 宿舍

drain [dreɪn] *n.* 排水；消耗(expenditure) *v.* (使)流走(flow away)

【记】分拆联想：d(看作dig, 挖)＋rain(雨水)→挖一条排雨水的沟→排水沟

【例】Water is let in or *drained* out until it reaches approximately the same level as the water ahead. 水被引进来或者排出去，直至达到与前面的水差不多的相同高度。

【派】drainage(*n.* 排水；排水装置)

drowsy [ˈdraʊzi] *a.* 昏昏欲睡的，使人昏昏欲睡的

【搭】make sb. drowsy 使某人昏昏欲睡

【例】A: We need to drive to the city tonight. But the doctor said this medicine might make me *drowsy*.

B: In that case, I'd better drive.

A: 我们需要今晚开车去那个城市。但是医生说这个药可能会让我昏昏欲睡。

B: 这样的话还是我来开吧。

A: How are you feeling?

B: The stuff the nurse gave me seemed to have helped. But it's making me awfully *drowsy*.

A: 你感觉如何？

B: 护士给我的药好像有效，但却让我感觉特别困。

edge [edʒ] *n.* 边(border)，棱；刀口，刃 *v.* 侧身移动，挤进

【搭】on the edge of 在…的边缘；on edge 紧张

【例】A: You seem on *edge* this morning.

B: I have to give a presentation in class this afternoon.

A: 你今天上午好像有点紧张。

B: 我下午要在班上做个报告。

efficiency [ɪˈfɪʃnsi] *n.* 效率，功效(effectiveness)

【记】词根记忆：ef(出)＋fic(做)＋iency→做出的成绩→功效

【例】Since the development of scientific technology, there has been a great improvement in energy *efficiency* at the factory. 自从科学技术得到了发展以来，工厂的能源利用效率得到了很大提高。

elevation [elɪˈveɪʃn] *n.* 提高；高度，海拔(altitude, height)

【搭】elevation of …的海拔；elevation to 升职为…

【例】Not long ago, some of you may have read about the team of mountain climbing scientists who helped to recalculate the *elevation* of the highest mountain in the world, Mount Everest. 不久以前，你们有些人可能读到一队登山科学家帮助重新测量世界最高的珠穆朗玛峰海拔的文章。

elongate [ɪˈlɔːŋɡeɪt] *vt.* 延长，伸长（lengthen, extend）
【记】词根记忆：e(加强) + long(长) + ate → 使不断变长 → 伸长
【例】The singer's face is too *elongated* in the photos. 在照片中歌手的脸被拉得太长了。
【派】elongation(*n.* 延长)

employ [ɪmˈplɔɪ] *vt.* 用，使用；雇佣（hire）
【例】For the past several years many graduates have been *employed* as a sales man or sales woman. 过去几年，很多毕业生都被雇用为销售人员。

erupt [ɪˈrʌpt] *vi.* 爆发（burst out）
【记】词根记忆：e(出) + rupt(断) → 断裂后喷出 → 爆发
【例】Kilauea is one of the world's most active volcanoes, having *erupted* dozens of times since 1952. Kilauea是世界上最活跃的火山之一，自1952年以来已爆发过几十次。
【派】eruption(*n.* 火山爆发，喷发)

extinct [ɪkˈstɪŋkt] *a.* 灭绝的
【记】词根记忆：ex(出) + tinct(看作stinct，刺) → 使不再长出刺，将刺灭光 → 灭绝的
【例】It is estimated that over 99 percent of all species that ever existed have become *extinct*. 据估计，在过去存在的物种中有超过99%都已灭绝。
【派】extinction(*n.* 灭绝)

fraction [ˈfrækʃn] *n.* 小部分（portion, segment）
【记】词根记忆：fract(碎裂) + ion → 整体碎裂成小部分 → 小部分
【例】Only a small *fraction* of all the organisms that have ever lived are preserved as fossils. 所有曾经存活的生物中只有一小部分以化石的形式保存了下来。

galaxy [ˈɡæləksi] *n.* 星系
【记】源自希腊文galaxias，字根gala的意思是"乳汁；乳状物"，可能因为古人仰望银河所见的一片银白很像乳汁的缘故。
【搭】the Galaxy 银河系，银河
【例】There are three main types of *galaxy*: spiral, elliptical, and irregular. 星系有三种主要类型：螺旋形、椭圆形和形状不规则的星系。

grace [ɡreɪs] *n.* 优美，优雅（elegance）
【记】发音记忆："格蕾斯"，著名的影星，最后成为王妃 → 她是美丽，优雅的代表 → 优美，优雅
【派】graceful(*a.* 优美的，优雅的); gracefully(*ad.* 优美地，优雅地)

hitherto [ˌhɪðər'tuː] *ad.* 迄今，至今

idle ['aɪdl] *a.* 懒散的（*inactive, lazy）；空闲的
（vacant）

【记】发音记忆："爱斗" → 无所事事的人
才爱斗 → 懒散的

【参】idol（*n.* 偶像）

idle

inanity [ɪ'nænəti] *n.* 空虚（emptiness）

【例】Their statement was a downright *inanity*. 他们的声明是彻头彻
尾的废话。

ingredient [ɪn'griːdiənt] *n.* 成分，要素（element）；（烹调的）原料

【记】词根记忆：ingr（=integr完整；进入）+ edi（吃）+ ent → 放入食
物内的东西 →（烹调的）原料

【例】The weather map became an essential *ingredient* in the redesign
of the American newspaper. 气象图成为了改版的美国报纸的基本
要素。//You can get all the *ingredients* at any supermarkets. 你可以
在任何超市买到所有的配料。

insulin ['ɪnsəlɪn] *n.* 胰岛素

【记】词根记忆：insul（岛）+ in → 胰岛素

interfere [ˌɪntər'fɪr] *v.* 干涉；妨碍（obstruct）

【记】词根记忆：inter（在…之间）+ fer（带来）+ e → 来到中间 →
干涉

【例】The government shouldn't *interfere* in private business. 政府不
应该干预私营企业。//Skyscrapers also *interfere* with television
reception. 摩天大楼也干扰电视信号的接收。

【派】interference（*n.* 干涉，干扰）

invitation [ˌɪnvɪ'teɪʃn] *n.* 邀请；请柬

【例】She'll consider the man's *invitation*. 她会考虑这位男子的邀请。//
They need to print more *invitations*. 他们需要印刷更多的请柬。

inviting [ɪn'vaɪtɪŋ] *a.* 动人的，诱人的（*attractive）

【例】The regions have become increasingly *inviting* playgrounds for
the growing number of recreation seekers. 这些地区已经日益成为了
吸引越来越多娱乐探索者的活动场所。

involve [ɪn'vɑːlv] *v.* 牵涉；包含（include）；使参与

【记】词根记忆：in（使…）+ volve（卷）→ 使卷入 → 牵涉

【例】Your main responsibilities will *involve* ensuring the safety of
everyone who skis here. 你主要的责任将是确保所有在这里滑雪的
人的安全。//I want to be *involved* from start to finish. 我想自始至终
地参与其中。

| □ hitherto | □ idle | □ inanity | □ ingredient | □ insulin | □ interfere |
| □ invitation | □ inviting | □ involve | | | |

item ['aɪtəm] *n.* 条，条款(clause)；项目

【搭】item on the agenda 议程条款；news item 新闻要点

keyboard ['ki:bɔ:rd] *n.* 键盘

【记】组合词：key(键) + board(板)→键盘

【例】Nowadays, children can successfully manipulate the *keyboard* or mouse of their home computers before they can even hold a pencil. 如今孩子们在能够握笔之前就可以成功地操作家用电脑的键盘或鼠标了。

A: $200 to fix my computer? I thought you said you could do it for 50.

B: I did, but it's not the *keyboard* after all. That's the major part inside the machine that will cost a lot more to replace.

A: 修我的电脑要200美元？我以为你说的是50美元。

B: 我是这么说的，但是问题不在键盘。电脑内部的主要部件需要换，这得花更多的钱。

lettuce ['letɪs] *n.* 生菜；莴苣

magnetic [mæɡ'netɪk] *a.* 磁(性)的

【搭】magnetic field 磁场；magnetic compass 磁盘指南针

【例】The electrons accelerated to nearly the speed of light move through *magnetic* fields. 几乎加速到光速的电子穿过磁场。

mason ['meɪsn] *n.* 泥瓦匠

【记】分拆联想：ma(音似：妈) + son(儿子)→妈妈希望儿子成为泥瓦匠→泥瓦匠

【派】masonry(*n.* 石建筑；石工)

meantime ['mi:ntaɪm] *ad./n.* 其时，其间(meanwhile)

【例】That will be fine, in the *meantime* you should try to take it easy. 那不会有问题，同时你应该放松。

merchant ['mɜ:rtʃənt] *n.* 商人

metallic [mə'tælɪk] *a.* 金属(性)的

【记】来自metal(*n.* 金属)

【例】The engineers are creating exotic new *metallic* substances. 工程师们正在创造奇异的新金属物质。

military ['mɪləteri] *a.* 军(事、用)的(martial) *n.* [the ~]军队(army, troops)

【记】词根记忆：milit(军事) + ary→军事的；军队

【例】The *military* stationed at the various forts. 军队驻扎在各个堡垒。

mode [moʊd] *n.* 方式(manner)；风格(style)；时尚(fashion)

monastery ['mɑ:nəsteri] *n.* 修道院，寺院；僧侣

【记】词根记忆：mon(=mono单个) + aster(星星) + y→孤星→孤独者所住之处→寺院

item	keyboard	lettuce	magnetic	mason	meantime
merchant	metallic	military	mode	monastery	

narrative [ˈnærətɪv] *n.* 叙述(depiction)；记叙文

【例】Oral *narratives* are a valid form of literature. 口述是文学的一种有效形式。

nourish [ˈnɜːrɪʃ] *vt.* 滋养(to promote the growth of)；养育(rear)

【记】词根记忆：nouri(=nutri滋养, 孕育)+(i)sh → 滋养；养育

【例】The rain *nourished* the crops. 雨水滋养了庄稼。

【派】nourishment(*n.* 营养品，食物)；nourishing(*a.* 有营养的)

optimistic [ˌɑːptɪˈmɪstɪk] *a.* 乐观的(affirmative)

【记】词根记忆：optim(最好) + istic → 最好的 → 乐观的

【例】Few people are *optimistic* about the team's chances of winning. 很少有人对该队获胜的可能性持乐观态度。

【参】optimization(*n.* 最优化)

天塌下来
高个顶着

optimistic

ornithology [ˌɔːrnɪˈθɑːlədʒi] *n.* 鸟类学

【例】I wish I'd seen it since that's what we're studying in my *ornithology* class. 我真希望自己看到了，因为那是我们在鸟类学课堂上正在学习的内容。

overnight [ˈoʊvərnaɪt] *a.* 通宵的，晚上的，前夜的

[ˌoʊvərˈnaɪt] *ad.* 在前一夜，整夜

【记】组合词：over(越过) + night(夜) → 通宵的

pale [peɪl] *a.* 苍白的；淡的

【例】I think I'd really rather have some *pale* yellow paper for my correspondence. 我想我宁愿用一些浅黄色纸当信纸。

penetrate [ˈpenətreɪt] *v.* 刺穿(*go through, pierce)；渗透；洞察(apperceive)

【记】分拆联想：pen(全部) + etr(看作enter, 进入) + ate → 全部进入 → 刺穿

【例】In a microwave oven, radiation *penetrates* food and is then absorbed primarily by water molecule, causing heat to spread through the food. 在微波炉中，热辐射穿透食物，然后主要被水分子吸收，使热量在食物中扩散。

【派】penetrating(*a.* 刺鼻的)

prominent [ˈprɑːmɪnənt] *a.* 卓著的(*distinguished, *famous)；突起的(protuberant)

【记】词根记忆：pro(向前) + min(伸) + ent → 向前伸出 → 突起的；卓著的

【例】Mercy Otis was born into a *prominent* family in Barnstable. 默西·奥蒂斯生于巴恩斯特布尔的一个显赫之家。

□ narrative	□ nourish	□ optimistic	□ ornithology	□ overnight	□ pale
□ penetrate	□ prominent				

154

proposal [prə'pouzl] *n.* 提议，建议(suggestion)；求婚

【记】来自propose(*v.* 提议，建议)

【搭】proposal for sth./doing sth. …的提议；a proposal to do sth. …的提议

【例】Scientists have put forward a *proposal* to reduce the emission of greenhouse gases since 1980s. 自20世纪80年代起，科学家们已经提出了一项减少温室气体排放的建议。

A: Bill Smith has volunteered to write a summary of the *proposals* we've agreed on.

B: Will I have a chance to review it?

A：比尔·史密斯自愿就我们达成一致的提议写一份总结。

B：我能有机会回顾一下吗？

A: We've been working on this *proposal* for so long that my eyes are starting to blur.

B: Why don't we get out of here? We can wrap it up later.

A：这份提议我们写了这么久，我的视线都开始模糊了。

B：我们为什么不出去？我们可以回头再写完。

qualify ['kwɑːlɪfaɪ] *v.* (使)具有资格，(使)合格(to fit by training, skill, or ability for a special purpose)

【搭】qualify... as 取得…资格

【例】The man isn't *qualified* for any of the jobs. 此人做任何工作都不合格。

【派】qualification(*n.* 资格，条件)；qualified(*a.* 有资格的，合格的)

realm [relm] *n.* 领域(region)；王国(kingdom)

【记】分拆联想：real(真正的) + m → 真正的好东西(如音乐、艺术)无国界 → 领域；王国

rug [rʌg] *n.* (小)地毯(carpet)；围毯

sac [sæk] *n.* 【生】囊，液囊

【记】联想记忆：神圣(sacred)中去掉了红色(red)，只剩下实质的囊(sac)

satiric [sə'tɪrɪk] *a.* 讽刺的(sarcastic)

【记】来自satir(e)(讽刺) + ic → 讽刺的

separate ['seprət] *a.* 分离的(*discrete)；个别的(*distinct)

['sepəreɪt] *v.* 分离(*split, *unravel)；划分；区别(*sort out)

【记】词根记忆：se(分开) + par(相等) + ate →(使)分成分 → 分离；划分

【例】Horse-powered threshing machines to *separate* the seeds from

□ proposal	□ qualify	□ realm	□ rug	□ sac	□ satiric
□ separate					

the plants were already in general use. 把种子与植株分离的马力脱粒机得到了普遍应用。

【派】separable(*a.* 可分离的)

shed [ʃed] *v.* 脱落(*discard, slough)；流出；散发 *n.* 小屋(hut, shanty)

【记】分拆联想：she(她)＋d → 女孩子容易流眼泪 → 流出

【例】The huge impact created a vapor that *shed* out into space and eventually condensed as the moon. 巨大的冲击产生了蒸汽，蒸汽喷射到了太空中并最终冷凝成了月球。

smother [ˈsmʌðər] *v.* (使)窒息

【记】分拆联想：s(看作she)＋mother(母亲) → 她快要被母亲的爱窒息了 → (使)窒息

so-called [ˌsoʊˈkɔːld] *a.* 所谓的(commonly named)

sore [sɔːr] *a.* 疼痛的(painful)；极度的(exceeding)

【记】联想记忆：做家务(chore)做得腰酸背痛(sore)

suspend [səˈspend] *v.* 吊，挂(*hang)；暂缓

【记】词根记忆：sus＋pend(挂) → 挂在下面 → 吊，挂

【例】Grain Exchange trading was *suspended*, and farmers sold at prices fixed by the board. 谷物交易所的交易被中止了，农民们按照委员会确定的价格出售谷物。

【派】suspended(*a.* 暂停的，缓期的)；suspender(*n.* [常 *pl.*] 吊裤带)

sustain [səˈsteɪn] *vt.* 保持，维持(生命)(*support, maintain)

【记】词根记忆：sus＋tain(拿住) → 保持，维持

【例】The hurricanes have *sustained* winds of 74 mph and up. 飓风维持时速74英里以上的风速。

【派】self-sustaining(*a.* 自给自足的)

【参】attain(*vt.* 达到)；retain(*vt.* 保持)

swarm [swɔːrm] *n.* (一大)群(crowd)

swarm

【记】分拆联想：s＋warm(暖的) → 大家挤成一群比较暖和 → 一群

【例】One of these migrating *swarms* was estimated to contain 124 billion locusts. 据估计这些迁徙的蝗虫一批就有1240亿只。

sweat [swet] *n.* 汗(水)

【记】联想记忆：辛勤的汗水(sweat)过后是甜蜜的(sweet)果实

【搭】sweat gland 汗腺

【派】sweaty(*a.* 出汗的；吃力的)；sweater(*n.* 毛衣；厚运动衫)

【参】sweatshirt(*n.* 运动衫)；sweatshop(*n.* 血汗工厂)

shed	smother	so-called	sore	suspend	sustain
swarm	sweat				

through [θru:] *prep.* 穿过，通过；从开始到结束；经由，以；因为，由于 *ad.* 从头到尾，自始至终

【搭】plough through 费力地阅读；be through 结束

【例】The broadcast can be heard by wireless operators on ships with a radio *through* several hundred miles. 在配有无线电的船只上，无线电报员能听到几百英里外的广播。

A: At the rate of its being used, the copier is not going to make it *through* the rest of the year.

B: The year? It's supposed to be good for five.

A：照现在的使用速度，没过今年复印机就会用坏。

B：今年？它应该能用5年呢。

A: You wouldn't believe the line at the auto inspection center. I waited more than two hours to get *through* it.

B: That's what you get for waiting until the last day of the month.

A：你不会相信车检中心排的长队。我等了两个多小时。

B：你等到月底最后一天才去就得排长队。

【参】thorough(*a.* 彻底的；完全的)

translucent [træns'lu:snt] *a.* (半)透明的(transparent)

【记】词根记忆：trans(穿过) + luc(光，照亮) + ent → 光线能穿过 →(半)透明的

【例】Glass can be colored or colorless, transparent, *translucent*, or opaque. 玻璃可以是有色或无色的、透明、半透明或不透明的。

【参】limpid(*a.* 清澈的；透明的)

untamed [ˌʌn'teɪmd] *a.* 难控驭的(wild)

【记】分拆联想：un + tame(驯服) + d → 未驯服的 → 难控驭的

【例】Robert S. Duncanson was considered a painter of the Hudson River school, which concentrated on scenes of America's *untamed* wilderness. 罗伯特·S·邓肯森被认为是哈德逊河流派的画家，这一画派专门描绘美国蛮荒之地的景色。

X-ray ['eksreɪ] *n.* X射线，X光

【例】I've just seen the *X-rays* and your teeth looked just fine. 我刚才看过X光片了，你的牙齿看上去没事。

Word List 15  MP3-15

词根、词缀预习表

vey	道路	convey	*vt.* 运送；传达
cline	倾斜	decline	*n./v.* 下降，衰退
lute	冲洗	dilute	*v.* 稀释，淡化
dur	持续	durable	*a.* 持久的
sit	坐	posit	*v.* 安排
gen	种，属	genre	*n.* 类型；流派
ciner	灰	incinerate	*v.* 焚化
hibit	拿住	inhibit	*vt.* 阻碍，抑制
nox	毒	noxious	*a.* 有害的
sacr	神圣的	sacred	*a.* 神圣不可侵犯的

awake [ə'weɪk] *a.* 醒着的；警觉的 *v.* 唤醒，唤起；醒（wake）；觉醒，醒悟到，认识到

【记】分拆联想：a + wake(醒) → 醒过来 → 醒着的

【搭】stay awake 保持清醒；awake sb. to do sth. 唤醒…做

【例】I stayed up all night cramming for my history exam. I couldn't keep my eyes open in my last class. I'm having this coffee so I can stay *awake* this afternoon. 我整夜没睡地为历史考试恶补。我在最后一节课上连眼睛都睁不开了。我喝点咖啡这样下午才能保持清醒。

A: You had met Prof. Johnson before, right? How would you describe his lectures?

B: Well, let me put in this way. I could never stay *awake* in one of his classes without first drinking at least two cups of coffee.

A：你已经见过约翰逊教授了，对不对？你觉得他的课怎么样？

B：这么说吧。如果不先喝至少两杯咖啡，我上他的课就会睡着。

code [koʊd] *n.* 密码；代码；法规(laws, rules) *v.* 把…编码

【搭】code of laws 法典；instruction code 指令(代)码；bar code 条形码

【例】They are specially *coded*. 它们是经过特别编码的。

【派】codify(*vt.* 编成法典)

commercial [kə'mɜ:rʃl] *a.* 商业的, 商务的, 贸易的

【记】来自commerce(商业) + ial(…的)→ 商业的

【搭】commercial success 商业成功

【例】A: Much to my surprise, Sidney is not interested in *commercial* art.

B: Me, too. After all, he has taken it for three years.

A: 真让我惊讶, 悉尼对商业美术不感兴趣。

B: 我也是。毕竟他已经学三年了。

【派】commercialized(*a.* 商业化的)

compliment ['kɑ:mplɪmənt] *n.* 赞美, 恭维(praise) *n.* [常 *pl.*]问候(regards)

['kɑ:mplɪment] *v.* 赞美, 恭维

【例】Thanks for the *compliment*. 谢谢您的赞誉。

【派】complimentary(*a.* 赞赏的)

【参】complement(*vt.* 补充); implement(*n.* 工具 *vt.* 实现)

concert ['kɑ:nsərt] *n.* 一致(agreement); 音乐会(musicale)

【派】concerted(*a.* 互相配合的)

convey [kən'veɪ] *vt.* 运(送、输)(carry, transport); 传达(communicate, transfer)

【记】词根记忆: con(共同) + vey(道路)→ 共同用路 → 运送; 传达

【例】I would *convey* the sense of adventure that cavers share. 我将传达一下洞穴探索者所共有的冒险意识。

deadly ['dedli] *a.* 致命的(deathful, fatal)

【例】They were bitten by *deadly* insects. 他们被致命的昆虫咬了。

decline [dɪ'klaɪn] *n./v.* 下降(descend); 衰退(decay)

【记】词根记忆: de(向下) + cline(倾斜)→ 向下倾斜 → 下降; 衰退

【例】After the peak year of 1957, the birth rate in Canada began to *decline*. 过了1957年这个高峰期, 加拿大的出生率开始下降了。

【派】declining(*a.* 下降的, 衰退的)

【参】recline(*v.* 放置); incline(*v.* 倾斜)

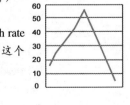

decline

devise [dɪ'vaɪz] *vt.* 设计(contrive); 发明(invent); 想出(think out)

【例】Every year the company *devises* a new plan. 公司每年都会设计出一项新计划。

differentiate [ˌdɪfəˈrenʃieɪt] *v.* (使)不同; 区别(distinguish)

【记】来自different(*a.* 不同的)

【例】Export merchants became *differentiated* from their importing counterparts. 出口商与进口商区分开了。

dilute [daɪˈluːt] *vt.* 稀释, 淡化(desalt)

【记】词根记忆: di + lute(冲洗) → 冲淡 → 稀释, 淡化

【例】Here the ocean is being *diluted* so that the salinity is decreased. 在这里海洋被稀释了, 这样盐度就降低了。

dismal [ˈdɪzməl] *a.* 阴沉的(gloomy); 忧郁的(blue)

【记】来自拉丁语dies mail, 意为"不吉利的日子", 后转变为"阴沉的, 悲伤的"

【例】The *dismal*, cold day depressed every one. 阴郁寒冷的天气令每个人都感到了压抑。

display [dɪˈspleɪ] *vt./n.* 陈列(*exhibit); 展示(demonstrate); 显示(show)

【搭】on display 展览

【例】Her artwork is *displayed* in a museum. 她的艺术品在博物馆展出。//Birds also *display* remarkable behavior in collecting building materials. 鸟类在搜集筑巢材料方面展示出了不同寻常的行为。

donate [ˈdoʊneɪt] *v.* 捐赠(contribute); 赠送(present)

【记】词根记忆: don(给予) + ate → 捐赠; 赠送

【例】A local business has *donated* these "Do Not Litter" signs to the club. 当地一家公司给俱乐部赠送了这些"请勿乱丢杂物"的标识。

【派】donation(*n.* 捐款, 捐赠物)

dubious [ˈduːbiəs] *a.* 可疑的(questionable)

【记】词根记忆: dub(二, 双) + ious → 前后两种态度的 → 有问题 → 可疑的

【例】I am *dubious* that a new stove will improve my cooking. 我对新炉子能提高我的烹饪技术持怀疑态度。

durable [ˈdʊrəbl] *a.* 持久的, 耐用的(*long-lasting, *lasting)

【记】词根记忆: dur(持续) + able → 持久的

【例】Beads were probably the first *durable* ornaments humans possessed. 珠子可能是人类最先拥有的耐用的装饰品。

【派】durability(*n.* 持久, 耐用)

dye [daɪ] *n.* 颜料, 染料 *vt.* 染色

【记】联想记忆: 劣质染料(dye)会导致人死亡(die)

elm [elm] *n.* 榆树

| ☐ differentiate | ☐ dilute | ☐ dismal | ☐ display | ☐ donate | ☐ dubious |
| ☐ durable | ☐ dye | ☐ elm | | | |

emotional [ɪ'mouʃnl] *a.* 感情(上)的, 情绪(上)的

【例】Very soon, these differences in adult stress and intonation can influence babies' *emotional* states and behavior. 很快, 成人话语中的重读和语调的不同能影响婴儿的情绪状态和行为。

【派】emotionally(*ad.* 在情绪上)

【参】emotive(*a.* 使感动的)

entrance ['entrəns] *n.* 入口

【记】来自enter(*v.* 进入)

【例】The huge stone over the *entrance* of the temple was cut away. 寺庙入口上方的大石头被切掉了。

environmental [ɪnˌvaɪrən'mentl] *a.* 由个人环境(产生)的, 个人环境的; 环境的

【搭】environmental science class 环境科学课

【例】Let's talk about an *environmental* issue that has to do with how common household products have changed. 让我们来谈论一个环境问题, 这与普通家庭用品如何改变有关。

A: Hi, Jim. What are you doing?

B: Oh. Hi, Linda. I'm working on a report on energy resources for my *environmental* science class.

A: 你好, 吉姆。你在干什么?

B: 哦。你好, 琳达。我在为环境科学课写一份能源资源报告。

exterior [ɪk'stɪrɪər] *n./a.* 外部(的), 外表(的)(outside)

【例】In day-to-day use, the potter smoothed the *exterior* surface of the pot with wet hands. 在日常使用中, 陶工用湿漉漉的手弄平了陶器的外表面。

【参】interior(*n.* 内部 *a.* 内部的)

extremity [ɪk'streməti] *n.* 末端; 极端, 极度

【例】The poor man was in an *extremity* of pain after being driven out of home. 这个穷人在被赶出家门后处于极度痛苦之中。

faint [feɪnt] *a.* 暗淡的, 模糊的(dizzy)

【例】Astronomers use sighting telescopes to study the motions of many of the *faint* stars. 天文学家使用瞄准望远镜来研究很多暗星的运动。

【参】feint(*vi.* 佯攻)

formation [fɔːr'meɪʃn] *n.* 形成, 构成; 编队

【记】分拆联想: form(形式) + at + ion → 固定的形式 → 形成, 构成

【例】I am reading an article about the *formation* of snowflakes. 我在读一篇关于雪花形成的文章。

genre [ˈʒɑːnrə] *n.* 类型(type)；流派(style)

【记】词根记忆：gen(种，属) + re → 类型；流派

【例】These writers can genuinely be said to have created a *genre*. 可以说这些作家真正创造了一个流派。

gravel [ˈɡrævl] *n.* 沙砾，砾石

【记】分拆联想：grav(重的) + el → 沙砾很重 → 沙砾

【参】engrave(*vt.* 雕刻)

hardy [ˈhɑːrdi] *a.* 强壮的(strong)；(植物等)耐寒的

【记】分拆联想：hard(硬的) + y(…的) → 强壮的；耐寒的

【例】The dachshund is a *hardy*, alert dog with a good sense of smell. 达克斯狗是一种身体强壮且警觉的狗，嗅觉非常灵敏。

hardy

hemp [hemp] *n.* 【植】大麻(纤维)；由大麻制成的麻醉药

【搭】grow hemp 种植大麻

【例】It is illegal to grow *hemp* in the United States, although some related medicines are legally imported. 在美国种植大麻非法，尽管相关药物可以合法进口。

impose [ɪmˈpouz] *vt.* 把…强加于(demand)；征(税)(levy)

【记】词根记忆：im(使…) + pos(放) + e → 强行放置 → 把…强加于

【搭】impose on sb. 占某人便宜(尤指施加不当的压力)

【例】New regulations were *imposed* on nontraditional education. 新规定被强加于非传统教育。//The government *imposed* a new tax on public entertainment. 政府对公共娱乐征收了一项新税。

【派】imposing(*a.* 壮观的；令人难忘的)

incinerate [ɪnˈsɪnəreɪt] *v.* 焚化(cremate)

【记】词根记忆：in(使) + ciner(灰) + ate → 使成灰 → 焚化

【例】Dry leaves *incinerate* easily. 干树叶很容易焚化。

【派】incinerator(*n.* 焚化炉)

incompatible [ˌɪnkəmˈpætəbl] *a.* 不协调的，合不来的；不兼容的，不能和谐共存的

【记】词根记忆：in(不) + com + pat(感情) + ible → 感情不一致的 → 合不来的，不能和谐共处的

【例】After a week together on a field trip, it is obvious that partners are totally *incompatible*. 共同进行校外旅行一周后，同组伙伴们之间明显完全合不来。

inevitably [ɪnˈevɪtəbli] *ad.* 不可避免地，必然地（*unavoidably, necessarily）

【记】来自inevitable（*a.* 不可避免的）

【例】The focus of educators and of laymen interested in education *inevitably* turned toward the lower grades. 教育家和对教育感兴趣的门外汉不可避免地将其关注点转向了更低的年级。

inherent [ɪnˈhɪrənt] *a.* 固有的；内在的；先天的

【记】词根记忆：in（内在）+ her（继承人）+ ent → 天生继承下来的 → 先天的；固有的

【例】Homing pigeons are not unique in this *inherent* skill. 并非只有信鸽才有这种先天的技能。

【派】inherently（*ad.* 天性地；固有地）

inhibit [ɪnˈhɪbɪt] *vt.* 阻碍，抑制（*hinder）

【记】词根记忆：in（不）+ hibit（拿住）→ 不让拿住 → 阻碍，抑制

【例】They may discipline group members who *inhibit* attainment of the group's goals. 他们可以处罚那些阻碍实现团队目标的成员。

【派】inhibition（*n.* 阻止，禁止）

intentionally [ɪnˈtenʃənəli] *ad.* 有意地，特意地

justice [ˈdʒʌstɪs] *n.* 法官；公正（equity）；司法

【记】来自just（*a.* 正义的，公正的）

【例】Martin Luther King Jr.'s magnificent speaking ability enabled him to effectively express the demands for social *justice* for Black Americans. 马丁·路德·金伟大的演说才能使他有效地表达了美国黑人对社会公平的要求。

kennel [ˈkenl] *n.* 狗舍，狗窝

【记】词根记忆：ken（=can 犬）+ nel → 狗窝；注意不要和kernel（*n.* 核心）相混

【例】When the dog escaped, the bird went into the *kennel* and ate its food. 这条狗逃跑之后，鸟钻进狗窝吃了它的食物。

librarian [laɪˈbreriən] *n.* 图书管理员

【记】分拆联想：librar(y)（图书馆）+ ian → 图书管理员。

lodge [lɑːdʒ] *n.* （海狸等的）巢穴

【记】发音记忆："落脚" → 落脚的地方 → 巢穴

【例】The beaver's penchant for building *lodges* and canals has got it into a lot of hot water lately. 海狸搭巢和筑坝的嗜好最近使其遇到了很多麻烦。

mast [mæst] *n.* 船桅

| inevitably | inherent | inhibit | intentionally | justice | kennel |
| librarian | lodge | mast | | | |

mercy ['mɜːrsi] *n.* 宽恕(*condone)；仁慈(sympathy)
【搭】at the mercy of 受…支配
【例】Our pilots are at the *mercy* of the winds, so who knows where they'll drift off to. 我们的飞行员受风的支配，所以谁知道他们会飘到哪里呢。

modest ['mɑːdɪst] *a.* 谦虚的；适度的(mild, decent)
【记】词根记忆：mod(方式，风度)＋est → 做事有风度 → 谦虚的；适度的
【例】The national debt had shot up from a *modest* \$65 million in 1861. 国债在1861年从适度的6500万美元猛增。
【派】modestly(*ad.* 谨慎地；适度地)

modest

naval ['neɪvl] *a.* 海军的
【记】词根记忆：nav(船)＋al → 船的 → 在海上的 → 海军的
【搭】naval academy 海军军官学校

needy ['niːdi] *a.* 贫穷的(poor)；生活艰苦的
【记】联想记忆：need(需要)＋y(…的) → 什么都需要的 → 贫穷的
【例】The two financially *needy* writers would receive enough money so they could devote themselves entirely to "prose literature". 两位经济拮据的作家会得到足够的资金，这样他们就能完全投入到"散文"创作中。

noxious ['nɑːkʃəs] *a.* 有害的(*harmful)；有毒的(poisonous)
【记】词根记忆：nox(毒)＋ious → 有毒的
【例】The result is an increased concentration of *noxious* chemicals in the air. 结果是空气中有毒化学品的浓度增加。

opponent [ə'poʊnənt] *n.* 对手，反对者(adversary, objector)
【记】词根记忆：op(相反)＋pon(放置)＋ent(人) → 立场不同的人 → 对手
【例】Our football team's *opponents* won the game. 我们足球队的对手赢得了比赛。

optional ['ɑːpʃənl] *a.* 随意的；非强制的(voluntary)
【记】分拆联想：option(选择)＋al → 可以任意选择的 → 随意的；非强制的
【例】In place of the usual Wednesday class, I've arranged an *optional* review session. Since it is *optional*, attendance will not be taken. 平时周三的课换了，我已经安排了可任选的复习课。既然是选修的，就不会记考勤。

| mercy | modest | naval | needy | noxious | opponent |
| optional |

A: Woo, are all those books you've got there required for the modern European history class?

B: No, a lot of these listed are *optional*, but you know me, when I do something, I do it 200 percent.

A：哇，你所有那些书都是现代欧洲历史课所需的吗？

B：不，很多列出的书都是可选的，但是你了解我，我做什么事都要付出百分之二百的努力。

ore [ɔːr] *n.* 矿物，矿石(mineral)

【记】联想记忆：矿石(ore)多一个m就是更多(more)

【参】roe(*n.* 鱼卵)

pants [pænts] *n.* 短裤(shorts)

part-time [ˌpɑːrt 'taɪm] *a.* 兼职的，部分时间的

【搭】part-time job 兼职工作

【例】A: You know that promotion I thought I was going to get at the bookstore? Well, I didn't, so I'm going to see my boss tomorrow and tell her I've had it.

B: Oh, I understand that you are upset, but, you know there just aren't a lot of *part-time* jobs out there right now. Try to keep that in mind before doing anything drastic, OK?

A：你知道我本以为我会在书店得到晋升的，结果我没被晋升，所以我明天要见见老板，告诉她我受够了。

B：哦，我理解你比较烦，但是你知道现在兼职工作不多。做极端的事情之前要记住这一点，好吗？

【参】full-time(*a.* 全职的)

permit [pər 'mɪt] *v.* 允许，许可(enable, allow)

['pɜːrmɪt] *n.* 许可证，执照(license)

【记】词根记忆：per + mit(送，放出) → 许可，允许

【例】She is not *permitted* to live off campus this year. 今年她没有获准住在校外。//His parking *permit* expired. 他的停车证过期了。

【派】permission(*n.* 许可)

photography [fə 'tɑːgrəfi] *n.* 摄影术，摄影

【记】词根记忆：photo(照片) + graph(图，写) + y → 摄影，摄影术

【搭】art photography 艺术摄影

【例】He became interested in *photography* and began to experiment with his camera. 他对摄影感兴趣，并且开始用他的相机做实验了。

【派】photographic(*a.* 摄影的，摄影用的)

popular ['pɑːpjələr] *a.* 通俗的；受欢迎的(*refreshing)；流行的(fashionable)

【记】词根记忆：popul(人民) + ar → 受广大人民喜欢的 → 受欢迎的

【搭】popular tune 流行歌曲

【派】popularize(*v.* 普及)；popularization(*n.* 普及)

posit ['pɑːzɪt] *v.* 安排(arrange)；假定(assume)

【记】分拆联想：po + sit(坐) → 坐下来 → 安置

precise [prɪˈsaɪs] *a.* 准确的，精确的(*accurate, exact)

【记】词根记忆：preci(价值，价格) + se → 定价一般都很准确 → 准确的

【例】The definition is not *precise*. 这个定义不准确。

【派】precisely(*ad.* 精确地；正好)

现在是北京时间 10点49分50秒25毫秒 39微秒6纳秒 52皮秒…

问询处

precise

provision [prəˈvɪʒn] *n.* 准备，预备(preparation)；供应(provision)

【记】来自provide(*v.* 提供)

【例】Standard music notation makes no *provision* for many of these innovations. 标准音符没有为很多创新作准备。

quantify ['kwɑːntɪfaɪ] *v.* 量化(to measure the quantity of)

【例】Scientists have tried to *quantify* this proportion of the Sun's energy. 科学家们已经试图量化太阳能的大小。

【派】quantitative(*a.* 数量的；定量的)；quantity(*n.* 量，数量)

receiver [rɪˈsiːvər] *n.* 接收器

recharge [ˌriːˈtʃɑːrdʒ] *vt.* 再充电；再装弹药

【搭】recharge batteries 为电池充电

【例】Swimming is a best way to relieve stress and *recharge* yourself. 游泳是缓解压力、养精蓄锐的最好办法。

rendition [renˈdɪʃn] *n.* 表演，演唱(performance)

reproduce [ˌriːprəˈduːs] *v.* 繁殖；复制(*copy)

reproduce

【记】re(再) + produce(生产) → 不断生产 → 繁殖；复制

【例】They've learned how to *reproduce* these cells. 他们已经学会了如何复制这些细胞。

【派】reproduction(*n.* 繁殖；复制品)；reproductive(*a.* 生殖的；再生的)

rub [rʌb] *n./v.* 擦，摩擦

【记】rubber(*n.* 橡皮)就是来自这个词

popular	posit	precise	provision	quantify	receiver
recharge	rendition	reproduce	rub		

【例】If you *rub* some soap on that drawer, it might stop sticking. 如果你在抽屉上擦点肥皂，抽屉可能就不会再卡住了。

sacred [ˈseɪkrɪd] *a.* 宗教(性)的(religious); 神圣不可侵犯的(holy)

【记】词根记忆: sacr(神圣的) + ed(…的) → 神圣不可侵犯的

scene [siːn] *n.* 地点，现场(location, spot); 景色(setting, spectacle)

【派】scenic(*a.* 风景如画的); scenery(*n.* 现场; 景色)

secrete [sɪˈkriːt] *vt.* 分泌(excrete)

【记】和secret(*a.* 秘密的)一起记

【例】This substance is *secreted* from cells in the intestinal walls. 这种物质是从肠壁的细胞中分泌出来的。

【派】secretion(*n.* 分泌，分泌物)

【参】secretin(*n.* 分泌素)

sedentary [ˈsednteri] *a.* 土生的，不移栖的(*unchangeable, settled)

【记】词根记忆: sed(坐) + entary → 久坐于此的 → 土生的

【例】These incursions disrupted the Old European *sedentary* farming lifestyle that had existed for 3,000 years. 这些入侵扰乱了持续了3000年的老欧式农业生活方式。

seem [siːm] *v.* 好像，似乎(appear)

【例】A: I was going to get something to eat at the cafeteria, but it *seems* to be closed.

B: Oh, that's because it's Sunday. Why don't you come with me to a place I know?

A: 我本来打算在餐厅弄点吃的，但是好像关门了。

B: 哦，那是因为今天是周日。你为什么不和我去个我知道的地方呢?

settlement [ˈsetlmənt] *n.* 住宅区

shatter [ˈʃætər] *v.* 使…粉碎，破碎(destroy, smash)

【记】发音记忆: "筛它" → 使…粉碎，破碎

【例】This is why glass *shatters* so easily. 这就是为什么玻璃这么容易碎的原因。

【参】shutter(*n.* 百叶窗; (照相机的)快门)

significance [sɪɡˈnɪfɪkəns] *n.* 意义，含义(sense); 重要性(importance)，重大

【记】来自significant(*a.* 有意义的，重大的)

【搭】historical significance 历史意义

【例】Nowadays the juvenile crime problems have great *significance* to social development. 现在，青少年犯罪问题对社会发展关系重大。

sour [ˈsaʊər] *a.* 酸(味)的(acid)

【记】发音记忆: "馊啊" → 酸的

| sacred | scene | secrete | sedentary | seem | settlement |
| shatter | significance | sour | | | |

staple [ˈsteɪpl] *n.* 主要(食品,产品); 原材料(*basic element) *vt.* 把…订起来(fasten) *a.* 主要的(*important)
【记】和stable(*a.* 稳定的)一起记
【搭】staple cotton 原棉

startling [ˈstɑːrtlɪŋ] *a.* 惊人的(astonishing)
【记】来自startle(*v.* 震惊)

stellar [ˈstelər] *a.* 恒星的

successive [səkˈsesɪv] *a.* 接连的, 连续的(subsequent)
【记】来自succeed(*v.* 接替)
【搭】successive generation 连续世代
【例】The team has won five *successive* games. 这个队已经连续赢了5场比赛。
【参】succession(*n.* 连续, 一系列)

tantalizing [ˈtæntəlaɪzɪŋ] *a.* 诱人的
【例】It was really a *tantalizing* night together with my classmates in the resort. 和同学们在度假胜地共度的那个夜晚真是美妙。

tantalizing

tectonics [tekˈtɑːnɪks] *n.* 构造地质学
【记】词根记忆: tect(遮蔽) + on + ics → 遮蔽在地球表面上的 → 构造地质学
【搭】the theory of plate tectonics 板块构造学说

torpor [ˈtɔːrpər] *n.* 迟钝, 不活泼(lethargy, inertia)

trigger [ˈtrɪgər] *vt.* 引发, 导致(cause, kindle)
【例】Pheromones are chemical signals *triggering* behavioral responses. 信息素是引发行为反应的化学信号。

Happiness, I have discovered, is nearly always a rebound from hard work.
我发现,辛勤工作的报酬几乎总是幸福。

——格雷森.D.(*David Grayson*)

☐ staple　　☐ startling　　☐ stellar　　☐ successive　　☐ tantalizing　　☐ tectonics
☐ torpor　　☐ trigger

词根、词缀预习表

proxim	接近	approximate	*v.* 近似 *a.* 大约的
archae	古	archaeology	*n.* 考古学
siege	包围	besiege	*vt.* 包围
flict	打击	conflict	*n.* 冲突
vict	征服	convict	*vt.* 定罪；宣告
licit	引导	elicit	*vt.* 得出，引出
viscer	内脏	eviscerate	*vt.* 取出内脏
integr	完整	integral	*a.* 不可分割的
neur	神经	neuron	*n.* 神经元
peri	周围的	periphery	*n.* 外围

absorption [əbˈsɔːrpʃn] *n.* 吸收(assimilation, reception)；专心

【例】Bosses really appreciate Jim's complete *absorption* in his work. 老板们很赏识吉姆对工作的全心投入。

accomplish [əˈkɑːmplɪʃ] *vt.* 达到(reach)；完成(complete)；实现(realize)

【记】词根记忆：ac + compl(满) + ish → 圆满 → 完成

【例】Human labor could still *accomplish* as much work as the first machines. 人工仍然可以完成最初的机器能完成的工作量。

【派】accomplishment(*n.* 成就)

adjunct [ˈædʒʌŋkt] *n.* 附加物，附件(*addition, accessory)

【记】词根记忆：ad + junct(结合，连接) → 连在上面的东西 → 附加物

【例】The garage is an *adjunct* to the house. 车库是房子的附加物。

appointment [əˈpɔɪntmənt] *n.* 约会(date)；约定(faith)

approximate [əˈprɑːksɪmeɪt] *v.* 近似(close to) *a.* [əˈprɑːksɪmət] 大约的(about)

【记】词根记忆：ap + proxim(接近) + ate → 近似；大约的

【例】The Greeks first calculated the *approximate* distance around the circumference of the earth. 希腊人首先计算出了地球圆周的大概距离。

absorption　accomplish　adjunct　appointment　approximate

【派】approximately(*ad.* 近似地，大约)

【参】proximity(*n.* 接近，邻近)

archaeology [ˌɑːrkiˈɑːlədʒi] *n.* 考古学

【记】词根记忆：archae(古) + ology(⋯学) → 考古学

【派】archaeological(*a.* 考古学上的); archaeologist(*n.* 考古学家)

attribute [ˈætrɪbjuːt] *n.* 属性(*characteristic, trait)

[əˈtrɪbjuːt] *vt.* 把⋯归结于(ascribe)

【记】词根记忆：at + tribute(付，赠与) → 把⋯归结于

【例】John has many good *attributes* that make him eligible for the job. 约翰有很多优点，这使得他能够胜任这份工作。//Jane *attributed* her lateness to the heavy traffic. 简把迟到归因于拥挤的交通。

【派】attribution(*n.* 归因)

【参】tribute(*n.* 产物; 贡物); distribute(*vt.* 分发); contribute(*v.* 捐助)

barter [ˈbɑːrtər] *n./v.* 实物交易(trade, deal)

【记】分拆联想：bar(酒吧) + ter → 酒吧可作为交易双方谈判易货的场所 → 实物交易

【例】Food could be *bartered* for other commodities long ago. 很久以前食物可以用来换取其他商品。

besiege [bɪˈsiːdʒ] *vt.* 包围(surround)

【记】分拆联想：be + siege(包围) → 包围

【例】Almost daily the public is *besieged* by claims for "no-aging" diets, new vitamins, and other wonder foods. 几乎每天公众都被"驻颜"膳食、新维生素和其他特效食品的宣称所包围。

boost [buːst] *vt.* 提高，推进(*raise, push)

【记】分拆联想：boo(看作boot，靴子) + st → 穿上靴子往高处走 → 提高

【例】These innovations in manufacturing *boosted* output and living standards to an unprecedented extent. 这些生产创新以前所未有的程度促进了产出，提高了生活水平。

【参】boast(*n./v.* 自夸)

bouquet [buˈkeɪ] *n.* 花束(bunch)

【搭】bouquet garni 香料包

【例】The students put a *bouquet* of roses and lilies in front of the monument. 学生们在纪念碑前献了一束玫瑰和百合花。

【参】banquet(*n.* 宴会，盛宴)

broadcast [ˈbrɔːdkæst] *n./v.* 广播

【例】A: We need to let everyone know about the benefit of the concert, but we don't have much money for advertising.

B: How about using the school radio station? They *broadcast* free public service announcements.

A：我们需要让每个人了解音乐会的益处，但是我们用于广告的资金不多。

B：使用学校电台如何？他们免费播放公共服务通知。

calm [kɑːm] *a.* (天气、海洋等)平静的；镇静的，沉着的(tranquil, cool, composed) *vt.* 使平静，使镇定，平息(tranquilize, soothe)

【记】联想记忆：她手(palm)心出汗，内心很不平静(calm)

【例】A majority of people take investment in stock market seriously because the financial markets are still not *calm* at the moment. 多数人都谨慎地投资股市，因为目前金融市场仍然不稳定。

chief [tʃiːf] *n.* 首领(leader, head) *a.* 主要的(*primary)；总的(total)

collision [kəˈlɪʒn] *n.* 碰撞，冲突

【记】来自collide(*vi.* 冲撞)

【搭】a collision of interests 利益冲突

【例】The biggest surprise is the role of air resistance in cushioning the shock of *collision*. 空气阻力在缓冲碰撞中起到的作用是令人惊奇的。

conflict [ˈkɑːnflɪkt] *n.* 冲突(clash)；不一致(disagreement)；争论(dispute)
[kənˈflɪkt] *vi.* 冲突(clash)；不一致(disagree)；争论(argue)

【记】词根记忆：con(共同) + flict(打击) → 互相打 → 冲突

【例】All the other work schedules *conflict* with his classes. 其他所有的工作安排都与他的课程冲突。

【参】afflict(*v.* 使痛苦，折磨)；inflict(*v.* 造成)

continent [ˈkɑːntɪnənt] *n.* 大陆(mainland)

【派】continental[*a.* 大陆(性)的]

convict [kənˈvɪkt] *vt.* 定罪，宣告…有罪(criminate)

【记】词根记忆：con + vict (征服；胜利) → 征服罪犯 → 定罪

【例】The jury *convicted* the man, and he was sentenced to twenty years in prison. 陪审团宣告此人有罪，他被判入狱20年。

【派】conviction(*n.* 确信)

【参】evict(*v.* 驱逐)；victorious(*a.* 胜利的)

cookout [ˈkʊkaʊt] *n.* 野外郊游时烹调的野餐，野烹食物 *a.* 野外烹饮聚会的

【例】Tom will bring food for the Friday night *cookout* for everyone. 汤姆周五晚上将给每个人带野外烹调的食物。

critical [ˈkrɪtɪkl] *a.* 批评的，非难的(disapproving)；非常重要的(*essential, crucial)；危急的

【派】uncritical(*a.* 不加批判的)

cylinder [ˈsɪlɪndər] *n.* 圆柱体；气缸

decay [dɪˈkeɪ] *v./n.* 腐烂(*rot)；衰落(decline)

【例】The rest of the organism has *decayed*. 生物体的其余部分已经腐烂。//The San Antonio project was designed to combat urban *decay*. 圣安东尼奥项目旨在防止城市衰落。

derive [dɪˈraɪv] *v.* 得自(from)，源于(originate)

【记】分拆联想：de + rive(r)(河水) → 黄河是中华文明的发源地 → 源于

【例】The subject of a sculpture should be *derived* from classical stories. 雕塑的主题可能源自古典故事。

dessert [dɪˈzɜːrt] *n.* (餐后)甜点

【参】desert(*n.* 沙漠 *v.* 放弃)；dissert(*vi.* 写论文)

dispersal [dɪˈspɜːsl] *n.* 疏散，散开

domesticate [dəˈmestɪkeɪt] *vt.* 驯养，驯化(cultivate)

【记】来自domestic(*a.* 家庭的)

【例】In ancient times, wild animals were caught and *domesticated* to serve human beings. 在古代，人们捕捉野生动物并将其驯化，使其为人类服务。

【派】domesticated(*a.* 驯养的，家养的)；domestication(*n.* 驯养，驯服)

drag [dræg] *vt.* 拖动(pull, move, haul)

【记】本身为词根，意为"拉"

due [duː] *a.* 到期的；由于(owe to)；预订的(scheduled)

【搭】due to 由于；due date 到期日；支付日

【例】I can't remember the *due* date for our final paper. 我想不起来论文的截止日期。

elicit [iˈlɪsɪt] *vt.* 得出，引出(*bring out, educe)

【记】词根记忆：e(出) + licit(引导) → 得出，引出

【例】Even questions that are less structured must be carefully phrased in order to *elicit* the type of information desired. 甚至设置得较差的问题都必须措辞严谨，以引出所想要的信息类型。

cookout	critical	cylinder	decay	derive	dessert
dispersal	domesticate	drag	due	elicit	

escape [ɪ'skeɪp] v. 逃脱, 逃走(flee); 避开, 避免(elude, avoid)

【例】There was no *escaping* the fact that the financial crisis had a great effect on global economy. 金融危机对全球经济产生了重大的影响, 这个事实不可回避。

【派】escapist[a./n. 逃避现实的(人)]

eviscerate [ɪ'vɪsəreɪt] vt. 取出内脏; 除去主要部分

【记】词根记忆: e + viscer(内脏) + ate → 取出内脏

fin [fɪn] n. 鳍

【搭】dorsal fin 背鳍

format ['fɔːrmæt] n. 设计; 安排; 样式 vt. 使格式化

【记】词根记忆: form(形式) + at → 固定的形式 → 样式

【搭】the format of a program 节目的编排

【例】Your presentation *format*, your grammar, all that stuff, they are looking at in your materials at the same time. 你的报告格式、语法等所有你材料里的这些东西, 他们都同时在研究。//The professor hopes to cover the entire process of writing a research paper, from selecting a topic to putting together the final *format* and presentation. 教授希望讲授撰写研究型论文的整个过程, 即从选题到组织最终的格式和作报告。

gorilla [gə'rɪlə] n. 大猩猩

【记】分拆联想: go(去) + rill(小河) + a → 到河边去看大猩猩 → 大猩猩

healthful ['helθfl] a. 有益健康的

hide [haɪd] vi. 躲藏; 掩藏(conceal), 掩盖(cover) n. 兽皮(skin)

【例】She couldn't *hide* her excitement. 她无法掩饰自己的兴奋。

hinterland ['hɪntərlænd] n. 内地, 腹地(backland); 内地贸易区(*region)

【记】组合词: hinter(=hinder, 后面的) + land(土地) → 内地, 腹地

【例】Dunhuang is located in the *hinterland* of the great desert. 敦煌处于大漠的腹地。

hypothesize [haɪ'pɑːθəsaɪz] vt. 假定(*speculate), 假设(suppose)

【记】词根记忆: hypo(在…下面) + thes(看作thet, 放) + ize → 放在下面, 不作为正式的 → 假定

【例】One researcher *hypothesized* that there were two parts to the explanation. 一位研究人员假设这个解释有两个部分。

【参】hypothesis(n. 假设; 前提); hypothetical(a. 假设的)

ignorant ['ɪgnərənt] a. 无知的(*naive); 不知道的(unaware)

【记】词根记忆: ig(不) + nor(看作gnor, 知道) + ant → 不知道的 → 无知的

| □ escape | □ eviscerate | □ fin | □ format | □ gorilla | □ healthful |
| □ hide | □ hinterland | □ hypothesize | □ ignorant | | |

173

【例】The scholar argues that without formal education people would remain *ignorant*. 这个学者辩称没有受过正规教育的人们会依旧无知。

【派】ignorance(*n.* 无知，不了解)

integral ['ɪntɪɡrəl] *a.* 构成整体所必需的；不可分割的(*fundamental)

【记】词根记忆：integr(完整) + al(…的) → 完整的 → 不可分割的

【例】Martha developed a powerful, expressive style that was *integral* to the foundations of modern dance. 玛莎形成了强大而富有表现力的风格，这是构成现代舞蹈中不可或缺的一部分。

lash [læʃ] *v.* 将(物品)系牢(fasten)；(风、雨等)猛烈打击

【记】分拆联想：l + ash(灰) → 敌人的鞭打似有挫骨扬灰之势 → 猛烈打击

【例】There are other drums that have skins *lashed* onto both sides. 有的鼓两面都绑有皮面。//Freak rainstorms once *lashed* in the central and southern sections of the state. 怪异的风暴曾在这个州的中南部肆虐。

layout ['leɪaʊt] *n.* 规划，布局(arrangement)

【记】来自词组lay out(布置，安排)

【例】Municipal planners deal chiefly with the physical *layout* of communities. 城市规划者主要负责社区的实体布局。

locally ['ləʊkəli] *ad.* 在本地

【记】来自local(地方的，当地的) + ly → 在本地

【例】Such sculpture is less expensive to produce *locally* than to import. 这种雕塑在本地生产要比进口便宜。

lure [lʊr] *vt.* 吸引，诱惑(*attract, tempt) *n.* 诱惑力

【记】联想记忆：纯(pure)属诱惑(lure)

【例】Many adults were *lured* to the cities by promises of steady employment. 很多成年人被稳定的就业前景吸引，纷纷来到城市。

magnet ['mægnət] *n.* 磁铁，磁体(lodestone)

【例】Both nickel and iron are whitish metals that are attracted by *magnets*. 镍和铁都是能被磁铁吸引的白色金属。

【派】magnetism (*n.* 磁力)；magnetize (*v.* 磁化)

magnet

minute [maɪ'njuːt] *a.* 微小的(*tiny)；详细的

【例】A snowfall consists of myriads of *minute* ice crystals that fall to the ground. 降雪由无数落到地上的极小的冰晶体构成。

□ integral	□ lash	□ layout	□ locally	□ lure	□ magnet
□ minute					

modem [ˈmoʊdem] *n.* 调制解调器

【例】She hooks up her telephone *modem* connections. 她连接上电话调制解调器。

neuron [ˈnʊrɑːn] *n.* 神经元，神经细胞

【记】词根记忆：neur(神经) + on(物) → 神经元

noticeable [ˈnoʊtɪsəbl] *a.* 明显的 (*conspicuous, outstanding)；值得注意的 (remarkable)

【记】来自notice(注意) + able → 值得注意的

【例】Red lettering on signs is much more *noticeable* than blue. 标识的红色字母比蓝色更加引人注目。

notwithstanding [ˌnɑːtwɪθˈstændɪŋ] *ad./prep.* 虽然，尽管如此 (despite)

【例】The teams played on, *notwithstanding* the rain. 尽管下着雨，两个队仍继续比赛。

opposite [ˈɑːpəzət] *a.* (to)对立的，相反的 (contrary) *n.* 相反的事物

【例】The window is *opposite* the heater. 窗户对着加热器。

【派】opposition(*n.* 反对)

overlap [ˌoʊvərˈlæp] *vt.* (与…)交叠

overlap

【例】The end of the first scene *over-lapped* the beginning of the second. 第一幕的结尾与第二幕的开始重合了。

【派】overlapping(*a.* 重叠的)

periphery [pəˈrɪfəri] *n.* 外围 (circumference, boundary)

【记】词根记忆：peri(周围的) + pher(带来) + y → 带到周围 → 外围

prairie [ˈpreri] *n.* 大草原

【记】分拆联想：pr + air(空气) + ie → 大草原上空气好 → 大草原

predator [ˈpredətər] *n.* 食肉动物

【记】词根记忆：predat(破坏；掠夺) + or → 掠夺者 → 食肉动物

【例】Some birds elevate their nests in branches perhaps to avoid *predators*. 一些鸟把窝建到高处的树枝，可能是为了躲避食肉动物。

【派】predatory(*a.* 食肉的)

predict [prɪˈdɪkt] *v.* 预言，预测 (expect, foretell)

【记】词根记忆：pre(在前的) + dict(说) → 预言，预测

【例】Experts *predict* that the gourmet coffee market in the United States is growing. 专家们预计美国的精品咖啡市场需求将会增长。

【派】predictable(*a.* 可预言的，可预报的)；predictability(*n.* 可预言)；prediction(*n.* 预言，预报)

【参】addict(*vt.* 使沉溺)；contradict(*vt.* 同…矛盾)；indict(*vt.* 起诉)

predictable [prɪˈdɪktəbl] *a.* 可预见的(expectable, likely)

【派】prediction(*n.* 预言，预报)；predictive(*a.* 预言性的，成为先兆的)；unpredictable(*a.* 不可预知的)

【例】To some degree, a *predictable* life is not very exciting. 在某种程度上说，可预知的生活缺少新鲜感。

prehistoric [ˌpriːhɪˈstɔːrɪk] *a.* 史前的；陈旧的

【记】词根记忆：pre(前)＋historic(历史的) → 史前的

【例】Archaeology has long been an accepted tool for studying *prehistoric* cultures. 考古学长期以来都是研究史前文化所普遍使用的工具。

previous [ˈpriːviəs] *a.* 先的，在前的(*past, preceding)

【记】词根记忆：pre(前)＋vi(道路)＋ous → 走路走在最前面的 → 在前的

【例】A library notice was sent to him at his *previous* address. 图书馆给他的通知寄到了他以前的地址。

【派】previously(*ad.* 先前，以前)

primitive [ˈprɪmətɪv] *a.* 原始的(original)，远古的(ancient)

【例】The origins of *primitive* sea life were explained. 远古海生物的起源得到了解释。

prodigious [prəˈdɪdʒəs] *a.* 巨大的(extraordinary in bulk, quantity, or degree)

【记】来自prodig(y)(惊人的事物)＋ious → 大得惊人 → 巨大的

【例】Desert animals can drink *prodigious* volumes of water in a short time. 沙漠动物可以在短时间内饮用大量的水。

professional [prəˈfeʃnl] *a.* 职业的(occupational, vocational)；专业的(*specialized) *n.* 专业人员

【例】The development of *professional* sports in the United States dates back to the nineteenth century. 美国职业运动的发展始于19世纪。

ration [ˈræʃn] *n.* 配给量，定量(quota)

【记】词根记忆：rat(理性)＋ion → 按照一定的量进行理性的配给 → 配给量，定量

raven [ˈreɪvn] *n.* 大乌鸦；掠夺 *v.* 掠夺

remark [rɪˈmɑːrk] *v.* 评论(comment)；谈论 *n.* 评论

【例】The customer agreed, and after drinking it, *remarked* how good it tasted. 这位顾客同意了，饮用之后评价味道不错。

| □ predictable | □ prehistoric | □ previous | □ primitive | □ prodigious | □ professional |
| □ ration | □ raven | □ remark | | | |

require [rɪˈkwaɪər] *vt.* 需要(need)，要求(demand)；规定

【记】词根记忆：re + quire(=quest追求)→对自己所需要的东西进行追求→需要

【例】Mechanized farming *requires* more capital and fewer laborers. 机械化农业需要更多的资金和更少的劳动力。

【派】required(*a.* 必需的)；requirement(*n.* 要求，需要)

resistance [rɪˈzɪstəns] *n.* 抵抗，反抗；抵抗力，阻力；电阻

【搭】resistance genes 抵抗基因；resistance to sth. 抵制…，抵抗…；disease resistance 抗病体

【例】The biggest surprise is the role of air *resistance* in cushioning the shock of collision. 空气阻力在缓冲碰撞中起到的作用是令人惊奇的。

responsible [rɪˈspɑːnsəbl] *a.* 有责任感的；负责的

【记】词根记忆：re + spons(约定) + ible →遵守约定→有责任感的

【例】Larry's roommate may be partly *responsible* for the problem. 拉里的室友可能对这个问题负有部分责任。

【派】responsibility(*n.* 责任，职责)

responsible

好汉做事
好汉当

Saturn [ˈsætɜːrn] *n.* 土星

save [seɪv] *vt.* 拯救(rescue)；保存(store)；节省(economize) *prep.* 除…之外(except)

【例】Similar materials will decay and vanish in dust in a few years or centuries, *save* under very exceptional conditions. 除非在非常特殊的环境下，否则类似的材料会在几年或几个世纪内腐烂消失。

seasonal [ˈsiːzənl] *a.* 季节的，季节性的

【搭】seasonal workers/employment 季工；seasonal variations 季节变更

【例】As a rule, there is a *seasonal* variation in unemployment figure. 通常来说，失业人数呈季节性变化。

【派】seasonally(*ad.* 季节性地)

sprout [spraʊt] *vi.* 萌芽，长出(grow, flourish)

【记】分拆联想：spr(看作spring，春天) + out(出)→春天来了，嫩芽长出来了→长出

【例】Its seeds cannot *sprout* on their own. 这些种子不能自己发芽。

stalk [stɔːk] *n.* 茎，柄(stem)

【记】和talk(*v.* 说话)一起记

【例】Its *stalk* is not strong enough to support its weight. 它的秸秆不够强壮，无法支撑起自身重量。

stiff [stɪf] *a.* 硬的，僵直的(rigid)；呆板的

【记】联想记忆：still(静止的)的ll变为ff就变成僵直的(stiff)

【搭】stiff paste 浓膏

【例】Her hands had become too *stiff* to sew. 她的手已变得过于僵硬，无法缝纫了。

【派】stiffen(*vt.* 使硬，使僵硬)

theory [ˈθɪri] *n.* 理论，原理；学说，见解，看法(notion)

【记】词根记忆：theo(神)+ ry → 把理论当成神来供奉 → 理论

【搭】in theory 理论上

【例】A: I might argue with some of the details, but I basically agree with managing the economy.

B: Sure it sounds great in *theory*. My concern is in practice.

A: 我可能会就一些细节有所争论，但是我基本上同意管理经济。

B: 理论上来说是不错。我关心的是实践问题。

A *theory* is that the moon was formed elsewhere in the solar system, and then it was captured, sort of speak, by earth. 一种理论认为，月亮在太阳系的其他地方形成，然后可以说被地球俘获了。

【派】theorize(*v.* 理论化，学说化)；theoretical(*a.* 理论的，理论上的)

transplant [trænsˈplænt] *v.* 迁移 (move)；移植 (transfer) *n.* [ˈtrænsplænt] 移植

【记】词根记忆：trans(转移)+ plant(种植)→ 移植

【例】The farmers gathered the baby oysters and *transplanted* them in waters to speed up their growth. 养殖户把牡蛎幼体集中起来，移植到水中以加速其生长。//The scientists might *transplant* specific genes to increase the release of the chemical signals. 科学家们可以移植特种基因来增加化学信号的释放。

tunnel [ˈtʌnl] *n.* 隧道(tube)，地道；风洞 *v.* 开(隧道)

【记】联想记忆：海峡(channel)像条长长的隧道(tunnel)

【例】These caves form a labyrinth of *tunnels*. 这些洞穴形成迷宫一般的隧道。//Did you know the proposal to *tunnel* through the silt under the Hudson River?你知道在哈德逊河下的淤泥中开挖隧道的提议吗?

undergo [ˌʌndərˈɡoʊ] *v.* 经历(*experience)；遭受(suffer)

【例】All forms of art were *undergoing* a revolution at that time. 所有的艺术形式在那个时候都在经历着革新。

velocity [vəˈlɑːsəti] *n.* 速度(speed)，速率(rate)

【记】分拆联想：velo(音似：未老) + city(城市) → 年轻的城市发展速度快 → 速度

【例】The *velocity* of a river is determined by the slope, the depth, and the roughness of the riverbed. 河流的速度由河床的坡度、深度和粗糙程度决定。

versatile [ˈvɜːrsətl] *a.* 多才多艺的(talented)；多用途的(all-purpose)

【记】词根记忆：vers (转) + atile → 在很多方面都玩得转 → 多才多艺的

【例】Her unique background made her into an unusually interesting and *versatile* human being. 独特的背景使她成为非常有趣和多才多艺的人。//It produced the *versatile* metal so crucial to the nation's growth. 这家工厂生产的多用途金属对国家的发展至关重要。

【派】versatility(*n.* 多才多艺；多功能性)

The key to the success of your career is that there are some people willing to help you and cooperate with you. This is my philosophy.

成就事业最关键的是要有人帮助你，乐意跟你工作，这就是我的哲学。

——李嘉诚(*Li Jiacheng*)

Word List 17  MP3-17

词根、词缀预习表

erg	起作用，工作	allergy	n. 过敏症
carn	肉	carnivore	n. 肉食动物
geo	地	geology	n. 地质学
grad	步，级	grading	n. 评分；等级
insul	岛	insulate	vt. 使隔离，使隔绝
milit	军事；打斗	militant	a. 好战的
uni	单一	unique	a. 唯一的
hypo	下	hypothesis	n. 假设，假说

action [ˈækʃn] n. 行为，活动（behavior）；作用（effect）

adjust [əˈdʒʌst] vt. 调整（alter, rectify）；使适合（adapt）

【记】分拆联想：ad + just（正确）→ 使正确 → 调整；使适合

【例】The basic idea is that insect pests can not *adjust* to temperatures much above normal. 基本的观点是害虫不能适应超出正常温度太高的温度。

【派】adjustment(n. 调整，调节)

allergy [ˈælərdʒi] n. 过敏症

【记】词根记忆：all + erg（起作用，工作）+ y → 这种药物对过敏症起作用 → 过敏症

【派】allergic(a. 过敏的；对…讨厌的)

arid [ˈærɪd] a. 干旱的（dry）；贫瘠的（barren）

【例】*Arid* America's soils are typically alkaline. 贫瘠的美国土壤往往都是碱性的。

aroma [əˈroʊmə] n. 香气

【记】发音记忆："爱罗马" →《罗马假日》中的奥黛丽·赫本如雏菊般芳香四溢 → 香气

【搭】aroma flavor 香气

□ action □ adjust □ allergy □ arid □ aroma

【例】The *aroma* of fresh pastry came to us from the kitchen. 我们闻到了从厨房飘来的新鲜糕点的香味。

assign [ə'saɪn] *vt.* 指派(*prescribe); 分配(apportion); 布置(作业)

【记】分拆联想: as + sign(签名, 做记号) → 考生在志愿表上签字以示服从分配 → 指派; 分配

【例】That novel she *assigned* us is so boring. 她指定我们读的小说特别无聊。

【派】assignment(*n.* 分派的任务; 作业)

associate [ə'souʃɪeɪt] *v.* 关联(relate); 结交(*consort) *a.* 副的
[ə'souʃɪət] *n.* 伙伴(companion, partner) *a.* 准的(比正式的低一级)

【记】分拆联想: as(加强) + soci(看作social, 社会的; 交际的) + ate(做) → 结合伙伴是一种社会交往方式 → 伙伴; 结交

【例】Our commercial art department doesn't give Bachelor's degrees, only *associate*. 我们的商业艺术系不授予本科学位, 只给专科学位。

【派】associated(*a.* 关联的; 联合的); association(*n.* 协会; 联合)

athlete ['æθliːt] *n.* 运动员

【记】发音记忆: "爱死你的" → 运动员体格健美让人喜爱 → 运动员

【派】athletic(*a.* 运动的); nonathletic(*a.* 非运动的)

aviation [ˌeɪvi'eɪʃn] *n.* 航空(navigation), 航空学; 飞行(fly)

【记】词根记忆: avi(鸟) + ation(表名词) → 像鸟一样飞 → 航空; 飞行

【参】aviator(*n.* 飞行家)

bedrock ['bedrɑːk] *n.* 基础, 根基; 基石(foundation, basis)

cardinal ['kɑːrdɪnl] *a.* 主要的, 最重要的(main, essential) *n.* 红衣凤头鸟

【记】词根记忆: card(心脏的) + inal → 心一样的 → 首要的, 最重要的

carnivore ['kɑːrnɪvɔːr] *n.* 肉食动物

【记】词根记忆: carn(肉) + i + vore(吃) → 肉食动物

【例】Wolves are classified as *carnivores*. 狼被列为肉食动物。

【派】carnivorous(*a.* 食肉类的)

census ['sensəs] *n.* 人口普查

【记】词根记忆: cens(评估) + us → 评估我们的数量 → 人口普查

【搭】census bureau 人口调查局

certificate

certificate [sər'tɪfɪkət] *n.* 证(明)书

【记】词根记忆: cert(搞清) + i + fic(做) + ate → 搞清身份 → 证(明)书

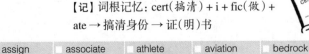

complex [kəm'pleks] *a.* 综合的；错综的；难以理解的（*intricate, complicated）['kɑːmpleks] *n.* 综合体

【记】词根记忆：com + plex（重叠，交叉）→ 重叠交叉的 → 错综的

【例】The decision involves a large number of variables with *complex* relationships. 这个决定涉及很多关系复杂的变量。//Have you inquired at the apartment *complex* down the street? 你询问过街道那边的公寓综合楼吗？

【派】complexity（*n.* 复杂性）

contract ['kɑːntrækt] *n.* 合同，契约（agreement, pact）

[kən'trækt] *v.* 订合同；收缩（shrink）

【例】In general, the *contracts* are often no more than verbal agreements. 一般而言，合同往往不过是口头协议。//The students paid for the meals they *contract* for. 学生们为订的饭付了钱。

【派】contraction（*n.* 收缩；压缩）

convex ['kɑːnveks] *a.* 凸出的（bulging）

【搭】convex lens 凸透镜

course [kɔːrs] *n.* 课程，教程；过程，进程（process）；路程，路线（route）；一道菜（dish）

【搭】required course 必修课；in the course of 在…过程中，在…期间；of course 当然，自然，无疑

【例】A: I already know what I want to take next semester. So why do I have to make an appointment to see my advisor? All I need is her signature on my *course* sheet.

B: I'm afraid it doesn't work that way. She has to talk with you to make sure everything is on the right track.

A: 我已经知道下学期想上什么课了。所以我为何还要约见我的指导教师呢？我只需要她在我的课程单上签字就可以了。

B: 恐怕不能这样。她要和你谈谈，确保一切正常。

criticize ['krɪtɪsaɪz] *v.* 批评，吹毛求疵，非难

【例】The decision to build permanent settlements on the beach was *criticized* by environmental groups. 环保组织批评了在海滩上建立永久居住区的决定。

dealer ['diːlər] *n.* 商人，小贩（businessman, peddler）

【记】来自deal（交易）+ er → 商人

defecate ['defəkeɪt] *vi.* 排粪；通大便

☐ complex	☐ contract	☐ convex	☐ course	☐ criticize	☐ dealer
☐ defecate					

dismay [dɪs'meɪ] v./n. (使)气馁,(使)沮丧(discourage, deject)
【记】分拆联想:dis(不)+ may(可能)→ 不可能做到 →(使)气馁
【例】I was *dismayed* by the news in the paper. 报纸上的消息让我十分沮丧。

drastic ['dræstɪk] a. 剧烈的(fierce, intense)
【例】What forms of life are able to make such a *drastic* change in lifestyle? 什么生命形式能在生活方式上做出如此剧烈的改变?
【派】drastically(ad. 激烈地;彻底地)

flake [fleɪk] n. 薄片(slice) v. 使成薄片(chip);雪片般落下
【记】分拆联想:f(看作fly,飞)+ lake(湖)→ 飞向湖中的薄片 → 雪片般落下

float [fləʊt] v. (使)漂浮(drift)
【记】联想记忆:船(boat)在水里漂浮(float)
【例】Some small local canals are able to *float* only small rafts of timber. 一些本地小的运河只能漂小木筏。
【派】floating(a. 漂浮的)

flourish ['flɜːrɪʃ] vi. 繁荣,茂盛(*thrive, boom)
【记】词根记忆:flour(=flor花)+ ish → 花一样开放 → 繁荣,茂盛
【例】The art movement really *flourished* in the 1930s, during the depression years. 艺术运动在20世纪30年代的大萧条时期真正兴盛起来了。

geology [dʒi'ɑːlədʒi] n. 地质学
【记】词根记忆:geo(地)+ logy(学科)→ 地质学
【例】I'm really looking forward to this trip with our *geology* class. 我非常盼望着与地理课同学的这次旅行。
【派】geologist(n. 地质学者);geological(a. 地质的,地质学的)

glaze [gleɪz] vt. 上釉(gloss) n. 釉
【记】和gaze(v. 盯,凝视)一起记
【例】It was created by adding a brown *glaze* to the fired clay. 这是通过给烧制好的黏土上褐色的釉而制成的。
【派】glazing(n. 上釉);glazed(a. 上过釉的;表面光滑的)

grading ['greɪdɪŋ] n. 评分;等级(rank)
【记】词根记忆:grad(步,级)+ ing → 评分;等级
【例】He doesn't know if Dr. Wilson has finished the *grading* of the midterm exams. 他不知道威尔逊博士是否已经批改完期中考试。

dismay	drastic	flake	float	flourish	geology
glaze	grading				

harsh [hɑːrʃ] *a.* 恶劣的（severe）；刺耳的（raspy）

【记】分拆联想：har(看作hard, 坚硬的)＋sh → 态度强硬 → 恶劣的

【例】They believe that iron offers less resistance to fire and *harsh* weather than traditional materials. 他们认为铁在抵抗火和严酷天气方面不如传统材料。//A constricted and harsh voice usually indicates anger. 一个紧迫并且刺耳的声音通常表示着愤怒。

【派】harshness(*n.* 严酷，恶劣)

hind [haɪnd] *a.* (成对的事物)后面的(back)，在后的

【记】联想记忆：后面的(behind)的后面(hind)

【例】The *hind* legs of the gerbil are particularly well adapted to leaping across its desert habitat. 沙鼠的后腿尤其适应于在沙漠栖息地跳跃。

hominid [ˈhɑːmɪnɪd] *n./a.* 原始人类(的)

【记】词根记忆：homi(=hom人)＋nid → 原始人类

【例】His study involves the eating and dietary habits of *hominids*. 他的研究涉及原始人类的饮食习惯。

hypothesis [haɪˈpɑːθəsɪs] *n.* 假设，假说(assumption, theory)

【记】词根记忆：hypo(下)＋thesis(论点) → 非真正论点 → 假说

【例】Professor Brown's *hypothesis* was that whale ate polluted fish, and this caused their death. 布朗教授的假设是鲸鱼食用了受到污染的鱼，这导致了其死亡。

illegible [ɪˈledʒəbl] *a.* 难以辨认的，(字迹)模糊的

【记】词根记忆：il(不)＋leg(读)＋ible → 不易读的 → 难以辨认的

【例】The letter on the monument was seriously worn and *illegible*. 纪念碑上的字母严重磨损，难以辨认。

incoming [ˈɪnkʌmɪŋ] *a.* 引入的，来临的

【记】来自income(*n.* 收入，所得)

【例】The traffic accident happened when a bus collided with an *incoming* truck. 公交车与迎面驶来的卡车相撞，造成了交通事故。

【参】forthcoming(*a.* 即将来临的)

individual [ˌɪndɪˈvɪdʒuəl] *a.* 单独的(separate)；独特的(special) *n.* 个人，个体(unit)

【记】分拆联想：in＋divid(e)(分割)＋ual → 分割开的 → 单独的；个人

□ harsh	□ hind	□ hominid	□ hypothesis	□ illegible	□ incoming
□ individual					

【例】How do *individual* ants adapt to specialized tasks? 蚂蚁个体如何适应特定工作?

【派】individually(*ad.* 个别地); individuality(*n.* 个性); individualize(*v.* 赋予个性)

inherit [ɪnˈherɪt] *vt.* 继承,遗传而得

【记】词根记忆: in + her(继承人) + it → 继承

【例】She *inherited* all her mother's beauty. 她承传了母亲的所有美貌。

【派】inheritance(*n.* 遗传)

instruct [ɪnˈstrʌkt] *vt.* 指示(direct); 教授(teach)

【记】词根记忆: in + struct(建筑) → 教授人如何建筑 → 教授

【例】His work is to *instruct* newcomers about bicycle maintenance. 他的工作是指导新来者如何维修自行车。

【派】instructive(*a.* 有益的; 知识丰富的); instructor(*n.* 教练)

insulate [ˈɪnsəleɪt] *vt.* 使隔离,使隔绝(isolate)

【记】词根记忆: insul(岛) + ate(使…) → 成为孤岛 → 使隔绝

【例】The ice shelves currently *insulate* the Antarctic continent from wind. 冰架目前使南极洲与风隔绝。

【派】insulation(*n.* 绝缘; 隔绝,孤立); insulator(*n.* 绝缘体,隔热或隔音的物质)

intellectual [ˌɪntəˈlektʃuəl] *n.* 知识分子 *a.* 智力的,有智力的

【记】词根记忆: intel(中间) + lect(选择) + ual → 能从中选择的 → 有智力的

【例】Plagiarism is a form of *intellectual* dishonesty. 抄袭是智力欺诈的一种形式。

【派】intellectualism(*n.* 智力活动; 知性主义); intellectually(*ad.* 智性上地,智力上地); intelligent(*a.* 聪明的); intellect(*n.* 智力)

legend [ˈledʒənd] *n.* 传奇故事,传说(tale)

【记】分拆联想: leg(腿) + end(终点) → 传说这条路没有终点 → 传说,传奇故事

【例】Cultures in the myths and *legends* passed down from one generation to another. 神话传奇的文化世代相传。

【参】legendary(*a.* 传奇的; 有名的)

legible [ˈledʒəbl] *a.* 清楚的(distinct); 易读的(readable)

【记】词根记忆: leg(读) + ible → 易读的

【例】The song she had written for the contest wasn't *legible*. 她为比赛所写的歌不容易懂。

【派】illegible(*a.* 难辨认的)

lime [laɪm] *n.* 石灰

【记】联想记忆: 石灰(lime)需要时间(time)来烧制

【参】limestone(*n.* 石灰石)

livelihood [ˈlaɪvlihʊd] *n.* 生计(living); 谋生手段

【例】The experts guard their knowledge to prevent others from stealing their *livelihood*. 专家守护自己的知识, 防止其他人偷走他们谋生的手段。

lizard [ˈlɪzərd] *n.* 蜥蜴

【记】联想记忆: 巫师(wizard)像蜥蜴(lizard)一样恶毒

male [meɪl] *a.* 男(雄)的 *n.* 男子; 雄性动物

【参】female(*n./a.* 雌性(的))

maturity [məˈtʃʊrəti] *n.* 成熟, 完备(full development)

【搭】at maturity 到期; 成熟时

【例】Blue whale may grow to 100 feet and weigh 150 tons at *maturity*. 蓝鲸成熟时可以长到100英尺, 重达150吨。

militant [ˈmɪlɪtənt] *a.* 好战的, 好暴力的

【记】词根记忆: milit(军事, 打斗) + ant → 好战的

mosaic [moʊˈzeɪɪk] *n.* 马赛克; 镶嵌细工

【记】发音记忆

【例】*Mosaic* is the art of closely setting small, colored pieces, such as stone or glass, into a surface to create a decorative design. 马赛克是把小块彩色石头或玻璃片紧密摆放到一个平面, 从而创作装饰图案的艺术。

motivation [ˌmoʊtɪˈveɪʃn] *n.* 动力; 动机(motive); 刺激

【搭】motivation for doing 做…的动机; one's motivation 某人的动机

【例】I'm going to introduce two current points of view about the *motivation* for writing the United States Constitution back in 1787. 我要介绍当前关于1787年制订美国宪法动机的两种观点。

overwhelm [ˌoʊvərˈwelm] *vt.* 淹没(submerge); 压倒(overcome)

【记】分拆联想: over + whelm(淹没) → 淹没; 压倒

【例】Extensive falls of volcanic ash and coarser particles *overwhelm* and bury all forms of life. 火山灰和更粗颗粒的大量降落, 淹没并埋葬了所有生命。

【派】overwhelmingly(*ad.* 压倒性地)

☐ lime　　☐ livelihood　　☐ lizard　　☐ male　　☐ maturity　　☐ militant
☐ mosaic　　☐ motivation　　☐ overwhelm

paraphrase [ˈpærəfreɪz] *n.* 释义（meaning）*vt.* 解释（explain）；改写（rewrite）

【记】词根记忆：para（辅助）+ phrase（短语）→ 帮助学习的短语 → 释义；解释

【例】The reporter *paraphrased* the president's comments. 记者解释了总统的评论。

pebble [ˈpebl] *n.* 小圆石，鹅卵石

posthumous [ˈpɑːstʃəməs] *a.* 死后的，身后的

preoccupation [priˌɑːkjuˈpeɪʃn] *n.* 主要考虑因素；全神贯注；抢先占据（concern, involvement）

【记】来自 preoccup(y)（占据）+ ation → 占据思想 → 全神贯注

【例】The beggar's main *preoccupation* at this time is getting some money and food. 乞讨者此时满脑子想着弄到一些钱和食物。

prepare [prɪˈper] *v.* 准备，预备

【搭】be prepared for 为…做准备，准备好

【例】The final exam is approaching. Students are busy *preparing* for it. 期末考试快到了。学生们正在忙着备考。//This vein cutting is just one method the beetles used to *prepare* a safe meal. 切断叶脉只是甲虫用来准备安全食物的一个方法。

A: What sorts of changes are you thinking of?

B: I'd like to make some changes in the way we *prepare* our food.

A：你在琢磨着怎样改变？

B：我想改变我们做饭的方式。

privilege [ˈprɪvəlɪdʒ] *vt.* 给予特权

【记】词根记忆：privi（分开；个人）+ lege（法律）→ 在法律上将人分等级，并给予高等级的人以特权 → 给予特权

【例】The Aliens and Hamiltons of Philadelphia introduced European art traditions to those colonists *privileged* to visit their galleries. 费城的外国人和汉密尔顿人向有权访问他们画廊的殖民者介绍了欧洲艺术传统。

publicize [ˈpʌblɪsaɪz] *vt.* 宣传（advertise, promote）；宣扬

【记】来自 public（公众）+ ize → 广告的作用就是向公众宣传某种产品 → 宣传

【例】He travels around to *publicize* his writings. 他四处游走宣传他的作品。//After a theory has been *publicized*, scientists design experiments to test the theory. 一个理论公布之后，科学家们设计实验来测试理论。

realistic [ˌriːə'lɪstɪk] *a.* 现实(主义)的

【记】来自 real(*a.* 真的, 真实的)

【搭】realistic movement 现实主义运动

【例】After reading the fiction, you'll get a *realistic* picture of the hard life people had on American frontier. 读完这个小说之后, 你会对人们在美国边疆的艰苦生活有个真实的了解。

【派】unrealistic(*a.* 不切实际的, 不实在的)

recipe ['resəpi] *n.* 食谱(cookbook); 方法(method)

region ['riːdʒən] *n.* 地区, 区域(district); (大气等的)层

【记】词根记忆: reg(统治)＋ion→统治的区域→地区, 区域

【派】regional(*a.* 地方的, 地域性的); regionalism(*n.* 地方分权主义); regionalization(*n.* 按地区安排)

rekindle [ˌriː'kɪndl] *vt.* 再点火; 使再振作

【记】词根记忆: re(重新)＋kindle(点燃)→重燃→再点火

【例】Nothing can *rekindle* the old singer's fading passion. 什么都无法重新燃起老歌手淡去的激情。

relevant ['reləvənt] *a.* 相关的, 有关的(relative)

【例】He doesn't have *relevant* resource material. 他没有相关的材料。

【派】relevance(*n.* 有关, 相关)

rental ['rentl] *n.* 租金额; 租赁, 出租

【搭】rental service 租赁服务

【例】I'll get in contact with a *rental* house company to rent an apartment. 我要联系一家房屋租赁公司租一间公寓。

rental

represent [ˌreprɪ'zent] *vt.* 代表; 表现(manifest); 描绘(portray)

【记】分拆联想: re＋present(出席)→他作为公司代表出席了这场大会→代表

【例】The picture below *represents* the addition of the red, green, and blue light. 下面的图画代表红色、绿色和蓝色光的增加。

【派】representation(*n.* 表现; 代表); representational (*a.* 表象的); representative[*n.* 代表 *a.* (of)有代表性的]

revision [rɪ'vɪʒn] *n.* 修订, 校订(modification, correction)

【记】来自 revise(*vt.* 修订, 修正)

【搭】make revisions 作修订

【例】A *revision* of that English book will be published in May this year. 那本英文书的修订版将于今年五月出版。

| □ realistic | □ recipe | □ region | □ rekindle | □ relevant | □ rental |
| □ represent | □ revision | | | | |

rite [raɪt] *n.* (宗教的)仪式(ritual)

rugged ['rʌgɪd] *a.* 崎岖的(uneven); (生活)艰难的(tough)
【例】Most of British Columbia is mountainous, with long, *rugged* ranges running north and south. 英属哥伦比亚大部分是山区, 有着从北向南延伸的绵长崎岖的山脉。

sanitation [ˌsænɪ'teɪʃn] *n.* 卫生(*health); 卫生设施
【记】词根记忆: sanit (=sanat健康) + ation → 要想健康, 得讲卫生 → 卫生

senior ['siːniər] *a.* 地位较高的(superior) *n.* 较年长者(elder); 四年级学生
【记】词根记忆: seni(=sen老) + or → 较年长者

skeletal ['skelətl] *a.* 骨骼的, 骸骨的
【记】来自skelet(on)(骨架) + al → 骨骼的, 骸骨的

stark [stɑːrk] *a.* 赤裸的(barren, bare); 十足的(utter, sheer)
【记】分拆联想: star(星球) + k → 宇宙中大部分星球表面是赤裸的 → 赤裸的
【例】The dark stones stand out in *stark* contrast to the white snow and ice. 深色的石头与洁白的冰雪形成鲜明对比。

strike [straɪk] *v.* 打, 敲(hit, smack); 侵袭(attack) *n.* 罢工(walkout)
【例】Volatile substances usually *strike* the bloodhound's nose as an entire constellation of distinctive scents. 猎犬的鼻子通常遇到易挥发性物质时能辨别出那是完全不同的一组气味。
【派】striking(*a.* 惹人注目的; 惊人的); strikingly(*ad.* 引人注目地)

sunset ['sʌnset] *n.* 日落(sundown)
【记】分拆联想: sun + set(落, 下沉) → 日落

swell [swel] *vt.* 增大, 膨胀(expand)
【记】分拆联想: s + well(泉) → 像泉水一样冒起来 → 增大, 膨胀
【例】The group of onlookers soon *swelled* to a crowd. 旁观者很快变成一大群人。
【派】swelling(*n.* 肿胀, 肿块)

tactic ['tæktɪk] *n.* 手段(means); [常*pl.*] 战术(strategy)
【记】词根记忆: tact(接触) + ic → 通过手段来接触 → 手段

tragedy ['trædʒədi] *n.* 灾难(disaster); 悲剧
【例】A protagonist of a play is what known in *tragedy* as the suffering main character. 戏剧的主角, 在悲剧中是指忍受痛苦的主要角色。

undertake [ˌʌndər'teɪk] *v.* 承担(take in hand); 进行, 从事(engage)
【例】The printer does not have the skills necessary to *undertake* large

publishing projects. 这个印刷商没有承接大规模印刷项目所需的技术。

【派】undertaking(*n.* 事业；任务)

unique [ju'niːk] *a.* 唯一的(sole, exclusive)；独特的(*rare)

【记】词根记忆：uni(单一) + que(…的) → 唯一的；独特的

【例】He considers each photograph to be *unique*. 他认为每张照片都很独特。

【派】uniquely(*ad.* 独特地；唯一地)；uniqueness(*n.* 独特，独一无二)

vestige ['vestɪdʒ] *n.* 痕迹，遗迹，残余(remnant, remains)

wax [wæks] *n.* 蜡；蜡状物

【派】waxy(*a.* 蜡色的；光滑的)

Almost everything I have done in my life attributes to my cooperation with others.

我一生中所做过的几乎每一件事情都与他人一起合作完成的。

——杰克·韦尔奇(*Jack Welch*)

Word List 18

ac	加强	accelerate	v. (使)加快, 加速
chron	时间	chronical	a. 慢性的
de	向下	decadent	a. 颓废的
tol	举起	extol	vt. 赞美, 颂扬
graph	写; 图	graphic	a. 文字的; 图解的
hydro	水	hydrogen	n. 氢
sight	眼光	insight	n. 洞察力
intim	内部	intimate	a. 亲密的

accelerate [əkˈseləreɪt] v. (使)加快, 加速 (*increase, quicken)
【记】词根记忆: ac(加强) + celer(快, 速) + ate(使…) → 加快, 加速
【例】Television *accelerates* the citizen's focus on character rather than issues. 电视使公民更加专注角色而非问题。
【派】acceleration(n. 加速(度))
【参】deceleration(n. 减速)

accessible [əkˈsesəbl] a. 易接近的; 可得到的 (*available); 可进入的
【例】Erosion on a hillside may make clay easily *accessible*. 山坡的腐蚀使人们可以轻易获得黏土。
【派】inaccessible(a. 难到达的, 不可及的); accessibility(n. 可得到)

accumulate [əˈkjuːmjəleɪt] v. 积累, 堆积 (*build up, *collect)
【记】词根记忆: ac(不断) + cumul(堆积) + ate(使…) → 堆积; 积累
【例】The glacier had formed as layer upon layer of snow *accumulated* year after year. 一层层的积雪经年累月之后就形成了冰川。
【派】accumulation(n. 堆积物; 积聚)

accumulate

adjacent [ə'dʒeɪsnt] *a.* 邻近的(*nearby, adjoining, bordering)

【记】分拆联想：ad + jacent(躺) → 躺在附近 → 邻近的

【例】Only in Pennsylvania and *adjacent* areas was stone widely used in dwellings. 只在宾夕法尼亚州及附近地区石头才被广泛应用于住所。

applicant ['æplɪkənt] *n.* 申请者

【记】来自apply(*v.* 申请)

【参】application(*n.* 申请)；applicability(*n.* 适用性)

aquatic [ə'kwætɪk] *a.* 水生的；水中(上)的(marine)

【记】词根记忆：aqu(水) + atic → 水中的

【例】Most *aquatic* animals breathe by means of gills. 多数水生动物都用鳃呼吸。

asteroid ['æstərɔɪd] *n.* 小行星

【记】词根记忆：aster(星星) + oid(像⋯⋯一样) → 小行星

chronical ['krɑːnɪkl] *a.* 慢性的，延续很长的(inveterate)

【记】词根记忆：chron(时间) + ic → 长时间的 → 慢性的

【例】Asthma is *chronical* and very common. 哮喘是慢性病，而且非常常见。

【参】chronology (*n.* 年代学)；synchronous (*a.* 同步的，同时的)；chronicle(*n.* 编年史)

clam [klæm] *n.* 蛤

【记】和claim(*v.* 宣称)一起记

【参】oysters(*n.* 牡蛎)；crab(*n.* 螃蟹)；abalone(*n.* 鲍鱼)；sponge(*n.* 海绵)；coral(*n.* 珊瑚)

complicated ['kɑːmplɪkeɪtɪd] *a.* 难懂的；复杂的(complex)

【例】This type of engine is expensive and *complicated*. 这种引擎昂贵并且复杂。

【派】uncomplicated(*a.* 简单的)

compound ['kɑːmpaʊnd] *n.* 混(化)合物(something formed by a union of elements or parts) *a.* 复合的

【记】词根记忆：com + pound(放置) → 放到一起的东西 → 混合物

【例】Kilns are used to dissolve carbons and iron *compounds*. 干燥炉用来分解碳铁化合物。//Not all insects have *compound* eyes. 并非所有昆虫都有复眼。

considerable [kən'sɪdərəbl] *a.* 相当大(或多)的(*great, *much, *substantial)；值得考虑的，重要的(significant)

【例】I bought the necklace at a *considerable* discount. 我以相当大的

□ adjacent	□ applicant	□ aquatic	□ asteroid	□ chronical	□ clam
□ complicated	□ compound	□ considerable			

折扣买了这条项链。//Powerful railroad barons made fortunes without having to be *considerable* to the customers. 实力强大的铁路大亨无需为顾客考虑很多就挣了大把钱。

【派】considerably(*ad.* 相当地)

consistent [kən'sɪstənt] *a.* 一致的(coherent); 稳定的(sustained); 调和的(compatible); 始终如一的(*constant)

【例】Now, keep in mind that a theory of the moon's origin has to be *consistent* with two important facts. 现在请记住,月球起源的理论必须与两个重要事实一致。//The quality of the cooking at Sullivan's is *consistent*. 苏利文那里的烹饪水平始终如一。

【派】consistency(*n.* 一致性; 坚固性); inconsistent(*a.* 不一致的); self-consistent(*a.* 首尾一致的)

constituent [kən'stɪtʃuənt] *n.* 要素, 组分(*component, element); 选民(electorate)

【记】词根记忆: con + stit(=stat站) + uent → 各种成分站在一起 → 要素, 组分

【例】Vitamins became recognized as essential food *constituents* necessary for health. 维生素被认为是健康所需的重要食物成分。

curve [kɜːrv] *n.* 曲线, 弯曲 *v.* 弄弯(bend)

【记】和carve(*v.* 雕刻)一起记

【例】The ballerina *curves* her arms above her head. 芭蕾舞女把胳膊弯曲在头上。

dazzling ['dæzlɪŋ] *a.* 眼花缭乱的; 耀眼的

【记】来自dazzle(*v.* 使眩目)

【例】Louis is playing the trumpet with *dazzling* originality. 路易斯在以令人眼花缭乱的技艺演奏小号。

decadent ['dekədənt] *a.* 颓废的(depraved)

【记】词根记忆: de(向下) + cad(落下) + ent → 向下落 → 颓废的

discrete [dɪ'skriːt] *a.* 分离的(*separate)

【记】词根记忆: dis(分离) + cre(生产) + te → 分离的

【例】Lisa's plan contains several *discrete* ideas. 利萨的计划包括几个独立的想法。

【参】discreet(*a.* 小心的)

displace [dɪs'pleɪs] *vt.* 取代(replace); 移置

【例】Many feared that radio would *displace* the newspaper industry altogether. 很多人担心广播会完全取代报纸行业。

【派】displacement(*n.* 取代; 排水量)

| consistent | constituent | curve | dazzling | decadent | discrete |
| displace |

drift [drɪft] *n./v.* 漂流；漂泊

【搭】drift wood 漂木；continental drift 大陆漂移

【例】The *drift* wood could have been drifting in the ocean currents for months or even years. 这块漂木可能已在洋流中漂流了数月或者几年。

【参】draft(*n.* 草稿)

executive [ɪɡˈzekjətɪv] *n.* 总经理，董事，行政负责人 *a.* 执行的，实施的

【搭】Chief Executive Officer 首席执行官；local business executives 本地商务主管

【例】Kate, a former teacher, is now an *executive* for a charity. 凯特从前是个教师，现在是一个慈善团体的管理者。

extol [ɪkˈstoʊl] *vt.* 赞美，颂扬(*praise, compliment)

【记】词根记忆：ex + tol(举起) → 举起来 → 赞美，颂扬

extrinsic [eksˈtrɪnsɪk] *a.* 外来的；外在的

【例】Today the professor will introduce a couple of technical terms: *extrinsic* value and intrinsic value. 今天教授将介绍一些技术词汇：外在价值和内在价值。

【参】intrinsic(*a.* 固有的，内在的)

flash [flæʃ] *n.* 闪光；闪现(flare, spark) *v.* 闪光(flare, glare, sparkle)；反射

【记】网络词汇"闪客"就是flash

【搭】in a flash 转瞬间；flash by 一闪而过

formulate [ˈfɔːrmjuleɪt] *v.* 阐明(clarify, illuminate)

【记】词根记忆：form(形成) + ulate → 形成自己的表达 → 阐明

【例】Possible solutions to the problem are *formulated*. 解决这个问题的合理方案已经被制订出来了。

fragment [ˈfrægmənt] *n.* 碎片，断片(*debris, patch)

【例】Snowflakes consist of broken *fragments* and clusters of adhering ice crystals. 雪花是由碎片和黏在一起的冰晶体团构成的。

【派】fragmentary(*a.* 由碎片组成的)；fragmented(*a.* 成碎片的)

frank [fræŋk] *a.* 坦白的，直率的

【记】联想记忆：弗兰克(Frank)是个很坦率的(frank)人

gear [gɪr] *n.* 齿轮；速度（pace）；设备（equipment）

【记】分拆联想：g + ear(耳朵) → 耳朵是身体上的设备 → 设备

【例】It must have several *gears*. 它肯定有好几个齿轮。

gibe [dʒaɪb] v. 嘲弄，讥笑

【记】也写作jibe，但jibe还有另一个意思"与…一致"

glean [gli:n] v. 点滴搜集；拾

【记】和clean(a. 干净的)一起记

【搭】glean sth. from sb./sth. 从…找到…

【例】Most of the methods he *gleaned* were of no practical use in our daily life. 他搜集的多数方法对我们的日常生活都没有实际用处。

【派】gleanings(n. 收集到的东西)

gourmet ['gʊrmeɪ] n. 美食家

【搭】gourmet coffee 极品咖啡；精制咖啡

【例】Over the last few years, a trend has been developing to introduce blended coffees known as *gourmet* coffee into the American market. 在过去短短几年兴起一个潮流，人们把被称作极品咖啡的混合咖啡引入了美国市场。

graphic ['græfɪk] a. 形象的(vivid)；文字的；图解的

【记】词根记忆：graph(写；图) + ic → 文字的；图解的

habit ['hæbɪt] n. 习惯(custom)；习性，脾性

【搭】habit forming 习惯的养成；have a habit of doing 有做…的习惯

【例】I've heard that playing cards is a *habit* forming, and it's hard to kick it off. 我听说打牌会养成一种习惯，很难戒掉。

A: Professor Johnson, for my sociology project this term I'm thinking of interviewing all the residents in town on their TV viewing *habit*.

B: Well that's quite an undertaking for such a short-time project. Maybe you should take a little while to think about what that would entail before making your final decision.

A：约翰逊教授，关于这个学期社会学的项目，我想就看电视的习惯采访镇里的所有居民。

B：对这样的短期项目而言这是项大工程。或许你在最终决定之前应该花时间想想这会涉及哪些工作。

herd [hɜːrd] n. 兽群(尤指牛群)

【记】联想记忆：兽群(herd)逐水草(herb)而居

hive [haɪv] n. 蜂房(cell)，蜂箱

【记】联想记忆：蜜蜂忙忙碌碌地生活(live)，建造蜂房(hive)

hydrogen ['haɪdrədʒən] n. 氢

【记】词根记忆：hydro(水) + gen(产生) → 参与生成水的物质 → 氢

□ gibe	□ glean	□ gourmet	□ graphic	■ habit	□ herd
□ hive	□ hydrogen				

identical [aɪˈdentɪkl] *a.* 相同的(*exactly alike)；同一的(selfsame)

【例】The director wants the songs in the Broadway version to be *identical* to the songs in the film. 导演想让百老汇版的歌曲与电影版的歌曲完全相同。

【参】identic(*a.* 同一的)

ignore [ɪgˈnɔːr] *vt.* 忽视(neglect)；不顾，不理

【记】分拆联想：ig + nore(看作nose，鼻子)→ 翘起鼻子不理睬 → 不理

【例】The accomplishments of women are *ignored* in most historical documents. 多数历史文献忽略女性的成就。

insight [ˈɪnsaɪt] *n.* 洞察力；领悟(perception)

【记】词根记忆：in(进入) + sight(眼光) → 眼光深入 → 洞察力

【例】Lillian Hellman's plays are marked by *insight* and finesse. 莉莲·赫尔曼的剧作从富有洞察力和写作技巧著称。

【派】insightful(*a.* 富有洞察力的，有深刻见解的)

insistence [ɪnˈsɪstəns] *n.* 坚持(adherence)

【记】来自insist(*v.* 坚持)

【例】There is much democratic *insistence* on the worthiness of every level of birth and work. 很多民众坚持认为每个层次的出身和工作都值得尊重。

intimate [ˈɪntɪmət] *a.* 亲密的(close)；详尽的；个人的(personal)

【记】词根记忆：intim(内部) + ate → 内部关系 → 亲密的

【例】The boss has *intimate* knowledge of the client's requirements. 老板非常熟悉客户的要求。

【派】intimacy(*n.* 熟悉；亲密)

ledge [ledʒ] *n.* (建筑物或岩石的)突出部分

【记】分拆联想：l + edge(边缘) → 位于边缘处的东西 → 突出部分

【例】McAdoo's men were forced to blast when they ran into an unexpected *ledge* of rock. 麦卡杜的士兵遇到了出乎意料突出的一块石头，不得不把它炸掉。

leisure [ˈliːʒər] *n.* 空闲，闲暇(spare time)

【例】She doesn't have much *leisure* time. 她没有多少空闲时间。

lore [lɔːr] *n.* 口头传说；学问，知识

【记】和lure(*v.* 诱惑)一起记

magma [ˈmægmə] *n.* 岩浆

【例】All *magma* consists basically of a variety of silicate minerals. 所有的岩浆基本上都由各种硅酸盐矿物质构成。

identical　ignore　insight　insistence　intimate　ledge
leisure　lore　magma

malnutrition [ˌmælnuːˈtrɪʃn] *n.* 营养不良

【记】分拆联想：mal(坏) + nutrition(营养) → 营养不好的 → 营养不良

【搭】suffer from malnutrition 患有营养不良；evidence/signs of malnutrition 营养不良的迹象

【例】Various disease often follows *malnutrition.* 营养不良往往引发各种疾病。

manipulate [məˈnɪpjuleɪt] *vt.* 操作(handle)，利用(use)

【记】分拆联想：mani(手) + pul(看作 pull，拉) + ate → 用手拉 → 操作；利用

【例】He accused the government of *manipulating* public opinion. 他谴责政府操纵公众舆论。

manipulate

【派】manipulation(*n.* 操纵)

massive [ˈmæsɪv] *a.* 大而重的，庞大的；可观的

【记】来自mass(*n.* 大多数，大量)

【例】There is a *massive* increase in spending on infrastructures this year. 今年基础设施的投资会大幅增加。

mess [mes] *n.* 混乱，混杂，脏乱 *v.* 弄脏，弄乱，搞糟

【搭】make a mess of 制造混乱；a mess of 很多；in a mess 混乱

【例】A: Sue, would you like to be my lab partner with the next experiment?

B: Sure. I just can't believe you still want to work with me after I *messed* up last time.

A: 苏，你愿意当我的实验室伙伴做下一个实验吗？

B: 当然愿意。我上次都搞砸了，真不敢相信你仍然想跟我合作。

mountainous [ˈmaʊntənəs] *a.* 多山的

【例】We traveled through wild *mountainous* country. 我们的旅行途经了一个荒凉多山的地方。

neon [ˈniːɑːn] *n.* 氖；霓虹灯

【记】发音记忆

【搭】neon sign 霓虹灯

path [pæθ] *n.* 道路(pathway)；路线(route)

【参】pathway(*n.* 路)

plantation [plænˈteɪʃn] *n.* 种植园

【记】来自plant(植物，种植) + ation(表状态、结果) → 种植园

malnutrition	manipulate	massive	mess	mountainous	neon
path	plantation				

197

【例】Back in the 17th and 18th century African and American women wove the baskets for use on the rice *plantations*. 早在17和18世纪，非洲和美洲女性编织篮子以供稻米种植园使用。

plastic ['plæstɪk] *n.* 塑料 *a.* 塑料的

【搭】plastic trash bags 塑料垃圾袋；plastic bead 塑料珠子

【例】The doors are made of *plastic*. 这些门是由塑料做的。

pocketbook ['pɑːkɪtbʊk] *n.* 钱袋，皮夹（purse, wallet）

portray [pɔːr'treɪ] *vt.* 描绘（picture, depict）

【记】分拆联想：por（看作pour，倒）+ tray（碟）→ 将（颜料）倒在碟子上 → 描绘

【例】Bret Harte achieved fame with stories that *portrayed* local life in the California mining camps. 布雷特·哈特因描写加州矿区当地生活的小说而成名。

【派】portrayal(*n.* 描述，表现)

presentation [ˌpriːzen'teɪʃn] *n.* 介绍，陈述

【记】来自present（*v.* 赠送；上演）

【例】I need to get in touch with Bill about tomorrow's *presentation*. 我需要和比尔联系来谈一下关于明天报告的事情。

A: Our history *presentation* is Thursday. When do you want to get together to work on it?

B: Well, how about Monday? That way we will still have enough time to figure out anything we are having trouble with.

A：我们的历史报告是在周四。你想什么时候凑在一起写这个报告？

B：周一怎么样？这样我们能有足够的时间来解决任何难点。

probe [proʊb] *vi.* 探查（explore）*n.* 探测器（detector）；探索

【记】词根记忆：prob（检查，试）+ e → 探查；探索

【例】Hummingbirds have stiletto-like bills to *probe* the deepest nectar-bearing flowers. 蜂鸟有钻孔锥一样的喙来探进有花蜜花朵的最深处。

proof [pruːf] *n.* 证据（evidence）；试验（examination）

【参】soundproof(*a.* 隔音的)；fireproof(*a.* 防火的)；waterproof(*a.* 防水的)；rustproof(*a.* 不生锈的)

purity ['pjʊrəti] *n.* 纯度（the quality or state of being pure）；纯净

reasonable ['riːznəbl] *a.* 合理的（fair），有道理的；适度的；通情达理的

【记】来自reason（道理）+ able → 懂道理的 → 通情达理的

【搭】a reasonable excuse 合理的借口

【例】A: What do you think would be a *reasonable* price to pay for a new computer?

B: You are asking the wrong person. My brother gave me mine.

A：你觉得一台新电脑付多少钱合理?

B：你问错人了。我这台电脑是我哥给的。

A: The job sounds great, but I'm a little worried about how much time it might take.

B: It's pretty *reasonable*. It never took me more than five hours a week to do all the grading and then another thirty to forty minutes to record the grades on the computer.

A：这份工作听起来不错，但是我担心它占用太多时间。

B：这很合理。我每周不超过5个小时用来打分，然后再用30到40分钟把分数输入电脑。

【派】unreasonable（*a.* 不合理的；不讲理的；过度的）；reasoned（*a.* 理性的）；reasoning（*n.* 推理，论证）

recruit [rɪˈkruːt] *v.* 招募(新兵)，征募(enlist)

【记】词根记忆：re + cruit(=cres成长) → 使部队成长壮大 → 招募(新兵)

recruit

【例】The Argentine ants can quickly *recruit* a huge army from their network of nests. 阿根廷的蚂蚁可以从巢穴网迅速募集一大批蚁群。//The team shouldn't *recruit* any more players. 这个队不应该再招募球员了。

【派】recruitment（*n.* 招聘；吸收新成员）

reservation [ˌrezərˈveɪʃn] *n.* 保留，保留意见；预订

【记】来自reserve（*vt.* 保留）

【搭】make reservation 预订

【例】A: I'm sorry. I need to work late tonight. So you should probably cancel our *reservation* at the restaurant.

B: Oh, actually I've never got round to making one in the first place.

A：对不起，今晚我得加班。你或许应该取消我们在饭店的预订。

B：哦，实际上是我先前一直都没空预订。

scarce [skers] *a.* 缺乏的，稀有的(*rare, lacking)

【记】分拆联想：scar(伤疤) + ce → 有伤疤，不完整的 → 缺乏的

【例】Watches and clocks were *scarce* in the United States until the late 1850s. 19世纪50年代之前钟表在美国很少见。

【派】scarcely（*ad.* 几乎不；刚刚）；scarcity（*n.* 缺乏，不足）

【参】scare（*v.* 惊吓）

shell [ʃel] *n.* 壳, 外壳(crust); 炮弹

【记】联想记忆: 坏蛋被一炮弹(shell)轰进地狱(hell)

【参】shellfish(*n.* 水生有壳动物)

simplify [ˈsɪmplɪfaɪ] *v.* 简化, 使简单, 使单纯

【记】来自simpl(e)(简单的)＋ify(使…化)→简化, 使单纯

【例】This technology can *simplify* network operations, significantly reducing recurring costs. 这项技术能够简化网络操作、大大降低重复的成本。

【派】simplicity(*n.* 简单, 简易; 朴素; 直率; 单纯)

smelting [ˈsmeltɪŋ] *n.* 冶炼

sound [saʊnd] *v.* 似乎(seem) *a.* 可靠的(secure); 健康的(healthy); 合理的(reasonable)

【派】soundly(*ad.* 非常好)

spoil [spɔɪl] *v.* 破坏(damage, destroy); 变质(decay)

【例】The bread can be stored a long time without *spoiling.* 面包可以长时间保存而不变质。

【派】spoilage(*n.* 变质)

stash [stæʃ] *vt.* 藏匿(conceal)

【记】分拆联想: st＋ash(灰)→躲在灰里→藏匿

【例】Garbage has been *stashed* in the building's basement despite sanitation laws to the contrary. 垃圾被藏到了这座建筑的地下室, 尽管卫生法规定不允许这么做。

submission [səbˈmɪʃn] *n.* 屈服, 服从; 提交; 呈递; 恭顺

【例】I was so excited to finally see my work in print. It was my third *submission.* 终于看到我的作品印刷出来了, 我特别兴奋。这是我第三次投稿了。

suppress [səˈpres] *vt.* 抑制, 阻止(restrain)

【记】词根记忆: sup(在…下面)＋press(压)→抑制, 阻止

【例】Alder trees can *suppress* the growth of nearby trees. 赤杨可能会抑制附近树木的生长。

【参】depress(*vt.* 使沮丧); oppress(*vt.* 压迫)

surpass [sərˈpæs] *vt.* 超过, 胜过(*exceed)

【记】词根记忆: sur(超过, 在上面)＋pass(通过)→在上面通过→超过

【例】Canada *surpassed* the United States in transportation improvements. 加拿大在运输改良方面超过了美国。

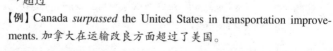

| shell | simplify | smelting | sound | spoil | stash |
| submission | suppress | surpass | | | |

tarnish [ˈtɑːrnɪʃ] *vt.* 失去光泽

【记】词根记忆：tarn(隐藏) + ish → 隐藏光泽 → 失去光泽

【例】Exposure to the open air *tarnished* the silver bowl. 暴露在空气中会使银碗失去光泽。

timber [ˈtɪmbər] *n.* 木材(wood, lumber)；原木(log)

【记】分拆联想：timb(看作time, 时间) + er → 树苗变成木材需要时间 → 木材

trait [treɪt] *n.* 特性，特点(characteristic, feature)

【记】联想记忆：要根据每位队员的特点(trait)进行训练(train)

【例】They share similar physical *traits.* 它们有相似的外形特征。

tube [tuːb] *n.* 管(pipe)；显像管

【记】联想记忆：立方形(cube)的管道(tube)

【搭】bronchial tube 支气管；vacuum tube 真空管，电子管

uneven [ʌnˈiːvn] *a.* 不平均的，不均匀的(unequal)

【例】Her hair has been badly cut and the ends are *uneven.* 她的头发剪得很糟，发端参差不齐。

【派】unevenly(*ad.* 不平坦地；不均衡地)

virtually [ˈvɜːrtʃuəli] *ad.* 事实上，实质上(actually, practically)

【例】We know *virtually* nothing about this man. 我们对此人几乎一无所知。

yogurt [ˈjoʊgərt] *n.* 酸奶(酪)

If you doubt yourself, then indeed you stand on shaky ground.
如果你怀疑自己，那么你的立足点确实不稳固了。 ——易卜生(*Ibsen*)

Word List 19 🔘 MP3-19

词根、词缀预习表

anti	反	antibiotic	*n.* 抗生素
di	二	dioxide	*n.* 二氧化物
cern	区分	discern	*vt.* 识别
dom	家	domestic	*a.* 国内的
spir	呼吸	inspire	*vt.* 鼓舞, 激励
liber	自由	liberate	*vt.* 解放, 释放
scribe	写	prescribe	*vt.* 开处方
vor	吃	voracious	*a.* 狼吞虎咽的

abrupt [əˈbrʌpt] *a.* 突然的, 意外的(unexpected)
【记】词根记忆: ab(离去) + rupt(断) → 他的断然离去令人很意外 → 突然的, 意外的
【例】Most paleontologists suspect that *abrupt* changes in climate led to the mass extinctions. 多数古生物学家怀疑是气候的突然变化才导致了古生物的大规模灭绝。

accessory [əkˈsesəri] *n.* 附件, 零件(adjunct)

accuse [əˈkjuːz] *vt.* 指责, 归咎(blame); 指控(charge)
【例】I *accused* John of hitting my dog. 我指责约翰打了我的狗。// The police *accused* Bill of being at the scene of the crime. 警方指控比尔曾在犯罪现场。
【派】accusation(*n.* 控告; 谴责)

aggressive [əˈɡresɪv] *a.* 挑衅的(combative, offensive); 强有力的(strong); 强有力的; 有进取心的, 有冲劲的
【记】词根记忆: ag (加强) + gress (行走) + ive → 到处乱走的 → 挑衅的
【例】A successful businessman must be *aggressive*. 成功的实业家必定是有闯劲的。
【派】aggressively(*ad.* 强劲地; 侵略地); aggressiveness(*n.* 争斗); aggression(*n.* 侵略)

alphabet [ˈælfəbet] *n.* 字母表

【记】由希腊字母表中的头两个字母alpha(阿尔法)和beta(贝它)组合而成，列出从前到后所有的字母就成了字母表

antibiotic [ˌæntibaɪˈɑːtɪk] *n.* [常*pl.*]抗生素 *a.* 抗生的

【记】词根记忆：anti(反) + bio(生命) + tic → 抗生素

【例】Now we have lots of *antibiotics* that kill bacteria. 现在我们有很多能消灭细菌的抗生素。

avoid [əˈvɔɪd] *vt.* 避免，规避(shy away from, prevent)

【记】分拆联想：a + void(空旷，空虚) → 使空旷 → 避免

【例】Listening to radio reports to *avoid* traffic jams. 听广播报道来避免碰上交通堵塞。

【派】avoidable(*a.* 可避免的); unavoidably(*ad.* 不得已，无可奈何); avoidance(*n.* 避免)

behavior [bɪˈheɪvjər] *n.* 举止，行为(conduct, manner)

【记】来自behave(*v.* 举动，举止)

【派】behavioral(*a.* 动作的); behaviorist(*n.* 行动主义者)

beneficial [ˌbeniˈfɪʃl] *a.* 有益的，有利的(advantageous)

bet [bet] *n./v.* 打赌

【搭】I bet that... 我敢肯定; You bet 的确，当然

【例】A: Hey, congratulations on winning the essay contest. That thousand-dollar prize money should really come in handy.

B: You *bet*! I've already put it aside to cover the increase my landlord just announced for next year.

A: 嗨，祝贺你赢得论文比赛。那1000元的奖金得的可真是时候。

B: 你说对了。我的房东刚宣布明年要涨租金，我已经留着奖金用来支付这部分费用了。

【参】bat(*n.* 蝙蝠; 球棒)

bond [bɑːnd] *n.* 联结，黏结; 债券; [化]键

【记】发音记忆："绑得" → 绑在一起 → 联结，黏结

【搭】chemical bond 化学黏合剂

【例】For any adhesive to make a really strong *bond*, the surfaces to be glued must be absolutely clean and free from moisture or grease. 要想让黏合剂真正牢靠，涂胶的表面必须非常干净，不能有任何潮湿或油脂。

cafeteria [ˌkæfəˈtɪriə] *n.* 自助餐厅(cafe)

cafeteria 小店要被吃穷啦

【记】分拆联想：cafe(咖啡馆) + teria → 自助餐厅

compete [kəmˈpiːt] *vi.* 比得上；竞争，对抗(rival)

【记】词根记忆：com(共同) + pet(追求，寻求) + e → 共同追求(一个目标) → 竞争，对抗

【例】They *compete* for the best seats in the class. 他们为班里最好的座位而竞争。//Magazines began to *compete* with newspapers. 杂志开始与报纸竞争了。

【派】competition (*n.* 竞争，竞赛)；competent (*a.* 能干的)；competitiveness(*n.* 竞争能力)

compromise [ˈkɑːmprəmaɪz] *n.* 妥协，折衷(yield)

【记】分拆联想：com + promise(保证) → 相互保证 → 妥协

【例】The two parties made an effort to reach a *compromise*. 两党努力达成妥协。

confusion [kənˈfjuːʒn] *n.* 混乱，混淆

【记】来自confuse(*vt.* 使困惑)

【搭】lead to confusion 导致混乱；in confusion 困惑地

【例】There is some *confusion* about what the exact definition of the theory should be. 关于这个理论的确切定义还存在着一些困惑。

consequently [ˈkɑːnsəkwentli] *ad.* 因此，从而(accordingly, therefore)

【记】来自consequent(*a.* 随之发生的)

【例】Her output was prodigious, and *consequently* her work is of varying quality. 她的著作太多了，结果作品的质量不一。

constricted [kənˈstrɪktɪd] *a.* 狭窄的(confined)；收缩的(contractive)

【记】来自constrict(*v.* 压缩)

【例】When asthmatic suffers an attack, the airway path was *constricted*, making it difficult for the person from breathing normally. 哮喘症患者发病时，呼吸道收缩使患者难以正常呼吸。

cultivated [ˈkʌltɪveɪtɪd] *a.* 栽植的(grown)；有修养的(educated)

【例】The preferred grass for forage was a *cultivated* plant. 草料首选的草是一种栽培植物。//The distinguished gentleman married a *cultivated* woman. 这位杰出的绅士娶了一位有修养的女子。

daisy [ˈdeɪzi] *n.* 雏菊

【搭】daisy chain 雏菊花环；as fresh as a daisy 精力充沛的

devote [dɪˈvoʊt] *vt.* (to)为…付出(时间、精力等)；献身于(dedicate)；作…之用

【记】分拆联想：de(加强) + vote(发誓) → 拼命发誓献身于革命事业 → 献身于

【例】They could *devote* themselves entirely to "prose literature". 他们

能完全投入到"散文"创作中。//This room is *devoted* to electric fish. 这个房间是用来养电鱼的。

【派】devoted(*a.* 投入的); devotion(*n.* 热爱, 投入)

dioxide [daɪˈɑːksaɪd] *n.* 二氧化物

【记】词根记忆: di(二) + oxide(氧化物) → 二氧化物

【搭】carbon dioxide 二氧化碳

discern [dɪˈsɜːrn] *vt.* 洞悉(ascertain); 识别(identify)

【记】词根记忆: dis (分开) + cern (区别) → 区别开来 → 洞悉; 识别

【例】The weather data allow computers to *discern* the subtle atmospheric changes. 气象资料使电脑可以识别细微的大气变化。

【派】discernible(*a.* 可识别的)

discrimination [dɪˌskrɪmɪˈneɪʃn] *n.* 识别, 辨别(discernment)

【例】Babies enter the world with the ability to make precisely those perceptual *discriminations* that are necessary if they are to acquire aural language. 婴儿生来就具有精确做出那些知觉辨别的能力, 这是他们习得听觉语言所必需的。

documentary [ˌdɑːkjuˈmentri] *a.* 文献的; 纪实的(realistic) *n.* 纪录片

【例】Most *documentary* filmmakers use neither actors nor studio setting. 多数纪录片摄制者既不使用演员, 也不用摄影棚的背景。// There was a really good *documentary* on television last night about bald eagles. 昨天晚上电视播放的纪录片很不错, 是关于秃头鹰的。

domestic [dəˈmestɪk] *a.* 国内的(internal); 家庭的 (household); 家养的

【记】词根记忆: dom (家) + estic(…的) → 家庭的; 家养的

domestic

【搭】domestic market 国内市场; domestic service 国内航线; 家政服务; domestic goods 国货

【例】At twelve she left home and was in *domestic* service until at twenty-seven. 她12岁离开家从事家政服务, 一直做到27岁。

【派】domestically (*ad.* 国内地); domesticate (*vt.* 驯养, 驯化); domestication(*n.* 驯养, 驯化)

draft [dræft] *n.* 草图(sketch), 草稿 *v.* 起草 *a.* 供役使的

【记】发音记忆: "抓夫" → 供役使的

【例】I've made a first *draft* of my speech for Friday, but it still needs a lot of work. 我已经写出了星期五演讲的初稿, 可是稿子还有许多地方需要加工。

【派】redraft(*vt.* 改写)；updraft(*n.* 上升气流)

elective [ɪˈlektɪv] *a.* 选修的(optional)

【搭】elective system 选课系统

element [ˈelɪmənt] *n.* 元素，要素(component)；[常 *pl.*]基础(foundation)

【派】elemental(*a.* 基本的；元素的)

enlightenment [ɪnˈlaɪtnmənt] *n.* 启发，启迪(illumination)

【记】来自 enlighten(*vt.* 启发，启蒙)

【搭】the Enlightenment 启蒙运动

equitable [ˈekwɪtəbl] *a.* 公平的，公正的(just, fair)

【搭】an equitable system 公正的制度

【例】It may be the most *equitable* solution to the international issue. 这可能是最公正的国际争端解决方法。

estate [ɪˈsteɪt] *n.* 地产(lands)

【记】词根记忆：est(存在) + ate → 实物 → 地产

【搭】real estate 房地产

ethics [ˈeθɪks] *n.* 道德规范；伦理学

【记】分拆联想：e(看作 east, 东方) + thics(看作 thick, 厚的) → 东方有深厚的道德规范 → 道德规范

【派】unethical(*a.* 不道德的)；ethically(*ad.* 伦理上)

federal [ˈfedərəl] *a.* 联邦(制、政府)的

【例】She is considered to be the first woman to hold a *federal* position. 她被认为是担任联邦职务的第一位女性。

【派】federalist(*n.* 联邦制拥护者)

finance [ˈfaɪnæns] *v.* 给…提供资金 (subsidize, supply funds to) *n.* 财政，金融

【记】分拆联想：fin (看作 fine, 好的) + ance → 一件好事 → 为…提供资金

【例】The troupe is *financed* by the elders. 剧团由老年人提供资金。

【派】financing(*n.* 融资，财务)；financial(*a.* 财政的，金融的)；financier(*n.* 金融家)

fossil [ˈfɑːsl] *n.* 化石 *a.* 陈腐的；化石的

【例】Even scratches found on *fossil* human teeth offer clues. 就连人类牙齿化石上的划痕都能提供线索。

【派】fossilize(*vt.* 使成化石)；fossilized(*a.* 成化石的；腐朽的)

fresco [ˈfreskoʊ] *n.* 壁画(mural)

【记】分拆联想：fres(看作 fresh, 新鲜的) + co(看作 cool, 凉爽的)

□ elective	□ element	□ enlightenment	□ equitable	□ estate	□ ethics
□ federal	□ finance	□ fossil	□ fresco		

→ 壁画的清新画面让人仿佛感受到了迎面而来的凉爽新鲜的气息 → 壁画

【例】A 19th century *fresco* was damaged beyond repair. 一幅19世纪的壁画遭到了破坏，无法修复。

frivolity [frɪˈvɑːləti] *n.* 轻浮(flippancy, levity)

fruitless [ˈfruːtləs] *a.* 不结果实的，无收获的

【例】The search for the missing old woman has been *fruitless* till now. 至今，对于那位失踪老年妇女的搜寻工作还是毫无进展。

fuel [ˈfjuːəl] *n.* 燃料 *v.* 激起

【记】联想记忆：加满(full)燃料(fuel)

【搭】a new type of fuel 新型燃料；alternative fuel 代用燃料；fuel efficiency 燃料效率

【例】Compare the new car to a moderately *fuel* efficient conventional car it can go 400-700 km on a tank of gas. 与燃油效率中等的传统汽车相比，这种新车一箱油能跑400到700公里。

gradient [ˈɡreɪdiənt] *n.* 梯度(change in quantity)

【记】词根记忆：gradi(步，级) + ent → 梯度

【搭】temperature gradient 温度梯度

hazel [heɪzl] *a.* 榛树的

herb [ɜːrb] *n.* 药草；(调味用的)香草；草本植物

【记】本身为词根：草

【参】herbicide(*n.* 除草剂)；herbivore(*n.* 草食动物)

huddle [ˈhʌdl] *vi.* 挤在一起(crowd together)

【记】联想记忆：聚集在一起(huddle)处理(handle)问题

【例】Horses and cows always seem to go to a protected area and *huddle* together. 马和牛好像总是要去一处受保护的区域，并聚在一起。

hue [hjuː] *n.* 颜色(color)；类型(type)

【例】They may be glassy blue, or in darker *hues*. 它们可能是玻璃蓝或更深的颜色。

inflation [ɪnˈfleɪʃn] *n.* 通货膨胀

【记】来自inflate(*vt.* 使膨胀)

【例】The governments in some countries have taken measures to control the *inflation* rate. 一些国家的政府已经采取了措施来控制通货膨胀率。

inspire [ɪnˈspaɪər] *vt.* 鼓舞，激励(stimulate)；给…以灵感
【记】词根记忆：in(使)＋spir(呼吸)＋e → 使…呼吸澎湃 → 鼓舞
【例】His stories are *inspired* by his travels. 他写小说的灵感来自他的游历。
【派】inspiration(*n.* 灵感；激励)；inspiring(*a.* 使人振奋的，鼓舞的)

instructor [ɪnˈstrʌktər] *n.* 教员(teacher)，教练，指导员
【例】Fred was asked to submit his term paper to the *instructor* in advance. 弗雷德被要求提前把学期论文交给导师。
【参】coach(*n.* 教练)；tutor(*n.* 家庭教师)

intrinsic [ɪnˈtrɪnsɪk] *a.* 固有的，本质的，内在的(inherent)
【记】分拆联想：intr(看作intro，向内)＋insic(看作inside，里面，内部) → 内在的，本质的
【例】During their growing period, many parents failed to teach children the *intrinsic* value of good behaviour. 在孩子的成长阶段，很多家长未能教导他们认识到良好品行的内在价值。

jogging [ˈdʒɑːgɪŋ] *n.* 慢跑
【例】A study shows that *jogging* for a short while every day is good for our health. 研究表明每天慢跑一段时间有益于健康。
【参】hiking(*n.* 徒步旅行)；cycling(*n.* 骑自行车兜风)

kernel [ˈkɜːrnl] *n.* (硬壳果)仁；(谷物去核后的)粒，子；(问题的)要点，核心
【记】词根记忆：kern(=corn，种子)＋el → 仁；子
【例】Squirrels bite through the shells to get at the nutritious inner *kernels*. 松鼠咬开果壳，吃里面营养丰富的果仁。

leather [ˈleðər] *n.* 皮革
【记】联想记忆：天气(weather)对皮革(leather)的保存有影响
【例】Hinges are often made of *leather*, but metal hinges are also used. 铰链通常是皮制的，但是人们也使用金属铰链。

liberate [ˈlɪbəreɪt] *vt.* 解放，释放(discharge, release)
【记】词根记忆：liber(自由)＋ate → 释放，解放
【例】This energy is *liberated* at the center of the Sun. 能量是从太阳的中心释放出来的。

mansion [ˈmænʃn] *n.* 公寓(flat)，府邸(dwelling)；大厦
【记】分拆联想：mans(看作manse，牧师住宅)＋ion → 大厦

mottled [ˈmɑːtld] *a.* 有杂色的，斑驳的(spotted)
【记】发音记忆："毛头的" → 头发颜色多的 → 有杂色的
【例】Drinking water containing excessive amounts of fluorides may

leave a *mottled* effect on the enamel of teeth. 含有过量氟化物的饮用水会在牙齿的珐琅质上留下斑点。

nail [neɪl] *n.* 指甲，爪；钉 *v.* 将…钉牢，钉住

【搭】as hard/tough as nails 像钉子一样硬；坚强

【例】A: Oh, my shirt sleeve. Must have gotten caught on that *nail*.

B: Here, let me take a look. Hmm, with a needle and thread, this can be mended—and look just like new.

A: 哦，我的衬衫袖子。肯定是被那个钉子挂住了。

B: 来，让我看看。嗯，用针线一缝就好了——看上去跟新的一样。

A: I think I need a new tire. I had to put air in it twice this week.

B: That happened to me once. It was just a *nail*, and they were able to repair it.

A: 我想我需要一个新轮胎。这周我打两次气了。

B: 这个问题我也遇到过一次。就是被钉子扎了，他们补好了它。

【参】hail(*n.* 冰雹)；mail(*n.* 邮件)；snail(*n.* 蜗牛)

noted [ˈnoʊtɪd] *a.* 著名的(famous)

【例】These journals contain essays by several *noted* historians. 这些杂志刊载几位著名历史学家的文章。

oceanographer [ˌoʊʃəˈnɑːɡrəfər] *n.* 海洋学者

paralyze [ˈpærəlaɪz] *vt.* 使麻痹

【记】词根记忆：para(在旁边) + lyze(分开) → 身体的一边像是分开了 → 使麻痹

【例】Those tiny poison threads can *paralyze* small sea animals. 这些细细的毒针能麻痹小型海洋动物。

【派】paralysis(*n.* 瘫痪)

parasite [ˈpærəsaɪt] *n.* 寄生物

【记】词根记忆：para(旁边) + site(吃) → 坐在旁边白吃的 → 寄生物

【例】The tachinid fly is a *parasite* of harmful insects. 寄蝇是一种有害的寄生昆虫。

【派】parasitic(*a.* 寄生的)

prescribe [prɪˈskraɪb] *vt.* 开处方；规定；指示(assign)

【记】词根记忆：pre (预先) + scribe (写) → 预先写好 → 规定

【例】The pills you *prescribed* are giving me a headache. 你开的药让我觉得头疼。

prescribe

【派】prescribed(*a.* 规定的，指定的)

【参】ascribe(*vt.* 归因于); inscribe(*v.* 记下)

regenerate [rɪˈdʒenəreɪt] *vt.* 使恢复(restore)

【记】词根记忆：re(又) + gener(制造，产生) + ate → 使又一次重生 → 使恢复

【例】The sea cucumber will *regenerate* itself if it is attacked. 海参被袭击后能够自我修复。

【派】regeneration(*n.* 再生，新生)

release [rɪˈliːs] *v./n.* 释放，解放(liberate); 发布

request [rɪˈkwest] *n. /vt.* 要求，请求

【记】分拆联想：re(一再) + quest(追求) → 要求，请求

【例】People from the television station have *requested* the viewers to send in their suggestions. 电台的工作人员要求观众把建议反馈给他们。

resilience [rɪˈzɪliəns] *n.* 弹力，弹性; 回弹能力

【记】分拆联想：resili(看作 resile，弹回; 恢复活力) + ence → 弹力，弹性

rhyme [raɪm] *n.* 韵，押韵(rhythm) *v.* 押韵

【记】分拆联想：r + hyme(看作 hymn，赞美诗) → 赞美诗一般是押韵的 → 押韵

【例】A poem usually *rhymes.* 诗通常都会押韵。

【派】rhyming(*n.* 押韵)

scale [skeɪl] *n.* 鳞; 规模; 比例(proportion); 刻度 *vt.* 攀登(climb)

【记】词根记忆：scal(登，爬) + e → 攀登

【搭】on a large scale 大规模地

【例】Foxes can't *scale* the sheer rocks. 狐狸不能攀爬陡峭的岩石。// Even in this current era of large *scale*, the interrelationships involved in this process are frequently misunderstood. 即使在目前这个大规模的时代，这个过程涉及的相互关系也常常被误解。

shade [ʃeɪd] *n.* 阴凉处，遮光物(shelter); 阴暗(shadow)

【例】These plants don't like the direct sunlight and little *shade* could help them immensely. 这些植物不喜欢阳光直晒，一点阴凉对它们大有裨益。

sort [sɔːrt] *n.* 种类，类别(type) *v.* 分类，挑选

【记】本身为词根：种类

【例】They *sorted* the apples into large ones and small ones. 他们把苹果分成了大小两类。

□ regenerate	□ release	□ request	□ resilience	□ rhyme	□ scale
□ shade	□ sort				

sow [soʊ] *vt.* 播种 (scatter, spread)

【派】sowing (*n.* 播种)

splash [splæʃ] *n.* 引人注目的事物 *v.* 溅，泼 (dash)

splash

【例】Early advertisements were quite small and subtle, not the *splash* sheet whole page spreads of today. 早期的广告篇幅很小，也很精巧，不像如今整版的广告那样引人注目。

sponsor ['spɑːnsər] *n.* 发起者 (source)；赞助人 (benefactor) *v.* 主办；赞助 (patronize)

【记】分拆联想：spons (音似：四帮四) + or → 以四帮四的形式资助别人 → 赞助

【例】Our museum membership will be *sponsored* by the professor. 我们的博物馆会员费将由教授赞助。

substitute ['sʌbstɪtuːt] *n.* 代替者，代替品 (replacement) *vt.* 代替 (replace)

【记】词根记忆：sub (下面) + stitut (站) + e → 站在下面的 → 代替品

【例】Radio is a *substitute* for newspapers in people's homes. 在家中，广播是报纸的一种替代品。

【派】substituted (*a.* 替代的)

sustained [sə'steɪnd] *a.* 持续的 (consistent)

【记】来自 sustain (*vt.* 保持)

【例】We just don't have the technology yet to do *sustained* research. 我们还不具备从事持续研究的技术。

taste [teɪst] *v.* 品尝，辨味；有…味道；体验，感到 *n.* 滋味 (flavor)；味觉；(趣) 味；鉴赏力

【搭】taste much better 尝起来更好

【例】A: This coffee never seems to *taste* quite right to me. Maybe we should buy a different brand.

B: Why not a new coffee pot?

A：这种咖啡喝起来总不对劲。或许我们应该买别的品牌。

B：为什么不买个新的咖啡壶呢？

【参】paste (*n.* 糨糊，面团)

traditional [trə'dɪʃənl] *a.* 传统的，惯例的 (conventional)；口传的，传说的

【搭】traditional view 传统观点

【例】I understand your troupe performs *traditional* music and dance from many different native American cultures. 我知道你的剧团可以表演来自不同美国土著文化的传统音乐和舞蹈。//The elevation of Mount Everest was determined many years ago using *traditional* surveying methods. 珠穆朗玛峰的海拔是多年前使用传统勘测手段测定的。

tundra [ˈtʌndrə] *n.* 苔原；冻土地带

【记】分拆联想：t + undra（看作 under，在…之下）→ 冰雪覆盖的草原 → 苔原

【例】In the Arctic *tundra*, ice fog may form under clear skies in winter. 在北极的冻土地带，冬季晴天时会形成冰雾。

underground [ˌʌndərˈɡraʊnd] *a.* 地下的，地面下的(subterranean, buried)

【记】组合词：under（在…下）+ ground（地面）→ 地面下的

【搭】underground water 地下水；underground garage 地下停车场；an underground passage 地下通道

【参】underestimate(*vt.* 低估)；understand(*v.* 理解)；undertake(*v.* 承担，担任)

universe [ˈjuːnɪvɜːrs] *n.* 宇宙(cosmos)；世界(world)

【记】词根记忆：uni（一个）+ vers（转）+ e → 一个旋转着的空间 → 宇宙

【例】The *universe* is filled with puzzling materials. 宇宙中充满了令人不解的物质。

【派】universal(*a.* 普遍的；宇宙的)；universally(*ad.* 普遍地，全体地)

vessel [ˈvesl] *n.* 船(cargo)；容器(container)；血管(vein)

【例】Canals are often classified by the size of *vessel* they can accommodate. 运河通常是按照其所能容纳的船只的尺寸来分类的。

voracious [vəˈreɪʃəs] *a.* 狼吞虎咽的；贪婪的(greedy, insatiable)

【记】词根记忆：vor（吃）+ acious → 吃得多的 → 狼吞虎咽的

Word List 20

词根、词缀预习表

bound	边界	abound	*vi.* 富于；充满
tract	拉	attract	*vt.* 吸引
mand	命令	command	*n. /v.* 命令；指挥
turb	搅乱	turbulent	*a.* 动乱的
vis	看	visible	*a.* 看得见的
bell	美	embellish	*vt.* 修饰

abound [ə'baʊnd] *vi.* (in)富于(flourish)；大量存在(teem)；充满(overflow)
【记】分拆联想：a + bound(边界) → 没有边界 → 大量存在；充满
【例】The state *abounds* in colonial architecture. 这个州有很多殖民时期的建筑。

amble ['æmbl] *vi.* 缓行，漫步(stroll, wander)
【记】amble本身就是一个词根=ambul(走路)

astronomical [ˌæstrə'nɑːmɪkl] *a.* 天文学的；极大的，庞大的
【记】词根记忆：astro(星星) + nomical → 星星的，星体的 → 天文学的
【搭】astronomical observation 天文观测；astronomical object 天体
【例】The natural colors of *astronomical* objects can be captured. 天体的自然颜色是可以捕捉到的。//Most *astronomical* objects are very remote and the light we receive from them is rather feeble. 多数天体都非常遥远，我们从它们那里接收到的光非常微弱。

attract [ə'trækt] *vt.* 吸引(lure, draw)
【记】词根记忆：at(加强) + tract(拉) → 拉过来 → 吸引
【例】The songs *attracted* only the young people in a community. 这些歌曲只吸引了社区里的年轻人。

attract

☐ abound　　☐ amble　　☐ astronomical　　☐ attract

213

【派】attraction(*n.* 吸引，诱惑); attractant(*n.* 引诱物)

basic [ˈbeɪsɪk] *a.* 基本的，基础的(fundamental)

【搭】basic rights 基本权利

【例】A: I'd really like to learn how to play chess, but it looks so complicated. It seems like it will take a really long time to learn.

B: Well, it takes a long time to get good at it. But we can learn the *basics* this afternoon if you want.

A: 我特想学下棋，但是它看上去太复杂了，好像要很长时间才能学会。

B: 下好需要很长时间。不过如果你想学，今天下午可以学点基本知识。

beam [biːm] *n.* 束；横梁(timber, bar)

【记】分拆联想：be + am → 做我自己，成为国家的栋梁 → 横梁

【搭】a beam of sunlight 一束阳光

bellows [ˈbeloʊz] *n.* 风箱

【记】和bellow(*v.* 吼叫)一起记

bloom [bluːm] *n.* 花 *vi.* 开花(blossom)

【例】The sun's shining, and the flowers are *blooming*. 阳光灿烂，花儿绽放。

cape [keɪp] *n.* 海角，岬

caterpillar [ˈkætərpɪlər] *n.* 毛虫，蝴蝶的幼虫

【记】源自法语词汇 chatepelose, 字面意思是"多毛的猫(hairy cat)"

characteristic [ˌkærəktəˈrɪstɪk] *a.* 特有的；典型的(typical) *n.* 特性(property)

【例】Different types of matter have different *characteristics*. 不同类型的物质有着不同的特点。

【派】characteristically(*ad.* 独特地)

collectively [kəˈlektɪvli] *ad.* 全体地，共同地(together)

【例】In early jazz, musicians often improvised melodies *collectively*. 早期的爵士乐手们常常一起进行即兴创作。

colonize [ˈkɑːlənaɪz] *vt.* 开拓(或建立)殖民地；移居于(settle)

【记】来自colony(*n.* 殖民地)

【派】colonization(*n.* 殖民；殖民地化)

command [kəˈmænd] *n. /v.* 命令；指挥；掌握(govern, control)

【记】词根记忆：com(共同) + mand(命令) → 命令大家一起做 → 命令；指挥

【例】Who issued the *command* to fire? 谁下令开枪的？

| □ basic | □ beam | □ bellows | □ bloom | □ cape | □ caterpillar |
| □ characteristic | □ collectively | □ colonize | □ command | | |

【派】commander(*n.* 司令官, 指挥); commandment(*n.* 戒律)

【参】demand(*n.* 要求)

continuum [kənˈtɪnjuəm] *n.* 连续统一体(a coherent whole)

【例】The development of jazz can be seen as part of the larger *continuum* of American popular music, especially dance music. 爵士乐的发展可被视为美国流行音乐,尤其是舞蹈音乐这一大的连续统一体中的一部分。

convenience [kənˈviːnɪəns] *n.* 便利(fitness or suitability); 便利设施

【记】词根记忆: con(共同) + ven(来) + i + ence → 共同行动来维护便民设施 → 便利设施

【例】For me the *convenience* of having a laundromat so close to where I live is worth the extra dollar. 对我而言,住处附近自助洗衣店带来的便利值得花更多的钱。

【派】inconvenience(*n.* 麻烦)

core [kɔːr] *n.* 中心, 核心; 地核(center)

daylight [ˈdeɪlaɪt] *n.* 日光(sunlight); 白昼; 黎明

【记】组合词: day(白天) + light(光) → 白天的光 → 日光

【搭】daylight hours 白天

【例】The African grass mouse is active during *daylight* hours. 非洲草鼠在白天很活跃。

delay [dɪˈleɪ] *vt./n.* 耽搁, 延迟(postpone)

【记】分拆联想: de + lay(放下) → 放下不管 → 耽搁

【例】A: They said the train won't arrive until nine.

B: Well, what that boils down to is yet another *delay* in our schedule.

A: 他们说火车9点才到。

B: 哦,这意味着我们的安排又要被耽误了。

A: The forecast calls for heavy snow again tonight. Aren't you glad we'll be getting away from this for a week?

B: I sure am. But let's call tomorrow morning before we leave for the airport to make sure our flight hasn't been *delayed* or cancelled.

A: 天气预报说今晚又有大雪。我们要远离这种天气一周,你难道不开心吗?

B: 我当然开心。但是明天早上去机场前要先打电话确认一下我们的航班没有晚点或取消。

depend [dɪˈpend] *vi.* (on)依靠, 依赖(rely); 取决于(lie on)

【记】词根记忆: de + pend(悬挂) → 悬挂着的 → 依靠, 依赖

【派】dependable(*a.* 可信赖的); dependence(*n.* 依赖); dependent

(*a.* 依赖的；取决于…的)

【参】interdependence (*n.* 互相依赖)；interdependent (*a.* 互相依赖的)

distract [dɪ'strækt] *vt.* 分散注意力，使…分心

【记】词根记忆：dis(分开) + tract(拉) → (精神)被拉开 → 使…分心

【例】The thunderstorm *distracted* the little boy from his homework. 雷电使小男孩无法专心写作业。

distract

【派】distracted (*a.* 心烦意乱的)

eclecticism [ɪ'klektɪsɪzəm] *n.* 折衷主义

elasticity [ˌiːlæ'stɪsəti] *n.* 弹力，弹性

【例】This kind of material eventually lost its *elasticity*. 这种材料最终失去了弹性。

embellish [ɪm'belɪʃ] *vt.* 修饰(decorate)；渲染(exaggerate)

【记】词根记忆：em + bell(美) + ish → 使…美 → 修饰；渲染

【例】Jimmy *embellished* the tale of his fishing trip to make it sound more exciting. 吉米给他的钓鱼之行添油加醋，使其听起来更加让人兴奋。

endangered [ɪn'deɪndʒərd] *a.* 濒临灭绝的(extinct)

【搭】endangered species 濒危物种

equal ['iːkwəl] *a.* 相同的(same) *vt.* 等于(amount)；相当于 *n.* 相等的事物、对手、同辈

【例】The pressure of the gases being breathed must *equal* the external pressure applied to the body. 吸进的气体压力必须等于施加在身体上的外部压力。

【派】equality (*n.* 平等)；equally (*ad.* 相等地；平等地)

era ['ɪrə] *n.* 纪元；时代(period of time, epoch)

【记】联想记忆：反过来拼写是are

【搭】Neolithic era 新石器时代；silent film era 无声电影时代

evacuation [ɪˌvækju'eɪʃn] *n.* 撤离(withdrawal)

【记】词根记忆：e(出) + vacu(空) + ation → 空出来 → 撤离

【例】The radio mentioned possible *evacuation* routes. 广播提到了可能的撤退路线。

exploit [ɪk'splɔɪt] *v.* 开发(tap)；利用(make use of)

【记】词根记忆：ex + ploit(利用) → 开发；利用

【例】As preeminent generalists, members of this species *exploit* a great range of habitats and resources. 作为著名的多面手，这个物种

| distract | eclecticism | elasticity | embellish | endangered | equal |
| era | evacuation | exploit | | | |

的成员有多种栖息地和资源。

【派】exploitation(*n.* 开发); over-exploitation(*n.* 过度开采)

facade [fə'sɑːd] *n.* 正面(front, face); 表面(surface); (喻)虚伪的外表

【记】分拆联想: fac(看作face, 正面) + ade → 正面; 表面

【例】The sound of a person may give a clue to the *facade* or mask of him. 一个人的声音可能是揭露其虚伪外表的线索。

fantastic [fæn'tæstɪk] *a.* 荒诞的, 奇异的; 极好的(terrific); 难以置信的

【记】来自fantasy(*n.* 幻想)

【例】My new neighbor has a *fantastic* collection of classical music. 我的新邻居有一批极好的古典音乐收藏品。

A: The concert pianist is fantastic.

B: And how!

A: 音乐会的钢琴演奏者棒极了。

B: 的确是这样!

fracture ['fræktʃər] *vt./n.* (使)破裂(*crack)

【记】词根记忆: fract(碎裂) + ure → 破裂

【例】*Fracture* on tools also indicates that a majority of ancient people were right-handed. 工具上的破裂处也表明古时大部分人都用右手。

guideline ['gaɪdlaɪn] *n.* [常*pl.*] 指导方针

【记】组合词: guide + line → 指导方针

haste [heɪst] *n.* 急忙, 匆忙(hurry)

【例】In my *haste* I forgot my books. 我一着急就把书给忘了。

【派】hasten(*vt.* 催促; 加速)

horn [hɔːrn] *n.* (牛、羊、鹿等的)角; 号角, 喇叭(speaker, trumpet)

【记】联想记忆: 牛、羊、鹿等天生(born)就有角(horn)

hurl [hɜːrl] *vt.* 猛投, 用力投掷(fling)

【例】The luxury express trains that *hurl* people over spots spotlight the romance of railroading. 把乘客载往各处的豪华快车突出了铁路旅行的浪漫。

indispensable [ˌɪndɪ'spensəbl] *a.* 必不可少的(necessary)

【记】分拆联想: in(不) + dispensable(可有可无的) → 不是可有可无的 → 必不可少的

【例】Surveys sometimes are *indispensable* sources of information. 调查有时候是信息必不可少的来源。

inferior [ɪn'fɪriə(r)] *a.* 差的; 次要的

【记】分拆联想: infer(推断) + ior → 推断的东西是次要的, 事实

☐ facade	☐ fantastic	☐ fracture	☐ guideline	☐ haste	☐ horn
☐ hurl	☐ indispensable	☐ inferior			

217

才是依据 → 次要的

【例】Vase painters sometimes produce *inferior* ware. 花瓶的绘画者有时会做出次品。

【派】inferiority(*n.* 下级；自卑感)

inflammation [ˌɪnfləˈmeɪʃn] *n.* 【医】炎症，发炎

informed [ɪnˈfɔːrmd] *a.* 受过教育的；见多识广的

【记】分拆联想：in(进入)＋form(形成)＋ed → 进入知识体系的形成 → 见多识广的

【参】learned(*a.* 有学问的)

install [ɪnˈstɔːl] *vt.* 安置，安装(fix)

【记】分拆联想：in(进入)＋stall(放) → 放进去 → 安置，安装

【例】This morning the carpenters *installed* the new kitchen cabinets. 今天上午木匠安装了新的橱柜。

【派】installation(*n.* 安装)

irreverent [ɪˈrevərənt] *a.* 不敬的

【记】词根记忆：ir＋re＋ver(真实)＋ent → 在神面前说假话 → 不敬的

【派】irreverence(*n.* 不敬；不敬的行为)

jeans [dʒiːnz] *n.* 牛仔裤

【例】It's all right to wear *jeans* for a class presentation, isn't it? 在课堂做报告可以穿牛仔裤，对吧？

irreverent

jewelry [ˈdʒuːəlri] *n.* [总称]首饰(ornament)；珠宝(gem)

maglev [ˈmæglev] *n.* 磁力悬浮火车

【例】*Maglev* will not actually ride on the tracks but will fly above tracks that are magnetically activated. 磁悬浮火车并不在轨道上行驶，而是漂浮在磁力驱动的轨道上快速行驶。

maize [meɪz] *n.* 玉米

【记】发音记忆："麦子" → 麦子和玉米都属于农作物 → 玉米

market [ˈmɑːrkɪt] *n.* 市场(mart)；股市 *v.* 销售(sell)

【搭】market day 集市日；market share 市场份额

【例】The two lens grinders first decided to *market* the telescope as a military invention. 这两个镜片磨光者起初决定把望远镜当作军事发明物来销售。

【派】marketable(*a.* 适于销售的)；marketing(*n.* 营销)

melt [melt] *v.* (使)融化，(使)熔化，(使)消散(dissolve, liquefy)

【例】If clay contains too much iron it will *melt* when fired. 如果黏土

| □ inflammation | □ informed | □ install | □ irreverent | □ jeans | □ jewelry |
| □ maglev | □ maize | □ market | □ melt | | |

含有过多的铁就会在烧制过程中熔化。

mime [maɪm] *vt.* 模拟(simulate) *n.* 喜剧(comedy); 模拟表演
【记】词根记忆: mim(假正经的)+e→假正经, 装模作样→模拟
【例】They often *mimed* the desired effect-success in hunt or battle. 他们经常模拟狩猎或战斗中想要的成功效果。//Next *mime* I'll be sure to call in advance and make a reservation. 下次的喜剧表演我一定会提前打电话预订。
【派】mimetic(*a.* 模仿的, 好模仿的)

mimic ['mɪmɪk] *vt.* 模仿(imitate)
【记】分拆联想: mimi(音似: 秘密)+c→偷偷摸摸地模仿→模仿
【例】People have always been fascinated by the parrot's ability to *mimic* human speech. 人们向来对鹦鹉模仿人类说话的能力惊叹不已。

molten ['moʊltən] *a.* 熔化的, 熔融的(melted)
【搭】molten glass 熔融态玻璃, 玻璃液
【例】Any rock that has cooled and solidified from a *molten* state is an igneous rock. 任何从熔化状态冷却固化的岩石都是火成岩。

notate ['noteɪt] *vt.* 以符号表示, 把…写成记号(或标志)
【记】词根记忆: not(标识)+ate(使…)→使…有标识→以符号表示
【例】Composers of Western music used a system of *notating* their compositions so they could be performed by musicians. 西方音乐的作曲家使用同一套符号系统, 这样音乐家就能演奏他们的作品了。
【派】notation(*n.* 符号)
【渗】notable(*a.* 明显的; 著名的)

oval ['oʊvl] *a.* 卵形的, 椭圆形的(elliptic)
【记】发音记忆: o(音似: 喔)+val(音似: 哇哦)→发哇哦这些声音, 嘴都张成椭圆形→椭圆的

pinpoint ['pɪnpɔɪnt] *vt.* 精准定位
【记】组合词: pin(钉, 针)+point(点, 尖端)→精准定位
【例】Radar can help *pinpoint* the location of an object within its range. 雷达可以帮助确定其监测范围内的物体的位置。

preference ['prefrəns] *n.* (for, to)偏爱(favoritism); 优先(权)(superiority)
【例】He has no reading *preferences*. 他在阅读方面没有特别的喜好。
【参】preferred(*a.* 首选的)

projector [prə'dʒektər] *n.* 放映机, 幻灯机, 投影仪
【例】*Projectors* have been widely used on class in developed countries. 发达国家已经在课堂上广泛使用投影仪了。

mime　mimic　molten　notate　oval　pinpoint
preference　projector

A: This *projector* is out of order and I need it for my presentation.

B: There's a spare in the storeroom.

A: 这台投影仪出问题了，我做报告要用。

B: 仓库有一台备用的。

pursuit [pər'suːt] *n.* 追求；[常 *pl.*] 花时间和精力等做的事、职业

【例】The peregrine falcon have been clocked at 140 to 200 miles per hour in successful *pursuit* of pray. 游隼成功追捕猎物时被记录的飞行速度为每小时140到200英里。

radioactive [ˌreɪdɪoʊ'æktɪv] *a.* 放射性的

【记】分拆联想：radi(光线) + o + active(活跃的) → 放射性的

rainbow ['reɪnboʊ] *n.* 虹

【记】组合词：rain + bow → 雨后的弓 → 虹

rattle ['rætl] *n.* 产生连续声音的器具；拨浪鼓

【参】rattlesnake(*n.* 响尾蛇)

rebellion [rɪ'beljən] *n.* 叛乱，反抗，起义(uprising)

【搭】crash the rebellion 平息叛乱

rattle

【例】In the 1950's, T-shirt became a sign of *rebellion* for teenagers. 在20世纪50年代，T恤衫成为了青少年反叛的标识。//The only way for a nation to survive is to crash the *rebellion*. 一个国家要想生存下去的唯一途径就是平息叛乱。

reconstruction [ˌriːkən'strʌkʃn] *n.* 复兴，改造，再建(restoration)

【搭】a reconstruction period 复兴时期

【例】The *reconstruction* of the tower is not a boy's play. 重建这座塔可不是儿戏。

reform [rɪ'fɔːrm] *v. /n.* 改革，革新(innovate)

【记】分拆联想：re(重新) + form(形成，形状) → 重新形成 → 改革，革新

【例】One of many *reforms* came in the area of public utilities. 众多改革中有一项涉及公共设施领域。

【派】reformer(*n.* 改革者)

relate [rɪ'leɪt] *v.* 叙述，讲述；使互相关联

【记】分拆联想：re + late (新近的) → 和新近的事件有关联 → 使相互关联

【搭】relate to 与…有关；be related to 与…有关，与…有亲缘关系，与…同一血统

【例】The report seeks to *relate* the rise in crime to the increase in unemployment. 这份报告试图把犯罪上升与失业增加联系起来。

【派】related(*a.* 有关的，相联系的)；unrelated(*a.* 无关的，不相干的)

scan [skæn] *vt.* 细察(examine, scrutinize)；扫描

【记】发音记忆："死看" → 四处看 → 扫描

scenery ['siːnəri] *n.* 风景，景色(landscape)；舞台布景

【记】分拆联想：scene(场面) + ry → 风景，景色

【例】Music and *scenery* are of little importance to the modern dance. 音乐和舞台布景对现代舞蹈来说并不重要。

【参】scenic(*a.* 景色优美的；布景的)

silicate ['sɪlɪkeɪt] *n.* [化] 硅酸盐

situated ['sɪtʃueɪtɪd] *a.* 坐落在…的(located)

【例】If a city is well *situated* in regard to its hinterland, its development is much more likely to continue. 一座城市腹地如果位置不错，就更有可能继续发展。

skull [skʌl] *n.* 颅骨；头脑

【记】和skill(*n.* 技能)一起记

slog [slɑːg] *v.* 艰难行进(tramp)

span [spæn] *n.* 跨度；一段时间(period) *vt.* 跨越

【搭】life span 寿命

stake [steɪk] *n.* 利害关系

【搭】at stake 在危险中；stake out a claim 坚持要求

【例】They hired people to *stake* out claims. 他们雇人来坚持这些要求。

tableland ['teɪbllænd] *n.* 高原(hill, plateau)

testimony ['testɪmoʊni] *n.* 证词

thread [θred] *n.* 线

【派】threadlike(*a.* 线状的)

thrifty ['θrɪfti] *a.* 节省的，节俭的(saving)

【记】来自thrift(*n.* 节约)

【例】The *thrifty* housewife only buys grocery items that are on sale. 那个节俭的家庭妇女只购买减价的杂货。

tinker ['tɪŋkər] *n.* 补锅工人 *v.* 做焊锅匠；做拙劣的修补

【例】In the past, only a few people who *tinkered* with wireless telegraphs as a hobby owned receivers. 过去，只有少数以鼓捣无线电报为嗜好的人拥有接收机。

| scan | scenery | silicate | situated | skull | slog | span |
| stake | tableland | testimony | thread | thrifty | tinker | |

221

【参】thinker(*n.* 思想家)

turbulent [ˈtɜːrbjələnt] *a.* 动乱的(disorderly)；狂暴的，汹涌的(violent)

【记】词根记忆：turb(搅乱) + ulent → 搅得厉害 → 动乱的；汹涌的

【例】The weather patterns are so *turbulent* here. 这里气候多变。

unconsolidated [ˌʌnkənˈsɑːlɪdeɪtɪd] *a.* 松散的，疏松的(loose)

【例】An *unconsolidated* aggregate of silt particles is also termed silt, whereas a consolidated aggregate is called siltstone. 一团没有固结的淤泥颗粒仍然叫作淤泥，而一团固结的淤泥就叫作粉砂石。

visible [ˈvɪzəbl] *a.* 看得见的，明显的(observable, noticeable)

【记】词根记忆：vis(看) + ible(可…的) → 看得见的，明显的

【例】The impact caused an explosion clearly *visible* from Earth. 碰撞造成了爆炸，在地球上清晰可见。

【派】visibility(*n.* 可见性；可见度)；visibly(*ad.* 明显地)；invisible(*a.* 看不见的，无形的)

The saying "Beginning is the hardest for everything" is reasonable sometimes. But generally speaking, the beginning period is the easiest, and the hardest period is the rush in the last period; only few can overcome the last barrier.

"凡事起头难"，这句话在某些时候的确有道理。但是一般而言，凡事起头易，最难的该是最后阶段的冲刺，能够克服这一关的人真是少之又少。

——歌德(*Goethe*)

Word List 21

词根、词缀预习表

greg	团体	aggregate	n. 聚成岩
ambi	在…周围	ambience	n. 周围环境, 气氛
arthr	连结; 关节	arthritis	n. 关节炎
calc	石头	calcium	n. 钙
pro	许多	proliferate	vi. 激增
feder	联盟	confederacy	n. 联盟
tag	接触	contagious	a. 传染性的
plete	满	deplete	v. (使)枯竭
spect	看	perspective	n. 远景; 角度

aggregate [ˈægrɪgət] n. 聚成岩; 聚集物

【记】词根记忆: ag + greg(团体) + ate → 成为一团 → 聚集物

【例】Marine mammals have the misfortune to be swimming *aggregates* of commodities that humans want: fur, oil, and meat. 海洋哺乳动物不幸成为人类需要的商品集合体: 皮毛、油脂和肉。

【派】aggregation(n. 集合; 集合体)

alternative [ɔːlˈtɜːrnətɪv] n. 选择(option) a. 其他可选用的

【例】So far the electric car seems to be the best *alternative*. 目前为止电动车好像是最好的替代品。

ambience [ˈæmbiəns] n. 周围环境, 气氛

【记】词根记忆: ambi(在…周围) + ence → 存在于四周的 → 气氛

【例】The manager tries to create a pleasant *ambience* in the office. 经理努力在办公室营造一种愉快的氛围。

ancestor [ˈænsestər] n. 祖先(forefather)

【记】分拆联想: ance(看作ante, 先) + st + or(人) → 祖先

【派】ancestral(a. 祖先的; 祖传的)

【参】ancestry(n. 世系, 血统)

anecdotal [ˌænɪkˈdoʊtl] *a.* 轶闻的，多轶闻趣事的

【记】来自 anecdote(*n.* 轶事)

【例】The scholar's findings are based on *anecdotal* evidences rather than formal researches. 这个学者的发现是基于轶事类的证据，而非正式的研究。

animation [ˌænɪˈmeɪʃn] *n.* 动画制作

【例】These topics will be illustrated with computer *animations* to make explanations easy to follow. 这些话题将辅以电脑动画，这样解释起来就很容易听懂了。

announcement [əˈnaʊnsmənt] *n.* 宣告；发表；通知(notice)

【记】来自 announce(*v.* 宣布，通告)

【例】A: I wish the plane would get here. It's already eight thirty.

B: There's no need to get nervous. The *announcement* said it would be fifteen minutes late.

A：但愿飞机能到。已经八点半了。

B：没有必要紧张。广播说会晚点十五分钟。

apartment [əˈpɑːrtmənt] *n.* 公寓住宅(flat, suite)

【记】分拆联想：a + part(部分，局部) + ment → 分成一栋一栋 → 公寓住宅

arthritis [ɑːrˈθraɪtɪs] *n.* 关节炎

【记】词根记忆：arthr(连结；关节) + itis(炎症) → 关节炎

authentic [ɔːˈθentɪk] *a.* 真正的，真实的(real, genuine)；可靠的

【例】A: I really enjoy the play. The students did a great job with the scenery. It looks so *authentic*. I felt like I was back in the 19th century.

B: I wish you could say the same thing about the costumes.

A：我很喜欢这部戏。学生们做的布景很棒，看上去很真实，感觉像是回到了19世纪。

B：我希望你对服装有同样的评价。

banner [ˈbænər] *n.* 横幅

【记】分拆联想：ban(禁止) + n + er → 禁止悬挂横幅 → 横幅

【参】ban(*n.* 禁令)

botany [ˈbɑːtəni] *n.* 植物学

【记】分拆联想：bot(看作about，关于) + any(任何) → 关于任何(植物) → 植物学

【派】botanical(*a.* 植物学的)；botanist(*n.* 植物学家)

calcium [ˈkælsiəm] *n.* 钙

【记】词根记忆：calc(石头) + ium → 像石头一样硬 → 钙

【搭】calcium carbonate 碳酸钙

☐ anecdotal ☐ animation ☐ announcement ☐ apartment ☐ arthritis ☐ authentic
☐ banner ☐ botany ☐ calcium

chaste [tʃeɪst] *a.* 贞洁的；朴素的；有道德的
【记】联想记忆：贞洁的(chaste)姑娘被追逐(chase)

classical [ˈklæsɪkl] *a.* 经典的；古典(文学)的
【记】分拆联想：classic(*n.* 经典，杰作)+al → 经典的
【例】Professor Lee will give a speech on *classical* literature in the hall this Friday. 李教授将于本周五在礼堂做古典文学的讲座。
【参】classic(*a.* 一流的)

client [ˈklaɪənt] *n.* 委托人，当事人；顾客(customer)

client

closet [ˈklɑːzət] *n.* 壁橱(cabinet) *a.* 隐蔽的(closely private)

commodity [kəˈmɑːdəti] *n.* 商品(article)；日用品
【记】词根记忆：com + mod (方式；范围) + ity → 各种各样的东西 → 商品
【例】By the 1940's her paintings had become a very precious *commodity*. 到20世纪40年代，她的绘画已成为非常珍贵的商品。

company [ˈkʌmpəni] *n.* 公司(corporation)，商号；陪伴，同伴；宾客，客人；连(队)，(一)群，(一)队，(一)伙
【搭】enjoy the company of sb./enjoy one's company 喜欢某人的陪伴；keep company with 与…交往，与…结伴
【例】A: We need a quiet place to study. My roommate's got *company*. Could we work over at your place?
B: Yeah, no problem, but I have to warn you: I haven't done much cleaning this week.
A: 我们需要安静的地方学习。有人来拜访我的室友。我们能在你那里学吗？
B: 可以，没问题。不过我得提醒你，我这个礼拜没怎么打扫卫生。

concise [kənˈsaɪs] *a.* 简明的，简练的(terse)
【记】词根记忆：con + cise(切掉) → 把(多余的)全部切掉 → 简练的
【例】Worksheets require defining the problem in a clear and *concise* way. 工作表要求清晰简要地给问题下定义。

confederacy [kənˈfedərəsi] *n.* 联盟(alliance)
【记】词根记忆：con + feder(联盟) + acy → 联盟
【例】She may have exerted even more influence on the *confederacy* than he did. 她对联盟产生的影响可能比他还多。
【派】confederate(*n.* 同盟)

| ☐ chaste | ☐ classical | ☐ client | ☐ closet | ☐ commodity | ☐ company |
| ☐ concise | ☐ confederacy | | | | |

contagious [kən'teɪdʒəs] *a.* 传染性的, 有感染力的(catching)

【记】词根记忆: con + tag(接触) + ious → 接触(疾病的) → 传染性的

【例】A hobby like collection of classical music can be *contagious* and expensive. 像收集古典音乐这样的嗜好会感染人, 花销也很大。

【参】contiguous(*a.* 邻近的)

convention [kən'venʃn] *n.* 惯例(custom); 公约(agreement); (正式)会议(conference)

【记】词根记忆: con(共同) + vent(来) + ion → 大家共同来遵守的东西 → 惯例; 公约

【例】In last week's films, we saw how Graffith ignored both these limiting *conventions*. 在上周的电影里, 我们看到了格拉菲斯是如何忽视这些限制性的传统的。//Have you any idea who will attend the convention? 你知道谁会参加会议吗?

【派】unconventional(*a.* 非传统的)

【参】同根词: intervention(*n.* 干预, 介入)

deplete [dɪ'pliːt] *v.* (使)枯竭, 耗尽(use up, exhaust)

【记】词根记忆: de + plete(满) → 倒空了, 不满 → (使)枯竭

【例】Food supplies are quickly *depleted*. 食物储备快耗尽了。

【派】depletion(*n.* 消耗, 用尽)

detail ['diːteɪl] *n.* 细节, 详情

【记】分拆联想: de(去掉) + tail(尾巴) → 去掉尾巴 → 对细枝末节的改动 → 细节

【搭】in detail 详细地; with details of 关于…的细节

【例】If you're interested in the job, I'll send you all the *details*. 如果你对这份工作感兴趣, 我将给你寄去全部的详细说明。

distinction [dɪ'stɪŋkʃn] *n.* 显赫, 声望(luster, honor); 差别, 特性(difference)

【搭】make a distinction 区分; distinction between …之间的差别; with distinction 优异地

【例】The music from the show *The Lion King* was used to summarize some of the technical *distinctions* between typical western music and the non-western music.《狮子王》的音乐被用来总结典型的西方音乐和非西方音乐之间的一些技术区别。

drive [draɪv] *v.* 开(车), 驾驶; 驱, 赶; 驱动; 把(钉、桩)打入 *n.* 驾驶, 驱车旅行

【搭】drive sb. up the wall 把某人逼到绝境; 使沮丧; drive home 开车回家; an hour's drive 开车一小时的行程

【例】A: Look at the time. I'm going to miss my bus.

B: Don't worry. I'll *drive* you to the stop. And if the bus has already left, I can get you to your apartment.

A: 看着点时间。我要赶不上公交车了。

B: 别担心。我开车送你去车站。如果车已经开走了，我就把你送到你的公寓。

【参】dive(*v.* 潜水)

emblem [ˈembləm] *n.* 徽章(badge)

【记】联想记忆：该词的字母组合(em + bl + em)本身像一个对称的徽章

energetic [ˌenərˈdʒetɪk] *a.* 精力充沛的(vigorous)；积极的(active)

【记】来自energy(*n.* 精神，活力)

【例】The interviewers are usually willing to offer posts to job applicants who are *energetic*, hardworking and responsible. 面试官一般愿意把职位提供给那些充满活力、工作勤奋和有责任心的求职人员。

existence [ɪgˈzɪstəns] *n.* 存在；实在；生存，生活(方式)

【记】来自exist(*v.* 存在；生存)

【例】People generally want portraits as evidence of their *existence* for future generations. 人们一般想要把画像留给后代，作为自己存在过的证据。//Scientists have established the *existence* of planets outside our own solar system. 科学家们已经证实我们所在的太阳系外存在着行星。

fix [fɪks] *v.* 使固定，安装；确定，决定；修理

【搭】fix the problem 解决问题；fix the heater 修理暖气

【例】A: Do you have hot water in your dorm? Because we haven't had any for three days and I hate cold showers.

B: Oh, sounds miserable. Since the gym's usually open, why don't you just go over there to *fix* the problem?

A: 你宿舍有热水吗？我们这里三天没热水了，我讨厌用冷水淋浴。

B: 哦，真可怜。健身房通常都会开着，你为什么不去那里解决呢？

A: Hi, hm... I think something's wrong with the washing machine. It works and I just did my laundry but it makes some strange noises. Maybe you should call somebody to *fix* it.

B: Oh, don't worry. Somebody from the repair shop is already on the way over to take a look at it.

A: 你好, 我觉得洗衣机出问题了。用是没问题, 我刚洗了衣服, 但是会出怪声。你或许可以打电话找人来修一下。

B: 哦, 别担心。修理人员已经在路上了。

flag [flæg] *n.* 旗帜(banner); 标记(sign)

flag

flexibility [ˌfleksə'bɪləti] *n.* 灵活性

【例】Computers provide employees with a great degree of *flexibility* in the way work is organized. 计算机在组织工作方面给雇员以很大的灵活性。

funding ['fʌndɪŋ] *n.* 用发行长期债券的方法来收回短期债券

【例】I think I'd like to bring up government *funding* for state universities. 我想我宁愿政府为州立大学提供资助。

garb [gɑːrb] *n.* 服装, 装束(costume, dress)

【例】A man in the *garb* of a priest went onto the stage and stood there silently. 一名穿着牧师服的男子走上了台, 并默默地站在那里。

gene [dʒiːn] *n.* 基因

【记】发音记忆

【例】This *gene* associated with particular nerve in brain. 这个基因与大脑特定的神经有关。

Gothic ['gɑːθɪk] *a.* 哥特式的

【例】It was famous for its use of *Gothic* decorative detail. 它因使用哥特式装饰细节而著名。

habitat ['hæbɪtæt] *n.* (动物或植物的)自然环境; 栖息地(home)

【记】词根记忆: hab(拥有) + itat → 所有地 → 栖息地

【例】One reason why the number of amphibians is declining is that their *habitats* have been destroyed. 两栖动物数量减少的原因之一是栖息地遭到破坏。

halt [hɔːlt] *n./v.* 停止

【记】词根记忆: h + alt(高) → 高处不胜寒, 该停住了 → 停止

【例】Work has to come to a *halt* when the machine goes wrong. 机器出问题时不得不停止工作。

humorous ['hjuːmərəs] *a.* 幽默的; 滑稽的

【记】分拆联想humor(幽默) + ous(…的) → 幽默的

【例】There are two sons and one daughter of Joe's marriage in the story: the daughter married a *humorous* artist and led a happy life in the end. 故事中乔婚后有两个儿子和一个女儿: 女儿嫁了一个幽默的艺术家, 最后过着幸福的生活。

| ☐ flag | ☐ flexibility | ☐ funding | ☐ garb | ☐ gene | ☐ Gothic |
| ☐ habitat | ☐ halt | ☐ humorous | | | |

incursion [ɪnˈkɜːrʒn] *n.* 袭击，入侵（raid）

inform [ɪnˈfɔːrm] *v.* 通知，告诉

【记】分拆联想：in(进入) + form(形成) → 形成文字进行通知 → 通知

【例】You should have *informed* me earlier. 你应该早点告诉我。

【派】informative(*a.* 提供大量资料或信息的)

inn [ɪn] *n.* 小旅馆，客栈（roadhouse）

internship [ˈɪntɜːrnʃɪp] *n.* 实习医师；实习医师期

【例】Why might the summer *internship* be a good opportunity for Jenise? 为什么夏天的实习医师期对詹尼斯而言可能是个好机会？

【参】memebership(*n.* 会员身份)

journalism [ˈdʒɜːrnəlɪzəm] *n.* 新闻业，报章杂志

lead [liːd] *v.* 领导，引导；领先，占首位；通向，导致，引起 *n.* 带领，引导 [led] *n.* 铅

【搭】lead to 导致；通向；lead the way 带路，引路

【例】For some students, these part-time jobs could *lead* to full-time work after graduation as they may offer experience in their own fields. 对一些学生而言，这些兼职为他们在各自的领域提供经验，帮助他们在毕业后找到全职工作。//What probably leads people to choose gourmet coffees over regular brands? 是什么可能使人们选择极品咖啡而非普通的品牌呢？

A: I can't believe that Prof. Lawrence is going to retire.

B: He's still going to *lead* a graduate seminar each semester though.

A：我不敢相信劳伦斯教授要退休了。

B：不过他还是会每个学期组织一次毕业生研讨会。

【参】head(*n.* 头)

linger [ˈlɪŋgər] *vi.* 徘徊（hover）

【记】联想记忆：那位歌手(singer)留恋徘徊(linger)于曾经的舞台

【例】Winter often *lingered*; autumn could be ushered in by severe frost. 冬季经常徘徊着不愿消逝；一次霜冻之后秋天就来了。

livestock [ˈlaɪvstɑːk] *n.* [总称] 家畜，牲畜

【记】分拆联想：live(活) + stock(东西) → 活物 → 家畜

【例】At the time Quebec was a major market for *livestock*, crops and fish. 当时魁北克是牲畜、谷物和鱼类的主要市场。

meaningful ['mi:nɪŋfl] *a.* 意味深长的（significant, important）

【记】分拆联想：meaning（含意，意义）+ ful → 意味深长的

【例】Learning to communicate with people from other countries was the most *meaningful* experiences I had in London. 学会与其他国家的人交流是我在伦敦最有意义的经历。

【参】meaningless（*a.* 无意义的，无价值的）

methane ['meθeɪn] *n.* 甲烷，沼气（firedamp）

mine [maɪn] *n.* 矿（山）*v.* 采矿

【派】miner（*n.* 矿工）

moth [mɔːθ] *n.* 蛾

【记】发音记忆："莫死" → 不畏死 → 飞蛾（moth）扑火哪畏死 → 蛾

ongoing ['ɑːngoʊɪŋ] *a.* 正在进行的

【记】分拆联想：on（进行地）+ going → 正在进行的

【例】Dr. Wilson gave me a few minutes to talk you about the biology department's *ongoing* turtle watching project down the south beach. 威尔逊博士，请您给我几分钟，我想和您谈谈生物系正在南海岸开展的海龟观察项目。

onslaught ['ɑːnslɔːt] *n.* 冲击（impact）

【记】分拆联想：on + slaught（打击）→ 冲击

【例】In the face of this *onslaught*, living things have evolved a variety of defense mechanisms. 面临这次冲击，生物演化出了各种防卫机制。

【参】slaughter（*n./v.* 屠杀）

outlying ['aʊtlaɪɪŋ] *a.* 边远的，偏僻的（remote, distant）

【记】分拆联想：out（出）+ ly（看作lie, 位于）+ ing → 位于外面的 → 边远的

【搭】outlying areas 边远地区

【例】In the nearby town, at least 2,000 people are trapped under the debris and huge rocks have buried roads to *outlying* villages. 在附近的镇子里，至少有2000人被困在废墟之下，大石块已经掩埋了去往偏僻村庄的道路。

patronizing ['petrənaɪzɪŋ] *a.* 要人领情的

【记】分拆联想：patroniz(e)（保护，以恩人自居）+ ing → 要人领情的

【例】Rudely, the waiter spoke to me in a *patronizing* tone. 这个服务员很粗鲁，用高高在上的口气跟我说话。

perspective [pər'spektɪv] *n.* 角度；远景；观点；前途

【记】词根记忆：per + spect（看）+ ive → 贯穿看 → 远景

【搭】perspective glass 望远镜

【例】The cost has also made such plants less attractive from a purely economic *perspective*. 从纯粹的经济角度考虑，这个成本也使这种作物没那么有吸引力。

pictorial [pɪkˈtɔːriəl] *a.* 图示的；图片的

【记】词根记忆：pict(描绘) + orial → 起描绘作用的 → 图示的

platelike [ˈpleɪtlaɪk] *a.* 层状的

poisonous [ˈpɔɪzənəs] *a.* 有毒的

【例】This recent scientific discovery is about a desert shrub whose leaves can shoot up a stream of *poisonous* resin a distance of six feet. 最近的科学发现是关于一种沙漠灌木的，其叶子能往6英尺外的地方喷射出有毒树脂。

premature [ˌpriːməˈtʃʊr] *a.* 早熟的；过早的 *n.* 早产儿

【记】分拆联想：pre(预先) + mature(成熟的) → 比预期时间成熟早的 → 早熟的

【例】The conclusion seemed to be *premature* that Wilson would be absent from election. 说威尔逊不会参加竞选好像有点言之过早。

proliferate [prəˈlɪfəreɪt] *vi.* 激增；繁殖(multiply；propagate, reproduce)

【记】分拆联想：pro(许多) + life(生命) + rate → 产生许多生命 → 繁殖

【派】proliferation(*n.* 增殖；分芽繁殖)

refine [rɪˈfaɪn] *vt.* 精炼，精制；使完善(improve)

【记】分拆联想：re(一再) + fine(纯的) → 不断地使变纯 → 精炼

【例】They do their best to *refine* their interviewing techniques. 他们尽全力完善其采访技巧。

【派】refinement(*n.* 改进；精巧)；refiner(*n.* 精炼者)；refining(*n.* 精炼)

remote [rɪˈmoʊt] *a.* 偏僻的，遥远的(*faraway)

【搭】remote control 遥控器

【例】He's confused by the *remote* controls. 他被遥控器弄糊涂了。

resin [ˈrezn] *n.* 树脂

revere [rɪˈvɪr] *vt.* 尊敬，敬畏(*respect)

【记】联想记忆：我们都很敬畏(revere)这位严厉(severe)的老师

【例】The movement *revered* craft as a form of art. 这场运动把工艺视为一种艺术形式。

【派】reverent(*a.* 虔敬的) reverently(*ad.* 虔诚地)

roll [roʊl] *v.* (使)滚动，转动 *n.* (一)卷，卷形物

【例】Icebergs may *roll* over unexpectedly. 冰山有可能会出人意料地滚动。

【派】roller(*n.* 滚筒，滚轴)；rolling(*a.* 起伏的，旋转的)

pictorial	platelike	poisonous	premature	proliferate	refine
remote	resin	revere	roll		

sole ［soʊl］ *a.* 单独的（*single）；唯一的（*only, individual）*n.* 鞋底

【记】词根记忆：sol(独特的) + e → 单独的；唯一的

【例】The rich investor is the *sole* owner of the office building. 这位富有的投资商是这幢写字楼的唯一所有人。

【派】solely(*ad.* 只，仅)

sparse ［spɑːrs］ *a.* 稀疏的，稀少的（rare）

【记】联想记忆：稀疏的(sparse)火星(spark)

【派】sparsely(*ad.* 稀少地，稀疏地)

sparse

special ［ˈspeʃl］ *a.* 特殊的（peculiar）；专门的（particular）*n.* 特别节目

【派】specialist(*n.* 专家)；specialty(*n.* 专业；特长)

【参】specific(*n.* 特效药 *a.* 特殊的；特定的)

spectacle ［ˈspektəkl］ *n.* 奇观；［*pl.*］眼镜(glasses)

【记】词根记忆：spect(看) + acle → 引人驻足观看 → 奇观

standard ［ˈstændərd］ *n.* 标准(model, rule) *a.* 标准的（*customary, normative）

【记】分拆联想：stand(站立) + ard → 按规则站好 → 标准

【搭】standard distance 标准间隔；standard practice(企业工艺过程的)标准练习

【例】They are working hard to meet these *standards.* 他们正努力地工作以满足这些标准。

【派】standardize(*vt.* 使…标准化)；standardized(*a.* 标准的，定型的)

strap ［stræp］ *n.* 带(strip) *vt.* 用带捆扎

【记】联想记忆：用皮带(strap)拍打(rap)

【例】This *strap* on my briefcase is broken. 我公事包的带子断了。// The drum skin was tightly *strapped* over the circle with rawhide laces. 鼓皮的一圈被生牛皮带紧紧地勒住了。

【参】strip(*n.* 条，带)；stripe(*n.* 斑纹，条纹)

synchronize ［ˈsɪŋkrənaɪz］ *v.* 同步，同时发生

【搭】synchronized waves 同步化波

【例】The title in a movie should *synchronize* with the action. 电影中的标题应该与剧情同步。

tariff ［ˈtærɪf］ *n.* 关税(tax, duty)；税率(tax rate)

【例】Their regulations keep *tariffs* high. 这些规定使关税一直居高不下。

□ sole	□ sparse	□ special	□ spectacle	□ standard	□ strap
□ synchronize	□ tariff				

thesis [ˈθiːsɪs] *n.* 论文（paper）

【例】A: Now that you've finished writing your *thesis*, do you think you will have time to sit back and take it easy? Maybe take a little bit vacation?

B: Believe me, that's exactly what I intend to do.

A：既然你把论文写完了，你觉得有时间放松吗？或许去度个假？

B：相信我，那正是我打算做的。

【派】hypothesis（*n.* 假设）

tide [taɪd] *n.* 潮，潮汐；潮流，趋势（trend）

【记】联想记忆：潮（tide）起潮落，岁月（time）如歌

【搭】tide sb. over 帮助某人渡过难关

【例】A: Could I borrow a twenty to *tide* me over till payday next Thursday?

B: You are in luck. I've just cashed the check.

A：我能借20块钱渡过难关吗？下周四就发工资了。

B：你真幸运。我刚兑现了这张支票。

【派】tidal（*a.* 潮汐的；潮流的）

【参】tidy（*a.* 简洁的）

tournament [ˈtʊrnəmənt] *n.* 比赛（game, match），锦标赛（title match）

【记】分拆联想：tour（巡回）+ nament → 到各处巡回比赛 → 比赛

【例】I almost forgot to tell you about the all-day volleyball *tournament* going on. 我差点忘了告诉你现在全天都在举行排球锦标赛。

turtle [ˈtɜːrtl] *n.* 海龟

【记】发音记忆："特逗" → 海龟（turtle）样子特逗 → 海龟

welfare [ˈwelfer] *n. /a.* 福利（的）（well-being）

【记】分拆联想：wel（看作well，好的）+ fare → 好的东西 → 福利

【搭】welfare state 福利国家

【例】The company's *welfare* officer deals with employees' personal problems. 公司负责福利的工作人员负责处理雇员的个人问题。

Word List 22 🔘 MP3-22

词根、词缀预习表

fect	做	defect	n. 瑕疵；过失
glor	光荣	glorify	v. 美化，赞扬
licen	允许	license	n. 许可证，执照
pute	想	repute	v.（被）称为，认为
mare	恶魔，妖怪	nightmare	n. 噩梦
vers	转	version	n. 译本

algebra ［'ældʒɪbrə］ n. 代数（学）

cascade ［kæ'skeɪd］ n. 小瀑布（steep small fall of water）
【记】词根记忆：cas(落下)＋cad(落下)＋e→水一再落下→小瀑布
同根词：casual(a. 偶然的)；decadent(a. 颓废的)

character ［'kærəktər］ n. 性格（nature）；特征（property）；角色（role）

chart ［tʃɑːrt］ n. 图表（map, graph）vt. 用图说明
(to make a map of)
【例】We can *chart* the history of innovation
in musical notation. 我们可以用图说明音乐
标记法的创新历史。
【派】uncharted(a. 地图上未标明的)

chart

circulation ［ˌsɜːrkjə'leɪʃn］ n. 发行额；循环（cycle）；
流通（flow）
【例】In 1872 only two daily newspapers could claim a *circulation* of
over 100,000. 在1872年，只有两份日报声称发行量超过10万份。

complement ［'kɑːmplɪmənt］ vt. 补充，使完善（*supplement, complete）；与…相
配（to match）
【记】词根记忆：com(加强)＋ple(满，填满)＋ment→补充，使
完善
【例】The myths and songs *complemented* our historical knowledge of

the lives of animals and of people here. 神话和歌曲补充了关于这里动物和人类生活的历史知识。//I think his new haircut really *complements* his beard. 我觉得他的新发型与胡子真的很配。

【参】compliment(*n.* 称赞); supplement(*n.* 补遗); implement(*n.* 工具)

conductor [kən'dʌktər] *n.* 导体;(乐队等的)指挥

【例】In the fall, the soil freezes first beneath stones because stones are a better *conductor* of heat than soil. 秋天土壤首先在石头下面冻结,因为石头比土壤的导热性好。

congress [ˈkɑːŋɡrəs] *n.* 议会,国会(parliament);(代表)大会(convention)

【记】分拆联想:con(共同)+ gress(行走)→ 走到一起开议会 → 大会

【派】congressional(*a.* 大会的,国会的)

【参】digress(*v.* 离题); transgress(*v.* 违反,犯罪)

couple [ˈkʌpl] *n.* (一)对,(一)双(pair);夫妇;[物]力偶,电偶 *v.* 连接,结合

【搭】a couple of 两个,几个

【例】I have already had a *couple* of ideas about how to do this experiment. 我对怎么做这个实验已经有了一些想法。

A: I think I'll get a *couple* of tickets to the play.

B: But don't just sit anywhere. You should get tickets in the orchestra section.

A:我想我要去买几张戏票。

B:但是要选好座位。你应该买正厅前座。

coupon [ˈkuːpɑːn] *n.* 礼券,优惠券(gift certificate)

【记】分拆联想:coup(意外行动)+ on → 意外得到优惠券 → 优惠券

【例】I've got a *coupon* for half-off diner at that new restaurant down the street. 我已搞到了街道那家新餐厅的半价优惠券。

critique [krɪˈtiːk] *n.* 批评,评论(criticism, comment)

【记】和 critic(*n.* 评论家)一起记

【搭】film critique 影评

【例】We'll talk more about the requirements of the *critique* later in the semester. 我们会在这学期晚些时候进一步讨论评论的要求。

crown [kraʊn] *n.* 王冠;顶,冠

【记】分拆联想:crow(乌鸦)+ n → 乌鸦戴顶帽子 → 王冠

cue [kjuː] *n.* 暗示,提示(hint)

【参】clue(*n.* 线索)

【搭】cue and timings sheet 电视节目安排时间表

| conductor | congress | couple | coupon | critique | crown |
| cue |

defect [ˈdiːfekt] *n.* 瑕疵(flaw); 过失

【记】词根记忆: de(变坏) + fect(做) → 没做好 → 过失

【例】The sweater could be a manufactures' *defect*, and we'll exchange it for you. 这个运动衫可能是有些瑕疵, 我们会为你换新的。

dehydrated [ˌdiːhaɪˈdreɪtɪd] *a.* 干燥的; 脱水的

【记】词根记忆: de + hydr(水) + ated → 去水的 → 脱水的

【搭】dehydrated climate 干燥的气候

【派】dehydrate(*vt.* 使脱水)

difference [ˈdɪfrəns] *n.* 差别, 差异, 分歧

【搭】make a difference 区分

【例】A: I don't know whether to ask Sandra or Carl to draw the poster.

B: What *difference* does it make? They are both excellent artists.

A: 我不知道让桑德拉还是卡尔来画张贴画。

B: 这有什么区别。他们都是优秀的艺术家。

disaster [dɪˈzæstər] *n.* 灾难(*catastrophe); 彻底的失败

【记】分拆联想: dis(离开) + aster(星星) → 离开星星, 星位不正 → 灾难

【例】The Mandans protected themselves against the *disaster* of crop failure and accompanying hunger. 曼丹人保护自己免受作物歉收以及由此引发的饥饿。

【派】disastrous(*a.* 灾难性的)

distinctive [dɪˈstɪŋktɪv] *a.* 出众的; 有特色的(unique)

【记】来自distinct(明显的) + ive → 显眼的 → 出众的; 有特色的

【搭】distinctive feature 特色

【例】American elms have *distinctive* dark green leaves that lock lopsided. 美国榆树有颇具特色的深绿色叶子, 看上去两侧还不均衡。// Green pepper has a very *distinctive* flavor. 青椒的味道很独特。

【参】distinct(*a.* 清楚的, 明显的; 截然不同的, 独特的)

drawback [ˈdrɔːbæk] *n.* 缺点, 障碍(disadvantage, shortcoming)

【记】组合词: draw(拉) + back(向后) → 拖后腿 → 缺点

【例】The main *drawback* of the new system is that it is hard to operate. 新系统的主要缺点是操作困难。

drop [drɑːp] *n.* 滴; 落下; 微量 *v.* 落下; 下降(fall); 失落; 放弃(quit); 退课

【搭】drop sth. 放弃…; drop by 顺便拜访…; drop a class 退课; drop off 把…放下; 让…下车; 掉下

【例】Movie attendance *dropped* when audience members chose to stay at home and be entertained. 观众选择待在家里娱乐时，去电影院的人就少了。//I'll plan on *dropping* my daughter off at your place on the way to work, around eleven. 我打算上班途中把女儿放到你那里，大约11点到。

A: Mary, did you *drop* off the roll of film for developing?

B: No. I got Susan to do it.

A：玛丽，你把胶卷拿去冲洗了吗?

B：没有，我让苏珊送去了。

evolve [ɪ'vɑːlv] *v.* 发展(develop); (使)进化

evolve

【记】词根记忆：e(出) + volve(卷，滚) → 卷出来 → 发展，进化

【例】The techniques of pottery manufacture had *evolved* well before the Greek period. 制陶技术早在希腊时期就已经发展起来了。

【派】evolution(*n.* 进化); evolutionary(*a.* 进化的)

expel [ɪk'spel] *vt.* 排出(discharge)

【记】词根记忆：ex(出) + pel(推) → 向外推 → 排出

【例】When you sneeze, you *expel* air from your lungs. 打喷嚏时会排出肺部的空气。

【参】impel(*v.* 推动，推进); compel(*v.* 强迫，驱使); repel(*vt.* 击退); impel(*vt.* 推动); dispel(*vt.* 驱散)

extract [ɪk'strækt] *vt.* 取出(*remove); 提取(distill)

['ekstrækt] *n.* 提出物(selection); 汁(juice)

【记】词根记忆：ex(出) + tract(拉) → 拉出 → 提出物

【例】Some fossils can be *extracted* from these sediments by putting the rocks in an acid bath. 把石头放到酸性液体里，就可以从一些化石中提取这些沉淀物。

fancy ['fænsi] *a.* 奇特的(peculiar); 异样的(unusual)

【记】分拆联想：fan(迷，狂热者) + cy → 着了迷的 → 异样的

【例】I'm taking John to that *fancy* new restaurant tonight. 我今晚要带约翰去那家花哨的新餐厅。

【参】infancy(*n.* 幼年)

fatal ['feɪtl] *a.* 致命的(*deadly); 毁灭性的(destructive)

【记】分拆联想：fat(看作fate，命运) + al(…的) → 致命的

【例】High temperatures are also *fatal* to the growing embryo. 高温对成长中的胚胎有致命的危险。

finalize [ˈfaɪnəlaɪz] *v.* 使完成; 把…最后定下来; 定稿

【搭】finalize papers 论文定稿

【例】A: Have you *finalized* your plans for spring break yet?

B: Well, I could visit some friends in Florida, or go to my roommate's home. It's a tough choice.

A: 你春季休假的计划定下来没有?

B: 嗯, 我可能会去看望佛罗里达的一些朋友, 或者去我室友的家里。二者很难选择。

flask [flæsk] *n.* 细颈瓶

【记】和 flash (*v.* 闪光) 一起记, something flashes in a flask (某物在细颈瓶中闪光)

fluctuate [ˈflʌktʃueɪt] *v.* 波动 (undulate); (使)变化

【记】词根记忆: fluct(=flu 流动) + uate → 波动; 变化

【例】The level of carbon dioxide in the atmosphere *fluctuated* between 190 and 280 parts per million. 大气中二氧化碳含量在每百万 190~280 之间波动。//Its temperature often *fluctuates* dramatically. 气温经常剧烈波动。

【派】fluctuation(*n.* 波动, 起伏)

frugal [ˈfruːgl] *a.* 节俭的 (thrifty)

【记】发音记忆: "腐乳过日" → 吃腐乳过日子 → 节俭的

【例】*Frugal* people save cash in kitchen pots and jars. 节俭的人把现金存放到厨房的锅和罐子里。

【派】frugality(*n.* 节省)

genetics [dʒəˈnetɪks] *n.* 遗传学

【记】来自 genetic (遗传的) + s → 遗传学

【例】He's interested in the *genetics* of mammals. 他对哺乳动物的遗传学感兴趣。

germinate [ˈdʒɜːrmɪneɪt] *v.* 发芽; 发展

【记】词根记忆: germ(种子) + inate → 让种子生长 → 发芽

【例】The idea of establishing her own enterprise started to *germinate* in her mind when she was just a college student. 上大学的时候她就萌生了建立自己的企业的想法。

glorify [ˈglɔːrɪfaɪ] *v.* 美化 (beautify); 赞扬 (praise)

【记】词根记忆: glor(光荣) + ify → 使光荣 → 美化; 赞扬

【例】Futurism rejected all traditions and attempted to *glorify* contemporary life by emphasizing the machine and motion. 未来学家拒绝一切传统, 通过强调机器和运动来试图美化现代生活。

☐ finalize ☐ flask ☐ fluctuate ☐ frugal ☐ genetics ☐ germinate
☐ glorify

hawk [hɔːk] *n.* 鹰(eagle)

【记】联想记忆：美国的两个党派：鹰派(Hawk)和鸽派(Dove)

humanity [hjuːˈmænəti] *n.* 人类(mankind), (总称)人

【记】来自human(人，人类) + ity(表性质) → 人类，人

【例】The soldiers devote their lives to unselfish service of *humanity*.
战士们把自己的一生献给了为人类无私的服务事业。

iceberg [ˈaɪsbɜːrg] *n.* 冰山

【记】组合词：ice + berg(大冰块) → 冰山

jot [dʒɑːt] *v.* 摘要记录；匆匆记下

【搭】jot down 记录

【例】A: Have you *jotted* down my telephone number?

B: Not yet. I'll do it at once.

A: 你记下我的电话号码了吗？

B: 还没有。我马上记。

【参】lot(*n.* 签); hot(*a.* 热的)

kid [kɪd] *n.* 小孩，儿童(child) *v.* 戏弄，取笑(tease)

【搭】be kidding 开玩笑

【例】A: How did the game go last night? Did your team win?

B: Are you *kidding*? We are just newcomers.

A: 昨晚比赛怎么样？你们队赢了吗？

B: 你在开玩笑吗？我们不过是新来的。

kingdom [ˈkɪŋdəm] *n.* 王国(realm, domain, empire)

【记】联想记忆：king(国王) + dom(领域) → 国王统治的领域 → 王国

【例】Many insects live in a colony in the *kingdom* of animals. 动物王国中很多昆虫都是群居动物。

【参】The United Kingdom 联合王国

lasting [ˈlæstɪŋ] *a.* 持久的，永久的(permanent)

【例】The rise of industrialization brought widespread and *lasting* change to the United States society. 工业化的崛起给美国社会带来了广泛而持久的变化。

license

我可不是无照行乞

license [ˈlaɪsns] *n.* 许可证，执照 (permit) *v.* 给执照

【记】词根记忆：licen(允许) + se → 许可证，执照

【搭】driver's license 驾驶执照

liquid ['lɪkwɪd] *n.* /*a.* 液体(的), 流体(的)

【记】分拆联想: liqu(液体) + id → 像液体一样

【例】The energy is used to convert *liquid* water to water vapor. 这个能量是用来把液体水转化为水蒸气的。

litter ['lɪtər] *n.* 垃圾(rubbish) *vi.* 乱丢垃圾使凌乱

【记】联想记忆: 把little的"l"乱丢, 错拿放成"r" → 乱丢; 注意: glitter(*v.* 闪光)

【例】We'll be putting the *litter* in these plastic trash bags. 我们要把这些垃圾扔到塑料垃圾袋里。//The ground under towing oaks is often *littered* with thousands of half-eaten acorns. 高大的橡树下经常有成千上万啃了一半的橡子。

machinery [mə'ʃiːnəri] *n.* [总称] 机器, 机械 (machines in general); 机构 (organization)

【记】来自machine(*n.* 机器, 机械)

【例】The use of farm *machinery* continued to increase. 农机工具的使用在继续增加。

magnitude ['mægnɪtuːd] *n.* 【天】等级; 巨大; 数量(quantity), 量级(*extent)

【记】词根记忆: magn(大) + itude(状态) → 巨大

【例】That star has a *magnitude* of 2. 那颗恒星的等级为2。//The decibel is a unit that expresses the ration of the *magnitude* of two electric voltages. 分贝是表示两个电压等级数量的单位。

【参】magnitude 震级; seismic wave 地震波

methanol ['meθənɔːl] *n.* 甲醇

【例】The impurities are washed out with *methanol*, I think, before this gas is sent on to reactors where it's changed into oil. 我认为, 在这个气体被送往反应器转变为油之前, 杂质就被甲醇清洗干净了。

microorganism [ˌmaɪkroʊ'ɔːrɡənɪzəm] *n.* 微生物, 细菌

【记】micro(微小) + organism(生物) → 微生物

negative ['neɡətɪv] *a.* 否定的; 消极的(passive); 负的(minus) *n.* 底片

【搭】negative reaction 负反力; glass negative 玻璃底片

【例】How do you usually explain our own *negative* behavior? 你通常如何解释我们自身的消极行为?

【派】negatively(*ad.* 否定地; 消极地)

| liquid | litter | machinery | magnitude | methanol | microorganism |
| negative | | | | | |

newsletter [ˈnuːzletər] *n.* 时事通讯

【例】The *newsletter* is published two times a month. 时事通讯一周印刷两次。

nightmare [ˈnaɪtmer] *n.* 噩梦；无法摆脱的恐惧；可怕的事

【记】词根记忆：night(夜晚) + mare(恶魔，妖怪) → 夜里遇恶魔 → 噩梦

【例】A: Why are you leaving so early? The movie doesn't start till seven.

B: I don't want to be at the traffic there. It's a *nightmare* on the express way during rush hour.

A：你为什么走这么早？电影7点才开始。

B：我不想把时间花在路上。高峰时高速路上简直是个噩梦。

observe [əbˈzɜːrv] *v.* 遵守，奉行；观察，注意到，看到(notice)

【记】词根记忆：ob(逆，反) + serv(服务) + e → 不予以服务却只是看 → 察觉；观察

【例】Like other behaviorists, John believed that psychologists should study only the behaviors they can *observe* and measure. 正如其他行为主义者，约翰认为心理学家应该只研究那些能观察和测量到的行为。

【派】observable(*a.* 应遵守的；看得见的)；observer(*n.* 遵守者；观察者)

【参】preserve(*v.* 保护，保存)；reserve(*v.* 储备；预定)

pertinent [ˈpɜːrtnənt] *a.* 相关的(*relevant)

【记】词根记忆：per(始终) + tin(拿住) + ent → 始终拿住与自己相关的东西 → 相关的

【例】The *pertinent* considerations that will be affected by each decision are listed. 受到每个决定影响的相关考虑被列了出来。

pin [pɪn] *n.* 钉，销，栓；大头针，别针，徽章 *v.* 钉住，别住

【搭】pin sb. down(通过加压或找其他借口)使某人不能离开

【例】A: It sounds like Karen isn't happy at all with her new roommate. Did she say why?

B: Believe me, I tried to find out. But I simply couldn't *pin* her down.

A：听起来卡伦对同屋的人不太满意。她说原因了吗？

B：相信我，我试着问过，但她就是不说。

pioneer [ˌpaɪəˈnɪr] *n.* 开拓者(settler) *v.* 开拓，开创(exploit)

【例】Local music store owners *pioneered* their own local recording industry. 当地音乐商店的店主开拓了自己的录制行业。

plunge [plʌndʒ] *vt.* 掉入（*drop, fall）

【记】发音记忆："扑浪急"→掉入海里，着急的扑打着浪花→掉入

【例】With the continued rise in sea level, more ice would *plunge* into the ocean. 随着海平面的继续上升，更多的冰会掉到海里。

plunge

prime [praɪm] *a.* 主要的（*chief）；最初的（original）；最好的

【记】词根记忆：prim(主要的) + e → 主要的

【例】In the railroads' *prime* years, there were a few individuals in the United States. 在使用铁路最初的岁月里，美国的人很少。

【派】primer(*n.* 初级读本)

quit [kwɪt] *v.* 停止；放弃（abandon）；离开（depart）；辞(职)（abdicate）

【例】She wants to *quit* her job in the chemistry lab. 她想辞去在化学实验室的工作。

【派】quitter(*n.* 轻易停止的人；懦夫)

random ['rændəm] *a.* 随机的，任意的（*unpredictable, arbitrary）

【记】分拆联想：ran(跑) + dom(领域) → 可以在各种领域跑的 → 任意的

【例】The effect of gravity at high altitude is *random*. 在高海拔的地方重力的影响是任意的。

【派】randomly(*ad.* 随便地)

reference ['refrəns] *n.* 提到；参考；介绍信

【例】The interviewer said that my *references* were full of praise. 面试官说我的介绍信里满是赞誉之词。

repute [rɪ'pjuːt] *v.* (被)称为，认为（consider）

【记】词根记忆：re + pute(想) → 反复想 → 认为

【例】The hotel was *reputed* to be the best in the country. 这家酒店据说是该国最好的。

【派】reputation(*n.* 名誉，名声)；reputedly(*ad.* 据说)；disrepute (*n.* 丧失名誉)

ridge [rɪdʒ] *n.* 脊，山脊

【记】联想记忆：桥梁(bridge)去掉b就只剩下脊(ridge) → 脊，山脊

【例】We drove up a hill side and finally stopped on a high *ridge*. 我们沿着山腰往上开，最后停在一个个高高的山脊上。

rodeo ['roʊdioʊ] *n.* 牛仔竞技表演

satellite ['sætəlaɪt] *n.* 卫星；人造卫星

| ☐ plunge | ☐ prime | ☐ quit | ☐ random | ☐ reference | ☐ repute |
| ☐ ridge | ☐ rodeo | ☐ satellite | | | |

satire ['sætaɪər] *n.* 讽刺文学；讽刺(irony)

【记】源自拉丁语，意为讽刺杂咏，现在在英语中多指"讽刺"或"讽刺文学"

【派】satirist(*n.* 创作讽刺作品的作家)

scarf [skɑːrf] *n.* 围巾，披巾(shawl)

【记】联想记忆：为了遮住脖子上的伤疤(scar)，围了条围巾(scarf)

simplicity [sɪm'plɪsəti] *n.* 简单；朴素(easiness; plainness)

【记】来自simpl(e)(简单的，直率的)+icity(表性质，状态)→简单

【例】The *simplicity* of this cartoon book makes it suitable for small children. 这本简单的卡通书适合小孩子阅读。

【派】simple(*a.* 简单的); simplification(*n.* 简化); simplify(*v.* 简化)

【参】explicitly(*ad.* 明确地，明白地)

somewhat ['sʌmwʌt] *ad.* 稍微，有点(*rather, slightly)

soothe [suːð] *vt.* 使(痛苦等)缓和或减轻(relieve)

【记】来自sooth(抚慰的)+e→抚慰→减轻

sophisticated [sə'fɪstɪkeɪtɪd] *a.* 老练的(worldly-wise); 精密的(exact); 复杂的；先进的

【记】分拆联想：sophisticat(e)(久经世故的人)+ed→老练的

【派】unsophisticated(*a.* 不懂世故的；单纯的)

【参】sophistication(*n.* 精密，复杂)

spin [spɪn] *v.* 旋转(twirl); 纺(纱)(reel) *n.* 旋转(whirl)

spinet ['spɪnət] *n.* 小型立式钢琴

spot [spɑːt] *n.* 地点 (position); 斑点 (dot) *v.* 认出，发现(*identify, recognize)

【例】Chick Webb *spotted* her in an amateur competition when she was sixteen. 在她16岁参加业余竞赛时奇克·韦伯发现了她。

【派】spotless(*a.* 没有污点的); spotted(*a.* 有斑点的，斑纹的)

【参】spotlight(*n.* 聚光灯)

station ['steɪʃn] *n.* 所；站；台

【搭】relay station 中继站; space station 太空站

suite [swiːt] *n.* 一批，一套，组

【记】联想记忆：这套家具很适合(suit)这个房间(suite)

【搭】a suite of rooms 一套房间

【派】suited(*a.* 适合的，匹配的)

token ['toʊkən] *n.* 表示；标志，象征(symbol); 记号(mark); 信物；纪念品；礼券，代价券；筹码 *a.* 象征性的

【记】联想记忆：拿走了(taken)代金券(token)

satire	scarf	simplicity	somewhat	soothe	sophisticated
spin	spinet	spot	station	suite	token

【搭】token reward 象征性奖励

【例】By the same *token*, the speech contest, I think, is a success. 出于同样的原因，我认为演讲比赛很成功。

trivial ['trɪvɪəl] *a.* 琐屑的，微不足道的(unimportant, trifling)

【记】词根记忆：tri(三) + via(路) + -l → 三条路的会合点，古罗马妇女喜欢停在十字路口同人闲聊些无关紧要或琐碎的事情，故 trivial 有"琐碎的、不重要的"意思

turn-out ['tɜːrnaʊt] *n.* (比赛、会议等的)全部参与人(数)；产量(output)，产额；清理，清除

【例】A: I heard that the *turn-out* for the opening of the new sculpture exhibit was kind of surprising.

B: I guess a lot of other people feel the way I do about modern art.

A：我听说参加新雕塑展开幕式的人很多，这让人颇感意外。

B：我猜很多人对现代艺术有着和我一样的感触。

turnpike ['tɜːrnpaɪk] *n.* 收费公路(toll road)

【记】分拆联想：turn(转动) + pike(收税栅栏，关卡) → 转动收费杆 → 收费公路

【例】These *turnpike* roads were still very slow, and traveling on them was too costly for farmers. 在收费公路上行驶不仅速度慢，而且对农民来说成本太高。

unaided [ʌn'eɪdɪd] *a.* 无助的；独立的(independent)

【搭】unaided eye 肉眼

【例】Eventually, the metal will crumple and uncrumple, totally *unaided*. 最后，在没有任何辅助的情况下，金属会变皱，然后恢复平整状态。

unsubstantiated [ˌʌnsəb'stænʃɪeɪtɪd] *a.* 未经证实的(*unverified)

【记】来自 substantiate(*vt.* 证实)

【例】There are numerous *unsubstantiated* reports. 有无数未经证实的报告。

version ['vɜːrʒn] *n.* 译文，译本(translation)；版本(edition)

【记】词根记忆：vers(转) + ion → 从原文转化而来 → 译本

【例】That rather romantic *version* of the story is not what actually happened. 那个相当浪漫的故事版本不符合实际发生的情况。

【参】vision(*n.* 视觉)

warp [wɔːrp] *n.* (织物的)经(线)

【例】The *warp* is always made of willow. 经线一般是用柳木做的。

| trivial | turn-out | turnpike | unaided | unsubstantiated | version |
| warp | | | | | |

Word List 23  MP3-23

词根、词缀预习表

acu	尖，锐利	acumen	*n.* 敏锐，聪明
mun	公共的	communal	*a.* 公共的
mens	测量	dimension	*n.* 维(数)，尺度
alt	高的	exalted	*a.* 崇高的
pauc	少	paucity	*n.* 极少量
horm	鼓动，冲动	hormone	*n.* 荷尔蒙
rig	水	irrigate	*vt.* 灌溉
medi	中间	media	*n.* 媒体
cur	发生	occur	*vi.* 发生，出现
trans	改变	transform	*vt.* 使变形

absence [ˈæbsəns] *n.* 缺席；缺乏(lack)，不存在
【记】来自absent(*a.* 缺席的；缺少的)
【例】I know your course has no *absence* policy. 我知道您的课不允许缺席。

activity [ækˈtɪvəti] *n.* 活动(movement)；活跃(fizz)
【搭】extracurricular activity 课外活动
【派】activist(*n.* 积极分子；活动家)

acumen [ˈækjəmən] *n.* 敏锐，聪明(acuteness, brightness)
【记】词根记忆：acu(尖，锐利)+men(表名词)→敏锐

allergic [əˈlɜːrdʒɪk] *a.* 过敏的；对…讨厌的
【记】联想记忆：aller(看作alert，警报)+gic→皮肤出现警报的→过敏的
【搭】be allergic to sth. 对…过敏；厌烦某事
【例】A: So are you going over to Cindy's after class?
B: I'd like to. But she has a pet cat and I'm very *allergic*.
A: 你下课后要去辛迪那里？

absence

B：我想去。但是她养了只猫，我很讨厌猫。

A: Oh, man! Something in this room is making my eyes itch. I must be *allergic* to something.

B: Hmm. I wonder what it is.

A：哦，天哪！屋子里有什么东西让我眼睛发痒，我肯定过敏了。

B：嗯，我想知道那是什么。

angle [ˈæŋgl] *n.* 角；角度（viewpoint）

【记】和 angel（*n.* 天使）一起记

【派】angular（*a.* 有角的；尖角的）

anomaly [əˈnɑːməli] *n.* 不规则；异常的人或物（aberration, abnormality）

【记】词根记忆：a（不）+ nomal（看作 normal，正常的）+ y → 不正常 → 异常的人或物

apparent [əˈpærənt] *a.* 显然的，明显的（*obvious, *evident, *detectable）

【记】分拆联想：ap + parent（父母）→ 父母对儿女的爱显而易见 → 显然的

【例】They noticed an *apparent* change in the position of the North Star. 他们注意到了北极星位置的明显变化。

【派】apparently（*ad.* 显然地）

ardent [ˈɑːrdnt] *a.* 热心的，热情洋溢的（enthusiastic, ardent）

【记】词根记忆：ard（热）+ ent → 热心的

【例】Christina was extremely *ardent* in her admiration for the professor. 克里斯蒂娜十分狂热地崇拜她的教授。

【参】impassive（*a.* 无动于衷的，无感情的，冷漠的）

artisan [ˈɑːrtəzn] *n.* 工匠，手艺人（workman, craftsman）

【记】词根记忆：art（技艺）+ is + an（人）→ 有技艺的人 → 工匠，手艺人

barbecue [ˈbɑːrbɪkjuː] *n.* 烧烤野餐

basin [ˈbeɪsn] *n.* 盆地

【参】bison（*n.* 野牛）

blade [bleɪd] *n.* 刃，刀片

【记】热门电影《刀锋战士》英文为 *Blade*

blast [blæst] *n.* 一股 *v.* 爆发（burst）；发出尖响

【记】分拆联想：b + last（最后）→ 最后一声 b → 爆发

【搭】blast furnace 鼓风炉

【例】Something about coal being set on fire *blasted* with a mixture of steam and oxygen. 煤被点着了，释放出蒸汽和氧气的混合体。//

angle	anomaly	apparent	ardent	artisan	barbecue
basin	blade	blast			

It's as though he *blasted* his stereo all night. 好像他整夜都开着立体声。

cell [sel] *n.* 细胞；单人房间（a single room usually for one person）；基层组织

cider ['saɪdər] *n.* 苹果酒

communal [kə'mjuːnl] *a.* 公共的；社区的（of or relating to a community）
【记】词根记忆：com + mun(公共) + al → 公共的
【例】His paintings depict the *communal* cultural experience of Mexican descended people in the U. S. 他的绘画描写了在美墨西哥后裔的社区文化体验。

conform [kən'fɔːrm] *vi.* 遵守，符合（comply, agree）；适应（adapt）
【记】词根记忆：con(共同) + form(形状) → 共同的形状 → 符合
【例】They should be designed to *conform* to the topography of the area. 它们的设计应该符合该地区的地貌。
【派】conformity(*n.* 符合，一致)；nonconformity(*n.* 不墨守成规)

congenial [kən'dʒiːniəl] *a.* 性格温和的（gentle）；相宜的（kindred）
【记】词根记忆：con + geni(=genius才能) + al → 有共同才能 → 相宜的
【例】Political liberty was *congenial* to the development of art taste. 政治自由有利于培养艺术品味。

conservation [ˌkɑːnsər'veɪʃn] *n.* 保守，保存，保持（preservation）；守恒
【记】来自conserve(*v.* 保存)
【例】Biological diversity has become widely recognized as a critical *conservation* issue only in the past two decades. 生物多样化在过去20年才被广泛认为是重要的环保议题。
【派】conservationist(*n.* 环保主义者)；conservatism(*n.* 保守主义)

delegate ['delɪɡət] *n.* 代表（representative）
['delɪɡeɪt] *vt.* 授权（authorize）
【记】和legate(*n.* 使者)一起记
【例】The town elected two *delegates* to attend the conference. 这个城镇选举了两名代表参加会议。//John *delegated* the job of mowing the lawn to his daughter. 约翰把割草的工作交给了女儿。

dimension [daɪ'menʃn] *n.* 维(数)；尺度（measure）；方面（aspect）；[常 *pl.*] 大小
【记】词根记忆：di + mens(测量) + ion → 尺度
【例】Another *dimension* of relationship banking is the development of highly personalized relationships between employee and client. 关系

cell	cider	communal	conform	congenial	conservation
delegate	dimension				

银行的另一个方面就是要在雇员和客户之间培养高度个人化的关系。// The *dimensions* of the cosmos are so large that using familiar units of distance would make little sense. 宇宙的尺寸太大了，使用常用的距离单位几乎没有意义。

【派】dimensional(*a.* 空间的)

【参】three-dimensional(*a.* 三维的)

diplomat	[ˈdɪpləmæt] *n.* 外交官

divert [daɪˈvɜːrt] *vt.* 转移(distract)；使娱乐(amuse, entertain)

【记】词根记忆：di(离开) + vert(转) → 转移

【例】The wind *diverted* the boat from its course. 风使船脱离了航线。// The first publisher to produce books aimed primarily at *diverting* a child audience. 最早的图书出版商的首要目的是娱乐儿童读者。

electricity [ɪˌlekˈtrɪsəti] *n.* 电；电流

【参】electric (*a.* 电动的，电的)；electrical (*a.* 电的，有关电的)；electrician(*n.* 电工)

errand [ˈerənd] *n.* 差事；差使(assignment, task)

【记】词根记忆：err(漫游) + and → 跑来跑去 → 差使

【例】I have to pick up my car and do a couple of *errands*. 我得去取我的车，跑一些差事。

ethnic [ˈeθnɪk] *a.* 种族的(racial)；民族的(national)

【记】词根记忆：ethn(种族) + ic → 种族的；民族的

【例】Massive waves of immigration brought new *ethnic* groups into the country. 大规模移民潮给这个国家带来了新的种族群体。

【参】ethics(*n.* 道德规范)

exalted [ɪgˈzɔːltɪd] *a.* 崇高的，高贵的(*superior)

【记】词根记忆：ex + alt(高的) + ed → 崇高的

【例】Their products, primarily silver plates and bowls, reflected their *exalted* status and testified to their customers' prominence. 这些产品——主要是银盘和银碗——反映了他们高贵的地位，证明了他们的客人的重要性。

exception [ɪkˈsepʃn] *n.* 除外，例外

【搭】without exception 无例外地；with the exception of 除…之外

【例】We've now discussed how most snakes move, but there are some notable *exceptions*. 我们已经讨论了多数蛇是如何移动的，但是有一些例外值得注意。

A: Prof, I know your course has no absence policy. But I have to have foot surgery next Friday and can't be here.

□ diplomat	□ divert	□ electricity	□ errand	□ ethnic	□ exalted
□ exception					

B: Medical excuses are one of the few *exceptions* I make.

A：教授，我知道您的课不允许缺席。但是我下周五脚要做手术，无法来上课了。

B：医治方面的理由是我允许的例外之一。

【参】reception(*n.* 接待，接收)

Fahrenheit ['færənhaɪt] *n.* 华氏温度计

【例】The temperature of the Sun is over 5,000 degrees *Fahrenheit* at the surface. 太阳表面的温度超过5000华氏度。

faucet ['fɔːsɪt] *n.* 水龙头；插口

【例】Did you fix the leaky *faucet*?你把滴漏的水龙头修好了吗？

【参】fauces(*n.* 咽喉)

flair [fler] *n.* 才能，本领

【记】和fair(公正的，美丽的)一起记

formal ['fɔːrml] *a.* 正(规、式)的(normal)；形式的

【例】Everyone was wearing *formal* suits or gowns. 所有人都身穿西装或礼服。//I'd rather not make the gardening club something *formal* and structured. 我不想把园艺俱乐部办得那么正式和结构分明。

【派】formally(*ad.* 正式地)

foster ['fɔːstər] *vt.* 鼓励(encourage)；培养(nurture)

【例】The sole purpose of the American Academy and Institute of Arts and Letters is to "*foster*, assist and sustain an interest" in literature, music, and art. 美国艺术和文学研究所的唯一目的是培养、帮助和维持人们对文学、音乐和艺术的兴趣。

genetically [dʒə'netɪkli] *ad.* 由基因决定地，与遗传有关地

【记】来自genetical(基因的)+ly→由基因决定地，与遗传有关地

【例】Researchers found that all the Argentine ants in California were very similar *genetically*. 研究人员发现加州所有的阿根廷蚂蚁的基因都非常相似。

gregarious [grɪ'geriəs] *a.* 群居的(social)

【记】词根记忆：greg (群体) + arious → 群居的

来张合影
gregarious

handy ['hændi] *a.* 可用的(available)；手边的

【搭】come in handy 迟早有用

【例】I really need to keep the book *handy* just in case. 这本书我真的要放在手边，以备不时之需。

harbor ['hɑ:rbər] *n.* 港口(port) *v.* 藏有
【搭】natural harbor 天然港

hormone ['hɔ:rmoun] *n.* 激素；荷尔蒙
【记】词根记忆：horm(鼓动，冲动) + one → 激素；荷尔蒙
【例】The short child of tall parents very likely had a *hormone* deficiency early in life. 高个子父母的孩子如果身材矮小，很有可能在小时候缺乏荷尔蒙。
【派】hormonal(*a.* 激素的；荷尔蒙的)

idiom ['ɪdiəm] *n.* 习惯用语；(在艺术上所表现的)风格，特色(style)
【例】Martha Graham's debut dance concert in her new *idiom* occurred on April 18, 1926. 1926年4月18日，玛莎·格雷汉姆首次举办了体现她新特色的舞蹈音乐会。

impact [ɪm'pækt] *v.* 影响(affect) *n.* ['ɪmpækt] 影响(力)(effect)；冲击，撞击(collision)
【记】词根记忆：im(进入) + pact(系紧) → 压进去的力量 → 影响力
【例】How did the agricultural societies *impact* people's family relationships? 农业社会如何影响人们的家庭关系？

incident ['ɪnsɪdənt] *n.* 事情，事件(happening)
【记】词根记忆：in + cid (落下) + ent (物) → 从天而降的东西 → 事件
【例】She isn't upset about the *incident*. 此事并没有让她不安。
【派】incidental(*a.* 偶然的)

infant ['ɪnfənt] *n.* 婴儿，幼儿(baby)

innovative ['ɪnəveɪtɪv] *a.* 创新的；富有革新精神的(*novel, inventive)
【例】Another *innovative* use for cold ocean water is to cool buildings. 冷海水的另一种创新用处是给建筑物降温。//The art community is *innovative*. 艺术团体是富有创新精神的。
【参】innovator(*n.* 创新者)

intersection [ˌɪntər'sekʃn] *n.* 交点；十字路口(crossroad)
【例】There was no left turn at the last *intersection*. 最后一个十字路口没有左转弯。

irrigate ['ɪrɪɡeɪt] *vt.* 灌溉
【记】词根记忆：ir(进入) + rig(水) + ate → 把水引进 → 灌溉
【派】irrigation(*n.* 灌溉)

manifestation [ˌmænɪfe'steɪʃn] *n.* 显示，表明(indication)，证明；[常 *pl.*]清楚表明某事的言行
【记】联想记忆：mani(手) + fest(仇恨) + ation → 用手打人，仇恨表现得够明显 → 表明

| □ harbor | □ hormone | □ idiom | □ impact | □ incident | □ infant |
| □ innovative | □ intersection | □ irrigate | □ manifestation | | |

【搭】manifestation of …的表现形式

【例】What Watson did was to observe muscular habits because he viewed them as a *manifestation* of thinking. 华生特别关注了（那个人）的肌肉习惯，因为他认为肌肉运动是思考的表现形式。

【派】manifest(*v.* 表明); manifestative(*a.* 显然的)

mate [meɪt] *n.* 配偶(spouse) *v.* 配对；交配(copulate)

【派】mating(*n.* 鸟兽等的交配，交尾)

【参】classmate(*n.* 同学); workmate(*n.* 同事); roommate(*n.* 室友)

media ['miːdiə] *n.* 媒介，媒体

【记】词根记忆：medi（中间）+ a → 媒体属中间的媒介 → 媒体；媒介

【例】Popular *media* often distort such stories. 大众媒体经常扭曲这种故事。

obtain [əb'teɪn] *vt.* 获得(*acquire, procure)

【记】词根记忆：ob(表加强) + tain(拿住) → 触手可及的 → 获得

【例】Desalination of water is the best way to *obtain* drinking water. 给水脱盐是获取纯净水的最佳方法。

【参】attain(*v.* 达到); abstain(*v.* 放弃)

occur [ə'kɜːr] *vi.* 发生，出现(happen, appear); 想到(think of)

【记】词根记忆：oc + cur(发生) → 发生，出现

【例】Most manufacturing *occurred* in relatively small plants. 多数生产活动是在相对较小的工厂进行的。

【派】occurrence(*n.* 事件；发生)

【参】recur(*vi.* 重现)

outrageously [aʊt'reɪdʒəsli] *ad.* 令人不可容忍地

【例】These watches are *outrageously* expensive. 这些手表贵得让人难以接受。

paucity ['pɔːsəti] *n.* 极小量

【记】词根记忆：pauc(少) + ity → 少量 → 极小量

personality [ˌpɜːrsə'næləti] *n.* 个性(individuality); 性格(character)

【例】A number of factors related to the voice reveal the *personality* of the speaker. 与声音有关的一些因素展示了说话者的个性。

proper ['prɑːpər] *a.* 正确的(accurate, correct); 适当的 (fitting); 特有的(peculiar)

【记】本身为词根，意为"适当的"

【例】The biologists did not have the *proper* equipment or the skill to handle the eggs. 生物学家没有合适的设备或技能来处理这些蛋。

【派】properly(*ad.* 适当地，正确地); improperly(*ad.* 不适当地，错误地)

quarry ['kwɔːri] *n.* 石矿；被追求的人或事物（prey）

【记】联想记忆：运送（carry）石矿（quarry）到工厂

【例】The police lost their *quarry* in the crowd. 警察在人群中找不到他们要追捕的人了。

rage [reidʒ] *n.* 风靡一时的事物，时尚（fashion）；狂怒（anger, fury）

【记】分拆联想：r + age（时代）→ 不同的时代有不同的时尚 → 时尚

【派】enrage（*vt.* 激怒）

reputation [ˌrepjuˈteiʃn] *n.* 名声，声望（fame）

【记】词根记忆：re（重新）+ put（想）+ ation（状态）→ 值得反复考虑 → 看重 → 名声，声望

【搭】a good/bad reputation 好/坏的名声；earn/gain/establish a reputation as something 作为…获得/建立好名声

【例】A: Professor Howl. Have you heard of him?

B: He does have a good *reputation* in the political science department.

A：你听说过豪尔教授吗？

B：他在政治科学系的声誉的确不错。

resemble [riˈzembl] *vt.* 与…相似，像（*look like）

【记】词根记忆：re + sembl（类似）+ e → 与…相似，像

【例】Giant pandas *resemble* bears in shape. 大熊猫体形像熊。

【派】resemblance（*n.* 相似，相像）

roam [rəum] *vi.* 漫游，漫步（wander）

【记】联想记忆：他的思绪漫游（roam）在广阔的空间里（room）

【例】Four male chimpanzees often *roam* together over a certain period. 四只雄猩猩在某个时间段经常一起漫游。

scarcely ['skersli] *ad.* 几乎不（hardly），简直没有，勉强；刚刚

【例】A: If you see your friend Julia in the next couple of days, would you mind asking her to give me a call? I was hoping she'd be able to help out with course registration next week.

B: Sure, if I see her. She *scarcely* come out lately.

A：今后几天如果见到你朋友朱丽叶，你能让她给我打个电话吗？我希望她下周能帮我登记课程。

B：如果见到她，我一定会转告。她最近很少露面。

scruffy ['skrʌfi] *a.* 不整洁的（unkempt）

☐ quarry	☐ rage	☐ reputation	☐ resemble	☐ roam	☐ scarcely
☐ scruffy					

severe [sɪˈvɪr] *a.* 严重的 (serious); 严厉的 (strict, harsh); 剧烈的 (drastic)

【记】联想记忆：曾经(ever)艰难(severe)的日子，一去不复返了

【派】severely(*ad.* 严重地，激烈地)

【参】sever(*v.* 切断)

shape [ʃeɪp] *n.* 形状，外形(form)；情况，状态；种类 *v.* 成型，塑造

【搭】in shape …的形状；健壮的体格，健美的体形

【例】A: Come on, we're almost there. I'll race you to the top of the hill.
B: I'm so out of *shape*; I might have to crawl the rest of the way.
A：加油，我们马上就到了。我和你比赛跑到山顶。
B：我状态太差，可能剩下的路我要爬着走了。

【参】shame(*n.* 羞耻，羞愧)

shovel [ˈʃʌvl] *n.* 铲子；挖掘机 *v.* 铲

【记】联想记忆：shove(推)+ l → 推开 → 铲

【例】It took some people several days to *shovel* the snow away from their homes. 这些人用了好几天的时间才把房前的雪铲走。

shroud [ʃraʊd] *vt.* 隐藏(conceal)

【例】The languages spoken by early Europeans are still *shrouded* in mystery. 早期欧洲人说的语言仍然很神秘。

signal [ˈsɪɡnəl] *n.* 信号，标志(sign, indication) *v.* 发信号

【记】词根记忆：sign(加上记号) + al → 信号，标志

【例】Pheromones *signal* the ants that the nest has been invaded and must be abandoned. 信息素向蚂蚁发信号，说巢穴遭到入侵，必须要放弃。

【派】signaling(*n.* 打信号，发信号)

silica [ˈsɪlɪkə] *n.* 硅石，硅土

【参】silicate(*n.* 硅酸盐)；siliceous(*a.* 硅酸的，硅土的)

slender [ˈslendər] *a.* 细长的(thin)；纤弱的(slim and weak)

【记】联想记忆：温柔(tender)和纤弱(slender)都是用来形容女孩子的

【派】slenderness(*n.* 苗条，纤细)

specify [ˈspesɪfaɪ] *vt.* 使具体化

【记】词根记忆：speci(外观) + fy → 体现其外观 → 使具体化

【派】specific(*a.* 详细而精确的，具体的)；specifically(*ad.* 特定地，明确地)；specification(*n.* 详述；规格，规范)

spontaneity [ˌspɑːntəˈneɪəti] *n.* 自发性(voluntary action)

【记】来自spontane(ous)(自发的) + ity → 自发性

severe	shape	shovel	shroud	signal	silica
slender	specify	spontaneity			

stain [steɪn] *n.* 污点，污渍(spot)

【记】联想记忆：一下雨(rain)，到处都是污点(stain)

【派】stained(*a.* 玷污的；着色的)

stout [staʊt] *a.* 结实的(strong)

【记】分拆联想：st + out(出来) → 肌肉都鼓出来了 → 结实的

【例】Crows have been seen to tear off *stout* green twig. 人们见到乌鸦已撕掉了结实的绿树枝。

stylized [ˈstaɪlaɪzd] *a.* 风格化的，程式化的(procedural)

【记】来自stylize(*v.* 使风格化)

【例】In her versions the figures became more *stylized* and the landscapes less naturalistic. 在她的版本里，人物更加脸谱化，风景不再那么写实。

sunlit [ˈsʌnlɪt] *a.* 阳光照射的

【记】分拆联想：sun + lit(light的过去分词，照亮) → 阳光照射的

【例】Icebergs are graceful, stately, inspiring in calm, *sunlit* seas. 在平静阳光照射的海洋上，冰山优雅壮观，令人鼓舞。

surgeon [ˈsɜːrdʒən] *n.* 外科医师

【记】分拆联想：surge(升起) + on → 外科医师举起手术刀 → 外科医师

【参】surgery(*n.* 外科手术；手术室)

susceptible [səˈseptəbl] *a.* 易受感染的，易受影响的(*subject to)

【记】词根记忆：sus(在…下面) + cept(接受) + ible → 在下面接受，容易接受 → 易受影响的

【例】Wheat was *susceptible* to many parasites. 麦子容易受到很多寄生虫的侵蚀。

transform [trænsˈfɔːrm] *vt.* 使变形(transfigure)；改(造、革)(reform)；转换(convert)

【记】词根记忆：trans(改变) + form(形状) → 使变形；转换

【例】The video equipment is capable of *transforming* raw weather data into words, symbols, and vivid graphic displays. 视频设备能把原始的气象资料转换成文字、标志和生动的图像显示。

【派】transformation(*n.* 变形；转变)；transformer(*n.* 变压器)

utensil [juːˈtensl] *n.* 用具(appliance)，器皿

【记】词根记忆：ut(用) + ensil → 用品 → 器皿

【搭】household utensil 家庭用具；kitchen utensil 厨房用具

【例】During the middle ages, mined metal was scarce and expensive, therefore was rarely used in the manufacture of household *utensils*. 中

世纪挖掘出的金属稀少而昂贵，所以它们很少用于制造家庭用具。

wear [wer] *v.* 穿戴

【例】I'm thinking about *wearing* a suit to the party tonight. 我想穿西装参加今晚的派对。

【参】fear(*n./v.* 恐惧)

willow [ˈwɪloʊ] *n.* 柳，柳树；柳木制品

【参】basketry 篮筐，篓编织品

Ordinary people merely think how they shall spend their time; a man of talent tries to use it.

普通人只想到如何度过时间，有才能的人设法利用时间。

——叔本华. *A.*(*Arthur Schopenhauer*)

Word List 24　 MP3-24

词根、词缀预习表

crit	判断	criterion	n. 标准
gest	运	digest	v. 消化，吸收
dorm	睡眠	dormant	a. 静止的；休眠的
eco	生态	ecology	n. 生态学
fid	相信	fidelity	n. 忠诚，忠实
govern	统治，管理	governor	n. 省长
pair	坏	impair	vt. 削弱
opt	视力	optical	a. 眼睛的；视力的；光学的
qui	安静的	quiescent	a. 静止的
sol	太阳	solar	a. 太阳的

adaptive [ə'dæptɪv] a. 适合的；适应的

【搭】adaptive behavior 适应行为

allegation [ˌælə'geɪʃn] n. 主张，断言

【记】来自allege(v. 宣称，断言)

【例】The celebrity demands the right of reply to the magazine's *allegation*. 这个名人要求行使回应杂志断言的权利。

boon [buːn] n. 恩惠，恩赐(blessing, benefit)

【记】联想记忆：从月亮(moon)得到恩惠(boon) → 恩惠

bulletin ['bʊlətɪn] n. 简明新闻；公告

【记】分拆联想：bullet（子弹）+ in → 简明新闻传播的速度如子弹 → 简明新闻

【搭】bulletin board 公告牌；news bulletin 新闻

campus ['kæmpəs] n. (大学)校园

【记】联想记忆：camp(野营地) + us(我们) → 校园是学生们学习的营地 → 校园

【搭】live on campus 住校

【例】The *campus* was so great and I loved it. 校园真大，我很喜欢。

☐ adaptive　　☐ allegation　　☐ boon　　☐ bulletin　　☐ campus

conceive [kən'siːv] *vt.* 以为；构思，设想(design, imagine)

【记】词根记忆：con(共同) + ceive(抓) → 一起抓(思想) → 构思，设想

【例】Gertrude had *conceived* it as a part of her mission. 格特鲁德认为这是她使命的一部分。//Mercy Warren *conceived* her plan to write a history of the American Revolution. 默西·沃伦构想了撰写美国革命历史的计划。

【参】deceive(*v.* 欺骗)；perceive(*vt.* 察觉)

conference ['kɑːnfərəns] *n.* 会议；讨论会(meeting, consultation)

【记】词根记忆：con(共同) + fer(带来) + ence → 带来问题和观点一起讨论 → 会议，讨论会

【参】inference(*n.* 推论；结论)

consistently [kən'sɪstəntli] *ad.* 一致地

【例】The artist was *consistently* praised by art critics. 这个艺术家受到了艺术评论家们的一致赞扬。

criterion [kraɪ'tɪriən] *n.* 标准(standard)

【记】词根记忆：crit(判断) + erion → 根据一定标准作判断 → 标准

decompose [ˌdiːkəm'pəʊz] *v.* 分解(disintegrate)；(使)腐烂(decay, rot)

【记】de(离开) + compose(组成) → 把组合在一起的东西分开 → 分解

【例】The Earth's surface is basically rock, and it is this rock that gradually *decomposes* into clay. 地球的表面主要是岩石，正是这些岩石逐渐分解成了黏土。

【派】decomposition(*n.* 分解；腐烂)

depredation [ˌdeprə'deɪʃn] *n.* 劫掠，掠夺，破坏(plunder, robbery)

【记】词根记忆：de + pred(=plunder掠夺) + ation → 劫掠

deter [dɪ't3ːr] *v.* 阻止(prevent)

【记】词根记忆：de + ter(=terr吓唬) → 威慑，吓住 → 阻止

【例】The cost of construction and the very high risk *deterred* private investment in this town. 建筑成本和高风险使私人不敢在这个镇子投资。

【参】defer(*vi.* 推迟)

dialect ['daɪəlekt] *n.* 方言(idiom)

【记】分拆联想：dia(相对) + lect(讲) → 站在两个山头对着讲方言 → 方言

digest [daɪˈdʒest] *v.* 消化，吸收(absorb)

【记】词根记忆：di(向下) + gest(运) → 带下去 → 消化

【例】The sea cucumber has the ability to *digest* whatever nutrients are present. 无论什么营养物海参都能够消化。

【派】digestion(*n.* 消化，吸收)

directory [dəˈrektəri] *n.* 人名地址录；目录

【记】分拆联想：direct（指引）+ ory（物）→ 指引人们查询的东西 → 人名地址录

【搭】telephone directory 电话簿

discard [dɪsˈkɑːrd] *v.* 丢弃(reject)

【记】分拆联想：dis(消失掉) + card(纸片) → 将废纸扔掉 → 丢弃

【例】I've *discarded* the old paper. 我已丢弃了用过的纸。

dissenter [dɪˈsentər] *n.* 不同意者；反对者(objector)

【参】proponent(*n.* 支持者)

dormant [ˈdɔːrmənt] *a.* 静止的(inactive)；休眠的(resting)

【记】词根记忆：dorm(睡眠) + ant → 休眠的

【例】When water is scarce, lichens may become *dormant*. 当水变少时，苔藓就可能休眠。

dump [dʌmp] *v.* 倾卸，倾倒

【记】发音记忆："当铺" → 到当铺去倾卸 → 倾卸

【例】The freighter was caught in a big storm and thousands of pairs of sneakers got *dumped* into the Pacific Ocean. 这艘货船遇到了大风暴，上千双运动鞋被卷进了太平洋。

【派】dumping(*n.* 倾倒)

ecology [iˈkɑːlədʒi] *n.* 生态，生态学

【记】词根记忆：eco(生态) + logy(…学) → 生态学

【派】ecological(*a.* 生态的，生态学的)；ecologist(*n.* 生态学家)

eliminate [ɪˈlɪmɪneɪt] *vt.* 消除；淘汰(*eradicate, remove)

【记】词根记忆：e + limin(门槛) + ate → 扔出门槛 → 消除；淘汰

【例】Certain species may be *eliminated* and others may survive for no particular reason. 不知什么原因，某些物种可能被淘汰，其他的可能存活。

【派】elimination(*n.* 消除，除去)

entry [ˈentri] *n.* 进入(权)；入口处(entrance)

【记】来自enter(*v.* 进入)

【例】I just admitted my *entry* for the art club's photography contest. 我刚入围艺术俱乐部的摄影竞赛。

258
□ digest □ directory □ discard □ dissenter □ dormant □ dump
□ ecology □ eliminate □ entry

exhibit [ɪg'zɪbɪt] *vt.* 显示(show); 展出(*display) *n.* 展览
【记】词根记忆: ex(出) + hibit(拥有) → 把有的拿出来 → 显示; 展出
【例】I'm trying to find someone to come with me to the new sculpture *exhibit* in the art museum on Saturday. 我正找人周六陪我去艺术博物馆看新的雕塑展览。
【派】exhibition(*n.* 展览会)

faculty ['fæklti] *n.* 全体教职员工; 能力(ability, capacity)
【搭】university/college faculty 大学教员
【例】The old man has a *faculty* for saying the right things. 这位老人有能力说出正确的话。

fiber ['faɪbər] *n.* 纤维; 光纤
【记】分拆联想: fi(看作five, 五) + ber → 由五种或更多的材料合成 → 纤维
【参】fibrous(*a.* 含纤维的)

fidelity [fɪ'deləti] *n.* 忠诚, 忠实(loyalty, allegiance)
【记】词根记忆: fid(相信) + elity → 值得相信 → 忠诚, 忠实
【例】With *fidelity* to real life and accurate representation without idealization, the authors studied local dialects. 作者们研究当地方言时, 忠于现实生活, 不美化任何东西, 客观反映现实。

focus ['foʊkəs] *n.* 焦点, (活动, 兴趣等的)中心 *v.* 使聚集, 集中
【记】分拆联想: foc(看作for, 为了) + us → 焦点访谈的口号是为人民大众服务 → 焦点
【搭】focus on 集中; be out focus 模糊的; 不聚焦的

franchise ['fræntʃaɪz] *n.* 特权(privilege), 公民权 *v.* 赋予特权, 赋予公民权
【搭】franchise store 连锁店
【例】That restaurant is expanding through the sale of *franchise*. 那家餐厅正在通过销售特许权进行业务扩展。

furry ['fɜːri] *a.* 毛皮的, 盖着毛皮的; 生苔的
【例】The African grass mouse's *furry* stripe's like a chipmunk's, which helps it blend in with its environment. 非洲草鼠毛茸茸的条纹就像金华鼠的条纹一样, 有助于它与环境很好地融合。

gallery ['gæləri] *n.* 画廊, 美术馆
【例】The *gallery* is a good place for the exhibition. 美术馆是举办这个展览的好场所。

gap [gæp] *n.* 缺口(*opening); 间隔(space)
【记】联想记忆: 地图(map)上它们的间隔(gap)没这么大

☐ exhibit	☐ faculty	☐ fiber	☐ fidelity	☐ focus	☐ franchise
☐ furry	☐ gallery	☐ gap			

【例】One of them might forget some of the words and make up new ones to fill the *gap*. 他们中有人可能会忘记一些词，于是就造新词来填空。

gin [dʒɪn] *n.* 轧棉机

【搭】the cotton gin 轧棉机

governor [ˈɡʌvərnər] *n.* 省长；州长；总督

【记】词根记忆：govern(统治，管理) + or → 省长；总督

haul [hɔːl] *v.* (用力)拖，拖运(pull, drag)

【记】联想记忆：hal(呼吸)中间加u → 拖东西累得喘气 → 拖，拖运

【例】Farm women had to *haul* large quantities of water into the house from wells. 农妇不得不从井里打水，然后挑回家里。

highlight [ˈhaɪlaɪt] *v.* 突出(stand out)；以强烈光线照射 *n.* 最精彩部分

【记】组合词：high(高的) + light(发光) → 突出；最精彩部分

【例】The light *highlights* the figures of the sailors. 灯光突出了水手们的身影。

ignition [ɪɡˈnɪʃn] *n.* 点火，点燃

【记】来自ignite(*v.* 点火，点燃)

【搭】ignition point 燃点

月亮
吾来也

ignition

万户

impair [ɪmˈper] *vt.* 削弱(weaken)；损害(damage)

【记】词根记忆：im (进入) + pair (坏) → 使…变坏 → 削弱；损害

【例】Without regular supplies of some hormones, our capacity to behave would be seriously *impaired*. 如果荷尔蒙不能有规律地供应，我们的行为能力就会严重受损。

imprecise [ˌɪmprɪˈsaɪs] *a.* 不精确的(inexact)，不严密的

【记】分拆联想：im(不) + precise(精确的，严密的) → 不精确的

【例】A: How did you check the scales before?

B: We have an old standard weight that we used to use. It had to be replaced because it was *imprecise*.

A：你以前是怎么检查秤的？

B：我们过去用一个旧的标准秤砣，但因为不准确被换掉了。

integrity [ɪnˈteɡrəti] *n.* 正直(honesty)；完整

【记】词根记忆：integr(整体) + ity → 一个正直的人才是完整的人 → 正直；完整

【例】People greatly admired Washington's *integrity*. 人们十分敬仰华盛顿的正直。//They questioned the artistic *integrity* of dancers. 他们质疑舞蹈者的艺术品质。

lawn [lɔːn] *n.* 草地，草坪（grassplot）

【记】分拆联想：law（法律）＋n（像一个门）→ 很多人乱踏草坪，所以要运用法律建一道保护的门 → 草坪

least [liːst] *a.* 最小的；最少的 *ad.* 最小；最少

【搭】at least

【参】feast（*n.* 节日，盛宴）

miserable [ˈmɪzrəbl] *a.* 痛苦的（tearing）；可怜的（wretched）

【记】分拆联想：miser(y)（痛苦）＋able → 痛苦的，可怜的

【例】I'm usually *miserable* for a week and the symptom ends up ruining my holidays. 我一般要难受一个星期，结果就把我的假期毁了。

myth [mɪθ] *n.* 神话，虚构的故事（legend, fiction）

nucleus [ˈnuːkliəs] [*pl.* nuclei] *n.* 核子，核心（core）

【例】At the core of every ice crystal is a minuscule *nucleus*. 每个冰晶体的核心是一个极小的核子。

odor [ˈoʊdər] *n.* 气味；香味（smell; fragrance）

【例】Each ant nest has its own *odor* as a result of its location, history, and local food supply. 每个蚁巢因位置、历史和当地食物供应的不同具有各自的味道。

【派】odorless（*a.* 无气味的）

optical [ˈɑːptɪkl] *a.* 眼的，视力（觉）的（visual）；光学的

【记】词根记忆：opt(视力)＋ical → 眼的，视力（觉）的

【参】optics（*n.* 光学）；optician（*n.* 眼镜商）

outstanding [aʊtˈstændɪŋ] *a.* 突出的，显著的（remarkable）

【记】分拆联想：out(出)＋stand(站)＋ing → 站出来的 → 鹤立鸡群的 → 杰出的

【搭】outstanding students 杰出的学生

【例】If you are interested in gymnastics, the university has an *outstanding* team. 如果你对体操感兴趣，大学有一个非常不错的体操队。

overcome [ˌoʊvərˈkʌm] *v.* 战胜，克服（conquer, defeat）

【记】来自词组come over 战胜，克服

【例】Fortunately, scientific and technological advances have *overcome* most of these problems. 幸运的是，科学技术进步已经克服了其中的大部分问题。

owl [aʊl] *n.* 猫头鹰

【记】发音记忆："嗷" → 像猫头鹰的叫声；注意不要和awl（*n.* 尖钻）相混

☐ lawn	☐ least	☐ miserable	☐ myth	☐ nucleus	☐ odor
☐ optical	☐ outstanding	☐ overcome	☐ owl		

permeate [ˈpɜːrmieɪt] v. 弥漫，渗透（*spread through, penetrate）

【记】词根记忆：per(贯穿)＋meat＋e → 贯穿进去 → 弥漫，渗透

【例】Water will *permeate* blotting paper. 水能够渗透吸水纸。

【参】permeable(a. 可渗透的)；impermeable(a. 不能渗透的)

personnel [ˌpɜːrsəˈnel] n. 全体人员；员工（crew）

【记】分拆联想：person(人)＋nel → 全体人员

【例】The fungus infections afflicted many military *personnel*. 很多军事人员遭受着真菌感染的折磨。

【参】personal(a. 个人的)

physiology [ˌfɪziˈɑːlədʒi] n. 生理学

【记】词根记忆：physio(生理的)＋logy(学科) → 生理学

【派】physiological(a. 生理的)

picky [ˈpɪki] a.【口】挑剔的；难以取悦的(fussy)

【例】The bees are *picky* about who comes to their family reunion. 蜜蜂对谁来参加家庭聚会比较挑剔。

【参】sticky(a. 黏的，黏性的)

picturesque [ˌpɪktʃəˈresk] a. 如画的；独特的(scenic, beautiful)

【搭】a picturesque village 风景如画的村庄；a picturesque style of architecture 别具一格的建筑风格

【例】The place is remarkable for its *picturesque* scenery. 这个地区因其风景如画而著名。

pointed [ˈpɔɪntɪd] a. 尖的；尖角的(sharp-angled)

【记】分拆联想：point(点；弄尖)＋ed → 尖角的

positive [ˈpɑːzətɪv] a. 肯定的(affirmative)；积极的(active)；实际的(actual)；【电】正的

【记】分拆联想：posit(断定)＋ive → 可以断定的 → 肯定的；积极的

【搭】positive charge 正电荷

【例】He believed writers should emphasize the *positive* aspects of life. 他认为作家应该强调生活的光明面。

【派】positively(ad. 明确地；带正电地；肯定地)

potter [ˈpɑːtər] n. 陶工，制陶工人

【记】分拆联想：pott(=pot 陶罐)＋er → 陶工

【例】In day-to-day use, the *potter* smoothed the exterior surface of the pot with wet hands. 在日常使用中，陶工用湿漉漉的手弄平了陶器的外表面。

【派】pottery(n. 陶器，制陶器术)

□ permeate	□ personnel	□ physiology	□ picky	□ picturesque	□ pointed
□ positive	□ potter				

predominate [prɪˈdɑːmɪneɪt] *vt.* 占优势（dominate）

【记】分拆联想：pre + dominate（统治）→ 处于统治地位 → 占优势

【例】Red and yellow *predominate* in these flowers. 这些花朵主要的颜色是红色和黄色。

【派】predominately(*ad.* 占优势地，主导地); predominant(*a.* 主要的)

principal [ˈprɪnsəpl] *a.* 主要的(*major, *main); 最重要的

【例】Coal became the *principal* source of electricity in the United States. 煤炭成了美国电力的主要来源。

【参】principle(*n.* 原则)

proprietor [prəˈpraɪətər] *n.* 所有者，业主（owner）

【例】My uncle is the *proprietor* of a chain of supermarkets. 我叔叔是一家连锁超市的业主。

quiescent [kwiˈesnt] *a.* 静止的；寂静的

【记】词根记忆：qui(=rest安静的) + escent(状态) → 安静的状态 → 静止的

raise [reɪz] *v.* 举起(lift)，提升；增加；饲养，养育；引起，惹起；竖起；提出，发起

【记】联想记忆：rise上升了一(a)点就是举起了raise

【搭】raise one's pay 涨工资

【例】A: Hey, did you hear that they're going to *raise* the dorm fees again?

B: Really? Am I glad I decide to move off campus?

A：嗨，你听说他们又要提高宿舍费用了吗？

B：真的？我该为我决定去校园外住而高兴吗？

A: I'm really glad our club decided to *raise* money for the children's hospital, and most of the people we'd phoned seemed happy to contribute.

B: Yeah, I agree. Now we've gone through all the numbers on our list now, so I guess we can call it a day.

A：我很高兴我们的俱乐部决定为儿童医院募集资金，接到我们电话的多数人都乐意捐赠。

B：是的，我同意。现在我们已经打完了名单上所有的号码，我想今天的工作可以告一段落了。

【参】rise(*v.* 升起，上升)

rally [ˈræli] *n.* 集会（assembly）

【记】分拆联想：r + all(所有) + y → 所有人都参加的大会 → 集会

relay ['riːleɪ] *n.* 补充物资

vt. 传达(convey)；转播(broadcast)

【例】Water is available at the relay station. 在中继站有水。//The pop festival was *relayed* all round the world. 流行节日在全球转播。

repertoire ['repərtwɑːr] *n.* (剧团等)常备剧目，保留剧目

【记】和report(*v.* 汇报)一起记 → 汇报演出需要常备剧目

shrimp [ʃrɪmp] *n.* 小虾

【记】联想记忆：sh(看作shui, 水) + rim(边) + p → 生活在水边的小虾 → 小虾

soccer ['sɑːkər] *n.* 足球

solar ['soʊlər] *a.* 太阳的；日光的

【记】词根记忆：sol(太阳) + ar → 太阳的；日光的

solid ['sɑːlɪd] *a.* 固体的；实心的；稳固的 (*substantial, firm) *n.* 固体 (substance)

【搭】solid mass 实体；solid particle 固体微粒

【派】solidarity(*n.* 团结)；solidify(*v.* 凝固)；solidly(*ad.* 牢固地)

starch [stɑːrtʃ] *n.* 淀粉(fecula)；[*pl.*] 淀粉类食物

【记】分拆联想：star (星星) + ch → 星星碎了，洒落下来成了淀粉 → 淀粉

sweeping ['swiːpɪŋ] *a.* 彻底的，广泛的(extensive)

【例】The Arts and Crafts Movement in the United States was responsible for *sweeping* changes in attitudes toward the decorative arts. 艺术和手工运动使人们对装饰艺术的态度彻底改变了。

swift [swɪft] *a.* 敏捷的，快的(rapid) *n.* 雨燕

【记】联想记忆：电梯(lift)因将l改成sw而变得飞快(swift)

【例】The current was too *swift* for boats to cross easily. 河水流得太快，船无法轻易穿过。

【派】swiftly(*ad.* 很快地)；swiftness(*n.* 迅速，快)

talent ['tælənt] *n.* 天赋(gift)；才干(ability)；人才(intellectual)

【记】分拆联想：tal(1) + ent(人) → 高人 → 人才

【例】Bonnie has a *talent* for expressing her ideas. 邦妮非常善于表达自己的观点。

【派】talented(*a.* 有才能的，天才的)

tendon ['tendən] *n.* 肌腱

trilogy ['trɪlədʒi] *n.* 三部剧，三部曲(three-part novel)

☐ relay ☐ repertoire ☐ shrimp ☐ soccer ☐ solar ☐ solid
☐ starch ☐ sweeping ☐ swift ☐ talent ☐ tendon ☐ trilogy

twinkling [ˈtwɪŋklɪŋ] *a.* 闪光的

unequal [ʌnˈiːkwəl] *a.* （在大小、数量等方面）不同的，不相等的（disproportionate）；（力量、能力等）不平等的，不相称的；（对做某事）不胜任的

unequal

【例】It's generally admitted that people with unequal talents should be paid *unequal* amounts. 一般认为为才智不同的人应该得到不同的报酬。

urgent [ˈɜːdʒənt] *a.* 急迫的，紧迫的

【记】词根记忆：urg(驱使) + ent(…的) → 不断驱使的 → 急迫的

【例】A: I need these articles photocopied and stapled. For my 4 clock meeting, do you think you could have it done by then?

B: There are several letters I need to type. They are not very *urgent* though. So I can make this top priority.

A: 我需要把这些文章复印装订，4点开会要用，你觉得你到时候弄得完吗？

B: 我需要录入几封信，不过这些信不太着急。所以，我可以先给你处理这件事。

utility [juːˈtɪləti] *n.* 功用，效用（function, avail）

【搭】utility company公用事业公司

【例】His *utility* bills are low. 他的公用事业账单费用不高。

vein [veɪn] *n.* 静脉；叶脉

【派】veining(*n.* 脉络分布)

You will achieve nothing if you place your hope merely on opportunity.
如果把一生的希望只寄托于"机遇"，则将一事无成。

——苏步青(*Su Buqing*)

Word List 25  MP3-25

词根、词缀预习表

vent	来	advent	n. 到来
portion	一部分	apportion	vt. 分配
civil	民间的	civilian	a. 平民的，民间的
dign	有价值的	dignity	n. 尊严，高贵
noc	伤害	innocent	a. 天真的
leth	死	lethargy	n. 死气沉沉
nov	新	novel	a. 新颖的
oper	工作	operate	v. 运转
solu	松的	soluble	a. 松的；可溶的
topo	地方	topography	n. 地形

additional [əˈdɪʃənl] *a.* 附加的(additive)，额外的(*further, extra)

【例】She needs the *additional* time to finish her paper. 她需要更多的时间完成论文。

admire [ədˈmaɪər] *vt.* 钦佩；欣赏(appreciate)

【记】词根记忆：ad(表加强) + mir(惊奇) + e → 让人很惊奇 → 钦佩，欣赏

【例】I *admire* your dedication. 我欣赏你的献身精神。

【派】admiration(*n.* 赞美；赞赏)

advance [ədˈvæns] *n./v.* 前进，提前

【搭】in advance 预先

【例】A: My parents need a place to stay when they come to the town next week. Do you have any suggestions?

B: I'd like to recommend the inn to visitors. But unlike the other places in town, they are usually filled months in *advance*.

A：我的父母下周来看我，他们得找个地方住。你有什么建议吗？

B：我想向他们推荐那家旅店。但是和这个镇子里其他地方不一样，那里通常几个月之前就订满了。

□ additional □ admire □ advance

A: Do we need to get the concert tickets in *advance*?

B: There may be some for sale at the door at a higher price.

A：我们需要提前订购音乐会门票吗？

B：门口可能会有卖高价票的。

【派】advanced(*a.* 高级的，先进的；前进的)

advent [ˈædvent] *n.* 到来(*arrival)，出现(emergence)

【记】词根记忆：ad + vent(来)→ 到来，出现

【例】With the *advent* of power-driven machinery, home industry began to give way to production in mills and factories. 随着动力驱动机的出现，家庭工业开始让位于磨坊和工厂的生产。

amusement [əˈmjuːzmənt] *n.* 娱乐(recreation)，消遣(*entertainment)

analysis [əˈnæləsɪs] *n.* 分析(study)

【例】They conducted a computer *analysis* of photographs. 他们对照片进行了电脑分析。

【参】analyst(*n.* 分析家)

ancient [ˈeɪnʃənt] *a.* 古代的(archaic)；古老的(*old)

【例】What does the professor say about *ancient* Greeks who traveled south?关于向南方旅游的古希腊人教授讲了什么？

apportion [əˈpɔːrʃn] *vt.* 分配(distribute, allot)

【记】词根记忆：ap + portion(一部分)→ 分成部分的 → 分配

appreciate [əˈpriːʃieɪt] *vt.* 赏识(*recognize)，鉴赏；感激

【例】She's learned to *appreciate* the sculptures. 她已经学会了欣赏雕塑。//I *appreciate* your getting my books, Bill. 感谢你帮我拿书，比尔。

【派】appreciation (*n.* 欣赏)；appreciative (*a.* 表示感激的)；appreciable(*a.* 值得重视的；可感知的)

【参】depreciation(*n.* 贬值)

auxiliary [ɔːɡˈzɪliəri] *a.* 辅助的；补充的(aiding; supplementary)

【记】词根记忆：aux(=aug提高) + iliary(形容词后缀)→ 促进提高的 → 辅助的

【搭】auxiliary machinery 辅助机器

【例】The factories in the region always have an *auxiliary* generator in event of power cuts. 这个地区的工厂总有一台备用发动机，以防断电。

bound [baʊnd] *a.* 被束缚的，被要求的(*obligated, enclose) *n.* [常*pl.*]界限(*limit, boundary)

【例】Music was closely *bound* up with religious beliefs. 音乐与宗教

信仰紧密相连。//Education knows no *bounds*. 教育无止境。

【派】unbound(*a.* 自由的，未绑的)

brand [brænd] *n.* 商标

buffalo [ˈbʌfəloʊ] *n.* 水牛

bump [bʌmp] *v.* 撞(破)(hit) *n.* 肿块

【记】象声词：物体碰撞的声音

【搭】bump into 偶然碰见

【例】I *bumped* into her at the market just last week. 我上周在市场碰巧遇到她。//Starfish's skin is covered with thorny *bumps*. 海星的皮肤上都是带刺的疙瘩。

【参】dump(*v.* 倾倒)；damp(*n.* 湿气)

butter [ˈbʌtər] *n.* 黄油，牛油

cannibalism [ˈkænɪbəlɪzəm] *n.* 嗜食同类

【记】来自cannibal(*n.* 食人者，食同类的动物)

characterize [ˈkærəktəraɪz] *vt.* 以…为特征；刻画…的性格(*distinguish, feature)

【例】The design elements have come to *characterize* the age of the skyscraper. 设计元素已经成为摩天大楼时代的特征。

civilian [səˈvɪliən] *a.* 平民的；民间的(folk)

【记】词根记忆：civil(民间的) + ian → 民间的

clay [kleɪ] *n.* 泥土，黏土(earth, mud)

【记】分拆联想：c + lay(层) → 泥土成一层一层分布 → 泥土

companion [kəmˈpæniən] *n.* 同伴，共事者(partner, comrade)

【记】来自company(*v.* 陪伴)

【例】Pierre and his *companions* did in fact reach the near vicinity of the North Pole. 皮埃尔和他的同伴的确到达了北极附近。

comparative [kəmˈpærətɪv] *a.* 比较的(relative)；相当的，接近的

【例】Bill is a *comparative* stranger in the town as he just moved here. 比尔刚来到这个镇子，相当于一个陌生人。

【参】compatible(*a.* 适宜的；符合的；兼容的)

competence [ˈkɑːmpɪtəns] *n.* 胜任；能力

【记】分拆联想：compet(e)(竞争) + ence → 竞争需要能力 → 胜任；能力

【例】By the age of three the babies will be well on their way to communicative *competence*. 三岁时孩子们就开始发展交流能力了。

concomitant [kənˈkɑːmɪtənt] *a.* 伴随的 *n.* 伴随物

【记】词根记忆：con(共同) + com(看作come) + itant → 一起来 →

伴随的

condense [kənˈdens] v. (使)压缩(compress); (使)凝结(contract)

【记】分拆联想: con + dense(密集的) → 变得密集的 →(使)压缩

【例】Eventually, the water stored as vapor in the atmosphere will *condense* to liquid again. 最后，大气中储存的水蒸气将再次凝缩为液体。

【派】condenser(n. 冷凝器)

crooked [ˈkrʊkɪd] a. 不诚实的; 欺诈的

【记】来自crook(v. 弯曲)

【搭】a crooked businessman 不诚实的商人

【例】Don't take *crooked* ways to solve the problem. 不要用歪门邪道解决这个问题。

cumbersome [ˈkʌmbərsəm] a. 笨重的(awkward); 麻烦的(troublesome)

【记】分拆联想: cumber(阻碍) + some → 受到阻碍的 → 笨重的

debut [deɪˈbjuː] n./v. 首次演出

【记】法语词: 开始, 初次露面 → 首次演出

【搭】film debut 电影首映式

descent [dɪˈsent] n. 血统(ancestry); 下降(drop)

【记】来自descend(v. 遗传; 下降)

【例】We watched the airplane's graceful *descent*. 我们看到飞机优雅地降落了。

【参】decent(a. 正派的)

descent

devastate [ˈdevəsteɪt] vt. 破坏(*ruin)

【记】词根记忆: de(变坏) + vast(大量) + ate → 大量弄坏 → 破坏

【例】The flood *devastated* countless houses. 洪水破坏了无数房屋。

development [dɪˈveləpmənt] n. 生长, 发育; 事态发展, 新情况; 研制, 培育

【例】I believe that social elements contributed to the *development* of bebop music. 我认为社会因素对比博普音乐的发展有贡献。// The focus of today's class is on an important element in the *development* of American cities. 今天的课主要是研究美国城市发展的一个重要因素。

dignity [ˈdɪgnəti] n. 尊严; 高贵(nobleness)

【记】词根记忆: dign(有价值的) + ity → 高贵

【例】Many poor people struggle to maintain their *dignity*. 很多穷人努力奋斗以维持他们的尊严。

【参】indignant(a. 愤慨的); dignify(vt. 使高贵)

dormancy [ˈdɔːrmənsi] *n.* 休眠；催眠状态；隐匿

【记】词根记忆：dorm(睡眠) + ancy → 睡眠的 → 催眠状态

【例】That huge volcano erupted after twenty years of *dormancy*. 那座巨大的火山休眠20年后又爆发了。

dress [dres] *n.* 服装，童装，女装 *v.* 穿衣，打扮

【搭】dress up 打扮，装饰

【例】In western countries, women should wear evening *dress* when attending the party. 在西方国家，女性参加聚会时应该穿晚装。

A: Which outfit should I wear to my job interview, the black *dress* or the navy blue suit?

B: Well, Jane, you've got to consider the image you want to present, and I say the suit is more professional looking.

A：我应该穿什么衣服去参加面试？黑色连衣裙还是海军蓝套装？

B：嗯，简，你要考虑自己想展现的形象。我觉得套装看上去更职业。

【参】mess(*n.* 混乱，肮脏)

endure [ɪnˈdʊr] *vt.* 忍受，忍耐(*tolerate, suffer)

【记】分拆联想：end(结束) + ure → 坚持到结束 → 忍受，维持

【例】I had to *endure* many painful shots because I'd been exposed to rabies. 我遭遇狂犬病，不得不忍受多次打针的疼痛。

【派】enduring(*a.* 持久的，持续的)；endurance(*n.* 忍耐力；持久力)

entrepreneur [ˌɑːntrəprəˈnɜːr] *n.* 企业家，主办人(business person)

【记】来自enterprise(*n.* 企业)

excavate [ˈekskəveɪt] *vt.* 挖掘(dig)，掘出(unearth)

【记】词根记忆：ex(出) + cav(看作cave，洞) + ate → 挖出洞 → 挖掘，掘出

【例】The deepest bone-bearing deposit was *excavated* in 1914. 最深的含有骨头的矿床于1914年被挖掘出来。

【派】excavation(*n.* 挖掘，[常*pl.*] 挖掘地)

excess [ɪkˈses] *n.* 过度，超过(superfluity)

[ˈekses] *a.* 过量的；额外的(extra)

【记】词根记忆：ex + cess(走) → 走出格 → 过量的

【派】excessive(*a.* 过多的，过度的)

exemplary [ɪgˈzempləri] *a.* 模范的，典型的

【记】来自example(*n.* 榜样)

□ dormancy　□ dress　□ endure　□ entrepreneur　□ excavate　□ excess
□ exemplary

【例】The *exemplary* function of the hero in literary works seems to remain constant. 文学作品中主人公的模范作用似乎是持久的。

exemplary

extent [ɪkˈstent] *n.* 程度，范围(*magnitude, *scale,*scope)

【例】These innovations in manufacturing boosted output and living standards to an unprecedented *extent*. 这些生产创新把产量和生活水平提高到了前所未有的程度。

【参】extend(*v.* 延伸); extant(*a.* 现存的)

favorable [ˈfeɪvərəbl] *a.* 良好的(pleasing); 赞成的(affirmative); 有利的 (advantageous)

【例】Her attitude toward the claims of health foods is somewhat *favorable*. 她对健康食品所宣称的持赞成态度。//Endotherms also regulate their temperature by choosing *favorable* environments. 恒温动物也通过选择有利的环境调节其体温。

female [ˈfiːmeɪl] *n.* 女性 *a.* 女(性)的; 母的, 雌性的

【记】联想记忆: 雌(female)雄(male)相吸

furnish [ˈfɜːrnɪʃ] *v.* 提供; 装备(*provide, supply)

【记】分拆联想: fur (皮毛) + nish → 卖了皮毛提供装备 → 提供; 装备

【例】Perhaps the dean's office can *furnish* the report. 或许系主任的办公室可以提供这份报告。

【派】furnishing(*n.* [常*pl.*]家具与陈设等)

grip [grɪp] *v.* 控制(control, command)

【记】和trip(*n.* 旅行)一起记

haircut [ˈheɪrkʌt] *n.* 理发

【搭】have/get a haircut 剪头发

【例】A: You look different today. Did you get a *haircut*?
B: That's funny. You're the third person to ask me that. But all I did was getting new frames for my eye glasses.
A: 你今天看上去有些不同。你理发了?
B: 真有意思, 你是第三个问我的人了。我只不过给眼镜换了个新框。

imitate [ˈɪmɪteɪt] *vt.* 模仿, 效仿(*copy)

【记】分拆联想: im + it(它) + ate(eat的过去式, 吃) → 它照着别人的样子吃 → 模仿

| extent | favorable | female | furnish | grip | haircut |
| imitate | | | | | |

【例】The author indicates that children *imitate* their parents. 作者指出儿童效仿其父母。//He had been trained to *imitate* the artist's style. 他受到训练去模仿这个艺术家的风格。

【派】imitation(*n.* 模仿，效法；仿制品)

innocent ['ɪnəsnt] *a.* 天真的(naive)

【记】词根记忆：in(无，非)＋noc(伤害)＋ent → 无害人之心的 → 天真的

【派】innocence(*n.* 天真纯洁)

inspection [ɪn'spekʃn] *n.* 检查，视察，细看

【记】来自inspect(*v.* 细看，视察)

【搭】the inspection of …的检查

【例】A: You wouldn't believe the line at the auto *inspection* center. I waited more than two hours to get through it.

B: That's what you get for waiting until the last day of the month.

A：你不会相信车检中心排的长队。我等了两个多小时。

B：月底最后一天去就得排长队。

lethargy ['leθərdʒi] *n.* 死气沉沉

【记】词根记忆：leth(死)＋argy → 像死了一样睡 → 死气沉沉

【例】A surprise military attack roused the nation from its *lethargy*. 一场突然的军事袭击使这个国家从死气沉沉的状态中清醒过来了。

lipid ['lɪpɪd] *n.* 油脂

mail [meɪl] *n.* 邮件 *v.* 邮寄(post)

【搭】mail carrier 邮差；by mail 通过邮件 internal mail 内部邮件

【例】A: I hear the post office hire two more students to work in the *mail* room.

B: They are just a little short of a full staff man.

A：我听说邮局又雇佣了两个学生在邮件室工作。

B：他们就是缺个全职人员。

medium ['mi:diəm] *n.* [*pl.* media] 媒介，媒体；方法 (*technique, way, means)

【记】词根记忆：medi(中间)＋um → 媒介

minor ['maɪnər] *a.* 较小的(lesser)；次要的(subordinate)

【记】词根记忆：min(小)＋or → 较小的；次要的

【例】Typing the essay is only a *minor* problem for me. 打论文对我来说只是个小问题。

mushroom ['mʌʃrʊm] *n.* 蘑菇(fungus)

【记】分拆联想：mush(软块)＋room(房子) → 蘑菇的样子很像软软的小房子 → 蘑菇

| ☐ innocent | ☐ inspection | ☐ lethargy | ☐ lipid | ☐ mail | ☐ medium |
| ☐ minor | ☐ mushroom | | | | |

navy ['neɪvi] *n.* 海军

【记】词根记忆：nav(船)+ y → 驾船保卫祖国 → 海军

novel ['nɑ:vl] *n.* 小说(fiction) *a.* 新颖的(innovative, new)

【记】词根记忆：nov(新)+ el → 新颖的

【例】The engine that became standard on western steamboats was of a different and *novel* design. 成为西方蒸汽船标准的引擎拥有一个不同的新颖设计。

【派】novelty(*n.* 新奇的事物；新鲜感)

nurture ['nɜ:rtʃər] *v.* 扶植，支持(support)

【记】联想记忆：大自然(nature)像母亲一样滋养(nurture)着人类

【例】We want to *nurture* the new project, not destroy it. 我们想支持新项目，而不是破坏它。

offensive [ə'fensɪv] *a.* 攻击性的(aggressive)

【例】The *offensive* team carried the ball closer to the goal. 进攻的球队把球带到了离球门更近的地方。

【派】inoffensive(*a.* 无害的)

operate ['ɑ:pəreɪt] *v.* 运转，开动（run）；动手术，开刀，(对…)施行手术

【记】词根记忆：oper（工作）+ ate → 工作着的 → 运转

【搭】operate the machine 操作机器

【例】It's important that you all understand that quartz heaters *operate* on a totally different principle with common convection heaters. 重要的是，你们要理解石英加热器与普通对流加热器的运行原理完全不同。

parachute ['pærəʃu:t] *n.* 降落伞

paste [peɪst] *n.* 面团，糨糊

【记】联想记忆：浆糊(paste)的味道(taste)不太好

perpetuate [pər'petʃueɪt] *vt.* 使…延续(last)

【记】词根记忆：per(贯穿)+ pet(追求)+ uate → 永远追求 → 使…延续

【例】Insects have many enemies, but they must *perpetuate* their kind. 昆虫有很多敌人，但是它们必须延续后代。

【参】perpetual(*a.* 永久的)

plank [plæŋk] *n.* 厚木板(board)

【记】联想记忆：plan（看作plant，植物）+ k → 厚木板来源于植物 → 厚木板

navy	novel	nurture	offensive	operate	parachute
paste	perpetuate	plank			

pollinate ['pɑ:ləneɪt] *v.* 给…传授花粉

【记】分拆联想: pollin(=pollen花粉) + ate → 给…传授花粉

【例】These moths continue to *pollinate* the flowers until well into September. 这些飞蛾继续给花朵授粉, 直至9月份才停止。

【派】pollination(*n.* 授粉); pollinator(*n.* 传粉媒介, 传粉昆虫)

【参】cross-pollinate(*v.* 异花授粉)

racket ['rækɪt] *n.* (网球等的)球拍

reach [ri:tʃ] *v.* 抵达(arrive), 达到; 伸手, 够到, 触到 *n.* 能达到的范围

【例】Cook told the world he had *reached* the Pole four years earlier. 库克告诉全世界他四年前就到达了极地。

reserve [rɪ'zɜ:rv] *n.* 储备(物); 自然保护区 *v.* 保留(save); 预订(book)

【记】分拆联想: re(反复) + serve(保存) → 保留

【例】The *reserve* section of the library is due to close in one hour. 图书馆的预订区要在一个小时后关闭。//She was asked to *reserve* a room. 她被要求预订房间。

【派】reservation(*n.* 预订); reserved(*a.* 预订的)

residue ['rezɪdu:] *n.* 剩余, 残余(remnant)

【记】词根记忆: re + sid(坐, 引申为"剩") + ue → 剩余

【例】The water can be drawn off and evaporated, leaving a *residue* of clay. 水可以排出来, 然后挥发, 留下一点黏土。

restraint [rɪ'streɪnt] *n.* 抑制, 限制(limitation)

【记】来自restrain(*v.* 克制)

【参】constraint(*n.* 约束, 强制)

scent [sent] *n.* 香气(odor, fragrance); 气味(smell)

snap [snæp] *v.* 突然折断(*break, burst); 突然抓住(snatch)

【记】分拆联想: s + nap(小睡) → 小睡时被老师抓住了 → 突然抓住

【搭】snap out of 突然摆脱不好的状态

soluble ['sɑ:ljəbl] *a.* 可溶的

【记】词根记忆: solu(松的) + ble → 可溶的

【派】insoluble(*a.* 不溶解的)

stick [stɪk] *n.* 棍, 棒; 手杖(wand) *v.* 黏住; 放置(put)

【搭】stick insect 竹节虫; stick around 逗留; stick with 坚持做

【例】*Stick* a message in a bottle and throw it in the water. 在瓶子里放一张纸条, 然后扔进大海。

【派】sticker(*n.* 胶粘物, 不干胶标签); sticky(*a.* 粘的, 有粘性的)

stylish ['staɪlɪʃ] *a.* 漂亮的; 时髦的(fashionable)

□ pollinate	□ racket	□ reach	□ reserve	□ residue	□ restraint
□ scent	□ snap	□ soluble	□ stick	□ stylish	

superintendent [ˌsuːpərɪnˈtendənt] *n.* 主管，负责人(principal)

【记】分拆联想：super(上等的) + intend(打算) + ent(人) → 作打算、写计划的人 → 主管，负责人

【例】At the time of the Revolution, the *Superintendent* of Indian Affairs had little power. 在革命时期，印第安人事负责人几乎没什么权力。

syrup [ˈsɪrəp] *n.* 糖浆；果汁(juice)

【记】分拆联想：sy + rup (看作cup, 杯) → 一杯一杯地喝糖浆 → 糖浆

tedious [ˈtiːdiəs] *a.* 乏味的(boring)，单调的，冗长的

【记】分拆联想：ted(看作tea, 茶) + i(我) + ous(…的) → 我一个人喝茶 → 乏味的

【搭】a tedious debate 单调乏味的辩论；a tedious fellow 令人生厌的家伙

【例】A: What do you think of Professor Lee's lecture?
B: So *tedious.*
A: 你觉得李教授的讲课如何？
B: 太乏味。

topography [təˈpɑːɡrəfi] *n.* 地形(terrain)

【记】词根记忆：topo(地方) + graph(图) + y → 地形

【例】The parks should be adapted to the local *topography.* 公园应该顺应当地的地形。

trend [trend] *n.* 趋势，倾向(*tendency)；[常*pl.*] 流行(fashion)

【记】联想记忆：tend(倾向)加r还是倾向(trend)

【搭】economic trend 经济趋势

【例】Other *trends* and inventions had also helped make it possible for Americans to vary their daily diets. 其他的趋势和发明也使美国人改变日常膳食成为了可能。

tug [tʌg] *n.* 牵引(pull)

【记】和bug(*n.* 臭虫)一起记

underneath [ˌʌndərˈniːθ] *prep.* 在…下面(beneath) *ad.* 在下面(below)

【例】The paper is *underneath* the book. 论文在书底下。

wasp [wɑːsp] *n.* 黄蜂

Word List 26  🎵 MP3-26

词根、词缀预习表

ile	易…	agile	a. 敏捷的
capt	抓	captive	n. 俘虏
eco	经济	economical	a. 节约的，节俭的
in	向内	intent	n. 意图，目的
seism	地震	seismograph	n. 地震仪
sequ	跟随	sequence	n. 顺序
err	错	erratic	a. 古怪的，反复无常的

absolutely ['æbsəluːtli] *ad.* 完全地；绝对地（utterly）

【记】来自absolute（*a.* 完全的，绝对的）

acid ['æsɪd] *n.* 酸 *a.* 酸的

【记】本身为词根：酸

【例】It's the *acid* that eventually eats away the paper. 最后让纸腐蚀的正是酸。

【派】acidic（*a.* 酸的，酸性的）；acidity（*n.* 酸度，酸性）

【参】arid（*a.* 干旱的）；avid（*a.* 渴望的）；avoid（*v.* 避免）

agile ['ædʒl] *a.* 敏捷的，轻快的（nimble, brisk）

【记】词根记忆：ag（做）+ ile（易…）→ 动作容易的 → 敏捷的

【搭】an agile mind 灵活的头脑

【例】The leader of a country needs an *agile* mind to solve sophisticated problems. 国家领导人需要敏捷的头脑来解决复杂的问题。

【派】agility（*n.* 敏捷，活泼）

allocation [ˌælə'keɪʃn] *n.* 配给，分配（apportion）

【记】来自allocate（*v.* 配给，分配）

【例】It does have the power to make laws and vote on the *allocation* of funds. 它的确有权力制定法律，并就资金的分配进行投票。

attorney [ə'tɜːrni] *n.* 代理人，辩护律师

【记】词根记忆：at + torn(转) + ey → 脑子转得快 → 能说会道的人 → 辩护律师

【例】When I was six years old, my father was selected as the district *attorney*. 我6岁时，父亲被选为了区检察官。

bias ['baɪəs] *n.* 偏见(prejudice)

【记】分拆联想：bi(两) + as → 两者只取其一 → 偏见

【例】Throughout the nineteenth century and into the twentieth, citizens of the United States maintained a *bias* against big cities. 整个19世纪和20世纪，美国公民对大城市一直有偏见。

bluff [blʌf] *n.* 悬崖，绝壁 *v.* 诈骗，吓唬

【记】和buffalo(美洲野牛)一起记，buffalo bluffs(野牛虚张声势)

【搭】bluff sb. into doing 欺骗某人做…

【例】The old man is kind and friendly despite his relatively *bluff* manners. 这个老人尽管有点虚张声势，但还是友善的。

bookstore ['bʊkstɔːr] *n.* 书店(bookshop)

【例】A: Did you say you were driving to town this morning?

B: Yes. I have to get a check cashed to pay my *bookstore* bill.

A：你说今天上午要开车进城吗？

B：是的。我要兑现一张支票来支付书店账单。

captive ['kæptɪv] *n.* 俘虏，猎物(quarry)

【记】词根记忆：capt(抓) + ive → 俘虏，猎物

cease [siːs] *v./n.* 结束，停止(stop, end)

【例】It *ceased* snowing. 雪停了。

ceremonial [ˌserɪ'moʊniəl] *n.* 仪式(ritual, ceremony) *a.* 正式的(formal)

charter ['tʃɑːrtər] *n.* 宪章(constitution) *vt.* 特许(certify)

【记】和chart(*n.* 航图；图表)一起记

【例】The states *chartered* manufacturing, baking, mining and transportation firms. 各州予以生产、烘烤、采矿和运输公司特许权。

claim [kleɪm] *v./n.* 声称；要求(request)；索赔 *n.* 断言(assertion)

【例】The farmers *claimed* that the iron poisoned the soil and made the weeds grow. 农民们声称铁使土壤有毒，还长野草。//Peary's *claim* was surrounded by controversy. 皮尔里的要求饱受争议。

club [klʌb] *n.* 俱乐部，夜总会；社团；棍棒，球棒

【例】A: I know you have a lot to do, but you were supposed to make those phone calls last night. You know about tomorrow's theater *club* meeting?

☐ attorney	☐ bias	☐ bluff	☐ bookstore	☐ captive	☐ cease
☐ ceremonial	☐ charter	☐ claim	☐ club		

B: Yeah.

A: 我知道你要做很多事情，但是你昨晚应该打这些电话。你知道明天剧院俱乐部的会议吗？

B: 是的。

concentration [ˌkɑːnsn'treɪʃn] *n.* 专心；集中（the act or process of concentrating）；浓度

【例】The music can help relieve depression and improve *concentration*. 音乐有助于缓解抑郁，提高注意力。//It's important to have the soil tested regularly to determine the lead *concentration*. 要定期检测土壤，确定铅含量，这很重要。

deciduous [dɪ'sɪdʒuəs] *a.* 脱落性的；落叶性的

【记】词根记忆：de + cid（落下）+ uous → 落叶性的

【搭】deciduous tree 落叶树

deduct [dɪ'dʌkt] *vt.* 扣除，减去（subtract）

【记】词根记忆：de（去掉）+ duct（引导）→ 引导去掉 → 减去，扣除

【例】The tax will be *deducted* from your salary later. 税随后会从你的工资里扣掉。

【派】deduction(*n.* 演绎；扣除)；deductive(*a.* 推论的，演绎的)

【参】conduct(*v.* 引导 *n.* 行为)

definite ['defɪnət] *a.* 清楚的，确切的(distinct, precise)

【记】来自define(*v.* 定义)

【例】He has no *definite* plans. 他没有明确的计划。

【派】definitely (*ad.* 确切地，肯定地)；definition (*n.* 定义)；indefinitely(*ad.* 不定地，无穷地)

【参】infinite(*a.* 无限的)

dense [dens] *a.* 密集的，浓厚的(thick)

【记】和tense(*a.* 紧张的)一起记

【派】densely(*ad.* 密度大地，浓密地)；density(*n.* 密度)

deteriorate [dɪ'tɪriəreɪt] *v.* 变坏；变质(erode)

【记】词根记忆：deterior(拉丁文：糟糕的)+ ate → 变糟糕 → 变坏

【例】Paper made from rags *deteriorated* quickly. 用破布做的纸很快就变质了。

【派】deterioration(*n.* 恶化)

discipline [ˈdɪsəplɪn] *n.* 纪律；学科（subject）*v.* 训练（drill）；惩罚（punish）

【记】分拆联想：dis + cip（拿）+ line（线）→ 让人站成一条线来训练 → 纪律

【例】He lacks *discipline* in his study habits. 他的学习习惯缺乏纪律。// They give orders and may *discipline* group members who inhibit attainment of the group's goals. 他们发号施令，可以处罚阻碍实现团队目标的成员。

【派】disciplined（*a.* 纪律的）

domain [doʊˈmeɪn] *n.* 领域（field）；领土（territory）

【记】词根记忆：dom（统治）+ ain → 领域；领土

【搭】public domain 公有土地

【例】All these lining things survived in the public *domain*. 这些生物在公有土地上存活下来了。

economical [ˌiːkəˈnɑːmɪkl] *a.* 节约的（thrifty），经济的

【记】词根记忆：eco（经济）+ nom（某一领域的知识）+ ical → 在某一方面节约的 → 节约的

【例】A: En, currently the only way to stop the books from decaying is to remove the binding and treat each page individually to remove the acid.

B: That doesn't sound very *economical*.

A：嗯，目前唯一一使书不腐烂的方法就是去掉封面，然后将每一页的酸性物质成分去掉。

B：那听起来不是太经济。

epic [ˈepɪk] *n.* 史诗 *a.* 英雄的

erratic [ɪˈrætɪk] *a.* 古怪的，反复无常的（eccentric）

【记】词根记忆：err（错）+ atic → 性格出错 → 反复无常的

evident [ˈevɪdənt] *a.* 明显的；清楚的（apparent）

【记】词根记忆：e + vid（看见）+ ent → 能够看得见的 → 明显的

【派】evidently（*ad.* 明显地）

evoke [ɪˈvoʊk] *vt.* 唤起，激起（stimulate, arouse）

【记】词根记忆：e（出）+ voke（喊）→ 喊出来 → 引起，激起

【例】The purpose of a poem need not be to inform the reader of anything, but rather to *evoke* feelings. 诗不需要让读者了解什么，其目的应该是激发情感，产生愉悦的体验。

【参】invoke（*v.* 调用）；provoke（*vt.* 激怒）；revoke（*vt.* 撤回）

experimental [ɪkˌsperɪˈmentl] *a.* 实验的

【记】来自experiment（*n.* 实验）

| discipline | domain | economical | epic | erratic | evident |
| evoke | experimental | | | | |

【搭】experimental station 实验站

【例】The *experimental* course which I registered for yesterday is Child Psychology. 我昨天登记的实验课是儿童心理学。

explosion [ɪkˈsploʊʒn] *n.* 爆炸(blast), 爆发; 激增

【记】来自explode(*v.* 爆炸)

【搭】a huge explosion 大爆炸

【例】Planets are a billion times dimmer than their parent stars. It would be like trying to see the light of a candle next to a huge *explosion*. 行星的亮度比母恒星暗10亿倍, 就好像大爆炸旁边的一抹烛光。

extraordinary [ɪkˈstrɔːdəneri] *a.* 特别的 (exceptional, special); 非凡的 (*remark-able)

【记】词根记忆: extra(超过的) + ordinary(平常的) → 特别的

【例】Nitinol is one of the most *extraordinary* metals to be discovered this century. 镍钛诺是本世纪发现的最特别的金属之一。

【派】extraordinarily(*ad.* 格外地)

foreshorten [fɔːrˈʃɔːrtn] *v.* (绘画中)按透视法缩短; 节略, 缩短

【记】词根记忆: fore(前面) + shorten(缩短) → 按照透视法缩短

【例】To get the perspective you want, you need to use what we call *foreshortening*. 要得到你想要的透视图, 你需要按照我们称之为透视法缩短的方法进行透视。

frustrate [ˈfrʌstreɪt] *v.* 使感到灰心, 挫败(thwart, confound)

【记】分拆联想: frust(一部分) + rate(费用) → 买东西只带了一部分钱, 买不成 → 挫败

【例】I'm *frustrated* with the computer. 电脑让我充满挫败感。

【派】frustration(*n.* 挫折); frustrating(*a.* 令人沮丧的)

germ [dʒɜːrm] *n.* 微生物(microorganism); 细菌(bacteria)

【记】本身就是词根: 种子, 引申为"微生物, 细菌"

【例】Some diseases are caused by *germ*-carrying insects. 一些疾病是由携带细菌的昆虫造成的。

gourd [ɡʊrd] *n.* 葫芦

groan [ɡroʊn] *v.* 呻吟(moan); 叹息(sigh)

【记】联想记忆: 长大后(grown)比小孩更爱叹息(groan)

hoe [hoʊ] *vt.* 用锄耕地, 锄

【记】联想记忆: 用锄头(hoe)挖洞(hole)

| ☐ explosion | ☐ extraordinary | ☐ foreshorten | ☐ frustrate | ☐ germ | ☐ gourd |
| ☐ groan | ☐ hoe | | | | |

【参】harrow(*n.* 耙)

hummingbird ['hʌmɪŋbɜːrd] *n.* 蜂鸟

【记】组合词：humming(嗡嗡叫) + bird(鸟) → 扇动翅膀发出嗡嗡声的鸟 → 蜂鸟

influx ['ɪnflʌks] *n.* 涌入(arrival)

【记】词根记忆：in(进入) + flu(流动) + x → 涌入

【例】The rapid growth of Boston during the mid-nineteenth century coincided with a large *influx* of European immigrants. 波士顿在19世纪中期迅速发展，这时正好从欧洲涌入了大量移民。

ingenious [ɪn'dʒiːnɪəs] *a.* (方法等)巧妙的；聪明的(clever)

【记】词根记忆：in(向内) + gen(产生) + ious → 聪明产生于内 → 聪明的；注意不要和ingenuous(*a.* 坦率的，天真的)相混

【例】By such *ingenious* adaptations to specific pollinators, orchids have avoided the hazards of rampant crossbreeding in the wild. 通过巧妙地适应具体传粉昆虫，兰花避免了在野外杂交泛滥的危险。

【派】ingeniously(*ad.* 有才能地，贤明地)

innovation [ˌɪnə'veɪʃn] *n.* 创新；改革

【记】来自innovate(*v.* 革新，创新)

【例】Duke Ellington's orchestra made many *innovations* in jazz. 埃林顿公爵的管弦乐队在爵士乐方面进行了很多创新。

intact [ɪn'tækt] *a.* 无损伤的，完整的(undamaged)

【记】词根记忆：in(不) + tact(接触) → 未接触过 → 完整的

【例】The ice shelf had remained *intact* for centuries despite the weather. 尽管天气变化，历经了几个世纪，冰架依然完好无损。

【参】contact(*v.* 接触，联系)

intent [ɪn'tent] *n.* 意图，目的(purpose, goal)

【记】分拆联想：in(向内) + tent(帐篷) → 深夜摸进帐篷，意欲何为？ → 意图，目的

【例】The man was charged with *intent* to kill. 那人被指控蓄意谋杀。

【派】intention(*n.* 意图，目的)；intentional(*a.* 存心的，故意的)；intentionally(*ad.* 故意地，存心地)

jeopardize ['dʒepərdaɪz] *v.* 破坏，危及(endanger)

【记】发音记忆："皆怕打死" → 当危及到自身安全时，谁都怕死 → 危及

【例】My boss keeps asking me to work overtime, but I always said no because I don't want to *jeopardize* my studies. 我的老板一直让我加班，不过我总说不行，因为我不想影响我的学业。

leading ['li:dɪŋ] *a.* 主要的; 排在前列的

【例】The *leading* cause of preventable hearing loss is excessive noise. 导致可预防听力损失的首要原因是过度的噪音。

literally ['lɪtərəli] *ad.* 照原文地; 确切地(exactly)

【记】来自 literal(文字的) + ly → 照原文地

【例】These were the pterosaurs, *literally* the "winged lizards". 这些是翼龙, 字面意思是"带翅膀的蜥蜴"。//Taken *literally*, this would seem to be an empty statement which gives us no information. 从字面理解, 这好像是个空洞陈述, 没有给我们什么信息。

luminosity [ˌlu:mɪ'nɑːsəti] *n.* 亮度, 发光度(light, radiance)

maintain [meɪn'teɪn] *v.* 维持, 保持(keep, preserve)

【例】Some consumers believe organic foods can *maintain* health. 一些消费者认为有机食品能够维持健康。

melodrama ['melədrɑːmə] *n.* 音乐剧; 情节剧

【记】来自 melody(旋律) + drama(戏剧) → 有旋律的戏剧 → 音乐剧

millennium [mɪ'leniəm] *n.* [*pl.* millennia] 一千年, 千禧年(a period of 1000 years)

【例】Over *millennia*, the sea has been getting saltier and saltier. 几千年来, 海水变得越来越咸了。

motor ['moʊtər] *n.* 发动机, 电动机(engine)

neolithic [ˌni:ə'lɪθɪk] *a.* 新石器时代的(of the latest period of the Stone Age)

【记】词根记忆: neo(新) + lith(石头) + ic → 新石器的 → 新石器时代的

nitrogen ['naɪtrədʒən] *n.* 氮

【记】词根记忆: nitro(含氮的) + gen(产生) → 氮

【例】*Nitrogen* composes 80 percent of the air we breathe. 我们呼吸的空气中80%为氮气。

notify ['noʊtɪfaɪ] *v.* 通报(inform)

【记】词根记忆: not(标识) + ify(使…) → 使…知道 → 通报

【例】I didn't *notify* them about camp registration. 我没有通知他们露营登记的事情。

poverty ['pɑːvərti] *n.* 贫困(poorness)

【例】These writers often focused on economic hardship, studying people struggling with *poverty*. 这些作家专注于经济困难, 研究那些与贫困作斗争的人们。

pretty ['prɪti] *a.* 漂亮的, 秀丽的(beautiful) *ad.* 相当地, 颇

【搭】a pretty heavy workload 非常繁重的工作量

| ☐ leading | ☐ literally | ☐ luminosity | ☐ maintain | ☐ melodrama | ☐ millennium |
| ☐ motor | ☐ neolithic | ☐ nitrogen | ☐ notify | ☐ poverty | ☐ pretty |

【例】A: This is such a great time to buy winter clothes. So many stores are having sales now and the price reductions are *pretty* substantial.

B: Yeah. It's just what I've been waiting for. There are so many things I need.

A: 现在真是买冬季衣服的好时候。这么多商店在打折，减价幅度很大。

B: 是啊。我就等着这一天呢。我需要很多东西。

A: I *pretty* much decide that I want to play on the soccer team next semester.

B: You are certainly good enough, but well, would you just tell me about how you really need to concentrate on improving your grades next semester?

A: 我决定下学期参加足球队了。

B: 你是不错，但是你能讲讲你怎样专注于提高下学期的成绩吗？

【参】petty(*a.* 小的；不重要的)

promising ['prɑ:mɪsɪŋ] *a.* 有希望的(hopeful)，有前途的

【记】和promise(*v.* 承诺)一起记，得到承诺感觉有希望

【例】One award subsidizes a *promising* American writer's visit to Rome. 这个奖项会资助一个有前途的美国作家访问罗马。

promptly ['prɑ:mptli] *ad.* 敏捷地，迅速地；立刻地

【例】The second carton of books was delivered *promptly.* 第二箱书立刻就递送了。

reception [rɪ'sepʃn] *n.* 招待会；接待；(无线电、电视等)接收效果

【搭】reception desk(旅馆、饭店的)接待处

refund [rɪ'fʌnd] *v.* 退还

['ri:fʌnd] *n.* 退款

【记】re(反) + fund(资金) → 返回资金 → 退款

【例】It's too late for the woman to get a *refund.* 对这个女子而言，现在要回退款为时已晚。

rely [rɪ'laɪ] *v.* 依赖，依靠(depend)；信赖，信任

【记】联想记忆：re(一再) + ly(音似："lie"撒谎) → 又撒谎了，不值得信赖 → 信赖

【搭】rely on 信任，依赖，指望

【例】A: I have to borrow enough money to buy a plane ticket. My archaeology class is taking a future trip to Alaska and I may never get another chance like this.

B: Look, when push comes to show, the people you can *rely* on most are your family.

A：我得借足够的钱购买机票。我的考古学课要组织去阿拉斯加实地考察，我可能再也得不到这样的机会了。

B：你瞧瞧，到了关键时刻，你最能依靠的人是你的家庭。

repertory [ˈrepərtɔːri] *n.* 保留剧目(repertoire)

【例】The *repertory* of a concert band includes marches, and other forms of music. 乐队的保留剧目包括进行曲和其他形式的音乐。

replace [rɪˈpleɪs] *v.* 替换，取代(substitute)；放回，归还

【记】联想记忆：re(重新)＋place(位置)→重新定位→替换，取代

【例】The old standard weight had to be *replaced* because it was imprecise. 旧的标准秤砣因为不精确只能被替换掉了。//I don't think even the most ardent supporters of electronic instruments expect them to completely *replace* acoustic instruments. 我觉得就算最支持电子设备的人也不期望它们完全替换声音设备。

A: $200 to fix my computer? I thought you said you could do it for 50.

B: I did, but it's not the keyboard after all. That's the major part inside the machine that will cost a lot more to *replace*.

A：修我的电脑要200美元？我以为你说的是50美元。

B：我是这么说的，但是问题不在键盘。电脑内部的主要部分需要替换，这得花更多的钱。

restore [rɪˈstɔːr] *vt.* 恢复，修复(renovate)

【记】re(重新)＋store(储存)→身体重新储存能量→恢复，修复

【例】The factory was *restored* to full working order. 工厂全部恢复了工作秩序。

【派】restoration(*n.* 恢复，修复)

retail [ˈriːteɪl] *a.* 零售的

【例】*Retail* merchants were not willing to sell goods at low prices. 零售商不愿意低价销售商品。

【派】retailer(*n.* 零售商人)

ripe [raɪp] *a.* 熟的，成熟的(mature)

【记】联想记忆：稻熟(ripe)米(rice)香

【例】Is the fruit at the snack bar *ripe*?小吃店的水果熟了吗？

【派】ripen(*vt.* 使…成熟)

saving [ˈseɪvɪŋ] *n.* 节省(economy)；[常 *pl.*] 存款，积蓄(deposit)

【搭】savings account 储蓄账户；National Saving Bank 国家储蓄银行

【例】He spent his *savings* on summer housing. 他把积蓄用在夏天的住房上了。

seismograph ['saɪzməɡræf] *n.* 地震仪

【记】词根记忆：seism(地震) + o + graph(写，图) → 能描绘地震情况的仪器 → 地震仪

sequence ['siːkwəns] *n.* 顺序，序列(order)

【记】词根记忆：sequ(跟随) + ence → 顺序，序列

sieve [sɪv] *n.* 筛子(boult)，漏勺(strainer) *v.* 筛，滤(sift)

【记】联想记忆：用筛子(sieve)过滤是为了保留(save)精华

soda ['soʊdə] *n.* 苏打；碳酸水

spectrum ['spektrəm] *n.* 谱，光谱(beam)；范围(extension, range)

【记】词根记忆：spectr(看) + um → 看到颜色 → 光谱

【例】The representatives are constitutionally elected by a broad *spectrum* of the population. 代表由广泛的人群根据宪法选举。

spew [spjuː] *v.* 喷涌(exude, vomit)

【例】We assume that volcanoes *spewed* out the same gasses. 我们认为火山喷发出了同样的气体。

sponge [spʌndʒ] *n.* 海绵；寄生虫(parasite)

【记】发音记忆："死胖子" → 海绵吸饱水活像个死胖子

【派】spongy(*a.* 柔软的)

stagecoach ['steɪdʒkoʊtʃ] *n.* 公共马车

【记】组合词：stage(驿站) + coach(马车) → 驿马用马车 → 公共马车

staggered ['stæɡərd] *a.* 交错的(interlaced)

stimulus ['stɪmjələs] *n.* 鼓励；刺激(物)[*pl.* stimuli]，促进因素(factor)

【记】联想记忆：stimul(刺激) + us → 刺激，鼓励

【搭】sensory stimulus 感官刺激；stimulus to 促进…，刺激…

【例】The invention of steamed engine acted as a *stimulus* to industrial development. 蒸汽机的发明促进了工业发展。

stream [striːm] *n.* 溪流(brook)；股(strand) *v.* 涌(flow)

【记】分拆联想：s + tream(看作dream，梦想) → 梦想的溪流

【例】Approximately 23 million immigrants *streamed* to the United States. 大约2300万移民涌入了美国。

sufficient [sə'fɪʃnt] *a.* 足够的，充分的(adequate)

【例】It takes only 10 to 20 minutes of exposure to sunlight a day to ensure *sufficient* vitamin D production. 每天只需10到20分钟日晒就能确保产生足够的维生素D。

☐ seismograph	☐ sequence	☐ sieve	☐ soda	☐ spectrum	☐ spew
☐ sponge	☐ stagecoach	☐ staggered	☐ stimulus	☐ stream	☐ sufficient

【派】sufficiency(*n.* 充足)；sufficiently(*ad.* 充分地，十分地)

unbridgeable [ʌnˈbrɪdʒəbl] *a.* 不能架桥的，不能逾越的（impassable, insurmountable）

【搭】unbridgeable differences 不可调和的分歧

volunteer [ˌvɑːlənˈtɪr] *n.* 志愿者(军) *v.* 自愿

【记】词根记忆：volunt(自愿) + eer(人)→志愿者

【例】I'm never going to *volunteer* to help Janet with the party again. 我再不会自愿帮助珍妮特搞派对了。

【派】voluntary(*a.* 自愿的，志愿的)；involuntary(*a.* 无意识的)

weathering [ˈweðərɪŋ] *n.* 侵蚀，风化(corrasion)

【例】Most of the fossils exposed on Earth's surface are destroyed by *weathering* processes. 多数暴露在地球表面的化石被风化作用毁坏了。

If you would go up high, then use your own legs! Do not let yourselves carried aloft; do not seat yourselves on other people's backs and heads.

如果你想走到高处，就要使用自己的两条腿！不要让别人把你抬到高处；不要坐在别人的背上和头上。

——尼采

Word List 27  MP3-27

词根、词缀预习表

cur	关心	accurate	a. 正确的
lud	玩，戏剧	allude	vi. 暗指
ampl	大	amplify	vt. 放大(声音等)
clam	喊	clamor	n. 吵闹，喧哗
syn	共同	synthesize	vt. 合成
order	顺序	disorder	n. 混乱，动乱
tort	扭曲	distort	n. 弄歪
foli	树叶	foliage	n. 树叶，植物
neg	否认	negate	vt. 否定，打消
ultim	最终	ultimate	a. 根本的 n. 最终

accurate [ˈækjərət] *a.* 正确的；精确的(precise, exact)

【记】词根记忆：ac + cur（关心）+ ate → 关心使之正确无误的 → 正确的

【例】Most scientists believe the theory to be *accurate*. 多数科学家认为这个理论是正确的。

【派】accurately(*ad.* 正确地，精确地)；inaccurate(*a.* 错误的，不准确的)

adopt [əˈdɑːpt] *vt.* 采用(assume)

【记】词根记忆：ad + opt(选择) → 采用

【例】Iron was rapidly *adopted* for the construction of bridges. 铁很快被用于来建造桥梁。

【派】adoption(*n.* 采用)

allude [əˈluːd] *vi.* 暗指，影射，间接提到(imply, refer to)

【记】词根记忆：al + lud(玩，戏剧) + e → 戏剧的内涵 → 暗指

【搭】allude to sb. /sth. 暗指…

alumnus [əˈlʌmnəs] *n.* 男校友[*pl.* alumni]

【例】We got the *alumni* to make donations. 我们让男校友进行捐赠。

accurate   adopt   allude   alumnus

amplify [ˈæmplɪfaɪ] *vt.* 放大(声音等); 增强(strengthen)
【记】词根记忆: ampl(大) + ify(使…) → 放大; 增强
【例】Can you *amplify* the sound so we can hear it better? 你能大声点让我们听得更清楚吗？ //Seeing the ballet *amplified* Jane's desire to learn to dance. 看到芭蕾舞让简学习跳舞的欲望更强了。
【派】amplification(*n.* 扩大); amplifier(*n.* 放大器; 扩音器)

anarchist [ˈænərkɪst] *n.* 无政府主义者
【派】anarchistic(*a.* 无政府主义的)

bleach [bliːtʃ] *n.* 漂白剂
【参】beach(*n.* 海滩); breach(*n.* 违背)

board [bɔːrd] *n.* 委员会; 膳食费用; 板
【搭】room and board 食宿; bulletin board 公告牌
【派】boarder(*n.* 寄膳者)

brilliance [ˈbrɪliəns] *n.* 光辉(radiance); 显赫
【记】分拆联想: brilli (看作bright, 明亮的) + ance → 光辉
【例】I was astounded by the *brilliance* of the sunlight on the ocean. 我被大海上灿烂的阳光惊呆了。//The scientist's *brilliance* is evident from these experiment. 从这些实验可以看出这个科学家的高明之处。

brilliance

checked [tʃekt] *a.* 格子花纹的; 棋盘状的
【例】A *checked* shirt won't look good on the man. 这个人穿格子花衬衫不好看。

choreograph [ˈkɔːriəgræf] *vt.* 设计舞蹈动作
【派】choreographic(*a.* 舞蹈术的, 舞台舞蹈的); choreography (*n.* 舞蹈编排)

clamor [ˈklæmər] *n.* 吵闹, 喧哗(sound, noise)
【记】词根记忆: clam(喊) + or → 吵闹, 喧哗
【例】The *clamor* from the backyard drew us out of the house. 后院的喧哗把我们引出了房子。
【参】claim(*n.* 要求); proclamation(*n.* 宣言); reclamation(*n.* 回收; 开垦)

collapse [kəˈlæps] *v./n.* 崩溃, 倒塌(crash)
【记】分拆联想: col + lapse(滑倒) → 全部滑倒 → 崩溃, 倒塌
【例】Numerous houses *collapsed* as a result of the Tangshan Earthquake in 1976. 1976年唐山大地震导致了无数房屋倒塌。

□ amplify　□ anarchist　□ bleach　□ board　□ brilliance　□ checked　□ choreograph　□ clamor　□ collapse

condensation [ˌkɑːndenˈseɪʃn] *n.* 浓缩, 凝结 (the act or process of condensing)
【记】来自 condense (*v.* 浓缩)
【例】 *Condensation* from the clouds provides the essential agent of continental erosion: rain. 云的凝结提供了侵蚀大陆的主要作用剂: 雨水。

contain [kənˈteɪn] *vt.* 包含 (include), 容纳 (admit); 控制 (control)
【记】词根记忆: con + tain (拿住) → 全部拿住 → 包含, 容纳
【例】 The committee's report *contains* mistakes. 委员会的报告有错误。//Starting in the late 18th century, the United States *contained* increasing numbers of such people. 从18世纪末开始, 美国有了越来越多的这种人。
【派】container (*n.* 容器, 集装箱); self-contained (*a.* 独立的)

contribute [kənˈtrɪbjuːt] *v.* 贡献, 捐赠 (donate); 有助于 (promote); 投稿 (to submit articles to)
【例】 I believe the social elements *contributed* to the development of bebop music. 我认为社会因素有助于比博普爵士音乐的发展。// She often *contributes* to the fashionable journal. 她经常给时尚杂志投稿。
【派】contribution (*n.* 贡献; 捐献物; 稿件)
【参】attribute (*n.* 属性); distribute (*vt.* 分发)

corrosion [kəˈrouʒn] *n.* 腐蚀 (状态), 侵蚀
【记】来自 corrode (*v.* 使腐蚀, 侵蚀)
【例】 If the beads are buried for long, the effects of *corrosion* can further change their outer appearance. 如果珠子埋时间长了, 腐蚀的作用会进一步改变其外观。

counter [ˈkaʊntər] *n.* 柜台; 计数器 *ad. /a.* 相反(的) *v.* 反对, 反击
【记】来自 count (*v.* 计算)
【搭】baggage counter 行李存放柜台
【例】 It may seem to run *counter* to common sense to say that introducing water into an area can cause it to become more like a desert. 往一个地区引水会导致该地更像沙漠, 这话好像有违常理。//Sometimes when it really gets busy, I work at the check-out *counter*. 有时真的忙起来, 我就在收银台工作。
A: Hey, Dan, do you think you might hurry up just a bit? You've been from that sandwich *counter* forever. And you know, I got class in ten minutes, and so do you, by the way...
B: Sorry, oh, I just wish they didn't give me so many choices.

A：喂，丹，你能快点吗？你在那个三明治柜台停这么久了。要知道，我10分钟后有课，你也有，再说了……

B：哦，对不起，他们要是不给我那么多选择就好了。

【参】encounter(v. 相遇)

creative [kriˈeɪtɪv] a. 有创造力的，创造性的

【例】A: I just found out at registration that the *creative* writing class is full. Now I have to wait another whole year to get in.

B: Why don't you check back after the first week? Somebody might drop it.

A：我刚在登记处发现创意写作课报满了。我只好再等一年报名。

B：你为何不等第一周过了再去查查？有人可能会取消报名。

【派】creativity(n. 创造力)

crust [krʌst] n. 硬壳，地壳；面包皮

【参】mantle(n. 地幔), core(n. 地核)

deliberate [dɪˈlɪbərət] a. 审慎的，深思熟虑的(careful, cogitative)

【记】词根记忆：de + liber(自由) + ate → 非自由的(非随意的) → 审慎的

【例】Every step in the process was slow and *deliberate*. 这个过程的每一步都稳扎稳打，深思熟虑。

【派】deliberately(ad. 故意地；深思熟虑地)

delicate [ˈdelɪkət] a. 易损的(fragile)；微妙的(subtle)；精巧的(exquisite)

【例】The tiny, *delicate* skeletons are usually destroyed by weathering before they can be fossilized. 小的易碎骨骼由于风化作用在能变成化石之前通常已被摧毁了。//Her photos were printed on *delicate* paper. 她的照片印刷在精巧的纸上。

【派】delicately(ad. 微妙地)

【参】dedicate(vt. 献身)

disorder [dɪsˈɔːrdər] n. 混乱，动乱(chaos)；失调(maladjustment)

【记】词根记忆：dis(不) + order(顺序) → 混乱；失调

【例】We have nothing to help us distinguish mental health from mental *disorder*. 没有任何东西能帮助我们区分精神健康和精神失常。

distort [dɪˈstɔːrt] v. 弄歪(形状等)(twist)；歪曲(misrepresent)

【记】词根记忆：dis(坏) + tort(扭曲) → 扭坏了 → 歪曲

【例】The old mirror *distorted* my reflection. 旧镜子扭曲了我的影子。//Mark *distorted* the story, trying to place the blame on his sister. 马克歪曲事实，想归罪于他的姐姐。

【派】distorted(a. 变形的); distortion(n. 歪曲，变形)

【参】contort(vt. 扭弯); retort(v. 反驳)

dragonfly [ˈdrægənflaɪ] *n.* 蜻蜓

ease [iːz] *n.* 不费力
【例】The *ease* of solving a jigsaw puzzle depends on the design of the picture. 解决智力拼图的难易程度取决于图画的设计。

ecological [ˌiːkəˈlɑːdʒɪkl] *a.* 生态学的，生态的
【搭】ecological balance 生态平衡; ecological disaster 生态灾难
【例】By enhancing this natural response in plants, researchers might reduce, some day even eliminate, the need for chemical pesticide, which can cause *ecological* damage. 通过提高植物的自然反应，研究人员可以减少，甚至某一天消除对破坏生态的化学杀虫剂的需要。

enterprise [ˈentərpraɪz] *n.* 公司(corporation); 事业
【记】词根记忆: enter(进入) + pris(握取) + e → 能够最先进入市场，把握先机 → 公司; 经营
【搭】private enterprise 私人企业，民营企业
【参】entrepreneur(*n.* 企业家，创业人)

exorbitant [ɪgˈzɔːrbɪtənt] *a.* (价格、索价)过高的，过分的
【记】词根记忆: ex + orbit(轨道，常规) + ant → 走出常规的 → 过分的

exponent [ɪkˈspoʊnənt] *n.* 拥护者(advocator)
【记】词根记忆: ex + pon(放) + ent → 放心的人 → 拥护者
【派】exponential(*a.* 指数的，幂的)

flavor [ˈfleɪvər] *n.* 风味，滋味(taste); 调味品 *v.* 给…调味
【搭】flavor of …的风味; a strong flavor 口味重; a bitter flavor 苦味
【例】A: This salad needs something to give it more *flavor*, don't you think?
B: You're right. Tell me what you'd like and I will run over to the corner store. I need to get a few other items anyway.
A: 这个色拉需要加点东西才更有味道，你觉得呢？
B: 你说对了。告诉我你想要什么，我去街拐角的商店买。反正我也需要买点别的东西。
A: I wonder what this new *flavor* of ice cream tastes like.
B: I tried it last week. If I were you, I would stick with an old favorite.
A: 我想知道冰激凌的新风味是怎么样的。
B: 我上周尝了。我要是你，我就吃老风味的。

foliage [ˈfoʊliɪdʒ] *n.* 树叶(leaf); 植物
【记】词根记忆: foli(树叶) + age → 树叶

【例】The insect is active at night and rests motionless amid *foliage* during the day. 昆虫夜间活跃，白天在树叶间一动不动地休息。

former [ˈfɔːrmər] *a.* 从前的 (previous) *n.* 前者

【记】来自 form (形成) + er (人，物) → 已形成的东西 → 前者

【例】I saw my *former* roommate a year ago. 我一年前见过以前的室友。//The *former* are called endotherms, and the latter are called ectotherms. 前者叫温血动物，后者叫冷血动物。

graphics [ˈɡræfɪks] *n.* (作单数用) 制图法，制图学

【记】联想记忆：graph (图表) + ics → 制图法，制图学

【例】Students are asked to prepare texts and *graphics* separately and then combine them. 要求学生分别准备课文和图片，然后将两者合并起来。

【参】mathematics (*n.* 数学)；physics (*n.* 物理学)

handle [ˈhændl] *v.* 处理 (deal)；对待 (treat)，操纵；触，摸，抚养 *n.* 柄，把手，拉手

【记】来自 hand (手) + le → 方便手操作的东西 → 柄，把手

【例】To start the machine, you need first read the handbook and then turn the *handle* left. 要想启动机器，首先需要阅读手册，然后再把手柄往左转。//I'm taking six classes and working a part-time job. That's about all I can *handle* right now. 我现在上六节课，做一份兼职。目前我只能应付这么多。

【参】candle (*n.* 蜡烛)

homing [ˈhoʊmɪŋ] *a.* 有自远处返回原地的本能的

【搭】homing pigeon 信鸽

imbibe [ɪmˈbaɪb] *vt.* 喝 (drink)

【记】词根记忆：im (进入) + bibe (=drink 喝) → 喝

【例】Camels have been known to *imbibe* over 100 liters in a few minutes. 公所周知，骆驼在几分钟之内可以喝 100 多升水。

indifference [ɪnˈdɪfrəns] *n.* 冷漠，不关心 (disinterest)

【记】来自 indifferent (*a.* 不关心的，冷漠的)

【例】What they feared most was *indifference*. 他们最害怕的是冷漠。

infectious [ɪnˈfekʃəs] *a.* 有传染性的 (contagious)

【搭】infectious disease 传染病

【例】Colds are *infectious*, and so are some eye diseases. 感冒传染，有些眼疾也传染。

infectious

别喝，我有肝炎

| former | graphics | handle | homing | imbibe | indifference |
| infectious | | | | | |

influenza [ˌɪnfluˈenzə] *n.* 流行性感冒
【记】记住它的简写形式 flu

invade [ɪnˈveɪd] *vt.* 侵入(move into, intrude); 侵略
【记】词根记忆: in(进入) + vad(走) + e → 未经允许走进来 → 侵入
【例】We are going to talk about a special way some plants respond to being *invaded* by pests. 我们要谈论一些植物对害虫入侵反应的特殊方式。
【派】invader(*n.* 侵略者); invasion(*n.* 入侵, 侵略)

meteor [ˈmiːtiər] *n.* 流星
【例】Wind motion can be observed in the mesosphere by watching the trails of *meteors* passing through it. 通过观察流星经过时留下的痕迹, 可以观测到中间层风的运动。
【派】meteoric(*a.* 疾速的)

microscopic [ˌmaɪkrəˈskɑːpɪk] *a.* 用显微镜可见的; 极小的
【记】词根记忆: micro(小) + scop(观察) + ic → 小的无法观察 → 极小的
【搭】a microscopic plant 极小的植物

mighty [ˈmaɪti] *a.* 强有力的, 巨大的(powerful)
【例】This circumstance was mitigated by the *mighty* river and lake systems. 大河和湖泊系统减轻了这种状况。

minimum [ˈmɪnɪməm] *a.* 最(小、低)的 *n.* 最小(值、化)
【记】词根记忆: minim(小) + um → 最小
【例】You seem to meet our *minimum* qualifications. 你好像满足我们最低的资历要求。

naturalist [ˈnætʃrəlɪst] *n.* 自然主义者; 博物学家
【例】*Naturalists* brought to their writing a passion for direct and honest experience. 博物学家给他们的写作带来了一种对直接客观经验的激情。
【派】naturalistic(*a.* 自然的; 自然主义的)

negate [nɪˈɡeɪt] *vt.* 打消, 否定(deny)
【记】词根记忆: neg(否认) + ate → 打消, 否定
【例】The new law *negated* the possibility of a reduction in taxes. 新的法律否定了减少税收的可能性。

nevertheless [ˌnevərðəˈles] *ad./conj.* 然而, 不过(however, still)
【例】She *nevertheless* urged men to educate their daughters and to treat their wives as equals. 她还是督促男性教育自己的女儿, 平等对待妻子。

novelty ['nɑːvlti] *n.* 新奇，新颖

【记】词根记忆：nov(新的) + elty → 新的 → 新奇，新颖

【例】There's no doubt that radio broadcasting was quite a *novelty* in those days. 毫无疑问，在那些岁月里无线电广播是个新鲜玩意。

occasional [əˈkeɪʒənl] *a.* 偶然的；非经常的(infrequent)

【记】来自occasion(*n.* 时机)

【例】Auctions were another popular form of *occasional* trade. 拍卖是不经常贸易的另一种流行形式。

origin ['ɔːrɪdʒɪn] *n.* 起源，由来

【记】词根记忆：ori(开始) + gin → 开始 → 起源，由来

【搭】the origins of civilization 文明的起源；the origin of a dispute 争端的起因

【例】To weather broadcasters, the *origin* of winds is more important than its destination. 对天气广播员而言，风的来源比其目的地更加重要。//The *origin* of earth's moon, the largest moon in the solar system, is still something of a mystery. 地球的卫星，月亮，是太阳系最大的卫星，其起源仍然是个谜。

palatable ['pælətəbl] *a.* 美味的(delicious)

【记】分拆联想：palat(看作plate，盘子) + able → 盘子里装着美味佳肴 → 美味的

【例】This soup isn't excellent, but it's *palatable*. 这个汤不算太好，不过味道不错。

【派】unpalatable(*a.* 不好吃的)

palatable

panel ['pænl] *n.* 面板，镶板 *vt.* 镶嵌 (to furnish or decorate)

【记】来自pan(面板) + el(小) → 面板

【例】The walls were made of plaster or wood, sometimes elaborately *paneled*. 墙由灰泥或木板做成，有时镶嵌得很精美。

patron ['peɪtrən] *n.* 赞助人(benefactor)；顾客(client)

【记】词根记忆：patr(父亲) + on → 像父亲一样进行资助 → 赞助人

penicillin [ˌpenɪˈsɪlɪn] *n.* 青霉素

pest [pest] *n.* 害虫；令人讨厌的人或物(nuisance)

【记】发音记忆："拍死它" → 见到害虫就拍死它 → 害虫

【参】pesticide(*n.* 杀虫剂)；insect(*n.* 昆虫)；bug(*n.* 小虫，臭虫)

phase [feɪz] *n.* 阶段，时期(period)【天】相位(One of the cyclically recurring apparent forms of the moon or a planet)

novelty | occasional | origin | palatable | panel | patron
penicillin | pest | phase

【例】The *phases* of the moon have served as primary divisions of time for thousands of years. 月相几千年来一直用以区分时间。

【参】phrase(*n.* 短语)

postage [ˈpoʊstɪdʒ] *n.* 邮资

【记】词根记忆：post(邮件) + age(费用) → 邮资

【例】How much is the *postage* for a letter to Vancouver? 往温哥华寄信邮资是多少？

preferable [ˈprefrəbl] *a.* 更好的，更优越的

【记】来自prefer(更喜欢，宁愿) + able → 更好的

【例】Apartments were *preferable* to tenements and cheaper than row houses. 公寓比廉租房更好，比联排式住宅更便宜。

quality [ˈkwɑːləti] *n.* 质量(degree of excellence)；品质(nature)；特性(property)

【搭】qualitative variable 定性变量

【例】Perhaps the most striking *quality* of satiric literature is its freshness, and its originality of perspective. 可能讽刺文学最显著的特点是视角新颖独特。

【派】qualitative(*a.* 定性的)

radically [ˈrædɪkli] *ad.* 根本上(drastically, completely)

【记】词根记忆：radi(根) + cally → 根本上

【例】The policies enacted two years ago should be changed *radically*. 两年前制订的政策应该从根本上改变。

【参】superficial(*a.* 肤浅的，浅薄的；表面的)

rear [rɪr] *n.* 后部；臀部 *v.* 养育；饲养(*raise)

【例】Later they developed a technique for feeding the larvae and *rearing* them to spat. 后来他们开发出一种喂养幼虫并养成蚝卵的技术。

review [rɪˈvjuː] *v.* 审查；复习 *n.* 复习；评论(comment)

【记】分拆联想：re(回) + view(看) → 回头反复看 → 复习

【例】The woman needs to *review* the report again. 这个女子需要再次审查这份报告。//Please *review* the first three chapters in the book. 请复习这本书的前三章内容。

【派】reviewer(*n.* 评论家)

ruin [ˈruːɪn] *v.* 破坏，毁灭(destroy) *n.* [常*pl.*] 废墟，遗迹(relic)

【记】联想记忆：大雨(rain)毁坏了(ruin)庄稼 → 破坏，毁灭

【例】A little rain never *ruined* a good picnic. 一点雨从来不会破坏一次好的野餐。

postage	preferable	quality	radically	rear	review
ruin					

scientific [ˌsaɪən'tɪfɪk] *a.* 科学上的

【记】来自 science（*n.* 科学）

【搭】scientific study 科学研究；scientific discovery 科学发现

【例】This morning I want to tell you about a recent *scientific* discovery dealing with the relation between plants and animals. 今天上午我想告诉你们关于动植物关系的一项新近的科学发现。//These plastic beads aren't for jewelry. They can be used for many *scientific* purposes, from conducting cancer research to calibrating microscopes. 这些塑料珠子不是用于制作首饰的，它们可以用于从开展癌症研究到校准显微镜的各种科学实验。

section ['sekʃn] *n.* 部分（part）；地区（region）；部门（division）

【记】词根记忆：sect（切割）+ ion → 部分

【例】Our library has a reserve *section* of fine books. 我们的图书馆有一个优秀图书存放区。

silversmith ['sɪlvərsmɪθ] *n.* 银器匠

statesman ['steɪtsmən] *n.* 政治家（politician）

【记】组合词：states（国家，政府）+ man（人）→ 管理国家事务的人 → 政治家

subject ['sʌbdʒɪkt] *n.* 主题（theme）；对象（object）*a.*（to）受…支配的（susceptible to）

[səb'dʒekt] *vt.*（to）使服从（submit）

【记】词根记忆：sub（在下面）+ ject（扔）→ 被扔在下面 → 受…支配的

【例】Organic material trapped in sediments is slowly buried and *subjected* to increased temperatures and pressures. 有机材料裹在沉淀物中，慢慢地被掩埋，继而会受到升温和增压的影响。//Plants are *subject* to attack and infection. 植物受到袭击和感染。

【派】subjective（*a.* 主观的）

sustenance ['sʌstənəns] *n.* 食物（food）；生计（living）

【记】分拆联想：susten（看作 sustain，维持）+ ance → 维持生命的东西 → 食物；生计

【例】During the Neolithic period, some hunters and gatherers began to rely chiefly on agriculture for their *sustenance*. 在新石器时代，一些猎人和采集者开始主要依靠农业来维生。

synthesize ['sɪnθəsaɪz] *vt.* 合成

【记】词根记忆：syn（共同，相同）+ thes（放）+ ize → 放到一起 → 合成

☐ scientific　☐ section　☐ silversmith　☐ statesman　☐ subject　☐ sustenance
☐ synthesize

【例】Vitamins are *synthesized* from foods. 维生素是从食物中合成的。

【派】synthesizer(*n.* 音响合成器); synthesis(*n.* 综合, 合成)

systematic [ˌsɪstəˈmætɪk] *a.* 系统的, 体系的(methodic)

【记】来自 system(*n.* 系统)

【例】While Edison's approach to invention was often cut-and-try, it was highly *systematic*. 虽然爱迪生搞发明的方法经常是试验性的, 但这个方法却非常具有系统性。

【参】systematize(*v.* 系统化, 使成制度或体系)

toed [toʊd] *a.* 有趾的

tolerant [ˈtɑːlərənt] *a.* 宽容的

【例】The prejudiced man is not at all *tolerant*. 这个怀有偏见的男子一点都不宽容。

【派】tolerance(*n.* 忍耐, 忍受)

tread [tred] *vi.* 踏, 践踏(trample)

【例】Please *tread* very quietly as the baby is asleep. 孩子睡觉呢, 脚步轻一点。

【参】treadmill(*n.* 踏车)

tribal [ˈtraɪbl] *a.* 部落的; 种族的(racial)

【记】来自 tribe(*n.* 部落)

tutor [ˈtuːtər] *n.* 家庭教师 *vt.* 辅导(coach)

【例】The man should hire a *tutor* before the midterm exam. 此人应该在期中考试之前聘请一个家庭教师。//Anna *tutored* the seven-year-old in math. 安娜给这个7岁孩子进行了数学辅导。

小学数学咋这么难

tutor

【派】tutorial (*a.* 私人教师的, 导师的 *n.* 指导课)

ultimate [ˈʌltɪmət] *a.* 根本的(fundamental, essential) *n.* 最终

【记】词根记忆: ultim(最后的) + ate(…的) → 最终

【例】It's the *ultimate* cause of winds. 这是产生风的根本原因。//Her discovery may help to answer some of our questions about the *ultimate* of the universe. 她的发现可能有助于回答我们关于宇宙终极的一些问题。

untapped [ˌʌnˈtæpt] *a.* 未使用的

【记】来自 tap(*vt.* 开发, 利用)

【例】Three-quarters of the Earth's fresh water supply is still tied up in glacial ice, a reservoir of *untapped* fresh water. 地球四分之三的淡水

供应仍然存在于冰川，那里蕴藏着未开发的淡水。

walnut [ˈwɔːlnʌt] *n.* 胡桃，胡桃木

【例】It's a black *walnut* that must be 80 feet tall. 那是一棵黑胡桃木，肯定有 80 英尺高。//As a matter of fact there is a plaque identifying the black *walnut* is the tallest black *walnut* in the state. 事实上，有个牌匾说明这就是该州最高的黑胡桃木。

【参】peanut(*n.* 花生)

I have but one lamp wait which my feet are guided; and that is the lamp of experience. I know of no way of judging of the future but by the past.

我只拿一盏灯来指引我的脚步，而那盏灯就是经验，对于未来，我只是能以过去来判断。

——帕特里克·亨利(*Patrick Henry*)

Word List 28  MP3-28

词根、词缀预习表

norm	规则	abnormal	*a.* 反常的
ben	好	beign	*a.* (病)良性的
circ	环绕	circuit	*n.* 电路，线路
stance	站	circumstance	*n.* 环境
dent	牙齿	dentist	*n.* 牙科医生
dif	不同	diffuse	*v.* 传播
em	使	embody	*vt.* 体现
fabric	构造	fabricate	*v.* 编造
in	向内	innate	*a.* 天生的
prud	小心的	prudent	*a.* 谨慎的

abnormal [æb'nɔːrml] *a.* 反常的，变态的（unusual, exceptional）

【记】词根记忆：ab(相反) + norm(规则) + al → 违反规则的 → 反常的

【搭】abnormal behavior 变态行为

【例】The warm December weather in northern Canada was *abnormal*. 加拿大北部12月份的温暖天气是不正常的。

absolute ['æbsəluːt] *a.* 完全的；绝对的

【记】词根记忆：ab(加强) + solut(松开) + e → 放开思想，完全接受 → 完全的

【搭】absolute zero 绝对零度；with absolute certainty 绝对肯定

air [er] *n.* 空气；大气（atmosphere）；天空；神气，架子 *vt.* 使通风

【搭】in the air 在流行中；在传播中；by air 乘坐飞机

【例】I had to put *air* in the tire twice this week. 这周我不得不给轮胎打了两次气。//A heater is using convection when it warms the *air* in a room. 加热器利用对流使房间变暖。

atrophy ['ætrəfi] *n.* 萎缩(症)（shrinkage）

【记】词根记忆：a(无)+troph(营养)+y→无营养会萎缩→萎缩(症)

☐ abnormal   ☐ absolute   ☐ air   ☐ atrophy

299

awkward [ˈɔːkwərd] *a.* 别扭的(unnatural)；笨拙的(clumsy)

【记】发音记忆："拗口的"→别扭的

【例】The tennis racket was too big and *awkward* for Jane. 网球拍对简来说太大了，用起来很别扭。//Tom was always a bit *awkward* when meeting new people. 汤姆见到生人时都会感到有点别扭。

【派】awkwardly(*ad.* 笨拙地；不协调地)

backlighting [ˈbæklaɪtɪŋ] *n.* 逆光

benign [bɪˈnaɪn] *a.* (病)良性的(innocuous)；和蔼的(kind)

【记】词根记忆：ben(好)＋ign(形容词后缀)→好的→良性的

【搭】a benign tumour 良性肿瘤

【例】The *benign* climate conditions brought this region a bumper crop. 良好的气候条件给这个地区带来了丰收。

bog [bɑːg] *n.* 沼泽(swamp)

celebrated [ˈselɪbreɪtɪd] *a.* 著名的(famous)；有名的(renowned)

【例】Grandma Moses is among the most *celebrated* twentieth-century painters of the United States. 摩西奶奶是美国20世纪最著名的画家之一。

【参】celebrity(*n.* 名人)

center [ˈsentər] *n.* 中心，中央

【搭】student recreation centre 学生娱乐中心

【例】A: I'm so frustrated. We are supposed to do our assignments for statistics on the computer. But the ones in the student *center* are always tied up.

B: I know what you mean. I'm looking forward to the day when I can afford to get my own.

A：我太沮丧了。我们要在电脑上做统计学的作业。但是学生中心的电脑总有人用。

B：我明白你的意思。我期盼着能买得起个人电脑的那一天。

challenge [ˈtʃælɪndʒ] *n.* 挑战(书)；艰巨任务，难题 *v.* 向…挑战

【记】联想记忆：美国"挑战者"号航天飞机的名字就是 *the shuttle Challenger*

【例】A: You were right about the puzzle you lent me last week. It really is a *challenge.* I want to try to get it myself though. So I'm going to work on it a little longer.

B: Well, if you get really stuck, remember I'm only a phone call away.

A：你说的没错，你上周借给我的难题的确是个挑战。不过我想自己解出来。所以我要再研究一段时间。

□ awkward	■ backlighting	■ benign	■ bog	■ celebrated	□ centre
□ challenge					

B: 好的，如果你真的解不出来，记住随时给我打电话。

【派】unchallenged(*a.* 未起争议的；未受过挑战的)；challenging (*a.* 具有挑战性的)

chew [tʃuː] *v.* 咀嚼；思量

【记】口香糖 chewing-gum

【搭】chew over 思量

【例】A: Linda, have you understood what the teacher said in class?

B: Maybe I need to *chew* it over for a few days.

A: 琳达，你理解老师课堂讲的内容吗？

B: 或许我要琢磨几天才能理解。

circuit [ˈsɜːrkɪt] *n.* 电路，线路(circular line)

【记】词根记忆：circ(环绕) + uit → 电路，线路

【搭】short circuit 短路；closed circuit 闭合电路

circumstance [ˈsɜːrkəmstæns] *n.* 环境(environment)；境况(condition, situation)

【记】词根记忆：circum(周围) + stance(站) → 周围的存在 → 环境

collect [kəˈlekt] *v.* 收集；聚集(accumulate, assemble) *ad. /a.* (打电话)由对方付费(的)

【派】collective(*a.* 共同的，集体的)

constitution [ˌkɑːnstəˈtuːʃn] *n.* 宪法，章程

【记】词根记忆：con + stitut(建立，放) + ion → 国无法不立 → 宪法

【派】constitutional(*a.* 章程的，宪法的)；constitutionally(*ad.* 按照宪法)

conventional [kənˈvenʃənl] *a.* 传统的，惯例的(traditional, customary)

【例】At that speed, *conventional* trains have trouble staying on the tracks. 以这样的速度前进，传统的火车很有可能脱轨。

dentist

cram [kræm] *v.* 填塞(pack)；匆忙准备

date [deɪt] *vt.* 注明…的日期(mark the time of)

dentist [ˈdentɪst] *n.* 牙科医生

【记】词根记忆：dent(牙齿) + ist(人) → 牙科医生

【派】dentistry(*n.* 牙科)

diffuse [dɪˈfjuːz] *v.* 传播(travel)；扩散(spread)

[dɪˈfjuːs] *a.* 散开的

【记】词根记忆：dif(不同) + fuse(流) → 扩散；传播

| ☐ chew | ☐ circuit | ☐ circumstance | ☐ collect | ☐ constitution | ☐ conventional |
| ☐ cram | ☐ date | ☐ dentist | ☐ diffuse | | |

【例】A gas forms no free surface but tends to *diffuse* throughout the space available. 气体并不形成自由的表面，而是会在现有的空间扩散。

【派】diffusely(*ad.* 广泛地); diffusion(*n.* 扩散；传播)

同根词: infusion(*n.* 注入；灌输)

disappoint [ˌdɪsəˈpɔɪnt] *vt.* 使失望；使扫兴

【记】联想记忆: dis(不) + appoint(任命) → 没被任命，所以失望 → 使失望；使扫兴

【例】A: I'm really *disappointed* about not getting that job.

B: An evening at the jazz club ought to make you feel better.

A: 我没有得到那份工作，真失望。

B: 去爵士乐俱乐部玩一晚上你就会感觉好点。

【参】appoint(*v.* 约定，指定；任命)

disease [dɪˈziːz] *n.* 疾病(illness, sickness)

【记】分拆联想: dis(不) + ease(安心) → 身心不安 → 疾病

【搭】viral disease 病毒病; heart disease 心脏病

【派】diseased(*a.*【植】有病害的；患病的)

embody [ɪmˈbɑːdi] *vt.* 体现(express); 含有(contain)

【记】词根记忆: em(使…) + body(形体) → 使有形 → 体现

【例】That's a national team that *embodies* competitive spirit and skill. 那是一支体现了竞争精神和技能的国家队。

even [ˈiːvn] *a.* 偶数的；平均的

【派】evenly(*ad.* 平坦地；均匀地); evenness(*n.* 平均)

fabricate [ˈfæbrɪkeɪt] *v.* 编造(create); 制造(construct, manufacture)

【记】词根记忆: fabric(构造) + ate → 构造出来 → 编造；制造

【例】She thought that writers should tell the truth about human affairs, not *fabricate* romance. 她认为作家对于人类事务应该讲真话，而不应编造传奇故事。

foment [foʊˈment] *v.* 煽动(instigate)

【记】分拆联想: fom(看作form，形成) + ent → 帮助形成 → 煽动；注意不要和ferment(*n.* 酶 *v.* 发酵)混淆

【例】Three sailors were *fomenting* a mutiny on the ship. 三名船员在船上煽动兵变。

geometry [dʒiˈɑːmətri] *n.* 几何(学)

【记】词根记忆: geo(地) + metr(测量) + y → 测量地表的有关学科 → 几何(学)

【例】I had the wrong date for my *geometry* test. 我把几何测试的日期记错了。

【派】geometric(*a.* 几何的); geometrically(*ad.* 几何学上地); geometricize(*v.* 做成几何图形)

gilding ['gɪldɪŋ] *n.* 贴金箔,镀金

gonna ['gɔːnə] *v.* 要去

【例】A: A group of us are *gonna* the park tomorrow. Do you want to go with us?

B: I'd like to, but I have some homework to do.

A: 我们一群人明天要去公园。你想和我们一起去吗?

B: 我想去,但是我要做家庭作业。

hydrothermal [ˌhaɪdroʊ'θɜːrməl] *a.* 热液的

【记】词根记忆: hydro(水) + therm(热) + al → 热液的

【例】There are *hydrothermal* vents, which are small cracks on the sea floor. 那儿有热液排放口,也就是海床上的小裂缝。

【参】thermal(*a.* 热的,热量的)

immunity [ɪ'mjuːnəti] *n.* 保护(*protection); 免除(exemption)

【例】The advantage of nesting on cliffs is the *immunity* seabirds give from foxes. 在悬崖上筑巢的优势是能使海鸟免于遭受狐狸的侵害。

initial [ɪ'nɪʃl] *a.* 开始的,最初的 *n.* (姓名的)首字母

【记】词根记忆: init(开始) + ial → 开始的,最初的

【例】The bank manager changed the date of the *initial* interview. 银行经理改变了最初面试的日期。//They are the *initials* of the person who created the penny's design. 它们是设计便士的人的姓名首字母。

innate [ɪ'neɪt] *a.* 天生的(inborn)

【记】词根记忆: in(向内) + nat(出生的) + e → 出生时带来的 → 天生的

【例】Most researchers assume that the ability to perform and encode the dance is *innate*. 多数研究者认为表演和编排舞蹈的能力是天生的。

insufficient [ˌɪnsə'fɪʃnt] *a.* 不足的,不够的(deficient)

【记】in + sufficient(充分的) → 不足的,不够的

【例】Funds for research were *insufficient*. 研究的经费不足。

intrude [ɪn'truːd] *v.* 强行进入(某地); 闯入; 侵入

【记】词根记忆: in(进入) + trude(突出) → 突进去 → 闯入

【派】intrusion(*n.* 入侵); intruder(*n.* 入侵者)

【参】extrude(*v.* 逐出); detrude(*vt.* 推倒,扔掉)

Jupiter ['dʒu:pɪtər] *n.* 木星

【例】The world anxiously watched as a hurtling chunk of comet plunged into the atmosphere of *Jupiter*. 全世界忧虑地看着一颗疾飞的彗星落入木星的大气层。

league [li:g] *n.* 联盟，同盟（alliance）

【记】联想记忆：联盟（league）成员都是同事（colleague）

lunar ['lu:nər] *a.* 月亮的

【搭】lunar eclipse 月蚀

match [mætʃ] *n.* 比赛（contest）；对手（opponent）*v.* 和…相配（suit）

【例】The man's socks *match* his shirt well. 那个人的袜子与他的衬衫很般配。

【派】matching（*a.* 匹配的）；unmatched（*a.* 无可匹敌的）

meager ['mi:gər] *a.* 不足的，贫乏的（deficient, scanty）

【记】分拆联想：m + eager（热心的）→ 光靠热心是不够的 → 不足的

【例】Prior to this report, Seattle's park development was very limited and funding *meager*. 在这个报告之前，西雅图的公园发展非常有限，资金很缺乏。

mechanism ['mekənɪzəm] *n.* 机械装置；机制

【搭】defense mechanism 防卫机制

【例】The religion, a variety of the Mennonite faith, provides the principal *mechanism* for maintaining-order. 这个宗教——门诺派教信仰的一种——为维持秩序提供了最重要的机制。

mesmerize ['mezməraɪz] *vt.* 施催眠术；使入迷，迷住

metropolis [mə'trɑːpəlɪs] *n.* 首府（capital）；大城市

【记】分拆联想：metro（铁）+ polis（城市）→ 有地铁的城市 → 大城市

【派】metropolitan（*a.* 首都的；大都市的）

mesmerize

mobile ['moʊbl] *a.* 可迅速移动的；多变的（changeable）*n.* 某些部分迎风转动的装饰性结构

【记】词根记忆：mob（动）+ ile → 可迅速移动的

【例】One of the sculptures is a *mobile* that is made of pieces of aluminum. 其中一个雕塑是用铝片做的，可以移动。

【派】mobility（*n.* 流动性；迁移率）；immobilize（*vt.* 使不动）

nest [nest] *n.* 巢，窝 *v.* 做窝，筑巢

【记】联想记忆：在巢（nest）里休息（rest）

【搭】to build nest 筑巢

| ☐ Jupiter | ☐ league | ☐ lunar | ☐ match | ☐ meager | ☐ mechanism |
| ☐ mesmerize | ☐ metropolis | ☐ mobile | ☐ nest | | |

【例】As many of you probably know, south beach is an important *nesting* site for the green turtle. 你们很多人可能知道，南海滩是海龟重要的筑巢地。

【参】west(*n.* 西方); east(*n.* 东方)

nonverbal [nɑːnˈvɜːrbl] *a.* 非语言的

【例】Body language such as gesture is the most important *nonverbal* expression. 像手势这种肢体语言是最重要的非语言表达。

obsess [əbˈses] *v.* 迷住(charm)

【例】Evans early became *obsessed* by the possibilities of mechanized production and steam power. 埃文斯早些时候对机械化生产和蒸汽动力的可能性很入迷。

【派】obsession(*n.* 入迷，困扰)

【参】obese(*a.* 肥胖的)

overview [ˈoʊvərvjuː] *n.* 梗概，概述

【例】Let me give you just an *overview* of Plato's ethical theory. 我来给你们概述一下柏拉图的道德理论。

【参】viewpoint(*n.* 观点)

perfume [pərˈfjuːm] *n.* 香味；香料，香水

【记】分拆联想：per(贯穿) + fume(气体) → 缭绕在身上的气体 → 香味

pique [piːk] *vt.* 激怒(provoke)；激起(arouse)

【记】piqu(刺激) + e → 因受刺激而不悦 → 激怒

【搭】pique one's interest/curiosity 激起某人的兴趣/好奇心

plaque [plæk] *n.* 金属板

【例】There is a rock behind the bushes with a rusty *plaque* riveted it. 灌木丛后面有一块石头，上面固定着一块生锈的金属板。

playwright [ˈpleɪraɪt] *n.* 剧作家(dramatist)

【记】组合词：play (戏剧) + wright (制造者) → 戏剧的创作者 → 剧作家

proficient [prəˈfɪʃnt] *a.* 熟练的，精通的(skilled, expert)

【记】分拆联想：pro(大量) + fic(做) + ient → 做得多了也就熟练了 → 熟练的，精通的

【例】The scrolls were written in a language that is really rare today. Only a few people are *proficient* at it. 卷轴上的语言现在非常罕见，只有很少的人才精通于此。

【参】efficient(*a.* 生效的); sufficient(*a.* 充分的)

prolonged [prə'lɔːŋd] *a.* 延长的（*extended）
【记】来自 prolong（*v.* 延长，拖延）

property ['prɑːpərti] *n.* 财产（possession）；特性（characteristic）；所有权（ownership）；房地产（real estate）
【例】Silver's most distinguishing *property* is its electrical conductivity. 银最显著的特性是其导电性。

prudent ['pruːdnt] *a.* 谨慎的（discreet）
【记】词根记忆：prud（小心的）+ ent → 谨慎的
【例】This was a colossal sum for those days but one that a *prudent* government could pay. 在那些日子，这是个巨大的数额，但是一个谨慎的政府还是能够支付的。

pulp [pʌlp] *n.* 纸浆
【记】发音记忆："啪扑" → 被砸成纸浆的声音

purchase ['pɜːrtʃəs] *n.* 购买；购买的物品 *v.* 购买（buy, shop）
【记】分拆联想：pur + chase（追逐）→ 为了得到紧俏的商品而竞相追逐 → 购买
【例】He's very pleased with his *purchase*. 他对购买的东西很满意。//She *purchased* a product for cleaning rugs. 她买了一个清洗地毯的产品。

刷卡 purchase

register ['redʒɪstər] *n. /v.* 登记，注册（enroll）
【例】There are two more days to *register* for the class. 登记报名这门课的时间还有两天。
【派】registrar（*n.* 登记员）；registration（*n.* 登记，注册）

republic [rɪ'pʌblɪk] *n.* 共和国，共和政体
【记】联想记忆：re + public（公共的）→ 公共利益的代表 → 共和国
【派】republican（*a.* 共和的，共和党的；*n.* 共和党人）

reside [rɪ'zaɪd] *vi.* 居住（live）
【记】词根记忆：re（再）+ side（坐）→ 再坐（之地）→ 居住
【例】Two species of these finches *reside* in the evergreen forests of North America. 这些雀的两个种类居住在北美的常青树林中。
【派】residence（*n.* 住处；居住）；residency（*n.* 住处）

respect [rɪ'spekt] *v.* 尊重 *n.* 尊重；方面（aspect）
【记】词根记忆：re + spect（看）→ 一再地看望 → 尊重
【搭】with respect to 关于…

□ prolonged	□ property	□ prudent	□ pulp	□ purchase	□ register
□ republic	□ reside	□ respect			

【例】In this *respect*, the North American migratory locusts resemble their African relatives. 从这个方面讲, 北美迁徙的蝗虫类似于非洲的蝗虫。

【派】respectable(*a.* 值得尊敬的)

【参】expect(*vt.* 期望); aspect(*n.* 方面); inspect(*v.* 视察); suspect(*v.* 怀疑; 猜想)

simultaneous [ˌsaɪml'teɪnɪəs] *a.* 同时的(at the same time, synchronous)

【记】词根记忆: simult(相同) + aneous(…的) → 时间相同的 → 同时的

【例】These ponderous machines reaped the grain, threshed it, and bagged it, all in one *simultaneous* operation. 这些沉重的机器收割谷子, 脱粒然后打包, 所有操作都在同一时间完成。

【派】simultaneously(*ad.* 同时地)

snowflake ['snoʊfleɪk] *n.* 雪花

【记】组合词: snow(雪) + flake(薄片) → 雪花

solder ['sɑːdər] *v.* 焊接(weld)

【记】联想记忆: 我们的战士(soldier)是钢铁焊接(solder)而成的

stage [steɪdʒ] *n.* 阶段(period); 舞台(platform); 戏剧(drama) *v.* 筹划(arrange)

【记】分拆联想: st + age(年龄; 时代) → 俗话说: 台上一分钟, 台下十年功 → 舞台

stimulation [ˌstɪmju'leɪʃn] *n.* 刺激, 激励, 鼓舞

【例】It's my guess that the lack of *stimulation* isn't a problem for students like you. 我猜对像你这样的学生而言缺乏激励不是问题。

subliminal [ˌsʌb'lɪmɪnl] *adj.* 下意识的, 潜意识的

【记】词根记忆: sub(下面) + limin(=limen最小限度的神经刺激) + al → 下意识的, 潜意识的

【搭】subliminal advertising 潜意识广告

【例】The form of *subliminal* advertising is illegal in some countries in Europe. 在欧洲一些国家, 潜意识广告这种形式是非法的。

subsidize ['sʌbsɪdaɪz] *v.* 补助, 资助(finance)

【记】来自subsidy(*n.* 补助金)

surgery ['sɜːrdʒəri] *n.* 外科手术治疗; 外科, 外科学; 手术室, 诊疗室

【记】词根记忆: sur(确定的, 安全的) + gery → 这个外科手术是安全的 → 外科手术治疗

【搭】Heart Bypass Surgery 心脏搭桥手术

【例】As a rule, doctors hold *surgeries* between 9 and 11:30 every day.

simultaneous	snowflake	solder	stage	stimulation	subliminal
subsidize	surgery				

一般来说，医生每天9点到11点半做手术。

【派】surgical(*a.* 外科的)

swamp [swɑːmp] *n.* 沼泽(marsh) *vt.* 使困窘；使应接不暇(overwhelm)

【例】Slogging through a *swamp* in the rain is not funny. 在大雨中穿过沼泽地可不是闹着玩的。// I have been *swamped* with other things. 我一直忙着别的事情。

【派】swampy(*a.* 沼泽的；湿地的)

swing [swɪŋ] *v.* (使)摇荡；转向(turn around) *n.* 摇摆

【记】分拆联想：s + wing(翅膀) → 摇摆翅膀，在风中转向

【搭】swing music 摇摆舞音乐

【例】The signal it receives causes it to *swing* to the left. 它收到的信号使它向左转。

texture ['tekstʃər] *n.* 质地(character)；纹理(vein)；结构(structure)

【记】词根记忆：text(编织) + ure → 质地；纹理

【例】Igneous rocks also vary in *texture* as well as chemistry. 火成岩在质地和化学成分上各有不同。

upheaval [ʌp'hiːvl] *n.* 剧变

【记】来自upheave(*v.* 举起；鼓起)

【例】As the Indo-Europeans encroached on Old Europe from the east, the continent underwent *upheavals*. 随着印欧人从东方侵占古欧洲，欧洲大陆经历了剧变。

upset [ʌp'set] *a.* 心烦意乱的(concerned, worried) [ʌp'set] *v.* 颠覆，推翻；扰乱(disturb, overturn)

【记】词根记忆：up(上) + set(放置) → 把上面的放在下面了 → 颠覆，推翻

【例】The new policy is likely to *upset* a lot of people engaged in retail industry. 新的政策很可能让很多从事零售业的人感到不安。

utilitarian [ˌjuːtɪlɪ'teriən] *a.* 实用的(functional)；功利(主义)的

【记】词根记忆：util(用) + itar + ian → 实用的；功利(主义)的

【例】Stoneware used to be simple, *utilitarian* kitchenware. 粗陶器过去是简单实用的厨房用品。//By our narrow standards, scrub doesn't meet our selfish *utilitarian* needs. 根据我们狭隘的标准，灌木丛不能满足我们自私的功利需求。

vacation [və'keɪʃn] *n.* 度假，休假

【记】词根记忆：vac(空的) + ation → 有空的 → 休假

【搭】on vacation 度假；summer vacation 暑假；paid vacation 带薪假期；take a vacation 度假

☐ swamp	☐ swing	☐ texture	☐ upheaval	☐ upset	☐ utilitarian
☐ vacation					

【例】During summer *vacation*, many white-collar people would like to go abroad to take a *vacation*. 暑假时，很多白领想去国外度假。

validate ['vælɪdeɪt] *vt.* 使有效，使生效

【记】词根记忆：val(价值) + id + ate(使) → 使有价值 → 使生效

【例】These two great poems are believed to have been written some time between 800BC and 700BC, partly because the poems refer to the social conditions of that time, conditions that have been *validated* by the findings of archeologists. 这两首伟大的诗篇被认为是写于公元前800年到700年，部分原因是诗篇提到当时的社会状况，这些状况已经被考古学家的发现所证实了。

【派】validation(*n.* 确认)

weird [wɪrd] *a.* 怪异的，神秘的(strange, mysterious)

【记】分拆联想：we(我们) + ird(看作bird, 鸟) → 如果我们都变成鸟该多怪异 → 怪异的

【例】Those modern sculptures over there are really *weird*. 那里的现代雕塑真怪异。

To conquer the hard, one must master the easy; to achieve greatness, one must begin from the triviality.

天下难事，必须于易；天下大事，必须于细。

——老聃(*Lao Dan*)

Word List 29  MP3-29

词根、词缀预习表

arbitr	判断	arbitrary	a. 任意的
choreo	舞蹈	choreographer	n. 舞蹈指导
ex	向外	expand	v. 扩张；膨胀
noct	夜	nocturnal	a. 夜间活动的
plic	重叠	replicate	v. 复制
speci	种	specific	a. 明确的；种的
nomin	名称	nominate	vt. 任命；提名

abandon [ə'bændən] v. 离弃；完全放弃（desert）

【例】She and her tribe had to *abandon* their lands and retreat to Canada. 她和她的部落不得不放弃他们的土地，撤退到加拿大。

【派】abandoned（a. 被抛弃的；废置的）；abandonment（n. 放弃，抛弃）

agitation [ˌædʒɪ'teɪʃn] n. 激动；煽动（disturbance）

ample ['æmpl] a. 充足的（abundant, enough）

【记】联想记忆：apple（苹果）很ample（充足）

【例】The state of New Jersey offers *ample* opportunities for bicyclists of all abilities. 新泽西州给各种水平的骑自行车的人很多机会。

【参】trample（vt. 踩，践踏）；amble（v. 缓行）

arbitrary ['ɑːrbətreri] a. 任意的，专断的（random）

【记】词根记忆：arbitr（判断）+ ary（…的）→ 自己做判断的 → 专断的

【搭】an arbitrary character 反复无常的性格；an arbitrary decision 武断的决定

【例】In the US, some people argue that a ban on some type of guns is *arbitrary*. 在美国，一些人认为禁止某些类型的枪支是专断的。

argument ['ɑːrgjumənt] *n.* 争论；辩论；论据，论点

【搭】support for the argument 支持论据

【例】A: Do you have a few minutes to look over this outline for next week's debate with me? I need to know if I have enough support for my *arguments*.

B: I'm tied up in the moment. Why don't you come back during my office hours.

A：你有时间跟我看看下周辩论的大纲吗？我需要知道我的论点是否有足够的支撑。

B：我现在很忙，你在我办公时间再来好吗？

asset ['æset] *n.* 有价值的人（或物）；优点（advantage），长处特性或技能；资产，财产

【记】词根记忆：as(加强) + set(放，置) → 不断置办财产 → 资产

【例】Sometimes a sense of humor is a great *asset.* 有时幽默感是很大的优点。

assignment [ə'saɪnmənt] *n.* 分配，委派；任务(task)，(课外)作业(home-work)

【记】来自assign(*v.* 指派，选派)

【搭】homework assignment 家庭作业

【例】A: I need to ask John about the chemistry *assignment* for tomor-row. But his phone's been busy for the last hour and a half. Who can he be talking to for so long?

B: It may not him, you know. It could be one of his housemates. Why don't you just hand on over there? Is that important?

A：我需要问约翰明天化学作业的事。但是他的电话在过去一个半小时内都占线。他和谁能讲这么长时间？

B：可能不是他，你知道。可能是他的同屋。你为何不等等呢？事情很重要吗？

bandanna [bæn'dænə] *n.* 大手帕

beat [biːt] *v.* 敲打 *n.* 拍子 *a.* 疲惫的

【例】The music had a steady *beat* that people could dance to. 音乐有稳定的节奏，人们可以随之起舞。//We were just *beat* after raking all the leaves. 我们用耙子耙完所有的树叶后都累坏了。

bison ['baɪsn] *n.* 美洲或欧洲的野牛

【记】发音记忆："拜神" → 印度人非常尊敬牛，美洲野牛去印度肯定也被当成神来拜

bland [blænd] *a.* 无味的

【记】发音记忆："布蓝的"→布是清淡的蓝色的→无味的；注意不要和blend(*n. /v.* 混合)相混

【例】This pizza tastes *bland*. There is not enough sauce. 这个比萨饼吃起来没味道，调味汁不够。

camouflage [ˈkæməflɑːʒ] *n. /v.* 掩饰，伪装(hide, disguise)

【例】Mammals rarely use this type of *camouflage*, but many fish and invertebrates do. 哺乳动物很少使用这种伪装，但是很多鱼和无脊椎动物会用。

canyon [ˈkænjən] *n.* 峡谷

【参】crayon(*n.* 蜡笔)

capacity [kəˈpæsəti] *n.* 能力(ability)；容量；身份(identity)

【记】词根记忆：cap(拿)+acity→能拿住→能力；容量

【例】Does human mental *capacity* has limitations? 人类脑容量有限度吗？

chlorine [ˈklɔːriːn] *n.* 【化】氯

choreographer [ˌkɔːriˈɑːɡrəfər] *n.* 舞蹈指导

【记】词根记忆：choreo(舞蹈)+graph(写)+er(人)→编写舞蹈的人→舞蹈指导

【例】She became the most sought-after *choreographer* on Broadway. 她成为了百老汇最受欢迎的舞蹈动作指导。

同根词：choreography(*n.* 舞蹈，舞蹈编排)

chunk [tʃʌŋk] *n.* 厚片，大块(lump)；相当大的部分(或数量)

【记】发音记忆："常客"→饭馆的常客占客人的一大部分→相当大的部分

【搭】a chunk of 一大块

【例】The impact caused the cores of the two planets to melt together and *chunks* of earth's crust to be thrown out into space. 这种影响使两个行星的核心融化在一起，大量的地球碎片飞进了太空。

clutch [klʌtʃ] *n.* 一次所孵的卵(或蛋) *v.* 企图抓住，抓紧(take, clench)

【记】分拆联想：clu(看作clue，线索)+tch→抓住线索→抓紧

【例】This species lays one and only one-*clutch* of forty eggs in a lifetime. 这个物种一生只孵一次蛋，共有40个。

codify [ˈkɑːdɪfaɪ] *vt.* 编成法典，编辑成书

【记】来自code(*n.* 法规)+ify→整理(法律)→编成法典

【例】The country is trying to *codify* the rules on outsourcing. 这个国家正在努力把外包规则编成法典。

□ bland □ camouflage □ canyon □ capacity □ chlorine □ choreographer □ chunk □ clutch □ codify

commerce ['kɑːmɜːrs] *n.* 贸易，商业（trade, business）
【派】commercial(*a.* 商业的；贸易的); commercialize(*vt.* 使商业化)
【参】commence(*v.* 开始，着手)

consistency [kən'sɪstənsi] *n.* 浓度，密度；一致性，协调；连接，结合
【记】来自consist(一致) + ency → 一致性
【搭】consistency of …的浓度；…的一致性
【例】Unitarian stress the *consistency* of the character portrayed in the poetry. 一神论者强调诗歌中描述人物的一致性。

constant ['kɑːnstənt] *a.* 稳定的（stable）; 不变的，持续的（consistent, continued, continuous）
【记】词根记忆：con(始终) + stant(站，立) → 始终站立 → 不变的
【搭】constant temperature 恒温
【例】The tuition remained *constant* in the past five years. 学费在过去5年保持不变。
【参】instant(*a.* 立即的)

continuity [ˌkɑːntə'nuːəti] *n.* 连贯性，连续性（consistency, succession）
【例】Some experts argue that school vacations interrupt the *continuity* of the school year. 一些专家辩称学校的假期打断了学年的连续性。
【派】discontinuity(*n.* 不连续，中断)

copper ['kɑːpər] *n.* 铜(币)
【记】分拆联想：cop（警察）+ per → 警察制服上的铜扣 → 铜

crater

crater ['kreɪtər] *n.* 火山口；(弹)坑
【参】curator(*n.* 馆长，监护人)

crucial ['kruːʃl] *a.* 至关重要的，决定性的（*important, essential）
【记】词根记忆：cruc(十字形) + ial → 十字路口 → 决定性的
【例】How salt became so *crucial* to our metabolism is a mystery. 盐如何对我们的新陈代谢如此重要仍然是个谜。

cubism ['kjuːbɪzəm] *n.* 立体主义

democratic [ˌdemə'krætɪk] *a.* 民主的
【搭】Democratic Party 民主党
【例】There is much *democratic* insistence on the worthiness of every level of birth and work. 大部分民众坚持认为各种出身和工作都值得尊重。

deposit [dɪ'pɑːzɪt] *v.* 沉淀（settle）; 堆积（accumulate）; 存款 *n.* 堆积物（accumulation）

□ commerce	□ consistency	□ constant	□ continuity	□ copper	□ crater
□ crucial	□ cubism	□ democratic	□ deposit		

【记】词根记忆：de + posit（放）→ 沉淀；堆积

【例】The sediments have been *deposited* over a comparable period of time. 沉淀物经过相当长的一段时间已经堆积起来了。//The *deposits* associated with present-day glaciers have been well studied. 对与当今冰河相关的沉淀物的研究已经很深入了。

【派】deposition(*n.* 沉积物，沉积作用)；depositor(*n.* 存款人)

deprive [dɪ'praɪv] *v.* (使)失去，剥夺(take away)

【记】词根记忆：de(去掉) + prive(单个) → 从个人身边拿走 → 剥夺

【例】Plant stems die when *deprived* of water. 植物茎秆缺水之后就会死。

【派】deprivation(*n.* 缺失)

disciple [dɪ'saɪpl] *n.* 门徒，弟子(follower, adherent)

【记】和discipline(纪律)一起记，学徒(disciple)必须有纪律

【例】Martin Luther King regarded himself as a real *disciple* of Gandhi. 马丁·路德·金把自己视为甘地的真正门徒。

discount ['dɪskaʊnt] *n.* 折扣

【记】分拆联想：dis(分离) + count(计算) → 不计算在内的部分 → 折扣

【搭】at a discount 打折扣

【例】She could stay at a hotel at a *discount*. 她可以待在打折酒店。

dozen ['dʌzn] *n.* 一打，十二个

【搭】dozens of 许多的

【例】There were *dozens* of people waiting in the hall for autographs. 门厅有几十人等着要签名。

A: Have you guys decided whether you are going to get an apartment off campus next year or are you staying in the dorm?

B: We are still talking about the pros and cons. I don't know. To me it seems like six of one and half of *dozen* of the other.

A：你们明年决定是在校外租公寓还是住在宿舍？

B：我们仍然在讨论利弊。我不知道。对我来说都可以。

exchange [ɪks'tʃeɪndʒ] *vt. /n.* 交换，兑换(change)；交易(trade)

【记】分拆联想：ex + change (变换) → 双方相互交换 → 交换

【搭】New York Stock Exchange 纽约证券交易所

expand [ɪk'spænd] *v.* 扩张(outspread)；膨胀(swell)

【记】词根记忆：ex(向外) + pand(分散) → 向外分散 → 扩张；膨胀

【例】The new university greatly *expanded* in size and course offerings,

breaking completely out of the old. 新的大学规模扩大和课程选择
增多，完全摆脱了旧的模式。

【派】expanding(*a.* 扩大的); expansion(*n.* 扩张)

feeble [ˈfiːbl] *a.* 虚弱的, 无力的(weak, frail)

【记】分拆联想: fee(费用) + ble → 看病需要花钱 → 虚弱的, 无
力的

【例】The national government made a *feeble* attempt to make larger
holdings available to homesteaders. 国民政府试图给自耕农更大的
股份, 但收效甚微。

fundamental [ˌfʌndəˈmentl] *a.* 基础的, 基本的 (integral, basic, essential, *primary)

【记】来自fundament(*n.* 基础)

【例】The society is undergoing *fundamental* change. 社会在经历根
本性的变化。

【派】fundamentally(*ad.* 根本地)

gallop [ˈɡæləp] *v.* (马)飞奔; 疾驰(spur)

【记】联想记忆: 汽车加了一加仑(gallon)的油, 于是疾驰(gallop)
起来

garbage [ˈɡɑːrbɪdʒ] *n.* 垃圾(rubbish); 废物(waste)

【例】We're going to be cleaning up all of the *garbage* here at the lake
area. 我们要清理干净湖区的所有垃圾。

gorgeous [ˈɡɔːrdʒəs] *a.* 漂亮的(beautiful); 令人愉快的

【记】分拆联想: gorge(峡谷) + ous → 峡谷是漂亮的 → 漂亮的

【例】What a *gorgeous* jacket! It must have cost a fortune. 多漂亮的夹
克啊! 肯定花了很多钱。//I just love walking through this park. The
tree is *gorgeous*. 我就喜欢在公园散步, 那里的树很漂亮。

incapacitate [ˌɪnkəˈpæsɪteɪt] *vt.* 使失去能力; 使不胜任

【记】词根记忆: in(无) + capac(=cap握住) + itate → 无力握住 →
使失去能力

【搭】be incapacitated for 不能胜任…; be incapacitated from 使失
去…资格

【例】Helen's poor sight *incapacitates* her for working as a taxi driver.
海伦视力不行, 这使她不能胜任出租车司机的工作。

【派】incapacitation(*n.* 无能; 不胜任)

indigestion [ˌɪndɪˈdʒestʃən] *n.* 消化不良

【记】来自indigest(*v.* 不消化)

【例】I get *indigestion*. 我消化不良。

lethal [ˈliːθl] *a.* 有害的，致命的(deadly)

【记】词根记忆：leth(死，僵) + al → 有害的，致命的

【例】Only about 25 kinds of scorpion are *lethal* to humans. 只有25种蝎子对人类是致命的。

list [lɪst] *n.* 表(table)，目录，名单 *v.* 把…编列成表，列入表内

【搭】reading list 阅读书目

【例】You must dial the number *listed* in the telephone book and contact us as soon as possible. 你必须拨打电话簿里的号码，尽快联系我们。

A: I have to look for a room to rent.

B: How about trying Carters? They usually have a long *list* of places.

A：我得租间房子。

B：试试卡特斯怎么样？他们通常有很多地方可供选择。

literature [ˈlɪtrətʃər] *n.* 文学；文学作品；文献

【记】词根记忆：liter(文字) + ature → 文学；文学作品

【搭】Nobel Prize for Literature 诺贝尔文学奖

【例】Maria had the strongest influence on this period of American children's *literature*. 玛利亚对这个时期的美国儿童文学影响力最大。

membrane [ˈmembreɪn] *n.* 薄膜；细胞膜

【记】分拆联想：mem(看作member) + brane(看作brain，头脑) → 人的头脑有保护膜 → 薄膜；细胞膜

meteorite [ˈmiːtiəraɪt] *n.* 流星，陨石

【例】As their name suggests, the iron *meteorites* consist almost entirely of metal. 正如其名称所表明的，铁陨星几乎全是金属构成的。

neglect [nɪˈglekt] *vt. /n.* 忘记，忽视(omit)

【记】词根记忆：neg(否定) + lect(选择) → 不去选它 → 忽视

【例】What I *neglected* to mention was the controversy around Peary's pioneering accomplishment. 我忘记提围绕皮尔里开创性成就的争议了。

nocturnal [nɑːkˈtɜːrnl] *a.* 夜行性的(active at night)

【记】词根记忆：noct(夜) + urnal → 夜行性的

【例】Most mice are *nocturnal*, but the African grass mouse is active during daylight hours. 多数老鼠是夜行性的，但是非洲草鼠在白天活跃。

nominate [ˈnɑːmɪneɪt] *vt.* 任命，提名(designate, name)

【记】词根记忆：nomin(名称) + ate → 任命，提名

lethal	list	literature	membrane	meteorite	neglect
nocturnal	nominate				

【例】You've been *nominated* for the committee. 你已经被提名为委员会成员了。

【派】nomination(*n.* 任命)

notch [nɑːtʃ] *n.* 刻痕

objective [əbˈdʒektɪv] *n.* 目标，目的（target, aim）
a. 客观的

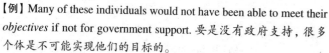

notch

【记】和object(*n.* 目标)一起记

【搭】strategic objective 战略目标；be objective about sth. 客观看待某事；achieve the objective 达到目的

【例】Many of these individuals would not have been able to meet their *objectives* if not for government support. 要是没有政府支持，很多个体是不可能实现他们的目标的。

【派】objectivity(*n.* 客观性，客观现实)

【参】subjective(*a.* 主观的)；optimistic(*a.* 乐观的)；neutral(*a.* 中立的)；critical(*a.* 批评的)；doubtful(*a.* 怀疑的)；approving(*a.* 赞成的)

outcome [ˈaʊtkʌm] *n.* 结果，成果(consequence, effect)

【记】来自词组come out 结果

particular [pərˈtɪkjələr] *a.* 特定的(selected)；独特的(unique)；详细的；挑剔的

【例】Each person is responsible for a *particular* part of the process. 每个人负责这个过程的特定部分。//Bill is very *particular* about his clothing. 比尔穿衣服很挑剔。

【派】particularly(*ad.* 特别，尤其)

【参】peculiar(*a.* 奇特的)

permanent [ˈpɜːrmənənt] *a.* 持久的(long-lasting)；固定不变的(stable)

【记】词根记忆：per(自始至终) + man(手) + ent(具…性质的) → 人一直靠自己的双手养活自己 → 持久的

【搭】permanent residence 固定住处

【例】Some of the baskets have been placed on *permanent* display at the Philadelphia museum of art. 在费城艺术博物馆一些篮子已经成为了永久展出的物品。

【派】permanency(*n.* 永存)；permanently(*ad.* 永久地)

persuasive [pərˈsweɪsɪv] *a.* 有说服力的

【记】来自persuade(*v.* 劝说)

【例】You'll have to be a lot more *persuasive* if you want to convince the committee to accept your proposal. 如果想说服委员会接受你的建议，你就得更加有说服力。

pigment ['pɪɡmənt] *n.* 颜料(paint)；色素

【派】pigmented(*a.* 有颜色的)；pigmentation(*n.* 天然颜色)

piracy ['paɪrəsi] *n.* 海上抢劫，海盗行为；盗版

【记】来自pirate(*v.* 盗版；掠夺)

【例】During periods of heavy *piracy* at sea, the amount of interest and the cost of the policy went up considerably. 在海盗活动猖獗期间，利益总数和政策成本成显著增长。

pivotal ['pɪvətl] *a.* 关键的；中枢的(central)

【记】来自pivot(枢轴；枢纽) + al → 极重要的

【例】Iry Lejeune became a *pivotal* figure in the revitalization of Cajun music. 艾里·勒琼成为复兴法裔美国人音乐的关键人物。

pose [pouz] *n.* 姿势 *v.* 造成；提出(frame)

【例】If this does *pose* a problem for you, you should contact my office as soon as possible. 如果这对你确实是个问题，你应该尽快联系我的办公室。

pottery ['pɑːtəri] *n.* (总称)陶器；陶器场；陶器制造术

【例】A: Have you seen the new *pottery* Lisa's made for the student's exhibition?

B: I know. She really outdid herself this time.

A: 你看到利萨给学生展览做的新陶器了吗？

B: 我知道，她这次的确超常发挥了。

【参】lottery(*n.* 抽奖给奖法)

predominantly [prɪ'dɑːmɪnəntli] *ad.* 主要地(primarily, mainly)

【例】Humans have been *predominantly* right-handed for more than 5,000 years. 人类在5000多年来主要都是用右手做事情。

range [reɪndʒ] *n.* 范围(extent)；山脉(mountain) *v.* (在某范围内)变动

【记】本身为词根，意为：排列，顺序

【例】He no longer believes short-*range* forecasts. 他不再相信短期预测。//My musical tastes *range* from jazz to country. 我的音乐品位不只局限于一种，从爵士乐到乡村音乐我都听。

【派】ranger(*n.* 护林员)

reliance [rɪ'laɪəns] *n.* 依靠；依靠的人或物(dependance)

【记】来自rely(*v.* 依赖)

replicate ['replɪkeɪt] *v.* 复制(duplicate)

【记】词根记忆：re + plic(重叠) + ate → 复制

【例】The virus *replicates* by attaching to a cell and injecting its nucleic acid. 病毒通过附着在细胞上，并往其中输入核酸来实现复制。

| pigment | piracy | pivotal | pose | pottery | predominantly |
| range | reliance | replicate | | | |

rumor [ˈruːmər] *n.* 传闻，谣言

【记】分拆联想：rum(看作run，跑) + or → 好事不出门，坏事传千里 → 传闻，谣言

saturation [ˌsætʃəˈreɪʃn] *n.* 饱和(状态)(satiety)

scrub [skrʌb] *n.* 灌木丛(shrub)

【记】和rub(*v.* 擦，摩擦)一起记

seashore [ˈsiːʃɔːr] *n.* 海岸，海滨(coast, beach, shore)

【例】Every day the old man goes to the *seashore* before daybreak. 这个老人每天日出前去海滩。

similar [ˈsɪmələr] *a.* (to)相似的，类似的(alike)

【记】词根记忆：simil(相类似) + ar → 相似的

【派】similarity(*n.* 类似，类似点)

skeleton [ˈskelɪtn] *n.* 梗概(sketch)；骨架，框架(framework)

sneaker [ˈsniːkər] *n.* 鬼鬼祟祟的人；卑鄙者；运动鞋

【例】There was a freighter carrying *sneakers* from a factory in Asia. 有一辆货船从亚洲某个工厂运送运动鞋。

A: Those are great *sneakers*. Were they very expensive?

B: I never could have bought them if the shoe store wasn't having a big sale.

A: 这些运动鞋真不错。贵不贵?

B: 要是鞋店不大幅度打折，我肯定买不起。

spare [sper] *a.* 备用的；空闲的 (free) *v.* 节约 (economize) *n.* 备用品(reserve)

【例】I don't know if I could *spare* the time. 我不知道能否抽出空来。

specific [spəˈsɪfɪk] *a.* 明确的，具体的；特定的，特有的

【记】词根记忆：speci (种) + fic → 一种的，某种的 → 特定的，特有的

【例】It's thought that *specific* genes in an animal's body have an influence on anxious behavior. 人们以为动物体内某些具体的基因对引起焦虑行为有影响。

【派】specifically(*ad.* 明确地；特定地)

【参】special(*adj.* 特别的)；especial(*adj.* 特别的)

stratum [ˈstreɪtəm] *n.* [*pl.* strata] 地层

stratum

stuff [stʌf] *n.* 原料，材料(material)，东西 *v.* 填满，塞满

【记】联想记忆：不能把职员(staff)充当原料(stuff)来使用

【例】Did you learn about this *stuff* in cooking school? 你在烹饪学校学过这个吗？

A: Hey Teresa! Thanks for agreeing to help me review all this history material.

B: No problem, Bob. So do you want to start with the *stuff* missed yesterday? They are part about urban problems in the colonial period.

A：你好，特蕾莎！感谢你同意帮我复习这些历史材料。

B：没问题，鲍勃。你想从昨天没学的内容开始吗？那是关于殖民时期城市问题的内容。

【参】staff(*n.* 员工)

supplant [sə'plænt] *vt.* 取代，代替(replace)

【记】词根记忆：sup(在…下面) + plant(种植) → 在下面种植 → 取代，代替

【例】Within a short time the trading company had *supplanted* the individual promoter of colonization. 在很短的时间内，这个贸易公司已经取代了个体殖民推动者。

symbolize ['sɪmbəlaɪz] *v.* 象征，作为…的象征(represent)

【记】分拆联想：symbol(象征) + ize → 象征

【例】In Europe, white *symbolizes* purity while in Asia it is usually the symbol of sadness. 在欧洲，白色象征着纯洁，而在亚洲白色通常是悲伤的象征。

wick [wɪk] *n.* (蜡烛、灯)芯

wonder ['wʌndər] *n.* 惊奇，惊异；奇迹，奇事 *v.* 诧异，奇怪；纳闷，想知道

【搭】no wonder 难怪，怪不得

【例】A: I've been running a mile every afternoon for the past month, but I still haven't been able to lose more than a pound or two. I *wonder* if it's worth it.

B: Oh, don't give up now. It always seems hard when you are just starting out.

A：过去一个月我一直坚持每天下午跑一英里，但是体重也就减轻不过一两磅。我不知道跑步到底值不值。

B：哦，现在不要放弃。万事总是开头难。

A: Tom and I are having a party next week. We *wonder* if you and Joe would be free to join us.

B: Sounds great. But I'd better talk to Joe before we say yes.

A：汤姆和我下周要开派对。不知道你和乔是否有空来参加。

B：听上去太好了。不过在同意之前我最好和乔说一声。

【参】wander(*v.* 徘徊)

□ supplant □ symbolize □ wick □ wonder

Word List 30  MP3-30

词根、词缀预习表

quire	追求	acquire	*vt.* 获得
aero	空气	aerobic	*n.* 有氧运动
chole	胆，胆汁	cholesterol	*n.* 胆固醇
ward	方向	downward	*ad./a.* 向下（的）
harmon	一致	harmony	*n.* 和声；协调
lingu	语言	linguistic	*a.* 语言的
miss	送，放出	mission	*n.* 代表团
octo	八	octopus	*n.* 章鱼

acquire [əˈkwaɪər] *vt.* 获得(*obtain, gain)；学到
【记】词根记忆：ac + quire(追求) → 不断追求才能够获得 → 获得
【例】They had begun to *acquire* and use capital. 他们已经开始获得资金并投入使用了。
【派】acquired(*a.* 后天习得的，已获得的)；acquisition(*n.* 获得，习得)
【参】require(*vt.* 需要)；inquire(*v.* 询问)

aerobic [eˈroʊbɪk] *a.* 增氧健身法的 [*pl.*] *n.* 有氧运动
【记】词根记忆：aero(空气) + bic → 增氧健身法的
【例】He jogs because he doesn't like *aerobics*. 他不喜欢有氧运动，所以就去慢跑。
【派】anaerobic(*a.* 厌氧性的)

amid [əˈmɪd] *prep.* 在…中
【记】词根记忆：a(在…) + mid(中间) → 在…中
【例】The katydid, a type of grasshopper, is active at night and rests motionless *amid* foliage during the day. 纺织娘是一种蚱蜢，夜里活跃，白天在树叶中一动不动地休息。

ammonia [əˈmoʊniə] *n.* 氨，氨水

☐ acquire ☐ aerobic ☐ amid ☐ ammonia

anthropology [ˌænθrəˈpɑːlədʒi] *n.* 人类学
【记】词根记忆: anthrop(人) + ology(…学) → 人类学
【派】anthropological(*a.* 人类学的); anthropologist(*n.* 人类学家)

arithmetic [əˈrɪθmətɪk] *n.* 算术

artificial [ˌɑːrtɪˈfɪʃl] *a.* 人造的(synthetic); 假的(false)
【记】词根记忆: arti(=skill技巧) + fic(面) + ial(…的) → 在表面使用技术的 → 人造的; 假的
【例】*Artificial* flowers are used for scientific as well as for decorative purposes. 假花既用于科学也用于装饰。
【派】artificially(*ad.* 人工地; 人为地)

bake [beɪk] *v.* 烘, 烤
【例】The cake was over *baked*. 蛋糕烤过头了。
【参】sunbaked(*a.* 晒裂的)

blip [blɪp] *n.* 雷达上显示的点

brittle [ˈbrɪtl] *a.* 易碎的(*easily broken, fragile)
【例】A lot of pages are turning brown and becoming *brittle*. 很多书页发黄变脆。

caribou [ˈkærɪbuː] *n.* 北美产驯鹿

cautious [ˈkɔːʃəs] *a.* 小心的, 谨慎的(discreet)
【例】Even the most *cautious* merchants became willing to risk shipping their goods over long distances. 甚至最谨慎的商人也愿意冒险长途运送他们的货物。
【参】precaution(*n.* 预防措施; 警惕)

channel [ˈtʃænl] *n.* [常*pl.*] 通道(path, way)

cholesterol [kəˈlestərɔːl] *n.* 胆固醇
【记】词根记忆: chole(胆, 胆汁) + sterol(固醇) → 胆固醇

coexist [ˌkoʊɪɡˈzɪst] *vi.* 共存(to exist together or at the same time)
【搭】coexist with 与…共存

constrain [kənˈstreɪn] *vt.* 束缚, 限制(confine, limit)
【记】词根记忆: con + strain(拉紧) → 使劲拉紧 → 束缚, 限制
【例】Their species' genetic makeup *constrains* them to be insects. 它们的物种基因构成限制了它们成为昆虫。
【派】constraint(*n.* 约束, 强制)

counselor [ˈkaʊnsələr] *n.* 顾问, 法律顾问(advisor)

court [kɔːrt] *n.* 法院; 球场(playground, field)
【搭】the Supreme Court 最高法院
【派】courtship(*n.* 求爱; 求爱期)

credit ['kredɪt] *n.* 荣誉；学分；信用；银行存款 *v.* (to)把…归给

【例】Watt should be *credited* with inventing the steam engine. 人们把蒸汽机的发明归功于瓦特。

【参】accredit(*vt.* 授权)；credence(*n.* 相信，信任)；credibility(*n.* 可信性，可靠性)

crystal ['krɪstl] *n.* 水晶；晶体 *a.* 透明的(clear)；结晶状的

【记】分拆联想：cry(哭泣) + stal(看作star，星星)→ 水晶像是星星哭泣掉下的眼泪 → 水晶

crystal

【例】Glass has an interlocking *crystal* network. 玻璃有一个连锁的晶体网络。

【派】crystalline (*a.* 水晶的；透明的)；crystallize (*v.* 结晶；明确)；crystallization(*n.* 结晶)

demonstrate ['demənstreɪt] *v.* 论证，表明(show)

【记】词根记忆：de(加强) + monstr(表示) + ate(做)→ 论证；表明

【例】The researchers have sought to *demonstrate* that their work can be a valuable tool of science. 研究人员试图证明，他们的工作可以成为科学的宝贵工具。//Peggy *demonstrated* her ability as a student. 佩吉证明了作为学生的能力。

【派】demonstration[*n.* 示威；(教学)示范]

downward ['daʊnwərd] *a.* 向下的 *ad.* 向下，往下(down)

【记】词根记忆：down(向下的) + ward(方向)→ 向下的

【例】Aristotle noted that when he released most objects, they would drop *downward*. 亚里士多德注意到，松开多数物体时，它们就会往下掉。

【参】upward(*a.* 向上的)；forward(*ad.* 向前地)

enclose [ɪn'kloʊz] *vt.* 围住；把…装入(信封、包裹等)

【记】词根记忆：en(进入) + close(关闭)→ 关闭在里面 → 围住

【例】The application instructions say to *enclose* a check or money order for twenty dollars. 申请指示说要往信封装一张20美元的支票或汇票。

【派】enclosed(*a.* 被围住的)；enclosure(*n.* 围栏)

entrepreneurial [ˌɑːntrəprə'nɜːriəl] *a.* 创业的

【例】As a rule, a leader's *entrepreneurial* spirit in a company encourages every staff at work. 通常公司领导的创业精神会鼓舞着工作的每位员工。

equator [ɪˈkweɪtər] *n.* 赤道
【记】词根记忆：equ(相等) + ator → 使(地球)平分 → 赤道

equator

evidence [ˈevɪdəns] *n.* 根据（basis）；证据(proof)；迹象 *v.* 证明(*indicate)
【记】词根记忆：e + vid（看见）+ ence → 看见的人或物 → 根据；证据
【例】Emotional health is *evidenced* in the voice by free and melodic sounds of the happy. 快乐的人畅所欲言，音调悠扬，证明其情绪健康。

explicit [ɪkˈsplɪsɪt] *a.* 清楚的，直率的(clear, direct)
【记】词根记忆：ex + plic(重叠) + it → 把重叠在一起的弄清楚 → 清楚的
【例】The directions Jane gave me to get to her home were very *explicit.* 简十分清楚地给我指路去她家。
【参】implicit(*a.* 含蓄的)；elicit(*vt.* 得出)

generation [ˌdʒenəˈreɪʃn] *n.* 一代人；发生
【搭】spontaneous generation 自然发生
【例】They've been weaving the baskets for *generations*, handing down the skill from mother to daughter. 她们世世代代都编织篮子，这个手艺从母亲传给女儿。

glimpse [glɪmps] *n.* 一看，一瞥(glance) *v.* 瞥见
【记】分拆联想：glim(灯光) + pse → 像灯光一闪 → 一瞥
【搭】catch a glimpse of 瞥见

gravitational [ˌɡrævɪˈteɪʃənl] *a.* 重力的，万有引力的
【记】来自gravitation(*n.* 引力；倾向)
【搭】gravitational force 引力，重力；gravitational field 引力场，重力场
【例】Jupiter has a weaker *gravitational* force than the other planets. 木星的引力比其他行星弱。//Mars was captured by the *gravitational* field of the Sun. 火星被太阳的引力场捕获了。

grocery [ˈɡroʊsəri] *n.* 杂货店
【例】It was sold in *grocery* stores and door-to-door. 它在杂货店有售，也上门售货。

hail [heɪl] *n.* 冰雹 *vt.* 热情地承认为…
【记】和sail(*v.* 航行)一起记
【例】Telecommuting has been *hailed* as a solution to all kinds of problems related to office work. 远程办公被认为能解决各种与办公相关的问题。

harmony [ˈhɑːrməni] *n.* 和声；协调 (accord)

【记】词根记忆：harmon(一致) + y → 和声；协调

【搭】in harmony with 协调一致

【例】The piano is able to play both the melody and its accompanying *harmony* at the same time. 钢琴能同时演奏音乐和伴奏的和声。

【派】harmonize (*v.* 协调；配和声)；harmonious (*a.* 和睦的；协调的)；harmoniously(*ad.* 和谐地，和睦地)

haven [ˈheɪvn] *n.* 庇护所 (shelter)；栖息处 (habitat)

【记】联想记忆：与天堂(heaven)只有一(e)步之遥的地方 → 庇护所(haven)

【例】Maine's abundant forests and rivers have made it a *haven* for many kinds of wildlife. 缅因州森林丰富，河流众多，使之成为很多种野生动物的栖息地。

hook [hʊk] *n.* 钩，吊钩 (clasp, hanger) *v.* 连接无线电设备以传送

【例】She often *hooks* up her telephone modem connections. 她经常连接上电话调制解调器。

hover [ˈhʌvər] *vi.* 徘徊 (wander)

【记】联想记忆：爱人(lover)在自己身边徘徊(hover)

【例】The criminal's *hovering* between life and death. 罪犯在生死之间徘徊。

【参】hovercraft(*n.* 气垫船)

identification [aɪˌdentɪfɪˈkeɪʃn] *n.* 辨认；鉴定

【记】来自identify(*v.* 鉴别)

【例】In modern world, fingerprinting as a means of *identification* have been widely used in many fields. 在当代社会，指纹是一种身份鉴定手段，广泛应用于很多领域。

immense [ɪˈmens] *a.* 巨大的；极大的 (vast, huge)

【记】词根记忆：im(不) + mens(测量) + e → 不能测量的 → 巨大的；极大的

【例】Horsetail rushes in prehistoric times grew to *immense* size. 史前的木贼灯心草长得很大。

impart [ɪmˈpɑːrt] *vt.* 传授 (initiate)；传达 (convey)；给予 (give)

【记】词根记忆：im(进入) + part(部分) → 成为(知识的)一部分 → 传授

【例】Parents rarely encourage this instinctive attraction by *imparting* a knowledge of nature to their children. 父母很少通过给孩子传授自然的知识来鼓励这种本能的吸引。

harmony	haven	hook	hover	identification	immense
impart					

325

inception [ɪn'sepʃn] *n.* 开端，开始(*beginning, start)

【记】词根记忆：in(进入) + cept(拿) + ion → 拿进来 → 开始

【例】From their *inception*, most rural neighborhoods in colonial North America included at least one carpenter, joiner, and sawyer. 一开始，北美殖民时期的农村地区包括至少一个木匠、工匠和锯工。

insanity [ɪn'sænəti] *n.* 精神错乱，疯狂(madness)

【记】来自insane(*a.* 疯狂的)

【例】Hers is a world of violence, *insanity*, fractured love, and hopeless loneliness. 她的世界充满了暴力、疯狂、破裂的爱情和无望的孤独。

interaction [ˌɪntər'ækʃn] *n.* 相互作用(communication)

【记】词根记忆：inter(在…中间) + act(作用) + ion → 相互作用

【例】Parents at work usually spend a small amount of time on *interaction* with their children. 上班的父母通常只花很少时间与孩子互动。

lengthen ['leŋθən] *vt.* 延长，使变长(extend, elongate)

【例】The daylight is *lengthening* as summer approaches. 随着夏天的临近，白天在变长。

linguistic [lɪŋ'gwɪstɪk] *a.* 语言的，语言学的

【记】词根记忆：lingu(语言) + istic → 语言的

【例】She was capable of resolving the differences between two distinct *linguistic* systems. 她能够解决两种显著不同语言系统之间的差异。

lumber ['lʌmbər] *n.* 木材，木料(timber)

【派】lumbering(*n.* 伐木业，采伐林木)

luminous ['lu:mɪnəs] *a.* 发光的，明亮的(light)

【记】词根记忆：lumin(光) + ous → 发光的

【例】The most distant *luminous* objects seen by telescopes are very far. 通过望远镜见到的最远的发光体离我们非常远。

magnify ['mægnɪfaɪ] *vt.* 放大，扩大(increase)

【记】词根记忆：magn(大) + ify(使…) → 使…大 → 放大，扩大

| inception | insanity | interaction | lengthen | linguistic | lumber |
| luminous | magnify | | | | |

【例】Industrialization and geographic mobility tended to *magnify* social distinctions. 工业化和地理流动性很可能扩大社会差别。

【派】magnification(*n.* 扩大，放大倍率)；magnifying(*a.* 放大的)

meridian [məˈrɪdiən] *n.* 子午线

mind [maɪnd] *n.* 头脑；精神；理智，智能；想法；意见；心情；记忆
v. 注意，留心；介意，反对

【搭】sth. on one's mind 脑子中有太多事情要记；keep in mind 记住；have in mind 记住，考虑到，想到；make up one's mind 下决心；never mind 不要紧，没关系

【例】A: Would you *mind* me closing the window? It's so cold.
B: Of course not.
A：你介意我关掉窗户吗？太冷了。
B：当然不介意。

mineral [ˈmɪnərəl] *n.* 矿(物、石)(ore) *a.* 矿物的

【例】These sources don't increase the actual *mineral* composition of the water. 这些来源不增加水中实际的矿物成分。

【派】mineralize(*vt.* 使矿化)；mineralization(*n.* 矿化)；mineralogy(*n.* 矿物学)

mission [ˈmɪʃn] *n.* 代表团(delegation)；任务，使命(task)

【记】词根记忆：miss(送，放出) + ion → 代表团

【例】The homing pigeon can be trained to carry out the *missions* that people demand. 信鸽可以训练用来执行人们所要求的任务。

multiple [ˈmʌltɪpl] *a.* 多样的；多重的(various, manifold) *n.* 倍数

【例】Beautiful glass can be decorated in *multiple* ways. 漂亮的玻璃可以用多种方式装饰。

octopus [ˈɑːktəpəs] *n.* 章鱼

【记】词根记忆：octo(八) + pus → 长八条腿的鱼 → 章鱼

outcry [ˈaʊtkraɪ] *n.* 大声疾呼，抗议(protest, shout)

【记】来自词组 cry out 大声呼喊；强烈抗议

【搭】outcry against/about/over 反对…

【例】If the government continues to build a large parking lot in this area, there'll be a great *outcry* among the local people. 如果政府继续在这个地区建造大型停车场，就会引发当地人强烈抗议。

painstaking [ˈpeɪnzteɪkɪŋ] *a.* 煞费苦心的(diligent, industrious)

【记】组合词：pains + taking → 煞费苦心的

【例】Panel painting involved a *painstaking*, laborious process. 镶板绘画是个费心费力的过程。

| meridian | mind | mineral | mission | multiple | octopus |
| outcry | painstaking | | | | |

patch [pætʃ] *n.* 片，块（scrap）；斑纹（stripe）
v. 弄成碎片（to make of fragments）
【例】Sometimes the corn was roasted or *patched*, but most of the corn was dried on the card. 有时候玉米被烘烤或压成碎片，但是多数玉米在纸板上晾干。

patch

pepper ['pepər] *n.* 胡椒粉，胡椒；辣椒 *v.* 大量给予
【记】发音记忆："拍拍" → 拿着小罐拍点胡椒粉 → 胡椒粉
【例】Many people like adding white *pepper* to their dishes. 很多人喜欢往菜里加白胡椒。

perceive [pər'siːv] *vt.* 感知；察觉（see, observe）
【记】词根记忆：per(全部)+ceive(拿住) → 全部拿住 → 感知；察觉
【例】Art deco in its many forms was largely *perceived* as thoroughly modern. 很多形式的艺术装饰在很大程度上都被认为是完全现代的。
【参】perceptive(*a.* 有理解的)

pronounced [prə'naʊnst] *a.* 非常明显的（marked, distinct）；明确的（definite）
【记】来自pronounce(宣称，发音)+d → 被宣布的 → 明确的
【例】A *pronounced* division of labor exists, leading to the establishment of many specialized professions. 因为存在非常明显的分工，所以有了很多特殊的行业。

provincialism [prə'vɪnʃlɪzəm] *n.* 地方主义（regionalism, localism）；心胸狭窄
【搭】narrow-minded provincialism 狭隘的地方主义

pump [pʌmp] *n.* 泵 *vt.* (用泵)抽
【例】The sequoia tree can *pump* water to its very top, more than 100 meters above the ground. 红杉树能把水抽到离地100多米高的树顶。

recruitment [rɪ'kruːtmənt] *n.* 征募新兵；补充
【例】We should check whether there any questions about *recruitment*. 我们应该检查对征募新兵是否有疑问。

remainder [rɪ'meɪndər] *n.* 剩余物，残余（remains）
【记】分拆联想：remain(保留)+der → 被保留下来的东西 → 剩余物

retain [rɪ'teɪn] *vt.* 保持，留住（keep）
【记】词根记忆：re(回)+tain(拿) → 拿回来 → 保持，留住
【例】If suddenly cooled, the object *retains* the shape achieved at that point. 如果突然冷却，这个物体会保留当时的形状。

| ☐ patch | ☐ pepper | ☐ perceive | ☐ pronounced | ☐ provincialism | ☐ pump |
| ☐ recruitment | ☐ remainder | ☐ retain | | | |

reverse [rɪ'vɜːrs] *vt.* 反转 *n.* 反面 *a.* 相反的(opposite)

【记】词根记忆：re + vers(移动，转向) + e → 向回转 → 反转

【例】Roughly every six hours the river *reverses* direction. 大约每六个小时河流就转向。//You are the *reverse* of polite. 你没礼貌。

【派】reversal(*n.* 颠倒，倒转); reversible(*a.* 可反转的，可逆的)

segment ['segmənt] *n.* 段，部分(part, section)

【记】词根记忆：seg(=sect切割) + ment → 段，部分

【例】Social atomization affected every *segment* of society. 社会分化影响了社会的所有部分。

sprawl [sprɔːl] *vi. /n.* 扩展(expand); 蔓延(overspread)

【记】联想记忆：伸展手脚趴在地上(sprawl)潦草地写(scrawl)

spring [sprɪŋ] *n.* 弹簧; 泉(stream) *v.* 跳跃(leap, jump)

【记】分拆联想：sp + ring(铃声) → 泉水叮咚似铃声 → 泉

【例】The dog *sprang* over the ditch. 狗跳过了沟渠。

stadium ['steɪdiəm] *n.* 运动场(playground)

【记】词根记忆：stad(站) + ium(场所) → 站着看比赛的地方 → 运动场

storage ['stɔːrɪdʒ] *n.* 库房(warehouse); 贮藏，存储

【记】来自store(*v.* 储存)

【搭】storage space 储藏室; storage shed 仓库; storage battery 蓄电池

【例】Some fungi can grow at 500℃, while others can grow at -5℃, so even food in cold *storage* may not be completely safe from them. 有些真菌能在500摄氏度生长，有些能在零下5摄氏度生长，所以甚至冷藏的食品都不能完全免于真菌。

submarine [ˌsʌbmə'riːn] *n.* 潜水艇，潜艇

【记】词根记忆：sub(在下面) + marine(海的) → 在海下面行进的 → 潜艇

telescope ['telɪskoʊp] *n.* 望远镜

【记】词根记忆：tele(远) + scope(视野) → 望远镜

【派】telescopic(*a.* 望远镜的; 眼力好的; 能见远处的)

tragic ['trædʒɪk] *a.* 悲惨的(miserable); 悲剧的

【记】分拆联想：t + rag(破旧衣服) + ic → 穿着破旧衣服的乞丐过着悲惨的日子 → 悲惨的

【例】Arthur Miller's play *Death of a Salesman* is a *tragic* story. 阿瑟·米勒的剧作《推销员之死》是一个悲剧故事。

□ reverse	□ segment	□ sprawl	□ spring	□ stadium	□ storage
□ submarine	□ telescope	□ tragic			

uppermost ['ʌpərmoʊst] *a.* 最高的

【例】Small mammals suffered hardship in the exposed and turbulent environment of the *uppermost* trees. 小哺乳动物在树顶暴露和混乱的环境里经受了磨难。

urge [ɜːrdʒ] *v.* 促进，力劝(impel) *n.* 迫切要求

【例】Do you think we should *urge* Bob to study Spanish?你觉得我们应该劝鲍勃学习西班牙语吗？

【派】urgent(*a.* 紧急的)；urgency(*n.* 紧急，紧急情况)

vascular ['væskjələr] *a.* 血管的，脉管的

【参】muscular(*a.* 肌肉的)

vegetarian [ˌvedʒə'teriən] *n.* 素食者

【例】Obtaining enough protein in the diet is especially important for *vegetarians.* 对素食者而言，从膳食中获得足够的蛋白质尤其重要。

verify ['verɪfaɪ] *v.* 检验(check)，核实

【记】词根记忆：ver(真实的)＋ify(使…)→ 使…真实 → 核实

【例】While a person could describe his thoughts, no one else can see or hear them to *verify* the accuracy of his report. 一个人可以描述他的想法，但是没有人能看到或听到这些想法，无法验证他报告的确切性。

wit [wɪt] *n.* 智力，才智(intellect, cleverness)

【记】联想记忆：运用才智(wit)取胜(win)

【搭】be at one's wits' end 山穷水尽

withstand [wɪð'stænd] *vt.* 经得住，耐(*tolerate, endure)

【例】A desert animal can *withstand* high body temperatures.沙漠动物耐高温。

□ uppermost	□ urge	□ vascular	□ vegetarian	□ verify	□ wit
□ withstand					

Word List 31  MP3-31

词根、词缀预习表

bas	基础	base	n. 基础
calcul	计算	calculate	v. 计算，推测
condi	隐藏	condiment	n. 调味品
rud	天然的，粗糙的	crude	a. 天然的
decor	装饰	decorate	v. 装饰
fascin	捆住	fascinate	v. 迷住
migr	迁移	immigrant	n. 移民
rect	直，正	rectangle	n. 矩形

abreast [ə'brest] *ad.* 并列地，并排地(side by side)

【记】分拆联想：a + breast(胸) → 胸和胸并排 → 并列地，并排地

【例】Edison kept *abreast* of recent scientific developments. 爱迪生了解最近科学发展的情况。

absurd [əb'sɜːrd] *a.* 可笑的，荒唐的(ridiculous)

【记】分拆联想：ab + surd(无道理的) → 不合理的 → 荒谬的

【例】Don Quixote makes chivalry seem *absurd*. 堂吉诃德使骑士精神显得荒唐。

absurd

admission [əd'mɪʃn] *n.* 准许进入；入场费；承认(acknowledgement)

【记】来自admit(*v.* 承认；接纳)

【例】It was the first rodeo to charge *admission*. 这是第一次收入场费的牛仔竞技表演。

amino [ə'miːnoʊ] *a.* 氨基的

【搭】amino acid 氨基酸

appliance [ə'plaɪəns] *n.* 用具，器具

【记】来自apply(*vt.* 应用)

【例】The *appliances* in the kitchen are all made of stainless steel. 厨房里的用具都是不锈钢做的。

atom [ˈætəm] *n.* 原子；微粒，微量

【搭】atom of …的原子

【例】Coal contains fewer hydrogen *atoms* than oil. 煤炭比石油包含的氢原子少。

attendance [əˈtendəns] *n.* 出席(presence)；出席人数

【例】Movie *attendance* dropped when audience members chose to stay at home and be entertained. 观众选择待在家里娱乐时，去电影院的人就少了。

augment [ɔːgˈment] *vt.* 增加，增大(increase)

【记】词根记忆：aug(增加)＋ment→增加，增大

【例】While searching for a way to *augment* the family income, she began making dolls. 她在想办法增加家庭收入方式时，开始做玩偶。

barren [ˈbærən] *a.* 贫瘠的，荒芜的(*infertile, unproductive)

【记】发音记忆："巴人"→巴山蜀水间早不见荒芜的景象

【例】The farmer's soil was overworked and *barren*. 这个农民的土壤由于过度使用而变得贫瘠了。

base [beɪs] *n.* 基础，底部；基地，根据地 *v.* 把…基于，以…为根据

【记】词根记忆：bas(基础)＋e→基础

【搭】base on 基于…

【例】For most social insects, membership in a colony is *based* on how closely related they are genetically. 对多数社会昆虫而言，一个群落里的成员身份与他们的基因有密切关系。

calculate [ˈkælkjuleɪt] *v.* 计算(count, figure)；推测(speculate)；打算(intend)

【记】词根记忆：calcul(计算)＋ate(做)→计算，推测

【例】They *calculated* the length of triangle sides. 他们计算了三角形各边的长度。

【派】calculation (*n.* 计算)；calculator (*n.* 计算器)；miscalculate (*v.* 误算)

cart [kɑːrt] *n.* 大车；手推车(a small wheeled vehicle)

cavity [ˈkævəti] *n.* 腔；洞(pit, crater)

【记】来自cave(*n.* 洞穴)

【搭】cranial cavity 颅腔；body cavity 体腔

atom　attendance　augment　barren　base　calculate　cart　cavity

celebrate [ˈselɪbreɪt] *vt.* 赞美 (praise); 庆祝 (commemorate, observe)

【例】He decided to *celebrate* his birthday some other time. 他决定在其他时间庆祝生日。

chance [tʃæns] *n.* 机会 (opportunity)

【搭】by any chance 可能, 或许; by chance 偶然

【例】A: I can't seem to find my calculator. Did I lend to you by any *chance*?

B: No, but you are welcome to mine if you need it, as long as I get it back by Thursday.

A: 我好像找不到计算器了。我是不是借给你了?

B: 没有, 不过如果你需要可以用我的, 只要周四还给我就行。

circular [ˈsɜːrkjələr] *a.* 圆形的 (round); 循环的 (intended for circulation)

【记】词根记忆: circ(圆) + ular → 圆形的, 循环的

clinic [ˈklɪnɪk] *n.* 门诊部 (dispensary)

【例】In America, patients have to make an appointment with doctors in the *clinic* first. 在美国, 病人看病时需要首先和诊所的医生预约。

condiment [ˈkɑːndɪmənt] *n.* 调味品 (dressing, flavoring)

【记】词根记忆: condi(隐藏) + ment → 隐藏(坏味道)的东西 → 调味品

【例】This kind of substance is recognized as a very precious *condiment* and food preservative. 这种物质被认为是非常珍贵的调味品和食物防腐剂。

counseling [ˈkaʊnsəlɪŋ] *n.* 咨询服务 (professional guidance of the individual)

【例】Vocational education and *counseling* extended the influence of public schools. 职业教育和咨询扩大了公立学校的影响。

craftsman [ˈkræftsmən] *n.* 工匠

【例】In 15th century, Paris, as the capital of arts, attracted a vast number of *craftsmen*, architects and musicians. 在15世纪, 巴黎作为艺术之都吸引了大量工匠、建筑师和音乐家。

crude [kruːd] *a.* 天然的, 未提炼的 (unrefined); 粗糙的 (rough)

【记】词根记忆: c + rud(天然的, 粗糙的) + e → 天然的; 粗糙的

【搭】crude oil 原油

【例】Even now many species still lay eggs in this sort of *crude* nests. 甚至到现在很多物种仍然在这样粗糙的巢穴中产卵。

【参】rude(*a.* 粗鲁的)

| celebrate | chance | circular | clinic | condiment | counseling |
| craftsman | crude | | | | |

333

decorate [ˈdekəreɪt] *v.* 装饰（*adorn, ornament）

【记】词根记忆：decor(装饰) + ate → 装饰

【例】The stoneware is *decorated* with simple, abstract designs. 粗陶器由简单抽象的图案所装饰。

【派】decoration〔*n.* 装饰（品）〕; decorative(*a.* 装饰的); decorator (*n.* 油漆工)

dedication [ˌdedɪˈkeɪʃn] *n.* 奉献；题献词；(教堂等的)启用典礼

【例】Abraham Lincoln delivered his most famous address at the *dedication* of the soldiers cemetery in Gettysburg. 亚伯拉罕·林肯在盖茨堡士兵墓地揭幕礼上发表了最著名的演说。

delight [dɪˈlaɪt] *n.* 使人高兴的东西 *v.* (使)愉快(please)

【记】分拆联想：de(向下) + light(阳光) → 沐浴在阳光下 → 使愉快

【例】Their basic aim is to *delight* and instruct. 他们最基本的目的是使人愉悦，并提供指导。

【派】delighted(*a.* 欣喜的); delightful(*a.* 令人愉快的)

destruction [dɪˈstrʌkʃn] *n.* 毁坏，毁灭(destroy)

【例】Some citizens in New York seek to rescue historic buildings from *destruction.* 纽约的一些市民试图抢救历史建筑使其免于毁灭。

dinosaur [ˈdaɪnəsɔːr] *n.* 恐龙

【记】分拆联想：dino(恐怖的) + saur(蜥蜴) → 恐龙

【参】tyrannosaur霸王龙; tyrannosaurus暴龙; pterosaur翼龙

distinct [dɪˈstɪŋkt] *a.* 明显的(*visible); 明确的(definite); 不同的(*separate, *different)

【记】词根记忆：di(分开) + stinct(刺) → 分开刺 → 明显的

【例】Two *distinct* processes are involved in molting. 蜕皮包括两个明显不同的过程。

【派】distinction (*n.* 差别；特性); distinctive (*a.* 与众不同的); distinctly(*ad.* 清楚地)

disturbance [dɪˈstɜːrbəns] *n.* 干扰(interference); 骚动(stir)

【记】词根记忆：dis + turb(扰乱) + ance → 干扰

【例】Noise, in the technical sense, implies a random chaotic *disturbance.* 从技术层面讲，噪音就是通常不需要的无序杂乱的干扰。

同根词：undisturbed(*a.* 没受干扰的，安静的)

dominate [ˈdɑːmɪneɪt] *vt.* 支配(*monopolize); 控制(control, rule) *vi.* 盛行 (*prevail)

【记】词根记忆：domin(=dom支配) + ate → 控制；支配

| □ decorate | □ dedication | □ delight | □ destruction | □ dinosaur | □ distinct |
| □ disturbance | □ dominate | | | | |

【例】The states *dominated* economic activity during this period. 在这期间, 各州在经济活动中起主导作用。

【派】dominant(*a.* 有统治权的, 占优势的); dominance(*n.* 优势, 统治)

doubt [daʊt] *n. /v.* 怀疑, 疑惑(suspect)

【例】I *doubt* we'll need one table for eight. 8个人的餐桌不知道行不行。

A: I'm having a few friends over for a lunch tomorrow. It'll be great if you can join us.

B: I *doubt* I'll be able to make it. My brother is leaving for Chicago tomorrow afternoon. And I promised to give him a ride to the airport.

A: 明天中午我有几个朋友来吃午饭。你如果能加入我们就好了。

B: 恐怕我去不了。我哥哥明天下午要去芝加哥, 我答应送他去机场。

exceptional [ɪkˈsepʃənl] *a.* 异常的; 杰出的

【记】来自except(*v.* 除…之外)

【搭】a man of exceptional talent 具有特殊才能的人

fascinate [ˈfæsɪneɪt] *v.* 迷住(charm); 使感兴趣(attract)

【记】词根记忆: fascin(捆住) + ate → 捆住 → 迷住

【例】He is so *fascinated* that he decides to study meteorology. 他十分感兴趣, 决定学习气象学。

【派】fascination(*n.* 迷恋); fascinating(*a.* 吸引人的)

framework [ˈfreɪmwɜːrk] *n.* 原则, 思想; 构架(structure)

【搭】framework of …的构架

【例】This law will provide a *framework* for employers and employees to sign a contract. 这部法律将给雇主和雇员提供一个签订合同的构架。

freight [freɪt] *n.* 货运(cargo)

【记】分拆联想: f(看作for, 为了) + reight(看作weight, 重量) → 运费一般是按照货物的重量计算

【例】The fish was shipped in refrigerated *freight* car. 鱼用冷藏货车运输。

【派】freighter(*n.* 货船)

gland [glænd] *n.* 【解】腺

【记】分拆联想: g + land(地带, 地区) → 体内的特殊地带 → 腺

【例】Examples of exocrine glands are the tear *glands* and the sweat *glands.* 外分泌腺体的例子有泪腺和汗腺。

【派】glandular(*a.* 腺的; 似腺的)

【参】exocrine gland 外分泌腺

☐ doubt　　☐ exceptional　　☐ fascinate　　☐ framework　　☐ freight　　☐ gland

guilty ['gɪlti] *a.* 内疚的

【例】You are washing your car even on vacation. It makes me feel *guilty*. 你假期都洗车, 这让我感到内疚。

idealize [aɪ'diːəlaɪz] *v.* 理想化(transfigure)

【例】This is how Thomas Jefferson *idealized* the farmers at the beginning of the 19th century. 这就是托马斯·杰斐逊在19世纪初把农民理想化的样子。

【派】idealization(*n.* 理想化)

immigrant ['ɪmɪɡrənt] *n.* (从外国移入的)移民 *a.* 移民的, (从外国)移来的

【记】词根记忆: im(在…内) + migr(迁移) + ant(人) → 向内迁移的人 → 移民

immigrant

【例】Looking after the house and family was familiar to *immigrant* women. 料理家务、照顾家人对移民女性而言很平常。

【参】immigration(*n.* 外来的移民); emigrant(*n.* 移居外国者)

integrate ['ɪntɪɡreɪt] *vt.* 使成整体, 使成为一体

【记】词根记忆: integr(完整) + ate → 完整化 → 使成整体

【例】She *integrated* dance and plot. 她使舞蹈和情节成为了一体。

【派】integrated(*a.* 综合的; 完整的); integration(*n.* 融合, 综合)

interstellar [ˌɪntər'stelər] *a.* 星际的

【记】词根记忆: inter(在…之间) + stell(星) + ar → 星际的

【例】Spiral galaxies are well supplied with the *interstellar* gas in which new stars form. 螺旋状星系有很多星际气体, 在气体里面会形成新的恒星。

laundry ['lɔːndri] *n.* 洗衣店; 洗熨

【记】分拆联想: laun(看作lau, 洗) + dry(干) → 干洗店 → 洗衣店

【例】The dormitory *laundry* service gives out clean sheets each week. 宿舍洗衣服务部每周都会发干净的床单。

liberty ['lɪbərti] *n.* 自主, 自由(freedom)

【记】词根记忆: liber(自由) + ty → 自由, 自主

【搭】at liberty 自由的, 有空的

【例】The children are left at *liberty* to exercise their activities. 孩子们被允许自由活动。

meteorological [ˌmiːtiərə'lɑːdʒɪkl] *a.* 气象学的; 气象的

【记】来自meteorology(*n.* 气象学; 气象状态)

□ guilty	□ idealize	□ immigrant	□ integrate	□ interstellar	□ laundry
□ liberty	□ meteorological				

【搭】meteorological data 气象数据；meteorological instrument 气象仪器

【例】Scientists have studied *meteorological* records for nearly ten years. 科学家已经研究了近10年的气象记录。

midterm [ˌmɪd'tɜːrm] *a.* 中间的，期中的 *n.* 期中考试；(任期)中期；学期期中

【例】Next Friday, a week from today, is the *midterm* exam, marking the half way point in the semester. 一周之后，也就是下周五就进行期中考试，这标志着这个学期已经过了一半。

A: How about seeing the new movie at the North Park Theater tonight?

B: Sounds great. But I got go over my notes for tomorrow's *midterm*.

A: 今天晚上在北公园剧院看新电影如何？

B: 好是好，但是我要为明天期中考试复习笔记。

nap [næp] *n.* 小睡(doze)

【搭】take naps/a nap 小睡一下，睡午觉

nonetheless [ˌnʌnðə'les] *ad.* 虽然如此，但是

【例】We're proud of our father's achievement, but *nonetheless* I sometimes find it useless. 我们为父亲的成就感到骄傲，但是有时候我发现那没什么用。

pancreas ['pæŋkriəs] *n.* 胰腺

【记】分拆联想：pan(全部) + cre(生长) + as → 给身体生长提供激素的器官 → 胰腺

【搭】pancreatic juice 胰液

【派】pancreatic(*a.* 胰腺的)

passive ['pæsɪv] *a.* 被动的，消极的(inactive)

【记】词根记忆：pass(感情) + ive(…的) → 感情用事 → 被动的，消极的

【例】I urged my *passive* friend to be more assertive. 我鼓励消极的朋友要更加自信。

peculiar [pɪ'kjuːliər] *a.* 独特的(*distinctive)；罕见的(unusual)

【例】Each product had its own *peculiar* characteristics. 每个产品都有其独特的特点。

【派】peculiarity(*n.* 特性)

perishable ['perɪʃəbl] *a.* 易腐的，易坏的 *n.* 易腐物品

【记】分拆联想：perish(毁灭，腐烂) + able → 易腐烂、毁灭的东西 → 易腐的

【例】Most organic materials are *perishable*. 大多有机材料都容易腐坏。

pitch [pɪtʃ] *n.* 高度；音调(tone)

【例】A brass or woodwind player may hum while playing, to produce two *pitches* at once. 铜管或木管乐器演奏者可以在演奏时哼唱，同时产生两个音调。

【参】pitcher(*n.* 大水罐)

plain [pleɪn] *a.* 平的(even)；简单的，朴素的(unadorned) *n.* 平原，草原(grassland)

【例】Larry certainly made a mess of that *plain* job. 拉里确实把简单的工作搞砸了。

pliable [ˈplaɪəbl] *a.* 易弯曲的，柔韧的(flexible, supple)

【记】词根记忆：pli(=ply 弯，折) + able → 能弯曲的 → 柔韧的

【例】The sheet of plastic becomes very *pliable* when it is warmed. 塑料片加热后变得非常柔韧。

position [pəˈzɪʃn] *n.* 位置(location)；职位(*job)；立场(*status) *v.* 安置(install)

【例】In the rising wind, the boys have *positioned* themselves to counter balance the tilt of the boat as it speeds along in a choppy sea. 风越来越大，男孩们摆好姿势，来平衡在波浪起伏的大海中急速行驶船的倾斜。

precede [prɪˈsiːd] *vt.* 在…之前，先于(prior, forerun)

【记】词根记忆：pre(前) + cede(走) → 走在前面 → 先于

【例】The idea of sea-floor spreading actually *preceded* the theory of plate tectonics. 海底扩展的认识实际上先于板块构造学理论。

【派】preceding(*a.* 前述的；前面的)；unprecedented(*a.* 空前的)

【参】proceed(*v.* 进行，继续)

prosper [ˈprɑːspər] *vi.* 繁荣(flourish)；成功(succeed)

【记】词根记忆：pro(向前) + sper(希望) → 希望在前面 → 繁荣；成功

radius [ˈreɪdiəs] *n.* 半径；半径范围

【记】词根记忆：radi(光线) + us → 半径；半径范围

【例】The roads reached out to more than 80 satellite villages within a 60-kilometer *radius*. 这些道路通向方圆60公里内的80多个卫星村。

reapply [ˌriːəˈplaɪ] *v.* 再申请

【搭】reapply for sth. 再申请某事

| □ pitch | □ plain | □ pliable | □ position | □ precede | □ prosper |
| □ radius | □ reapply | | | | |

rectangle [ˈrektæŋgl] *n.* 矩形

【记】词根记忆：rect(直，正) + angle(角) → 矩形

【例】My garage is in the shape of a *rectangle*. 我的车库形状是矩形。

【派】rectangular(*a.* 长方形的，矩形的)；rectangularly(*ad.* 矩形地)

remaining [rɪˈmeɪnɪŋ] *n.* 剩余，残余(residue) *a.* 剩余的

【例】Their children were crowded into the few *remaining* classrooms in the school. 他们的孩子挤进了学校剩余的几间教室。

repel [rɪˈpel] *vt.* 驱除；排斥(exclude)

【记】词根记忆：re(反) + pel(推) → 反推 → 驱除；排斥

【例】The gravitation force makes stars *repel* each other rather than attract. 万有引力使恒星相互排斥而非吸引。

ridiculous [rɪˈdɪkjələs] *a.* 荒唐的，可笑的(absurd)

【记】词根记忆：rid(笑) + icul + ous(…的) → 被人嘲笑的 → 荒唐的，可笑的

【例】Never have I heard such a *ridiculous* excuse. 我从来没有听过这么荒唐的借口。

rotate [ˈrəʊteɪt] *v.* (使)转动(revolve)；(使)轮流(*alternate)

【记】词根记忆：rot(旋转) + ate(使…) → 转动

【例】It was difficult to move or *rotate*. 这很难移动或转动。

【派】rotation(*n.* 旋转)

scheme [skiːm] *n.* 计划，方案(plan, design)

【记】分拆联想：sch(看作school, 学校) + eme(看作theme, 作文) → 学校作文 → 计划，方案；注意不要和schema(*n.* 图表)相混淆

【搭】propose a scheme 拟定计划

【例】One of the earliest of these *schemes* was patterned on the human eye. 最初方案之一就是模仿人类的眼睛。

sensory [ˈsensəri] *a.* 感觉的(esthetic)；感官的

【记】词根记忆：sens(感觉) + ory → 感觉的

significantly [sɪgˈnɪfɪkəntli] *ad.* 值得注目地；相当地(considerably, profoundly, substantially)

【记】来自significant(*a.* 有意义的；重大的)

【例】The majority of farmers did not benefit *significantly* from it. 多数农民没有从中获得很大益处。

signify [ˈsɪgnɪfaɪ] *vt.* 意味(mean)

【记】词根记忆：sign(信号) + ify → 意味

rectangle	remaining	repel	ridiculous	rotate	scheme
sensory	significantly	signify			

【例】Dark clouds *signify* that it will rain soon. 乌云意味着很快会下雨。

【派】significant (*a.* 意义重大的；数量巨大的)；significance (*n.* 意义；重要性)

statistic [stə'tɪstɪk] *n.* 统计数值；[*pl.*] 统计学

【记】分拆联想：stat(看作 state，国家) + istic → 统计数值一般都是由国家或政府部门完成并公之于众 → 统计数字

【派】statistician(*n.* 统计员，统计学家)

stir [stɜ:r] *v.* 搅拌；煽动，刺激(provoke)

【记】本身是词根，意为：刺激

【搭】stir up 激起，鼓动，煽动

strict [strɪkt] *a.* 严格的(rigid)；精确的(precise)

【例】Dr. White enforces *strict* deadlines on lab work. 怀特博士对实验工作实施着严格的日期限制。

【派】strictly(*ad.* 严格地)

strict

subsist [səb'sɪst] *vi.* 存活，生存(exist)

【记】词根记忆：sub(下面) + sist(站) → 站下去，活下去 → 生存

【例】Many prehistoric people *subsisted* as hunters and gatherers. 很多史前的人靠狩猎和采集生存。

【派】subsistence(*n.* 生存，生计；存活)

tangle ['tæŋgl] *v.* (使)缠结(*twist) *n.* 混乱(mess)

【记】联想记忆：俩人缠结(tangle)在一起跳探戈(tango)

tornado [tɔ:r'neɪdoʊ] *n.* 飓风，龙卷风(whirlwind, gale)

【记】词根记忆：torn(转动) + ado → 转动的风 → 飓风，龙卷风

【搭】tornado cellar 飓风避难地下室

【例】The pressure at the center of a *tornado* is usually 13 pounds per square inch. 龙卷风中心的压力通常是每平方英寸 13 磅。

vehicle ['vi:əkl] *n.* 交通工具，车辆(carriage, conveyance)

【记】词根记忆：veh(带来) + icle(东西) → 载人的东西 → 交通工具

【例】Private companies built the roads, and collected fees from all *vehicles* traveled on them. 私营企业修建了道路，向路过的所有车辆征收费用。

vivid ['vɪvɪd] *a.* 鲜明的(bright)；生动的(lively)

【记】词根记忆：viv(生命) + id → 生动的；鲜明的

【例】Garlen gave a *vivid* description of Julie Peterson. 加林生动地描写了朱莉·彼得森。

【派】vividly(*ad.* 生动地，鲜明地)

wanna ['wɔ:nə] *v.* (=want to)想要

【例】Hey, Larry. *Wanna* meet a few of us for coffee in a little while? 你好，拉里。一会儿想和我们几个喝点咖啡吗？

wedge-shaped ['wedʒʃeɪpt] *a.* 楔形的

whereby [wer'baɪ] *ad. /conj.* 借以，凭

【例】There should be a compensation arrangement *whereby* workers cooperate. 应该有一个补偿安排，以使人们合作工作。

wispy ['wɪspi] *a.* 像小束状的，纤细的(slight)

【例】Objects in the universe show a variety of shapes: round planets (some with rings), tailed comets, *wispy* cosmic gas and dust clouds. 宇宙中的物体呈现各种形状（圆的行星（有些带环状物）、带尾巴的彗星、束状的宇宙气体和灰尘云。

yarn [jɑːrn] *n.* 纱，纱线(thread, wool)

【记】联想记忆：纱线(yarn)是论码(yard)卖吗？

Experience keeps a dear school, yet fools will learn in no other.
经验始终是收费高的学校，然而，笨汉非进此学校不可。

——富兰克林.*B.*(*Benjamin Franklin*)

Word List 32

MP3-32

词根、词缀预习表

clinic	门诊	clinical	*a.* 临床的
tempor	时间	contemporary	*a.* 当代的
drain	排水	drainage	*n.* 排出物
imper	命令	imperative	*a.* 必要的
term	术语	terminology	*n.* 术语，术语学
medic	医疗	medication	*n.* 药物治疗
myria	许多	myriad	*n.* 无数
pest	害虫	pesticide	*n.* 杀虫剂
potent	潜力	potential	*a.* 潜在的；可能的

abolition [ˌæbəˈlɪʃn] *n.* 废除，废止

【记】来自 abolish(*v.* 废除，废止)

【例】During the 1850s, reform movements advocating temperance and the *abolition* of slavery gained strength in the United States. 在19世纪50年代，提倡禁酒和废除奴隶制的改革运动在美国获得了发展。

【派】abolitionist(*n.* 废奴主义者)

accordion [əˈkɔːrdiən] *n.* 手风琴

advocate [ˈædvəkeɪt] *vt.* 提倡(recommend publicly)

[ˈædvəkət] *n.* 倡导者(*proponent)

【记】词根记忆：ad + voc (叫喊，声音) + ate → 为其摇旗呐喊 → 提倡

【例】They *advocate* the use of masonry in the construction of skyscrapers. 他们提倡在建造摩天大楼时使用石工。

【派】advocacy(*n.* 拥护，支持)

aria [ˈɑːriə] *n.* 独唱曲，咏叹调

arouse [əˈraʊz] *v.* 唤醒，唤起(awake)；激起，引起(evoke)

【记】联想记忆：a + rouse(唤醒，激起) → 引起，唤起，唤醒

□ abolition   □ accordion   □ advocate   □ aria   □ arouse

【搭】arouse one's anxiety/curiosity/interest 引起不安/好奇/兴趣；arouse sb.(from sth.)唤醒某人

【例】The strange behavior of the neighbor *aroused* Mike's curiosity. 邻居奇怪的举止引起了迈克的好奇。//Mary is *aroused* by clock alarm at 9 o'clock every morning. 玛丽每天早上9点被闹钟叫醒。

【参】arise(v. 出现，发生)

assert [əˈsɜːrt] vt. 断言，声称(affirm, declare)

【记】词根记忆：as + sert(插入) → 强行插入观点 → 断言，声称

【例】The new generation *asserts* its own style as the representative American art. 新一代声称自己的风格代表着美国艺术。

bagel [ˈbeɪgl] n. 一种圈状硬面包

【例】A: We'd better make sure we get to the presentation early tomorrow morning. The dean said there'll be *bagels* and pastries and fruit at party. But I have a feeling that they're going to go quickly.

B: I guess I'll bring my appetite.

A：我们最好确保明天上午早点去听报告。系主任说派对上会有硬面包圈、糕点和水果。但是我觉得它们会很快被吃光。

B：我想我会很有胃口的。

barber [ˈbɑːrbər] n. 理发师(haircutter)

【记】发音记忆："爸爸" → 爸爸是理发师

【例】I remembered to ask the *barber* not to cut my son's hair too short. 我记得告诉了理发师不要把我儿子的头发理得太短了。

barber

circumference [sərˈkʌmfərəns] n. 周边(periphery)；圆周 (the perimeter of a circle)

【记】词根记忆：circum(环绕，周围) + fer(带来) + ence → 带来一圈 → 圆周

【例】They have calculated the approximate *circumference* of the earth. 他们已经计算出了地球圆周的大概长度。

civil [ˈsɪvl] a. 公民的；市民的(civic)；国内的

【记】词根记忆：civ(公民) + il(…的) → 公民的

【搭】civil rights 公民权；civil war 内战；civil service 文职；行政事务

【派】civilian(n. 平民)

clinical [ˈklɪnɪkl] a. 临床的

【记】词根记忆：clinic(门诊) + al(…的) → 临床的

【搭】clinical trials 临床试验

【例】It's said the new drug against AIDS has reached the stage of *clinical* trials. 据说治疗艾滋病的新药已经到了临床试验阶段。

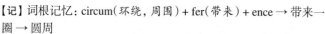

coalition [ˌkoʊəˈlɪʃn] *n.* 结合体，同盟；结合，联合（combination）

【记】联想记忆：co(共同) + ali(看作ally，结盟) + tion → 联合，结合

【搭】in coalition with 与…联合；the student action coalition 学生运动联盟

【例】I'm going door to door tonight to tell people about the student action *coalition*. 我今晚要挨家挨户告诉人们关于学生行动同盟的事情。//The environmental groups advocate healthy life in *coalition* with consumer groups. 环保组织与消费者组织联合倡导健康生活的方式。

competing [kəmˈpiːtɪŋ] *a.* 有竞争力的，不相上下的

【例】If one enterprise wants to survive the economic crisis, it must have its own *competing* products. 如果一个企业想在经济危机中生存，必须要有有竞争力的产品。

confine [kənˈfaɪn] *vt.* (to)限制(*restrict, *limit)

【记】词根记忆：con(加强) + fine(限制) → 限制

【例】The other early apartment buildings were *confined* to the typical New York building lot. 其他早期的公寓楼分布局限于典型的纽约建筑用地。

【派】confinement(*n.* 限制，禁闭)

confused [kənˈfjuːzd] *a.* 困惑的，不了解的(bewildered)

【例】Scientists are still *confused* with the virus killing many people. 科学家们仍然对杀死很多人的病毒感到困惑。

A: I'm so *confused* by my notes from Professor Johnson's lectures.

B: How about reviewing them now over a cup of coffee?

A: 我很头疼我在约翰逊教授课上记的笔记。

B: 边喝咖啡边复习如何？

consider [kənˈsɪdər] *v.* 认为(think)，把…看作；考虑，细想；体谅，照顾

【搭】consider sth. done 当作…做完了；consider to be 认为是

【例】Today we'll cover what we *consider* to be the two great periods of Wright's career. 今天我们将学习我们认为是赖特职业生涯的两个伟大阶段。

A: Which outfit should I wear to my job interview, the black dress or the navy blue suit?

B: Well, Jane, you've got to *consider* the image you want to present, and I say the suit is more professional looking.

A: 我应该穿什么衣服去参加面试？黑连衣裙还是海军蓝套装？

B: 嗯，简，你要考虑自己想展示的形象。我觉得套装看上去更职业一些。

contamination [kənˌtæmɪ'neɪʃn] *n.* 污染(pollution)，玷污

【记】联想记忆：conta(看作contra，反对) + min(最小) + ation → 污染再小也要反对，所谓"勿以恶小而为之，勿以善小而不为" → 污染

【例】In the 1970s, the peregrine falcons almost disappeared as a result of the *contamination* of the food chain by the DDT in pesticide. 在20世纪70年代，由于杀虫剂中的DDT污染了食物链，游隼几乎消失了。

contemporary [kən'tempəreri] *a.* 当代的，现在的（*existing, current) *n.* 同时代的人

【记】词根记忆：con(共同) + tempor(时间) + ary(人) → 同时代的人

【例】Her style is imitative of other *contemporary* authors. 她的风格模仿了其他当代作者。//At Harvard, he was a *contemporary* of Santayana. 在哈佛大学，他是与桑塔亚那同时代的人。

contest ['kɑːntest] *n.* 竞赛(game)；辩论(debate)

【记】词根记忆：con (共同) + test (测试，证据) → 共同接受测试 → 比赛

【派】uncontested(*a.* 无竞争的；无异议的)

deceptive [dɪ'septɪv] *a.* 欺骗性的(fraudulent)

【记】来自deceive(*v.* 欺骗)

【例】Its simplicity of appearance is *deceptive*. 它淳朴的外表具有欺骗性。

disguise [dɪs'ɡaɪz] *v./n.* 掩饰(mask)；伪装(pretend)

【记】dis + guise(姿态，伪装) → 掩饰；伪装

【例】These songs' origins cannot be *disguised* and therefore they belong primarily to the composer. 这些歌曲的起源不能被掩饰，所以它们主要属于这个作曲家。

drainage ['dreɪnɪdʒ] *n.* 排水；排泄；排出物

【记】词根记忆：drain(排水) + age(表集合名词) → 排水(系统)

【例】When the city was unearthed, archaeologists found that it had a perfect *drainage* system. 这个城市被发掘出来之后，考古学家发现它有完美的排水系统。

dull [dʌl] *a.* 单调的(*drab)；迟钝的(slow)

envision [ɪn'vɪʒn] *v.* 想象(imagine)

【记】词根记忆：en + vis (看) + ion → 用心去看 → 想象

【例】It wasn't until the 1920s that someone *envisioned* mass appeal for radio. 直到20世

纪20年代，才有人预见出广播对大众的吸引力。

factor [ˈfæktər] *n.* 要素，因素(element, ingredient)；因数；变量(variable)

factual [ˈfæktʃuəl] *a.* 实际的，真实的

【记】来自fact(*n.* 事实，真相)

【例】The story of the train may not be completely *factual*. 这辆列车的故事可能并非完全符合事实。

familiarize [fəˈmɪliəraɪz] *vt.* 使熟悉

【记】来自familiar(*a.* 熟悉的)

【例】They don't *familiarize* themselves with the campus. 他们对校园不熟悉。

fatigue [fəˈtiːg] *n.* 劳累(tire)；(金属材料等)疲劳

【记】分拆联想：fat(胖的)＋igue → 胖人容易劳累

【例】Metal *fatigue* is the tendency of metal to break under repeated stress. 金属疲劳是指金属容易在反复压力之下断裂。

flavoring [ˈfleɪvərɪŋ] *n.* 调味(品、料)

【记】来自flavor(*n.* 味道)

【例】The *flavorings* are added to give the fish some taste. 给鱼加了一些调料来提味。

homestead [ˈhoʊmsted] *n.* 家园；田产(lands)

【搭】the Homestead Act《宅地法》

【派】homesteader(*n.* 农场所有人)

hospitable [hɑːˈspɪtəbl] *a.* (气候、环境等)宜人的(pleasant)

【例】The climate is more *hospitable* in the sea. 海洋的气候更加宜人。

【参】hospital(*n.* 医院)

imperative [ɪmˈperətɪv] *a.* 必要的(necessary) *n.* 必要的事

【记】词根记忆：imper(命令)＋ative → 命令的 → 必要的

【例】With the gradual evolution of society, simple counting became *imperative*. 随着社会的逐渐演变，简单的计算变得有必要了。

independent [ˌɪndɪˈpendənt] *a.* 独立的；自立的(*autonomous) *n.* 无党派者

【例】She is very *independent*. 她非常独立。

【派】independently(*ad.* 独立地)

initiate [ɪˈnɪʃieɪt] *vt.* 开始(*begin)；开始实施

【记】词根记忆：init(开始)＋iate → 开始

【例】Those organizations *initiated* a rescue program. 那些组织开始实施了一项救援计划。

intelligent [ɪnˈtelɪdʒənt] *a.* 有才智的，聪明的(clever)

【例】He didn't realize how *intelligent* Mary really was. 他没有认识

| ☐ factor | ☐ factual | ☐ familiarize | ☐ fatigue | ☐ flavoring | ☐ homestead |
| ☐ hospitable | ☐ imperative | ☐ independent | ☐ initiate | ☐ intelligent | |

到玛丽有多聪明。

【派】intelligence(*n.* 智力)

ironically [aɪˈrɑːnɪkli] *ad.* 具有讽刺意味地，嘲讽地

【例】*Ironically*, a newspaper's richest, most instructive weather maps often are comparatively small and inconspicuous. 具有讽刺意味的是，报纸上最丰富、最有教育意义的气象图相对较小，也不起眼。

jar [dʒɑːr] *n.* 坛子；广口瓶 *vt.* 使震动

【记】联想记忆：酒吧(bar)里摆满了酒坛子(jar)

【例】Satire *jars* us out of complacence into a pleasantly shocked realization that many of the values we unquestioningly accept are false. 讽刺使我们受到震撼，摆脱自满，并且愉快地意识到我们不加怀疑地接受的很多价值观都是错的。

【参】ajar(*a.* 门窗等微开的)

labyrinth [ˈlæbərɪnθ] *n.* 迷宫；错综复杂的事件

【记】词根记忆：labyr（=labour努力）+ inth（里面）→ 在里面努力 → 迷宫

【例】In reality, the old castle itself is a *labyrinth* with dark corridors. 实际上，这座古老的城堡本身就是一座由黑暗走廊构成的迷宫。

line [laɪn] *n.* 线，绳；台词；路线，航线；排，行；线路，电线；界线，边线 *v.* 排队；加衬，作里

【搭】in line 成一直线，排成一行；in line with 和…成直线；与…一致，按照；line up 排队，使排成一行；hard line 强硬路线

【例】You'd better find another actor to play this role. The *lines* are so long. 你最好找别的演员表演这个角色。台词太长了。

A: Waiting in *line* to copy just one page of an article wastes so much time.

B: Have you ever tried the photocopier on the third floor of the library? I don't think many people know about it.

A：排队只复印一页文章太浪费时间。

B：你试过图书馆三楼的复印机吗？我觉得那个地方的人不多。

A: Look at all those cars *lined* up for the ferry. There must be forty ahead of us.

B: Yeah. I think it's going to be a while.

A：你看有那么多车排队等待轮渡。我们前面得有40辆车。

B：是啊。我想得等一会儿了。

【参】fine(*a.* 好的)；mine(*n.* 矿 *v.* 开采)

margin [ˈmɑːrdʒən] n. 边缘（*edge, rim）

【例】Predators find it easier to catch small birds perching at the *margins* of the roost. 食肉动物发现捕捉在栖息处边缘休息的小鸟更加容易。

marsh [mɑːrʃ] n. 沼泽，湿地（swamp）

【记】联想记忆：红军长征（march）过沼泽（marsh）

【派】marshy（a. 沼泽般的，沼泽的）

medication [ˌmedɪˈkeɪʃn] n. 药物治疗；药物（medicine）

【记】词根记忆：medic（医疗）＋ation（表物）→ 药物治疗

【搭】be on medication (for sth.)（为…病）而吃药

【例】A: Are your allergies acting up again? I thought your doctor gave you *medication* for that last week.

B: He did, but so far, it isn't helping much. I'm going to have to go back to try to get it changed.

A: 你又过敏了吗？我以为医生上周给你开过药了。

B: 药是开了，但是到目前为止用处不大。我要再去一趟让他换种药。

mild [maɪld] a. 【冶】低碳的；轻微的（slight）；温和的（temperate）

【记】联想记忆：温柔（mild）的 m 颠倒过来就是野蛮的（wild）

【例】The southwestern coastal region has a humid *mild* marine climate. 西南沿海地区是湿润温和的海洋性气候。

miracle [ˈmɪrəkl] n. 奇事，奇迹（wonder）

【记】词根记忆：mir（惊奇）＋acle（物）→ 奇事

【派】miraculous（a. 奇迹的；不可思议的）

motif [moʊˈtiːf] n. 主题，主旨（subject, mythos）；图形（*design）

【例】The sky seen from an airplane became one of her favorite *motifs* and the subject of her largest work. 在飞机上看到的天空成为了她最喜欢的主题之一，也是她巨著的主题。

multitude [ˈmʌltɪtud] n. 大群（a great number）

【记】词根记忆：multi（多）＋tude → 多的状态 → 大群

【搭】a multitude of 大量，许多

【例】The man used to have a *multitude* of friends. 这个男子过去有很多朋友。

mundane [mʌnˈdeɪn] a. 世俗的（earthly），平凡的（*ordinary）

【记】来自拉丁语 mundus（世界），联想记忆：mund（看作 mud，泥，尘）＋(d)ane（音似：淡）→ 来自尘土，归于尘土 → 世俗的，平凡的

【例】The thinker or philosopher stood apart from this *mundane* world. 思想家或哲学家与世俗世界有点格格不入。

myriad ['mɪriəd] *n.* 无数（innumerability）*a.* 无数的（numerous）；种种的（*many）

【记】词根记忆：myria（许多）+ d → 无数的；种种的

【例】A snowfall consists of *myriads* of minute ice crystals. 雪是由无数细小的冰晶体构成的。//In all its *myriad* forms, glass represents a major achievement in the history of technological developments. 玻璃有多种形式，这代表着技术发展的主要成就。

nectar ['nektər] *n.* 花蜜

【记】原指希腊和罗马神话中如花蜜般的神酒 → 花蜜

【例】Honeybees communicate the sources of *nectar* to one another by doing a dance in a figure-eight pattern. 蜜蜂通过跳8字舞相互交流花蜜的源头。

oasis [oʊ'eɪsɪs] *n.* 绿洲

olfactory [ɑːl'fæktəri] *a.* 嗅觉的

【例】The poisonous gas damaged my *olfactory* nerves. 毒气破坏了我的嗅觉神经。

optimal ['ɑːptɪməl] *a.* 最佳的，最理想的（optimum）

【记】词根记忆：optim（最好）+ al → 最好的 → 最佳的，最理想的

【例】This is the *optimal* time for harvesting apples. 这是收获苹果的最佳时机。

particle ['pɑːrtɪkl] *n.* 微粒，颗粒（fragment, grain）

【记】分拆联想：part（部分）+ icle（看作article，物品）→ 物品的一部分 → 颗粒

【例】The smoke *particles* are so small that they cool rapidly. 烟的微粒非常小，所以能迅速冷却。

pesticide ['pestɪsaɪd] *n.* 杀虫剂，农药

【记】词根记忆：pest（害虫）+ i + cide（杀）→ 杀虫剂

【搭】pesticide-free 无农药的

plight [plaɪt] *n.* 困境

【记】分拆联想：p（音似：不）+ light（轻松的）→ 不轻松的处境 → 困境

【例】Max sympathized with Bill, who was in a horrible *plight*. 马克思同情陷入可怕困境的比尔。

potassium [pə'tæsiəm] *n.* 钾

potential [pə'tenʃl] *a.* 潜在的；可能的（*possible）*n.* 潜能

【记】词根记忆：potent（潜力的）+ ial → 潜在的；潜能

【例】The agricultural *potential* of the area was enormous if water for irrigation could be found. 如果能找到灌溉用水，该地区的农业潜力就会很大。

【派】potentially(ad. 潜在地)

【参】patent(n. 专利)；potent(a. 有力的)

practical ['præktɪkl] a. 实用的；现实的(realistic)

【例】Her new hairstyle is more *practical*. 她的新发型更加实用。

refined [rɪ'faɪnd] a. 精致的(perfect, exquisite)

【记】来自refine(精制，精炼)＋d→精致的

【例】The higher the clay content in a sample, the more *refined* and durable the shapes into which it can be molded. 样品中黏土的含量越高，它能塑造的形状就越精致持久。

reflect [rɪ'flekt] v. 反射；反映(mirror)

【记】词根记忆：re＋flect(弯曲)→产生弯曲→反射

【例】What an insulator does is to *reflect* back the heat of burning fuel. 隔热装置的作用是反射燃烧燃料的热量。//Partly this decline *reflected* the low level of births during the depression and the war. 这种下降部分反映了大萧条和战争期间的低生育水平。

【派】reflection(n. 反映；考虑)；reflective(a. 反射的)；reflector(n. 反射体)

【参】self-reflective(a. 自省的)

revitalize [riː'vaɪtəlaɪz] vt. 使恢复生机 (*bring new life to)

【记】词根记忆：re＋vital (有活力的)＋ize →使恢复生机

【例】In numerous cities, art is being raised as a symbol of the commitment to *revitalize* urban areas. 在很多城市，人们把艺术提升为使城区恢复生机象征的保证。

复活吧

revitalize

roe [rou] n. 雌鱼腹中的鱼卵

【记】发音记忆："肉" → 鱼卵也是鱼妈妈身上的一块肉

【例】Sturgeons are prized for their blackish *roe*. 鲟鱼因其黑色鱼卵而受到珍视。

sake [seɪk] n. 缘故，理由(purpose)

【搭】for the sake of 为了

sample ['sæmpl] n. 样品，标本(specimen) v. 抽样调查

【记】联想记忆：简单的(simple)样本(sample)

【例】Fossils provide a limited *sample* of ancient organisms. 化石提供

| ☐ practical | ☐ refined | ☐ reflect | ☐ revitalize | ☐ roe | ☐ sake |
| ☐ sample | | | | | |

了古代生物有限的样品。

【派】sampling(*n.* 取样)

sequoia [sɪˈkwɔɪə] *n.* 美洲杉(redwood)

shallow [ˈʃæloʊ] *a.* 浅的(superficial)

【例】The beautifully preserved fossil fish lived in a vast *shallow* lake. 保存完美的化石鱼曾生活在一片广阔的浅水湖中。

statistics [stəˈtɪstɪks] *n.* 统计;统计数字;统计学

【例】According to the latest *statistics*, there are 23 million people who lose their jobs in Asia due to financial crisis. 根据最新的统计数字,由于金融危机,亚洲有2300万人失业。

statue [ˈstætʃuː] *n.* 雕像(sculpture)

【记】词根记忆:sta(站,立)+ tue → 雕像

【派】statuette(*n.* 小雕像)

【参】status(*n.* 身份,地位);statute(*n.* 法令);stature(*n.* 身长)

steer [stɪr] *v.* 驾驶;引导(guide)

【记】联想记忆:驾驶着(steer)一艘钢铁(steel)打造的大船

【例】Some of them *steer* by the position of the sun. 他们中一些人通过观察太阳的位置来驾驶。

【派】steering(*n.* 操纵,控制)

stock [stɑːk] *n.* 库存;股票(share) *v.* 储存(store)

【搭】stock market 股票市场;stock exchange 证券交易所;stock company 股份公司;stock up 备货,囤积

【例】The farmer *stocked* his ponds with fish. 这个农民在他的鱼塘里养了鱼。

submerge [səbˈmɜːrdʒ] *v.* 浸没,淹没(immerge)

【记】词根记忆:sub(在下面)+ merge(吞没)→ 被吞没下去 → 沉没,淹没

【例】The rest of the peninsula was *submerged*. 剩下的半岛被水淹没了。

【派】submerged(*a.* 淹没的;在水中的)

subsidy [ˈsʌbsədi] *n.* 补助金,津贴(*financing, allowance)

【记】分拆联想:sub(下面)+ sid(坐)+ y → 坐下来领补助金 → 补助金

subsistence [səbˈsɪstəns] *n.* 生存,生计,存活

【记】subsist(生存)+ ence → 生存,生计

【搭】minimum subsistence 最低生活必需

【例】*Subsistence* is impossible in such extreme conditions. 在这种极端的条件下生存是不可能的。

summit [ˈsʌmɪt] *n.* 峰顶，极点（peak）

【例】Scientists need to put a special receiver on the *summit* to receive signals from the satellites. 科学家们需要在山顶放置一个特殊的接收器来接收卫星发出的信号。

tarnish [ˈtɑːrnɪʃ] *v.* 使失去光泽，使变暗淡；败坏，玷污 *n.* 失去光泽，光泽变暗

【例】Sometimes, you can see a kind of *tarnish* color in the sky. 有时候，你可以在天空看到一种浅褐色。

technique [tekˈniːk] *n.* 技术（technology）；技能，技巧（skill）

【记】词根记忆：tech（技艺，技术）+ nique → 技术；技能

【例】He gave her some advice on painting *techniques*. 他给了她一些绘画技巧方面的建议。

telegraph [ˈtelɪɡræf] *n.* 电报（机）

【例】They tinkered with wireless *telegraphs* as a hobby. 他们把修理无线电报机当成了一种爱好。

temper [ˈtempər] *n.* 脾气，性情（mood, disposition）*vt.* 缓和，调节（modulate, moderate）

【记】联想记忆：情绪（temper）会影响体温（temperature）

【例】An excellent movie can lessen the girl's *temper*. 一部好电影能使这个女孩的脾气变得缓和。

tempt [tempt] *vt.* 诱使（entice, allure）

【记】本身为词根，意为：尝试 → 因为引起兴趣，所以要尝试

【派】temptation（*a.* 诱惑物）

【例】The government designs a new program to *tempt* young people into teaching in poor area. 政府设计了一项新的规划，旨在吸引年轻人去贫困地区执教。

【参】attempt（*n./vt.* 尝试，企图）

terminology [ˌtɜːrməˈnɑːlədʒi] *n.* 术语（term）；术语学

【记】词根记忆：term（术语）+ in + ology（…学）→ 术语（学）

【例】You're familiar with basic film *terminology*. 你熟悉基本的电影术语。

violently [ˈvaɪələntli] *ad.* 猛（激）烈地，极端地（awfully, extremely）

【例】The movie was *violently* criticized in the first show. 这部电影在第一场演出中受到了强烈批评。

词根、词缀预习表

quaint	知道	acquaint	vt. 使认识
her	粘连	coherent	a. 有黏性的;黏合在一起的
contra	反	contradict	v. 反驳
scend	爬	descend	v. 遗传
flu	流	effluent	n. 流出物,污水
hier	神圣	hierarchy	n. 等级制度
de	变慢	decrease	v. 减少

academy [əˈkædəmi] n. 研究会,学术团体;专门院校

【记】哲学家柏拉图常在园林小径上对向他求教的学生边走边讲,这种讲学方式被称为Academia,以后的教学机构沿用此名。

【派】academic(a. 学院的;学术的);academician(n. 学者;学会会员)

accident [ˈæksɪdənt] n. 意外事件,事故

【记】词根记忆: ac(加强) + cid(切,杀) + ent(表名词) → 不小心切了手 → 意外事件

【例】According to the new statistics, one in seven *accidents* is caused by drunken drivers. 根据最新的统计数据,7起事故中有1起是醉酒驾驶造成的。

【派】accidental(a. 意外的,偶然的);accidentally(ad. 意外地,偶然地)

accompany [əˈkʌmpəni] vt. 陪伴(attend);为…伴奏

【记】分拆联想: ac(加强) + company(公司;陪伴) → 陪伴

【例】She will *accompany* the man to the restaurant. 她会陪那名男子去饭店。//I need someone to *accompany* me while I play the piano. 我弹奏钢琴时需要人伴奏。

【派】accompanying(a. 陪伴的,附随的);accompaniment(n. 伴奏)

☐ academy ☐ accident ☐ accompany

acquaint [ə'kweɪnt] *vt.* 使认识(inform); 使熟悉(familiarize)

【记】词根记忆：ac + quaint(知道)→ 知道的很多 → 使熟悉

【例】She's well *acquainted* with the subject. 她对这个主题非常熟悉。

【派】acquaintance(*n.* 了解; 熟人)

adobe [ə'doʊbi] *n.* 泥砖，土坯

【记】分拆联想：a + do + be → 一次做完的土坯 → 土坯，泥砖

【参】abode(*n.* 住处)

amateur ['æmətər] *n.* 业余爱好者(non-professional)

【记】词根记忆：amat(=amor爱) + eur(人)→ 爱好的人 → 业余爱好者

【例】Chick Webb spotted her in an *amateur* competition when she was sixteen. 她16岁参加业余竞赛时，奇克·韦伯发现了她。

articulate [ɑːr'tɪkjələt] *a.* 有关节的

[ɑːr'tɪkjuleɪt] *vt.* 明确有力地表达(utter distinctly)

【记】词根记忆：art(关节) + icul + ate(…的)→ 有关节的

【例】Some species, such as ants, seem to be very *articulate* creatures. 一些物种，比如蚂蚁，好像是非常有表达能力的动物。

aspect ['æspekt] *n.* 方面(*facet)

asthma ['æzmə] *n.* 哮喘

【记】分拆联想：as + th(看作the) + ma(拼音：妈)→ 像大妈一样有哮喘病 → 哮喘

【搭】nasal asthma 鼻性哮喘; mild asthma 轻度哮喘

【例】Now I want to answer a question one of you asked me yesterday about *asthma*. 现在，我来回答昨天你们有人提的一个关于哮喘的问题。

avenue ['ævənuː] *n.* 途径(approach); 大街

barb [bɑːrb] *n.* 鱼钩，倒钩

【记】barb原也指倒翘的胡子，后来胡子一词变为beard

barb

barrel ['bærəl] *n.* 桶

【记】分拆联想：bar（横木）+ rel → 横木围住的桶 → 桶

【派】barrelful(*n.* 一桶之量)

bead [biːd] *n.* 珠子，水珠

【例】The Homestead Act of 1862 gave *beads* of families or individuals the right to own 160 acres of public land. 1862年的《公地放领法》保证了很多家庭和个人拥有160英亩公共土地的权利。

| ☐ acquaint | ☐ adobe | ☐ amateur | ☐ articulate | ☐ aspect | ☐ asthma |
| ☐ avenue | ☐ barb | ☐ barrel | ☐ bead | | |

clumsy [ˈklʌmzi] *a.* 笨拙的(awkward)

coherent [koʊˈhɪrənt] *a.* 有条理的；一致的；有黏性的；黏合在一起的

【记】词根记忆：co + her(粘连) + ent → 黏连在一起 → 有黏性的

【搭】coherent light 相干光(relating to or composed of waves having a constant difference in phase)

【例】Ethics is the branch of philosophy that deals with the values of life in a *coherent*, systematic, and scientific manner. 伦理学是哲学的一个分支，以连贯、系统和科学的方式研究人生的价值。

【派】cohesive(*a.* 凝聚的)；incoherence(*n.* 不连贯，语无伦次)

compass [ˈkʌmpəs] *n.* 罗盘；[*pl.*] 圆规；范围(range, scope)

【记】词根记忆：com(共同) + pass(通过) → 共同通过的地方 → 范围

【例】The television station broadcasts over a wide *compass*. 电视台播送节目的范围很广。

compose [kəmˈpoʊz] *vt.* 创作 (*create, devise)；组成 (constitute)；使安定 (calm, pacify)

【记】词根记忆：com(一起) + pose(放) → 放到一起 → 组成

【例】From these early sources she then began to *compose* original paintings. 之后，她就根据这些早期素材开始创作绘画作品了。// The nervous system is *composed* of many millions of nerve and glial cells. 神经系统由数百万的神经和神经胶质细胞构成。

concept [ˈkɑːnsept] *n.* 概念，思想(notion, thought)

【例】I'll give a lecture on the different *concept* of political thought. 我会就政治思想的不同概念做一次讲座。

【派】conceptual(*a.* 概念上的)

【参】conception(*n.* 观念)；misconception(*n.* 误解)；precept(*n.* 规则)

configuration [kənˌfɪɡjəˈreɪʃn] *n.* 构造，外形(structure, shape)

【记】来自configure(*vt.* 使成形)

【例】The awkward *configuration* of the kitchen is very inefficient. 厨房的布局别扭，很不实用。

consort [kənˈsɔːrt] *vi.* 结交(associate)

【记】词根记忆：con(共同) + sort(类型) → 同类相聚 → 结交

【例】Some colonial urban portraitists *consorted* with affluent patrons. 一些殖民时期的城市肖像画家与富有的赞助人结交。

【派】consortium(*n.* 协会，联盟)

【参】assorted(*a.* 各式各样的)；resort(*n.* 度假胜地；*v.* 采用)

| ☐ clumsy | ☐ coherent | ☐ compass | ☐ compose | ☐ concept | ☐ configuration |
| ☐ consort | | | | | |

constantly [ˈkɑːnstəntli] *ad.* 不断地，坚持不懈地（continually）；经常地（regularly, always）

【例】They ran back and forth *constantly*. 他们不断地来回跑。

contact [ˈkɑːntækt] *n.* 接触，联系 *v.* 接触（touch），联系

【记】词根记忆：con(共同)＋tact(接触)→接触，联系

【搭】in contact with 与…接触；与…保持联系；come into contact with 接触…

【例】Nowadays, more and more young people like wearing *contact* lens, but they don't know it may do harm to their eyes. 如今，越来越多的年轻人喜欢戴隐形眼镜，但是他们不知道这对眼睛有害。//If the deadline of leaving the dorm poses a problem for you, you should *contact* my office as soon as possible. 如果离开宿舍的最终期限对你来说是个问题，你应该尽快联系我的办公室。

A: Have you seen John since he started wearing *contact* lenses?

B: I almost didn't recognize him at first.

A：约翰开始戴隐形眼镜以来你见过他没有？

B：一开始我几乎没有认出他。

【参】contract(*n.* 合同)

contradict [ˌkɑːntrəˈdɪkt] *v.* 反驳（refute）；同…矛盾，同…抵触

【记】词根记忆：contra(反)＋dict(说话，断言)→说反对的话→反驳

【例】Newton's idea of gravity *contradicted* the idea of a universe that is static, unchanging. 牛顿关于引力的思想与宇宙是静止不变的观点相抵触。

【派】contradictory(*a.* 反驳的，反对的)；self-contradictory(*a.* 自相矛盾的)

correspond [ˌkɔːrəˈspɑːnd] *v.* 相符合（accord）；相应（match）

【记】词根记忆：cor(共同)＋respond(作出反应)→作出相同的反应→相应

【例】The majority of films made after 1927 *corresponded* to specific musical compositions. 1927年以后摄制的大部分影片与具体的音乐作品相对应。

【派】corresponding(*a.* 相应的；通讯的)

curiosity [ˌkjuriˈɑːsəti] *n.* 好奇心（desire to know）

【例】You really pick my *curiosity*. 你确实激起了我的好奇心。

declaration [ˌdekləˈreɪʃn] *n.* 宣言

【搭】Declaration of Independence《独立宣言》

【例】The president issued a *declaration* of war. 总统发布了战争宣言。

decrease [dɪ'kriːs] *v.* 减少(diminish, reduce)

['diːkriːs] *n.* 减少

【记】词根记忆: de(变慢)+ cre(生长)+ ase → 减少

【例】He thinks clothing prices will *decrease* even further. 他认为衣服的价格会进一步下降。

delectable [dɪ'lektəbl] *a.* 美味的; 使人愉快的(tasty, delicious)

【记】联想记忆: d+elect(选)+able → 能被选出来的 → 使人愉快的

【例】It is extremely *delectable* for us to have accepted your application for the membership of Student Union. 我们非常高兴接受了你加入学生会的申请。

dependable [dɪ'pendəbl] *a.* 可靠的, 可信赖的(reliable, trustworthy)

【搭】a dependable companion 可信赖的朋友

【参】affordable(*a.* 负担得起的; 提供得起的); changeable(*a.* 可改变的)

descend [dɪ'send] *v.* 遗传(inherit); 下降(fall)

【记】词根记忆: de(向下)+ scend(爬) → 向下爬 → 下降

【搭】be descended from 是…的后裔

【例】The octopus and the squid *descended* from earlier creatures with shells. 章鱼和鱿鱼是早期有壳生物的后代。

【派】descendant(*n.* 后代, 后裔); descendent(*a.* 派生的)

【参】decent(*a.* 正派的); descent(*n.* 下降; 衰落; 血统)

disrepute [ˌdɪsrɪ'pjuːt] *n.* 坏名声, 不光彩(discredit, dishonor)

【记】dis(否定)+ repute(名声) → 坏名声

diversion [daɪ'vɜːrʒn] *n.* 消遣, 娱乐(recreation, entertainment); 转移, 转换

【记】词根记忆: di(离开)+ vers(转)+ ion → 转移

【搭】created a diversion 分散注意力, 声东击西; diversion of …的转移

【例】Statistics showed that there was a *diversion* of funds from the manufacture to food industry in March. 统计数据显示, 三月份有资金从制造业转向了食品工业。

efficient [ɪ'fɪʃnt] *a.* 有效的, 有效率的(effective); 有能力的, 能胜任的

【记】词根记忆: ef(出)+ fic(做)+ ient(…的) → 能做出来的 → 有能力的

【搭】efficient energy 高效能量

【例】Comparing the new car to a moderately fuel *efficient*

conventional car, it can go 400~700 km on a tank of gas. 把这辆新车与燃油效率适中的传统车相比，它用一箱油能跑400到700公里。

【派】inefficient(*a.* 效率低的); efficiently(*ad.* 有效地)

【参】effective(*a.* 有效的)

effluent ['efluənt] *n.* 流出物，污水

【记】词根记忆: ef(出) + flu(流) + ent → 流出来的 → 流出物

【参】fluent(*a.* 流利的，流畅的)

emergence [ɪ'mɜːrdʒəns] *n.* 出现，浮现(appearance)

【记】来自emerge(*v.* 显现)

【派】emerging(*a.* 正在不断出现的)

entrenched [ɪn'trentʃt] *a.* 确立的; (风俗习惯) 不容易改的 (established, rooted)

exciting [ɪk'saɪtɪŋ] *a.* 令人兴奋的，刺激的

extra ['ekstrə] *a.* 额外的，附加的(additional) *n.* 附加物，额外的东西

【记】本身为词根: 额外的; 特别的

【搭】an extra day's time 再一天的时间

【例】A: Say, Richard. If you like antique cars, we've got an *extra* ticket for the auto show on Saturday. Care to join us?

B: Gee. How could I turn down an offer like that?

A: 理查德，如果你喜欢古董车，我们多一张周六车展的票。想跟我们一起去吗？

B: 太好了。我怎么能拒绝这样的邀请呢？

A: This is the second time this month that my boss's asked me to work *extra* hours. I am glad to get a bigger paycheck, but I just don't want her to give me such a heavy schedule.

B: Better watch your step. A lot of people would like to trade places with you.

A: 老板这个月第二次要我加班，多发工资我很高兴，但是我不想让她把我的工作安排得这么满。

B: 你还是小心为好。很多人都愿意和你换位置。

feat [fiːt] *n.* 功绩; 壮举(achievement, act, deed)

【记】分拆联想: f + eat(吃) → 取得了功绩，要好好吃一顿，犒劳一下 → 功绩; 壮举

【例】Acquiring their language is a most impressive intellectual *feat* for children. 习得语言是孩子们最了不起的智力成就。

filter ['fɪltər] *n.* 过滤器(strainer) *vt.* 过滤(percolate, screen)

【例】Springwater is clean, since it has been *filtered* through permeable

effluent　emergence　entrenched　exciting　extra　feat　filter

rocks. 泉水很干净，因为是由具有渗透性的岩石过滤的。

fragrant [ˈfreɪgrənt] *a.* 芬芳的，香的(aromatic, spicy)

【记】和flagrant(*a.* 恶名昭著的)一起记，fragrant中有两个"r"像两朵花，所以是"芳香的"

【例】The flowers emit a *fragrant* odor. 花朵散发出芳香。

【派】fragrance(*n.* 芬芳，香气)

gigantic [dʒaɪˈgæntɪk] *a.* 巨大的，庞大的(*huge, *enormous)

【记】联想记忆：gigant(看作giant，巨人) + ic(…的) → 巨大的

【例】Scientists speculate it might be a *gigantic* hurricane. 科学家们猜测那可能是一个大型飓风。

grain [greɪn] *n.* 谷物；颗粒(particle)；少量(a little)

【记】联想记忆：食用谷物(grain)对大脑(brain)的发育十分有益

【搭】go against the grain 与自己的性格、意愿格格不入

【例】There was at least a *grain* of truth in this. 这至少还有一点道理。

【派】grainy(*a.* 有明显颗粒的)

grudge [grʌdʒ] *n.* 怨恨(malice)

【记】联想记忆：去做苦工(drudge)肯定会怨恨(grudge)

gull [gʌl] *n.* 鸥，海鸥

【记】联想记忆：一只海鸥(gull)落在一只呆呆的(dull)公牛(bull)背上

【例】Most *gulls* keep the nest area clear. 多数海鸥保持鸟巢区域的清洁。

grudge

harness [ˈhɑːrnɪs] *n.* 马具 *vt.* 利用…产生动力

【记】分拆联想：har(看作hard，结实的) + ness → 马具通常都很结实 → 马具

【例】The waterwheel is a mechanism designed to *harness* energy from a source instead of animals. 水车是利用能源而非动物的机械装置。

henceforth [ˌhens ˈfɔːrθ] *ad.* 从此以后(*from that time on)

【记】组合词：hence(因此) + forth(往前) → 从此以后

【例】In 1926 he announced that *henceforth* his factories would close for the entire day on Saturday. 1926年，他宣布自己的工厂从此以后在周六都全天停工。

hierarchy [ˈhaɪərɑːrki] *n.* 等级制度；阶层(rank)

【记】词根记忆：hier(神圣) + archy(统治) → 僧侣统治 → 等级制度

【搭】social hierarchy 社会阶层

【例】The author puts honesty first in her *hierarchy* of values. 作者在

她的价值观体系中把诚实列于首位。

hint [hɪnt] *n.* 提示(cue)；[常*pl.*] 忠告(advice)

【记】分拆联想：hi(嗨) + nt → 向你打招呼，给你提示

【例】Our counselors will give you *hints* about successful interviewing. 我们的顾问将给你一些关于成功采访的建议。

hostile ['hɑːstl] *a.* 不友好的，敌意的(unamiable, unfriendly)

【记】分拆联想：host（主人）+ ile → 鸿门宴的主人 → 不友好的，敌意的

【例】The citizens were *hostile* to the report's conclusions. 公民们对报告的结论充满了敌意。

【派】hostility(*n.* 敌意，敌对)

implicit [ɪm'plɪsɪt] *a.* 含蓄的(implied)；绝对的(absolute)

【记】词根记忆：im(进入) + plic(重叠) + it →（意义）叠在里面 → 含蓄的

【例】The doctor gave an *implicit* answer. 医生给出了一个含蓄的回答。

【参】explicit(*a.* 清楚的；外在的)

infrastructure ['ɪnfrəstrʌktʃər] *n.* 基础设施

【记】词根记忆：infra(在…下) + struct(建筑) + ure → 基础设施

【例】Both the national and state governments developed transportation *infrastructure*. 国家和州政府都发展了运输基础设施。

jaw [dʒɔː] *n.* 颌，颚；[常*pl.*] 嘴(包括颌骨和牙齿)

【记】发音记忆："嚼" → 他下颌脱臼了，没法嚼东西

legislation [ˌledʒɪs'leɪʃn] *n.* 法律，法规(law)；立法(lawmaking)

【例】The intent of this *legislation* was to provide protection to selected coastal habitats. 该立法的目的是保护所选择范围内的沿海栖息地。

level ['levl] *n.* 水平(高度)(altitude)；级别 *a.* 水平的(horizontal) *vt.* 夷平，使平坦

【例】I just had to get his signature to take an upper *level* seminar. 我必须得到他的签名，才能参加高水平的研讨会。//The mountains were *leveled* and their debris dumped into the oceans. 山脉被夷平，碎片被投入了海中。

locomotive [ˌloʊkə'moʊtɪv] *n.* 机车(engine) *a.* 运动的(kinetic)

【例】In the nineteenth century, North American *locomotives* ran on hardwood fuel. 在19世纪，北美的机车依靠硬木燃料运行。//The "railroad novel" offers the ambience of station yards and *locomotive* cabs. "铁路小说"描绘了站台和机车驾驶室的氛围。

lubricant ['luːbrɪkənt] *n.* 润滑剂

| hint | hostile | implicit | infrastructure | jaw | legislation |
| level | locomotive | lubricant | | | |

【记】词根记忆：lubric(光滑) + ant(表物) →(使)变光滑的东西 →
润滑剂

mediate [ˈmiːdieɪt] v. 调解，调停(reconcile)

【记】词根记忆：medi(中间) + ate → 在中间做调停，调解
注意不要和meditate(v. 沉思)相混淆

【例】The National Academy of Design *mediated* conflicts between
artists. 国家设计研究院调解了艺术家之间的冲突。

mosquito [məˈskiːtoʊ] n. 蚊子(skeeter)

【记】发音记忆："貌似黑头" → 像鼻子上的黑头 → 蚊子

participate [pɑːrˈtɪsɪpeɪt] v. (in)参与，参加(take part in)

【记】分拆联想：parti(看作party, 晚会) + cip(抓，拿) + ate(做) →
找人参加派对 → 参与

【例】They *participated* in the last three races. 他们参加了最后三项
比赛。

【派】participation(n. 参与)；participator(n. 参与者)
同根词：participant(n. 参与者)

patronage [ˈpætrənɪdʒ] n. 赞助，支持(sponsor, support)；保护

【记】来自patron(赞助人) + age(行为) → 赞助；支持

【例】The antique shop wanted to encourage *patronage* by wealthy
customers. 古董店想鼓励富有的顾客光顾。

perform [pərˈfɔːrm] vt. 表演；执行(enact, execute)

【记】分拆联想：per + form(形式) → 综合各种艺术形式 → 表演

【例】They *perform* their music as a means of individual self-
expression. 他们把演奏音乐当作自我表现的一种方式。

【派】performance(n. 表演；执行；绩效)；performer(n. 表演者)

prize [praɪz] v. 珍视(value)；估价(rate) n. 奖品(award)；奖金(premium)

【例】Sturgeons are *prized* for their blackish roe. 鲟鱼因其黑色的鱼
卵而受到珍视。

radar [ˈreɪdɑːr] n. 雷达

【记】发音记忆

reciprocity [ˌresɪˈprɑːsəti] n. 互惠

【例】It can be approached only when the agreement is based on the
reciprocity. 只有当协议基于互惠互利时才能处理这个问题。

refer [rɪˈfɜːr] v. (to)提到，涉及到(relate to)；参考(consult)

【记】词根记忆：re + fer(带来，拿来) → 提到，涉及到

rigor [ˈrɪɡər] n. 严格(strictness)

【例】Everyone has to understand the utmost *rigor* of the law. 每个人

mediate　mosquito　participate　patronage　perform　prize
radar　reciprocity　refer　rigor
361

都得理解法律最严格的规定。

【派】rigorous(*a.* 严格的)

sculpture [ˈskʌlptʃər] *n.* 雕刻术(engraving)；雕塑品(carving)

【搭】sculpture painting 浅浮雕

sew [soʊ] *v.* 缝(纫)

【记】和sow(*v.* 播种)一起记

【派】sewing(*n.* 缝纫)

sharpen [ˈʃɑːrpən] *v.* 削尖；使敏锐，使敏捷；陡峭；清晰

【记】来自sharp(锋利的)＋en → 使锋利 → 使尖锐

【例】A: I'm having trouble slicing the bread with this knife.

B: Oh. Sorry about that. I haven't gotten around to *sharpening* it yet.

A: 我用这把刀切面包有困难。

B: 噢。对不起。我一直没空磨那把刀。

【参】shorten(*v.* 缩短)；strengthen(*v.* 加强，巩固)；lengthen(*v.* 延长)

spawn [spɔːn] *v.* 产(卵)(fertilize)；产生，促成(*create, bring forth)

【记】联想记忆：大虾(prawn)产卵(spawn)

【例】They could induce oysters to *spawn* not only in the summer but also in the fall. 他们可以诱使牡蛎不仅在夏天还在秋天产卵。

speculate [ˈspekjuleɪt] *v.* 推测(*hypothesize)

【记】词根记忆：spec(看)＋ulate → 看了以后再推测 → 推测

【例】Although scientists can *speculate* about its nature, neither humans nor machines will ever be able to visit it. 尽管科学家们能猜测其性质，但人类和机器都不可能造访那里。

【派】speculation(*n.* 推测)；speculative(*a.* 推测的；投机的)；speculator(*n.* 投机者)

squabble [ˈskwɑːbl] *v. /n.* 口角；争吵(quarrel)

【例】A: It's not fun being around Debbie and Mike these days. All they do is quarrel.

B: I've noticed it too. I wish they would keep their *squabbles* to themselves.

A: 这些日子跟德比和迈克在一起不好玩，他们老吵架。

B: 我也注意到了。希望他们的争吵不要影响别人。

stress [stres] *n.* 压力(pressure)；强调(emphasis) *v.* 强调(*emphasize)

【派】stressful(*a.* 充满压力的)

subversive [səbˈvɜːrsɪv] *a.* 颠覆性的，破坏性的

sculpture	sew	sharpen	spawn	speculate	squabble
stress	subversive				

symmetry [ˈsɪmətri] *n.* 对称(性), 均衡

【记】词根记忆: sym(共同) + metr(测量) + y → 测量结果相同 → 对称, 均衡

【搭】radial symmetry 径向对称, 放射对称

track [træk] *n.* 跑道, 小路(path); 轨迹, 轮迹 *v.* 跟踪, 追踪

【记】联想记忆: 原声大碟 Original Sound Track

【例】A: You certainly have a lot of clocks. There seems to be one in every room.

B: My family gave them to me because I have trouble keeping *track* of the time.

A: 你的钟表真多。好像每个房间都有一个。

B: 都是我家人给的, 因为我老忘时间。

The speeds of these birds can be *tracked* by orbiting satellites, by means of transmitters attached to the bird. 环绕轨道运行的卫星通过绑在鸟身上的发射机跟踪它们的飞行速度。

【参】trace(*n.* 痕迹, 踪迹 *v.* 追踪)

turkey [ˈtɜːrki] *n.* 火鸡(肉)

【记】联想记忆: 土耳其(Turkey)的火鸡(turkey)最好吃

unify [ˈjuːnɪfaɪ] *vt.* 统一(unite)

【记】词根记忆: uni(单一) + fy(表动词) → 统一

【例】The area was economically *unified*. 这个地区在经济上实现了统一。

visualize [ˈvɪʒuəlaɪz] *v.* 想象, 形象化

【记】词根记忆: vis(看) + ual + ize → 使…看见 → 想象

【搭】visualize sb. doing sth. 设想某人做某事

【例】An architect can take a look at a drawing and *visualizes* the shape of the building. 建筑师看一眼设计图, 就能想象出建筑物的形状。

zone [zoʊn] *n.* 地域, 地带(region, area)

【派】zoning(*n.* 分区制)

Word List 34  MP3-34

词根、词缀预习表

esthe	感觉	aesthetic	*a.* 美学的；审美的
pile	堆	compile	*vt.* 汇编；编辑
ate	表示动作	cultivate	*vt.* 耕种；培养
kine	动	kinetic	*a.* 运动的
mechan	机械	mechanic	*n.* 机修工
pan	全部	panorama	*n.* 全景
sedi	坐	sediment	*n.* 沉淀物
soci	结交	sociable	*a.* 好交际的

accomplished [əˈkɑːmplɪʃt] *a.* 多才多艺的（all-round）；完成了的（*achieved）
【例】They were *accomplished* musicians. 他们是多才多艺的音乐家。

aesthetic [esˈθetɪk] *a.* 美学的（artistic）；审美的
【记】词根记忆：a + esthe(感觉) + tic(…的) → 美学的；审美的
【例】One of the oldest types of *aesthetic* theory is that of formalism.
最古老的美学理论类型之一就是形式主义。
【派】aesthetically(*ad.* 审美地)；aesthetics(*n.* 美学)

alert [əˈlɜːrt] *a.* 机警的（*vigilant, watchful）*vt.* 提醒（*ware, remind）
【记】Red Alert"红色警戒"，20世纪90年代风靡全球的电脑游戏
【例】I want something that will keep me *alert* in class. 我想要能让我
上课提神的东西。//Fire ants make use of an alarm pheromone to
alert workers to an emergency. 火蚁利用一种报警信息素来提醒工
蚁会出现的紧急情况。

approach [əˈproutʃ] *vt. /n.* 接近（near）*n.* 方法（way），手段（measure）
【记】词根记忆：ap + proach(接近) → 接近；方法
【例】Our bus is *approaching* Cambridge where we'll be stopping to
eat. 我们的公交车快到剑桥了，我们要在那里停下来吃饭。//to
change students' *approach* to writing 改变学生写作的方法

audition [ɔːˈdɪʃn] *n.* 旁听；试演(rehearsal)

【例】You won't need a text for the *audition*. 你旁听不需要课本。// He plans to sing a song at the *audition*. 他计划在试镜时唱一首歌。

biography [baɪˈɑːɡrəfi] *n.* 传记

【记】词根记忆：bio(生命) + graph(写) + y → 记录生命 → 传记

【派】biographical(*a.* 传记的)；biographer(*n.* 传记作者)

brighten [ˈbraɪtn] *vt.* 使快活

【例】The flowers in the window really *brighten* my spirits. 橱窗里的花确实让我精神愉快。

【派】brightly(*ad.* 明亮地)；brightness(*n.* 光亮，明亮)

buck [bʌk] *n.* 美元

burgeon [ˈbɜːrdʒən] *vi.* 迅速成长，发展(bloom, flourish)

【记】词根记忆：burg(=bud 花蕾) + eon → 花蕾迅速成长 → 迅速成长；注意burg本身一个是单词，意为"城，镇"

【例】As the number of wage earners in manufacturing rose, the number of huge plants in Philadelphia *burgeoned*. 随着制造业雇佣劳动者数量的增加，在费城大型工厂的数量也在迅速增长。

campaign [kæmˈpeɪn] *n.* 竞选活动 *vi.* 竞选；参加战斗

【记】分拆联想：camp(野营地，引申为军队行军) + aign → 参加战斗

【例】Mary shouldn't have *campaigned* against Steve. 玛丽本不应该开展反史蒂夫的运动的。

carbon [ˈkɑːrbən] *n.* 碳

【搭】carbon dioxide 二氧化碳；carbon monoxide 一氧化碳

【参】carbonate(*n.* 碳酸盐)

career [kəˈrɪr] *n.* 生涯，经历；职业(profession)，专业

【记】和同音词Korea(*n.* 韩国)一起记

【例】The *career* advisory service here on campus can help you prepare your cover letters. 校园里的职业咨询服务能帮助你准备求职附函。

A: The conference on *career* planning is only a month away, but there are still a few things that our organizing committee needs to work out.

B: Then it's clear that we'd better meet again and soon, would you mind setting it up?

A：还有一个月就要召开职业规划会议了，但是我们组委会还有一些事情需要解决。

B：显然，我们最好尽快再开一次会。你介意安排一下吗？

【参】cancer(*n.* 癌症)

centric [ˈsentrɪk] *a.* 中心的，中央的

【搭】ego centric 以自我为中心的

【例】Anyone who wants to make friends with others should not be ego *centric*. 任何想和他人交朋友的人都不应该以自我为中心。

chaos [ˈkeɪɑːs] *n.* 混乱（muddle, disorder）

【记】发音记忆：音近似汉语"吵死" → 混乱

【例】Unprecedented change in the nation's economy would bring social *chaos*. 这个国家前所未有的经济变化将会导致社会动乱。

【派】chaotic(*a.* 混乱的，无秩序的); chaotically(*ad.* 混乱地)

climate [ˈklaɪmət] *n.* 气候；社会风气

【例】Economic globalization has become a trend in the current economic *climate*. 经济全球化已经成为了当前经济气候的一个趋势。

compile [kəmˈpaɪl] *vt.* 收集(资料等)；汇编(*put together)；编辑(edit)

【记】词根记忆：com + pile(堆) → 堆积一起 → 汇编

【例】Computers can quickly *compile* and analyze this large volume of weather information. 电脑能快速收集并分析大量的气象信息。

consequence [ˈkɑːnsəkwens] *n.* 结果(outcome)；影响(influence)；推理(inference)

【记】词根记忆：con + sequ(跟随) + ence → 跟随其后 → 结果；影响

【搭】in consequence of 由于…的缘故

【例】The extinction of a few species is a *consequence* of human progress. 一些物种灭绝是人类发展过程的结果。//The relative importance of each consideration or *consequence* is determined. 每种考虑或后果的相对重要性都是确定的。

【派】consequent(*a.* 随之发生的)

controversy [ˈkɑːntrəvɜːrsi] *n.* 争论，辩论(dispute, argument)

【记】词根记忆：contro(相反) + vers(转) + y → 意见转向相反的方向 → 争论，辩论

【例】Peary's claim was surrounded by *controversy*. 皮尔里的声明饱受争议。

【派】controversial(*a.* 争议的)

controversy

conversational [ˌkɑːnvərˈseɪʃənl] *a.* 对话的，会话的

【例】The freshman valued himself on his *conversational* power when he first came to the college. 这位一年级学生刚到学院时，以他的对话能力而自诩。

corona [kə'rəʊnə] *n.* 日冕（sunglow），光环（aura）

【例】By the time the Sun's *corona* rays reach the Earth, they are weak and invisible. 日冕的光线到达地球时已经微弱得看不见了。

crazy ['kreɪzi] *a.* 疯狂的，狂热的（insane, deranged）

【派】craze(*n.* 狂热)

cultivate ['kʌltɪveɪt] *v.* 耕种；培养（bring up, foster）；建立；加强；结交

【记】词根记忆：cult(培养，种植) + iv + ate(表动作) → 耕种；培养

【例】Expressive leaders *cultivate* a personal relationship with staff in the group. 富有表现力的领导与小组成员建立了一种私人关系。

【派】cultivation(*n.* 耕种；培养)

diameter [daɪ'æmɪtər] *n.* 直径

【记】词根记忆：dia(对面) + meter(计量，测量) → 量到对面的线 → 直径

equivalent [ɪ'kwɪvələnt] *a.* 相同的（identical）；相当的（*interchangeable）*n.* 对等物（equal）

【记】词根记忆：equi(平等) + val(强壮的) + ent → 力量平等 → 相同的

【例】American children's stories differed from their British *equivalents*. 美国儿童故事与英国的儿童故事不同。

fragile ['frædʒl] *a.* 易碎的（brittle）；脆弱的（delicate, frail）

【例】His muscle fibers were short and *fragile*. 他的肌肉纤维短而脆弱。

【派】fragility(*n.* 脆弱)

generous ['dʒenərəs] *a.* 慷慨的（unselfish）；大量的（plentiful）

【记】词根记忆：gener(产生) + ous → 产生很多的 → 大量的

【例】After the Civil War, politicians rarely opposed the government's *generous* support to business owners. 内战之后，政客们很少反对政府对企业家的慷慨支持。

【派】generosity(*n.* 慷慨，大方)

giant ['dʒaɪənt] *a.* 巨大的（immense）；超群的（outstanding）*n.* 巨大的动植物

【记】分拆联想：gi + ant(蚂蚁) → 蚂蚁虽小，团结的力量却是巨大的 → 巨大的

【例】A galaxy is *giant* family of many millions of stars. 星系是成千上百万恒星组成的一个巨大家族。

glacier ['gleɪʃər] *n.* 冰川；冰河

【例】The *glaciers* that reached the Pacific Coast were valley *glaciers*. 延伸到太平洋沿岸的冰川是山谷冰川。

corona	crazy	cultivate	diameter	equivalent	fragile
generous	giant	glacier			

gnaw [nɔː] *v.* 啃(nibble)；咬(bite)
【派】gnawing(*a.* 咬的；折磨人的)

gulf [gʌlf] *n.* 海湾(bay)；分歧(branching, divergence)
【记】联想记忆：海湾(gulf)国家的富豪们喜欢玩高尔夫(golf)
【例】Did you know that 90% of the coast is eroding the *Gulf* of Mexico?你知道墨西哥湾90%的海岸都正受到侵蚀吗？//A *gulf* that seemed unbridgeable was created between husbands and wives at times. 丈夫和妻子之间不时会出现似乎无法逾越的鸿沟。

host [houst] *n.* 主人(master)；【生】寄主(a living animal or plant on or in which a parasite lives)
【搭】be host to(作为主人)招待或款待
【例】The parasite lives on its *host*'s blood. 寄生虫以宿主的血液为生。

humidity [hjuːˈmɪdəti] *n.* 湿气，湿度
【记】humid(*a.* 潮湿的)的名词形式
【搭】relative humidity 相对湿度
【例】People living in this area have to endure the relatively high *humidity* in summer. 在这个地区生活的人们不得不忍受夏天很重的湿气。
【派】humid(*a.* 潮湿的)

initially [ɪˈnɪʃəli] *ad.* 开头，最初；首先(*at first)
【例】One characteristic of jazz is a rhythmic drive that was *initially* called "hot" and later "swing". 爵士乐的一个特点是节奏感强，富有活力，这起初被称为"热辣"，后来被称为"摇摆"。

intellect [ˈɪntəlekt] *n.* 智力，理解力
【记】词根记忆：intel(在…之间) + lect(选择) → 能在很多事物中做出选择的能力 → 智力，理解力
【例】As a child, sculptor Anne Whitney showed a high-level *intellect* and artistic talent. 雕塑家安妮·惠特尼小时候就表现出了极强的理解能力和艺术天赋。
【派】intellectual(*a.* 智力的 *n.* 知识分子)

internal [ɪnˈtɜːrnl] *a.* 内在的，内部的(interior)
【例】There are two categories of reasons: *internal* factors and external factors. 存在两类原因：内部原因和外部原因。
【派】internally(*ad.* 在内，在中心)
【参】external(*a.* 外在的，外部的)

irregular [ɪˈregjələr] *a.* 不规则的，不整齐的
【搭】an irregular coast line 曲折的海岸线

| □ gnaw | □ gulf | □ host | □ humidity | □ initially | □ intellect |
| □ internal | □ irregular | | | | |

【派】irregularity(*n.* 不规则性，无规律性)

jumble ['dʒʌmbl] *vt.* 混杂(mix)

【记】分拆联想：jum(看作jump，跳) + ble → 上蹿下跳，群魔乱舞 → 混杂

【例】Swift currents and waves *jumble* and carry away small bones of the dead animals. 湍急的水流和波浪裹挟着死亡动物的小块骨头。

kinetic [kɪ'netɪk] *a.* 运动的，运动引起的

【记】词根记忆：kine(动) + tic → 运动的

【搭】kinetic energy 动能；kinetic molecular theory 分子运动论

【例】Each fragment's immense *kinetic* energy was transformed into heat. 每个碎片产生的巨大动能被转化为热能。

libel ['laɪbl] *vt.* 以文字损害名誉，诽谤 *n.* 诽谤(罪)；诽谤的文字(或图画等)

【记】词根记忆：lib(文字) + el → 用文字的 → 诽谤

【参】label(*n.* 标签)

lightning ['laɪtnɪŋ] *n.* 闪电

【记】light(光) + ning → 极强的光 → 闪电

【例】Although thunder and *lightning* are produced at the same time, light waves travel faster than sound waves do. 尽管雷鸣和闪电同时产生，但光波传播速度要快于声波。

linear ['lɪniər] *a.* 线的，直线的；线性的

【记】分拆联想：line(直线) + ar → 线的，直线的

【搭】linear algebra 线性代数

maneuver [mə'nuːvər] *vt.* 操纵(manipulate) *n.* 策略(strategy)；花招(trick)

【记】词根记忆：man(手) + euver(工作) → 用手来做 → 操纵

【例】It is critical for *maneuvering* them between the scales and spreading the scales apart. 在秤之间操纵它们以及把秤展开都很重要。//Similar municipal *maneuvers* took place in Chicago and in New York. 芝加哥和纽约也曾采取类似的市政政策。

mechanic [mə'kænɪk] *n.* 机修工(machinist, technician)；[*pl.*]力学，机械学

【记】词根记忆：mechan(机械) + ic(表人) → 机修工

【例】She knows a *mechanic* who can fix the man's car. 她认识一个机修工，能修理此人的车。

【派】mechanical(*a.* 机械的；物理上的)

muscular ['mʌskjələr] *a.* 肌肉的；肌肉发达的；强健的(strong, well-built)

【记】muscul(看作muscle，肌肉) + ar → 肌肉的，强健的

【搭】muscular cell 肌细胞；muscular dystrophy 肌肉萎缩；muscular

tissue 肌肉组织

muscular

【例】The athletes kept their *muscular* bodies in shape with three hours' swimming every morning. 运动员每天上午游泳三个小时以保持其强健的体形。

naked	[ˈneɪkɪd] *a.* 裸露的，无遮盖的(bare)

【搭】naked eye 肉眼

nickel	[ˈnɪkl] *n.* 镍

【记】发音记忆："你抠" → 连五分镍币都舍不得给 → 镍

oak	[oʊk] *n.* 橡树，橡木

outgas	[ˌaʊtˈgæs] *vt.* 除去…的气

panorama	[ˌpænəˈræmə] *n.* 全景

【记】词根记忆：pan(全部) + orama(看) → 全部看得到 → 全景

partnership	[ˈpɑːrtnərʃɪp] *n.* 合伙关系，合股关系；伙伴关系

【记】词根记忆：partner(合伙人) + ship(表身份) → 合伙身份

【例】Henry built up his own business in *partnership* with an American expert. 亨利与一个美国专家合伙创立了自己的公司。

【参】relationship(*n.* 关系)

patriarch	[ˈpeɪtriɑːrk] *n.* 家长，族长(master, chief)

pattern	[ˈpætərn] *n.* 样式，图案 *v.* 仿制(imitate)

【例】World trade *patterns* are indicative of the important economic issues that confront the world today. 世界贸易模式影射了当今世界面临的重要经济议题。

【派】patterned(*a.* 被组成图案的)

perish	[ˈperɪʃ] *v.* 灭亡(die out)

【记】联想记忆：珍惜(cherish)生命，不应随意毁灭(perish)

【例】When a species is no longer adapted to a changed environment, it may *perish*. 一个物种不能再适应变化的环境时就会灭亡。

precursor	[priːˈkɜːrsər] *n.* 初期形式

【记】词根记忆：pre(前) + curs(跑) + or → 跑在前面的 → 初期形式

【例】Carbon compounds might have been the *precursors* of life on Earth. 碳化合物可能是地球上生命的最初形式。

primate	[ˈpraɪmeɪt] *n.* 灵长类动物

【搭】erect bipedal *primate* 直立两足灵长类动物(早期人类)

pueblo	[ˈpweblou] *n.* 印第安人村庄

【记】分拆联想：pue(看作pure，纯洁的) + blo(音似：部落) → 纯

☐ naked	☐ nickel	☐ oak	☐ outgas	☐ panorama	☐ partnership
☐ patriarch	☐ pattern	☐ perish	☐ precursor	☐ primate	☐ pueblo

洁的部落 → 印第安人村庄

【例】The largest *pueblos* had five stories and more than 800 rooms. 最大的印第安村庄有五层，共800多个房间。

quartz [kwɔːrts] *n.* 石英

ratify ['rætɪfaɪ] *vt.* 正式批准（approve）

【记】词根记忆：rat（推定）+ ify（使…）→ 推定后批准 → 正式批准

receptor [rɪ'septər] *n.* 【生理】感受器

【记】词根记忆：recept（感受，接受）+ or → 感受器

record ['rekərd] *n.* 记录；唱片

[rɪ'kɔːrd] *v.* 记录

【搭】set a record 记录

【例】A: You know that summer internship I apply for. They want an official copy of all my grades. But the *records* office charges 50 dollars for an official grade report. That's a lot, don't you think?

B: It really is. I only had to pay six for mine last year.

A：你知道我申请的暑假实习工作。他们要我所有成绩的正式复印件。但是档案室出具一份正式成绩单要收50美元。这要的钱太多了，你觉得呢？

B：的确如此。我去年只需要付6美元。

【参】concord（*n.* 和谐）

recycle [ˌriː'saɪkl] *vt.* 回收利用

【记】词根记忆：re（重新）+ cycle（循环）→ 回收利用

【例】Old buildings in many cities were *recycled* for modern use. 很多城市的旧建筑在现代又被重新利用起来。

reluctant [rɪ'lʌktənt] *a.* 不情愿的，勉强的（unwilling）

【记】发音记忆："驴拉坦克"→ 不情愿的，勉强的

respond [rɪ'spɑːnd] *vi.* 回答（reply）；做出反应

【记】词根记忆：re + spond（约定）→ 按约定回答 → 回答；做出反应

【例】They don't *respond* to stress well. 他们不能很好地应对压力。

【派】respondent（*n.* 回答者）

revise [rɪ'vaɪz] *vt.* 修订，修改（change）*n.* 再校样

【记】词根记忆：re（一再）+ vis（看）+ e → 反复看 → 修订

【例】Experience led workers to *revise* their techniques. 经验促使工人们改进了技术。// What I expect you to do with your *revise* is to improve the effectiveness of your paper. 我期望你修改时提高论文的有效性。

【派】revision（*n.* 修订，修改）

rigid [ˈrɪdʒɪd] *a.* 严格的 (strict)；刚硬的，不易弯曲的 (stiff)

【记】词根记忆：rig (=rog 要求) + id → 不断要求 → 严格的

【例】It progressively stiffens until *rigid*. 它逐渐变硬，直至不易弯曲。

【派】rigidity (*n.* 坚硬)；rigidly (*ad.* 严格地)

rustproof [ˈrʌstpruːf] *a.* 不锈的

sediment [ˈsedɪmənt] *n.* 沉淀物，沉积物 (deposit)

【记】词根记忆：sedi (坐) + ment → 坐下去的东西 → 沉淀物

【派】sedimentation (*n.* 沉淀，沉降)；sedimentary (*a.* 沉积的，沉淀性的)

sense [sens] *n.* 感官，官能；感觉；判断力；见识；意义，意思 (meaning) *v.* 觉得，意识到

【记】词根记忆：sens (感觉) + e → 感觉

【搭】make sense 明白，理解；解释清楚，言之有理；in a sense 从某种意义上说

【例】Bees use their *sense* of smell to recognize whether another bee is related to them. 蜜蜂使用嗅觉来辨认另外一只蜜蜂是否跟它们有关系。

A: I'm getting worried about Jennifer. All she talks about these days is her volleyball team and all she does is practice.

B: Her grades will fall for sure. Let's try to find her after dinner and talk some *sense* into her.

A：我开始担心詹妮弗了。这些天她只谈论她所在的排球队，什么都不干只练球。

B：她的成绩肯定会下降。晚饭后咱们去找找她，给她讲讲道理。

A: Did you like the movie?

B: I couldn't make any *sense* out of it.

A：你喜欢这部影片吗？

B：我一点都看不懂。

setting [ˈsetɪŋ] *n.* 环境 (surroundings)；背景 (context)；布景；[常 *pl.*] 设置，安装 (fixing)

【例】*Setting* can influence literary style. 场景能够影响文学风格。

sharply [ˈʃɑːrpli] *ad.* 急剧地 (severely)

sociable [ˈsouʃəbl] *a.* 好交际的，合群的；友善的，友好的 (outgoing)

【记】词根记忆：soci (结交) + able → 好交际的

【例】A good *sociable* ability is good for one's growth. 良好的交际能力对一个人的发展有好处。

A: Have you noticed how John's changed since he became student

rigid	rustproof	sediment	sense	setting	sharply
sociable					

government president?

B: I think the whole thing's gone to his head, and he used to be so *sociable* and open.

A：你注意到约翰成为学生自治会主席以来的变化吗?

B：我觉得这让他有点自满，他以前很友善坦率的。

souvenir [ˌsuːvəˈnɪr] *n.* 纪念品 (reminder, memento)

【记】联想记忆：sou(看作south) + ven(来) + ir → 从南方带回来的东西 → 纪念品

【搭】as a souvenir of 作为…的纪念；a souvenir shop 纪念品商店

【例】The shop along the street sells the *souvenirs* of the famous tourist attraction. 沿街的商店销售著名旅游景点的纪念品。

spiny [ˈspaɪni] *a.* 长满刺的，带刺的

【例】Starfish are not really fish, they belong to the family of echinoderms which are *spiny* skinned sea animal. 海星其实不是鱼，它属于棘皮类动物，一种皮长满刺的海洋动物。

stardom [ˈstɑːrdəm] *n.* 明星的身份或地位 (fame)

subspecies [ˈsʌbspiːʃiːz] *n.* 【生】亚种 (subgroup)

【记】词根记忆：sub(次一等) + species(物种) → 亚种

summary [ˈsʌməri] *n.* 摘要，概要 (abstract)

【派】summarize(*v.* 概括，总结)；summarization(*n.* 摘要，概要)

switch [swɪtʃ] *n.* 开关 *v.* 转换 (transform)

【搭】switch off 切断；switch to 转到，转变成；switch over 转变

【例】I couldn't make myself *switch* off the TV. 我无法让自己关掉电视。

【派】switching(*n.* 转换)

teem [tiːm] *v.* 充满 (abound)

【搭】teem with 富于，充满

【例】The food was found to be *teeming* with bacteria. 食物被发现充满了细菌。

thorough [ˈθɜːroʊ] *a.* 彻底的 (exhaustive)；详尽的 (elaborate)；一丝不苟的 (careful about detail)

【例】The investigation of Peary's expedition wasn't *thorough*. 对皮尔里远征的调查是不彻底的。//My report wasn't so good because I wasn't *thorough*. 我的报告不是太好，因为我不太细心。

【派】thoroughly(*ad.* 十分地，彻底地)

violent [ˈvaɪələnt] *a.* 暴力的 (forcible)

【例】The American Revolution was not a sudden and *violent*

overturning of the political and social framework. 美国革命不是以暴力方式突然推翻政治和社会框架。

【派】violence(*n.* 暴力行为); nonviolence(*n.* 非暴力)

【参】violin(*n.* 小提琴); violet(*n.* 紫罗兰); violate(*v.* 违反)

wholesome [ˈhoʊlsəm] *a.* 有利于健康的(healthful)

【记】分拆联想: whole(完整; 健康) + some(…的) → 有利于健康的

Doing something is like playing football. You will never stop until you score a goal.

做一件事就像踢足球, 你一定要拼命达到自己的目标, 要入球才罢休。

——霍英东(*Huo Yingdong*)

Word List 35 MP3-35

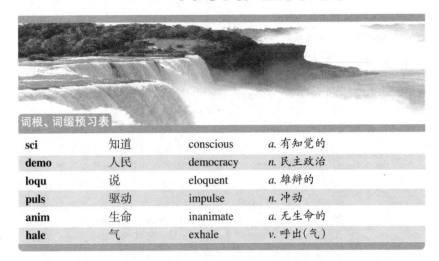

词根、词缀预习表

sci	知道	conscious	a. 有知觉的
demo	人民	democracy	n. 民主政治
loqu	说	eloquent	a. 雄辩的
puls	驱动	impulse	n. 冲动
anim	生命	inanimate	a. 无生命的
hale	气	exhale	v. 呼出(气)

abut [ə'bʌt] *vi.* 邻接，毗邻(adjoin, border on)

【记】分拆联想：a(无)+but(但是)→ 没有转折 → 不需要经过绕弯就能直接到达 → 邻接，毗连

【搭】abut against 紧靠；abut on 接连，邻接

acoustic [ə'kuːstɪk] *a.* 非电声乐器的；听觉的

【例】I don't think the most ardent supporters of electronic instruments expect them to completely replace *acoustic* instruments. 我觉得就算最支持电子设备的人也不希望它们完全替代声音设备。

adolescence [ˌædə'lesns] *n.* 青春期(youthhood)

【记】分拆联想：ado(看作adult, 成人)+lescence (看作licence, 许可证)→ 青少年即将拿到成年的许可证 → 青春期

【派】adolescent(*n.* 青少年)

我长胡子了　我长喉结了

adolescence

affinity [ə'fɪnəti] *n.* 密切关系；吸引；喜爱

【记】词根记忆：af + fin (范围)+ ity → 在范围内 → 密切关系

【例】There is an *affinity* between the cultures of the two countries. 两国文化之间存在着密切关系。

【参】infinity(*n.* 无限的时间或空间；无穷大，无穷)

alga ['ælgə] *n.* [*pl.* algae]藻类，海藻(seaweed)

anchor ['æŋkər] *vt.* 紧固，使固定(fix)

☐ abut　☐ acoustic　☐ adolescence　☐ affinity　☐ alga　☐ anchor

【例】The framework of a lichen is usually a network of minute hairlike fungus that *anchors* the plant. 苔藓的结构通常是附在植物上细如发丝的真菌构成的。

appetite ['æpɪtaɪt] *n.* 胃口，食欲（savor）

【例】I don't have an *appetite*. 我没有胃口。

【派】appetizer（*n.* 开胃品）；appetizing（*a.* 美味可口的）

argue ['ɑːrgjuː] *v.* 争论，辩论（debate）；主张，论证；说服，坚持，劝说

【记】发音记忆："阿Q" → 阿Q喜欢和人争论

【例】Idealists *argue* that the representatives needed to control a series of problems in order for the United States to survive. 理想主义者认为，代表们需要对一系列问题进行调控以使美国渡过难关。

A: I might *argue* with some of the details, but I basically agree with managing the economy.

B: Sure it sounds great in theory. My concern is in practice.

A：我可能对一些细节有异议，但对此经济管理模式基本同意。

B：理论上听起来不错，但我关心的是实践。

【派】argument（*n.* 争论，辩认；论据，论点）

assemble [ə'sembl] *vt.* 集合（gather）；装配（fit together）

【记】分拆联想：as（表加强）+ semble（类似）→ 物以类聚 → 集合

【例】When a nest intruder is too large for one individual to handle, nestmates can be quickly *assembled* by alarm signals. 鸟巢侵犯者太大，一只鸟无法应付时，报警信号可以迅速聚集鸟巢其他的成员。The clerk *assembled* the bicycle for a $25 charge. 这个职员组装这辆自行车收费25美元。

【参】resemble（*v.* 象，类似）

average ['ævərɪdʒ] *a.* 一般的；平庸的 *n.* 平均水平；平均数 *vt.* 平均为

【搭】average person 常人；the average per capita 人均

【例】The new designed train runs at an *average* speed of 120 miles per hour. 新设计的火车平均时速120英里。

belt [belt] *n.* 地带；腰带

【例】The southern states are sometimes referred to be the *Bible Belt*. 南方州有时被称为《圣经》地带。

bicameral [ˌbaɪ'kæmərəl] *a.* 两院制的，有两个议院的

boast [boʊst] *n./v.* 自我夸耀（brag）

boast

【记】和roast（*v.* 烤，烘）一起记

【例】Anne made many *boasts* about her business. 安妮大肆夸耀自己的生意。

| ☐ appetite | ☐ argue | ☐ assemble | ☐ average | ☐ belt | ☐ bicameral |
| ☐ boast | | | | | |

braid [breɪd] *vt.* 编织(weave)

bruise [bruːz] *vt.* 使…受挫伤 *n.* 伤痕,擦痕,青肿

【记】发音记忆:"不如死" → 对她来说,脸上有伤痕还不如死 → 伤痕

【例】A: It looks like you've just *bruised* the bone in your foot. 好像你伤到你的脚骨头了.

canvas [ˈkænvəs] *n.* 帆布(sail);画布

casual [ˈkæʒuəl] *a.* 非正式的,随便的;漫不经心的(informal, purposeless)

【记】联想记忆:平常的(usual)时候可以穿非正式的(casual)服装

【搭】casual clothes 便装;a casual remark 漫不经心的话

【例】Nowadays, more and more young students prefer *casual* clothes to school uniforms. 如今越来越多的青年学生喜欢便装而非校服。

【参】causal(*a.* 原因的)

catalog [ˈkætəlɔːg] *n.* 目录(list)

【记】词根记忆:cata(下面)+ log(说话)→ 下面要说的话 → 目录

chain [tʃeɪn] *n.* 链(条)[*pl.*]镣铐;一连串,一系列(serial),连锁 *v.* 用链条拴住

【搭】food chain 食物链

【例】Algae are the base of the aquatic food *chain*, which means the other organisms depend on them for food. 水藻是水生食物链的基础,也就是说其他生物以水藻为食。//With bicycle *chains* covered, cyclists would need to clean and oil their chains only once every six months instead of once a week. 盖住自行车链条,骑车的人只需半年而非一周给链条清洗上油一次。

A: If that toad became extinct, we'd lose an important link in the *chain* of revolution, right?

B: Exactly.

A: 如果那种蟾蜍灭绝了,我们将失去进化链上重要的一环,对不对?

B: 没错。

cliff [klɪf] *n.* 悬崖,绝壁(precipice, bluff)

【参】bluff(*n.* 断崖,绝壁;诈骗)

conscious [ˈkɑːnʃəs] *a.* 有知觉的(perceptual);有意识的(awake)

【记】词根记忆:con + sci(知道)+ ous → 知道的 → 有知觉的

cliff

【例】Humans should be more *conscious* of the influence they have on ecosystems. 人类应更清楚地认识到自己对生态系统的影响。

【派】consciousness(*n.* 知觉；意识)；self-consciousness(*n.* 自觉，自我)；unconscious(*a.* 无意识的)

【参】conscientious(*a.* 尽责的)

conserve [kən'sɜːrv] *vt.* 保存，保藏(*retain, preserve)

【记】词根记忆：con(全部) + serve(保持) → 保存，保藏

【例】We're trying to protect and *conserve* some of the open spaces on campus. 我们正在试图保护校园里的一些空地。

【派】conservative(*a.* 保守的 *n.* 保守派)

craft [kræft] *n.* 工艺(art) *v.* 手工制作

【例】It is wonderful to see this disappearing *craft* to return to popularity. 很高兴看到这种消失的工艺重新流行起来。//The men wove textile and *crafted* tortoise jewelry. 这些人编织物品，手工制作玳瑁首饰。

crest [krest] *n.* 顶部(peak)

【记】分拆联想：c + rest(休息) → 到了顶峰，该休息了 → 顶部

【例】Small craters have rim *crests* that are elevated above the surrounding terrain. 小火山口边缘顶部比周围的地形要高。

crustacean [krʌ'steɪʃn] *n.* 甲壳类动物

【记】分拆联想：crust(外壳) + acean(看作ocean，海洋) → 海洋中有甲壳类动物 → 甲壳类动物

dam [dæm] *n.* 坝，堤

【记】发音记忆："担" → 堤坝担负着阻隔洪水的责任 → 坝，堤

democracy [dɪ'mɑːkrəsi] *n.* 民主政治，民主主义

【记】词根记忆：demo(人民) + cracy(统治) → 人民统治 → 民主政治

【例】We always stick to the principles of *democracy* and serve the public. 我们向来坚持民主的原则并服务于大众。

dent [dent] *n.* 缺口，凹痕(cavity) *v.* 使凹下，凹进

disintegrate [dɪs'ɪntɪɡreɪt] *v.* (使)瓦解(collapse)；(使)碎裂(smash)

【记】词根记忆：dis(不) + integrate(使一体化，使完整) → (使)瓦解

【例】The books printed less than one hundred years ago are beginning to *disintegrate*. 这些印刷还不到100年的书开始散了。

downtown [ˌdaʊn'taʊn] *ad. /a.* 在市区(的)，往市区(的)

【例】I just got back from the new art gallery *downtown*. 我刚从市中心新开的艺术画廊回来。

conserve	craft	crest	crustacean	dam	democracy
dent	disintegrate	downtown			

effectiveness [ɪˈfektɪvnɪs] *n.* 效力(efficiency)

eloquent [ˈeləkwənt] *a.* 雄辩的(expressive); 传神的

【记】词根记忆: e + loqu(说) + ent(…的)
→ 能说会道的 → 雄辩的

舌战群儒

eloquent

【例】Camen Lomas Garza's *eloquent* etchings depict primal images of the rural environment. 卡门·洛马斯·加尔扎生动的铜版画描绘了农村环境的原貌。

【派】eloquently(*ad.* 善辩地)

encounter [ɪnˈkaʊntər] *vt.* 偶然碰到(come across); 遭遇(meet)

【记】词根记忆: en(使…) + counter(相反) → 使从两个相反方面来 → 偶然碰到

【例】Abstract art *encountered* much opposition in its early years. 抽象艺术在早期遭遇到了很多反对。

equality [iˈkwɑːləti] *n.* 同等, 平等(parity)

【记】来自equal(*a.* 相等的)

【搭】sexual equality 性别平等

【例】Women have been struggling to achieve full *equality* with men in the workplace. 女性一直为在工作场所实现与男性平等而斗争。

establish [ɪˈstæblɪʃ] *v.* 建立(*set, *enact), 安置

【例】She helped *establish* peace between her tribe and the colonists. 她帮助在自己的部落与殖民者之间建立和平局面。//How long does it take for lichens to *establish* themselves?青苔多长时间才能扎根?

【派】established(*a.* 确定的); establishment(*n.* 建立; 机构)

exhale [eksˈheɪl] *v.* 呼出(气)(breathe out)

【记】词根记忆: ex(出) + hale(气) → 呼出(气)

【例】A diver must ascend slowly, never at a rate exceeding the rise of the *exhaled* air bubbles, and must *exhale* during ascent. 潜水者必须缓慢上升, 速度不能超过呼出气泡上升的速度, 上升过程中还必须呼气。

fauna [ˈfɔːnə] *n.* 动物群

【记】来自Fannus(潘纳斯), 罗马神话中的动物之神

【参】flora(*n.* 植物群)

fertilize [ˈfɜːrtəlaɪz] *vt.* 使…受精, 使受粉, 施肥(make fertile)

【记】拆分联想: fertil(看作fertile, 能繁殖的) + ize → 要能繁殖, 就要受精、受粉 → 使…受精, 使受粉

【例】The soil loses its nutrients, so it needs either to be *fertilized* or to be left unused for at least a season. 土壤失去了养分，要么施肥，要么至少休耕一季。

【派】fertilization(n. 施肥); fertilized(a. 已受精的); fertilizer(n. 肥料)

formidable [ˈfɔːrmɪdəbl] a. 艰难的(*difficult, rough); 强大的(mighty, powerful)

【记】分拆联想: for + mid(中间) + able → 作为中间的力量 → 强大的

【例】They faced *formidable* difficulties in their attempt to reach the mountain summit. 他们在试图抵达山顶的过程中面临着巨大困难。

gaseous [ˈɡæsiəs] a. (含)气体的, 气态的

【记】来自gas(气体) + eous → 气体的, 气态的

【例】Like Jupiter, Saturn is a large, *gaseous* planet. 土星与木星一样, 是个巨大的气态行星。

grant [ɡrænt] vt. 给予, 授予(award); 同意(approve); 承认(admit) n. 拨款

【记】联想记忆: 授予(grant)显赫的(grand)贵族爵位

【搭】take... for granted 认为…理所当然

【例】The bank *granted* her a loan to cover her school expenses. 银行为她提供贷款来支付上学费用。//Mary seems surprised that she got a research *grant*. 玛丽对得到研究经费好像感到很惊讶。

handful [ˈhændfʊl] n. 一把; 少数

household [ˈhaʊshoʊld] n. 家庭(family) a. 家庭的, 家用的; 家喻户晓的

【记】分拆联想: house(家) + hold → 家庭

【搭】household appliance 家用电器; household word 家喻户晓的词语

【例】She was almost *household* throughout much of her lifetime because of her prolific literary output. 她创作了大量文学作品, 所以她一生大部分时间都是个家喻户晓的人物。

imagist [ˈɪmədʒɪst] a. 意象派的 n. 意象派诗人

【例】The *imagist* movement in poetry arose during the second decade of the twentieth century. 诗歌领域的意象主义运动在20世纪20年代兴起。

impulse [ˈɪmpʌls] n. 冲动(urge); 脉冲(pulse)

【记】词根记忆: im(使…) + puls(驱动) + e → 冲动

【例】Fish also uses such ability to produce and detect electrical *impulses* to communicate. 鱼类也通过它们这种产生和探测电脉冲的能力来进行交流。

【参】propulsion(n. 推进力)

inanimate [ɪnˈænɪmət] *a.* 无生命的；无生气的(dull)
【记】词根记忆：in(无) + anim(生命) + ate → 无生命的
【例】A fable is usually a short tale featuring animals or *inanimate* objects that can talk and think like humans. 寓言通常是关于能像人类那样说话和思考的动物或无生命物体的短小故事。

incentive [ɪnˈsentɪv] *n.* 刺激(stimulus)；动机(motive)
【记】词根记忆：in + cent(=cant, 唱, 说) + ive → 使人说话、唱歌 → 刺激
【例】There was *incentive* for American potters to replace the imports with comparable domestic goods. 美国制陶工人用与进口商品相当的国产商品替代进口商品是有一定动机的。

inject [ɪnˈdʒekt] *vt.* 注射(药物等)；注入
【记】词根记忆：in(进) + ject(扔) → 扔到里面 → 注射(药物等)
【例】Snakes frequently subdue their prey without *injecting* poison. 蛇经常无需注射毒液就能制服它们的猎物。

inscribe [ɪnˈskraɪb] *v.* 铭刻(engrave)；在某物上写
【记】词根记忆：in(进入) + scribe(写) → 刻写进去 → 铭刻
【例】They *inscribed* vocabulary and other study aids on tables. 他们把单词和其他学习资料刻在了桌子上。
【派】inscription(*n.* 铭刻, 碑文)

kiln [kɪln] *n.* (砖、石灰等的)窑，炉(furnace)
【记】联想记忆：煤窑(kiln)倒塌杀死(kill)了许多人
【例】More and more large *kilns* were built to create the high-fired stoneware. 为了制造高温焙烧的陶器，建造了越来越多的大型窑炉。

laser [ˈleɪzər] *n.* 激光；激光器
【记】发音记忆："镭射" → 激光
【例】The word *laser* was coined as an acronym for Light Amplification by the Stimulated Emission of Radiation. 激光这个词是根据受激辐射式光频放大器的首字母缩略词而造的。

loan [loʊn] *n.* 贷款；暂借的东西；出借，借出 *v.* 借出(lend)
【记】发音记忆："漏" → 因为把钱借出去了，所以账本有漏洞 → 出借，借出
【搭】student loan 学生贷款；loan application 贷款申请
【例】Martin is looking into the possibility of getting a *loan*. 马丁正在调查获得贷款的可能性。
A: Janet, here's the book you *loan* me. I'm a bit embarrassed I can't

seem to find the jacket for it.

B: I would never even notice this. You are the few people who actually returned books to me.

A: 珍妮特，这是你借给我的书。不好意思，我好像找不到书套了。

B: 我都没注意到。很少有人会把书还给我。

【参】moan(*n./v.* 呻吟)

minimal [ˈmɪnɪməl] *a.* 最小的(minimum)；最低限度的(the least possible)

【例】Are you aware that you can go to that school at a *minimal* cost? 你知道你能以最低的花费去那所学校上学吗?

【派】minimalist(*n.* 最简单派艺术家)

opaque [oʊˈpeɪk] *a.* 不透明的

【记】分拆联想: opa(cus)(遮蔽阳光的) + que → 不透明的

【例】Quartz may be transparent, translucent, or *opaque*. 石英可以是透明、半透明或不透明的。

pedagogy [ˈpedəgɑːdʒi] *n.* 教育学，教学法(education)

【记】词根记忆: ped(儿童) + agog(引导) + y → 引导儿童之学 → 教育学

【派】pedagogic(*a.* 教育的)

"...第三章 别打孩子"

pedagogy

polish [ˈpɑːlɪʃ] *vt.* 磨光(burnish, gloss) *n.* 上光剂

【记】联想记忆: 波兰的(Polish)擦光剂(polish)

【例】The shoe *polish* doesn't match the shoes. 鞋油与鞋子不匹配。

【派】polished(*a.* 磨光的，光亮的)

pollinator [ˈpɑːləneɪtər] *n.* 传粉媒介，传粉昆虫

progressive [prəˈgresɪv] *a.* 进步的(ascensive)；渐进的(gradual)

【记】分拆联想: progress(进步) + ive → 进步的

【例】Although based on feudal models, the colony of Pennsylvania developed a reputation for a *progressive* political and social outlook. 尽管基于封建模式，宾夕法尼亚殖民地却因进步的政治和社会观点而颇受好评。

【派】progressively(*ad.* 逐渐地)

rank [ræŋk] *n.* 等级(grade)；头衔(title) *v.* 属于某等级，归类(class)

【例】For a long time cotton *ranked* first among Alabama's crops, but today it accounts for only a fraction of the agricultural production. 长期以来，棉花在亚拉巴马州的农作物中头等重要，但是如今只占农业生产的一小部分。

【派】ranking(*a.* 高级的)

reinforce [ˌriːɪnˈfɔːrs] *vt.* 加固，加强(strengthen)

【记】组合词：rein(统治) + force(强制，强加) → 加固，加强

【例】I guess they wanted to *reinforce* the stuff we learned in school about history. 我猜他们想巩固我们在学校学习的历史知识。

【派】reinforcement(*n.* 增援，加强)

restrict [rɪˈstrɪkt] *vt.* 限制，约束(limit, restrain)

【记】分拆联想：re(一再) + strict(严格的) → 一再对其严格 → 限制，约束

【例】The girl's parents were blamed for *restricting* her activities. 女孩的父母因限制其活动而受到了指责。

【派】restriction(*n.* 限制，约束)；restrictive(*a.* 限制性的)

revival [rɪˈvaɪvl] *n.* 复兴(renewal)；复活；恢复

【记】词根记忆：re(又) + viv(生命) + al → 生命重现 → 复兴

【例】Our economy is undergoing a *revival*. 我们的经济在复兴。

【派】revive(*vt.* 使复苏，再流行)

ritual [ˈrɪtʃuəl] *n.* 典礼，(宗教等的)仪式；固定方式 *a.* 仪式的(ceremonial)

【记】来自rit(e)(典礼，仪式) + ual → 仪式的

【例】*Ritual* ceremonies were conducted by the brother or son. 典礼仪式是由兄弟或儿子主持的。

routine [ruːˈtiːn] *n.* 惯例，常规(convention) *a.* 例行的

【记】联想记忆：例行公事(routine)就是按常规路线(route)走

【例】Farmers relieved the burden of the daily *routine* with such relaxation as hunting. 农民以狩猎这种娱乐活动来缓解日常劳作的艰辛。

【派】routinely(*ad.* 例行公事地)

saddle [ˈsædl] *n.* 鞍子，马鞍

【记】联想记忆：骑马上鞍(saddle)，划船用桨(paddle)

seasoning [ˈsiːzənɪŋ] *n.* 调味品，调料(flavoring, spice)

seasoning

【例】The fruit of this kind of plant can be used for *seasoning*, such as in chili powders. 这种植物的果实可以用作调料，比如可以加入辣椒粉中。

shift [ʃɪft] *n./v.* 转移(transfer)；改变(change)

【记】联想记忆：电脑键盘上的切换键即shift键

【例】Builders of tunnels was beginning to *shift* from Europe to the United States. 隧道建造者开始从欧洲转向美国。

| reinforce | restrict | revival | ritual | routine | saddle |
| seasoning | shift | | | | |

【派】shifting(*a.* 运动的 *n.* 移位)

soloist ['soulouɪst] *n.* 独奏者；独唱者

【例】After the concert, all those people were crowding around the back stage to see Jackson and the *soloist*. 音乐会结束后，这些人都拥挤在后台周围，想目睹杰克逊和独奏者的风采。

space [speɪs] *n.* 空地；空间(vacuum)；太空(firmament) *v.* 隔开(separate)

【例】We're planning to *space* out payments for a house over twenty years. 我们计划分期付款20年还清房贷。

【派】spacing(*n.* 间隔，间距)；spacious(*a.* 广阔的，宽敞的)

【参】spacecraft(*n.* 宇宙飞船)；spaceship(*n.* 宇宙飞船)；spacesuit(*n.* 太空服)

split [splɪt] *v.* 分开，分裂(divide, separate) *n.* 分化

【记】发音记忆："死劈了它" → 劈开 → 分开

【例】A lighting bolt *split* the sky. 一道闪电划破长空。

squirt [skwɜːrt] *vi.* 喷出(spout, spurt)

【记】联想记忆：喷出(squirt)的东西全喷到裙子(skirt)上

static ['stætɪk] *a.* 静止的(stationary) *n.* 静电噪声

【记】词根记忆：stat(站，立) + ic → 静止的

【搭】static electricity 静电绝缘体上电荷的积聚

【例】There was so much *static* that I couldn't make out what he was saying. 静电噪音太大，以致于我听不清他在说什么。

steep [stiːp] *a.* 陡峭的；急剧的(sharp)

【记】联想记忆：阶梯(step)中又加一个e就更陡峭(steep)

【例】The traditional organizations went into *steep* decline during the 1950's and 1960's. 在二十世纪五、六十年代，传统组织急剧衰退。

strategy ['strætədʒi] *n.* 战略，策略(tactics)

【记】分拆联想：str(看作strange，奇怪的) + ate(吃) + gy → 用奇怪的方法吃掉对手 → 战略，策略

【派】strategic(*a.* 战略的)

thaw [θɔː] *v.* (使)融化，(使)解冻(melt, defrost)

【记】分拆联想：t + haw(看作hoe，锄地) → 冰雪融化便可以锄地了 → (使)融化，(使)解冻

【例】Even when the ice *thaws*, the stones do not return to their original positions. 甚至冰融化时，石头也不会恢复原本的位置。// He often *thaws* out the fish in a bucket of water. 他经常把鱼放在一桶水中解冻。

☐ soloist	☐ space	☐ split	☐ squirt	☐ static	☐ steep
☐ strategy	☐ thaw				

thorny [ˈθɔːrni] *a.* 多刺的

【记】分拆联想: t + horn(角)+y → 尖尖的角 → 刺 → 多刺的

【搭】thorny bumps 带刺的凸起处

【例】There are many *thorny* rosebushes growing in the *tropical* rainforest. 在热带雨林中, 生长着很多多刺的玫瑰丛。

【参】irony(*n.* 反话, 讽刺)

toxic [ˈtɑːksɪk] *a.* 有毒的(poisonous)

【记】词根记忆: tox(毒)+ic → 有毒的

【例】Some plant tissues contain a diverse array of *toxic* or potentially toxic substances. 某些植物组织含有各种有毒或可能有毒的物质。

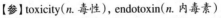

【参】toxicity(*n.* 毒性), endotoxin(*n.* 内毒素)

typify [ˈtɪpɪfaɪ] *v.* 是…的典型

【例】These houses which were popular in the early 1900s *typify* what's known as the unique style. 20世纪初流行的这些房子是当时独特风格的典范。

virtue [ˈvɜːrtʃuː] *n.* 美德(excellence); 优点(merit)

【搭】by virtue of 依靠, 由于

【例】I'll be focusing on the *virtues* of his designs. 我将关注他设计上的优点。

virtuous [ˈvɜːrtʃuəs] *a.* 有道德的, 品性好的, 品德高的

【记】来自virtue(*n.* 美德)

【例】If we are going to discuss goodness and justice—what makes an individual good or a society just or *virtuous*—then we need to start with the ancient Greeks. 如果我们讨论善良与正义——能使一个人品德高尚或使一个社会正义的东西——我们需要从古希腊讲起。

Word List 36 🔘 MP3-36

auto	自动	automatic	a. 自动的
flam	火	flame	n. 火焰，光辉
flor	花	flora	n. 植物（群）
ure	表状态	stature	n. 地位
volat	飞	volatile	a. 不稳定性的

accommodate [əˈkɑːrmədeɪt] *vt.* 供应（住宿或房间）(supply)；使适应(conform, adjust to)

【记】分拆联想：ac + commo（看作common，普通的）+ date（日子）→ 人们适应了过普通的日子 → 使适应

【例】His house can *accommodate* a meeting of the entire committee. 他的房子可以容纳整个委员会开会。

【派】accommodation(*n.* [常*pl.*] 住处，膳宿)

accustom [əˈkʌstəm] *vt.* 使习惯于(familiarize)

【记】分拆联想：ac（一再）+ custom（习惯）→ 使习惯于

【例】I'm not *accustomed* to using a gas stove. 我不习惯使用煤气炉。

【派】accustomed(*a.* 惯常的，习惯的)

admiration [ˌædməˈreɪʃn] *n.* 钦佩，赞美

afflict [əˈflɪkt] *vt.* 使苦恼，折磨(torture)

【记】词根记忆：af + flict（打击）→ 一再打击 → 使苦恼，折磨

【例】Financial difficulties *afflicted* the Smiths. 经济困难困扰着史密斯一家。

analyze [ˈænəlaɪz] *vt.* 分析，研究

【例】Experts *analyze* spider webs using a computer program. 专家们用电脑程序分析蜘蛛网。

aquarium [əˈkweriəm] *n.* 养鱼池；水族馆

【记】词根记忆：aqu（水）+ arium → 水族馆

☐ accommodate ☐ accustom ☐ admiration ☐ afflict ☐ analyze ☐ aquarium

attend [ə'tend] v. 出席，参加(be present at)；入学；照顾，护理
【记】联想记忆：at + tend(伸展) → 伸长脖子看 → 专心于
【搭】attend the tournament 出席比赛；attend the conference 出席会议
【例】Some of the representatives hadn't planned to *attend* the international conference. 一些代表没有打算参加这次国际会议。
A: Well, what did you think of the theater director?
B: You mean Emily Thompson? She was away *attending* a conference.
A：嗯，你觉得剧院的导演如何？
B：你是说艾米丽·汤普森吗？她去外地参加会议了。
【参】tend(v. 趋向；照顾)

audit ['ɔːdɪt] vt. 旁听
【例】If you *audit* a course, you don't have to take the tests. 如果你仅是旁听一门课，就不需要参加考试。

authorize ['ɔːθəraɪz] vt. 授权(empower)，批准(sanction)，许可(permit)
【例】I'm not *authorized* to give out that kind of information. 我无权发布此类信息。// It should be *authorized* by the source. 这应该由资料提供者授权。
【派】authorization(n. 授权；认可)；unauthorized(a. 未授权的)

automatic [ˌɔːtə'mætɪk] a. 自动的(self-acting)
【记】词根记忆：auto(自动) + matic → 自动的
【例】My new camera is supposed to be completely *automatic*. 我的新照相机应该是全自动的。
【派】automation(n. 自动装置)

belie [bɪ'laɪ] vt. 给人错觉(misrepresent)；掩饰(disguise)
【记】be + lie(谎言) → 使…成谎言 → 给人错觉
【例】The boy's cheerful manner *belied* his real thoughts. 男孩开心的样子掩饰了他真实的想法。

cactus ['kæktəs] n. [pl. cacti] 仙人掌

capability [ˌkeɪpə'bɪləti] n. 能力(ability, potentiality)；性能；容量
【例】The limited mining *capability* made iron very expensive. 有限的矿产容量致使铁非常昂贵。

离我远点
cactus

choir ['kwaɪər] n. 唱诗班，合唱队
【记】和chair(n. 椅子)一起记
【参】choral(a. 合唱队的)

citadel ['sɪtədəl] n. 堡垒，要塞(fort, fortress)
【例】The place was once a *citadel* in the First World War. 此地曾是第一次世界大战中的一个要塞。

| ☐ attend | ☐ audit | ☐ authorize | ☐ automatic | ☐ belie | ☐ cactus |
| ☐ capability | ☐ choir | ☐ citadel | | | |

combination [ˌkɑːmbɪˈneɪʃn] *n.* 结合(体)(mixture); 化合; 组合(compounding)

commission [kəˈmɪʃn] *n.* 委任(charge) *vt.* 委托, 授命(appoint, assign)

【记】词根记忆: com(表加强)+ miss(送)+ ion → 送交给某人 → 委任; 委托

【搭】public commission 社会工作(任务)

【例】Artists are taking the distinction between public and private spaces into account when executing their public *commissions*. 艺术家在执行公众委任的事务时, 会考虑到公开场合与私人空间的区别。

【派】commissioner(*n.* 委员, 专员)

community [kəˈmjuːnəti] *n.* 社团(corporation); 社会(society at large); 群落

【记】com + mun (看作muni, 服务)+ ity → 为大家服务的社团 → 社团

【搭】community service 社区服务

contaminate [kənˈtæmɪneɪt] *vt.* 污染(pollute)

【记】词根记忆: con + tamin(接触)+ ate → 接触脏东西 → 污染

【例】They are so *contaminated* with lead that they shouldn't be used. 它们受到了严重的铅污染, 不能再用了。

【派】contamination(*n.* 污染)

contrary [ˈkɑːntreri] *a.* 相反的, 逆的(in conflict with, opposite) *n.* 相反, 相反的事物

【记】词根记忆: contra(相反)+ ry → 相反的

【例】If there is no evidence to the *contrary*, we ought to believe the witness. 如果没有反面证据, 我们应该相信这个证人。

convection [kənˈvekʃn] *n.* 对流; 传送(conveying, transmission)

【例】A heater is using *convection* when it warms the air in a room. 加热器给屋子空气加热时, 利用了对流原理。

conversion [kənˈvɜːrʒn] *n.* 转变; 改变信仰

【记】词根记忆: con + vers(转)+ ion → 转变

【例】The *conversion* of steam-powered engines into battery-powered ones can improve energy efficiency. 把蒸气引擎换成电池驱动的引擎能提高能源的使用效率。

correspondence [ˌkɔːrəˈspɑːndəns] *n.* 信件; 通信 (communication by letters); 相当; 相似处

【例】There are many *correspondences* between the two novels. 这两部小说之间有许多相似之处。

□ combination □ commission □ community □ contaminate □ contrary □ convection
□ conversion □ correspondence

counteract [ˌkaʊntərˈækt] *vt.* 消除(clear up), 抵消(neutralize)

【记】词根记忆: counter(反) + act(动作) → 做相反的动作 → 消除, 抵消

【例】Antacid will *counteract* the excess acid in your stomach. 解酸剂会消除胃里过剩的酸。

delirium [dɪˈlɪriəm] *n.* 精神错乱(insanity, madness)

depart [dɪˈpɑːrt] *v.* 离开(leave, exit); 背离(deviate)

【记】词根记忆: de(去掉, 离开) + part(离开) → 离开; 背离

【例】Some musicians consciously *depart* from strict meter to create a relaxed sense of phrasing that also emphasizes the underlying rhythms. 一些音乐家有意摆脱严格的韵律, 试图在强调基本旋律的同时创造一种宽松的编排方式。

【派】departure(*n.* 离开, 出发)

diminish [dɪˈmɪnɪʃ] *v.* 减低重要性(debase, devalue); (使)变小(decrease)

【记】词根记忆: di + mini(小) + sh →(使)变小

【例】I don't mean to *diminish* Revere's role. 我并不打算降低里维尔的职位。//Those animals' ability to survive is *diminished*. 这些动物的生存能力降低了。

dispose [dɪˈspoʊz] *v.* 使愿意做; 除掉(get rid of)

【例】Contemporary readers are easily *disposed* to think of "literature" only as something written. 当代读者很容易认为"文学"只是书面的东西。//Irresponsible people often *dispose* of the waste in ponds. 没有责任感的人经常把垃圾扔到池塘里。

【派】disposal(*n.* 处理; 垃圾倾倒); disposable(*a.* 一次性的) disposed(*a.* 愿意的); disposition(*n.* 部署)

earnest [ˈɜːrnɪst] *n.* 诚挚, 认真 *a.* 热心的; 重要的

【记】联想记忆: earn(挣钱) + est → 要想挣钱就得认真地干 → 认真

edible [ˈedəbl] *a.* 可食用的(eatable)

【例】Codfish is a kind of *edible* fish that lives in cold water. 鳕鱼是一种生活在冷水中的可食用鱼。

【派】inedible(*a.* 不能吃的)

elliptical [ɪˈlɪptɪkl] *a.* 椭圆的

【记】来自ellipse(*n.* 椭圆, 椭圆形)

enroll [ɪnˈroʊl] *v.* 登记(check in); 注册(register)

【记】词根记忆: en(进入) + roll(名单) → 上名单 → 登记; 注册

【例】He didn't know that she was *enrolled* in a linear algebra course. 他不知道她选了线性代数课程。

counteract　delirium　depart　diminish　dispose　earnest
edible　elliptical　enroll
389

exposition [ˌekspəˈzɪʃn] *n.* 展览会，博览会（exhibition）

【记】词根记忆：ex + pos（放）+ ition → 放出来（让人看）→ 展览会；博览会

flame [fleɪm] *n.* 火焰（blaze）；光辉（brilliance）

v. 闪耀（*burn, shine）

【记】词根记忆：flam（火）+ e → 火焰

【例】The candles *flamed* brighter. 蜡烛燃烧得更亮了。

【派】flaming（*a.* 燃烧的）

flame

flora [ˈflɔːrə] *n.* 植物（群）

【记】词根记忆：flor（花）+ a → 植物群

【派】floral（*a.* 植物的）

frost [frɒst] *n.* 霜；结霜

【记】分拆联想：fr(看作freeze, 冰冻) + ost(看作lost, 失去) → 霜冻的来临使春意消失 → 霜

greeting [ˈɡriːtɪŋ] *n.* 问候（regard），致敬

【搭】brief holiday greeting 简短的假日问候；exchange greetings 互相问候；birthday/Christmas greeting 生日/圣诞祝福；greeting card 贺卡

【例】The first actual radio broadcast was made on Christmas Eve of 1906, arranged the program of two short musical selections of poem and brief holiday *greeting*. 第一次广播是在1906年圣诞节前夕播出的，节目包括两首短小的配乐诗和一段简短的节日祝福。

【参】meeting(*n.* 会议)

hardly [ˈhɑːrdli] *ad.* 几乎不，简直不；仅仅（barely）

【例】I hardly ever use the dictionary anyway. 反正我几乎不用字典。

A: That movie was awful. And yet it got such great reviews.

B: It was *hardly* worth the price of admission.

A: 那部电影太差了，可还是得到了好评。

B: 花钱买那个电影票都不值。

【参】rarely(*ad.* 很少地)；scarcely(*ad.* 几乎不)；nearly(*ad.* 几乎)；barely(*ad.* 仅仅)

instrument [ˈɪnstrəmənt] *n.* 仪器，器械；乐器

【例】Some alarmists believe these new *instruments* will bring an end to classical music. 一些杞人忧天的人认为这些新乐器会给古典音乐带来灭顶之灾。

【派】instrumental(*a.* 有帮助的；乐器的)；instrumentalist(*n.* 器乐演奏者，器乐家)

☐ exposition ☐ flame ☐ flora ☐ frost ☐ greeting ☐ hardly
☐ instrument

【参】percussion (*n.* 打击乐器)

lichen [ˈlaɪkən] *n.* 青苔，地衣

【例】*Lichens* are famous for their ability to survive a water shortage. 青苔以其在缺水环境下仍然富有顽强的生命力而著称。

likewise [ˈlaɪkwaɪz] *ad.* 同样地 (similarly)；也

【例】*Likewise*, when a football game was shown on the air, the stands were often empty because fans chose to watch the game at home. 同样地，在转播足球赛时，看台上往往是空的。这是因为球迷们更愿意在家观看比赛。

marine [məˈriːn] *a.* (航)海的；海生的

【记】词根记忆：mari(海) + ne → 海的；海生的

【例】The southwestern coastal region has a humid mild *marine* climate. 西南沿海地区是湿润的温带海洋气候。

【派】mariner(*n.* 水手)；submarine(*n.* 潜水艇)

measure [ˈmeʒər] *n.* 尺寸 (size)；测量；[常 *pl.*] 措施 (step) *v.* (测)量 (ascertain)

【例】The biologists realized that if new *measures* were not taken, oysters would become extinct. 生物学家意识到，如果不采取新的措施，牡蛎就会灭绝。//The energy content of food is *measured* in calories. 食物包含的能量用卡路里来度量。

【派】measurement(*n.* 测量)

mechanize [ˈmekənaɪz] *vt.* 使机械化

【记】词根记忆：mechan(机械) + ize → 使机械化

【例】*Mechanized* farming required more capital and fewer laborers. 机械化农业需要投入更多的资本，使用更少的劳动力。

【派】mechanization(*n.* 机械化)

novice [ˈnɑːvɪs] *n.* 生手，新手 (tyro)

【记】分拆联想：no + vice(副的，第二的) → 连副的都不是 → 新手

【例】Selina is a complete *novice* as a journalist. 塞丽娜作为记者完全是个新手。

【参】dab(*v.* 轻拍，轻触)

obedience [əˈbiːdiəns] *n.* 服从，顺从 (submittal, compliance)

【记】来自obey(*v.* 服从，顺从)

【例】The unruly children showed no *obedience* to their parents. 任性的孩子不会服从他们的父母。

【派】disobedience(*n.* 不服从，违抗)

obsolete [ɑ:bsə'li:t] *a.* 过时的（old-fashioned）

【记】词根记忆：ob(不) + solete(使用) → 不再使用 → 过时的

obsolete

【例】The astronomers consider the study of cosmic jets to be an *obsolete* scientific field. 天文学家认为关于宇宙喷射流的研究是过时的。

occupy ['ɑ:kjupai] *vt.* 占用；占据（take up）

【例】Wish I'd brought a book or something to *occupy* my time. 我真该带本书或一些别的东西来打发时间。//Landmasses *occupy* only one third of the Earth's surface. 陆地只占地球表面的三分之一。

【派】occupation(*n.* 职业); occupant(*n.* 居住者); occupancy(*n.* 居住)

outermost ['autərmoust] *a.* 最外面的, 离中心最远的（farmost, utmost）

【参】innermost(*a.* 最里面的, 内心的)

parliament ['pɑ:rləmənt] *n.* 国会, 议会（congress）

【记】分拆联想：parlia(看作parle, 谈话) + ment → 谈论政务的地方 → 议会

【派】parliamentary(*a.* 议会的)

pheromone ['ferəmoun] *n.*【生化】信息素

【例】*Pheromones* play numerous roles in the activities of insects. 信息素在昆虫的活动中起重要的作用。

porous ['pɔ:rəs] *a.* 能渗透的；多孔的

【例】Some bones are not *porous* enough to be effectively grafted. 有些骨头渗透性不强, 无法对其进行有效嫁接。

possess [pə'zes] *vt.* 具有, 拥有（own）

【记】分拆联想：poss(看作boss, 老板) + ess → 老板占有很多财产 → 具有, 拥有

【例】They *possess* detailed knowledge of the rules of jazz performers. 他们对爵士乐演奏者的规则有很详细的了解。

【派】possessed(*a.* 着迷的, 疯狂的); possession(*n.* 拥有；财产)

powder ['paudər] *n.* 粉末（dust）

prior ['praiər] *ad. /a.* 在…之前（的）（*preceding, former); 优先（的）（taking precedence）

【记】词根记忆：pri(=prim, 第一的, 首要的) + or → 优先的

【例】*Prior* to this report, Seattle's park development was very limited and funding meager. 在这个报告之前, 西雅图公园的开发非常有限, 资金很缺乏。

| □ obsolete | □ occupy | □ outermost | □ parliament | □ pheromone | □ porous |
| □ possess | □ powder | □ prior | | | |

puddle ['pʌdl] *n.* 水坑(sump)

【记】注意不要和peddle(*v.* 沿街叫卖)相混

pure [pjʊr] *a.* 纯洁的(virgin); 纯净的(free from dust); 完全的(absolute)

puddle

【例】Is the cup made of *pure* gold? 这只杯子是纯金的吗?

【派】purely(*ad.* 纯粹地, 完全地)

rarely ['rerli] *ad.* 很少(seldom), 难得, 非常地

【例】A: You know the noise in my dorm has really gotten out of control. My roommate and I can *rarely* get to sleep before midnight.

B: Why don't you take the problem up with the dorm supervisor?

A: 我宿舍的噪音太大, 我和室友在午夜前很难入睡。

B: 你为什么不向宿舍管理员反映这个问题?

recoil [rɪ'kɔɪl] *vi.* 弹回, 反冲(rebound, resile)

【记】词根记忆: re + coil(卷, 盘绕) → 卷回去 → 弹回

【搭】recoil from doing sth. 对做⋯畏缩不前

recommend [ˌrekə'mend] *vt.* 推荐(nominate); 建议(suggest)

【记】分拆联想: re(一再) + com(共同) + mend(修) → 这本书是大家一修再修的成果, 强力推荐 → 推荐

【例】He doesn't *recommend* going to Central Mountain. 他不推荐去中部山区。

【派】recommendation(*n.* 推荐; 介绍信)

recover [rɪ'kʌvər] *vt.* 使复原, 使恢复(renew); 恢复健康

【例】She has almost *recovered* from her cough. 她的咳嗽快好了。

【派】recovery(*n.* 恢复)

regulate ['regjuleɪt] *vt.* 管理, 控制(control); 调节(adjust)

【记】词根记忆: regul(=reg, 统治) + ate → 管理, 控制

【例】They *regulate* their temperature by making a variety of internal adjustments. 它们通过各种体内调节来控制体温。

【派】regulation(*n.* 规章, 规则); regulator(*n.* 调节器); regulatory(*a.* 调整的)

relatively ['relətɪvli] *ad.* 相对地; 相当地(comparatively)

【例】She began her career as a writer *relatively* late in her life. 她的作家生涯开始得相对较晚。

relieve [rɪ'liːv] *vi.* 缓解, 减轻(ease)

【记】词根记忆: re + liev(=lev, 轻) + e → 缓解, 减轻

【派】relieved(*a.* 放心的); reliever(*n.* 缓解物)

□ puddle	□ pure	□ rarely	□ recoil	□ recommend	□ recover
□ regulate	□ relatively	□ relieve			

reservoir [ˈrezərvwɑːr] *n.* 水库, 蓄水池
【记】分拆联想: reserv(e)(保存, 储备) + oir(地方) → 保存水的地方 → 水库, 蓄水池

second [ˈsekənd] *a.* 第二的; 次等的, 二等的 *n.* 秒 *vt.* 赞成, 附和
【例】A: Is there a discount if I take a student ID card?
B: Oh, let me see. I need to check. Just a *second*.
A: 如果我用学生证是否能打折?
B: 让我看看, 我需要核实一下, 请稍等片刻。
A: That's a long line. Do you think there'll be any tickets left?
B: I doubt it. Guess we'll wind up going to the *second* show.
A: 排的队太长。你觉得我们能买到票吗?
B: 不能确定。或许我们只看下一场演出。

seminar [ˈsemɪnɑːr] *n.* 研讨会(workshop)
【记】分拆联想: semi(半) + nar → 研讨会每半年举行一次 → 研讨会

sentimental [ˌsentɪˈmentl] *a.* 伤感的(emotional)
【记】分拆联想: sentiment(情感) + al → 伤感的
【派】sentimentalism(*n.* 感伤主义); sentimentalize(*v.* 感伤)

sentimental
无可奈何花落去

source [sɔːrs] *n.* 源, 源泉; 来源, 出处(origin)
【搭】energy source 能源
【例】A: Excuse me, does this library have anything on the international arts festival coming this summer or should I go to the art library for that?
B: If you give a minute, I think we have a few *sources* for that kind of information.
A: 打扰一下, 这个图书馆有关于今年夏天国际艺术节的信息吗? 还是我该去艺术图书馆问问?
B: 请稍等, 我想我们有一些这方面的信息。
【参】resource(*n.* 资源)

statistical [stəˈtɪstɪkl] *a.* 统计(学)的
【记】和statistic(*a.* 统计的, 统计学的)一起记
【搭】statistical mechanics 统计力学

stature [ˈstætʃər] *n.* 身材(natural height); 地位(status)
【记】词根记忆: stat(站) + ure(表状态) → 站的状态 → 身材

sting [stɪŋ] *n.* (昆虫的)尾刺; 刺痛
【记】发音记忆: "死叮" → 刺痛

suitcase [ˈsuːtkeɪs] *n.* 手提箱, 衣箱

□ reservoir	□ second	□ seminar	□ sentimental	□ source	□ statistical
□ stature	□ sting	□ suitcase			

【记】合成词: suit(一套衣服)+ case(箱子)→ 衣箱

topographical [ˌtɑːpəˈɡræfɪkl] *a.* 地形学的

【派】topography(*n.* 地形)

validity [vəˈlɪdəti] *n.* 有效性，正确性

【记】分拆联想: valid(有效的)+ ity → 有效性

【搭】the validity of a contract 合同的有效性

【例】Employees must confirm the *validity* of a contract when signing it with employers. 雇员与雇主签订合同时必须确认其有效性。

varied [ˈverid] *a.* 各式各样的(*different, diverse)

【记】词根记忆: vari(不同的)+ ed → 各式各样的

【例】There are several levels, dotted with kiosks and fountains, which offer *varied* prospects of San Francisco Bay. 这里有好多楼层，其间星罗棋布地点缀着大大小小的亭子和喷泉。在那里可以欣赏旧金山湾的各种风光。

【派】variety (*n.* 种类；变化); various (*a.* 各种各样的); variation (*n.* 变化；变异)

volatile [ˈvɑːlətl] *a.* 不稳定性的(unstable); 挥发性的

【记】词根记忆: volat(飞)+ ile → 挥发性的

【例】These bacteria release *volatile* substances. 这些细菌会释放挥发性物质。

【派】volatility(*n.* 挥发性)

ware [wer] *n.* 陶器(pottery), 器皿(vessel)

【参】glassware(*n.* 玻璃器具)

wary [ˈweri] *a.* 小心翼翼的(*cautious); 机警的(alert)

【派】unwary(*a.* 粗心的)

weed [wiːd] *n.* 杂草

【记】联想记忆: 种子(seed)在杂草(weed)中顽强生长

If winter comes, can spring be far behind?
冬天来了，春天还会远吗？　　　　　　　——雪莱.*P.B.*(*P. B. Shelley*)

Word List 37  MP3-37

词根、词缀预习表

chrom	颜色	chromosome	*n.* 染色体
son	声音	consonant	*a.* 协调的 *n.* 辅音
cour	跑	courier	*n.* 信使
rept	爬行	reptile	*n.* 爬行动物
dia	相对	diagonal	*a.* 斜的；斜纹的
philo	爱	philosophy	*n.* 哲学；人生观
plat	平	plateau	*n.* 高原

adjustment [ə'dʒʌstmənt] *n.* 调整

【例】The government should make a slight *adjustment* for inflation, when the drop in interest rates is quite small. 在利率降低幅度非常小时，政府应该对通货膨胀做轻微调整。

appropriate [ə'prəupriət] *a.* 适当的(suitable)

[ə'prəuprieit] *vt.* 拨款；占用(engross)

【记】词根记忆：ap + propri(自己的) + ate → 变为自己的 → 占用

【例】The United States Congress *appropriates* some four million dollars a year for the upkeep of the White House. 美国国会每年为白宫的维修拨款大约400万美元。

【派】appropriately(*ad.* 适当地)；inappropriate(*a.* 不适合的)

ascribe [ə'skraib] *vt.* (to)把…归于(attribute)

【记】词根记忆：a + scribe(写) → 把…写上去 → 把…归于

【例】Tradition *ascribes* these works to a man named Homer. 一直以来人们都认为这些作品是一个叫荷马的人写的。

assign [ə'sain] *v.* 分配，分派；指定，选派

【搭】assigned books 指定的书

【例】I was *assigned* to look after the freshmen on the first day of school. 开学第一天我被委派去照顾新生。

A: That novel the professor *assigned* us is so boring.

B: Really? I started it yesterday afternoon, and I couldn't put it down until I finished it.

A：教授指定我们读的小说太无聊了。

B：真的吗？我昨天下午开始看的，直到读完了我才舍得放下。

avert [ə'vɜːrt] *vt.* 避免，规避（avoid）

【记】词根记忆：a + vert（转）→ 转开 → 避免，规避

【例】A fresh tragedy was narrowly *averted* yesterday. 昨天差点又发生了一场悲剧。

【派】aversion（*n.* 厌恶）

awful ['ɔːfl] *a.* 不舒服的（unwell）；糟糕的（terrible）；可怕的（awesome）

【记】来自awe（*n.* 敬畏；惧怕）

【例】I feel *awful*. I think I'm coming down with that flu. 我感觉特难受，觉得自己得了流感。//The cafeteria food was *awful*. 自助餐厅的饭糟糕透了。

【派】awfully（*ad.* 非常，很）

blend [blend] *vt./n.* 混合（mix, combine）

【记】发音记忆："不论的" → 不论什么东西都放在一起 → 混合

【例】Many birds have feathers whose colors *blend* with their surroundings. 很多鸟的羽毛颜色与周围环境相混杂难分。

【派】blended（*a.* 混合的）

breakthrough ['breɪkθruː] *n.* 突破（improving）

【记】来自词组break through（突破）

【例】In fact important *breakthroughs* in the field of astronomy can come from students' work. 事实上，很多天文学领域中的重要突破可能来自学生的工作。

canopy ['kænəpi] *n.* 天篷，遮篷（awning, covering）

【记】分拆联想：can（能）+ opy（看作copy，复制）→ 能被复制的遮篷 → 遮篷；来自希腊语konopeion（蚊帐），后指天篷

cascara [kæ'skærə] *n.* 缓泻剂

chafe [tʃeɪf] *vt.* 擦热；擦破；擦痛（abrade, rub）

【例】He rarely uses suspenders, since they may *chafe* him. 他很少穿吊裤带，因为会擦得身上痛。

【参】chase（*v./n.* 追逐）

chromosome ['kroʊməsoʊm] *n.* 染色体

avert	awful	blend	breakthrough	canopy	cascara
chafe	chromosome				

【记】词根记忆：chrom(颜色)＋o＋some(体) → 染色体

classify [ˈklæsɪfaɪ] *vt.* 分类(categorize, sort)；分等(to arrange in classes)

【例】We have difficulty in *classifying* all of the varieties of owls. 我们很难给各种猫头鹰分类。

【派】classification(*n.* 分类；级别)

combat [ˈkɑːmbæt] *n./v.* 格斗，战斗(conflict, battle)

【记】词根记忆：com(共同)＋bat(打，击) → 共同打 → 战斗

【例】San Antonio, Texas, offers an objective lesson for numerous other cities *combating* urban decay. 得克萨斯州的圣安东尼奥市给很多与城区衰落作斗争的城市提供了客观的经验。

comparison [kəmˈpærɪsn] *n.* 比较(the act or process of comparing)；比喻

【例】The passage mainly discusses a *comparison* of urban and rural life in the early twentieth century. 这一段主要是探讨20世纪初城市与乡村生活的比较。//The *comparison* is quite appropriate. 这个比喻很恰当。

compatible [kəmˈpætəbl] *a.* 协调的，一致的(harmonious, coherent)

【记】词根记忆：com＋pat(=path感情)＋ible → 他们的感情生活很协调 → 协调的

【例】This project is not *compatible* with the company's long-term plans. 这个方案与公司的长远计划不一致。

【派】incompatible(*a.* 不协调的，合不来的；不兼容的)

confidence [ˈkɑːnfɪdəns] *n.* 信心(faith, belief)

【记】词根记忆：con(加强)＋fid(相信)＋ence → 信心

【例】When speaking before a group, a person's tone may indicate unsureness or fright, *confidence* or calm. 在一群人面前讲话时，一个人的语气可能表现出犹疑、恐惧、自信或镇静。

【参】self-confidence(*n.* 自信)；overconfident(*a.* 过于自信的)

consonant [ˈkɑːnsənənt] *a.* 协调的(harmonious) *n.* 辅音

【记】词根记忆：con(共同)＋son(声音)＋ant → 同声的 → 协调的

【例】The man is behaving with a dignity *consonant* with his rank. 此人举止得体，与其身份相符。

constitute [ˈkɑːnstətuːt] *vt.* 组成(make up)；设立(set up, establish)；制定(enact)

【记】词根记忆：con＋stitute(建立，放) → 组成；设立

【例】Governments should be *constituted* by the will of the people. 政府应依人民的意愿而设立。

【参】institute(*n.* 学会)；substitute(*n.* 代用品)

courier [ˈkʊriər] *n.* 送急件的人，信使

【记】词根记忆：cour(跑) + ier → 跑着送信的人 → 送急件的人

【例】A *courier* can deliver the parcels and letters to our office. 信使可以将包裹和信件递送到我们的办公室。

creep [kriːp] *vi.* 慢慢行进；爬行(crawl)

【记】联想记忆：兔子偷懒睡觉(sleep)时乌龟缓慢地行进(creep)

【搭】creep along 沿着…爬；creep into/over 爬进/过

【例】I *crept* up the stairs in case I woke up my roommates. 我悄悄地走上楼梯，生怕吵醒我的室友。

【派】creepy(*a.* 爬行的，匍匐的)

deficient [dɪˈfɪʃnt] *a.* 不足的，缺乏的(*inadequate)

【记】词根记忆：de(变坏) + fic(做) + ient → 做得不好的 → 缺乏的，不足的

【例】John's diet is *deficient* in fiber and vitamin E. 约翰的膳食中缺少纤维和维生素E。

delicious [dɪˈlɪʃəs] *a.* 美味的，可口的(tasty, savory)

devour [dɪˈvaʊər] *vt.* 贪婪地吃；吞食(consume)

【记】词根记忆：de + vour(=vor吞吃) → 贪婪地吃；吞食

【例】It is not surprising that each whale *devours* more than one ton of krill daily. 每只鲸鱼一天吞吃一吨多磷虾，这不足为奇。

diagonal [daɪˈæɡənl] *a.* 倾斜的 *n.* 斜线

【记】词根记忆：dia(相对) + gon(角) + al → 对角 → 斜线

【派】diagonally(*ad.* 对角地)

diagram [ˈdaɪəɡræm] *n.* 图表(graph, chart)

【记】词根记忆：dia + gram(写；图) → 图表

【例】The *diagram* indicates that there has been a sharp increase in unemployment rate for three months. 图表显示三个月来失业率急剧上升。

【参】signal (*n.* 信号)；label (*n.* 标签)；mark (*n.* 标记)

distress [dɪˈstres] *n.* 痛苦，不幸(pain, grief)

【记】分拆联想：dis(分开) + tress(看作dress, 衣服) → 看到衣服睹物思人，悲从中来 → 痛苦，不幸

【例】Two in *distress* makes sorrow less. 同病相怜。

eclipse [ɪˈklɪps] *n.* (日、月)食 *vt.* 使相形见绌；使黯然失色

【记】词根记忆：ec + lipse(看作lapse, 滑走) → 日月的光华滑走 → (日、月)食

【搭】lunar/solar eclipse 月/日食

| courier | creep | deficient | delicious | devour | diagonal |
| diagram | distress | eclipse | | | |

【例】The desperate plight of the South has *eclipsed* the fact that reconstruction had to be undertaken also in the North. 南方极糟的情况掩盖了另一实际情况，即北方也需要重建。

【参】ellipse(*n.* 椭圆，椭圆形); lapse(*v.* 流逝)

eject [iˈdʒekt] *vt.* 逐出(expel); 喷出(erupt)

【记】词根记忆：e(出来)＋ject(扔)→被扔出来→逐出；喷出

【例】Some artists came to truly embrace the life in small towns and to *eject* city life in so called "sophisticated society". 一些艺术家开始真正接受小城镇的生活，拒绝所谓"复杂社会"的城市生活。//A superheated fireball was *ejected* back through the tunnel. 一个超热的火球通过隧道喷射了出去。

【参】reject(*vt.* 拒绝); object(*v.* 反对); inject(*vt.* 注射); deject(*vt.* 使沮丧)

entertain [ˌentərˈteɪn] *vt.* 招待; 使娱乐(amuse)

【记】词根记忆：enter(进入)＋tain(拿住)→拿着东西进去，一般是请客时送礼或要招待别人→招待；使娱乐

【例】Movie attendance dropped when audience members chose to stay at home and be *entertained.* 观众选择待在家里娱乐时，去电影院的人就少了。

【派】entertainer(*n.* 表演艺人); entertainment(*n.* 娱乐)

evergreen [ˈevərgriːn] *a.* 常绿的 *n.* 常绿树；常绿植物

【搭】evergreen trees 常青树

furious [ˈfjʊriəs] *a.* 狂怒的(angry); 狂暴的，猛烈的

evergreen

【搭】furious with sb. at sth. 因为…对…大发雷霆; in a furious way 以一种狂怒的方式

【例】A: I feel horrible. Deborah was *furious* that I lost her notes. Do you think I should apologize again?
B: If I were you, I'd let her cool off a few days before I talked to her.
A: 我感觉很糟糕。我丢了德波拉的笔记，她十分恼火。你觉得我需要再次道歉吗？
B: 我要是你，我就让她冷静几天，然后再和她谈谈。

【参】curious(*a.* 好奇的)

genial [ˈdʒiːniəl] *a.* 亲切的，和蔼的(amiable, kindly)

【记】联想记忆：做个和蔼(genial)的天才(genius); 注意不要和genital(*a.* 生殖的)相混

【参】congenial(*a.* 性格相似的)

gentle ['dʒentl] *a.* 温柔的(soft); 温和的(mild)

【例】If the flow of the beaches is *gentle*, the water energy is lessened as it washes up along the shore. 如果海滩涨潮和缓, 海水冲刷上岸时水能就会减少。

【派】gentility(*n.* 文雅, 有教养); gently(*ad.* 轻轻地; 柔和地)

govern ['gʌvərn] *vt.* 治理, 管理(administrate); 决定(decide)

【记】government的动词形式

【例】Laws are *governing* the printing industry. 依法治理印刷行业。

【派】governing(*a.* 控制的, 管理的)

gymnasium/gym [dʒɪm'neɪziəm] *n.* 体育馆; 健身房

【记】该词源自希腊语gymnazo(赤身训练), 古希腊运动员训练时要求赤身裸体, 据说能使全身最大限度地自由活动, 本词即源于此。

hum [hʌm] *v.* 发嗡嗡声(buzz) *interj.* 嗯嗯(表示犹豫)

【例】A brass or woodwind player may *hum* while playing, to produce two pitches at once. 铜管或木管乐器演奏者可以在演奏时哼唱, 用来同时产生两个音调。

incessant [ɪn'sesnt] *a.* 不断的, 不停的(unceasing)

【记】词根记忆: in(不) + cess(停止) + ant → 不停的

【例】I'm tired of his *incessant* complaining. 他无休止的抱怨让我厌烦。

【派】incessantly(*ad.* 不断地, 不停地)

inquire [ɪn'kwaɪər] *v.* 打听, 询问(ask)

【记】词根记忆: in + quire(追求) → 追着询问 → 打听, 询问

【例】The applicant *inquired* about meeting the other manager. 申请人询问了一下与另一位经理会面的事宜。

【派】inquiry(*n.* 调查)

ivory ['aɪvəri] *n.* 象牙

【记】词根记忆: i + vor(吃) + y → 象牙

【例】Today what little fossil *ivory* remains comes from Alaska. 如今少数象牙化石来自阿拉斯加。

loathsome ['loʊðsəm] *a.* 令人讨厌的

lounge [laʊndʒ] *n.* 等候室, 休息室(lobby)

【记】分拆联想: loung(看作long, 长的) + e → 放长条(东北方言) → 在休息室里(懒洋洋地)倚或躺 → 休息室

loathsome

marble ['mɑːrbl] *n.* 大理石；雕塑品（sculpture）

【记】分拆联想：mar（三月）+ ble → 大理三月好风光 → 大理石

【例】The Minnesota State Capitol building is made of white granite and *marble*. 明尼苏达州的州议会建筑是由白色花岗岩和大理石建成的。

melodic [mə'lɑːdɪk] *a.* 旋律的，曲调的；音调优美的（tuneful）

【记】来自 melod(y)（旋律）+ ic → 旋律的

【例】Emotional health is evidenced in the voice by free and *melodic* sounds of the happy. 快乐者自由并有旋律的声音证明其情绪健康。// In jazz music, a riff is a simple *melodic* figure. 在爵士乐中，即兴反复片段是一个简单的曲调音型。

mount [maʊnt] *n.* 山，峰（mountain）*v.* 增加（increase）

【例】Blankets of snow and ice grains *mounted* layer upon layer. 厚厚的雪与冰粒层层相叠。

musicologist [ˌmjuːzɪ'kɑːlədʒɪst] *n.* 音乐学者

navigate ['nævɪgeɪt] *vi.* 航行；飞行（fly）；测定位置和路线

【记】词根记忆：nav（船）+ ig（走）+ ate → 坐船走 → 航行

【例】Researchers have found that migrating animals use a variety of inner compasses to help them *navigate*. 研究人员发现迁徙的动物使用各种体内指南针帮助其导航。

【派】navigation(*n.* 航行；导航)；navigable(*a.* 适于航行的)

nicotine ['nɪkətiːn] *n.* 尼古丁

【记】来自人名 Nicot，此人于 1560 年将烟草引入法国

【搭】nicotine patch 尼古丁贴剂

philosophy [fə'lɑːsəfi] *n.* 哲学；人生观

【记】词根记忆：philo（爱）+ soph（聪明的，智慧）+ y → 爱思考的聪明人 → 有学问 → 哲学；人生观

【搭】metaphysical philosophy 形而上学哲学

【派】philosopher(*n.* 哲学家)；philosophic(*a.* 哲学的)

【参】psychology(*n.* 心理学)；philology(*n.* 语文学)

plateau [plæ'toʊ] *n.* 高原（tableland）

【记】词根记忆：plat（平）+ eau → 高出平地的地 → 高原

prey

prey [preɪ] *n.* 猎物；受害者 *vi.* (on)捕食；掠夺

【记】联想记忆：心中暗自祈祷(pray)不要成为受害者(prey)

【例】Some human hunters *prey* on animals of

| marble | melodic | mount | musicologist | navigate | nicotine |
| philosophy | plateau | prey | | | |

all ages, but gray wolves concentrate their efforts on young animals. 一些猎人捕捉各个年龄段的动物，但是灰狼专门捕食年幼的动物。

【参】pray(*v.* 祈祷)

primordial [praɪˈmɔːrdiəl] *a.* 原始的，最初的(primeval, primitive, fundamental)

【记】词根记忆：prim(第一)+ ord(顺序)+ ial → 处于第一顺序的 → 最初的

process [ˈprɑːses] *n.* 过程(*circle);程序，手续(procedure) *vt.* 处理(dispose)

【记】词根记忆：pro(向前)+ cess(走)→ 向前走 → 过程

【例】The women used their tools to *process* all of the fish and marine mammals brought in by the men. 女人用工具加工所有男人带回来的鱼和海洋哺乳动物。

【派】processing(*n.* 处理)

productive [prəˈdʌktɪv] *a.* 生产(性)的；能产的，多产的

【记】词根记忆：pro + duct(带来)+ ive → 带来产品的 → 多产的

【搭】expand productive forces 发展生产力；a productive writer 多产的作家；a productive meeting 卓有成效的会议

【例】Health is important to me as a means to a *productive* life. 健康对我很重要，只有这样我的人生才能有所建树。

【派】productively(*ad.* 有结果地，有成果地)

【参】conductive(*a.* 传导的)

prosperous [ˈprɑːspərəs] *a.* 繁荣富强的，兴旺的(fortunate, thriving)

【例】Historians who wrote during the calm and *prosperous* 1950s found reasons to believe the idealist view. 在20世纪50年代平稳繁荣环境下写作的历史学家有理由相信唯心主义观点。

pursue [pərˈsuː] *v.* 继续(hold on);从事(engage);追击(*chase);追踪(trace)

【例】Few predators fail to *pursue* such obviously vulnerable prey. 很少有肉食动物不能追捕到如此明显易受攻击的猎物。

quote [kwoʊt] *n.* 引文(quotation) *v.* 引用(cite);报价

【记】联想记忆：记录(note)报价(quote)

【例】The author *quotes* public opinion to support the argument for farming plankton. 作者引用舆论来支持养殖浮游生物的论点。

【派】quotation(*n.* 引文；报价)

recline [rɪˈklaɪn] *v.* 靠在，斜倚

【记】词根记忆：re(回)+ cline(倾斜，斜坡)→ 斜回去 → 斜倚

【例】If anyone is tired during the visit, he or she can *recline* on the lounge chair for tourists. 如果有人在参观期间感到疲惫，可以斜躺在为游客准备的安乐椅上。

【参】incline[*v.* (使)倾斜]

primordial　process　productive　prosperous　pursue　quote
recline

recreation [ˌrekriˈeɪʃn] *n.* 娱乐活动, 消遣(amusement)
【记】来自recreat(e)(再创造) + ion → 一遍遍地制造娱乐新闻 → 娱乐活动
【派】recreational(*a.* 消遣的, 娱乐的)

repetition [ˌrepəˈtɪʃn] *n.* 重复
【记】来自repe(a)t(重复) + ition → 重复
【参】repetitive(*a.* 重复的, 反复性的)

reptile [ˈreptaɪl] *n.* 爬行动物
【记】词根记忆: rept(爬行) + ile(物) → 爬行动物
【派】reptilian(*a.* 爬虫类的)

rinse [rɪns] *v.* 用清水冲洗; 漱
【记】联想记忆: rin(=rain下雨) + se → 雨水冲刷着地面 → 用清水冲洗

scorch [skɔːrtʃ] *v.* 烤焦(*burn, sear)
【记】联想记忆: 用火把(torch)烤焦(scorch)
【派】scorcher(*n.* 大热天)

scorch

secure [səˈkjʊr] *vt.* 获得(*obtain, *acquire); 保护 *a.* 安全的, 有保障的(*safe); 确定的
【记】分拆联想: se(看作see, 看) + cure(治愈) → 亲眼看到治愈, 确定其是安全的 → 确定的; 安全的
【例】Agriculture made possible a more stable and *secure* life. 农业使更加稳定和安全的生活成为可能。
【派】securely(*ad.* 安全地); security(*n.* 安全, 保障)

seismic [ˈsaɪzmɪk] *a.* 地震(引起)的
【记】词根记忆: seism(地震) + ic → 地震的
【搭】seismic waves 震波

shame [ʃeɪm] *n.* 羞耻, 羞愧, 耻辱; 可耻的人(或事物); 遗憾的事 *vt.* 使羞愧, 玷辱
【例】A: Just as Sarah was opening the present I realized the camera wasn't working.
B: What a *shame*!
A: 萨拉正要打开礼物, 我发现照相机不能用了。
B: 真遗憾!
It's a real *shame* that most people today don't realize how strong and long-lasting a thatched roof is. 如今多数人不知道茅草屋顶有多结实耐用, 这真是个遗憾。
【参】ashamed(*a.* 羞耻的, 羞愧的); shave(*v.* 刮)

shore [ʃɔːr] *n.* 海滨，岸(coast, beach)

slightly ['slaɪtli] *ad.* 苗条地；轻微地，些微地

【例】A: Dr. Eliot, I'd like you to check the way you calculated my grade for this test. I think you may have made a mistake in adding up the number of questions I got right. When I added them up I came up with this *slightly* higher grade than you did.

B: I'd be happy to check it for you. And if I made a mistake in determining the grade I'll be sure to correct it. Don't worry.

A: 艾略特博士，我想让您核查一下计算我的测验成绩的方法。我认为您在计算我做对的题目的数量时出了差错。我总计之后得的分数比您给的稍微高一点。

B: 我乐意为你查一下。如果算成绩时出了差错，我肯定会改正。不要担心。

subdue [səb'duː] *v.* 制服，征服(conquer)

【记】分拆联想：sub(在下面) + due(音似：丢) → 打得敌人丢盔弃甲 → 制服，征服

【例】Snakes frequently *subdue* their prey with injecting poison. 蛇经常通过注射毒液来制服被捕食的动物。

【派】subdued(*a.* 缓和的；被抑制的)

submit [səb'mɪt] *v.* 提交，呈递

【记】词根记忆：sub(下面的) + mit(送，放出) → 从下面送上 → 提交，呈递

swear [swer] *v.* 诅咒(curse)；郑重地说

【例】You'd better take your mind off the math problem that you were *swearing* over for the last two hours. 这道数学题你都琢磨两个小时了，你最好放松一下自己。

symbolic [sɪm'bɑːlɪk] *a.* 象征的；符号的

【搭】symbolic language 符号语言；symbolic instruction 符号指令

【例】Many paintings are rich in *symbolic* overtones. 很多绘画作品都富含象征寓义。

synonym ['sɪnənɪm] *n.* 同义词

【记】词根记忆：syn(共同) + onym(名字) → 同义词

【派】synonymous(*a.* 同义的)

tavern ['tævərn] *n.* 小旅馆，客栈，小酒店(inn)

【例】The news are read loud every root in homes, workshops and *taverns*. 无论在家里、车间还是小酒馆，处处都在大声朗读这条消息。

theoretical [ˌθiːəˈretɪkl] *a.* 不切实际的(unrealistic)；理论(上)的(abstract)

【例】They devoted a lot of time to *theoretical* problems. 他们在理论问题上投入了大量时间。

【派】theoretically(*ad.* 理论上)

transition [trænˈzɪʃn] *n.* 过渡；转变(conversion)

【记】来自transit(*v.* 通过 *n.* 转变)

【例】The *transition* to settled life also has a profound impact on the family. 向稳定生活的转变对这个家庭也有着深远的影响。

【派】transitional(*a.* 过渡期的)

transportation [ˌtrænspɔːrˈteɪʃn] *n.* 运输，运送

【搭】public transportation 公共交通

【例】Today I want to mention an even earlier form of *transportation*, one that brought the first European settlers to America. 今天我想提一种更早的交通形式，是它把第一批欧洲殖民者带到了美洲。

A: I think the whole class is going on the field trip next Friday.

B: I'm not so sure. Not everyone has paid the *transportation* fee.

A: 我认为下周五全班都要去进行实地考察旅行。

B: 我不太肯定。并非每个人都交了交通费。

utterly [ˈʌtərli] *ad.* 完全地，绝对地(absolutely, completely)

vault [vɔːlt] *n.* 拱顶

【例】Previously the poor quality of the iron had restricted its use in architecture to items such as *vaults* and walls. 以前铁的质量不好，限制了其在建筑中如拱顶和墙壁中的使用。

【派】vaulted(*a.* 拱状的)

vision [ˈvɪʒn] *n.* 视觉(seeing, sight)

【记】词根记忆：vis(看)＋ion → 视觉

【搭】human vision 人类视觉；good/normal/poor vision 视力好/正常/差；night vision 夜视；field/line of vision 视野

【例】Animals such as cats and dogs have better night *vision* than human beings. 猫狗这些动物在夜间的视力比人类好。

yeast [jiːst] *n.* 酵母，发酵粉

【记】分拆联想：y＋east(东方) → 据说酵母最先是由东方人发明的 → 酵母

Word List 38

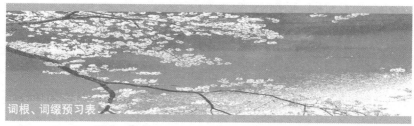

词根、词缀预习表

apt	适应；能力	adapt	v. (使)适应
pens	花费	compensate	vt. 赔偿
sper	希望	desperate	a. 令人绝望的
irrit	痒	irritable	a. 急躁的
patri	父亲	patriot	n. 爱国者
proto	首先	prototype	n. 原型
friger	冷	refrigerate	vt. 冷藏

ablaze [ə'bleɪz] a. 着火的, 燃烧的(burning); 闪耀的(bright)

【记】分拆联想: a(…的) + blaze(火焰) → 火焰般的 → 燃烧的

academic [ˌækə'demɪk] a. 学术的(scholarly); 学院的; 理论的(theoretical)

【记】来自academy(n. 学院, 学术团体)

【搭】academic status 学术地位; a purely academic question 一个纯理论问题; academic conference 学术会议; academic calendar 校历

【例】Recently, universities have become involved with students' emotional lives and their *academic* lives. 最近, 大学已开始关注学生的情感生活和学术活动。

【派】academician(n. 学者; 学会会员)

accuracy ['ækjərəsi] n. 准确(性), 精确(性)(nicety, precision)

【记】来自accurate(a. 准确的, 精确的)

【例】Those companies rely on high *accuracy* scales to manufacture and package medicine. 这些公司依靠高精度标准来生产和包装药品。

adapt [ə'dæpt] v. (使)适合(adjust); 调整(alter)

【记】词根记忆: ad + apt(适应; 能力) → 使适合

【例】When we moved to France, the children *adapted* to the change very well. 我们家搬到法国之后, 孩子们很容易便适应了这个变化。

☐ ablaze　☐ academic　☐ accuracy　☐ adapt

【派】adaptation(*n.* 适应)；adaptable(*a.* 能适应的)；adaptive(*a.* 适应的；适合的)

【参】adopt(*vt.* 采用；收养)；adept(*a.* 熟练的)

aloft [əˈlɒft] *ad.* 在高处；在空中

【记】词根记忆：a + loft(阁楼；鸽房)→ 阁楼在高处 → 在高处

【例】As the bell is ringing, the students are immediately sent *aloft* to bed. 铃声一响，学生们立刻上床睡觉。

attain [əˈteɪn] *vt.* 达到(*reach)；获得(*achieve, gain)

【记】词根记忆：at + tain(拿住)→ 稳稳拿住 → 获得

【例】Mango trees grow rapidly and can *attain* heights of up to 90 feet. 芒果树生长得很快，高度可达90英尺。

【派】attainment [*n.* 达到；(常*pl.*)成就]

attention [əˈtenʃn] *n.* 注意(力)，留心；立正

【记】联想记忆：at + tent(伸展) + ion(表名词)→ 伸长了脖子 → 注意

【搭】pay attention to 注意

【例】*Attention*, please, Ladies and Gentlemen. Our bus is approaching Cambridge, Massachusetts, where we'll be stopping to eat. 女士们，先生们，请注意，我们的公交车快到剑桥了，我们要在那里停下来就餐。

A: I'd think twice about taking a history class next year. There's not a single good professor in all history department.

B: Look, that's what you said last term about the sociology department and I'm very glad I didn't pay any *attention* to what you said.

A: 明年修历史课我要三思了。历史系就没有一个好教授。

B: 你瞧，你上学期对社会学系也这么说。我很高兴我没理睬你的评价。

backhand [ˈbækhænd] *n.* 反手击球

【例】A: After two weeks of tennis lessons, I think I finally managed to improve my *backhand*.

B: Like my mom always says, "Practice makes perfect."

A: 上了两周的网球课后，我觉得我的反手击球终于有进步了。

B: 正如我妈妈常说的："熟能生巧。"

band [bænd] *n.* 乐队；队；(光或颜色的)带；带子 *v.* 联合，集合(unite, ally)

【记】和hand(*n.* 手)一起记

besides [bɪˈsaɪdz] *prep.* 除…之外 *ad.* 而且，还有

【例】I'm not sure what else I could say, *besides* I don't think they will reject it. 我不肯定我还能说什么，此外我觉得他们不会拒绝。

bill [bɪl] *n.* 账单，票据；议案；钞票；(似)鸟嘴

breed [briːd] *n.* 品种 *vt.* 饲养(raise)；繁殖(reproduce)

【例】Our dog is a rare *breed*. 我们的狗是稀有品种。//The songbirds have finished *breeding*. 鸣禽完成了繁殖。

【参】inbreeding(*n.* 同系繁殖，近亲交配)

burrow ['bɜːrou] *v.* 挖地洞(dig, tunnel) *n.* 洞穴

【记】和borrow(*v.* 借)一起记

【例】The aardvark is a mammal that *burrows* into the ground to catch ants and termites. 土豚是一种哺乳动物，它们挖地洞捕食蚂蚁和白蚁。

category ['kætəgɔːri] *n.* 种类(kind)；范畴

【记】词根记忆：cata(下面) + gory → 向下细分 → 种类

【例】The common broad leaf trees we have on campus fall into this *category*. 我们校园常见的宽叶树属于这个类别。

【派】categorize(*vt.* 分类)

compensate ['kɑːmpenseɪt] *vt.* 赔偿，弥补(pay for, make up)

【记】词根记忆：com + pens(挂；花费) + ate → 负责全部花费 → 赔偿

【例】How do humans *compensate* for an underdeveloped sense of smell? 人类如何弥补不够发达的嗅觉？

compensate

【派】compensatory(*a.* 补偿性的)

concern [kən'sɜːrn] *vt.* 涉及，关系到 *vt./n.* 关心，挂念 *n.* (利害)关系

【记】词根记忆：con(共同) + cern(搞清) → 都想搞清楚 → 关心

【搭】as/so far as... be concerned 就…来说；concern oneself with 关心；be concerned with 关心

【例】The main factors to be particularly *concerned* about writing are the structure of essays and collection of written material. 写作时尤其要关注的主要因素是论文结构和书面材料的搜集。

【派】unconcerned(*a.* 不关心的，不关注的)；concerned(*a.* 关切的，关注的)

conclusive [kən'kluːsɪv] *a.* 确定的(*definitive)；最后的

【例】Is the research about the link between coffee and heart disease *conclusive*? 关于咖啡和心脏病之间存在联系的研究确定吗？

□ bill	□ breed	□ burrow	□ category	□ compensate	□ concern
□ conclusive					

【参】inclusive(*a.* 包含的，包括的)；inconclusive(*a.* 非决定的)

cooperative [koʊˈɑːpərətɪv] *a.* 合作的，协力的

【例】He is not *cooperative.* 他不是太合作。

cube [kjuːb] *n.* 立方体，立方

【记】和tube(*n.* 管，显像管)一起记

dawn [dɔːn] *n.* 黎明；开端(outset)

【派】dawning(*n.* 拂晓，黎明)

debt [det] *n.* 债务(liability)

【记】发音记忆："贷的" → 贷款 → 债务

【例】Many small-and-middle-sized companies went bankrupt during the financial crisis. 经济危机期间很多中小型公司都破产了。

【派】debtor(*n.* 债务人)

describe [dɪˈskraɪb] *v.* 描写，描述(portray, depict)；称作(call)

【记】词根记忆：de(加强) + scribe(写) → 描写

【例】Let's move on and I'll *describe* what we see as we go. 我们接着走，我会边走边描述我们所见到的东西。

【派】description(*n.* 描述；性质)

【参】subscribe(*v.* 赞成)

desperate [ˈdespərət] *a.* 令人绝望的(despairing)

【记】词根记忆：de(去掉) + sper(希望) + ate → 去掉希望 → 令人绝望的

【例】His failure made him *desperate.* 他的失败令他绝望了。

【参】prosperous(*a.* 繁荣的)

destination [ˌdestɪˈneɪʃn] *n.* 目的地(termini, end)

【记】联想记忆：destin(看作destine，预定) + ation → 预定的地方 → 目的地

【例】The travel agency will provide a variety of *destinations* and flight times for their customers. 旅行社将为顾客提供各种旅游景点和各个时段的航班。

disrupt [dɪsˈrʌpt] *v.* (使)中断(interrupt)；扰乱(disturb)

【记】词根记忆：dis(分开) + rupt(断) → 使断裂开 → 中断

【例】An accident has *disrupted* railway services into and out of the city. 一场事故使得进出城市的铁路交通陷入混乱。

endow [ɪnˈdaʊ] *vt.* 使天生具有

【例】Nature *endowed* Jane with a pleasant smile. 简天生就有迷人的笑容。

【派】endowment(*n.* 天赋)

□ cooperative	□ cube	□ dawn	□ debt	□ describe	□ desperate
□ destination	□ disrupt	□ endow			

ethical ['eθɪkl] *a.* 道德的(moral)

【例】In his positive *ethical* viewpoint, George tries to support the opinion that human being should live in harmony with nature. 乔治具有积极的道德观，他尽力支持人类应该与自然和谐共处的观点。

【参】ethnic(*n.* 人种的，种族的)

fumigate ['fjuːmɪgeɪt] *vt.* 烟熏；用香薰

【记】词根记忆：fum(=fume烟)+igate(用…的)→烟熏

gentility [dʒen'tɪləti] *n.* 有教养，文雅

【记】来自gent(le)(温和的，文雅的)+ility→有教养，文雅

【例】Many people think fine clothes are a mark of *gentility.* 很多人认为精致的服饰是文雅的标志。

grasshopper ['græshɑːpər] *n.* 蚂蚱，蝗虫(locust)

【记】组合词：grass(草地)+hopper(跳跃者)→草地上的跳跃者→蚂蚱

humanitarian [hjuːˌmænɪ'teriən] *n./a.* 人道主义者；人道主义的

【搭】humanitarian aid 人道主义援助

husk [hʌsk] *n.* (果类或谷物的)外壳；皮(shell, outer covering) *vt.* 剥…的壳；削皮(remove the husk from)

implication [ˌɪmplɪ'keɪʃn] *n.* 含意(*significance)；暗示(suggestion)

【例】What are the social *implications* of meat eating? 食肉的社会含义是什么？

inhabit [ɪn'hæbɪt] *vt.* 居住于，(动物)栖居于(*live)

【记】词根记忆：in(进入)+habit(居住)→住在里面→居住于，栖居于

【例】The archaeological evidence indicates that Native Americans first *inhabited* the area. 考古学证据显示，美洲土著人最初在这个区域居住。

【派】inhabitant(*n.* 居民；栖息的动物)；uninhabited(*a.* 无人居住的，杳无人迹的)；uninhabitable(*a.* 不适于人居住的)

insect ['ɪnsekt] *n.* 昆虫，虫

interact [ˌɪntər'ækt] *vi.* 相互作用；互相配合

【记】词根记忆：inter(在…之间)+act(行动)→互动→相互作用

【例】The people in the office should *interact* with each other and with outside clients. 办公室人员应该互相交流，也应该与外面的客户交流。

insect

【派】interaction(*n.* 相互作用，相互影响)；interactive(*a.* 交互式的；

相互合作的)

interval [ˈɪntərvl] *n.* 间隔时间; 间距(*distance); 音程

【记】词根记忆: inter(在…之间) + val → 间距

【搭】at intervals 不时; 相隔一定距离

【例】The earliest road markers were stones piled at *intervals*. 最早的道路标记是相隔一段距离摆放的石头。// Non-western music produces a greater number of distinct tones within the same *interval*. 非西方音乐在同一个音程中产生数量更多的不同音调。

irritable [ˈɪrɪtəbl] *a.* 急躁的, 易怒的

【记】词根记忆: irrit(痒) + able → 身上瘙痒时, 人很容易变得急躁 → 急躁的, 易怒的

【例】She is *irritable* when she is unhappy. 她不开心时容易急躁。

landing [ˈlændɪŋ] *n.* 登陆; 着陆, 降落

【例】The voyage lasted 46 minutes, from its departure in Philadelphia to its *landing* across the Delaware River. 从费城出发抵达特拉华河对面的旅程持续了46分钟。

limb [lɪm] *n.* 肢

【记】联想记忆: 如果没有四肢(limb)就不能攀爬了(climb)

【参】limp(*v.* 跛行)

mask [mæsk] *n.* 化装舞会; 面具

【记】分拆联想: m(看作must, 必须) + ask(问) → 被掩盖的事物必须通过询问方可弄清 → 面具

mass [mæs] *n.* 块, 团(block); 【物】质量(the property of a body) *a.* 大量的(large-scale)

【搭】mass communication 大众传播

【派】massive(*a.* 雄伟的; 巨大的)

microprocessor [ˌmaɪkroʊˈprousesər] *n.* 微处理器

morale [məˈræl] *n.* 士气, 斗志(spirit)

【记】和moral(*n.* 道德)一起记

【例】Throughout the wilderness, post bands provided entertainment and boosted *morale*. 四周一片荒芜, 哨所乐队提供了娱乐, 鼓舞了士气。

musical [ˈmjuːzɪkl] *a.* 音乐的; 悦耳的 (melodious, tuneful); 有音乐天赋的 *n.* 音乐喜剧(comedy)

【例】Ella is the perfect *musical* partner for her friend. 艾拉是她朋友的完美音乐搭档。

【派】musicality(*n.* 音感, 音乐性); musically(*ad.* 音乐上)

| ☐ interval | ☐ irritable | ☐ landing | ☐ limb | ☐ mask | ☐ mass |
| ☐ microprocessor | ☐ morale | ☐ musical | | | |

oversleep [ˌoʊvərˈsliːp] *v.* (使)睡过头; (使)睡得过久

【例】I *overslept* this morning, so I ran out of the house without listening to the forecast. 我今天早晨睡过头了，没听天气预报就出门了。

A: I hope I don't *oversleep*; I've simply got to catch the first flight out.

B: If I were you, I'd request the wake-up call from the front desk.

A: 我希望自己别睡过头。我要赶第一趟航班。

B: 我要是你，我就要前台安排电话叫醒服务。

oxide [ˈɑːksaɪd] *n.* 氧化物

【记】词根记忆: oxi(=oxy氧) + de → 氧化物

patriot [ˈpeɪtriət] *n.* 爱国者

【记】词根记忆: patri(父亲) + ot → 把祖国当父亲看待的人 → 爱国者

【派】patriotic(*a.* 爱国的)

誓死不降

patriot

periodic [ˌpɪriˈɑːdɪk] *a.* 周期的; 定期的(regular)

【记】来自period(周期) + ic → 周期的, 定期的

【搭】periodic table 元素周期表

【例】This *periodic* extinction might be due to intersection of the Earth's orbit with a cloud of comets. 这种周期性灭绝可能是因为地球轨道和彗星的云交叉。

【派】periodical(*n.* 期刊, 杂志); periodically(*ad.* 定期地; 周期地)

pierce [pɪrs] *vt.* 刺穿(*puncture, penetrate)

【记】联想记忆: r从一片(piece)中穿过 → 刺穿

【例】The bullet *pierced* the police officer's vest. 子弹打穿了警官的防弹衣。

pine [paɪn] *n.* 松树

【参】pineapple(*n.* 凤梨, 菠萝)

pipe [paɪp] *n.* 管子(tube, hose)

planetary [ˈplænəteri] *a.* (似)行星的

【搭】planetary motions 行星运动

【例】Many *planetary* orbits are not circles. 很多行星轨道都不是圆形的。

platitude [ˈplætɪtuːd] *n.* 陈词滥调

【记】词根记忆: plat(平) + itude → 平庸之词 → 陈词滥调

【例】My advisor's hollow *platitudes* aren't very helpful. 我的指导教

师的空洞的陈词滥调用处不大。

【派】platitudinous(*a.* 陈腐的；乏味的)

propensity [prə'pensəti] *n.* 倾向，癖好(inclination, tendency, disposition)

【记】词根记忆：pro(提前) + pens(花费) + ity → 他有用信用卡提前消费的癖好 → 癖好

【搭】have a propensity for sth. 有…的倾向；a propensity to do sth. 喜欢做…，有做…的倾向

【派】propend(*vi.* 倾向于)

prosperity [prɑː'sperəti] *n.* 繁荣，兴旺(flourish, blossom)

【例】The *prosperity* of the Erie encouraged the state to enlarge its canal system by building several branches. 伊利湖的繁荣促使了这个州通过挖掘支流来扩大运河系统。

prototype ['prəʊtətaɪp] *n.* 原型(archetype)

【记】词根记忆：proto(首先) + type(形状) → 首先的形状 → 原型

【例】The water of the early oceans might thus have become the chemical *prototype* for the fluids of all animal life. 早期海水可能是所有动物体液的化学原型。

publication [ˌpʌblɪ'keɪʃn] *n.* 出版，发行(emit)；出版物(a published work)

【例】When she was eighty years old, some twenty-five volumes were awaiting *publication*. 时至80岁高龄，她仍有25卷书等待出版。

quiz [kwɪz] *n.* 小测验

【记】联想记忆：他最终放弃(quit)了智力竞赛(quiz)

refrigerate [rɪ'frɪdʒəreɪt] *vt.* 冷藏；使变冷

【记】词根记忆：re + friger(冷) + ate → 冷藏；使变冷

【例】Ice was used to *refrigerate* freight cars. 货车冷藏时用冰。

【派】refrigerator(*n.* 冰箱；冷藏库)；refrigerated(*a.* 冷冻的)；refrigeration(*n.* 冷藏，冷冻)

reject [rɪ'dʒekt] *vt.* 拒绝，抵制(exclude)

【记】词根记忆：re(反) + ject(扔) → 被扔回来 → 拒绝

【例】It reflects poetic techniques that were *rejected* by modern poets. 它反映了现代诗人不再采用了的写诗技巧。

【派】rejection(*n.* 拒绝)

relief [rɪ'liːf] *n.* 浮雕；缓解

【例】Molds are used to create particular effects for some products, such as *relief*-decorated vessels and figurines. 模子用来为一些产品制造特殊效果，例如有浮雕装饰的器皿和小雕像。//We should have some *relief* by the end of the week. 这个周末我们应该轻松一下。

□ propensity	□ prosperity	□ prototype	□ publication	□ quiz	□ refrigerate
□ reject	□ relief				

restricted [rɪˈstrɪktɪd] *a.* 受约束的，限制的（*limited）

【例】They can only go to this week's lecture during the next three weeks, the admission will be *restricted* to engineering students. 在接下来的三周里，他们只有本周的讲座可听，其余讲座只限工程系的学生入场。

revenue [ˈrevənuː] *n.* 收入（income）

【记】词根记忆：re + ven(来) + ue → 回来的东西 → 收入

【例】The tourist attraction does not generate any *revenue* for the town. 旅游景点没有给镇子带来任何收入。

revert [rɪˈvɜːrt] *v.* 恢复（原状）

【记】词根记忆：re(重新) + vert(转) → 转回去 → 恢复

【例】A glacier can *revert* to a fluffy mass. 冰川能够重新变回成蓬松的一团。

revoke [rɪˈvoʊk] *v.* 撤销，撤回；取消，废除

【记】词根记忆：re(反) + vok(呼喊) + e → 高喊反对 → 撤销

【例】John's work permit was *revoked* after six months. 半年之后，约翰的工作证被吊销了。

【参】provoke(*vt.* 激怒)；evoke(*vt.* 引起)

rudimentary [ˌruːdɪˈmentri] *a.* 未充分发展的（*undeveloped）；基本的（fundamental）

【记】词根记忆：rudi (天然的；粗糙的) + ment + ary → 未充分发展的

【例】Many animals are capable of using objects in the natural environment as *rudimentary* tools. 很多动物能够把自然界的物体当作基本工具使用。

scope [skoʊp] *n.* 范围，界限（*extent, range）

【参】telescope(*n.* 望远镜)；microscope(*n.* 显微镜)

settle [ˈsetl] *v.* 安定，安顿；停息；定居；解决；调停

【记】联想记忆：set(放置) + tle → 安放，放置

【搭】settle down 平静；定居，过安定的生活

【例】A: I'm sort of upset with my brother. He hasn't answered either of my letters.

B: Well, just remember how hectic your freshman year was. Give him a chance to get *settled*.

A: 我的弟弟有点让我不安。我给他写的两封信都没有回复。

B: 想想你大学第一年有多忙吧。给他一个机会安顿下来。

shortly ['ʃɔːrtli] *ad.* 不久 (soon); 简要地 (briefly)
【例】He caught a cold *shortly* after the tournament. 锦标赛之后不久他就感冒了。

slope [sloʊp] *n.* 斜坡, 斜面 (slant, inclination)
【记】分拆联想: slo (看作slow, 慢的) + pe → 慢慢地走下斜坡 → 斜坡
【派】sloping (*a.* 倾斜的, 有坡度的)

slope

squeeze [skwiːz] *vt.* 挤压 (press); 挤入 (crush)
【记】分拆联想: s + quee (看作queen, 女王) + ze → 很想挤进去与女王握手 → 挤压; 挤入
【搭】squeeze into 挤进

staggering ['stægərɪŋ] *a.* 巨大的; 势不可挡的 (*overwhelming)

stimulate ['stɪmjuleɪt] *vt.* 刺激; 激励, 激发 (*motivate, evoke)
【记】词根记忆: stimul (刺; 刺激) + ate → 刺激; 激励
【派】stimulus (*n.* 促进因素; 刺激物); stimulant (*n.* 刺激物; 兴奋剂)

technical ['teknɪkl] *a.* 技术的, 工艺的; 专业的
【记】来自techn (技艺) + ical (…的) → 技术的
【搭】technical innovation 技术革新
【例】I have to admit the word "ethnography" scared me a little at first. It seems so *technical*. 我得承认"人种史"这个词一开始有点吓着我了。它看起来如此专业。
【派】technically (*ad.* 技术上; 专业上)

textile ['tekstaɪl] *n.* 纺织品 (fabric) *a.* 纺织的
【记】词根记忆: text (编织) + ile → 纺织品
【例】The European *textile* industry increased its demand for American export products then. 欧洲纺织业那时增加了对美国出口产品的需求。//The men weave textile and craft jewelry. 这些人编织纺织品, 并用手工制作首饰。

transaction [træn'zækʃn] *n.* 交易 (deal)
【记】词根记忆: trans (变换) + act (行为) + ion → 交易
【例】There has been a sharp decrease in commercial *transactions* between companies since financial crisis. 金融危机以来, 公司之间的商业交易大幅度减少。
【参】transfer (*v.* 转移); transport (*vt.* 运输); transmit (*v.* 传输)

transfer [træns'fɜːr] *v.* 转移 (move); 转学 *n.* ['trænsfɜːr] 转移; 换乘
【记】词根记忆: trans (转移) + fer (带来) → 转移
【例】Pollen can be *transferred* by birds that come into contact with

□ shortly	□ slope	□ squeeze	□ staggering	□ stimulate	□ technical
□ textile	□ transaction	□ transfer			

flowers. 花粉可以通过接触花朵的鸟来传播。//She isn't planning to transfer to a different university. 她没有打算转到另外一所大学。

transparent [træns'pærənt] *a.* 透明的

【记】词根记忆：trans(穿过) + par(平等，相等) + ent →(光线)均匀地穿过 → 透明的

【例】Jellyfish may be large enough to be seen, but they are *transparent*. 水母可以大得能被看到，但是它们是透明的。

【派】transparency(*n.* 透明；透明度)

vaccine [væk'si:n] *n.* 疫苗(bacterin)

【记】词根记忆：vacc(牛) + ine → 牛痘苗 → 疫苗

【例】She was criticized for developing the risky *vaccine*. 她因开发危险的疫苗而受到了批评。

【派】vaccinate(*v.* 预防接种)；vaccination(*n.* 接种疫苗)

vertebrate ['vɜːrtɪbrət] *n.* 脊椎动物 *a.* 有脊柱的(having a spinal column)

【记】来自vertebra(*n.* 脊椎骨)

【例】The nervous system of *vertebrates* is characterized by a nerve cord. 脊椎动物神经系统的特点是具有神经索。

I find life an exciting business and most exciting when it is lived for others.
我发现生活是令人激动的事情，尤其是为别人活着时。

——海伦·凯勒(*Helen Keller*)

☐ transparent ☐ vaccine ☐ vertebrate

Word List 39 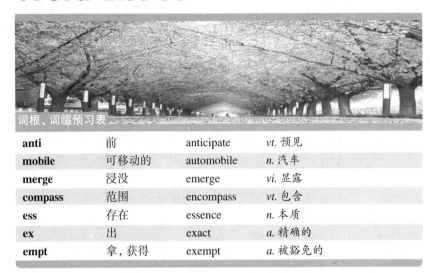 MP3-39

词根、词缀预习表

anti	前	anticipate	vt. 预见
mobile	可移动的	automobile	n. 汽车
merge	浸没	emerge	vi. 显露
compass	范围	encompass	vt. 包含
ess	存在	essence	n. 本质
ex	出	exact	a. 精确的
empt	拿，获得	exempt	a. 被豁免的

allay [əˈleɪ] vt. 减轻，减少(*reduce, alleviate)

【例】Maria wrote stories interesting enough to attract children and morally instructive enough to *allay* adult distrust of fiction. 玛利亚写的故事足够有趣，能吸引儿童，也具有道德指导意义，能减少成年人对小说的怀疑。

aluminum [ˌæljəˈmɪniəm] n. 铝

anticipate [ænˈtɪsɪpeɪt] vt. 预见(foresee)，预期(*look forward to, expect)

【记】词根记忆：anti(前)+ cip(落下)+ ate → 提前想到苹果会落下 → 预见

【例】The test was harder than he had *anticipated*. 测验比他预期的要难。

【派】anticipated(a. 预期的)

assortment [əˈsɔːrtmənt] n. 分类；各类物品的聚集，混合物

assume [əˈsuːm] vt. 假定(premise, suppose)；承担(bear)

【记】词根记忆：as + sume(拿，取) → 他拿起包袱背在了肩上 → 承担

【例】I *assume* everyone here is a sophomore, since this is the Nursing Department second-year physiology course. 我假定在座的每位都是二年级学生，因为这是护理系二年级的生理学课程。

【派】assumption(n. 假定；担任)

☐ allay ☐ aluminum ☐ anticipate ☐ assortment ☐ assume

【参】presume(v. 假定；认为)；consume(v. 消耗，消费)；resume(vt. 恢复)

automobile ['ɔːtəməbiːl] n. 汽车(motor)

【记】词根记忆：auto(自动) + mobile(可移动的)→ 汽车

【派】automotive(a. 汽车的)

【参】immobile(a. 固定的；不活动的)

blizzard

beaver ['biːvər] n. 海狸

blizzard ['blɪzərd] n. 大风雪

【参】bazaar(n. 集市)；bizarre(a. 古怪的)

blues [bluːz] n. 抑郁，沮丧(gloom, depressed spirits)；布鲁斯音乐

brush [brʌʃ] n. 毛笔 vt. 刷，拂(wipe)

【搭】brush up on sth 奋起直追(重温生疏了的技术等)

【例】I really need to *brush* up on my math. 我确实需要复习数学。

by-product ['baɪˌprɑːdʌkt] n. 副产品

cabinet ['kæbɪnət] n. 内阁；贮藏橱；陈列柜

chapel ['tʃæpl] n. 小礼堂(a subordinate or private place of worship)

【记】分拆联想：c + hap(运气) + el → 人们在小礼堂祈祷自己好运 → 小礼堂

【参】cathedral(n. 大教堂)

comedy ['kɑːmədi] n. 喜剧

completion [kəm'pliːʃn] n. 完成，实现(accomplishment, realization)

【例】They do not need to carry each task to *completion* from start to finish. 他们不需要从头到尾完成每项任务。

coral ['kɔːrəl] n. 珊瑚(虫) a. 珊瑚色的，珊瑚红的

【记】分拆联想：cor(看作core，核心) + al → 大海的核心之处有珊瑚 → 珊瑚

【搭】coral reef 珊瑚礁

declare [dɪ'kler] v. 表明(announce)；宣称(assert)

【记】分拆联想：de(加强) + clare(清楚) → 说清楚 → 表明；宣称

【例】"My flight was done with no expectation of reward," she *declared*, "just purely for the love of accomplishment." "我飞行没有期望得奖，"她宣称，"纯粹是为了有所成就。"

demobilize [diː'moʊbəlaɪz] vt. 遣散，使复员

【例】The child soldiers in the country have been *demobilized* recently. 该国的娃娃兵最近被遣散了。

devoid [dɪ'vɔɪd] a. 全无的(empty)

| automobile | beaver | blizzard | blues | brush | by-product | cabinet |
| chapel | comedy | completion | coral | declare | demobilize | devoid |

419

【记】词根记忆：de + void(空) → 全无的

【例】The hot air is *devoid* of even the slightest amount of moisture. 热空气中没有一点水汽。

【参】void(*a.* 空的); voidance(*n.* 排泄，放出); avoid(*vt.* 避免)

dilemma [dɪˈlemə] *n.* 进退两难的局面

【记】发音记忆："地雷嘛" → 陷入雷区 → 进退两难的局面

【例】I have the *dilemma* of choosing a new car or a computer. 我面临选择新车或电脑的两难局面。

dwarf [dwɔːrf] *n.* 侏儒；矮小的东西 *v.* 使…显得矮小(outshine)；萎缩

【搭】dwarf star 矮星

【例】Cotton became the main American export, *dwarfing* all other products. 棉花成为了美国主要的出口商品，超过所有其他产品。

elevate [ˈelɪveɪt] *vt.* 举起，抬高(lift, raise)

【记】词根记忆：e(出) + lev(举起) + ate(使…) → 举起，抬高

【例】The birds began to *elevate* their nests in branches perhaps to avoid predators. 一些鸟把窝建在了高处的树枝上，可能是为了躲开食肉动物。

【派】elevation(*n.* 提高；海拔); elevator(*n.* 电梯，升降机)

【参】escalator(*n.* 自动扶梯)

emerge [iˈmɜːrdʒ] *vi.* 显露，暴露(*appear)

【记】词根记忆：e(出) + merge(浸没) → 从浸没之中出来 → 显露，暴露

【例】Several outstanding musicians *emerged* as leading jazz artists in Chicago. 几位音乐家脱颖而出成为了芝加哥引领风骚的爵士乐艺术家。

【派】emergence(*n.* 形成；出现); emergency(*n.* 紧急情况，突发事件)

encase [ɪnˈkeɪs] *vt.* 包住(*embed)

【记】分拆联想：en(进入) + case(容器) → 被装入容器中 → 包住

【例】Floating on the oceans every year are 7, 659 trillion metric tons of ice *encased* in 10,000 icebergs. 每年有1万座冰山包裹着7659兆公吨的冰漂浮在海洋上。

encompass [ɪnˈkʌmpəs] *vt.* 包含 (*include)；环绕(encircle)

【记】词根记忆：en (进入) + compass (范围) → 进入范围 → 包含；环绕

【例】The term "art deco" has come to *encompass* three distinct but related design

encompass

trends of the 1920's and 1930's. "艺术装饰"这个词涵盖了二十世纪二、三十年代三个明显不同但又相关的设计潮流。

epoch [ˈepək] *n.* 新纪元；时代(era)
【记】和echo(*v./n.* 回响)一起记

essence [ˈesns] *n.* 本质(*nature)；精髓
【记】词根记忆：ess(存在) + ence → 存在的根本 → 本质；精髓
【搭】of the essence 非常重要的，不可缺少的
【例】This constant reshaping and recreation is the *essence* of folk music. 这种不断的重塑和再创造是民间音乐的精髓。

exact [ɪɡˈzækt] *a.* 精确的，准确的(precise)
【记】词根记忆：ex(出) + act(做) → 做出精确的结果 → 精确的
【搭】to be exact 准确说来
【例】To be *exact*, the assignments must be handed in on time by the end of next Monday. 准确地说，必须在下周一准时交作业。

exempt [ɪɡˈzempt] *a.* 被免除的，被豁免的
【记】词根记忆：ex + empt(拿，获得) → 拿出去 → 被免除的
【例】You are not *exempt* from the rules! 你没有被免于遵守这些规定！
【派】exemption(*n.* 免除)

fountain [ˈfaʊntn] *n.* 喷泉
【记】联想记忆：山(mountain)里有喷泉(fountain)

generate [ˈdʒenəreɪt] *vt.* 产生(produce)；引起(*cause)
【记】词根记忆：gener(产生) + ate → 产生；引起
【例】The smoke it *generated* went out through the main chimney. 它所产生的烟通过主烟道飘出去了。
【派】generator(*n.* 发电机)

glamorous [ˈɡlæmərəs] *a.* 富有魅力的，迷人的(attractive, charming)
【记】来自glamor(*n.* 魅力)

glare [ɡler] *n.* 耀眼的光(shine)
【例】The *glare* was so intense even my sunglasses didn't help. 光太强烈，我的墨镜都不管用了。

gross [ɡroʊs] *v.* 总计；获得…总收入(或毛利)*n.* 箩(计算单位，等于12打144个)*a.* 总的；毛的
【例】The company *grossed* $4 million. 该公司获得了400万美元毛利。

hinder [ˈhɪndər] *vt.* 阻碍，妨碍(*inhibit, obstruct)
【记】分拆联想：hind(后面) + er → 被挡在后面 → 阻碍，妨碍
【例】The government shouldn't create regulations that might *hinder*

business growth. 政府不应该制订妨碍商业发展的规定。

【派】unhindered(*a.* 不受妨碍的，不受阻碍的)

immediate [ɪ'miːdiət] *a.* 即刻的(instant)；最接近的(proximal)

【记】分拆联想：im(不，无) + mediate(居中的) → 省去中间过程 → 即刻的

【例】Reaction from the public and press was *immediate*, and derisive. 公众和媒体立即作出了反应，给予了讥讽。

【参】intermediate(*a.* 中间的；中级的)

incorporate [ɪn'kɔːrpəreɪt] *v.* 纳入；合并(combine)

【记】词根记忆：in(进入) + corpor(团体) + ate → 进入团体 → 纳入；合并

【例】When hypotheses are confirmed, they are *incorporated* into theories. 当假定被证实时，就可以纳入理论了。

【派】incorporation(*n.* 结合，合并)

insulation [ˌɪnsə'leɪʃn] *n.* 绝缘；隔离；孤立(isolation, separation)

【例】If you want to reduce your heating bills, good *insulation* of your home will be effective. 如果你想减少取暖费账单，在家里安装好的隔热材料会有效果。

intrusion [ɪn'truːʒn] *n.* 侵扰，干扰

【搭】intrusion into/on/upon 侵入，干涉

irony ['aɪrəni] *n.* 嘲讽

【记】分拆联想：iron(铁) + y → 像铁一样冷冰冰的话 → 嘲讽

issue ['ɪʃuː] *n.* 问题；(报刊的)一期 *vi.* 颁布；发行

【例】He and Dr. Johnson disagree on basic economic *issues*. 他和约翰逊博士对基本的经济问题持不同意见。//No silver coins were *issued* until 1794. 直到1794年才发行银币。

您真苗条

irony

kerosene ['kerəsiːn] *n.* 煤油，火油

【例】*Kerosene* was used to light lamps. 过去用煤油点灯。

lava ['lɑːvə] *n.* 岩浆，熔岩(magma)

【记】联想记忆：幼虫(larva)被岩浆(lava)熔化掉了

【例】Evidence of this is the molten *lava* that flows out of volcanoes. 流出火山的熔岩证实了这一点。

limitation [ˌlɪmɪ'teɪʃn] *n.* 限制，局限性(limit)

【例】Any *limitation* to the king's power could be permanent. 对国王权力的任何限制都是永久性的。

☐ immediate	☐ incorporate	☐ insulation	☐ intrusion	☐ irony	☐ issue
☐ kerosene	☐ lava	☐ limitation			

linen ['lɪnɪn] *n.* 亚麻织品，亚麻布 *a.* 亚麻(布制)的

【记】分拆联想：line(线) + n → 亚麻布是用一根根的线织成的 → 亚麻布

【例】Fine handmade lace is traditionally made of *linen* thread. 精美的手工蕾丝传统上是用亚麻丝做成的。

mannerism ['mænərɪzəm] *n.* 特殊习惯，怪癖(idiosyncrasy, peculiarity, habit)

【记】词根记忆：manner(风格，方式) + ism(表风格、特征) → 个人独有的言行 → 怪癖

mere [mɪr] *a.* 仅仅的，纯粹的(pure, absolute)

【记】联想记忆：要想抓住爱情，仅仅(mere)在这(here)徘徊是不行的

【例】From *mere* spectators, they became willing passengers and finally pilots in their own right. 他们开始只是旁观者，后来心甘情愿地成为乘客，并最终凭自身的努力成为了飞行员。

【派】merely(*ad.* 仅仅，只不过)

migrate ['maɪgreɪt] *vi.* 迁徙(flight)，移居(transplant)

【记】词根记忆：migr(移动) + ate → 迁徙，移居

【例】When these people *migrated* from the countryside, they carried their fears and suspicious with them. 这些人从乡村迁徙时，心里不乏担忧和疑虑。

【派】migrant(*n.* 移居者)；migratory(*a.* 迁移的；流浪的)

neutral ['nuːtrəl] *a.* 中性的；中立的(indifferent)

【记】词根记忆：neutr(两者都不) + al → 两者都不偏向的 → 中立的

【搭】neutral particle 中性粒子

【例】His attitude toward the claims made by advocates of health foods is *neutral*. 他对健康食品支持者的主张持中立态度。

【派】neutrality(*n.* 中性)；neutralize(*vt.* 中和)

output ['aʊtpʊt] *n.* 产量(yield)；输出(export)；产品(production)

【记】来自词组put out (产生)

overseas [ˌoʊvər'siːz] *ad./a.* 在海外(的)；在国外(的)(abroad)

panic ['pænɪk] *n./v.* 惊慌(alarm)

【记】来自Pan(潘)，是希腊神话中的山林、畜牧之神。它的怪叫声会使人产生极大的恐惧感，panic就是指Pan出现时给人们带来的恐惧感。

【例】The class presentation started half an hour ago and I was just beginning to *panic*. 课堂报告半个小时前一开始，我就惊慌起来。

| ☐ linen | ☐ mannerism | ☐ mere | ☐ migrate | ☐ neutral | ☐ output |
| ☐ overseas | ☐ panic | | | | |

passion [ˈpæʃn] *n.* 激情, 热情(emotion, enthusiasm)

【记】词根记忆: pass(感情) + ion → 激情, 热情

【例】It's been my *passion* since I collected my first Lincoln dime in 1971. 自从我1971 年收藏第一枚林肯十分硬币以来, 这就成了我的嗜好。

pervasive [pərˈveɪsɪv] *a.* 普遍深入的

【记】来自pervade(*v.* 遍及)

【派】This basic fact has been the most *pervasive* influence in determining the social arrangements and cultural practices of the people. 这一基本事实已普遍影响了人们对社交安排和文化实践的决定。

photosynthesis [ˌfoʊtoʊˈsɪnθəsɪs] *n.* 光合作用

【记】词根记忆: photo(光) + synthesis(综合) → 光合作用

press [pres] *n.* 报刊; 新闻界; 通讯社; 挤压 *v.* 挤压; 催促

【例】I'll be really *pressed* to get it done. 办这件事情我会顶着很大的压力。

pressure [ˈpreʃər] *n.* 压力(compression); 压强; 压迫(oppress)

【例】The deposits harden under conditions of heat and *pressure*. 沉淀物在高温高压条件下变硬。

proliferation [prəˌlɪfəˈreɪʃn] *n.* 繁殖, 大量增殖

【记】来自proliferat(e)(增生) + ion → 繁殖

prospect [ˈprɑːspekt] *n.* 前景(outlook); 可能性(*possibility); 景色; 期望(expectation)

v. 寻找(seek)

【记】词根记忆: pro(向前) + spect(看) → 向前看 → 前景; 寻找

【例】In Nevada, Twain *prospected* for sister and gold without much luck, but did succeed as a writer. 在内华达州, 吐温在寻找姐姐和金子时, 运气都不太好, 不过作为作家他的确成功了。

【派】prospector(*n.* 探勘者; 采矿者); prospective(*a.* 未来的; 可能的)

questionnaire [ˌkwestʃəˈner] *n.* 问卷, 调查表

【记】来自question(*n.* 问题)

【例】The professor wants them to fill in a research *questionnaire*. 教授想让他们填写一份研究调查表。

☐ passion ☐ pervasive ☐ photosynthesis ☐ press ☐ pressure ☐ proliferation
☐ prospect ☐ questionnaire

ray [reɪ] *n.* 光线 (beam); 射线

reflection [rɪˈflekʃn] *n.* 反映 (expression); 思考，想法

ray

【搭】without reflection 轻率; on reflection 再三思考

【例】After a few days of *reflection* the little girl decided to leave the city with her mother. 小女孩思考几天之后决定与母亲离开这座城市。

【派】reflect (*v.* 反射; 反映); reflected (*a.* 反射的); reflectionism (*n.* 反映论); reflectional (*a.* 反射的; 反映的)

resolve [rɪˈzɑːlv] *vt.* 解决 (*find a solution for, solve); 分辨 (distinguish)

【记】词根记忆: re(再) + solve(解决) → 解决

【例】It took forever to *resolve* the problem with the account. 解决这个客户的问题用了很长时间。//Earth-based telescopes can *resolve* objects as small as a few hundred meters on the lunar surface. 放置在地球上的高倍望远镜能分辨出月球表面几百米大小的物体。

【派】resolution(*n.* 分辨率，清晰度)

rival [ˈraɪvl] *vt.* 与…相匹敌 (match)

【记】分拆联想: ri + val(强壮的) → 差不多强壮的 → 与…相匹敌

【例】Ships can't *rival* aircraft for speed. 船只在速度上无法同飞机相比。

rotation [roʊˈteɪʃn] *n.* 旋转 (revolution)

salient [ˈseɪliənt] *a.* 显著的，突出的 (distinct, outstanding)

【记】词根记忆: sal(跳) + ient → 跳出来 → 突出的

scavenger [ˈskævɪndʒər] *n.* 清道夫 (ashman); 食腐动物

【记】来自 scaveng(e)(*v.* 打扫; 以腐肉为食) + er → 食腐动物

【参】revenge(*vt.* 报仇); avenge(*vt.* 为…报仇)

soybean [ˈsɔɪbiːn] *n.* 大豆 (legume, soy)

【记】组合词: soy(大豆) + bean(豆) → 大豆

spaghetti [spəˈgeti] *n.* 意大利式细面条

【例】A: Did you hear what George did last night? He was cooking dinner for the members of the drama club and he spilled *spaghetti* sauce all over the kitchen.
B: Doesn't surprise me one bit, he did the same thing last semester.
A: 你听说乔治昨天晚上干什么了吗? 他在给戏剧俱乐部的会员做饭时，把意大利面酱弄得满厨房都是。
B: 我一点都不奇怪。他上学期也这么做了。

sum [sʌm] *n.* 总和，数额（*amount）；算术 *v.* 合计（total）

【例】We have *summed* up the most important single fact about it at this moment in time. 此时此刻我们已经及时地对与它相关的最重要的一条事实进行了总结。//Ask them to work out a *sum*. 让他们算出总额。

【派】summing（*a.* 求和的）

terminate ['tɜːrmɪneɪt] *v.* 停止，结束（stop, end）

【记】词根记忆：termin（结束）+ ate → 结束

【例】In America, a woman's decision to *terminate* the pregnancy is involved in human rights and moral problems. 在美国，女性终止妊娠的决定涉及人权和道德问题。

【派】termination（*n.* 终止，结束）

terrestrial [təˈrestriəl] *a.* 陆地的，陆生的；地球的

【记】词根记忆：terr（地）+ estr + ial → 陆地的，陆生的

【例】Ichthyosaurs had a higher chance of being preserved than *terrestrial* creatures did. 鱼龙比陆生生物被保存下来的几率要大。//The highest *terrestrial* mountain is Mount Everest. 陆地上最高的山是珠穆朗玛峰。

tract [trækt] *n.* 地域（area）；领域（field）

【例】Despite the intent of the law, speculators often manage to obtain large *tracts*. 尽管法律有意禁止，但投机者仍常常设法获得大片土地。

【参】traction（*n.* 牵引）；tractor（*n.* 拖拉机）

twig [twɪg] *n.* 嫩枝

【例】Large mammals also have their own tactics for browsing among food-rich *twigs*. 大型哺乳动物在吃富含食料的嫩枝时也有自己的策略。

uniform ['juːnɪfɔːrm] *n.* 制服（costume）*a.* 统一的（unitive）；均匀的（homogeneous）

【记】词根记忆：uni（单一）+ form（形式）→ 他们都穿着形式单一的制服 → 制服；统一的

【例】Textile mills turn to wool for blankets and *uniforms*. 纺织厂需要用羊毛做毯子和制服。//*Uniform* limits should be established for all air pollutants. 应该对所有的空气污染物设定统一的限制。

【派】uniformly（*ad.* 一律地，均一地）；uniformity（*n.* 同样，一致）

uniformity [ˌjuːnɪˈfɔːməti] *n.* 同样，一致（性）

【例】Students should avoid a lack of *uniformity* in evidences when writing their papers. 学生在撰写论文时应该避免论据不一致。

vacuum ['vækjuəm] *n.* 真空；空间(room) *a.* 真空的

【记】词根记忆：vacu(空) + um → 真空

【搭】vacuum cleaner 真空吸尘器

vibrate ['vaɪbreɪt] *vt.* 颤动，振动(swing)

【记】词根记忆：vibr(振动) + ate → 颤动，振动

【例】The quartz crystal in a heater *vibrates* at a particular frequency. 加热器的水晶振子按照某个特定频率振动。

vocation [voʊ'keɪʃn] *n.* 职业(occupation, profession)

【搭】vocational education 职业教育

【例】The guidance counselor helps the student choose a *vocation*. 指导老师帮助学生选择职业。

【派】vocational(*a.* 职业的；业务的)

【参】avocation(*n.* 业余爱好)

wrinkle ['rɪŋkl] *n.* 皱纹 *v.* 起皱；皱眉

【记】联想记忆：眨眼(twinkle)容易起皱纹(wrinkle)

【例】What Galileo has shown us is that Ganymede's surface is deeply *wrinkled* with ridges and fissures, a sign that it experiences some of the same dynamic forces that move continents and cause quakes on earth. 伽利略向我们表明，木卫三表面布满山脊和裂缝，沟壑丛生，这标志着它上面存在着与地球上导致大陆漂移、引发地震的同样的动力。

Try not to become a man of success but rather try to become a man of value.

不要为成功而努力，要为做一个有价值的人而努力。

——爱因斯坦(*A. Einstein*)

Word List 40  MP3-40

词根、词缀预习表

ad	做	advertise	v. 为…做广告
itude	表状态	altitude	n. 海拔，高度
cede	割让	concede	v. 承认；让步
system	系统	ecosystem	n. 生态系统
sinu	弯曲	sinuous	a. 弯曲的
vapor	水汽	evaporate	v. (使)蒸发
fac	脸，面	facet	n. 面
ible	能…的	incredible	a. 惊人的
orig	升起，开始	originate	v. 起源，发起

advertise [ˈædvərtaɪz] v. 为…做广告，宣传(promote)

【记】词根记忆：ad(做) + vert(转) + ise(使…) → 通过做来转变人们的看法 → 宣传

【例】I'd like to enroll in the free seminar you *advertised* in newspaper. 我想报名参加你在报纸上宣传的免费研讨会。

【派】advertisement(n. 广告，公告)

alloy [ˈælɔɪ] n. 合金

[əˈlɔɪ] vt. 使成合金

【记】分拆联想：all(所有的) + oy → 把所有的金属混在一起 → 合金

altitude [ˈæltɪtuːd] n. (海拔)高度(height)；[常pl.]海拔甚高的地方

【记】词根记忆：alt(高) + itude(表状态) → 高度

【例】Plants cannot move water to high *altitudes*. 工厂无法把水运到高海拔地区。

arrange [əˈreɪndʒ] vt. 布置，安排(plan)；筹备(prepare)

【记】分拆联想：ar(加强) + range(排列) → 有顺序地排列 → 布置，安排

【例】Help the man *arrange* his trip. 帮助此人安排他的行程。

【派】arrangement(*n.*［常*pl.*］安排，布置)；rearrange(*vt.* 重新安排)

backup [ˈbækʌp] *n.* 后援；后备 *v.* 备份

【例】A: I know I promised to drive you to the airport next Tuesday. But I am afraid that something has come up. And they've called a special meeting at work.

B: No big deal. Jenny said she was available as a *backup*.

A：我知道我答应了下周二开车送你去机场。不过我恐怕有事去不了。我上班的地方要召开一个特别会议。

B：没关系。珍妮说她有空作为后备。

You'd better *backup* your files when you edit them. 你编辑文档时最好备份一下。

blame [bleɪm] *vt.* 谴责，责备(condemn, rebuke) *n.* 过失；责备(condemnation, reprehension)

【例】The report *blames* leaders' neglect of duty for milk powder with poor quality. 报道谴责领导人在劣质奶粉问题上玩忽职守。

blink [blɪŋk] *v.* 眨眼

【记】联想记忆：b + link(连接) → 用眨眼睛来联络感情 → 眨眼

blur [blɜːr] *vt.* 使…模糊(make indistinct)

boulder [ˈboʊldər] *n.* 大石头

boulder

【记】联想记忆：shoulder(*n.* 肩膀)上扛大石头(boulder)

cancel [ˈkænsl] *vt.* 取消，把…作废(abolish)；删去，删除(revoke, call off)，划掉；相互抵消

【记】词源记忆：源自拉丁文cancelli(斜条格钩)，据说罗马书写员在抄写错误时会用斜条格钩状来表明注销，后被引入英语，作"取消，撤销"讲。

【搭】cancel out 抵偿；抵消

【例】A: When are you going to have your eyes checked?

B: I had to *cancel* my appointment. I couldn't fit it in.

A：你什么时候去检查眼睛?

B：我得取消预约。我安排不过来。

【派】cancellation(*n.* 取消)

cashier [kæˈʃɪr] *n.* 收银员，出纳员

【例】The petrol station *cashier* was threatened by the armed robbers at mid-night. 加油站的收银员在午夜时受到了持械抢劫犯的威胁。

□ backup	□ blame	□ blink	□ blur	□ boulder	□ cancel
□ cashier					

centigrade [ˈsentɪɡreɪd] *a.* 摄氏温度的

【记】词根记忆：centi(一百) + grade(等级) → 百分度的 → 摄氏温度的

chip [tʃɪp] *n.* 碎片(piece, bit)；芯片(integrated circuit) *v.* 削(或凿)下(break off)

【搭】silicon chip 硅片

【例】Early settlers used to *chip* our blocks of ice to melt for drinking water. 早期移民常常凿下冰块，把它们融化成饮用水。

cipher [ˈsaɪfər] *n.* 密码(code)

clear [klɪr] *a.* 清晰的，明白的；清朗的，清澈的；明亮的；畅通的，无阻的 *ad.* 清楚地，清晰地

【搭】clear away 扫除，收拾；消除；clear up 整理，收拾；清除，解除；解释，澄清；(天气)变晴

【例】A: Can you see the lake today?

B: You could if this fog would only *clear*.

A：你今天能看到湖吗？

B：只有雾散去之后才能看到。

You must make sure that all of your personal property has been *cleared* out of your room. 你必须确保你的所有个人物品都已从房间里清除出去了。

clump [klʌmp] *n.* 土块 *vi.* 丛生，成群(cluster)

【例】He got a *clump* of soil from the edge of a cow pasture. 他从奶牛牧场的边缘处取了一块土。

concede [kənˈsiːd] *v.* 承认(grant)；让步(yield)

【记】词根记忆：con + cede(割让) → 割让出去 → 让步

【例】The author *conceded* that individual chimpanzees may have a preference for certain companions. 作者承认猩猩个体可能对特定同伴有偏好。

【参】cede(*v.* 割让，放弃)；accede(*v.* 同意)；recede(*v.* 后退)；precede(*v.* 领先)

conservationist [ˌkɑːnsərˈveɪʃənɪst] *n.* (天然资源的)保护管理论者

conservative [kənˈsɜːrvətɪv] *a.* 保守的，谨慎的；守旧的(traditional, conventional)

【记】来自conserve(*vt.* 保存，保守)

【搭】conservative views 保守的观点；a dark conservative suit 一套黑色的传统西服；conservative society 守旧的社会

☐ centigrade	☐ chip	☐ cipher	☐ clear	☐ clump	☐ concede
☐ conservationist	☐ conservative				

【例】At a *conservative* estimate, the visit to Paris for five days will cost about £2,000. 保守地估计，到巴黎旅游5天要花费大约2000英镑。

【派】conservatively(*ad.* 保守地)

context ['kɑːntekst] *n.* 上下文；背景(setting)；环境(environment)

【记】分拆联想：con(共同) + text(编织) → 共同编织在一起 → 上下文

【例】Beads are often valuable in their original cultural *context* as well as in today's market. 珠子项链无论是在最初的文化背景下还是在当今的市场上往往都很值钱。

crack [kræk] *v.* (使)破裂(break) *n.* 裂(缝、纹)(split)

【例】The otter uses a stone to *crack* mussel shells. 海獭用石头敲碎贝壳。

【参】crush(*v.* 压碎)；crash(*n.* 碰撞)；craft(*n.* 工艺)

crack

culture ['kʌltʃər] *n.* 文化，文明；培养 *vt.* 培养

【搭】popular culture 通俗文化

【例】Hazen methodically screened and *cultured* scores of soil samples. 黑曾有条不紊地筛选并培养出了几十个土壤样本。

deform [dɪ'fɔːrm] *v.* (使)变形(distort)

【记】词根记忆：de(变坏) + form(形状) → (使)形状变坏 → (使)变形

【例】The intense heat from the fire *deformed* the metal chair. 火产生的高温使金属椅子变形了。

【派】deformation(*n.* 变形)；deformed(*a.* 不成形的)

degree [dɪ'griː] *n.* 程度；度数；学位；等级(grade)

【搭】to some degree 从某种程度上来说

【例】Some studies done with mice indicate that mammals do inherit fearfulness to some *degree*. 用老鼠做的一些研究表明，哺乳动物的确在一定程度上继承恐惧。

A: You're taking another computer class? I thought you'd already had a *degree* in computer science.

B: I do, but the technology keeps changing all the time, this is the best way to keep up with it.

A: 你还要再上电脑课？我以为你已经有了计算机科学学位。

B: 我的确有，但是技术一直在变。这是与技术保持同步的最佳方式。

context crack culture deform degree

distribution [ˌdɪstrɪˈbjuːʃn] *n.* 分发，分配；配给物；散布，分布

【搭】the distribution of …的分配；population distribution 人口分布；distribution center 分销中心

【例】The *distribution* of marine organisms depends on the chemical and physical properties of seawater. 海洋生物的分布取决于海水的化学和物理特征。

disturb [dɪˈstɜːrb] *vt.* 打扰，扰乱（upset, bother）

【记】词根记忆：dis（分开）＋turb（搅动）→ 搅开了 → 扰乱

drought [draʊt] *n.* 干旱（期）

【记】分拆联想：dr（看作 dry）＋ought（应该）→ 应该干 → 干旱

【例】The businessman stored large quantities of grain during periods of *drought*. 这个商人在旱灾期间囤积了大量粮食。

【参】draught（*n.* 气流；拖，拉）

economic [ˌiːkəˈnɑːmɪk] *a.* 经济（上）的；经济学的

【记】词根记忆：eco（经济）＋nom（某一领域的知识）＋ic → 经济学的

【搭】economic conditions 经济情况

【例】In the *economic* sense, laisser faire meant that while the government should be responsible for things like maintaining peace and protecting property rights, it should not interfere with private business. 从经济学上讲，自由主义指政府应该为诸如维护秩序和保护产权这些事务负责，而不应该干预私营企业。

【派】uneconomic（*a.* 非经济的）；socioeconomic（*a.* 社会经济学的）

ecosystem [ˈiːkoʊsɪstəm] *n.* 生态系统

【记】词根记忆：eco（生态）＋system（系统）→ 生态系统

engineering [ˌendʒɪˈnɪrɪŋ] *n.* 工程学

【记】来自 engineer（*n.* 工程师）

【搭】electronics engineering 电子工程学

【例】A: Could you give me a ride to the *engineering* building?

B: I would. But I'm late for the appointment on the other side of the town.

A: 你能开车送我去工程系大楼吗？

B: 我想送你去。但是我在镇另一头有个约会，就要迟到了。

A: What's the problem, Paul? You really look panicked.

B: I am speaking to a group of high school students about *engineering* this afternoon. But I have no idea how I am going to simplify some of the concepts for them.

A: 保罗，出什么事情了？你看上去真够慌张的。

B: 我今天下午要给一群高中生讲工程方面的东西。但是我不知道如何把一些概念讲得浅显易懂。

entail [ɪnˈteɪl] *vt.* 牵涉(involve)

【记】分拆联想：en + tail(尾巴) → 被人抓住尾巴 → 牵涉

【例】You should take a little while to think about what that would *entail* before making your final decision. 在做最后决定之前，你应该花点时间想想这会牵涉到什么。

essential [ɪˈsenʃl] *a.* 基本的，本质的(substaintial)；重要的

【记】词根记忆：ess(存在) + ential → 存在的东西 → 基本的，本质的

【例】Calcium is *essential* for maintaining bones and teeth healthy. 钙对保持骨骼和牙齿健康至关重要。

【派】essentially(*ad.* 本质上)

evaluate [ɪˈvæljueɪt] *vt.* 评价，估计(assess, estimate)

【记】词根记忆：e(出) + valu(=val价值) + ate → 给出价值 → 评价，估计

【例】What I expect you to do with your revise is to *evaluate* and improve the overall effectiveness of your paper. 我期望你修改时能客观评价并加强论文的整体效果。

【派】evaluation(*n.* 评估，评价)；evaluative(*a.* 可评估的)

evaporate [ɪˈvæpəreɪt] *v.* (使)蒸发；消失(disappear, vanish)

【记】词根记忆：e(出) + vapor(水汽) + ate(使…) → 使水汽出去 → 蒸发

【例】Ices have *evaporated* from its outer layers to leave a crust of nearly black dust all over the surface. 冰已经从外层融化，在表面留下一层几乎是黑色的灰尘。

【派】evaporation(*n.* 蒸发)；evaporated(*a.* 浓缩的，脱水的)；evaporating(*a.* 蒸发作用的)

exert [ɪgˈzɜːrt] *vt.* 发挥；施加(*cause, *influence)

【记】词根记忆：ex(出) + ert(能量，活动) → 发挥出能量 → 发挥；施加

【例】The pressure *exerted* on the human body increases by an atmosphere for every 10 meters of depth in seawater. 人体在海水中每下降10米，所受的压强就增加一个大气压。

【派】exertion(*n.* 发挥；行使)

explode [ɪk'sploʊd] *vi.* 爆炸（burst）

【记】联想记忆：探险（explore）遭遇爆炸（explode）

【例】How a star becomes unstable and *explodes* as a supernova is not known. 人们不了解恒星是如何变得不稳定并爆炸成超新星的。

【派】explosion（*n.* 爆炸）; explosive（*n.* 炸药; *a.* 爆炸的）; explosively（*ad.* 爆发地）

extravagant [ɪk'strævəgənt] *a.*（言行等）放肆的, 过度的（excessive）

【记】由拉丁文 extra（在外）+ vagor（游荡）组合而成, 故意思应该是"离开正道的", "游离不定的", 后来转变为"过度的, 放肆的"

【派】extravagantly（*ad.* 挥霍无度地）

facet ['fæsɪt] *n.* 面;（问题等的）方面

【记】词根记忆：fac（脸, 面）+ et → 方面

falcon ['fælkən] *n.* 猎鹰

【搭】peregrine falcon 游隼

【派】falconer（*n.* 养猎鹰者, 放鹰狩猎人）

fiction ['fɪkʃn] *n.* 小说; 虚构, 编造

【记】发音记忆："费口舌" → 别费口舌瞎编了 → 小说

【例】Such claim makes it difficult for the general public to separate fact from *fiction*. 这种声称使一般公众很难分辨虚实。

【派】fictional（*a.* 虚构的; 小说式的）

fray [freɪ] *vi.* 磨（损、破）（rub, fret）

【记】分拆联想：f + ray（光线）→ 时光催人老 → 磨（损、破）

【例】His woolen pants were sometimes fortified with buckskin to keep them from *fraying*. 为免磨破, 他的羊毛裤子有时缝上了鹿皮。

fuse [fjuːz] *v.* 熔合（mix, melt）; 合并（combine）

【例】The resulting mass was further heated to *fuse* the mass into what was called potash. 生成的物质被进一步加热了, 熔合成所谓的碳酸钾。

【派】fusion（*n.* 熔解; 核聚变）

image ['ɪmɪdʒ] *n.* 形象; 肖像; 影像, 映像

【记】联想记忆：网页上的图片都是 image 这个单词

【例】A: Which outfit should I wear to my job interview, the black dress or the navy blue suit?

B: Well, Jane, you've got to consider the *image* you want to present, and I say the suit is more professional looking.

A: 我应该穿什么衣服去参加面试？黑连衣裙还是藏青色套装？

explode	extravagant	facet	falcon	fiction	fray
fuse	image				

B：嗯，简，你得考虑自己想展示的形象。我觉得套装看上去更职业一些。

incredible [ɪnˈkredəbl] *a.* 惊人的，难以置信的(unbelievable)

【记】词根记忆：in(不) + cred(相信) + ible(能…的) → 难以置信的

【例】He must get an *incredible* phone bill every month. 他每个月的电话费账单肯定很惊人。

【派】incredibly(*ad.* 惊人地)

insert [ɪnˈsɜːrt] *vt.* 插入；放入

【例】Now use your hands to *insert* the keys in the locks. 现在用手把钥匙插到锁里。

我是两孔的

insert

instead [ɪnˈsted] *ad.* 代替，顶替

【例】A: This casserole really tastes good. I guess that's because the vegetables in it are fresh *instead* of canned.

B: I know. Kind of a rare treat in this cafeteria.

A：这个砂锅味道真不错。我猜这是因为里面是新鲜蔬菜，而不是罐装蔬菜。

B：我知道。在这个餐厅里难得吃到。

instrumental [ˌɪnstrəˈmentl] *a.* 起作用的，有帮助的；乐器的

【记】分拆联想：instrument (器具，手段) + al → 像工具一样的 → 有帮助的

【例】The government collected money on performances that included any types of acting, dancing or singing, but not *instrumental* music. 政府对包括任何种类的表演、舞蹈或演唱的演出进行了收费，但是不包括器乐。

interrupt [ˌɪntəˈrʌpt] *vt.* 打扰；使中断；阻碍(hinder)

【记】词根记忆：inter(在…之间) + rupt(断裂) → 在中间断裂 → 使中断；阻碍

【例】When you *interrupted* me, you made me lose my train of thought. 你打断我的时候，我失去了思绪。

【派】interruption(*n.* 打扰)

isolate [ˈaɪsəleɪt] *vt.* 使隔离，使孤立(separate)

【记】词根记忆：i + sol(孤独的) + ate(使…) → 使孤独 → 使隔离，使孤立

【搭】isolate from 与…隔离

【例】Studies show that non-readers tend to *isolate* themselves from the community. 研究表明不会阅读的人倾向于把自己和社会隔离开。

【派】isolated(*a.* 隔离的, 孤立的)

landscape ['lændskeɪp] *n.* 风景；风景画；地形(landform)

【记】组合词：land + scape(景色) → 风景

【例】In her versions the figures become more stylized and the *landscapes* less naturalistic. 在她的版本里, 人物更加程式化, 而风景不再那么写实。

larynx ['lærɪŋks] *n.* 【解】喉

lobby ['lɑːbi] *n.* 休息室, 大厅(hall)

【记】和hobby(*n.* 爱好)一起记

【例】Sally is waiting for the man in the *lobby*. 萨莉正在大厅等待那位男子。

mechanical [məˈkænɪkl] *a.* 机械的；机械性的(automatic)；呆板的(monotonous)

【派】mechanist(*n.* 机械论者)

mechanics [məˈkænɪks] *n.* 机械学；力学；过程；方法

【例】We've been talking about *mechanics* and then we still have a few minutes. 我们一直在讨论力学, 之后我们还有几分钟时间。

【派】mechanist(*n.* 机械论者)；mechanician(*n.* 机械师)；mechanic (*n.* 技工)

mercantile ['mɜːrkəntaɪl] *a.* 商业的(commercial)

【记】词根记忆：merc(贸易, 商业) + antile → 商业的

【例】Beads can often be used to designate the degree of *mercantile*, technological, and cultural sophistication. 珠子工艺经常被用来体现商业、技术和文化的高超水平。

mercury ['mɜːrkjəri] *n.* [M-] 水星；水银

【记】分拆联想：mer(音似：没) + cury(看作cure, 治愈) → 水银中毒没治了 → 水银

opal ['oʊpl] *n.* 猫眼石

originate [əˈrɪdʒɪneɪt] *v.* 起源, 发起(initiate, launch)

【记】词根记忆：orig(升起, 开始) + inate → 起源, 发起

【例】Life *originated* in the early seas less than a billion years after the Earth was formed. 地球形成之后不到10亿年, 就在早期的海洋中找到了生命体。

【派】origination(*n.* 发源)；originator(*n.* 创始人；发明人)

patent ['pætnt] *n.* 专利权(privilege) *a.* 专利的 *vt.* 申请专利

【例】He never tried to *patent* his discoveries or get wealth from them. 他从未试图为自己的发明申请专利或从中牟利。

【派】copatent(*vt.* 联合取得专利)

peak [pi:k] *n.* 最高点, 顶峰(*maximum, summit) *a.* 最高的

【记】发音记忆: "匹克" → 奥林匹克的精神之一就是挑战极限, 达到顶峰 → 顶峰

【例】After the *peak* year of 1957, the birth rate in Canada began to decline. 过了1957年这个高峰期后, 加拿大的出生率就开始下降了。

pertain [pər'teɪn] *vi.* (to)依附于或从属于某事物

【记】词根记忆: per(贯穿, 自始至终) + tain(拿住) → 始终拿着 → 始终拿着自己的东西 → 从属于某事物

【例】Almanacs provided the perfect steady seller because their information *pertains* to the locale in which they would be used. 年鉴的销量非常稳定, 因为其信息与所使用的地区相关。

plankton ['plæŋktən] *n.* 浮游生物

【例】Most *planktons* have transparent tissues as a protective camouflage. 多数浮游生物有透明的组织作为保护性伪装。

plate [pleɪt] *n.* 盘子; 版图(territory)

polar ['poulər] *a.* (南、北)极的

【搭】polar bear 北极熊; polar expedition 极地探险

【派】polarity(*n.* 极性); polarize(*vt.* 使极化)

pollutant [pə'lu:tənt] *n.* 污染物质

【记】来自pollute(*vt.* 污染)

【例】These cars must put no *pollutants* whatsoever into the atmosphere. 这些车不能往大气排放任何污染物。

procedure [prə'si:dʒər] *n.* 程序, 步骤(approach, course); 手续

【搭】graduate school application procedure 读研申请程序

profession [prə'feʃn] *n.* 职业(occupation); 同行; 专业(specialty)

pupil ['pju:pl] *n.* 瞳孔; 小学生(schoolchild)

reef [ri:f] *n.* 礁, 暗礁

respective [rɪ'spektɪv] *a.* 分别的, 各自的

【记】词根记忆: re + spect(看) + ive → 从各个方向看 → 分别的

【例】Northerners and Southerners alike threw themselves into the task of supplying their *respective* armies. 北方人和南方人一样投入到了供给各自军队的任务中去。

【派】respectively(*ad.* 各自地, 分别地)

☐ peak ☐ pertain ☐ plankton ☐ plate ☐ polar ☐ pollutant
☐ procedure ☐ profession ☐ pupil ☐ reef ☐ respective
437

rush [rʌʃ] v. (使)冲，(使)突进；奔，急速流动 n. 冲，急速行进 a. (交通)繁忙的

【搭】rush hour 高峰期；rush out of sth. 快速从…出来

【例】When gold was discovered in California in the mid-1800's, hundreds of people *rushed* in, hoping to get a part of the wealth. 19世纪中叶在加州发现黄金之后，成百上千的人蜂拥而至，希望得到一部分财富。

A: Are you OK? You are all out of breath.

B: I was running late this morning and had to *rush* to get here for the meeting.

A：你没事吧？上气不接下气的。

B：我今天上午迟到了，只能赶忙过来开会。

A: Why don't we drive downtown now?

B: Wouldn't it be better to wait until *rush* hour?

A：我们为什么不现在开车去城里呢？

B：等车流高峰期过了再去不更好吗？

【派】rushed(a. 匆忙的)

【参】bush(n. 矮树丛)

scratch

scratch [skrætʃ] vt. 刮擦(scrape) n. 划痕(mark, nick)

【例】Mind you don't s*cratch* the table with those scissors! 小心别用剪刀划坏桌面！

shrivel [ˈʃrɪvl] v. (使)枯萎

【记】联想记忆：sh(音似：使) + rivel(看作river, 河流) → 天气干旱使河流无水, 树木枯萎 → (使)枯萎

【派】shriveled(a. 满是皱纹的)

sinuous [ˈsɪnjuəs] a. 蜿蜒的(winding)

【记】词根记忆：sinu(弯曲) + ous → 弯曲的 → 蜿蜒的

stack [stæk] n. 堆(pile, heap) v. 堆积(pile)

【记】联想记忆：库存(stock)一堆(stack)商品

【搭】stack up 堆起

【例】There's room to *stack* up the cans of coffee. 有地方堆放咖啡罐。

stew [stu:] n. 炖(煨或焖)的食物 v. 炖，焖

【记】发音记忆："死丢" → 拼命往锅里丢东西 → 炖，焖

【派】stewing(n. 炖，煨)

subtract [səbˈtrækt] v. 减(去)

☐ rush　☐ scratch　☐ shrivel　☐ sinuous　☐ stack　☐ stew　☐ subtract

【记】词根记忆：sub(下面) + tract(拉) → 拉下去 → 减去

【例】Most photographic filters work by *subtracting* portions of visible light from the subject. 多数摄影滤光器的作用是把部分可见光从摄影对象中滤掉。

supply [səˈplaɪ] *vt.* 供给，供应(provide)；满足(需要)，补足 *n.* 供应，供应量

【记】词根记忆：sup + ply(重叠) → 重复给出物品 → 供给

【搭】supply sth. to sb. 为…提供…

【例】Take water with you. It is available at the relay stations but it helps to have an additional *supply*. 带上水。虽然中继站提供水，但是多带些水对你有好处。

A: I'm driving downtown this afternoon. I have to stop by the art *supply* store to get some paints for my art class.

B: It moved to Smithville.

A: 我下午要去市中心。我会在美术用品商店停一下，为我的美术课买一些颜料。

B: 那商店搬到史密斯威尔去了。

survive [sərˈvaɪv] *vi.* 幸免，幸存

【记】词根记忆：sur + vive(生命) → 在(事故)下面活下来 → 幸存

【例】The tailed toad may not *survive* without special efforts of conservationists. 没有生态环境保护者付出的特殊努力，有尾蟾蜍可能无法生存。

survive

【派】survival(*n.* 生存，幸免)；survivor(*n.* 幸存者，生还者)

willful [ˈwɪlfl] *a.* 任性的(unruly)

wreck [rek] *vt.* 破坏，毁坏(destroy)

【例】The scandal *wrecked* the politician's chances of being elected. 丑闻使这个政客失去了当选的可能。

【参】shipwreck(*n.* 船只失事)

Word List 41 MP3-41

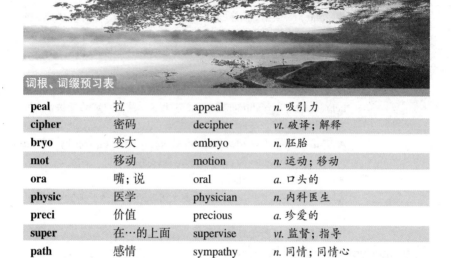

词根、词缀预习表

peal	拉	appeal	n. 吸引力
cipher	密码	decipher	vt. 破译；解释
bryo	变大	embryo	n. 胚胎
mot	移动	motion	n. 运动；移动
ora	嘴；说	oral	a. 口头的
physic	医学	physician	n. 内科医生
preci	价值	precious	a. 珍爱的
super	在…的上面	supervise	vt. 监督；指导
path	感情	sympathy	n. 同情；同情心
terr	使…惊吓	terrific	a. 极好的

account [ə'kaʊnt] *n.* 解释(interpretation)；账户(record) *v.* 说明…的原因
【搭】take... into account 考虑；重视；account for 说明；占；on account of 由于
【例】The three main television networks in the United States *account* for more advertising dollars than any other medium. 美国三大电视网络占有的广告费比其他任何媒体都要多。
【派】accounting(*n.* 会计学)；accountant(*n.* 会计师)；accountable (*a.* 应作解释的；应负责的)

appeal [ə'piːl] *n.* 吸引力(*attraction) *vi.* 吸引；上诉
【记】词根记忆：ap + peal(=pull 拉)→ 拉过去 → 吸引
【例】This modern wildlife art *appeals* to large numbers of nature lovers. 这一现代野生动物艺术吸引大量热爱自然的人。
【派】appealing(*a.* 吸引人的；打动人心的)

apprenticeship [ə'prentɪʃɪp] *n.* 学徒工作；学徒的年限
【例】During their mid teens a number of young people leave home to serve as an *apprenticeship* in the factories. 许多年轻人在十五、六岁时就离家去工厂当学徒。

□ account □ appeal □ apprenticeship

attach [əˈtætʃ] *vt.* 连接（fix, connect）；贴上；依附于（affix）

【例】They *attach* themselves to the mother's leg joints. 他们抱着母亲的腿。

【派】attached（*a.* 附加的，附属的）；attachment（*n.* 附加装置；依恋）

barge [bɑːrdʒ] *n.* 驳船；游艇

【记】发音记忆：“八只”→八只驳船→驳船

beak [biːk] *n.* 鸟嘴，喙

breeze [briːz] *n.* 微风

【记】和freeze(*v.* 冷冻)一起记

bronze [brɑːnz] *n.* 青铜

【搭】Bronze Age 青铜器时代

bundle [ˈbʌndl] *n.* 捆，束（package, bale）*vt.* 推搡；匆匆赶往

【记】发音记忆：“绑到”→把散的东西捆到一起→捆，束

【例】Mary gave a *bundle* of clothes to charity. 玛丽给了慈善组织一捆衣服。//The farmers *bundled* the husks of corn together for fuel. 农民们把玉米皮绑起来用作燃料。

canoe [kəˈnuː] *n.* 独木舟；小游艇

cartilage [ˈkɑːrtɪlɪdʒ] *n.* 【解】软骨

【例】The *cartilage* in John's nose was broken when it was hit. 约翰鼻子里面的软骨在受到撞击后断了。

cast [kæst] *n.* 铸件 *vt.* 浇铸（mold）；投掷（throw）

【例】They had invented bronze, an alloy that could be *cast* in molds, out of which they made tools and weapons. 他们已经发明了青铜，这种合金可以在模子里浇注，做成工具和武器。

chamber [ˈtʃeɪmbər] *n.* 房间（room, compartment）；洞穴（cavity）

chorus [ˈkɔːrəs] *n.* 合唱队

clipper [ˈklɪpər] *n.* 快速帆船

compact [ˈkɑːmpækt] *a.* 紧凑的；简洁的（concise）[kəmˈpækt] *vt.* 压缩（compress）

【搭】the compact industrial city 工业密集型城市

【例】Native plants in these areas are becoming more *compact*. 这些地

| attach | barge | beak | breeze | bronze | bundle | canoe |
| cartilage | cast | chamber | chorus | clipper | compact | |

441

区的本土植物变得更加密集。//The layers of granular snow further *compact* to form firm, a much denser kind of snow. 一层层的雪粒进一步压缩，形成结实并且密度更大的雪。

【参】impact(*n.* 碰撞)

confront [kən'frʌnt] *vt.* 使面临(face, encounter)；对抗(oppose)

【记】词根记忆：con + front(前面) → 面对面 → 使面临；对抗

【例】Staggering tasks *confronted* the people of the United States, North and South, when the Civil War ended. 内战结束后，美国南北方的人民都面临着艰巨的任务。

congratulation [kən,grætʃu'leɪʃn] *n.* 祝贺，道喜

considerate [kən'sɪdərət] *a.* 考虑周到的；体贴的(thoughtful)

【例】What we need is a roommate who is neat and *considerate*. 我们需要一位爱整洁、体贴的室友。

【派】consideration(*n.* 考虑；体贴)；inconsiderate(*a.* 不体贴的；轻率的)

considering [kən'sɪdərɪŋ] *prep.* 就…而论；照…说来；鉴于(regarding)

【例】A: I was just complaining about the hot sand. *Considering* what the water's like, I wonder how the sand can be so hot.

B: Well, professor's lecture on specific heat might give you a clue. Water has a higher specific heat than sand.

A: 我刚才在抱怨沙子太烫。想想水的温度，我奇怪怎么沙子可以这么烫。

B: 嗯，教授关于比热容的课会给你一点启发。水的比热比沙子高。

A: I'm sorry I forgot to return your physics book last night.

B: I'll forgive you *considering* the test isn't until Friday.

A: 对不起，昨晚忘还你物理书了。

B: 考虑到周五才考试，我会原谅你的。

decipher [dɪ'saɪfər] *vt.* 破译(decode)

【记】词根记忆：de(去掉) + cipher(密码) → 解开密码 → 破译

【例】Ancient Egyptian hieroglyphic script was finally *deciphered*. 古埃及的象形文字终于被破译了。

detective [dɪ'tektɪv] *n.* 侦探

【搭】detective story 侦探小说

【例】My *detective* solved a jewelry store robbery. 我的侦探破获了一起珠宝店抢劫案。

downside ['daʊnsaɪd] *n.* 缺点；负面

【例】The *downside* of my part-time job is that the company is too far away from my dorm. 我兼职工作不好的一面是，公司离宿舍太远。

【参】upside(*n.* 上边，上面)

eager ['iːgər] *a.* 渴望的；热切的(keen)

【搭】eager to do 渴望做…；eager for 渴望…

【例】A crowd of *eager* shareholders are waiting outside the big company. 一群急不可耐的股东正在大公司外面等待。

【参】eagle(*n.* 鹰)

electron [ɪ'lektrɑːn] *n.* 【物理】电子

【派】electronic(*a.* 电子的); electronics(*n.* 电子学)

【参】electrocardiogram(*n.* 心电图)

embryo ['embrɪoʊ] *n.* 胚胎；雏形

【记】词根记忆：em + bryo(变大) → 种子等变大 → 胚胎

【派】embryonic(*a.* 开始的)

exaggerate [ɪg'zædʒəreɪt] *v.* 夸张，夸大(overstate)

【记】词根记忆：ex(出) + agger(堆积) + ate → 越堆越高 → 夸张，夸大

【例】I tend to discount anything that Sally says. She *exaggerates* so much! 萨莉说什么我都不会信了。她太夸张了!

【派】exaggeration(*n.* 夸张); exaggerated(*a.* 夸张的)

exclude [ɪk'skluːd] *vt.* 把…排除在外

【记】词根记忆：ex(出) + clude(关闭) → 关出去 → 把…排除在外

【例】Please don't *exclude* grains from your diet. 请不要把谷物排除在你的膳食之外。

【派】exclusion(*n.* 排斥); exclusive(*a.* 排他的)

【参】conclude(*v.* 结束；作结论)

graph [græf] *n.* 图表(diagram); 坐标图(plotting)

【记】本身为词根，意为：书写；画图

【例】They should look for another *graph* immediately. 他们应该立刻去另找另一张图表。

heyday ['heɪdeɪ] *n.* 全盛期(climax)

【记】组合词：hey(惊喜声) + day → 充满惊喜声的日子 → 全盛期

【搭】in sb's heyday …的全盛时期

【例】In his *heyday*, David was a great movie director. 戴维在他的顶峰期是位了不起的电影导演。

ideal [aɪ'diːəl] *a.* 理想的；完美的(*perfect) *n.* 理想

☐ downside	eager	electron	embryo	☐ exaggerate	☐ exclude
☐ graph	heyday	ideal			

【记】分拆联想: i + deal(看作dear, 亲爱的) → 我亲爱的人是最理想、最完美的 → 理想的; 完美的

【例】They say that arm exercises are an *ideal* way to become physically fit. 他们说锻炼胳臂是使身体健康的理想方式。

【派】idealist(*n.* 理想主义者); idealistic(*a.* 理想主义者的)

imaginary [ɪ'mædʒɪneri] *a.* 想象中的, 虚构的

【搭】an imaginary world 虚构的世界

【例】The so-called equator, which we often mention, is actually an *imaginary* line around the middle of the earth. 我们经常提到的所谓的赤道, 其实是地球中间一条虚构的线。

【参】imaginative(*a.* 富有想象力的; 创新的)

inclined [ɪn'klaɪnd] *a.* 有…倾向的; 倾斜的

【记】来自incline(*v.* 倾向于)

【例】Some people are *inclined* to jump to hasty conclusion. 一些人倾向于草率下结论。

infancy ['ɪnfənsi] *n.* 幼年(babyhood); (发展或生长的)初期(beginning)

【记】来自infant(*n.* 婴儿, 幼儿)

【例】In Earth's *infancy*, its surface was warm enough for life. 地球形成初期, 其表面对生命而言足够温暖。

instance ['ɪnstəns] *n.* 例子; 事例(*case)

【记】分拆联想: in + stan(看作stand, 站立) + ce → 模特站在那就是最好的例子 → 例子

interplay ['ɪntərpleɪ] *n.* 相互作用, 相互影响(interact)

【记】词根记忆: inter(在…之间) + play(起作用) → 相互作用

【例】She combines cultural documentation with invention in an *interplay* of fact and fiction. 她通过事实与虚构的相互作用, 把文化记录与虚构结合起来。

legendary ['ledʒənderi] *a.* 传奇的(mythical, fabled)

【记】来自legend(*n.* 传奇; 传说)

【搭】a legendary hero 传奇英雄

limestone ['laɪmstoʊn] *n.* 石灰岩

【记】组合词: lime(石灰) + stone(石头) → 石灰岩

melting ['meltɪŋ] *a.* 融化的; 熔化的(thawy)

【搭】melting point 熔点

【例】The seeds in the soil are watered by the *melting* snows of winter. 融化的冬雪浇灌了土壤里的种子。

melting

□ imaginary □ inclined □ infancy □ instance □ interplay □ legendary
□ limestone □ melting

metabolic [ˌmetəˈbɑːlɪk] *a.* 新陈代谢的

【记】来自 metabol(ism)(新陈代谢)+ ic → 新陈代谢的

【例】Sea cucumbers have the capacity to become quiescent and live at a low *metabolic* rate. 海参能够休眠，并以很低的新陈代谢率生存。

【参】metabolism(*n.* 新陈代谢)

milieu [miːˈljɜː] *n.* 环境；出身背景

【记】联想记忆：mi(d)(中间)+ lieu(地方)→ 在一个地方里 → 在一个环境中 → 环境

motion [ˈmoʊʃn] *n.* 运动，移动(*movement)

【记】词根记忆：mot(移动)+ ion → 运动，移动

【例】The fish pushes water aside by the forward *motion* of its head and with a curve of its body and its flexible tall. 鱼通过头向前运动以及身体曲线和灵活的尾巴而把水推向两侧。

【派】motionless(*a.* 不动的，静止的)

oblivious [əˈblɪviəs] *a.* 遗忘的(forgetful)

【记】词根记忆：ob(反)+ liv(=live 活)+ ious → 不再活的 → 不再活着的东西很快就会被人遗忘 → 遗忘的

【例】The lad stretched full length by the mast seems *oblivious* to the spray of the bow waves. 桅杆旁全身伸展的小伙子好像没有察觉船首的浪花。

official [əˈfɪʃl] *a.* 官方的；正式的

【记】来自 office(*n.* 政府机关；部)

【搭】official copy 正式文本

【例】A: You know that summer internship I applied for. They want an *official* copy of all my grades. But the records office charges 20 dollars for an *official* grade report. That's a lot, don't you think?

B: It really is. I only had to pay six for mine last year.

A: 你知道我申请的暑假实习工作。他们要我所有成绩的正式复印件。但是档案室出具一份正式成绩单要收20美元。这也太贵了，你觉得呢？

B: 的确如此。我去年只需要付6美元。

oral [ˈɔːrəl] *a.* 口头的，口述的(spoken)

【记】词根记忆：ora(嘴，说)+ l(…的)→ 口头的，口述的

passage [ˈpæsɪdʒ] *n.* 文章；一段(paragraph, chapter)

【记】分拆联想：pass(通过)+ age → 通过的部分 → 一段

pasture [ˈpæstʃər] *n.* 牧场，草原(grassland, meadow)

【记】分拆联想：pas(看作 pass，通过)+ ture → 牛羊通过的地方 →

牧场，草原

【搭】far-flung pasture 广袤的草原

percussion [pərˈkʌʃn] *n.* 打击乐器

【记】来自 percuss（轻敲）+ ion → 需要敲打的乐器 → 打击乐器

physician [fɪˈzɪʃn] *n.* 内科医生

【记】词根记忆：physic（医学）+ ian → 内科医生

portraiture [ˈpɔːrtrətʃər] *n.* 肖像画法

【参】landscape(*n.* 风景画)

poster [ˈpoustər] *n.* 招贴；海报

【记】来自 post（邮政；张贴）+ er → 海报；招贴

precious [ˈpreʃəs] *a.* 珍爱的（cherished）；贵重的（valuable）

【记】词根记忆：preci（价值）+ ous → 有价值的 → 贵重的

【例】I know this is *precious* to you, and I'll take good care of it. 我知道这对你来说很珍贵，我会好好保管的。

【派】semiprecious(*a.* 半宝石的)

prescription [prɪˈskrɪpʃn] *n.* 处方，药方

【记】来自 prescribe(*v.* 开处方)

【搭】prescription drug 处方药

【例】Pharmacists fill drug *prescriptions*, keep records of the drugs their patients are taking to make sure that harmful combinations are not prescribed. 药剂师填写医药处方，记录病人要服用的药物，确保没有开出有害的药物组合。

【参】school infirmary 学校医务室

pretension [prɪˈtenʃn] *n.* 要求；主张（claim）

【记】分拆联想：pre（预先）+ tension（紧张，压力）→ 预先感到了压力，主张放松一下 → 要求；主张

propagate [ˈprɑːpəgeɪt] *vt.* 繁殖（raise, reproduce）；散布；传播（spread, disperse）

【记】词根记忆：pro + pag（砍；切）+ ate → 繁殖；原意是把树的旁枝剪掉使主干成长，引申为繁殖

【例】Some tropical plants can only be *propagated* from seeds. 一些热带植物只能通过种子进行繁殖。

prose [prouz] *n.* 散文

【记】分拆联想：p + rose（玫瑰）→ 散文如玫瑰花瓣，形散而神不散 → 散文

【例】Now Gertrude Stein is better known for her *prose* than for her poems. 现在格特鲁德·斯坦的散文比她的诗歌更加有名。

| percussion | physician | portraiture | poster | precious | prescription |
| pretension | propagate | prose | | | |

pulse [pʌls] *n.* 脉搏(throb); 脉冲(an electromagnetic wave)
【记】词根记忆：puls(驱动)+e → 脉搏；脉冲
【搭】electronic pulse 电冲

raft [ræft] *n.* 木筏
【记】联想记忆：坐木筏(raft)漂流(drift)

ravine [rə'viːn] *n.* 沟壑；峡谷(gorge)

rayon ['reɪɑːn] *n.* 人造丝；人造纤维

residential [ˌrezɪ'denʃl] *a.* 住宅的，与居住有关的
【记】来自resident(*n.* 居民)
【搭】residential block/district 住宅区；a residential school 寄宿学校
【派】residentiary(*n.* 居住者)

romantic [roʊ'mæntɪk] *a.* 浪漫的
【例】That rather *romantic* version of the story is not what actually happened that night. 那件事相当浪漫的版本不符合当晚发生的实际情况。
【派】romanticism(*n.* 浪漫主义); romanticize (*v.* 浪漫化；传奇化)

roughly ['rʌfli] *ad.* 大致地(*approximately); 粗糙地
【记】来自rough(粗糙的)+ly → 粗糙地
【例】In recent years, the United States' population had increased *roughly* five times. 近些年，美国的人口大概增加了五倍。

season ['siːzn] *n.* 季(节)；时期(period)
【派】seasonal(*a.* 季节的；季节性的)

seismology [saɪz'mɑːlədʒi] *n.* 地震学
【记】词根记忆：seism(地震)+ology(…学) → 地震学

shrub [ʃrʌb] *n.* 灌木(丛)
【记】分析联想：sh+rub(摩擦) → 灌木擦伤皮肤 → 灌木

sidewalk ['saɪdwɔːk] *n.* 人行道(sideway, pavement)
【例】A: It's a bit warm out today.
B: Warm? You could fry an egg on the *sidewalk*.
A: 今天外面比较暖和。
B: 暖和？你都可以在人行道上煎鸡蛋了。

soak [soʊk] *v.* 浸泡，浸湿，浸透
【记】和soap(*n.* 肥皂)一起记
【搭】soak up the sun 沐浴阳光

| pulse | raft | ravine | rayon | residential | romantic |
| roughly | season | seismology | shrub | sidewalk | soak |

447

【例】A: I'm so *soaked* from the rain. I'd go back to my room to change my clothes if there were more time before the performance.

B: I don't want to miss even a few minutes of this concert.

A：雨水把我浇透了。演出前要是时间充裕的话，我就回屋换件衣服。

B：我可不想错过这场演出，哪怕只有几分钟。

【参】soap(*n.* 肥皂)

sociology [ˌsoʊsiˈɑːlədʒi] *n.* 社会学

【记】词根记忆：soci(同伴；结交) + ology(学科) → 社会学

【派】sociological(*a.* 社会学的；社会学上的)；sociologist(*n.* 社会学家)

spectacular [spekˈtækjələr] *a.* 壮观的；引人注目的(striking, remarkable)

【记】来自spectac(le)(景象；奇观) + ular → 壮观的；引人注目的

【例】The most *spectacular* thing about the sea cucumber is the way it defends itself. 海参最了不起的是它自卫的方式。

stationary [ˈsteɪʃəneri] *a.* 静止的(immobile)；固定的(*fixed, immovable)

【记】词根记忆：sta (站；立) + tion + ary → 总站在一个地方的 → 静止的

【参】stationery(*n.* 文具)

strategic [strəˈtiːdʒɪk] *a.* 对全局有重要意义的；关键的；战略(上)的(tactical)

【例】The bridge is one of the most *strategic* card games. 桥牌是最具有战略意义的纸牌游戏之一。

sulfur [ˈsʌlfər] *n.* 硫磺

【记】联想记忆：吸入了过多的硫磺(sulfur)让人痛苦(suffer)

【派】sulfuric(*a.* 硫磺的，含硫磺的)

supervise [ˈsuːpərvaɪz] *vt.* 监督(oversee)；指导

【记】词根记忆：super(在…上面) + vise(看) → 在上面看 → 监督

【例】The National Academy of Design for the painters *supervised* the incorporation of new artistic techniques. 针对画家的国家设计研究院指导新艺术技巧的融合。

【派】supervision(*n.* 监督)；supervisor(*n.* 主管，监督员)

surround [səˈraʊnd] *v.* 包围；环绕(circle)

【记】联想记忆：sur + round(圆) → 在圆的外边 → 环绕；包围

【例】Nowadays we are constantly *surrounded* by news and information. 现在我们时刻都被新闻和信息所包围着。

【参】surrounding(*n.* 环境)

□ sociology	□ spectacular	□ stationary	□ strategic	□ sulfur	□ supervise
□ surround					

sympathy ['sɪmpəθi] *n.* 同情；同情心 (pity)；(感情上的) 支持和赞同

【记】词根记忆：sym (相同) + path (感情) + y → 怀有相同的感情 → 同情

【例】Expressive leaders often offer *sympathy* when someone experiences difficulties. 富于感情的领导者经常向身处困境的人给予支持。

【派】sympathize (*vi.* 体谅)

symphony ['sɪmfəni] *n.* 交响乐

【记】词根记忆：sym (共同) + phon (声音) + y → 奏出共同的声音 → 交响乐

【搭】symphony orchestra 交响乐团

【派】symphonic (*a.* 交响乐的)

temperate ['tempərət] *a.* (气候) 温和的 (benign)

【记】词根记忆：temper (时间) + ate → 时间推移气候逐渐温和 → 温和的

【搭】temperate climate 温带气候

【例】This early comparison of tropical and *temperate* butterfly's richness has been well confirmed. 热带和温带蝴蝶之间种类多少的早期比较已经得到充分证实。

temperate

【参】tropical (*a.* 热带的；炎热的)

terrific [tə'rɪfɪk] *a.* 极好的 (wonderful)；非常的，极度的

【记】词根记忆：terr (使…惊吓) + ific → 大得吓人 → 非常的

【例】A: Isn't this a *terrific* painting? It looks great on the wall in my office.

B: To be honest, I don't know what you see in it.

A：这幅画难道不漂亮吗？挂在我办公室的墙上很好看。

B：说实话，我不知道你在这幅画上看到了什么。

A: Good news. I'm not going to need surgery after all. The doctor says I can start working out again soon. And maybe play soccer again in a few weeks.

B: That's *terrific*. It would be great if you could get back in shape in time for the state tournament.

A：好消息。我不需要动手术了。医生说我很快就能开始训练。或许几周之后就能踢足球了。

B：太棒了。如果你能及时恢复参加州锦标赛就好了。

torrent ['tɔːrənt] *n.* 迸发 (rush)

【记】词根记忆：tor (=torn 转动) + rent → 水流转动不停地前进 → 迸发

【例】His article brought a *torrent* of criticism. 他的文章招来很多非议。

【派】torrential(*a.* 奔流的)

vital [ˈvaɪtl] *a.* 致命的(mortal)；至关重要的(of the utmost importance)

【记】词根记忆：vit(生命) + al → 致命的

【例】This temperature gradient may be *vital* to successful hatching. 这种温度梯度可能对孵化的成功至关重要。

【派】vitalism (*n.* 活力论；生机说)；vitalist (*n.* 活力论者)；vitality (*n.* 生命力；活力)

How many persons in the world would have scored achievement, if they did not waste the valuable time.

世界上不知有多少能够建立功业的人，却因为把宝贵的时间轻易放过，以致默默无闻。　　　　　　　　　　　　　　　——莫泊桑(*Maupassant*)

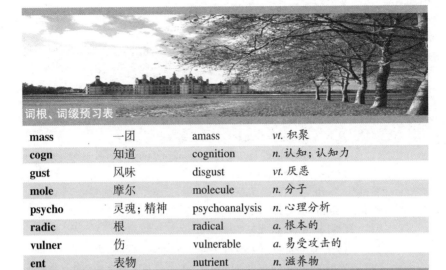

词根、词缀预习表

mass	一团	amass	*vt.* 积聚
cogn	知道	cognition	*n.* 认知;认知力
gust	风味	disgust	*vt.* 厌恶
mole	摩尔	molecule	*n.* 分子
psycho	灵魂;精神	psychoanalysis	*n.* 心理分析
radic	根	radical	*a.* 根本的
vulner	伤	vulnerable	*a.* 易受攻击的
ent	表物	nutrient	*n.* 滋养物

adaptable [əˈdæptəbl] *a.* 能适应的;可修改的(flexible, revisable)

【记】词根记忆:ad + apt(能力) + able(能…的)→ 有适应能力的 → 能适应的

【例】The twins are always *adaptable* to fit new conditions. 这对双胞胎总能适应新的环境。

alter [ˈɔːltər] *vt.* 改变(*change, vary)

【记】本身为词根,意为:改变状态

【例】The effect of super saturation is simply to *alter* the growth rate. 过饱和的效果不过是改变生长速度。

【派】alteration(*n.* 改变,改造);unaltered(*a.* 未被改变的;不变的)

【参】altar(*n.* 祭坛)

amass [əˈmæs] *vt.* 积聚(accumulate)

【记】分拆联想:a + mass(一团)→ 变成一团 → 积聚

【例】The shellfish *amass* around the rocks in the shallow water. 贝类聚集在浅水区的岩石周围。

anthropologist [ˌænθrəˈpɑːlədʒɪst] *n.* 人类学家

【记】词根记忆:anthrop(人) + ologist(学家)→ 人类学家

【例】Recently some *anthropologists* conducted an interesting case study in ethnology. 最近,一些人类学家开展了一项有趣的民族学

案例研究。//*Anthropologists* are interested in the ordinary aspects of life. 人类学家对人类生活中的普通方面感兴趣。

artesian [ɑːrˈtiːʒn] *a.* 自流水的；喷水的

【搭】artesian spring 自流泉；artesian well 自流井

【例】Some natural springs geographers are interested in *artesian* spring. 一些研究天然泉的地理学家对自流泉感兴趣。

attempt [əˈtempt] *n./vi.* 尝试(try)；努力(strive)

【记】词根记忆：at(加强)＋tempt(尝试)→尝试；努力

【例】The bird flaps one wing in an apparent *attempt* to take to the air. 这只鸟扇动着一只翅膀，明显是想飞起来。

【参】contemplate (*v.* 凝视)；contemporary (*n.* 同时代的人)；tempting(*a.* 吸引人的)

barely [ˈberli] *ad.* 仅仅；几乎不能

boom [buːm] *n.* 繁荣(*expansion) *vi.* 迅速增长

【搭】baby boom 生育高峰

【例】Agriculture *boomed*, with machinery doing the job of farm workers drawn into the army. 随着机器被用于从事被应召入伍的农民们的工作，农业迅速发展了起来。

【派】booming(*a.* 急速发展的)

bureau [ˈbjʊroʊ] *n.* 局，署

【记】法语词，意为：办公室

calculus [ˈkælkjələs] *n.* 微积分

【记】词根记忆：calcul(计算)＋us→微积分

cognition [kɑːgˈnɪʃn] *n.* 认知，认识(力)(perception)

【记】词根记忆：cogn(知道)＋ition→认知，认识

【例】Tool use may indicate that animals have some *cognition.* 对工具的使用或许表明动物具有一定的认知能力。

【参】cognitive(*a.* 认知的；感知的)

combine [kəmˈbaɪn] *v.* (使)联合；(使)结合(*fuse, unite)

【记】词根记忆：com(共同)＋bi(两个)＋ne→使两个在一起→(使)结合

【例】In public ceremonies singing is *combined* with dancing and with music from a variety of instruments. 在公共仪式上，歌唱与舞蹈以及各种乐器演奏的音乐结合在一起。

concentric [kənˈsentrɪk] *a.* 同心的

【记】词根记忆：con(共同的)＋centr(中心)＋ic→有着共同中心的→同心的

artesian　attempt　barely　boom　bureau　calculus　cognition　combine　concentric

【搭】concentric circle 同心圆

【例】Many *concentric* circles were formed in the pond. 池塘里形成了很多同心圆。

【派】concentricity(*n.* 同心；集中)

copier [ˈkɑːpiər] *n.* 影印机；复印机

【例】A: Have the parts we need for the *copier* arrived yet?

B: I ordered them last week, but something's holding them up.

A：我们需要的复印机零件到了吗？

B：我上周订的货，但是有事耽误着还没送到。

cowhand [ˈkaʊhænd] *n.* 牛仔；牧牛工

crush [krʌʃ] *v.* 碾碎(grind)；使变皱

【例】The weight of a tornado can *crush* a building's roof when it passes overhead. 龙卷风经过时能将建筑物的屋顶摧毁。

【参】crash(*v./n.* 碰撞)

dated [ˈdeɪtɪd] *a.* 过时的(old-fashioned)

【例】Your boots are a little *dated*. 你的靴子有点过时了。

debatable [dɪˈbeɪtəbl] *a.* 有争议的(disputable, unsettled)

【搭】debatable viewpoint 有争议的观点

【例】It's *debatable* whether or not the policies have changed the messed situation. 这些政策是否改变了混乱局面，对此还存有争议。

decimal [ˈdesɪml] *a.* 十进的；小数的；十进制的 *n.* 小数

【记】词根记忆：deci(十分之一)+ mal → 十进的

【例】You should treat *decimals* as the whole number to solve the mathematical problem. 解这道数学题时，你应该把小数算作整数。

delta [ˈdeltə] *n.* (河流的)三角洲

【记】和Delta Force(三角洲)一起记，著名PC射击游戏

demolish [dɪˈmɑːlɪʃ] *vt.* 拆除(dismantle)；破坏(destroy)

【例】The human species is altering the physical and chemical world and *demolishing* the environment. 人类正在改变物理和化学世界，并破坏着环境。

depression [dɪˈpreʃn] *n.* 萧条(期)(recession)；低气压；沮丧(dejection)

【搭】economic depression 经济萧条

【例】Economic *depressions* lowered the prices of farm products. 经济萧条降低了农产品价格。// Some interesting topics that will be discussed are dreaming, memory and *depression*. 届时将会讨论一些有趣的话题：做梦、记忆和抑郁。

【参】depressed(*a.* 沮丧的)

| copier | cowhand | crush | dated | debatable | decimal |
| delta | demolish | depression |

diet [ˈdaɪət] *n.* 饮食; 食物 *vi.* 节食

【搭】on a diet 节食

【例】People who're *dieting* need a variety of foods to assure a constant supply of nutrients their bodies need. 节食的人需要各种食物, 以确保身体所需的营养能得到持续的供应。

【派】dietary(*a.* 饮食的); dieter(*n.* 节食者; 减肥者); dietitian(*n.* 饮食学家)

digestive [daɪˈdʒestɪv] *a.* 消化的; 和消化有关的

【搭】digestive system 消化系统; digestive function 消化功能

disgust [dɪsˈɡʌst] *vt.* 厌恶; 嫌恶(detest, loathe)

【记】词根记忆: dis(不) + gust(风味) → 不喜欢这个味道 → 厌恶

【例】The raw fish *disgusted* me, so I left the table. 生鱼让我感到恶心, 所以我离开了餐桌。

【派】disgusted(*a.* 厌烦的, 厌恶的)

【参】gusto(*n.* 爱好, 嗜好); degust(*v.* 品尝)

displacement [dɪsˈpleɪsmənt] *n.* 移置, 转移

【例】*Displacement* of an organ to other location will arouse complicated disease. 器官移位会引起复杂的疾病。

educated [ˈedʒukeɪtɪd] *a.* 受过教育的; 有教养的(informed, learned)

【例】Gifford, a highly *educated* man who suffered from inward struggle, died of depression at last. 吉福德是个非常有教养的人, 他遭受着内心的挣扎, 最终抑郁而死。

emission [iˈmɪʃn] *n.* 散发(物); 发出; 射出

【记】词根记忆: e(出) + miss(放出) + ion → 放出 → 发出; 散发(物)

【搭】zero-emission 零排放; 无污染

enzyme [ˈenzaɪm] *n.* 酶

【记】来自希腊语, en(在…里) + zyme(发酵) → 酶在发酵过程中起着至关重要的作用 → 酶

erode [ɪˈroʊd] *v.* 侵蚀, 腐蚀(corrode, rot)

【记】词根记忆: e + rod(咬) + e → 咬掉 → 侵蚀, 腐蚀

【例】Melting ice *erodes* the soil around them. 融化的冰侵蚀着它们周围的土壤。

【派】erosion(*n.* 侵蚀, 腐蚀)

exotic

exotic [ɪɡˈzɑːtɪk] *a.* 外来的 (foreign); 奇异的(strange)

【记】词根记忆: exo(外面) + tic → 外来的

| □ diet | □ digestive | □ disgust | □ displacement | □ educated | □ emission |
| □ enzyme | □ erode | □ exotic | | | |

【例】Leopold is to create a botanical garden where only *exotic* flowers grew. 利奥波德要建造一个植物园，只种植奇花异草。

extinction [ɪk ˈstɪŋkʃn] *n.* 灭绝，绝种；熄灭

【记】来自extinct(*a.* 灭绝的)

【搭】in danger of extinction 处于灭绝的危险中

【例】Conservationists are making efforts to save the rare species from *extinction*. 环境保护主义者正在努力抢救稀有物种，使其免于灭绝。

fabric [ˈfæbrɪk] *n.* 布(cloth)；织品(textile)；结构(framework)

【例】Mass transportation revised the social and economic *fabric* of the American city in three fundamental ways. 公共交通以三个基本的方式改变了美国城市的社会、经济结构。

fashion [ˈfæʃn] *n.* 方式；流行，风尚 *v.* 形成，把…塑造成(*create)

【例】Quilt-making originated as a means of *fashioning* bed covers from bits of fabric. 棉被制作源自一种用小块布制作床罩的方式。

【派】fashioned(*a.* …式的，…风格的)

feasible [ˈfiːzəbl] *a.* 可行的(practical, workable)

【记】词根记忆：feas(=fac做) + ible → 能做的 → 可行的

【例】It is not *feasible* to build sea defenses to protect against erosion. 修建海防避免侵蚀是不可行的。

fervor [ˈfɜːrvər] *n.* 热情；热烈

【例】The political leaders are always speaking with great *fervor*. 政治领导人演说时总是满腔热情。

【参】apathy(*n.* 冷漠)

figure [ˈfɪɡjər] *n.* 体形(shape)；数字(number)；图形；人物 *v.* 算出(calculate)；估计(estimate)；推测

【记】发音记忆："菲戈"(西班牙皇马著名球星) → 人物

【搭】figure out 确定…

【例】First I want to go over some basics about hearing, then we can take a look at our school's environment and see if we can *figure* out some ways to protect hearing. 首先，我想介绍一下关于听力的基本知识，然后我们可以观察学校的环境，看看是否能想些办法来保护听力。

A: This is hopeless. These *figures* still don't add up right. Let's do the calculations over again.

B: Yes, but why not do them tomorrow? It's very late now.

A：这太糟糕了。这些数字加起来还是不对。我们再算一遍吧。

B：是的，不过为什么不明天算呢，现在很晚了。

functional ['fʌŋkʃənl] *a.* 功能的；可起作用的

【记】联想记忆：function(作用，功能) + al → 可起作用的；功能的

【搭】a functional organ 机能器官

【例】With the increase in people's needs, buildings are sensitively designed, not purely *functional*. 随着人们需求的增加，建筑物的设计日益精妙，不再纯粹为实用而设计。

【派】multifunctional(*a.* 多功能的); functionalism(*n.* 机能主义)

fungus ['fʌŋɡəs] *n.* [*pl.* fungi] 真菌；霉菌

【记】分拆联想：fun(有趣) + g + us → 我们第一次看到这么有趣的真菌 → 真菌

【参】fungicide(*n.* 杀真菌剂)

gemstone ['dʒemstoʊn] *n.* (经雕琢的)宝石

【记】组合词：gem(宝石) + stone(石头) → 宝石

genuine ['dʒenjuɪn] *a.* 真正的(true)；真实的(actual)

【记】词根记忆：genu (出生；产生) + ine → 他出生于真正的书香门第 → 真正的

【派】genuinely(*ad.* 真正地)

【参】genius(*n.* 天才)

granular ['ɡrænjələr] *a.* 粒状的

【记】分拆联想：gran(看作grain，颗粒) + ular → 粒状的

grimly ['ɡrɪmli] *ad.* 冷酷地(ruthlessly)

hammer ['hæmər] *n.* 槌(pestle)；锤子(mallet) *v.* 锤打(pound)

【例】Silversmiths *hammer* these ingots to the appropriate thickness by hand. 银匠用手工把这些纯铁锤打到合适的厚度。

heritage ['herɪtɪdʒ] *n.* 遗产(legacy)；传统(tradition)

【记】词根记忆：her(继承人) + it + age(物) → 继承下来的东西 → 遗产

【搭】World Cultural Heritage 世界文化遗产

【例】African Americans were urged by Locke to promote their own cultural *heritage*. 洛克鼓励美国黑人发扬他们自己的文化传统。

impermeable [ɪm'pɜːrmiəbl] *a.* 不可渗透的；不透水的

【记】词根记忆：im(不) + permeable(可渗透的) → 不可渗透的

【例】The objects are covered with *impermeable* decorative coatings of glasslike material. 这些物体上覆盖着玻璃状不透水的装饰涂层。

impersonal [ɪm'pɜːrsənl] *a.* 冷淡的(indifferent); 客观的(objective)

【记】分拆联想: im(不) + personal(个人的) → 不牵涉个人感情的 → 冷淡的

【例】The relationships tend to be *impersonal*. 这种关系往往会很冷淡。

inflate [ɪn'fleɪt] *vt.* 使充气; 使膨胀(expand)

【派】inflation(*n.* 通货膨胀)

【例】The yellow balloon is *inflated* with helium. 黄气球里充的是氦气。

influential [ˌɪnflu'enʃl] *a.* 有影响的; 有权势的

【记】和influent(*a.* 流动的)一起记

【例】Who is the most *influential* watercolor painters in the mid-1800's? 谁是19世纪中叶最有影响力的水彩画家? // They all have *influential* families. 他们的家庭都很有权势。

informative [ɪn'fɔːrmətɪv] *a.* 提供消息的; 见闻广博的

joint [dʒɔɪnt] *n.* 关节; 接合处

【记】词根记忆: join(结合; 连接) + t → 关节

【例】They can cause severe pains, particularly around the *joints*. 它们能导致严重的疼痛, 尤其在关节部位。

journalist ['dʒɜːrnəlɪst] *n.* 新闻记者

【搭】work as a journalist 做一名记者

【例】*Journalists*, I think, should take responsibility to report the truth, not distort it. 我认为记者应该有责任报道真相, 而非扭曲真相。

【派】journalistic(*a.* 新闻事业的)

leak [liːk] *v.* 漏; (使)泄漏

【例】The faucet started *leaking*. 水龙头开始漏水了。

lens [lenz] *n.* 透镜; 镜头; 镜片

【记】联想记忆: 借(lend)给你透镜(lens)看

mint [mɪnt] *v.* 铸造(硬币)(coin) *n.* 造币厂

【例】They identified the city where the penny was *minted*. 他们确认了铸造便士的城市。

molecule ['mɑːlɪkjuːl] *n.* 分子

【记】词根记忆: mole(摩尔, 克分子) + cule → 分子

【派】molecular(*a.* 分子的; 分子组成的)

nutrient ['nuːtriənt] *n.* 滋养物, 营养品(nourishment) *a.* 有营养的

【记】词根记忆: nutri(滋养) + ent(表物) → 滋养物, 营养品

□ impersonal	□ inflate	□ influential	□ informative	□ joint	□ journalist
□ leak	□ lens	□ mint	□ molecule	□ nutrient	

457

【例】The soil loses its *nutrients*, so it needs to be fertilized. 土壤失去了养分，需要施肥。

peninsula [pəˈnɪnsələ] *n.* 半岛

【记】词根记忆: pen(接近) + insula(岛) → 接近岛的 → 半岛

pilot [ˈpaɪlət] *n.* 飞行员; 领航员 *a.* 试验性的

【例】In a *pilot* reclamation project, they tested the growth possibilities of eight species of plants. 在一个实验性开垦项目中，他们检测了 8 个植物物种生长的可能性。

【派】piloted(*a.* 有人驾驶的)

plasma [ˈplæzmə] *n.* 血浆

psychoanalysis [ˌsaɪkoʊəˈnæləsɪs] *n.* 心理分析; 精神分析

【记】词根记忆: psycho(灵魂; 精神) + analysis(分析) → 精神分析

【参】psychoanalyst(*n.* 心理分析学者); psychogenic(*a.* 心理的; 精神上的)

purple [ˈpɜːrpl] *n./a.* 紫色(的)

【记】联想记忆: 很多人(people)喜欢紫色(purple)

quasar [ˈkweɪzɑːr] *n.*【天】类星体(any of a class of celestial objects that resemble stars)

【记】分拆联想: qu + a + sar(看作 star, 星星) → 类星体

racing [ˈreɪsɪŋ] *n.* 比赛, 竞赛(game)

radical [ˈrædɪkl] *a.* 根本的(fundamental); 激进的(drastic) *n.* 原子团; 激进分子

【记】词根记忆: radic(根) + al → 根本的

【搭】free radical 自由基; 游离基

【例】Cities had undergone *radical* social change. 城市经历了根本的社会变革。

【派】radically(*ad.* 根本上地)

rainfall [ˈreɪnfɔːl] *n.* 降雨; 降雨量

【记】组合词: rain + fall → 降雨

reason [ˈriːzn] *n.* 原因, 理由(cause) *v.* 推断(conclude)

【例】The detective *reasoned* that David had been murdered for his money. 侦探推断戴维被人谋财害命了。

【派】reasonable(*a.* 合情合理的; 适度的; 公道的); reasonably (*ad.* 合理地; 相当地); reasoning(*n.* 推理)

robust [roʊˈbʌst] *a.* 健壮的, 强壮的(*strong)

【记】联想记忆: "乐百氏"(Robust)矿泉水

【例】This bird has a large, *robust* bill. 这只鸟的喙大而结实。

| peninsula | pilot | plasma | psychoanalysis | purple | quasar |
| racing | radical | rainfall | reason | robust | |

sap [sæp] *n.* 树液；汁液(fluid) *vt.* 使衰竭(drain, exhaust)

solicit [sə'lɪsɪt] *vt.* 恳请(entreat)；乞求(beg)

【记】词根记忆：soli(=sole唯一；全部) + cit(引出) → 引出某人做事 → 恳请；乞求

【例】Bill *solicited* my opinion. 比尔征求了我的意见。

species ['spi:ʃi:z] *n.* 种类；类群(group, class)

【记】词根记忆：speci(种类) + es → 种类；类群

spread [spred] *v./n.* 展开(unfold, extend)；蔓延；散布(distribute)

【记】联想记忆：散布(spread)传单给人们看(read)

【派】spreading(*a.* 扩展的 *n.* 扩展；伸展)

temple ['templ] *n.* 寺庙

【记】发音记忆："淡泊" → 神殿中人淡泊名利 → 寺庙

terminal ['tɜ:rmɪnl] *a.* 末端的（endmost）*n.* 终点站(destination)

【记】词根记忆：term(边界) + inal → 末端的

【搭】passenger terminal 客运枢纽站

【例】You'd be better off calling the *terminal* for new schedule. 你最好给终点站打电话索取新的时刻表。

【参】terminus(*n.* 终点站)；terminate(*v.* 终止，结束)

terrain [tə'reɪn] *n.* 地势，地形

【记】词根记忆：terr(地) + ain → 地势，地形

【例】The moon may be divided into two major *terrains*. 月球可以分为两种主要地形。

transmit [trænz'mɪt] *v.* 传输(transfer)；传播(spread)

【记】词根记忆：trans(穿过) + mit(送) → 传输

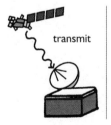

transmit

【例】Communications satellites can *transmit* data around the world. 通讯卫星可以在全世界传输数据。//Liz insists that only female wasps *transmit* diseases. 利兹坚持认为只有母黄蜂才会传播疾病。

【派】transmitter(*n.* 发射机)；transmission(*n.* 发射；传送)

tycoon [taɪ'ku:n] *n.* (商界)巨头(magnate)

【记】发音记忆："太酷" → 那些有钱的巨头太酷 → 巨头

【例】For every crooked *tycoon* there are thousands of ordinary citizens living on fixed incomes. 有一个奸诈的商界巨头，就有成千上万靠固定收入为生的普通市民。

sap	solicit	species	spread	temple	terminal
terrain	transmit	tycoon			

vegetation [ˌvedʒəˈteɪʃn] *n.* 植物（plant）；植被

【例】They feed almost exclusively on dead *vegetation*. 它们几乎只吃死了的植物。

【参】vegetable（*n.* 蔬菜；植物）

vulnerable [ˈvʌlnərəbl] *a.* 易受攻击的；易受伤害的（*unprotected）

【记】词根记忆：vulner（伤）+ able → 易受伤害的

【例】Amphibians are especially *vulnerable* to pesticides dissolved in the water. 两栖类动物尤其容易受到溶解在水中的杀虫剂的伤害。

weave [wiːv] *vi.* 迂回行进（swing）*vt.* 编织；组合（knit, interlace）

【记】联想记忆：老板就希望工人织（weave）好布赶快走（leave）人

【搭】weave sth. together 编织；编造

【例】The history of baskets *woven* from strips of willow in the area can date back to 18th century. 该地区用柳条编织篮子的历史可以追溯到18世纪。

【派】weaver（*n.* 织布者；织工）

The fireworks that jump high and go far are beautiful.
凡是能冲上去的，能散发出来的焰火，都是美丽的。

——安徒生（*Andersen*）

Word List 43  MP3-43

词根、词缀预习表

clar	清楚；明白	clarify	*vt.* 澄清
hance	高	enhance	*vt.* 提高
enthus	热心	enthusiasm	*n.* 热情
cub	睡	incubate	*v.* 孵卵
monu	提醒；警告	monument	*n.* 纪念碑
poly	多	polygon	*n.* 多角形
ratio	理性；理由	rational	*a.* 理性的
tenu	薄；细	tenuous	*a.* 细的

abbreviate [əˈbriːvieɪt] *vt.* 缩短；缩写(shorten)

【派】abbreviation(*n.* 缩写；缩写词)；abbreviated(*a.* 简短的)

aerial [ˈeriəl] *a.* 空中的

【记】词根记忆：aer(空气) + ial(…的) → 空中的

annex [əˈneks] *vt.* 兼并；附加(append, add)

【记】联想记忆：an + nex(看作next，与…邻接的) → 邻接建筑物 → 附加

【例】Money and reputation are not always *annexed* to happy life. 金钱和名气并非总是与幸福的生活有关。

assistant [əˈsɪstənt] *n.* 助手(helper, aide)；助教 *a.* 辅助的；助理的

【搭】teaching assistant 助教；personal assistant 私人助理；librarian assistant 图书管理员助理；sales assistant 销售助理

【例】Bob was quickly sacked, and one week later Friedman chose Joe as *assistant* general manager. 鲍勃很快被开除了，一周之后弗里德曼选择了乔为副总经理。

A: Are you going home for winter vacation?

B: I've agreed to stay on here as a research *assistant*.

A：你寒假回家吗？

B：我已经同意留下来当助理研究员了。

【派】assist(*v.* 帮助，援助); assistance (*n.* 协助，援助)

【参】tutor(*n.* 指导教师); professor (*n.* 教授); instructor(*n.* 讲师)

bare [ber] *a.* 赤裸的(naked, bald)

【派】barely(*ad.* 几乎不能)

哇!
我衣服呢?

bare

battery ['bætəri] *n.* 电池

【记】分拆联想: batt(看作bat, 蝙蝠) + ery → 给蝙蝠飞行提供能量 → 电池

【例】The calculator needs a new *battery*. 计算器需要一块新电池。

beach [biːtʃ] *n.* 海滩; 湖滩; 河滩

【搭】a beach person 常去海滩的人; 海滩迷

【例】Geologists have found that seawalls actually speed up the destruction of the *beaches*. 地质学家发现，海堤其实会加速对海滩的破坏。

【参】reach(*v.* 到达)

behave [bɪˈheɪv] *v.* 行为; 表现(conduct)

【记】分拆联想: be + have(有) → 他有着不错的表现 → 行为; 表现

【例】Tim isn't well *behaved* for his age. 蒂姆的行为不符合他的年龄。

blanket ['blæŋkɪt] *n.* 毛毯; 覆盖物

【记】分拆联想: blank(空的) + et(小) → 铺在一小块空地上 → 毛毯; 覆盖物

bunch [bʌntʃ] *n.* (一)簇; 束, 捆; 串, 一串; 一帮, 一伙(gang) *vi.* 捆成一束(pack); 聚集(crowd)

【记】联想记忆: 一群(bunch)人在吃午餐(lunch)

【例】A: A *bunch* of us are going out for pizza.

B: Count me out, but have a good time.

A: 我们一帮人要出去吃比萨饼。

B: 不要把我算进去，但是祝你们开心。

A: These carrots look so good and they are only 29 cents a pound.

B: Let's get a *bunch*, and how about some lettuce too?

A: 这些胡萝卜看着真不错，一磅才29美分。

B: 咱们买一捆，再来点生菜怎么样?

【参】lunch(*n.* 午餐); bundle(*n.* 捆, 束)

bush [bʊʃ] *n.* 矮树丛(shrub)

【搭】beat about the bush 旁敲侧击

□ bare	■ battery	■ beach	■ behave	■ blanket	■ bunch
□ bush					

【例】There is an abundance of wild lives in the *bushes*, such as snakes, mushrooms. 灌木丛中有很多野生动植物，例如蛇和蘑菇。

cassette [kə'set] *n.* 盒式录音(或录像)带

cite [saɪt] *vt.* 引用，引证(quote)；举例

【例】Where in the passage does the author *cite* the goal of the Academy-Institute? 作者在这篇文章的什么地方引用了研究院的目标？

clarify ['klærəfaɪ] *vt.* 澄清；阐明(identify, explain)

【记】词根记忆：clar(清楚；明白)+ ify(…化)→ 澄清；阐明

【例】He tries to *clarify* his position. 他试图澄清自己的立场。

concrete ['kɑːŋkriːt] *n.* 混凝土(cement) *a.* 具体的(material)

confession [kən'feʃn] *n.* 供认；承认(admission)

【例】My *confession* won't solve anything. 我坦白了也解决不了任何问题。

consciously ['kɑːnʃəsli] *ad.* 有意识地(*on purpose)；自觉地

【例】The mothers observed by the researchers are *consciously* teaching their babies to speak. 研究人员所观察的母亲在有意识地教婴儿说话。

consist [kən'sɪst] *v.* 在于；存在于；由…组成，由…构成(compose)

【记】词根记忆：con(共同)+ sist(站)→ 站在一起 → 由…组成，由…构成

【搭】consist of 由…组成

【例】Ancient Greek philosopher thought the earth was *consisted* of five elements. 古希腊哲学家认为地球由五种元素构成。// A balanced meal *consists* of five key elements: proteins, carbohydrates, fats, vitamins and minerals. 平衡的膳食包括5个关键的要素：蛋白质、碳水化合物、脂肪、维生素和矿物质。

【参】insist(*v.* 坚持)；persist(*v.* 坚持)

cosmic ['kɑːzmɪk] *a.* 宇宙的(of or relating to the universe)

【记】词根记忆：cosm(宇宙)+ ic → 宇宙的

【搭】cosmic dust 宇宙尘埃；cosmic ray 宇宙射线

【例】The extinction of the dinosaurs was caused by some physical event, either climatic or *cosmic*. 恐龙灭绝是由某种气候或宇宙的物理事件造成的。

crisscross ['krɪskrɔːs] *vt.* 交叉往来

【例】Coaches and wagons continued to *crisscross* the West. 马车和货车继续交叉往来于西部。

☐ cassette	☐ cite	☐ clarify	☐ concrete	☐ confession	☐ consciously
☐ consist	☐ cosmic	☐ crisscross			

damp [dæmp] *a.* 潮湿的(moist)

【记】分拆联想：dam(水坝) + p → 水坝上是很潮湿的 → 潮湿的

【例】Farmers often squeeze the *damp* soil into three basic shapes. 农民们经常把潮湿的土捏成三种基本形状。

【派】dampen(*vt.* 使潮湿)

definitive [dɪ'fɪnətɪv] *a.* 决定性的；最后的

【派】definitively(*ad.* 决定性地；最后地)

deliver [dɪ'lɪvər] *v.* 传送，传递(transmit, pass)；陈述(state)

【记】词根记忆：de(离开) + live(举起) + r → 举起拿走 → 传送

【例】They'll *deliver* a bucket at no charge. 他们将免费递送一桶。

【派】delivery(*n.* 投递；送交)

descriptive [dɪ'skrɪptɪv] *a.* 描述性的

【搭】descriptive statistics 描述性统计

【例】*Descriptive* statistics involves tabulating, depicting, and describing collections of data. 描述性统计包括制表以及描绘一系列的数据。

dive [daɪv] *n./v.* 跳水；潜水(submerge)

【派】diver(*n.* 潜水者)

enhance [ɪn'hæns] *vt.* 提高(*increase, improve)；增强

【记】词根记忆：en(使…) + hance(高) → 提高；增强

dive

【例】Many poets *enhance* their work by creating a contrast between realism and symbolism in a given poem. 很多诗人通过在一首诗中制造现实主义与象征主义间的反差，来提升他们的作品。

【派】enhancement(*n.* 增加)；enhanced(*a.* 增强的；提高的)

enthusiasm [ɪn'θuːziæzəm] *n.* 热情(passion)；积极性(positivity)

【记】词根记忆：enthus(热心) + iasm → 热情；积极性

【参】enthusiastic(*a.* 热情的)；enthusiastically(*ad.* 狂热地)；enthusiast (*n.* 狂热者)

evolution [ˌiːvə'luːʃn] *n.* 发展，演变(development, progression)

【记】来自evolve [*v.* (使)进化]

【例】In the 19th century, the theory of *evolution*, put forward by Darwin, was violently criticized by religious people. 19世纪，达尔文提出的进化论受到了宗教人士的强烈批判。

expedition [ˌekspə'dɪʃn] *n.* 远征(队)；探险(队)(exploration)

【记】词根记忆：ex(出) + ped(脚) + ition → 靠脚进行长途跋涉 →

| ☐ damp | ☐ definitive | ☐ deliver | ☐ descriptive | ☐ dive | ☐ enhance |
| ☐ enthusiasm | ☐ evolution | ☐ expedition | | | |

远征; 探险。注意不要和expenditure(*n.* 支出, 花费)相混

【例】His initial *expedition,* which sailed in 1578 with a patent granted by Queen Elizabeth was defeated by the Spanish. 他在1578年的首次远征获得了伊丽莎白女王的批准, 但是被西班牙人击败了。

facial [ˈfeɪʃl] *a.* 面部的

【例】Fear, happiness, sadness, and surprise are universally reflected in *facial* expressions. 恐惧、开心、悲伤和惊讶都由面部表情所反映。

fault [fɔːlt] *n.* 过错(error, defect);【地质学】断层(a fracture in the crust of a planet)

【搭】fault plane断层面; fault zone断层带

【例】*Faults* in the Earth's crust are most evident in sedimentary formations, where they interrupt previously continuous layers. 地壳的断层在沉积层最明显, 在那它们中断了之前连续的地层。

【参】layer/stratum 地层; plate 板块

flock [flɑːk] *n.* 群(group, crowd); 大量 *vi.* 聚结(gather)

【记】分拆联想: fl +(bl)ock(一批)→ 群

【例】Many spectators *flocked* to the farm to catch a glimpse of Mrs. Stowe. 很多观众聚集到了这个农场一睹斯托女士的风采。

frame [freɪm] *n.* 框架 *v.* 设计; 构成(*pose)

【记】联想记忆: 他很有名望(fame), 所以人们将其照片镶在框(frame)里表示尊敬

【参】framework(*n.* 构架; 框架)

gem [dʒem] *n.* 宝石

girder [ˈɡɜːrdər] *n.* 大梁(crossbeam)

【记】分拆联想: gird(围梁; 方框支柱)+ er → 支撑物 → 大梁

glue [gluː] *n.* 胶, 胶水(gumwater) *v.* 黏合(cement); 紧附于(attach)

【记】联想记忆: 警方终于从那瓶蓝色(blue)胶水(glue)中, 找到了线索(clue)

hieroglyph

hieroglyph [ˈhaɪərəɡlɪf] *n.* 象形文字

【派】hieroglyphic(*a.* 象形文字的)

immune [ɪˈmjuːn] *a.* 免疫的; 不受影响的

【记】词根记忆: im(没有)+ mune(公共)→ 不得公共病 → 免疫的

【搭】immune system 免疫系统

【例】They were *immune* to drought. 他们未受旱灾影响。

【派】immunize(*vt.* 使免疫)

【参】immure(*vt.* 监禁)

incubate ['ɪŋkjubeɪt] *v.* 孵卵(hatch)
【记】词根记忆：in(里面) + cub(睡) + ate → 睡在里面 → 孵卵
【例】The researchers remove eggs from the nests of parrots and *incubate* them under laboratory conditions. 研究人员从鹦鹉巢里取走鸟蛋，并在实验室环境下将其孵化。
【派】incubation(*n.* 孵卵); incubator(*n.* 孵化器)

insurance [ɪn'ʃʊrəns] *n.* 保险；保险业
【记】来自insure(*vt.* 给…投保险)
【例】You can see how *insurance* helped encourage international trade. 你可以看到保险在促进国际贸易中的作用。

ironical [aɪ'rɑːnɪkl] *a.* 讽刺的；用反语的
【例】The young actor has found the *ironical* looks on audiences' faces. 年轻的演员已发现观众脸上讽刺的神情。

irresistible [ˌɪrɪ'zɪstəbl] *a.* 诱人的，无法抗拒的
【记】分拆联想：ir(不) + resistible(可抵抗的) → 不可抵抗的 → 诱人的，无法抗拒的

leap [liːp] *vi.* 跳跃(jump) *n.* 跳跃；骤变
【搭】by leaps and bounds 飞跃地
【例】Your little nephew is growing by *leaps* and bounds. 你的小外甥长得真快。//A number of insects rely on *leaping* or jumping as a way of escaping from enemies. 很多昆虫依靠跳跃逃脱天敌。

loyal ['lɔɪəl] *a.* 忠诚的，忠贞的(faithful)
【记】联想记忆：对皇家的(royal)事情是忠诚的(loyal)
【例】The *loyal* fans enjoyed the chilly weather. 忠实的粉丝享受着寒冷的天气。
【派】loyalty(*n.* 忠诚，忠心); loyalist(*n.* 忠诚分子)

microbe ['maɪkroʊb] *n.* 微生物；细菌(bacteria, germ)
【记】词根记忆：micro(小) + be(=bio生命) → 微生物
【派】microbial(*a.* 由细菌引起的); microbiology(*n.* 微生物学)

microwave ['maɪkrəweɪv] *n.* 微波(炉)

monument ['mɑːnjumənt] *n.* 纪念碑
【记】词根记忆：monu(提醒；警告) + ment(表物) → 提醒人们的标志物 → 纪念碑
【例】This is a *monument* to all those who died in the revolution war. 这座纪念碑是为所有在革命战争中献身的人而立的。

muscle ['mʌsl] *n.* 肌肉(brawn)；体力；力量(strength)
【派】muscular(*a.* 肌肉的；强健的)

| incubate | insurance | ironical | irresistible | leap | loyal |
| microbe | microwave | monument | muscle | | |

negotiation [nɪˌɡoʊʃiˈeɪʃn] n. 商议；谈判(treaty)

【记】来自negotiate(v. 商议；谈判)

【例】At the peace *negotiations* with Britain, Americans demanded, and got what they wanted. 与英国和平谈判时，美国人提出了要求并得到了满足。

nerve-cell [ˈnɜːrv ˈsel] n. 神经细胞；神经元细胞

【例】These are genes that are associated with particular *nerve-cell* receptors in the brain. 这些基因与大脑中特定神经元感受器相关。// The degree of overall fearfulness in the mammal seems to depend in large part on the presence or absence of these *nerve-cell* receptors. 哺乳动物总体恐惧程度似乎很大部分取决于这些神经元感受器的存在与否。

obstacle [ˈɑːbstəkl] n. 障碍(handicap)；妨害物(barrier, obstruction)

【记】词根记忆：ob(反) + st(=stand站) + acle(物) → 反着站的物体 → 障碍；妨碍物

【例】Shortage of materials posed the biggest *obstacle* to the development of military forts. 原料匮乏构成了军事堡垒建设的最大障碍。

oratorio [ˌɔːrəˈtɔːrioʊ] n. 宗教剧

【记】词根记忆：orat(演讲) + orio(表示音乐类) → 配以音乐的演讲 → 宗教剧

photograph [ˈfoʊtəɡræf] n. 照片

【搭】take a photograph 拍照

【例】Our professor took *photographs* of small oceanic snails. 我们的教授给小型海洋蜗牛拍了照。

【参】paragraph(n. 段)

pivot [ˈpɪvət] n. 枢轴；中心点；重点

plump [plʌmp] a. 圆胖的

【记】发音记忆："拨浪鼓" → 像拨浪鼓一样圆胖的 → 圆胖的；注意不要和plumb(v. 深入了解)相混

【例】The man is so short and *plump* that he has to be lifted up on his horse. 此人身材又矮又胖，只能被人抬上马。

polygon [ˈpɑːliɡɑːn] n.【数】多角形；多边形

【记】词根记忆：poly(多) + gon(角) → 多角形

【搭】convex polygon 凸多边形

【派】polygonal(a. 多边形的；多角形的)

ponderous [ˈpɑːndərəs] a. 笨重的(*heavy)

【记】分拆联想：ponder(音似：胖的) + ous → 笨重的

【例】These *ponderous* machines reaped the grain, and bagged it. 这些笨重的机器收割谷子，然后打包。

predecessor ['predəsesər] *n.* 前辈(*antecedent); 前任; (被取代的)原有事物

【记】词根记忆：pre(前) + de + cess(走) + or → 前面走的人 → 前辈

【例】The eighteenth-century houses showed great interior improvements over their *predecessors*. 18世纪的房屋内部改进很大，胜过之前的房屋。

proportion [prə'pɔːrʃn] *n.* 部分(share); 比例(ratio); 均衡(equipoise)

【记】词根记忆：pro(许多) + portion(一部分) → 部分; 比例

【例】Scientists have tried to quantify this *proportion* of the Sun's energy. 科学家们已经试图量化太阳能的这部分。

【派】proportionally(*ad.* 按比例地); proportionately(*ad.* 成比例地); disproportionately(*ad.* 不成比例地)

puppet ['pʌpɪt] *n.* 木偶(marionette)

【记】分拆联想：pup(小狗) + pet(宠物) → 宠物小狗被控制 → 木偶

puppet

rational ['ræʃnəl] *a.* 理性的; 合理的(reasonable)

【记】词根记忆：ratio(理性; 理由) + nal → 理性的; 合理的

【例】*Rational* people will not be fooled by the demagogue's rhetoric. 理性的人们不会被蛊惑民心的政客的说辞愚弄。

【派】rationalism(*n.* 唯理论)

readily ['redɪli] *ad.* 欣然地(willingly); 容易地(*easily)

【记】和ready(*a.* 有准备的; 情愿的)一起记

【例】It is made of wood not *readily* available. 它是由珍稀的木材制成的。

regular ['reɡjələr] *a.* 有规律的; 正常的(normal); 经常的(usual)

【例】They occur at *regular* intervals. 它们有规律地间歇发生。

【派】regularity(*n.* 规律性); regularly(*ad.* 有规律地; 经常地)

rejuvenate [rɪ'dʒuːvəneɪt] *vt.* 使恢复活力(refresh)

【记】词根记忆：re(重新) + juven(年轻) + ate → 使重新年轻 → 使恢复活力

【例】Music can help *rejuvenate* or soothe the patient. 音乐有助于患者恢复活力，或者减轻其痛苦。

resident ['rezɪdənt] *n.* 居民(dweller) *a.* 常驻的; 定居的

【记】来自resid(e)(居住; 定居) + ent → 居民; 定居的

【例】Each nest has a distinct odor that allows its inhabitants to distinguish foreign ants from *resident* ants. 每个蚁穴都有独特的气味, 使居住在其中的蚂蚁能够分辨外来蚂蚁和常驻蚂蚁。

【派】residential(*a.* 居住的; 住宅的)

resource ['riːsɔːrs] *n.* [常*pl.*]资源; 财力

【记】分拆联想: re(再) + source(源泉) → 可一再使用的源泉 → 资源

【派】resourcefulness(*n.* 足智多谋)

【参】source(*n.* 水源); sauce(*n.* 酱油); saucer(*n.* 茶托); recourse(*n.* 求援)

reward [rɪ'wɔːrd] *n.* 奖赏(prize); 报酬(pay) *vt.* 奖赏

【例】My flight was done with no expectation of *reward*. 我飞行不是为了期待奖赏。//The winner will be *rewarded*. 优胜者将会获奖。

【派】rewarding(*a.* 有报酬的)

【参】award(*vt.* 授予)

scrape [skreɪp] *v.* 刮; 擦掉(rub, brush) *n.* 擦痕(abrasion)

【搭】scrape off 擦去

【派】scraping(*n.* 刮削下的碎屑)

series ['sɪriːz] *n.* 系列; 连续(succession); 连续剧

shuffle ['ʃʌfl] *v./n.* 拖着脚步走; 洗(纸牌); 蒙混; 搅乱

【记】发音记忆: "杀否" → 输了, 再杀一盘可否 → 洗(纸牌)

【搭】shuffle the deck 在甲板上散步

【例】With sore throat and aching chest the patient *shuffled* over to the ward. 患者喉咙和胸口发痛, 拖着脚步走到了病房。

【参】muffle(*v.* 压抑)

simmer ['sɪmər] *v.* 充满(难以控制的怒火等)

【记】联想记忆: 夏天(summer)的时候, 人往往容易充满(simmer)难以控制的怒火

【例】You are not going to like your new neighbors when you do meet them if you keep on *simmering*. 如果你一肚子气, 那么当你见到新邻居时你就不会喜欢他们。

specialized ['speʃəlaɪzd] *a.* 专门的; 专业的(professional)

【例】Each person develops one *specialized* skill. 每人培养一项专门技能。

spur [spɜːr] *n.* 马刺 *vt.* 刺激(provoke); 促进(urge)

【记】联想记忆: 美国NBA中2003赛季的总冠军马刺队(Spurs)

□ resident □ resource □ reward □ scrape □ series □ shuffle
□ simmer □ specialized □ spur
469

substance [ˈsʌbstəns] *n.* 物质；要旨；实质（matter）

【例】The moon isn't much like the earth in terms of *substance*. 从物质方面来看，月亮不太像地球。

symbol [ˈsɪmbl] *n.* 符号；标志（sign）；象征

【例】The common meal served at a common hearth is a powerful *symbol*, a mark of social unity. 公共壁炉旁共同就餐是社会团结的一个有力象征。

【派】symbolism（*n.* 象征主义）；symbolize（*vt.* 象征）；symbology（*n.* 象征学）

tenant [ˈtenənt] *n.* 房客；承租人（dweller, occupant）

【记】分拆联想：ten + ant（蚂蚁）→ 十只蚂蚁来住店 → 它们虽小可也是房客 → 房客

【例】The *tenant* can use any space in the parking area. 房客可以使用停车区的任何空间。

tentacle [ˈtentəkl] *n.* 触角；触须（antenna）

【记】词根记忆：tent（张开）+ acle（物）→ 张开去接受信息之物 → 触角

【例】The *tentacles* drag this prey into the sea anemone's mouth. 触角把捕获物拽进海葵的嘴里。

tenuous [ˈtenjʊəs] *a.* 细的（slender）

【记】词根记忆：tenu（薄；细）+ ous → 细的

【例】The cord tying the boat to the rock is *tenuous*. 把船绑在岩石上的绳子很细。

twist [twɪst] *v./n.* 缠绕，扭曲（tangle, wind）

【记】分拆联想：tw（看作two，两个）+ ist（人）→ 两个人扭打在一起 → 缠绕

twist

【例】I heard Dan *twisted* his ankle during basketball practice yesterday. 听说丹昨天练篮球时把脚踝扭了。//I think they *twisted* the meaning of what the mayor said. 我想他们曲解了市长的意思。

ultraviolet [ˌʌltrəˈvaɪələt] *a.* 紫外（线）的

【记】词根记忆：ultra（超出）+ violet（紫罗兰；紫色）→ 紫外（线）的

【搭】ultraviolet ray 紫外（射）线

【例】Lichens are little affected by the strong *ultraviolet* rays in the mountains. 苔藓几乎不受山区强烈紫外线的影响。

□ substance □ symbol □ tenant □ tentacle □ tenuous □ twist □ ultraviolet

urban ['ɜːrbən] *a.* 城市的；市内的

【记】词根记忆：urb(城市) + an → 城市的

【例】The *urban* population decreased rapidly. 城市人口迅速减少。

【派】urbanism(*n.* 都市化；都市生活)；urbanize(*vt.* 使…都市化)；urbanization(*n.* 都市化)

variation [ˌverɪ'eɪʃn] *n.* 变化，变动；变种，变异

【记】词根记忆：vari(改变) + ation(状态) → 变化，变动

【搭】climate variations 气候变化

【例】The study showed that the *variation* between the two animals was very small. 研究表明，这两种动物之间的变异非常小。

Experience keeps a dear school, yet fools will learn in no other.

经验始终是收费高的学校，然而，笨汉非进此学校不可。

——本杰明·富兰克林(*Benjamin Franklin*)

Word List 44  MP3-44

词根、词缀预习表

tomy	切	anatomy	n. 解剖构造
orium	场所；地点	auditorium	n. 礼堂
dors	背	dorsal	a. 背部的
velope	包	envelope	n. 信封
grav	重	gravity	n. 重力
mur	墙	mural	n. 壁画
alg	痛	nostalgia	n. 怀旧感
organ	器官	organism	n. 有机物

abiding [ə'baɪdɪŋ] *a.* 持久的(enduring, permanent)

【记】来自abide(*v.* 坚持；容忍)

【搭】abiding friendship 持久的友谊

【例】The old man has an *abiding* love for music and drama. 这位老人一直热爱音乐和戏剧。

【参】temporal(*a.* 世俗的); temporary(*a.* 临时的)

abundant [ə'bʌndənt] *a.* 充足的，丰富的(*rich, *plentiful)

【记】和abound(*v.* 大量存在；充满)一起记

【例】Feldspar is the most *abundant* mineral on the Earth's surface. 长石是地球表面最丰富的矿物质。

【派】abundantly(*ad.* 丰富地，充裕地)

across [ə'krɔːs] *ad.* 横过；在对面 *prep.* 越过

【搭】go/walk/run across 穿过

【例】I happened to be looking through some of my roommate's science magazines and I came *across* an article on phrenology. 我碰巧在看室友的科学杂志，遇到一篇关于颅相学的文章。

A: My parents are taking me to a really fancy restaurant tonight. So I'm wearing this new cologne. I got a sample of it from the magazine. Can you smell it?

□ abiding   □ abundant   □ across

B: From *across* the room!

A: 我父母今晚要带我去一家高级餐厅。所以我用了这个新的古龙水，是从杂志上得到一份样品。你能闻到吗？

B: 从房间对面都能闻到！

不理他　aloof

aloof	[əˈluːf] *a.* 远离的(remote)；冷淡的(indifferent)

amuse [əˈmjuːz] *v.* 逗乐，逗笑(delight, entertain)

【例】The department chair was *amused* by my letter. 系主任被我的信逗乐了。

【派】amused(*a.* 愉快的，开心的)

anatomy [əˈnætəmi] *n.* 解剖构造；解剖(dissection)

【记】词根记忆：ana(分开) + tomy(切) → 切开身体 → 解剖

【例】We will discuss other features of the Neanderthal *anatomy*. 我们将讨论穴居人解剖构造的其他特点。

【派】anatomical(*a.* 解剖的)

antique [ænˈtiːk] *n.* 古董(an object of ancient times)

【记】词根记忆：anti(前) + que → 以前的东西 → 古董

【参】antiquated(*a.* 陈旧的；过时的)；antiquity(*n.* 古迹；古物)

applicable [əˈplɪkəbl] *a.* 可应用的；可实施的

【记】分拆联想：appli(看作apply，运用) + cable(能…的) → 能运用的 → 可应用的；可实施的

application [ˌæplɪˈkeɪʃn] *n.* 请求；申请(书，表)；应用，运用；施用，敷用；作用，影响

【记】来自apply(*vt.* 申请；应用)

【搭】application for 申请…；the application of …的申请

【例】Many overseas students' *applications* for full scholarship are turned down every year in the US. 在美国，每年都有很多海外学生的全额奖学金申请遭到拒绝。

A: Excuse me, I heard that there were a couple of jobs available in the library. So I'd like to apply for one of them. Can I fill out the *application* form at home and bring it back next week?

B: Sure, but you should know that we're about to start looking at the *applications*, and we hope to make some job offers in a few days.

A: 打扰一下，我听说图书馆有几个工作机会。我想申请一个。我能在家填写申请表，下周再带回来吗？

B: 当然可以，但是你应该知道我们要开始看这些申请了，我们希望几天之内确定一些工作的人选。

☐ aloof	☐ amuse	☐ anatomy	☐ antique	☐ applicable	☐ application

assistance [əˈsɪstəns] *n.* 帮助，援助（help, aid）

【例】A: I'm really having trouble with this calculus course. If I can't start doing better soon, I'm going to have to drop it.

B: Why don't you get some help from the graduate *assistance*? That's what it is there for.

A：微积分课真难。如果不能很快学好，我就打算不上这门课了。

B：你为何不从研究生援助会那里寻求帮助呢？那是设立援助会的目的。

auditorium [ˌɔːdɪˈtɔːriəm] *n.* 礼堂（hall）；观众席

【记】词根记忆：audit(听)＋orium(场所；地点)→礼堂

aware [əˈwer] *a.* 知道的（perceptible）；意识到的

【例】People are becoming increasingly *aware* of national and international issues. 人们越来越关注国家和国际事务了。

【派】unaware(*a.* 未意识到的)

barn [bɑːrn] *n.* 谷仓；牲口棚

【记】和bar(*n.* 酒吧)一起记

blossom [ˈblɑːsəm] *n.* 花 *vi.* 开花（bloom）

【记】联想记忆：bloom中间开出两个s形的花

【例】You may have noticed trees in your area *blossoming* and their fruit ripening. 你或许已经注意到，你所在地区的树木已经开花，果实在成熟。

cling [klɪŋ] *vi.* 附着；紧贴（adhere, stick）

【例】The baby *clung* to its mother. 那个婴儿紧紧贴在母亲身上。

coax [koʊks] *vt.* (巧妙地)处理

【记】分拆联想：co(看作coke, 可乐)＋ax(看作axe, 斧头)→用可乐和斧头来威逼利诱→(巧妙地)处理

【例】The hammers that hit the strings have to be *coaxed* not to sound like percussion. 打击弦的小锤必须巧妙处理，这样听起来才不像打击乐。

【参】hoax(*vt.* 欺骗)；coaxal(*a.* 同轴的)

commentary [ˈkɑːmənteri] *n.* 评论；注释（comment）

【搭】social commentary 社会评论

【例】I prefer non-fiction: history, social *commentary* and stuff like that. 我喜欢纪实性读物：历史、社会评论以及此类读物。

【参】commentator(*n.* 评论员)

commentary

conversation [ˌkɑːnvərˈseɪʃn] *n.* 交谈，会话
【记】来自converse(*v.* 交谈，会话)
【派】conversational(*a.* 适于交谈的)

cramped [ˈkræmpt] *a.* (指空间)狭小的，狭窄的(limited)
【记】联想记忆：在狭窄的(cramped)纸上写字显得密密麻麻的(crammed)
【例】This place is nice but it seems pretty *cramped*. 这个地方不错，但是似乎有点挤。

crippling [ˈkrɪplɪŋ] *a.* 导致瘫痪的；严重的
【记】来自cripple(*vt.* 使残废)

decent [ˈdiːsnt] *a.* 体面的(honorable)；适当的(suitable)；令人满意的(satisfactory)
【例】What I'd like to do is to find a *decent* job. 我想做的就是找到一份体面的工作。//It's hard work, but I get to be outdoors and the pay is *decent*. 这是个辛苦活，但是我可以在户外，而且报酬也不错。

dedicate [ˈdedɪkeɪt] *v.* (to)(使)致力于(*devote)；奉献
【记】分拆联想：de + dic(宣称) + ate → 宣称为祖国献身 → 奉献；致力于
【例】The mayor was *dedicated* to fighting crime in the city. 市长致力于和城市中的犯罪行为作斗争。

defense [dɪˈfens] *n.* 防御，防卫(protection)
【记】来自defend(*v.* 防护；辩护)
【搭】defense machanism 防卫机制；defense against 对…的防御
【派】defenseless(*a.* 无防御的)；defensible(*a.* 可防御的)；defensive (*n.* 防御 *a.* 保卫的)

dissolve [dɪˈzɑːlv] *v.* (使)溶解(melt, liquefy)；清除(eliminate)
【记】词根记忆：dis(分开) + solve(=solv松开) → 松开；分散 → 溶解
【例】Kilns are also used for *dissolving* carbons and iron compounds. 窑也用来分解碳和铁的化合物。

dissolve

dorsal [ˈdɔːrsl] *a.* 背部的；背脊的(back)
【记】词根记忆：dors(背) + al → 背部的
【搭】dorsal fin 背鳍
【例】The fishes' *dorsal* fins are usually cut off by the fishermen. 鱼类的背鳍通常被渔民切掉。
【参】tail fin 尾鳍

elusive [iˈluːsɪv] *a.* 难懂的；难捕捉的

【记】来自elude(*v.* 逃避；困惑)

embarrass [ɪmˈbærəs] *v.* (使)尴尬，(使)困窘

【记】分拆联想：em + barr(看作bar, 酒吧) + ass(蠢驴) → 在酒吧喝醉了表现得像头蠢驴 → (使)尴尬

【例】I just get so *embarrassed* and nervous whenever I have to speak in front of a group of people. 我只要在一群人面前说话，就会特别尴尬紧张。

encourage [ɪnˈkɜːrɪdʒ] *vt.* 鼓励；促进(*urge, stimulate)

【记】词根记忆：en(使…) + courage(精神) → 使有精神 → 鼓励；促进

【例】We *encourage* all students to volunteer for at least one community activity before they graduate. 我们鼓励所有学生毕业之前自愿参与至少一项社区活动。

【派】encouragement(*n.* 鼓励，激励)

envelope [ˈenvəloup] *n.* 信封

【记】词根记忆：en + velope(包) → 用纸包起来 → 信封

【例】A: Look, I got a letter from my cousin Jeff in Alaska.

B: Can I get the return address from the *envelope*?

A：你瞧，我收到了在阿拉斯加的堂兄杰夫的一封信。

B：能给我信封上的寄信人地址吗？

【参】develop(*v.* 发展)

epitomize [ɪˈpɪtəmaɪz] *v.* 成为…的缩影

【记】词根记忆：epi(在…后) + tom(看作tome, 一卷书) + ize → 写在一卷书后面的话 → 成为…的缩影

excessive [ɪkˈsesɪv] *a.* 过多的；过分的

【记】词根记忆：ex(出) + cess(走) + ive → 走出了；走过了 → 过分的

【例】In the 18th century French economists protested the *excessive* regulation of business by the government. 18世纪，法国经济学家抗议政府对商业的过度管制。//The leading cause of preventable hearing loss is *excessive* noise. 可预防性听力丧失的首要原因是过多的噪音。

【派】excessively(*ad.* 过分地)

【参】excess(*a.* 过度的)

exercise [ˈeksərsaɪz] *n.* 练习；习题；训练，锻炼 *v.* 训练，锻炼；行使

【例】A: Dr. Smith, this is Hill, those stretching *exercises* that you

□ elusive　■ embarrass　■ encourage　■ envelope　■ epitomize　■ excessive
■ exercise

recommended are really helping with my back pain. But the pills you prescribed, I think, they are giving me a headache.

B: That's not unusual. Let's try cutting back two, just one a day, all right?

A: 史密斯医生，我是希尔。你推荐的伸展运动的确缓解了我背部的疼痛。但是我觉得你开的药让我头痛。

B: 是有这种情况。咱们试着减少两片，一天只吃一片，好吗？

exhilarating [ɪgˈzɪləreɪtɪŋ] *a.* 令人高兴的，使人兴奋的(exciting)

【记】来自exhilarate(*vt.* 使高兴，使愉快)，ex + hilar(高兴) + ate → 使高兴

【例】The children screamed with delight on the *exhilarating* carnival ride. 在令人兴奋的狂欢旅程上，孩子们开心地喊叫着。

fortuitous [fɔːrˈtuːɪtəs] *a.* 偶然的(*lucky, sudden, casual*)

【例】They fell in love with each other in a *fortuitous* meeting. 他们偶然相遇后就双双坠入了爱河。

【派】fortuitously(*ad.* 偶然地)

fortune [ˈfɔːrtʃən] *n.* 财富(riches, wealth); 运气(luck)

【记】分拆联想：for + tune(调子) → 一个人有了大量的财富，说话的调子也不同了 → 财富

【派】fortunate(*a.* 幸运的)

fund [fʌnd] *n.* [常*pl.*]基金; 资金(capital); 储备

【记】发音记忆："放的" → 国家发放的资金 → 资金

gravity [ˈɡrævəti] *n.* 重力

【记】词根记忆：grav(重) + ity(表性质) → 重力

【例】There is more *gravity* on the Mars than on Moon. 火星上的重力比月球上的大。

horizontal [ˌhɔːrəˈzɑːntl] *a.* 水平的(level)

【记】来自horizon(*n.* 地平线)

【搭】horizontal movement 水平运动

illusion [ɪˈluːʒn] *n.* 幻觉，错觉(delusion)

【记】词根记忆：il(不，无) + lus(看作lust，光) + ion → 看到根本没有的光 → 幻觉，错觉

【例】They brush away *illusions* and secondhand opinions. 他们不理会幻觉和二手评价。//Many workers are seduced by rosy *illusions* of life as a telecommuter. 很多员工被远程办公生活的美好幻觉所诱惑。

【派】disillusioned（*a.* 对…幻想破灭的）；illusive（*a.* 错觉的；幻觉的）

【参】allusion（*n.* 提及，暗示）；delusion（*n.* 错觉）；elusion（*n.* 逃避）

inspect [ɪnˈspekt] *vt.* 检查（check）；调查；视察

【记】词根记忆：in（进入）+ spect（看）→ 进去看 → 检查；视察

【搭】inspect the damage 检查损坏；inspect sth. for sth. 为…而检查…

【例】Experts suggest car owners should have their cars *inspected* regularly. 专家建议车主应该定期找人检查车辆。

【派】inspector〔*n.* 检查员；巡视员；（警察）巡官〕

【参】aspect（*n.* 方面）；respect（*vt.* 尊重，尊敬）；prospect（*n.* 景色；前景）

major [ˈmeɪdʒər] *a.* 较大的；主要的（principal）*n.* 专业（an academic subject）*v.* 主修（to pursue an academic subject）

【记】词根记忆：maj（大）+ or → 较大的

【搭】major category 主要范畴；major course 主修课

【例】At that time Quebec was a *major* market for livestock, crops and fish. 当时魁北克是牲畜、谷物和鱼的主要市场。//I'm going to *major* in criminal law. 我将主修刑法专业。

【派】majority（*n.* 多数，大半）

mention [ˈmenʃn] *vt.* 提及，说起（remark）

【例】Today I want to *mention* an even earlier form of transportation. 今天我想谈一个更早期的运输形式。

menu [ˈmenjuː] *n.* 菜单（list）

monster [ˈmɑːnstər] *n.* 怪物；巨兽

【记】分拆联想：mon（音似：猛）+ ster → 凶猛可怕的怪物 → 怪物；巨兽

motive [ˈmoʊtɪv] *n.* 动机，目的（incentive）

【记】词根记忆：mot（移动）+ ive → 移动的用意 → 动机，目的

mural [ˈmjʊrəl] *n.* 壁画；壁饰（fresco）

【记】词根记忆：mur（墙）+ al → 墙上的画 → 壁画

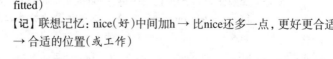

mural

niche [niːʃ] *n.* 壁龛（a recess in a wall）；合适的位置（或工作）（a place or status for which a person or thing is best fitted）

【记】联想记忆：nice（好）中间加 h → 比 nice 还多一点，更好更合适 → 合适的位置（或工作）

inspect	major	mention	menu	monster	motive
mural	niche				

【例】Late ancestral horse types moved from their forest *niche* out onto the grassy plains. 此后的马的祖先离开了森林环境，来到了长满草的旷野。

nostalgia [nəˈstældʒə] *n.* 怀旧感；思乡病(homesickness)

【记】词根记忆：nost(家) + alg(痛) + ia → 想到家就心痛 → 思乡病

【例】The female novelist's work is pervaded by *nostalgia* for her hometown. 这位女小说家的作品弥漫着思乡之情。

opportunity [ˌɑːpərˈtuːnəti] *n.* 机会，时机(chance, occasion)

organism [ˈɔːrɡənɪzəm] *n.* 生物(a living being)；有机物

【记】词根记忆：organ(器官) + ism → 生物一般都有器官 → 生物

【例】All living *organisms* have to adapt to it when environment has changed. 所有活的生物都必须适应环境的变化。

oxygen [ˈɑːksɪdʒən] *n.* 氧；氧气

【记】词根记忆：oxy(氧的) + gen(产生) → 氧气

【例】The professor said something about coal being set on fire and blasted with a mixture of steam and *oxygen*. This process produces a gas made up of hydrogen and carbon, the... hum, the basic elements of oil. 教授讲到了将煤点燃之后向上面喷射蒸汽和氧气的混合物。这个过程产生的气体由氢气和碳构成…嗯，就是石油的基本元素。

【参】hydrogen(*n.* 氢)

perpendicular [ˌpɜːrpənˈdɪkjələr] *a.* 垂直的(vertical)；直立的(upright)

【记】词根记忆：per(自始至终) + pend(挂) + icular → 自始至终挂着 → 垂直的

【例】It will take extreme courage to climb up the *perpendicular* mountain. 攀爬上垂直的山峰需要很大的勇气。

【参】horizontal(*a.* 水平的)

philosopher [fəˈlɑːsəfər] *n.* 哲学家；哲人

【记】来自philosophy(*n.* 哲学)

【例】The lecture mainly talks about how the ancient *philosophers* measured the distance between heavenly bodies. 这堂课主要讲古代哲学家如何测量天体之间的距离。

politics [ˈpɑːlətɪks] *n.* 政治；政见

【记】联想记忆：政治(politics)要讲政策(policy)

【派】political(*a.* 政治的；行政上的)

prestigious [preˈstɪdʒəs] *a.* 有威望的，有声望的(honored)

【例】The Nobel Prize for Literature is the most *prestigious* form of literary recognition in the world. 诺贝尔文学奖是文学界最高的奖项。

primary ['praɪmeri] *a.* 最初的；首要的(dominant, chief)；根本的(*funda-mental)

【例】The phases of the Moon have served as *primary* divisions of time for thousands of years. 月相几千年来都被用来区分时间。

【派】primarily(*ad.* 主要地)

pyramid ['pɪrəmɪd] *n.* 金字塔

【例】Plants are the basis of the food *pyramid* for all living things, even for other plants. 植物是所有生物，甚至其他植物的食物金字塔的基础。

pyramid

quaint [kweɪnt] *a.* 古色古香的

【例】The museum displayed *quaint* advertisements from the 1920s. 博物馆展出了20世纪20年代以来古色古香的广告。

rate [reɪt] *n.* 速率；比率；价格；费用；等级 *v.* 估价；评级；评价

【记】词根记忆：rat(计算)＋e→计算的结果→比率

【搭】at any rate 无论如何；至少；at the rate of 以…速度；at this rate 这样的话；interest rate 利率

【例】Freight trains have an accident *rate* that is only 1/3 that of the trucking industry. 货运火车的事故率只是卡车业的三分之一。

A: Another one of the letters I mailed last week has been returned!

B: Didn't you realize the airmail *rates* went up a month ago?

A：又一封我上周寄的信被退回来了！

B：你不知道航空邮件的资费上个月涨了吗？

recollection [ˌrekə'lekʃn] *n.* 回忆；记忆(memory, remembrance)

【记】来自recollect(*vt.* 回想)；re＋col(一起)＋lect(收集)＋ion→将过去的回忆收集在一起→回忆

【搭】beyond recollection 不记得；within one's recollection 在…的记忆中

【例】After the accident, the little boy had no *recollection* at all of his childhood. 这起事故之后，小男孩全然回忆不起他的童年了。

【派】recollect(*vt.* 回忆，想起)

rhinoceros [raɪ'nɑːsərəs] *n.* 犀牛

rivalry ['raɪvlri] *n.* 竞争(competition, contest)；敌对状态

【记】来自rival(*vt.* 竞争)

【例】Due to the financial crisis, the *rivalry* between the two

| primary | pyramid | quaint | rate | recollection | rhinoceros |
| rivalry | | | | | |

companies grew much more intense. 由于金融危机，两家公司之间的竞争更加激烈了。

senator ['senətər] *n.* 参议员

【记】来自senate(*n.* 参议院)

sensitive ['sensətɪv] *a.* 敏感的；灵敏的(delicate)

【记】词根记忆：sens(感觉) + itive → 敏感的

【例】Ants can be extremely *sensitive* to these signals. 蚂蚁会对这些信号十分敏感。

【派】sensitively(*ad.* 敏感地)；hypersensitive(*a.* 非常敏感的)；sensitivity(*n.* 灵敏性；敏感)

shield [ʃiːld] *n.* 防护物(defense)；盾 *vt.* 保护(*protect, defend)

【例】The mountains surrounding Los Angeles effectively *shield* the city from the hot. 围绕洛杉矶的这些山脉有效地使这个城市免受酷热。

slight [slaɪt] *a.* 轻微的，微弱的(subtle, tiny)

【记】分拆联想：s + light(轻的) → 轻微的

【例】Life resembles in only a *slight* degree the popular image of it. 人生只在很小程度上与其通俗的表象相似。

【派】slightly(*ad.* 稍微地；稍稍)

snack [snæk] *n.* 快餐；小吃

【搭】snack food 点心；小吃；snack bar 快餐店

spinning ['spɪnɪŋ] *a.* 旋转的(revolving) *n.* 纺纱

【记】来自spin(*v.* 旋转；纺纱)

spray [spreɪ] *n.* 飞沫 *vt.* 喷(射)(sprinkle, splash)

【记】分拆联想：sp(音似：四波) + ray(光线) → 光线向四面射去 → 喷(射)

【例】An insulating material was *sprayed* on engine parts. 引擎上喷上了绝缘材料。

square [skwer] *a.* 正方形的(foursquare)；平方的 *n.* 广场(plaza)

【派】squarely(*ad.* 正对着地；明确无误地)

squirrel ['skwɜːrəl] *n.* 松鼠

sumptuous ['sʌmptʃuəs] *a.* 奢侈的(luxurious)；华丽的(magnificent, splendid)

【记】词根记忆：sumpt(拿；取) + uous → (把钱)拿出去 → 奢侈的

tremendous [trə'mendəs] *a.* 惊人的(striking)；巨大的

【记】词根记忆：trem(颤抖) + endous → 让人发抖的 → 惊人的

【例】He has a *tremendous* skill for placing his buildings in harmony with nature. 他技艺高超，能使他的建筑与自然和谐统一。//

Tremendous amounts of food supplies and artifacts have been found there. 那里发现了大量的食物给养和手工艺品。

【派】tremendously(*ad.* 巨大地；非常地)

trench [trentʃ] *n.* 壕沟(ditch)

【记】分拆联想：tr + ench(看作bench，长凳) → 像长凳一样狭长的地区 → 壕沟

【例】The oceanic crust is remelted beneath the ocean *trenches*. 海洋底壳在海沟下又一次融化。

trip [trɪp] *n.* 旅行；远足(excursion) *v.* 绊倒；失足

【搭】make a trip 旅行；a special trip 特殊的旅行

【例】Pick up that box, or someone will *trip* over it. 把那个箱子捡起来，不然会把人绊倒的。

tropical [ˈtrɑːpɪkl] *a.* 热带的

【记】词根记忆：trop(转) + ical(…的) → 热得人晕头转向的 → 热带的

【搭】tropical environment 热带环境

【例】A: Do you think that the *tropical* storm is on the way?

B: Too early to tell, but we need to be prepared. The radio mentioned possible evacuation routes.

A：你认为热带风暴快到了吗？

B：现在说还为时过早，但是我们需要有所准备。广播提到了可能的撤退路线。

The new method stimulates plant growth and enables gardeners in *tropical* climates to grow crops from cooler climates. 新方法会刺激植物的生长，使园丁能够在热带气候下种植来自较冷气候的作物。

【参】typical(*a.* 典型的)

ultimatum [ˌʌltɪˈmeɪtəm] *n.* 最后通牒

【记】分拆联想：ultim (最后的) + a + tum (看作term，期限) → 最后的期限 → 最后通牒

最后三天 ultimatum

【例】If George misses one more meeting, we'd better give him an *ultimatum*. 如果乔治再错过一次会议，我们最好给他下最后通牒。

utter [ˈʌtər] *v.* 说(speak, express) *a.* 完全的

【派】utterance(*n.* 发声；表达)；utterly(*ad.* 完全地)

vacate [vəˈkeɪt] *vt.* 腾出，空出

【记】词根记忆：vac(空) + ate → 腾出，空出

【例】You must *vacate* your room by June 3rd. 你必须在7月3日前腾出你的房间。

variable ['veriəbl] *n.* 变数；变量 *a.* 易变的(inconstant)

【例】Our weather has been *variable* the last three months. 最近三个月的天气变化无常。//The decision involves a large number of *variables* with complex relationships. 这个决定涉及很多关系复杂的变量。

【派】invariably(*ad.* 不变地；总是)

withdraw [wɪð'drɔ:] *v.* 取消(cancel)；撤销(retreat, recede)

【记】词根记忆：with(向后) + draw(拉) → 拉回；收回 → 取消；撤销

【例】Is it too late for me to *withdraw* from my music class? 我现在取消音乐课是不是太晚了？

【派】withdrawal(*n.* 收回；撤回；撤退)

The most promising successor is not the talented, but those who are good at seizing every opportunity to explore.

最有希望的成功者，并不是才干出众的人，而是那些最善于利用每一时机去发掘开拓的人。

——苏格拉底(*Socrates*)

Word List 45  MP3-45

词根、词缀预习表

ate	使	activate	vt. 使活动
corpor	团体	corporate	a. 共同的
flu	流动	flux	n. 变迁
metic	害怕的	meticulous	a. 细心的
peri	周围的	peripheral	a. 不重要的
luxur	丰富；精美	luxury	n. 奢侈品

abstract ['æbstrækt] *a.* 抽象的(unconcrete)；抽象派的(nonrepresentational)
【记】词根记忆：abs + tract(拉；抽) → 抽象的
【例】I really like those *abstract* paintings we saw in our history class today. 我确实很喜欢今天历史课上看到的抽象绘画作品。
【派】abstracted(*a.* 出神的，心不在焉的)；abstraction(*n.* 抽象概念；抽象化状态)

activate ['æktɪveɪt] *vt.* 刺激(stimulate)；使活动
【记】词根记忆：activ(e)(活跃的) + ate(使) → 使活跃 → 使活动
【例】If you press the red button near the bottom it will *activate* the washing machine. 按靠近底部的红色按钮，就会启动洗衣机。

adjoining [ə'dʒɔɪnɪŋ] *a.* 毗邻的(neighboring, adjacent)
【搭】adjoining countries 毗邻的国家
【例】During weekend we usually heard noises in the *adjoining* apartment. 周末我们通常会听到来自毗邻公寓的噪音。

affect [ə'fekt] *vt.* 影响(influence)；感动；感染
【记】词根记忆：af(加强) + fect(做) → 反复做就会有影响 → 影响
【例】Let's take a look at Parry's research and how it *affects* what modern day scholars think about Homer. 让我们看看帕里的研究，看它如何影响当代学者对荷马的认识。

How will the tax affect people on low incomes?税收会如何影响低收入人群?

【派】unaffected(*a.* 未受影响的)

【参】effect(*n.* 作用；影响)；infect(*vt.* 传染；感染)

affirm [əˈfɜːrm] *vt.* 断言；坚持声称(assert)

【记】词根记忆：af(加强)+firm(坚定的)→断言；坚持声称

【例】The scholar *affirmed* Shakespeare's authorship of the plays. 这位学者断言莎士比亚是这些剧本的作者。

alignment [əˈlaɪnmənt] *n.* 排列(arrangement)；联合，联盟(association, alliance)

【记】来自align(*vt.* 使成一行；使结盟)

array [əˈreɪ] *n.* 一系列(series)

【记】分拆联想：ar+ray(光线)→像光线一样→一系列

Babylonian [ˌbæbɪˈloʊnjən] *a.* 巴比伦的

basement [ˈbeɪsmənt] *n.* 建筑物的底部；地下室；地窖(cellar)

【记】联想记忆：base(底部)+ment→房子的底部就是地下室→地下室

【例】A: Wendy is in the *basement* trying to repair the washing machine.

B: Shouldn't she be working on her engineering paper?

A：温迪正在地下室试着修理洗衣机。

B：她不是应该在写工程论文吗？

basement

bonanza [bəˈnænzə] *n.* 富矿带；带来好运的事

brilliant [ˈbrɪliənt] *a.* 闪耀的(bright)；杰出的(outstanding)

【例】Scientists predicted the comet would be a *brilliant* spectacle. 科学家预言彗星将成为奇观。//Tiffany is a *brilliant* designer. 蒂法尼是个杰出的设计师。

【派】brilliantly(*ad.* 辉煌地；灿烂地)

bulk [bʌlk] *n.* (大)体积；大部分(majority)

【例】Most of their *bulk* is hidden below the water. 它们的主体都隐藏在水下。//Airmail began to constitute the *bulk* of the United States' mail. 航空邮件开始成为美国邮件的主要部分。

chant [tʃænt] *n.* 圣歌

【记】联想记忆：形似拼音"chang"(唱)→咏唱→圣歌

【例】We've been studying Zulu *chants* of South Africa. 我们一直在研究南非祖鲁人的圣歌。

charcoal [ˈtʃɑːrkoʊl] *n.* 木炭

【记】组合词：char(烧焦) + coal(煤炭) → 像烧焦的煤炭 → 木炭

confirm [kənˈfɜːrm] *vt.* 证实(validate, verify)；使巩固(strengthen)；批准(approve)

【记】词根记忆：con(加强) + firm(坚定) → 使巩固

【例】They *confirmed* earlier theories about the Moon's surface. 他们证实了早期关于月球表面的理论。//Has tomorrow's meeting been *confirmed*? 明天的会议得到批准了吗？

【派】confirmation(*n.* 确认；证明)

【参】conform(*vt.* 使顺从)

continuation [kənˌtɪnjuˈeɪʃn] *n.* 延长；延续(prolongation)

【例】Which topic will most probably be included in the *continuation* of today's lecture? 今天这堂课接下来的部分最有可能包含哪个话题？

corporate [ˈkɔːrpərət] *a.* 共同的；公司的(incorporated)

【记】词根记忆：corpor(团体) + ate → 共同的；公司的

【例】Sarah used to teach psychology, but now she is a *corporate* statistician. 萨拉过去教过心理学，不过现在她是一个公司的统计员。

deny [dɪˈnaɪ] *vt.* 否认(negate)；拒绝(refuse)

【记】发音记忆："抵赖" → 否认

diffusion [dɪˈfjuːʒn] *n.* 散布，扩散，传播

【搭】air diffusion 空气扩散；cultural diffusion 文化扩散

【例】A series of reaction *diffusion* system is involved in the new equipment. 新设备包括一系列的反应扩散系统。

distasteful [dɪsˈteɪstfl] *a.* (令人)不愉快的(displeasing)；讨厌的(disagreeable)

【例】The teacher's manners were *distasteful* to every student in the class. 老师的态度令班里的每个学生讨厌。

district [ˈdɪstrɪkt] *n.* 区域，管区(section, area, region)

endeavor [ɪnˈdevər] *vi./n.* 努力，尽力(strive, effort)

【记】分拆联想：end(尽头) + eav(看作eager, 热情) + or → 用尽了我们的热情 → 努力，尽力

【例】Susan *endeavors* to get better grades in college. 苏珊尽力在大学取得更好的成绩。

enterprising [ˈentərpraɪzɪŋ] *a.* 有事业心的；有进取心的(ambitious)

【例】Forts serve as bases where *enterprising* entrepreneurs could bring commerce to the West. 要塞是有创业精神的企业家的基地，他们可以由此把贸易带到西部。

| □ charcoal | □ confirm | □ continuation | □ corporate | □ deny | □ diffusion |
| □ distasteful | □ district | □ endeavor | □ enterprising | | |

ephemeral [ɪ'femərəl] *a.* 短暂的, 转瞬即逝的 (transient)

【记】词根记忆: e + phem (出现) + eral → 出现就消失 → 短暂的

eruption [ɪ'rʌpʃn] *n.* 爆发 (outbreak); 喷发

【记】来自 erupt (*v.* 爆发)

essay ['eseɪ] *n.* 散文 (prose); 短文; 评论 (comment)

【记】分拆联想: es (看作 easy, 随意的) + say → 随意地说; 随意地写 → 散文; 短文

【例】We'll begin our study by reading the first *essay* listed in the syllabus. 我们将通过阅读提纲列出的第一篇文章来开始我们的学习。

execute ['eksɪkjuːt] *vt.* 执行 (*create, perform); 处死; 完成 (complete)

【派】execution (*n.* 执行; 完成); executive (*a.* 行政的 *n.* 执行者; 经理人员)

expose [ɪk'spoʊz] *vt.* 使暴露; 使曝光

【记】词根记忆: ex (出) + pos (放) + e → 放出来 → 使暴露

【搭】be exposed to 暴露于

【例】A group of mice was placed in a brightly lit open box with no hiding places. Some of the mice wandered around the box and didn't appear to be bothered about being so *exposed*. 一群老鼠被放在了照亮的无盖的盒子里, 里面没有躲藏的地方。有些老鼠在盒子里转来转去, 好像并不介意暴露在灯光之下。

familiar [fə'mɪliər] *a.* 熟悉的; 通晓的; 亲近的

【搭】be familiar with 与…熟悉; 通晓; look familiar 看起来很像; be familiar to 为…所熟悉的

【例】Many of you are *familiar* with this huge tree. It's found in many areas of the US and Canada in cities and small towns. 你们很多人都熟悉这种大树。美国和加拿大的城市和小镇的很多地区都有这种树。

far-fetched [ˌfɑːr'fetʃt] *a.* 牵强的

【例】The proposal the president had put forward seemed a little *far-fetched*. 董事长的提议似乎有点牵强。

A: How did you like yesterday's astronomy class?

B: It was interesting. But the point the teacher was trying to make seemed a little *far-fetched*.

A: 你觉得昨天的天文课怎么样?

B: 有意思。但是老师提出的观点似乎有点牵强。

ephemeral	eruption	essay	execute	expose	familiar
far-fetched					

487

firm [fɜːrm] *n.* 公司（corporation）*a.* 结实的（*hard, fixed）；坚定的（steadfast）

【例】Children with parents whose guidance is *firm*, consistent, and rational are inclined to possess high levels of self-confidence. 从父母那里得到坚定、一致和理性指导的孩子们自信心更强。

【派】firmly(*ad.* 稳固地)

flap [flæp] *n.* 拍打 *v.*（使）摆动（sway）；拍打（lap）；飘动

【记】分拆联想：f(看作fly，飞) + lap(拍打)→拍打

【例】The flags are *flapping* in the breeze. 旗帜正在微风中飘扬。

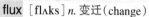
flap

flux [flʌks] *n.* 变迁（change）

【记】词根记忆：flu(流动) + x → 变动 → 变迁

【例】Life on Earth has continually been in *flux* as slow physical and chemical changes have occurred on Earth. 随着地球上缓慢发生的物理和化学变化，生命也一直在变化。

【派】influx(*n.* 流入)

fort [fɔːrt] *n.* 要塞；堡垒（stronghold）

【记】联想记忆：在重要港口(port)建筑堡垒(fort)

【参】fortress(*n.* 要塞；堡垒)

giraffe [dʒəˈræf] *n.* 长颈鹿

grazing [ˈɡreɪzɪŋ] *n.* 放牧；牧场（pasture）

【搭】over grazing 过度放牧

harmonic [hɑːrˈmɑːnɪk] *a.* 和声的

【记】联想记忆：harm(适合) + onic → 都合适 → 和声的

ideomotor [ˌaɪdiəˈmoʊtə] *a.* 观念运动的

【搭】ideomotor action 观念运动；ideomotor theory 念动说

【例】As we all know, *ideomotor* action is a term of psychology. 众所周知，观念运动是一个心理学术语。

idyllic [aɪˈdɪlɪk] *a.* 田园诗的

【记】来自idyll(田园诗) + ic → 田园诗般的 → 田园诗的

illustrate [ˈɪləstreɪt] *vt.* 阐明（clarify）；举例说明

【记】词根记忆：il(不断) + lust(照亮；光) + rate → 不断给光明 → 阐明

【例】These topics will be *illustrated* with computer animations to make explanations easy to follow. 电脑动画将用来说明这些话题，

| firm | flap | flux | fort | giraffe | grazing |
| harmonic | ideomotor | idyllic | illustrate | | |

这样解释起来就容易听懂了。

【派】illustration(*n.* 说明；例证；插图)

inclination [ˌɪnklɪˈneɪʃn] *n.* 爱好(*preference)；趋向(tendency)

【记】词根记忆：in(内向)+clin(倾斜)+ation→倾向→爱好；趋向

【例】They had neither the skills nor the *inclination* to become farmers. 他们既无技能也不愿成为农民。// Individual birds have markedly different interests and *inclinations*. 鸟类个体有明显不同的兴趣和爱好。

instinct [ˈɪnstɪŋkt] *n.* 本能；天性(nature)

【记】词根记忆：in(内)+stinct(刺)→内在的刺激→本能；天性

【例】The *instinct* drives green turtles to always return to the beach where they were hatched. 本能使绿海龟总是回到它们的孵化地所在的海滩。

【派】instinctive(*a.* 本能的；天生的；直觉的)；instinctively(*ad.* 本能地)

【参】extinct(*a.* 灭绝的)；distinct(*a.* 清楚的)；extinguish(*vt.* 熄灭)

introduction [ˌɪntrəˈdʌkʃn] *n.* 介绍；传入，引进；导言，导论，绪论

【记】词根记忆：intro(入内)+duct(引导)+ion→引导入内→介绍

【例】I've got to take an *introduction* to poetry before. 我之前学习过诗歌导论。

A: Did I hear that right? Our reports are due next Friday?

B: Just the *introduction*, the rest will find out about today in class.

A：我没听错吧？我们的报告下周五就要交？

B：只是交绪论，剩下的今天上课才能知道。

ironic [aɪˈrɑːnɪk] *a.* 讽刺的(sarcastic)

【记】来自irony(*n.* 反话；讽刺)

【例】Maybe the most *ironic* example of human behavior that can lead to desertification is irrigation. 或许导致沙漠化的最具讽刺意味的人类行为就是灌溉。

luxury [ˈlʌkʃəri] *n.* 奢侈(品)

【记】词根记忆：luxur(丰富；精美)+y→奢侈品一般都很精美→奢侈(品)

【例】Goods that had once been *luxury* items became part of everyday life. 曾经的奢侈品已成为今天日常生活中的一部分。

啊！我的爱…

lyric

【派】luxurious(*a.* 奢侈的)

lyric [ˈlɪrɪk] *a.* 抒情的 *n.* 抒情诗；[常*pl.*]歌词

【记】分拆联想：ly(看作lying，躺)＋ric → 躺在星空下 → 抒情的

【例】Margaret wrote the *lyrics* for 21 children's records. 玛格丽特给21张儿童唱片创作了歌词。

【派】lyricism(*n.* 抒情)；lyrically(*ad.* 抒情地)

mantle [ˈmæntl] *n.* 覆盖物(cloak)；【地】地幔

【记】分拆联想：man(词根：手)＋tle → 一手遮天 → 覆盖物

【例】He concluded that the depth marked the boundary between a solid *mantle* and the liquid core. 他推断这个深度标明了固态地幔和液态地核之间的界限。

meticulous [məˈtɪkjələs] *a.* 细心的，很注意细节的(*careful)

【记】词根记忆：metic(害怕的)＋ulous(多…的) → 经常害怕出错的 → 细心的

【例】Champagne is typical in its brilliance of color, *meticulous* rendering of detail, compact composition, and unabashed abundance. 香槟酒具有独特的色泽、一丝不苟的细节、紧凑的构成和不加掩饰的丰富。

【派】meticulously(*ad.* 小心翼翼地)

migration [maɪˈɡreɪʃn] *n.* 迁居，迁徙；迁徙的人、动物等的数量；【化】【物】移动

【记】来自migrate(*v.* 迁移)

【搭】bird migration 鸟类迁徙

【例】With the development of the global warming, *migration* patterns of some birds have changed. 随着全球变暖的发展，一些鸟类的迁徙模式也改变了。

moderate [ˈmɑːdərət] *a.* 适度的(mild)；温和的(temperate)；普通的(ordinary)

【记】词根记忆：mod(方式)＋erate → 有方式的；不过分的 → 适度的

【例】Flies breed prolifically when temperatures are warm, food is abundant, and humidity is *moderate*. 当天气暖和、食物充足、湿度适宜时，苍蝇会大量繁殖。//It is a common experience in people that appetite is lost even under conditions of *moderate* thirst. 人们经常有这种体验，那就是适度口渴时也会失去胃口。

【派】moderately(*ad.* 适度地)；moderation(*n.* 适度)

moisture [ˈmɔɪstʃər] *n.* 潮湿；湿气(humidity)

【例】This *moisture* is supplied by the passage of an airstream over a water surface. 气流经过水面，带来了湿气。

mantle　meticulous　migration　moderate　moisture

municipal [mjuːˈnɪsɪpl] *a.* 市（政）的；地方性的（local）
【记】联想记忆：muni(服务)+cip(看作city，城市)+al → 提供城市公共服务的 → 市（政）的
【例】The *municipal* government ordered landlords to roll back their rents to the levels charged in 1978. 市政府下令让房东们把房租降到1978年的收取水平。

nauseous [ˈnɔːʃəs] *a.* 令人作呕的；厌恶的
【例】A: This prescription is supposed to be effective from paining, but it's maybe too strong for me. I took it when I woke up in pain in the middle of the night, and now I feel *nauseous*.
B: You should read the label first. It says right here on the bottom to be taken with meals only.
A：这个处方应该能缓解疼痛，但是可能对我来说太猛了。我半夜疼醒吃了一片，现在觉得恶心。
B：你应该先看看标签。底下明明白白写着只能饭后服用。

odd [ɑːd] *a.* 奇异的（bizarre）；奇数的（singular）*n.*［常 *pl.*］可能性（possibility）
【记】联想记忆：奇奇(odd)相加(add)为偶

oppose [əˈpoʊz] *v.* 反对，对抗（object, resist）
【例】Politicians rarely *opposed* the government's generous support of business owners. 政客们很少反对政府对企业家的慷慨支持。
【派】opposed(*a.* 反对的)；opposing(*a.* 反向的；相反的)

orbital [ˈɔːrbɪtl] *a.* 轨道的
【记】来自：orbit(*n.* 轨道)

orchestra [ˈɔːrkɪstrə] *n.* 管弦乐队（band）
【记】分拆联想：or+chest(胸腔)+ra → 管弦乐队的成员大都需要借助胸腔的力量来演奏乐器 → 管弦乐队
【搭】symphony orchestra 交响乐队
【派】orchestral(*a.* 管弦乐的)；orchestration(*n.* 管弦乐编曲)

pensive [ˈpensɪv] *a.* 沉思的（meditative）
【记】词根记忆：pens（挂）+ive → 挂在心上 → 沉思的

pensive

peripheral [pəˈrɪfərəl] *a.* 不重要的（unimportant）；外围的
【记】词根记忆：peri(周围的)+pheral → 外围的
【搭】peripheral nerves 外围神经
【例】However, the dispute between the colonists and England was *peripheral*. 然而，殖民者和英国之间的争议是不重要的。

pole [poʊl] *n.* 地极；磁极；杆

pound [paʊnd] *vt.* 猛击(strike)；捣碎(mash) *n.* 磅；英镑
【例】After drying the fish, the women *pounded* some of them into fish meal. 这些女人把鱼晾干之后，捣碎了其中的一部分做成鱼肉饭。

practically ['præktɪkli] *ad.* 几乎(nearly)；实际上(virtually, actually)
【记】来自practical(实际的) + ly → 实际上
【例】I've *practically* spent my entire budget for the semester. 我几乎花完了这学期的所有预算。

prestige [pre'stiːʒ] *n.* 影响力(influence)；威望，声望(reputation)
【记】分拆联想：pres(看作president, 总统) + tige(看作tiger, 老虎) → 总统和老虎两者都是有威信、威望的 → 威望，声望
【例】No other colonial artisans rivaled the silversmiths' *prestige.* 殖民地其他的工匠都无法与银匠的声望匹敌。

relic ['relɪk] *n.* 遗迹
【记】分拆联想：reli(看作rely, 依靠) + c → 依靠遗产生活 → 遗迹

resort [rɪ'zɔːrt] *n.* 度假胜地；(to)求助
【记】联想记忆：向上级打报告(report)求助(resort)
【例】A woodworker can join a chest together without *resort* to nails or glue. 木工无需钉子或胶水就能打造一个箱子。

rough [rʌf] *a.* 粗糙不平的(coarse)；粗暴的(tough)；艰难的 *n.* (高尔夫球场的)深草区；草图
【记】和tough(*a.* 强硬的)一起记
【例】Life in nineteenth-century forts was very *rough.* 19世纪要塞里的生活非常艰苦。
【派】roughness(*n.* 粗糙)

sauce [sɔːs] *n.* 沙司；调味汁；佐料(condiment, relish)
【记】联想记忆：调味汁(sauce)是香味的来源(source)

scout [skaʊt] *n.* 侦察；侦察机
【记】分拆联想：sc + out(外面) → 在外面巡逻的侦察员 → 侦察

seclusion [sɪ'kluːʒn] *n.* 独处；隐居

slide [slaɪd] *v.* 滑动 (glide, slip) *n.* 滑动(slippage)；幻灯片
【记】分拆联想：s + lid(盖子) + e → 盖子太滑，从桌子上掉了下去 → 滑动

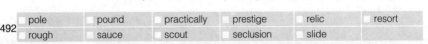

seclusion

【搭】slide projector 幻灯机；slide rule 计算尺
【例】They *slide* on a more yielding layer at the base of the lithosphere.

它们在岩石圈底部更柔软的一层滑动。

【派】slider(*n.* 滑雪者；滑冰者)；sliding(*a.* 滑行的)

studio ['stuːdɪoʊ] *n.* 工作室；录音室

supplement ['sʌplɪmənt] *n.* 补充，增补(*extension)

['sʌplɪment] *vt.* 补充，增补(*add to)

【记】词根记忆：supple (=supply提供) + ment → 提供所缺物资 → 补充

【例】This kind of pottery was produced to *supplement* imported European pottery. 这种陶器生产出来以补充进口的欧洲陶器。

【派】supplementary(*a.* 增补的)；supplementation(*n.* 增补，补充)

therefore ['ðerfɔːr] *ad.* 因此；从而(consequently)

【例】The transplanted bone may not be compatible with the patient's body, and *therefore* runs the risk of rejection. 移植的骨头可能与病人的身体不匹配，所以存在被排斥的风险。

tough [tʌf] *a.* 坚韧的；棘手的，困难的(hard)；强健的；吃苦耐劳的；粗暴的(rough)；凶恶的

【记】发音记忆："塔夫" → 像塔一样的壮夫 → 强健的

【搭】a tough job 棘手的工作；tough luck 真倒霉；tough choice 艰难的抉择；tough guy 硬汉

【例】He's as *tough* as nails—a good man to have on the mountain rescue team. 他很能吃苦——是山区营救队的得力成员。

【参】rough(*a.* 粗糙的；粗暴的)

transmitter [træns'mɪtər] *n.* 发射台；传送者，传输者

【搭】neural transmitter 神经介质

【例】These vegetables are all rich in the amino acid that helps produce in the brain a neural *transmitter* that induces sleep. 这些蔬菜富含氨基酸，帮助大脑产生诱导睡眠的神经介质。//This neural *transmitter* will help you relax, and you'll be on the way to get a good night's sleep. 这种神经介质会帮助你放松，你会睡上一个好觉。

tropic ['trɑːpɪk] *n.* 回归线；热带

【记】源自希腊根词trope (= turn转向；转动)，即太阳直射点每年在南北回归线间来回移动

【例】Heat is transported from the *tropics* to the middle and high latitudes. 热量从热带被传输到中高纬度地区。

【派】tropical(*a.* 热带的)；subtropical(*a.* 亚热带的)

ultimately [ˈʌltɪmətli] *ad.* 最终 (eventually, finally); 基本上 (fundamentally)

【例】This herculean task was *ultimately* completed, but with discouraging slowness. 这个极为艰巨的任务最终完成了，但是速度之慢令人沮丧。

vent [vent] *n.* 通风口; 排出口

【记】本身为词根，意为: 来; 风

【搭】air vent 气孔

【例】All along the *vents* there are these unusual microorganisms. 沿着整个通风口都是这些罕见的微生物。

【派】ventilate(*vt.* 使通风); ventilation(*n.* 通风)

volume [ˈvɑːljuːm] *n.* 卷 (book); 体积; 容量 (amount, capacity); 音量

【例】Joyce's first publication was a *volume* of short fiction. 乔伊斯第一次出版的是一卷短篇小说。

zinc [zɪŋk] *n.* 锌

Doubt is our traitor, often making us lose the possible victory for fear of trying.

疑惑是我们的叛徒，往往使我们因害怕尝试而输掉了可能会赢得的战果。

——莎士比亚(*William Shakespeare*)

索引

abandon /310
abbreviate /461
abiding /472
ability /12
ablaze /407
abnormal /299
abolition /342
abort /103
abound /213
abrasion /147
abreast /331
abrupt /202
absence /245
absenteeism /147
absolute /299
absolutely /276
absorb /114
absorption /169
abstract /484
absurd /331
abundant /472
abut /375
academic /407
academy /353
accelerate /191
accent /24
access /93
accessible /191
accessory /202
accident /353
acclaim /147
accommodate /386
accompany /353
accomplish /169
accomplished /364
accomplishment /1
accord /12
accordion /342
account /440
accounting /71

accredit /93
accumulate /191
accuracy /407
accurate /287
accuse /202
accustom /386
acid /276
acidic /103
acidity /71
acknowledge /114
acoustic /375
acquaint /354
acquire /321
acronym /1
across /472
acting /71
action /180
activate /484
activity /245
acumen /245
acute /1
adapt /407
adaptable /451
adaptive /256
addictive /136
addition /125
additional /266
additive /12
address /125
adequate /103
adhere /2
adhesive /125
adjacent /192
adjoining /484
adjunct /169
adjust /180
adjustment /396
administer /82
admiration /386
admire /266

admission /331
admit /24
adobe /354
adolescence /375
adopt /287
adoption /71
adorn /103
advance /266
advanced /93
advent /267
adventure /36
adverse /93
advertise /428
advisable /126
advocate /342
aerial /461
aerobic /321
aesthetic /364
affect /484
affection /13
affinity /375
affirm /485
afflict /386
afford /94
agency /136
aggregate /223
aggression /2
aggressive /202
agile /276
agitation /310
agreeable /60
ailment /48
air /299
airborne /136
alarm /71
alchemist /126
alert /364
alga /375
algebra /234
alien /136

alignment /485
alike /13
alkali /24
allay /418
allegation /256
allegiance /60
allergic /245
allergy /180
alleviate /60
allocation /276
alloy /428
allude /287
aloft /408
along /82
aloof /473
alphabet /203
alter /451
alternate /72
alternately /13
alternative /223
altitude /428
aluminum /418
alumnus /287
amass /451
amateur /354
ambience /223
ambitious /114
amble /213
amenity /115
amid /321
amino /331
ammonia /321
amount /83
ample /310
amplify /288
amuse /473
amusement /267
analogy /36
analysis /267
analyze /386

anarchist /288
anatomy /473
ancestor /223
anchor /375
ancient /267
anecdotal /223
angiosperm /72
angle /246
angular /61
animation /224
annex /461
announce /126
announcement /224
annoyed /61
annoying /94
annual /83
anomaly /246
anthropologist /451
anthropology /322
antibiotic /203
anticipate /418
antique /473
anxious /137
apartment /224
apologize /83
apparent /246
appeal /440
appetite /376
applaud /115
appliance /331
applicable /473
applicant /192
application /473
apply /36
appointment /169
apportion /267
appraisal /37
appreciate /267
appreciation /94
apprenticeship /440
approach /364
appropriate /396
approve /104
approximate /169
aquarium /386
aquatic /192
aquifer /72
arbitrary /310
arboreal /72
archaeology /170
architect /61
ardent /246
argue /376
argument /311
aria /342

arid /180
arithmetic /322
aroma /180
arouse /342
arrange /428
array /485
artesian /452
arthritis /224
articulate /354
artifact /37
artificial /322
artisan /246
artistic /2
ascending /61
ascribe /396
aspect /354
assemble /376
assembly /94
assert /343
asset /311
assign /181
assigned /396
assignment /311
assimilate /48
assistance /474
assistant /461
associate /181
assortment /418
assume /418
assure /37
asteroid /192
asthma /354
astronomical /213
astronomy /147
astute /83
asymmetrical /24
athlete /181
atmosphere /137
atom /332
atomic /104
atrophy /299
attach /441
attain /408
attempt /452
attend /387
attendance /332
attention /408
attire /37
attorney /277
attract /213
attractive /137
attribute /170
auction /126
audience /137
audio /48

audit /387
audition /365
auditorium /474
augment /332
aurora /72
authentic /224
authority /24
authorize /387
automatic /387
automobile /419
auxiliary /267
available /72
avalanche /115
avenue /354
average /376
avert /397
aviation /181
avoid /203
awake /158
aware /474
awareness /2
awesome /72
awful /397
awkward /300
axis /49
Babylonian /485
backhand /408
backlighting /300
backup /429
bacon /72
bacteria /104
bagel /343
bake /322
balance /2
balcony /73
bald /115
band /408
bandanna /311
banner /224
barb /354
barbecue /246
barber /343
bare /462
barely /452
bargain /25
barge /441
bark /137
barn /474
barrel /354
barren /332
barrier /115
barter /170
base /332
basement /485
basic /214

basin /246
battery /462
beach /462
bead /354
beak /441
beam /214
beat /311
beaver /419
bedrock /181
behave /462
behavior /203
behaviorism /13
belie /387
bellows /214
belt /376
beneficial /203
benefit /94
benign /300
besides /408
besiege /170
bet /203
beverage /137
bias /277
bicameral /376
bill /409
bind /83
biochemical /37
biography /365
biologist /13
bison /311
blade /246
blame /429
bland /312
blanket /462
blast /246
bleach /288
blend /397
blink /429
blip /322
blizzard /419
block /84
bloom /214
blossom /474
blues /419
bluff /277
blur /429
blush /73
board /288
boast /376
bog /300
bold /137
bolster /115
bonanza /485
bond /203
bony /25

bookstore /277
boom /452
boon /256
boost /170
botany /224
boulder /429
bounce /61
bound /267
boundary /148
bouquet /170
braid /377
brand /268
brass /148
break /73
breakthrough /397
breathing /104
breed /409
breeze /441
brief /25
brighten /365
brilliance /288
brilliant /485
brittle /322
broadcast /171
brochure /2
bronze /441
bruise /377
brush /419
bubble /104
buck /365
buckle /73
bud /84
buddy /25
budget /13
buffalo /268
bulb /104
bulk /485
bulletin /256
bump /268
bunch /462
bundle /441
bureau /452
burgeon /365
burrow /409
bush /462
butter /268
by-product /419
cabin /61
cabinet /419
cable /49
cactus /387
cafeteria /203
calcium /224
calculate /332
calculus /452

calendar /13
calm /171
camouflage /312
campaign /365
campus /256
canal /84
cancel /429
candidate /148
cannibalism /268
canoe /441
canopy /397
canvas /377
canyon /312
capability /387
capacity /312
cape /214
captive /277
captivity /94
carbon /365
cardiac /73
cardinal /181
care /137
career /365
careless /2
cargo /115
caribou /322
carnivore /181
carp /61
cart /332
cartilage /441
carve /115
cascade /234
cascara /397
cashier /429
cassette /463
cast /441
casual /377
catalog /377
catalyst /38
catastrophe /25
category /409
caterpillar /214
cautious /322
cavity /332
cease /277
celebrate /332
celebrated /300
celestial /61
cell /247
cellist /126
census /181
centennial /73
centigrade /430
centre /300
centric /366

ceramic /115
cereal /126
ceremonial /277
ceremony /61
certificate /181
chafe /397
chagrin /73
chain /377
challenge /300
chamber /441
champion /84
championship /94
chance /333
channel /322
chant /485
chaos /366
chapel /419
character /234
characteristic /214
characterize /268
charcoal /486
chart /234
charter /277
chaste /225
check/cheque /126
checked /288
chew /301
chief /171
chill /84
chilled /94
chimpanzee /3
chip /430
chlorine /312
choir /387
cholesterol /322
choreograph /288
choreographer /312
chorus /441
chromosome /397
chronical /192
chubby /49
chunk /312
cider /247
cipher /430
circuit /301
circular /333
circulation /234
circumference /343
circumstance /301
citadel /387
cite /463
civil /343
civilian /268
claim /277
clam /192

clamor /288
clarify /463
classic /26
classical /225
classify /398
clay /268
clear /430
client /225
cliff /377
climate /366
cling /474
clinic /333
clinical /343
clipper /441
clog /73
closet /225
club /277
clue /95
clump /430
clumsy /355
cluster /104
clutch /312
coalition /344
coarse /26
coax /474
code /158
codify /312
coexist /322
cognition /452
coherent /355
cohesion /38
coil /13
coincide /148
collaborator /73
collapse /288
colleague /13
collect /301
collective /3
collectively /214
collide /73
collision /171
colonial /61
colonize /214
colony /148
column /95
combat /398
combination /388
combine /452
combustible /38
comedy /419
comet /74
comic /148
command /214
commemorate /95
comment /137

commentary /474
commerce /313
commercial /159
commission /388
commit /126
commitment /116
committee /49
commodity /225
common /138
communal /247
communicate /26
community /388
commute /49
compact /441
companion /268
company /225
comparable /62
comparative /268
compare /26
comparison /398
compass /355
compatible /398
compel /26
compensate /409
compete /204
competence /268
competing /344
compile /366
complacence /127
complain /38
complement /234
complementary /62
completion /419
complex /182
complicated /192
compliment /159
comply /138
component /95
compose /355
composer /14
composition /14
compound /192
comprehend /26
comprehensive /148
compress /127
comprise /138
compromise /204
compute /127
concave /148
conceal /138
concede /430
conceive /257
concentrate /26
concentration /278
concentric /452

concept /355
concern /409
concert /159
concise /225
conclude /116
conclusive /409
concomitant /268
concrete /463
condensation /289
condense /269
condiment /333
conduct /138
conductivity /3
conductor /235
confederacy /225
confer /116
conference /257
confession /463
confidence /398
configuration /355
confine /344
confirm /486
conflict /171
conform /247
confront /442
confused /344
confusion /204
congenial /247
congestion /3
congratulation /442
congress /235
congressional /62
conscious /377
consciously /463
consent /27
consequence /366
consequently /204
conservation /247
conservationist /430
conservative /430
conserve /378
consider /344
considerable /192
considerate /442
consideration /27
considering /442
consist /463
consistency /313
consistent /193
consistently /257
consonant /398
consort /355
constant /313
constantly /356
constituent /193

constitute /398
constitution /301
constrain /322
constricted /204
construct /84
construction /127
consult /49
consume /104
consumption /84
contact /356
contagious /226
contain /289
contaminate /388
contamination /345
contemporary /345
content /74
contest /345
context /431
continent /171
continuation /486
continuity /313
continuum /215
contour /139
contract /182
contradict /356
contrary /388
contrast /27
contribute /289
controversy /366
convection /388
convenience /215
convention /226
conventional /301
converge /74
conversation /475
conversational /366
converse /49
conversion /388
convex /182
convey /159
convict /171
convince /3
cookout /172
cooperation /148
cooperative /410
coordinate /27
copier /453
copious /27
copper /313
coral /419
core /215
cornerstone /62
corona /367
corporate /486
corps /127

correspond /356
correspondence /388
corrosion /289
corrosive /49
cosmic /463
cosmos /95
cost /74
costume /74
council /3
counseling /333
counselor /322
count /27
counter /289
counteract /389
counterpart /38
couple /235
coupon /235
courageous /49
courier /399
course /182
court /322
cousin /49
cowhand /453
crab /139
crack /431
craft /378
craftsman /333
cram /301
cramped /475
crater /313
crawl /116
crazy /367
creative /290
creativity /84
credential /50
credit /323
creep /399
crest /378
crevice /3
crew /62
crippling /475
crisscross /463
criterion /257
critic /95
critical /172
criticize /182
critique /235
crooked /269
crossing /3
crow /62
crown /235
crucial /313
crude /333
crumple /139
crusade /28

crush /453
crust /290
crustacean /378
crystal /323
cube /410
cubism /313
cue /235
cultivate /367
cultivated /204
culture /431
cumbersome /269
cuneiform /84
curiosity /356
curious /148
curl /74
current /84
curriculum /3
curve /193
cushion /28
custom /28
cylinder /172
dairy /14
daisy /204
dam /378
damp /464
data /38
date /301
dated /453
dawn /410
daylight /215
dazzling /193
deadline /14
deadly /159
deal /14
dealer /182
debatable /453
debate /3
debris /105
debt /410
debut /269
decade /38
decadent /193
decay /172
deceive /14
decent /475
deception /116
deceptive /345
deciduous /278
decimal /453
decipher /442
declaration /356
declare /419
decline /159
decode /149
decompose /257

decorate /333
decrease /357
dedicate /475
dedication /334
deduct /278
defecate /182
defect /236
defense /475
deficiency /3
deficient /399
define /50
definite /278
definitive /464
deform /431
degree /431
dehydrate /95
dehydrated /236
delay /215
delectable /357
delegate /247
deliberate /290
delicate /290
delicious /399
delight /334
delirium /389
deliver /464
delta /453
demanding /149
demobilize /419
democracy /378
democrat /84
democratic /313
demolish /453
demonstrate /323
denote /50
dense /278
dent /378
dentist /301
deny /486
depart /389
department /62
depend /215
dependable /357
depict /127
deplete /226
deposit /313
depot /139
depredation /257
depression /453
deprive /314
derive /172
descend /357
descent /269
describe /410
descriptive /464

deserted /139
deserve /62
designate /149
desire /63
desolate /75
desperate /410
despoil /95
dessert /172
destination /410
destined /105
destruction /334
destructive /116
detail /226
detect /85
detectable /28
detective /442
deter /257
detergent /50
deteriorate /278
determine /85
detest /75
devastate /269
development /269
device /50
devise /159
devoid /419
devote /204
devotion /4
devour /399
diagnose /139
diagonal /399
diagram /399
dialect /257
diameter /367
dictate /116
diction /95
diet /454
difference /236
differentiate /160
diffuse /301
diffusion /486
digest /258
digestive /454
dignity /269
digression /63
dilate /139
dilemma /420
dilute /160
dim /96
dimension /247
dimensional /39
diminish /389
dinosaur /334
dioxide /205
diplomat /248

diplomatic /39
director /63
directory /258
disadvantage /63
disappoint /302
disaster /236
discard /258
discern /205
discharge /4
disciple /314
discipline /279
discount /314
discrete /193
discrimination /205
disease /302
disguise /345
disgust /454
disintegrate /378
dismal /160
dismay /183
disorder /290
dispersal /172
displace /193
displacement /454
display /160
disposal /39
dispose /389
dispute /4
disrepute /357
disrupt /410
disseminate /85
dissenter /258
dissolve /475
distant /15
distasteful /486
distinct /334
distinction /226
distinctive /236
distinguish /63
distort /290
distract /216
distress /399
distribute /105
distribution /432
district /486
disturb /432
disturbance /334
dive /464
diverse /4
diversification /139
diversion /357
diversity /149
divert /248
division /117
doctrine /4

documentary /205
documentation /39
dogged /149
dolphin /105
domain /279
domestic /205
domesticate /172
dominant /50
dominate /334
donate /160
donation /149
dormancy /270
dormant /258
dormitory /149
dorsal /475
dot /139
doubt /335
downside /443
downtown /378
downward /323
dozen /314
draft /205
drag /172
dragonfly /291
drain /150
drainage /345
dramatic /15
drastic /183
draw /28
drawback /236
dress /270
drift /194
drill /105
drive /226
drop /236
drought /432
drowsy /150
dubious /160
ductile /39
due /172
dull /345
dump /258
durable /160
dwarf /420
dye /160
eager /443
earnest /389
ease /291
Easter /85
eccentric /63
eclecticism /216
eclipse /399
ecological /291
ecology /258
economic /432

economical /279
economy /75
ecosystem /432
edge /150
edible /389
edifice /28
editorial /117
educated /454
effective /140
effectiveness /379
efficiency /150
efficient /357
effluent /358
eject /400
elaborate /96
elasticity /216
elective /206
electricity /248
electrode /117
electron /443
elegant /85
element /206
elementary /105
elevate /420
elevation /150
elicit /172
eligible /63
eliminate /258
elliptical /389
elm /160
elongate /151
eloquent /379
elusive /476
embarrass /476
embellish /216
emblem /227
embody /302
embryo /443
emerald /75
emerge /420
emergence /358
eminent /127
emission /454
emit /117
emotion /75
emotional /161
emphasize /28
employ /151
enactment /117
encase /420
enclose /323
encompass /420
encounter /379
encourage /476
endangered /216

endeavor /486
endless /4
endow /410
endure /270
energetic /227
enforce /4
engage /39
engaging /85
engine /29
engineering /432
engraving /105
engulf /96
enhance /464
enlightenment /206
enormous /85
enrich /40
enroll /389
enrollment /85
entail /433
enterprise /291
enterprising /486
entertain /400
enthusiasm /464
entitle /105
entrance /161
entrenched /358
entrepreneur /270
entrepreneurial /323
entry /258
envelop /29
envelope /476
environmental /161
envision /345
enzyme /454
ephemeral /487
epic /279
epidemic /40
episode /29
epitomize /476
epoch /421
equal /216
equality /379
equation /29
equator /324
equitable /206
equivalent /367
era /216
erect /117
erode /454
erosion /15
errand /248
erratic /279
erupt /151
eruption /487
escape /173

essay /487
essence /421
essential /433
essentially /5
establish /379
estate /206
estimate /51
eternal /96
ethical /411
ethics /206
ethnic /248
ethnology /75
evacuation /216
evaluate /433
evaporate /433
evaporation /40
even /302
evergreen /400
evidence /324
evident /279
eviscerate /173
evoke /279
evolution /464
evolve /237
exact /421
exaggerate /443
exalted /248
excavate /270
excavation /51
exceed /75
exception /248
exceptional /335
excess /270
excessive /476
exchange /314
exciting /358
exclude /443
excursion /117
execute /487
executive /194
exemplary /270
exempt /421
exercise /476
exert /433
exhale /379
exhaust /117
exhibit /259
exhilarating /477
existence /227
exorbitant /291
exotic /454
expand /314
expansion /105
expect /75
expedition /464

expel /237
experimental /279
expertise /40
expire /5
explicit /324
explode /434
exploit /216
exploration /40
explore /40
explosion /280
explosive /15
exponent /291
expose /487
exposition /390
exposure /105
expressive /76
expressly /140
extend /85
extension /40
extent /271
exterior /161
external /29
extinct /151
extinction /455
extol /194
extra /358
extract /237
extraordinary /280
extravagant /434
extreme /86
extremity /161
extrinsic /194
fabric /455
fabricate /302
facade /217
facet /434
facial /465
facilitate /51
facility /140
factor /346
factual /346
faculty /259
fade /29
Fahrenheit /249
faint /161
fair /96
fairly /96
falcon /434
familiar /487
familiarize /346
fancy /237
fantastic /217
fantasy /128
farce /106
fare /5

far-fetched /487
fascinate /335
fascinating /128
fashion /455
fashionable /128
fasten /86
fatal /237
fatigue /346
faucet /249
fault /465
fauna /379
favor /118
favorable /271
favored /118
feasible /455
feat /358
federal /206
feeble /315
fellow /51
fellowship /29
female /271
feminist /76
ferment /118
fertile /118
fertilize /379
fertilizer /118
fervor /455
feudal /96
fiber /259
fiction /434
fidelity /259
field /140
fierce /29
figurative /40
figure /455
file /64
film /86
filter /358
fin /173
finalize /238
finance /206
financial /76
finch /140
firm /488
fitness /86
fix /227
flag /228
flagellum /64
flair /249
flake /183
flamboyant /86
flame /390
flap /488
flash /194
flask /238

flat /5
flavor /291
flavoring /346
flexibility /228
flexible /106
flint /30
float /183
flock /465
flora /390
flourish /183
flu /128
fluctuate /238
flux /488
focus /259
fold /64
foliage /291
folklore /86
foment /302
foolish /64
forage /40
forecast /118
forefront /30
foremost /51
forerunner /76
foreshorten /280
forestall /15
formal /249
format /173
formation /161
former /292
formidable /380
formulate /194
fort /488
fortuitous /477
fortune /477
forward /5
fossil /206
foster /249
foul /5
fountain /421
fraction /151
fracture /217
fragile /367
fragment /194
fragrant /359
frame /465
framework /335
franchise /259
frank /194
fray /434
freeze /30
freight /335
frenzy /51
fresco /206
friction /51

frigid /140
frivolity /207
frost /390
frugal /238
fruitless /207
frustrate /280
fuel /207
fulfill /106
fume /15
fumigate /411
function /96
functional /456
fund /477
fundamental /315
funding /228
fungi /64
fungus /456
furious /400
furnace /140
furnish /271
furry /259
fuse /434
galaxy /151
gallery /259
gallop /315
gap /259
garb /228
garbage /315
gaseous /380
gasoline /141
gear /194
gem /465
gemstone /456
gender /106
gene /228
generalization /86
generalize /141
generate /421
generation /324
generous /368
genesis /118
genetic /86
genetically /249
genetics /238
genial /400
genius /106
genre /162
gentility /411
gentle /401
genuine /456
geology /183
geometry /302
germ /280
germinate /238
giant /368

gibe /195
gigantic /359
gilding /303
gin /260
giraffe /488
girder /465
given /141
glacial /64
glacier /368
glamorous /421
gland /335
glare /421
glaze /183
glean /195
glimpse /324
glorify /238
glossy /128
glow /5
glue /465
gnaw /368
gonna /303
gorgeous /315
gorilla /173
gospel /106
Gothic /228
gourd /280
gourmet /195
govern /401
governor /260
grab /64
grace /151
gradient /207
grading /183
gradual /96
grain /359
granite /128
grant /380
granular /456
graph /443
graphic /195
graphics /292
graphite /128
grasp /64
grasshopper /411
gravel /162
gravitational /324
gravity /477
grazing /488
greeting /390
gregarious /249
grimly /456
grind /30
grip /271
groan /280
grocery /324

groom /30
gross /421
grudge /359
guarantee /128
guideline /217
guilty /335
gulf /368
gull /359
gym /5
gymnasium/gym /401
habit /195
habitat /228
hail /324
haircut /271
halt /228
hammer /456
hamper /106
handful /380
handle /292
handy /249
harbor /250
hardly /390
hardware /51
hardy /162
harmonic /488
harmony /325
harness /359
harsh /184
haste /217
hatch /87
haul /260
haunt /41
haven /325
hawk /239
hay /141
hazard /129
hazel /207
heading /30
healing /119
healthful /173
heed /97
hemisphere /141
hemp /162
henceforth /359
herald /129
herb /207
herd /195
heritage /456
heyday /443
hibernation /97
hide /173
hierarchy /359
hieratic /141
hieroglyph /465
highlight /260

hike /76
hind /184
hinder /421
hint /360
hinterland /173
hitherto /152
hive /195
hockey /129
hoe /280
hollow /97
homestead /346
homing /292
hominid /184
homogeneous /41
honest /6
hook /325
horde /30
horizon /97
horizontal /477
hormone /250
horn /217
hospitable /346
host /368
hostile /360
household /380
hover /325
huddle /207
hue /207
hum /401
humanitarian /411
humanity /239
humid /129
humidity /368
hummingbird /281
humorous /228
hurl /217
hurricane /41
hurry /76
husk /411
hydrogen /195
hydrothermal /303
hygiene /107
hypothesis /184
hypothesize /173
iceberg /239
ideal /443
idealize /336
identical /196
identification /325
identify /129
identity /76
ideology /107
ideomotor /488
idiom /250
idle /152

idyllic /488
igneous /15
ignition /260
ignorant /173
ignore /196
illegible /184
illuminate /97
illusion /477
illustrate /488
illustration /129
image /434
imaginary /444
imagist /380
imbibe /292
imitate /271
imitation /141
immature /141
immediate /422
immense /325
immigrant /336
immune /465
immunity /303
immutable /15
impact /250
impair /260
impart /325
impending /77
imperative /346
impermeable /456
impersonal /457
impetus /16
implement /97
implication /411
implicit /360
imply /41
impose /162
imprecise /260
impressive /141
imprint /51
improve /6
improvise /64
impulse /380
inaccessible /77
inactivate /119
inactive /30
inanimate /381
inanity /152
incapacitate /315
incense /97
incentive /381
inception /326
incessant /401
incessantly /87
incident /250
incinerate /162

inclination /489
inclined /444
incoming /184
incompatible /162
incongruity /129
inconspicuous /65
inconvenient /107
incorporate /422
incredible /435
incubate /466
incursion /229
independent /346
indicate /16
indicative /77
indifference /292
indigestion /315
indispensable /217
individual /184
induce /52
industry /16
inert /52
inevitably /163
infancy /444
infant /250
infection /52
infectious /292
inferior /217
infest /31
inflammation /218
inflate /457
inflation /207
influential /457
influenza /293
influx /281
inform /229
informative /457
informed /218
infrared /107
infrastructure /360
ingenious /281
ingredient /152
inhabit /411
inherent /163
inherit /185
inheritance /142
inhibit /163
initial /303
initially /368
initiate /346
inject /381
inn /229
innate /303
inner /129
innocent /272
innovation /281

innovative /250
inquire /401
insanity /326
inscribe /381
insect /411
insert /435
insight /196
insist /97
insistence /196
inspect /478
inspection /272
inspire /208
install /218
instance /444
instead /435
instinct /489
institute /65
instruct /185
instruction /87
instructor /208
instrument /390
instrumental /435
insufficient /303
insulate /185
insulation /422
insulin /152
insult /119
insurance /466
intact /281
integral /174
integrate /336
integrity /260
intellect /368
intellectual /185
intelligence /16
intelligent /346
intense /52
intent /281
intentionally /163
interact /411
interaction /326
interactive /142
interest /6
interfere /152
interior /31
internal /368
internship /229
interplay /444
interpret /16
interrupt /435
intersection /250
interstellar /336
interval /412
intimate /196
intoxication /41

intrepid /130
intricate /130
intriguing /16
intrinsic /208
introduction /489
intrude /303
intrusion /422
intuitive /52
invade /293
invasion /107
inventory /77
invertebrate /119
investigate /6
invitation /
inviting /152
involve /152
ironic /489
ironical /466
ironically /347
irony /422
irregular /368
irresistible /466
irreverent /218
irrigate /250
irritable /412
isolate /435
isolated /52
issue /422
item /153
ivory /401
jar /347
jaw /360
jeans /218
jelly /53
jeopardize /281
jewelry /218
jog /31
jogging /208
joint /457
jolt /53
jot /239
journal /65
journalism /229
journalist /457
juice /87
jumble /369
jumble /369
junction /107
Jupiter /303
justice /163
justify /17
juvenile /6
keen /77
kennel /163
kernel /208
kerosene /422

keyboard /153
kid /239
kiln /381
kinetic /369
kingdom /239
label /41
laboratory /53
labyrinth /347
lace /142
lack /87
lament /53
landing /412
landmark /65
landmass /77
landscape /436
larva /87
larynx /436
laser /381
lash /174
lasting /239
latent /77
Latin /31
latitude /142
latter /119
launch /98
laundry /336
laureate /107
lava /422
lawn /261
lay /142
layer /78
layout /174
lead /229
leading /282
league /304
leak /457
leap /466
lease /87
least /261
leather /208
ledge /196
leftover /53
legend /185
legendary /444
legible /185
legislation /360
legislative /17
legislature /142
legitimate /17
leisure /196
lengthen /326
lens /457
lethal /316
lethargy /272
lettuce /153

level /360
libel /369
liberate /208
liberty /336
librarian /163
license /239
lichen /391
lightning /369
likewise /391
limb /412
lime /186
limestone /444
limitation /422
line /347
linear /369
linen /423
linger /229
linguist /98
linguistic /326
lipid /272
liquid /240
list /316
listless /119
literacy /17
literally /282
literary /107
literature /316
lithosphere /53
litter /240
livelihood /186
livestock /229
lizard /186
load /6
loan /381
loathsome /401
lobby /436
locality /130
locally /174
locate /42
locomotion /17
locomotive /360
lodge /163
log /7
logical /42
longevity /98
longitude /17
loose /65
lore /196
lounge /401
lower /18
loyal /466
lubricant /360
lumber /326
luminosity /282
luminous /326

lunar /304
lure /174
lush /66
luster /130
luxury /489
lyric /489
machinery /240
maglev /218
magma /196
magnesium /130
magnet /174
magnetic /153
magnificent /87
magnify /326
magnitude /240
mail /272
maintain /282
maintenance /42
maize /218
major /478
male /186
malnutrition /197
mammal /31
mammoth /108
manage /7
management /98
maneuver /369
mania /108
manifest /42
manifestation /250
manipulate /197
manner /78
mannerism /423
mansion /208
mantle /490
manual /108
manufacture /53
marble /402
march /142
margin /348
marine /391
maritime /7
marked /18
market /218
marsh /348
marvel /142
mask /412
mason /153
mass /412
massive /197
mast /163
mat /7
match /304
mate /251
material /42

mathematics /42
mature /119
maturity /186
maximum /42
meager /304
meaningful /229
meantime /153
measure /391
mechanic /369
mechanical /436
mechanics /436
mechanism /304
mechanist /119
mechanize /391
medal /98
media /251
mediate /361
medication /348
medieval /98
medium /272
melanin /31
melodic /402
melodie /88
melodrama /282
melody /108
melt /218
melting /444
membrane /316
memo /42
mental /66
mention /478
menu /478
mercantile /436
merchandise /119
merchant /153
mercury /436
mercy /164
mere /423
meridian /327
mesmerize /304
mess /197
metabolic /445
metallic /153
meteor /293
meteorite /316
meteorological /336
meteorologist /88
meteorology /99
methane /230
methanol /240
method /78
meticulous /490
metric /142
metropolis /304
metropolitan /143

microbe /466
microorganism /240
microprocessor /412
microscope /99
microscopic /293
microwave /466
midterm /337
mighty /293
migrate /423
migration /490
mild /348
milieu /445
militant /186
military /153
millennium /282
mime /219
mimic /219
mind /327
mine /230
mineral /327
minimal /382
minimize /78
minimum /293
minor /272
minority /119
mint /457
minute /174
miracle /348
miserable /261
mission /327
mobile /304
mock /99
mode /153
modeling /143
modem /175
moderate /490
modest /164
modify /130
modulate /18
moist /66
moisture /490
mold /43
molecule /457
molten /219
monarch /18
monastery /153
monitor /143
monotonous /130
monster /478
monument /466
monumental /78
moral /108
morale /412
mosaic /186
mosquito /361

moth /230
motif /348
motion /445
motivate /130
motivation /186
motive /478
motor /282
mottled /208
motto /18
mount /402
mountainous /197
muggy /108
multiple /327
multiply /143
multitude /348
mundane /348
municipal /491
mural /478
muscle /466
muscular /369
mushroom /272
musical /412
musician /88
musicologist /402
mutual /18
myriad /349
myth /261
mythical /143
mythology /131
nail /209
naive /108
naked /370
nap /337
narrate /109
narrative /154
nationalism /66
naturalist /293
nauseous /491
naval /164
navigate /402
navigation /131
navy /273
nectar /349
needy /164
negate /293
negative /240
neglect /316
negotiation /467
neoclassical /43
neolithic /282
neon /197
nerve-cell /467
nest /304
neuron /175
neutral /423

neutron /78
nevertheless /293
newsletter /241
niche /478
nickel /370
nicotine /402
nightmare /241
nitrogen /282
nocturnal /316
nomadic /31
nominate /316
nominee /66
nonetheless /337
nonsense /66
nonverbal /305
normally /88
nostalgia /479
notate /219
notation /66
notch /317
noted /209
noticeable /175
notify /282
notion /109
notorious /32
notwithstanding /175
nourish /154
nourishment /99
novel /273
novelty /294
novice /391
noxious /164
nucleus /261
numerous /99
nurture /273
nutrient /457
nutrition /88
oak /370
oasis /349
obedience /391
objective /317
oblivious /445
obscure /99
observe /241
obsess /305
obsolete /392
obstacle /467
obstruct /7
obtain /251
occasional /294
occupy /392
occur /251
oceanographer /209
octopus /327
odd /491

odor /261
offensive /273
offer /109
official /445
offspring /143
olfactory /349
omit /88
ongoing /230
onslaught /230
ooze /131
opal /436
opaque /382
operate /273
opponent /164
opportunity /479
oppose /491
opposed /53
opposite /175
optical /261
optimal /349
optimistic /154
optional /164
oral /445
oratorio /467
orbit /120
orbital /491
orchestra /491
orchid /78
ore /165
organic /131
organism /479
orientation /88
origin /294
original /43
originate /436
ornament /43
ornithology /154
otherwise /66
outbreak /109
outcome /317
outcry /327
outermost /392
outfit /131
outgas /370
outline /43
outlying /230
output /423
outrageously /251
outspoken /131
outstanding /261
oval /219
overall /19
overcharge /7
overcome /261
overdue /131

overhaul /54
overlap /175
overload /109
overlook /19
overnight /154
overseas /423
oversleep /413
overtime /54
overview /305
overwhelm /186
owl /261
oxide /413
oxygen /479
oyster /43
pack /54
packed /120
paddle /43
painstaking /327
palatable /294
palate /67
pale /154
pamphlet /143
pancreas /337
panel /294
panic /423
panorama /370
pants /165
parachute /273
parallel /19
paralyze /209
parameter /32
paramount /19
paraphrase /187
parasite /209
parking /120
parliament /392
partial /109
participant /19
participate /361
particle /349
particular /317
partly /7
partnership /370
part-time /165
passage /445
passion /424
passive /337
paste /273
pastel /131
pasture /445
patch /328
patent /436
path /197
pathology /32
patient /78

patriarch /370
patriot /413
patron /294
patronage /361
patronizing /230
pattern /370
paucity /251
pause /143
pave /120
pay /54
peak /437
pebble /187
peculiar /337
pedagogy /382
pendant /19
penetrate /154
penicillin /294
peninsula /458
penmanship /79
pensive /491
pepper /328
perceive /328
perception /43
perceptive /44
percussion /446
perfect /54
perform /361
perfume /305
periodic /413
peripheral /491
periphery /175
perish /370
perishable /337
permanent /317
permeate /262
permission /79
permit /165
perpendicular /479
perpetuate /273
persist /131
personal /120
personality /251
personnel /262
perspective /230
persuasive /317
pertain /437
pertinent /241
pervasive /424
pest /294
pesticide /349
petition /143
petroleum /143
pharmacy /144
phase /294
phenomena /32

phenomenon /99
pheromone /392
philosopher /479
philosophy /402
photodissociation /54
photograph /467
photography /165
photosynthesis /424
physical /67
physician /446
physiology /262
picky /262
pictorial /231
picturesque /262
pierce /413
pigeon /54
pigment /318
pilot /458
pin /241
pine /413
pinpoint /219
pioneer /241
pipe /413
pique /305
piracy /318
pit /99
pitch /337
pivot /467
pivotal /318
plain /338
planet /19
planetary /413
plank /274
plankton /437
plantation /197
plaque /305
plasma /458
plaster /32
plastic /198
plate /437
plateau /402
platelike /231
platitude /413
plausible /20
playwright /305
pleasing /132
pliable /338
plight /349
plot /20
plow /79
plumage /100
plump /467
plunge /242
pocketbook /198
poetry /54

pointed /262
poisonous /231
polar /437
pole /492
policy /32
polish /382
politics /479
pollen /7
pollinate /274
pollinator /382
pollutant /437
polygon /467
ponderous /467
popular /166
populate /109
porcelain /100
pore /88
porous /392
portable /132
portion /100
portrait /89
portraiture /446
portray /198
pose /318
posit /166
position /338
positive /262
possess /392
postage /295
postcard /67
poster /446
posthumous /187
postpone /100
potassium /349
potential /349
potter /262
pottery /318
pound /492
poverty /282
powder /392
practical /350
practically /492
prairie /175
precede /338
precious /446
precipitate /20
precise /166
precursor /370
predator /175
predecessor /468
predict /175
predictable /176
predominant /7
predominantly /318
predominate /263

prefer /89
preferable /295
preference /219
prehistoric /176
preliminary /120
premature /231
preoccupation /187
prepare /187
preponderance /79
prerequisite /89
prescribe /209
prescription /446
presentation /198
preserve /144
presidency /100
president /67
press /424
pressure /424
prestige /492
prestigious /479
pretension /446
pretentious /44
pretty /282
prevail /132
prevailing /110
prevalent /8
previous /176
prey /402
primal /79
primary /480
primate /370
prime /242
primitive /176
primordial /403
principal /263
principle /55
prior /392
priority /144
privilege /187
prize /361
probe /198
procedure /437
proceed /44
process /403
proclaim /132
prodigious /176
productive /403
productivity /100
profession /437
professional /176
proficient /305
profound /55
progressive /382
prohibitively /110
project /79

projector /219
proliferate /231
proliferation /424
prolific /89
prolonged /306
prominent /154
promising /283
promote /55
prompt /55
promptly /283
pronounced /328
proof /198
proofread /110
propagate /446
propel /79
propensity /414
proper /251
property /306
proponent /100
proportion /468
proposal /155
propose /55
proprietor /263
prose /446
prospect /424
prosper /338
prosperity /414
prosperous /403
protagonist /8
protein /100
protest /110
prototype /414
provincialism /328
provision /166
prudent /306
psychoanalysis /458
psychology /120
publication /414
publicize /187
puddle /393
pueblo /370
pulp /306
pulse /447
pump /328
punctual /89
puncture /44
pupil /437
puppet /468
purchase /306
pure /393
purity /198
purple /458
pursue /403
pursuit /220
puzzle /144

pyramid /480
quaint /480
qualify /155
quality /295
quantify /166
quarry /252
quartz /371
quasar /458
quench /32
questionnaire /424
quiescent /263
quilt /67
quit /242
quiz /414
quota /110
quotation /80
quote /403
racing /458
racket /274
radar /361
radiate /20
radiation /8
radical /458
radically /295
radioactive /220
radius /338
raft /447
rage /252
rainbow /220
rainfall /458
raise /263
rally /263
rampant /110
ranch /80
rancher /67
random /242
range /318
rank /382
rare /67
rarely /393
rash /80
rate /480
ratify /371
ratio /110
ration /176
rational /468
rattle /220
raven /176
ravine /447
raw /67
ray /425
rayon /447
reach /274
reactor /55
readily /468

realistic /188
realization /56
realm /155
reapply /338
rear /295
reason /458
reasonable /198
rebel /44
rebellion /220
recall /44
receiver /166
receptacle /121
reception /283
receptor /371
recession /56
recharge /166
recipe /188
reciprocity /361
recital /110
reckless /110
recline /403
recognition /144
recognize /100
recoil /393
recollection /480
recommend /393
reconstruction /220
record /371
recover /393
recreation /404
recruit /199
recruitment /328
rectangle /338
recurring /144
recycle /371
reddish /67
reef /437
refer /361
reference /242
refine /231
refined /350
reflect /350
reflection /425
reform /220
refraction /144
refreshing /68
refrigerate /414
refund /283
refurbish /132
regardless /89
regenerate /210
region /188
register /306
regular /468
regulate /393

rehabilitate /8
rehearse /121
reinforce /383
reject /414
rejuvenate /468
rekindle /188
relate /220
relative /90
relatively /393
relay /264
release /210
relevance /44
relevant /188
reliable /56
reliance /318
relic /492
relief /414
relieve /393
reliever /121
religion /132
reluctant /371
rely /283
remainder /328
remaining /339
remains /44
remark /176
remarkable /56
remind /133
remnant /20
remodel /80
remote /231
removal /20
renaissance /20
render /80
rendition /166
renew /32
renovate /8
rental /188
repel /339
repertoire /264
repertory /284
repetition /404
replace /284
replenish /56
replicate /318
report /133
represent /188
representative /90
reproduce /166
reptile /404
republic /306
reputation /252
repute /242
request /210
require /177

reschedule /90
rescue /68
resemble /252
reservation /199
reserve /274
reservoir /394
reside /306
resident /469
residential /447
residue /274
resign /68
resilience /210
resin /231
resist /121
resistance /177
resistant /44
resolve /425
resonance /133
resort /492
resource /469
respect /306
respective /437
respond /371
response /56
responsible /177
restoration /110
restore /284
restraint /274
restrict /383
restricted /415
resume /133
retail /284
retain /328
retire /20
retreat /144
reunion /133
reveal /145
revenue /415
revere /231
reverse /329
revert /415
review /295
revise /371
revision /188
revitalize /350
revival /383
revoke /415
revolt /121
revolution /56
reward /469
rhinoceros /480
rhyme /210
rhythm /121
ribbon /121
ridge /242

ridiculous /339
rigid /372
rigor /361
rinse /404
ripe /284
ripen /33
rite /189
ritual /383
rival /425
rivalry /480
roam /252
robust /458
rod /21
rodent /111
rodeo /242
roe /350
roll /231
romantic /447
roost /33
rotate /339
rotation /425
rough /492
roughly /447
routine /383
rub /166
rudimentary /415
rug /155
rugged /189
ruin /295
rumor /319
rupture /68
rural /45
rush /438
rust /90
rustic /45
rustproof /372
sac /155
sacred /167
sacrificial /80
saddle /383
sake /350
salamander /100
salient /425
salmon /33
salon /21
sample /350
sanctuary /145
sanitation /189
sap /459
sapphire /8
satellite /242
satire /242
satiric /155
saturate /90
saturation /319

Saturn /177
sauce /492
save /177
saving /284
scale /210
scan /221
scar /21
scarce /199
scarcely /252
scarf /243
scatter /8
scavenger /425
scene /167
scenery /221
scent /274
schedule /68
scheme /339
scholar /68
scholarship /111
scientific /296
scope /415
scorch /404
score /80
scout /492
scrape /469
scratch /438
screen /90
script /33
scrub /319
scruffy /252
scuba /111
sculpt /45
sculpture /362
scurry /56
seal /69
seashore /319
season /447
seasonal /177
seasoning /383
seclusion /492
second /394
secrete /167
section /296
secure /404
sedentary /167
sediment /372
sedimentary /111
seem /167
seep /101
segment /329
segregate /122
seismic /404
seismograph /285
seismology /447
selection /91

selective /45
semester /134
seminar /394
senate /101
senator /481
senior /189
sense /372
sensible /56
sensitive /481
sensory /339
sensual /8
sentimental /394
separate /155
sequence /285
sequoia /351
series /469
session /101
setting /372
settle /415
settlement /167
severe /253
sew /362
sewage /134
sewerage /111
shade /210
shallow /351
shame /404
shape /253
sharpen /362
sharply /372
shatter /167
sheath /69
shed /156
sheer /33
shell /200
shellfish /9
shelter /69
shield /481
shift /383
shipwright /21
shore /405
shortage /101
shortly /416
shovel /253
shower /111
shrimp /264
shrink /45
shrivel /438
shroud /253
shrub /447
shuffle /469
shuttle /9
sidewalk /447
sieve /285
signal /253

significance /167
significant /122
significantly /339
signify /339
silica /253
silicate /221
silicon /80
silt /111
silversmith /296
similar /319
simmer /469
simplicity /243
simplify /200
simply /80
simulate /57
simultaneous /307
sinuous /438
situated /221
skeletal /189
skeleton /319
skeptical /122
sketch /145
skip /101
skull /221
skyscraper /91
sled /91
sledding /45
slender /253
slice /101
slide /492
slight /481
slightly /405
slip /101
slog /221
slope /416
sloth /21
sluggish /57
slumber /91
smelting /200
smoothly /91
smother /156
snack /481
snap /274
sneaker /319
snowflake /307
soak /447
so-called /156
soccer /264
sociable /372
sociology /448
soda /285
sodium /9
soft /57
solar /264
solder /307

sole /232
solicit /459
solid /264
solitary /21
solo /9
soloist /384
soluble /274
solution /122
somewhat /243
soothe /243
sophisticated /243
soprano /122
sore /156
sort /210
sound /200
sour /167
source /394
souvenir /373
sow /211
soybean /425
space /384
spacecraft /69
spaghetti /425
span /221
spare /319
spark /134
sparse /232
spawn /362
special /232
specialize /21
specialized /469
species /459
specific /319
specify /253
specimen /21
spectacle /232
spectacular /448
spectator /21
spectrum /285
speculate /362
spew /285
sphere /80
spherical /69
spice /9
spill /21
spin /243
spinet /243
spinning /481
spiny /373
spiral /33
splash /211
split /384
spoil /200
sponge /285
sponsor /211

spontaneity /253
spontaneous /45
spot /243
sprawl /329
spray /481
spread /459
spring /329
sprout /177
spun /122
spur /469
squabble /362
square /481
squash /57
squeeze /416
squid /134
squirrel /481
squirt /384
stable /69
stack /438
stadium /329
staff /33
stage /307
stagecoach /285
staggered /285
staggering /416
stain /254
stake /221
stalk /177
standard /232
stanza /145
staple /168
starch /264
stardom /373
stark /189
startling /168
stash /200
state /21
statesman /296
static /384
station /243
stationary /448
statistic /340
statistical /394
statistics /351
statue /351
stature /394
status /101
steady /33
steep /384
steer /351
stellar /168
stem /22
stereo /91
sterile /122
stew /438

stick /274
sticky /45
stiff /178
stimulate /416
stimulation /307
stimulus /285
sting /394
stir /340
stock /351
storage /329
stout /254
strain /101
strand /91
strap /232
strata /34
strategic /448
strategy /384
stratigraphy /134
stratum /319
stream /285
stress /362
stretch /9
strict /340
stride /101
strike /189
string /22
strip /134
stripe /111
strive /9
stuck /57
studio /493
stuff /319
stun /134
stunt /134
sturdy /22
stylish /275
stylistic /9
stylized /254
subdue /405
subject /296
subliminal /307
submarine /329
submerge /351
submission /200
submit /405
subsequent /57
subsidize /307
subsidy /351
subsist /340
subsistence /351
subspecies /373
substance /470
substantial /22
substantiate /57
substantive /145

substitute /211
subtle /122
subtract /438
suburb /57
subversive /362
subway /101
successive /168
sufficient /285
suffragist /134
suitcase /394
suiten. /243
sulfur /448
sum /426
summarize /91
summary /373
summit /352
sumptuous /481
sunlit /254
sunset /189
superficial /45
superintendent /275
superior /34
supervise /448
supplant /320
supplement /493
supply /439
suppose /111
suppress /200
supreme /57
surge /102
surgeon /254
surgery /307
surpass /200
surplus /9
surrender /34
surround /448
survey /122
survive /439
susceptible /254
suspect /91
suspend /156
suspension /34
sustain /156
sustained /211
sustenance /296
swallow /122
swamp /308
swan /91
swarm /156
swear /405
sweat /156
sweep /9
sweeping /264
swell /189
swift /264

swing /308
switch /373
syllable /9
symbol /470
symbolic /405
symbolize /320
symmetry /363
sympathetic /69
sympathy /449
symphony /449
symptom /111
synchronize /232
synonym /405
synthesize /296
synthetic /46
syrup /275
systematic /297
tableland /221
tactic /189
talent /264
tally /69
tangle /340
tannish /352
tantalizing /168
target /145
tariff /232
tarnish /201
taste /211
tavern /405
technical /416
technique /352
technological /134
tectonics /168
tedious /275
tedium /135
teem /373
telegraph /352
telescope /329
temper /352
temperate /449
temple /459
temporary /10
tempt /352
tenant /470
tend /91
tendency /10
tendon /264
tenement /70
tension /111
tentacle /470
tenuous /470
term /10
terminal /459
terminate /426
terminology /352

terminus /102
terrain /459
terrestrial /426
terrific /449
territory /102
testimony /221
textile /416
texture /308
thaw /384
theoretical /406
theory /178
therapy /34
thereby /102
therefore /493
thesis /232
thorn /122
thorny /385
thorough /373
thread /221
threaten /135
thrifty /221
thrive /123
through /157
throw /46
thwart /135
tide /233
tile /34
timber /201
tinker /221
tissue /70
toed /297
token /243
tolerant /297
tolerate /92
topographical /395
topography /275
topsoil /102
tornado /340
torpor /168
torrent /449
tough /493
tournament /233
tow /10
towering /22
toxic /385
trace /57
track /363
tract /426
trade /46
traditional /211
tragedy /189
tragic /329
trait /201
transaction /416
transcend /81

transfer /416
transform /254
transit /102
transition /406
translucent /157
transmit /459
transmitter /493
transparent /417
transplant /178
transportation /406
trash /123
tread /297
treadmill /112
tremendous /481
trench /482
trend /275
trial /10
triangle /81
tribal /297
tributary /112
trigger /168
trilogy /264
trip /482
trivial /244
tropic /493
tropical /482
troupe /123
tube /201
tug /275
tuition /92
tundra /212
tunnel /178
turbulent /222
turkey /363
turn-out /244
turnpike /244
turtle /233
tutor /297
twig /426
twine /123
twinkling /264
twist /470
tycoon /459
typical /81
typify /385
ultimate /297
ultimately /494
ultimatum /482
ultraviolet /470
unadorned /34
unaided /244
unbridgeable /286
unconsolidated /222
undergo /178
undergraduate /46

underground /212
underlying /135
underneath /275
underscore /92
undertake /189
undertaking /112
unearth /10
unequal /265
uneven /201
uniform /426
uniformity /426
unify /363
unique /190
unity /146
universe /212
unparalleled /112
unprecedented /34
unpredictable /102
unravel /146
unsubstantiated /244
untamed /157
untapped /297
upheaval /308
uppermost /329
upset /308
urban /471
urge /330
urgent /265
utensil /254
utilitarian /308
utility /265
utilize /34
utmost /123
utter /482
utterly /406
vacancy /123
vacant /70

vacate /482
vacation /308
vaccine /417
vacuum /427
vague /57
valid /124
validate /309
validity /395
vanish /46
vapor /124
variable /483
variation /471
varied /395
varnish /11
vary /135
vascular /330
vast /57
vault /406
vegetarian /330
vegetation /460
vegetative /135
vehicle /340
veil /146
vein /265
velocity /179
venom /47
vent /494
venture /47
verbal /124
verify /330
versatile /179
verse /70
version /244
versus /22
vertebrate /417
vertical /112
vessel /212

vestige /190
veto /47
viable /92
vibrate /427
vibration /47
vicinity /47
vigilance /112
vigorous /34
violent /373
violently /352
viral /81
virtually /201
virtue /385
virtuous /385
virus /57
visible /222
vision /406
visual /58
visualize /363
vital /450
vivid /340
vocal /113
vocation /427
volatile /395
volcano /92
volume /494
volunteer /286
voracious /212
voyage /124
vulnerable /460
wagon /135
walnut /298
wane /113
wanna /340
ware /395
warehouse /92
warp /244

wary /395
wasp /275
waste /70
watercourse /59
wax /190
wear /255
weathering /286
weave /460
wedge-shaped /341
weed /395
weird /309
welfare /233
whereby /341
wholesome /374
wick /320
willful /439
willow /255
wipe /11
wispy /341
wit /330
withdraw /483
wither /135
withstand /330
wonder /320
worth /22
wrap /23
wreck /439
wrinkle /427
X-ray /157
yarn /341
yeast /406
yield /124
yogurt /201
zealous /70
zinc/494
zone /363

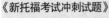

《ETS新托福考试官方指南》

（第4版）（含光盘1张）

ETS（美国教育考试服务中心）编著

◎ ETS中国唯一授权版本

◎ 新托福考试的必备权威辅导书

◎ 数百道托福考试题目及写作题库

定价：118元　开本：16开　页码：664页

《新托福考试官方指南词汇必备》

（附MP3）　余仁唐 编著

◎ 页码为序，合理编排方便查找

◎ 选词科学，根据语境精准释义

◎ 重点词汇，循环出现加深记忆

◎ 一书多用，全面攻克托福词汇

定价：25元　开本：32开　页码：268页

《新托福考试综合教程》

（含互动模考光盘1张 + 9张CD）

Deborah Phillips 著　张洪伟 等译

◎ 8套专项训练题目，全方位强化应试技能

◎ 2套完整的全真模拟试题，帮助考生熟悉真实考试形式

定价：148元　开本：16开　页码：672页

《托福考试备考策略与模拟试题》

（含光盘1张）

Nancy Gallagher 著

◎ 35个包含阅读、听力、口语及写作的语言技能训练单元

◎ 4套完整的全真强化试题

◎ 为考生设置了15周的学习计划，提供大量练习资料

定价：108元　开本：16开　页码：720页

《新托福考试全真模考题与精解》（含MP3和模考盘各1张）

Pamela J. Sharpe 著

◎ 详细说明听说读写四部分的特点及有效的应试策略

◎ 含650分钟录音光盘1张，包含书中所有音频内容

◎ 含模考光盘1张，模拟真实考试情景

定价：118元　开本：16开　页码：832页

《新托福考试冲刺试题》

（含光盘1张）　**Nancy Gallagher** 著

◎ 6套完整全真冲刺试题，600道经典测试题目，体现托福考试的最新特色

◎ 文章题材、出题角度、考题类型以及话题内容等与实际考试一致

◎ 随书配有360分钟录音光盘1张，语境逼真，契合真实考场情景

定价：58元　开本：16开　页码：396页

《TOEFL官方题库范文精讲》

（附MP3）　**Lin Lougheed** 编著

◎ 提供TOEFL写作三步法，详解写作技巧和策略

◎ 精编大量练习题目，针对性极强

◎ 10篇综合写作参考例文 + 185篇独立写作题库范文

定价：58元　开本：16开　页码：432页

《新托福考试口语胜经》

翟少成 编著

◎ 深入剖析各个口语题型，点拨回答技巧

◎ 3份真题详解 + 4套模拟试题 + 5个核心章节 + 6大实用模板 = 实现托福口语高分

定价：49元　开本：16开　页码：320页

《托福主题词汇与阅读》

（附CD-ROM）　赖水信 编著

◎ 以历年真题为蓝本，精编48个Advanced Test

◎ 每个Advanced Test包含50道词汇题目，全书共计2400道

◎ 全书涉及的主题广泛而多样，充满知识性与趣味性

定价：55元　开本：16开　页码：524页

《新托福考试写作高分速成》

陈向东 著

- 详细阐述托福综合写作解答的7大步骤及5大写作原则，给出独立写作3大写作策略和5大解题原则
- 深刻剖析写作思路，并提供解题策略及思维训练，解读真题
- 精心打造托福写作题型、解答原则与黄金模板

定价: 35元 开本: 16开 页码: 280页

《TOEFL 写作／口语论证论据素材大全》 韦晓亮 编著

- 全面性: 全面补充TOEFL写作和口语英文论证论据素材
- 权威性: 汇集世界优秀外文期刊、报纸、书籍、检索数据库和权威新闻网站的英文内容
- 指导性: 汇集新东方TOEFL考试培训项目数年教学经验和写作、口语教学成果

定价: 25元 开本: 16开 页码: 248页

《新托福考试核心语法》

（含光盘 1 张）

Nancy Gallagher 编著

- 全书涵盖20个重要的英语语法点，紧扣新托福考试语法要点
- 结合经典的例子，对各个语法点进行精深入的讲解
- 提供大量模考练习，设有计时测验

定价: 50元 开本: 16开 页码: 308页

《新托福考试阅读特训》

（第二版） **Ji-Yeon Lee 著**

- 62篇精选文章，题材广泛，全面满足备考需求
- 特设仿真阅读试题，体验真实考试情境
- 全书结构编排科学合理，实用性强

定价: 55元 开本: 16开 页码: 472页

《新托福考试口语特训》

（另配光盘／磁带4盘）

Ji-Yeon Lee 著

- 大量真实练习语料，全面满足备考需求
- 提供多种练习方式，逐步掌握答题技巧
- 特设口语模拟试题，体验真实考试情景

定价: 48元 开本: 16开 页码: 380页

《新托福考试听力特训》

（第二版）（含光盘 1 张）

Ji-Yeon Lee 著

- 59篇精选听力练习语料，题材广泛，全面满足备考需求
- 提供多种练习方式，逐步掌握答题技巧
- 特设听力模拟试题，体验真实考试情景

定价: 58元 开本: 16开 页码: 452页

《新托福考试写作特训》

（第二版）（含光盘 1 张）

Ji-Yeon Lee 著

- 三个章节精练详解，两种题型各个击破
- 提供多种练习方式，逐步掌握写作技巧
- 特设仿真写作测试，体验真实考试情境

定价: 46元 开本: 16开 页码: 304页

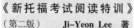

《TOEFL 巴朗词表》（附 MP3）

Steven J. Matthiesen 编著

- 系统研究真题，提炼高频词汇
- 收录双语词义，遴选同义派生
- 提供经典例句，加深理解记忆

定价: 35元 开本: 16开 页码: 256页

《托福词组必备》

俞敏洪　编著

◎ 紧扣真题，选词科学
◎ 例句经典，原汁原味
◎ 收录同义词组，扩充词汇量
◎ 幽默插图，巧妙助记

定价：22元　开本：32开　页码：256页

《TOEFL词汇词根＋联想记忆法：45天突破版》

（含光盘1张）　俞敏洪　编著

◎ "词根＋联想记忆法"实用有趣，有效提升词汇量
◎ 甄选重点词汇，紧跟TOEFL考试趋势
◎ 增加单词返记菜单，有助于复习和自测
◎ 再现真题例句，直击TOEFL考试要点

定价：45元　开本：32开　页码：528页

《TOEFL iBT 词汇10000》

（含光盘1张）张洪伟　戴云　编著

◎ 源于真题目——收录托福真题的必备词汇与经典例句
◎ 奉献真经典——凝结托福名师的教学感悟与智慧结晶

定价：45元　开本：16开　页码：444页

《TOEFL iBT 听力词汇小伴侣》邱政政　戴懿德　编著

◎ 紧跟TOEFL考试趋势，权威指点
◎ 精选考核心词汇，针对性强
◎ 分类词汇专业全面，重点突出
◎ 精选TOEFL常用短语与习惯搭配，实用性佳

定价：18元　开本：32开　页码：388页

《TOEFL iBT 口语词汇小伴侣》　张洪伟　翟少成　编著

◎ 应试导向——紧扣新托福口语考试趋势，给出三类词汇供考生掌握
◎ 科学统计——所涉及学术类专业词汇来自真实词频统计数据

定价：15元　开本：32开　页码：280页

《TOEFL iBT 阅读词汇小伴侣》　张洪伟　蔡青　编著

◎ 针对性强——囊括托福阅读全部话题及学科领域词汇
◎ 实用性佳——精选托福阅读词汇及同义词，在语境中真正融会贯通
◎ 分类清晰——囊括托福阅读基础、核心、高频及次高频分类词汇

定价：15元　开本：32开　页码：204页

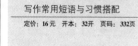

《托福写作词汇小伴侣》

张洪伟　戴云　编著

◎ 针对性强——浓缩托福独立写作和综合写作最常用词汇
◎ 实用性佳——精选鲜活的托福写作常用短语与习惯搭配

定价：16元　开本：32开　页码：332页

《TOEFL 核心词汇21天突破》　李笑来　编著

◎ 21天不长——如果不背单词的话一如既往，21天会很快过去——无所事事的日子总是轻松愉快
◎ 21天不短——如果去背单词的话然而最终，21天还是会很快过去——不同的是你已经脱胎换骨

定价：38元　开本：32开　页码：544页

《词以类记：TOEFL iBT 词汇》

（含光盘1张）　张红岩　编著

◎ TOEFL iBT 最新词汇：覆盖听说读写
◎ 按学科和意群分类：细分至最小同义词区间

定价：35元 开本：32开 页码：424页

《新托福考试专项进阶——初级听力》（附 MP3 光盘）

定价：42元 开本：16开 页码：288页

《新托福考试专项进阶——中级听力》（附 MP3 光盘）

定价：45元 开本：16开 页码：340页

《新托福考试专项进阶——高级听力》（附 MP3 光盘）

定价：45元 开本：16开 页码：348页

《新托福考试专项进阶——初级口语》（附 MP3 光盘）

定价：42元 开本：16开 页码：296页

《新托福考试专项进阶——中级口语》（附 MP3 光盘）

定价：38元 开本：16开 页码：244页

《新托福考试专项进阶——高级口语》（附 MP3 光盘）

定价：42元 开本：16开 页码：288页

《新托福考试专项进阶——初级阅读》

定价：35元 开本：16开 页码：308页

《新托福考试专项进阶——中级阅读》

定价：38元 开本：16开 页码：344页

《新托福考试专项进阶——高级阅读》

定价：40元 开本：16开 页码：368页

《新托福考试专项进阶——阅读模拟试题（上）》

定价：36元 开本：16开 页码：252页

《新托福考试专项进阶——阅读模拟试题（下）》

定价：36元 开本：16开 页码：252页

《新托福考试专项进阶——初级写作》（附 MP3 光盘）

定价：40元 开本：16开 页码：268页

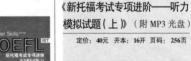

《新托福考试专项进阶——中级写作》（附 MP3 光盘）

定价：38元 开本：16开 页码：248页

《新托福考试专项进阶——高级写作》（附 MP3 光盘）

定价：42元 开本：16开 页码：304页

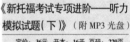

《新托福考试专项进阶——听力模拟试题（上）》（附 MP3 光盘）

定价：40元 开本：16开 页码：256页

《新托福考试专项进阶——听力模拟试题（下）》（附 MP3 光盘）

定价：36元 开本：16开 页码：220页

◎ 《新托福考试专项进阶》系列丛书从托福考试所考查的听、说、读、写四项技能入手，为考生提供了详尽的考试指导，并将各技能分为初、中、高三级，通过独特的"进阶训练"方式，再辅以大量练习，让考生逐步掌握托福实考的技巧，同时切实提高英语实际运用能力，从而在短期内轻松取得托福高分。本丛书内容编排由易到难，循序渐进，实战性强，是不可多得的托福备考资料。

◎ 本丛书引进自韩国多乐园出版社。该社成立于1977年，在韩国英语教育出版领域始终处于领军地位。本丛书被韩国众多学校和培训机构指定为课堂教材，在托福考生中享有较高声誉。

读者反馈表

尊敬的读者：

　　您好！非常感谢您对**新东方大愚图书**的信赖与支持，希望您抽出宝贵的时间填写这份反馈表，以便帮助我们改进工作，今后能为您提供更优秀的图书。谢谢！

　　为了答谢您对我们的支持，我们将对反馈的信息进行随机抽奖活动，当月将有20位幸运读者可获赠**《新东方英语》**期刊一份。我们将定期在新东方大愚图书网站www. dogwood. com. cn公布获奖者名单并及时寄出奖品，敬请关注。

来信请寄：

　　　　北京市海淀区海淀东三街2号新东方南楼19层
　　　　北京新东方大愚文化传播有限公司
　　　　　　　　图书部收
　　　　邮编：100080　　　　E-mail：bj62605588@163. com

姓名：_____　年龄：_____　职业：_____　教育背景：_____

邮编：_____　通讯地址：_____

联系电话：_____　E-mail：_____

您所购买的书籍的名称是：_____

1. 您是通过何种渠道得知本书的（可多选）：
   □书店　□新东方网站　□大愚网站　□朋友推荐　□老师推荐
   □@新东方大愚图书(http://weibo. com/dogwood)　□其他_____

2. 您是从何处购买到此书的？
   □书店　□新东方大愚淘宝网　□其他网上书店　□其他_____

3. 您购买此书的原因（可多选）：
   □封面设计　□书评广告　□正文内容　□图书价格　□新东方品牌
   □新东方名师　□其他_____

4. 您对本书的封面设计满意程度：
   □很满意　□比较满意　□一般　□不满意
   改进建议_____

5. 您认为本书的内文在哪些方面还需改进？
   □结构编排　□难易程度　□内容丰富性　□内文版式　□其他_____

6. 本书最令您满意的地方：□内文　□封面　□价格　□纸张

7. 您对本书的推荐率：□没有　□1人　□1—3人　□3—5人　□5人以上

8. 您更希望我们为您提供哪些方面的英语类图书？
   □四六级类　□考研类　□IELTS类　□TOEFL类　□GRE、GMAT类
   □SAT、SSAT类　□留学申请类　□BEC、TOEIC类　□英语读物类
   □初高中英语类　□少儿英语类　□其他_____
   您目前最希望我们为您出版的图书是：_____

9. 您在学习英语过程中最需要哪些方面的帮助？（可多选）
   □词汇　□听力　□口语　□阅读　□写作　□翻译　□语法　□其他_____

10. 您最喜欢的英语图书品牌：_____
    理由是(可多选)：□版式漂亮　□内容实用　□难度适宜　□价格适中
    □对考试有帮助　□其他_____

11. 您对新东方图书品牌的评价：_____

12. 您对本书(或其他新东方图书)的意见和建议：_____
    _____
    _____
    _____
    _____

13. 填表时间：_____年_____月____日